THE PERFECT PICKLE

Pickling made easy

Naturally preserved

1000 Varieties

Kitchen Fundamentals on
VEGETABLE CRAFT
PICKLING TECHNIQUES
AND BASE PREPARATIONS

Guides on
BUYING, STORAGE, NUTRIENT SAVER
AND MICROWAVE OVEN COOKING

Features on
SPICES, VEGETABLES,
OILS, PRESSURE COOKING
AND SUBSTITUTES

Usha's PICKLE DIGEST

Usha R Prabakaran

Usha's
PICKLE DIGEST
THE PERFECT PICKLE RECIPE BOOK

Usha R Prabakaran

PEBBLE GREEN Publications
Chennai, INDIA

PEBBLE GREEN Publications
Chennai, INDIA

Usha's
PICKLE DIGEST
THE PERFECT PICKLE RECIPE BOOK

© Usha R Prabakaran 1998
First Published at Chennai INDIA 1998

Recipes Copyright © Usha R Prabakaran 1998

Computer setting
Preethi C

Layout Assistance
Vedha Anbu Kumar A
Murali S
Krithivasan G

Pagesetting
REPLIKA, Chennai

Printing
Sudarsan Graphics, Chennai

Cover design
Raja Rahul

Publication & Design Advisor
Ramachandrananda, Swami

This book is copyright.

Apart from any fair dealing for the purposes of private study, research, criticism or review, as permitted under the Copyright Act, no part of the publication may be reproduced, stored in a retrieval system, or transmitted, in any form or by any means, electronic, mechanical, photocopying, recording or otherwise, without prior permission of the author.

Dedicated to
all pickle lovers

SPECIAL FEATURE

Recipes in this book are naturally preserved, free from additives

---

Contents

Foreword	Padmashree Thangam E Philip	vi
Introduction	Usha R Prabakaran	vii

KITCHEN FUNDAMENTALS

Vegetable Craft	Cooking basics / Cleaning basics / Staining / Discolouration / Bitterness / Itching / Insects / Economy	3
Pickling Techniques	Preparation basics / Pickling basics	7
Base Preparations	Curd setting / Tamarind pulp / Lime juice / Vinegar / Sugar syrup / Spice powders / Sprouting / Sprout chart	12

HOME GUIDES

Buying Guide	The art of selecting vegetables & fruits	19
Storage Guide	Preservation of vegetables & fruits	22
Nutrient Saver Guide	Nutrient savings through peeling, cutting, salting, washing, soaking & cooking	24
Microwave Oven Guide	General features / Cooking instructions / Special features / Dishes	26

RECIPES

Classique	Traditional favourites, commonly prepared in every Indian home	29
Unique Flavours	Popular and typical preparations of different regions, presenting varied styles	43
Exclusive	Unusual creations	55
Exotic	Rare collections for the adventurous	73
Quick serve	Instant, time-saving, no-nonsense recipes	97

Contents

Assorted	A wide range of hot, sweet & tart imaginative recipes of familiar and unfamiliar vegetables	137
Oil Free	Opens up a staggering variety of fabulous, low-calorie but tasty delicacies for the health conscious	263
Dietary	Full of the goodness of vitamin & mineral-rich fruits and vegetables, skillfully combined	285
Anti Waste	unforgettable, tasty, tangy, nutritious morsels combining skins, peels, rinds and seeds, with aromatic spices	307

APPENDIX

Adulterants Chart	Methods of adulterants detection	318
Cooking Methods Chart	Various cooking forms	320
Goodness Chart	Vitamins / Minerals etc.,	323
Multi-Language Chart	Names of foodstuff in 10 languages	326

GLOSSARY

Pickling Vocabulary	Cooking terminology	342

INDEX

Vegetable Category	A – Z Vegetables	344
Acknowledgements	Credits	355

Other Features

Measurements	6	*The Leafy Way*	148
Sprout Chart	16	*All About Pressure Cooking*	284
Kitchen Spices	42 / 72 / 96	*The Oil Range*	306
Sun-dried Vegetables	76	*Preparation of Spice Powders*	309
Vegetable Smart	101	*Substitutes*	322

Padmashree Thangam, E. Philip
M.S., F.H.C.I.M.A.,
F.C.F.A., M.R.S.H.

PRINCIPAL EMERITUS
INSTITUTE OF HOTEL MANAGEMENT, CATERING
TECHNOLOGY & APPLIED NUTRITION

SHALOM, PAKKIL P.O.,
KOTTAYAM - 686 012.
KERALA.
TEL. : 0481-430514
FAX : 0481-563086

DATE : 26.10.1998

Foreword

The world's largest repetoire of pickles and preserves is found in India. The variety is truly mind boggling! Regrettably many of these are lost to posterity due to inadequate documentation. Usha R. Prabakaran must be commended for meticulously gathering, selecting, standardising, testing and cataloguing the recipes into her book *Usha's PICKLE DIGEST* using her reputed skills and knowledge in this field. It is a pleasure for me to write the foreword to such a labour of love.

I am sure, all users will find the book immensely helpful as no Indian meal is complete without the appropriate pickle or chutney as accompaniment.

Wishing Usha success in her venture to spread the experience of generations and with warm regards.

THANGAM E PHILIP

Padmashree Thangam E Philip has been continuously engaged in food education and food research. Her rich experience in food education, love for cookery and deep appreciation of foods won her several laurels. She has to her credit a number of books in this field, notably Modern Cooking for Teaching and the Trade, in 2 Volumes. Every one of her books deals with scientific methods of cooking, planning of meals and improvement of a sense of taste & flavour.

Introduction

THE INDIAN ART OF PICKLING has raised culinary art to such a high level of sophistication that it has acquired an exotic, almost legendary reputation. One of the most striking aspects of Indian pickling is the great variety and range it offers for all seasons and occasions. Even the humblest of vegetables is transformed into a delicacy, through the subtle use of spices.

This book is dedicated as much to the passionate cook as to the ardent beginner. This book is a labour of love. It is the culmination of painstaking efforts at collecting recipes from Indian homes as well as interior villages. It is a result of improving existing recipes as well as discovering new ones.

The *PICKLE DIGEST* brings to you tried and tested recipes, as well as out-of-the way exotic ones – all are not only tasty but also aid digestion. This work has been made possible all the more because of the tremendous variety of fruits and vegetables to choose from, starting from the humble potato to the lowly cabbage. India, the spice shell, makes pickle-making thoroughly exciting and a continuous process of self-discovery.

Pickle making remains a mystery to most. The purpose of this work is to demystify. I've never found it neccessary to overcomplicate the preparation of any pickle. Almost all the recipes can be prepared in the average kitchen – No fuss – No mystique. Only rewarding authenticity.

Take any page and you will first meet the title, which itself will be self-explanatory, followed by the ingredients, then directions on preparation and finally instructions on cooking. At the end of this book you will find the **Appendix** containing some useful charts, viz., an *Adulterants Chart* detailing commonly used adulterants and their detection; a *Cooking Methods Chart* comparing various cooking forms from a nutrition angle, a *Goodness Chart*, highlighting the mineral and vitamin content of commonly pickled fruits, vegetables, grains etc., and finally ending with a *Multi-Language Chart*, containing the names of fruits, vegetables etc., appearing in the book in ten different languages.

Before attempting pickling it will be useful to read through the first part of the book containing the **Kitchen Fundamentals** and the **Home Guides,** rather than take to pickling straightaway. Kitchen Fundamentals sets the ground by explaining how vegetables are to be cleaned and cooked without much loss of nutrients and flavour in addition to details regarding *Base Preparations*. Home Guides provides in a nutshell generations of experience with respect to selecting, storing vegetables and fruits plus a guide to nutrition saving and cooking in Microwave Ovens. At the end of the book you will find the **Glossary** containing the list of cooking terminology, titled *Pickling Vocabulary*. The **Index** is set out alphabetically to facilitate easy tracking of any recipe for your chosen fruit or vegetable.

The notable feature of the book is that the recipes have been categorised as *Classique, Unique Flavours, Exclusive, Exotic, Quick Serve, Assorted, Oil Free, Dietary and Anti Waste*. The *Classique* varieties are Traditional and the most popular. Unique flavours brings to you certain *Unique Flavours* like Gonkura of Andhra Pradesh and Chhundo of Gujarat. *Exclusives* reflect my experience. *Exotic* lists out the unusuals. *Quick Serve* is self-explanatory – instant varieties. *Assorted* is a large group containing every known fruit and vegetable pickle. *Oil Free* and *Dietary* are for the weight-watchers and health-freaks. *Anti Waste* pickles as the name indicates converts peels, skins and seeds, into mouth-watering delicacies.

Every recipe in this book has been tested and refined in my own kitchen. I hope you enjoy the pages ahead and the discovery of the most exciting, varied pickling techniques in the world. It is the pickle that adds to the allure of tongue-tickling dishes, creating a complete, memorable meal. The special feature of these pickles is that generally, no preservative is used. Most of the pickles keep for a few months, some for years.

The incredible variety of pickles has been made possible because of foreign influence on Indian cusine as also due to cross-fertilisation between sub-cuisines. Difference in the produce of each region, religious practices, geographic location, climatic variation, customs, tradition and beliefs has made this more possible.

As I began collecting my recipes I was amazed to find that, in India, the most ordinary vegetable can be pickled in hundreds of ways. Spices and seasonings can also transform the same pickle, so it tastes different.

Pickles not only perk up a meal. The spices and seasoning used in pickling, have clearly defined attributes that help the body in specific functions. Spices are anti-oxidants, so they act as free-radical scavengers. Moreover they contain essential oils which help to kill bacteria in the intestinal tract.

Ginger, asafoetida, turmeric are all considered digestives. They are pickled with beans or split peas to fight off their hard-to-digest stubborness. Mint does the same thing. It also kills germs. Asafoetida is considered a nerve tonic. Cummin and green cardamom are cooling, clove and cinnamon are warming, ginger is good for cold, while raw garlic is good for circulatory ailments and jangled nerves. Red chillies in small doses have an antiseptic action. Black pepper livens the appetite and acts as a tonic for new mothers.

One of the exciting aspects of Indian pickling is its wide choice. Every pickle becomes more of an adventure this way and it gets imbued with possibilities of many added tastes. Part of the fun is that you may indeed put together anything that strikes your fancy. You will find here some of the commonest vegetables pickled in the most uncommon ways. There is a recipe for watermelon rind. There is a recipe for woodapple.

The use of different oils can make such a difference to the pickle. In some parts of India only mustard oil is used for pickling. This fiery pungent oil turns sweet and docile when heated. It envelops pickles in its gentle warmth.

While every effort has been taken to ensure that pickling quantities are accurate in each of the recipes, this may not be so when you try them out. The quantities may change slightly. And for a host of reasons. All these affect the end result. If these things are kept in mind, one will get a good idea as to how to vary the quantities and timing, even if they don't vary very much.

Pickle making is very fast and very easy. It can be prepared with a minimum of fuss and effort. These recipes are just a beginning. And will serve their full purpose, when they have managed to show you, how you can let your imagination, work wonders for you. HAPPY PICKLING.

Chennai, 2 Nov., 1998   **Usha R Prabakaran**

Kitchen Fundamentals

Vegetable Craft

COOKING BASICS
CLEANING
STAINING
DISCOLOURATION
BITTERNESS
ITCHING
INSECTS
ECONOMY

The Indian art of pickling is uniquely refined, fastidious and subtle. There are a host of vegetables, fruits and grains waiting to be pickled. The matter is further complicated by the astonishing range of spices and the innumerable ways in which they may be skilfully blended. One has to learn how these vegetables need to be treated to get of their best. This has to be done at various stages of pickling, from buying to storing, from cleaning to cutting, from washing to cooking.

The following instructions provide a practical guidance aiming to fill-in the gaps, by imparting the knowledge that most recipe books take for granted. It is not intented for the experts but for the enthusiasts, who want to learn more about pickling. Let's hope they can discover why!

With these fundamentals, it should be easy to put together the combination of your skills and knowledge, to use any reliable recipe book, not just this book, with success.

COOKING BASICS

BOILING CABBAGE
- While boiling cabbage or cauliflower, add 2 teaspoons vinegar to avoid its unpleasant smell.

CUTTING CHILLIES
- Instead of using a knife to cut chillies, use scissors. This way you can avoid getting cuts on your fingers.

COOKING PEAS OR BEANS
- Dried peas or beans require very little cooking if put in a vacuum flask with boiling water, the night before they are required.

COVERING FRIED FOODS
- Avoid covering fried foods with a lid while keeping them hot, because the trapped steam will make them go soft.

FRYING FOOD
- Frying temperatures vary from 340° - 400°F. If the fat is too hot, the outside of the foods will brown before the inside is cooked : if too cold, the food will absorb the fat, becoming greasy and indigestible. It is important to avoid over-filling the pan with food, otherwise the temperature of the fat will drop too low.

- Reheat fat before frying a second batch of food, to bring back to the required temperature.

STEAMING FOOD
- Use minimum water while steaming food.

COOKING LADY'S FINGER
- To eliminate the stickiness when lady's finger is cooked, wash and dry each with a cloth separately.

- If you want to cook lady's finger quickly, add the spices and squeeze the juice of a lime over it.

BOILING LENTILS, GRAMS & PULSES
- Cook lentils, grams, pulses in a little over double the quantity of warm water.

- Lentils, grams, pulses should be soaked in warm water and then cooked in the same water. Grams take 3 to 4 hours and whole pulses 12 hours, when no sprouting is needed. Do not stir or the grams will take longer to cook. Add a little turmeric to soften it quickly.

- Add a few drops of lime juice to lentils, grams, pulses while cooking, instead of tomatoes for best results.

- Lentils, pulses and rice, soaked for about 30 minutes before cooking, need much less cooking time.

- In boiling all kinds of lentils, pulses, rice and vegetables, skimming is most important. As the white frothy scum rises it should be taken off with the help of a spoon as both the flavour and appearance of the food are injured by it.

Vegetables should be put into boiling water immediately they are cut, to inactivate the enzymes.

SPROUTING LENTILS, GRAMS AND PULSES

• Sprouted lentils, grams and pulses are ideal in both summer and winter, though they take much longer to sprout roots in the cold weather. The best way is to clean, wash thoroughly and then put them into a pan half-filled with water. Cover the pan and keep in a warm place for about 24 hours. After this period uncover the pan and drain out the excess water by tilting it, without disturbing the gram. Leave it covered for another 24 hours - it could be less in summer and more in winter - by which time the gram should have all sprouted little white roots. In case they are not properly sprouted you can add a bit of water and leave the gram covered for another 12 hours or so. Wash gently before use. Once the gram has sprouted refrigerate until use. Only whole gram can be sprouted (ie. whole green gram, whole black gram, whole pink lentils, whole bengal gram).

PEELING MANGOES

• Immerse mangoes in cold water for some time before peeling them. This hastens the process of peeling and makes the process rather neat too!

COOKING MUSHROOM

• Minimize the use of salts and heavy spices while cooking mushroom as it kills its delicate flavour as well.

CLEANING MUSTARD & CORIANDER

• To remove stones from mustard and coriander seeds, roll the seeds on a slightly slanted vegetable board.

PEELING ONIONS

• A quick and easy way to peel onions is to cut-off one end and quickly immerse them in hot water for a few seconds. Then make a cross-shaped cut on the other end and the skin will come off very easily.

COOKING GREEN PEAS

• If a little coconut oil is added to green peas while cooking, the peas will turn out softer and tastier.

BOILING POTATOES

• Always cook potatoes over a slow fire. Fast cooking causes them to break up but remain hard inside.

• To prevent the cooker from turning black on boiling potatoes, add a little turmeric to the water in which you have put the potatoes.

• To get firmly boiled potatoes, add a dash of salt to them while boiling.

SALTING SPINACH

• Be cautious while salting spinach as it is naturally quite salty.

PEELING TOMATOES

• Instead of boiling tomatoes in water and then peeling the skins off, toast them directly on the gas flame. The skin will come off in seconds when cool.

PEELING ROOT VEGETABLES

• Scrub and scrape root vegetables or peel thinly, if tough-skinned.

SALTING VEGETABLES

• Salt should be added to the vegetables only after they are cooked, to hasten cooking. The vegetable will then be cooked in a few minutes.

HEATING FAT

• Never heat oil or any fat in a wet pan or it will splutter. Before frying, make sure that the fat is very hot. Wait till the fat begins to smoke before you put in the food, then reduce the flame. Transfer the fried food to a piece of absorbent paper before serving, to get off the excess fat.

COOKING IN IRON PANS

• Cooking in iron pans is said to be good for the health, as it gives you added iron!

CLEANING

USE OF KNIVES

• Use knives, used for cutting brinjal/raw plantain only after washing as they will discolour the other vegetables.

• Use knives used for cutting onions only after washing, as they will smell of onion.

• To remove the strong smell of onions from the fingers and knives, rub them with lime peel.

• To prevent rust on knives, rub with glycerine or machine oil from time to time.

MIXER CARE

• To clean the mixer, put a slice of bread into the machine and run it. The bread will absorb the smell of the spices as well as the grease.

• To remove the smells of onion and garlic in the mixer, rub the inside of the bowl with a small piece of potato and wash.

• To sharpen the blades of a mixer jar, grind crystal salt in it.

POT & PAN MAINTENANCE

• To clean frying pans after use, sprinkle a little salt into the frying pan, keep on the fire till it is just hot and then wipe with paper.

- To keep your pots and pans gleaming on the outside, clean them occasionally with a paste made of cream of tartar and a little water. Rub all over and then rinse-off after a couple of minutes.

- To clean stained pots and pans, boil a teaspoon of cream of tartar in them half-filled with water. They will come up sparkling.

STERILIZING BOTTLES

- To clean used and empty pickle bottles fill-in with warm water, add three tablespoons synthetic vinegar, a tablespoon washing powder and shake at intervals. Leave overnight. Rinse in the morning. The bottles will be odour-free.

STAINING

- While cutting colocasia (arbi), yam, kovakkai, raw plantain, brinjal, plantain flower and jackfruit, rub oil over the hands to prevent staining.

DISCOLOURATION

COOKING VEGETABLES

- Vegetables cooked in aluminium pots and pans tend to be darker in colour. Therefore cook vegetables only in stainless steel, enamel pans or in mud pots.

COOKING CAULIFLOWER

- To retain the brightness of raw cauliflower even after cooking, add a small strip of lime peel or a teaspoon of sugar to the water.

COOKING GREEN VEGETABLES

- To retain the colour of green vegetables sprinkle some sugar on them while cooking.

- To prevent green vegetables from turning an unattractive greenish brown colour after they have been cooked, add a little salt and a few drops of lime juice or a pinch of cooking soda.

BOILING GREENS

- Boil greens with a teaspoon of rice flour to retain their green colour.

COOKING LEAFY VEGETABLES

- To preserve the natural colour of leafy vegetables always cook them in an uncovered pan with less water.

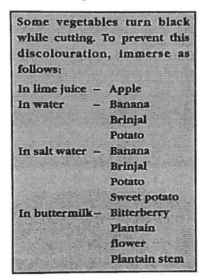

Some vegetables turn black while cutting. To prevent this discolouration, immerse as follows:

In lime juice	— Apple
In water	— Banana
	Brinjal
	Potato
In salt water	— Banana
	Brinjal
	Potato
	Sweet potato
In buttermilk	— Bitterberry
	Plantain flower
	Plantain stem

BOILING POTATOES

- Add a few drops of vinegar to the water while boiling potatoes and cauliflower to keep their original white colour.

GRINDING RED CHILLIES

- Add a few drops of mustard oil while grinding red chillies to obtain an attractive red colour.

BITTERNESS

BITTERNESS IN BITTER GOURD

- To remove the bitterness of bitter gourd remove the seeds and rub the inner layer with salt, a day before preparation.

- Excessive bitterness in bitter gourd pieces can be got rid off, by soaking them for a few minutes before preparation in salt and turmeric or sour buttermilk.

- To reduce the bitterness of bitter gourd and plantain flower cook in lightly salted dilute tamarind water.

BITTERNESS IN CUCUMBER

- If a cucumber is broken at its centre, the bitterness if any gets eliminated.

- To remove the bitterness from cucumber, slice and immerse in rice-washed water for half an hour. Drain out and use the cucumbers which will no longer be bitter.

- Cut a small piece from the top of the cucumber and rub the two pieces together. A sort of foam will emerge and the bitterness, if any, will disappear.

BITTERNESS IN FENUGREEK LEAVES

- To remove the bitterness from fenugreek leaves, sprinkle the leaves with salt and set aside for 15 minutes. Squeeze out all the water and wash thoroughly before cooking.

ITCHING

HANDLING CHILLIES

- To remove the burning sensation on the hands after handling chillies, apply a solution of tamarind juice and sugar.

HANDLING YAM

- To prevent itching sensation on the hands while handling yam and colocasia (arbi), rub the fingers with tamarind water or oil before cutting.

- To prevent itching sensation in the mouth caused by cooked yam or colacasia soak the peeled chopped pieces in thin tamarind water or in salt water before cooking or cook in rice-washed water.

INSECTS

PREPARING CAULIFLOWER

• Before preparing cauliflower put it in water, to which a little vinegar or salt has been added. Set aside for 15 minutes and it will be free of all dirt and insects. Rinse well under running water before cutting.

STORING GRAINS, LENTILS & PULSES

• Add a few dried red chillies to stored grains to keep them insect-free.

• Place dried neem leaves in lentils and pulses to prevent insect-formation.

PROTECTING SPICES

• To protect spices from insects, store in airtight tins or jars with a few salt crystals and peppercorns or mercury trapped in dried cement balls.

PEST-FREE TAMARIND

• Remove seeds from tamarind and sun-dry to prevent insect-formation.

• Combine tamarind with a little coarse salt to prevent insect-formation and darkening.

ECONOMY

FREEZING PEAS

• To freeze peas, drop shelled peas into boiling water. As soon as the peas are put in, the water will stop bubbling. Allow it to come back to a rolling boil and let stand for a minute. Remove the peas from the water and plunge into ice-cold water for one more minute. Drain, dry thoroughly with a towel, and pack into freezer bags. When you want to use them, thaw out and cook. Frozen peas take less time to cook as they have already been parboiled. Carrots may be similarly freezed.

MORE JUICE FROM CITRUS FRUITS

• All citrus fruits will give very little juice if used straight out of the refrigerator. Allow them to thaw and come to room temperature before squeezing.

• Roll the citrus fruits (like limes or oranges) on a hard surface firmly for a minute or two to get more juice with less squeezing.

• Immerse citrus fruits in warm water for 15 minutes before cutting them to obtain maximum juice.

MORE JUICE FROM TAMARIND

• **To get the maximum quantity of juice from tamarind, soak the desired quantity of tamarind in lukewarm water for 10 minutes before squeezing. Alternatively it may be blended in the mixer for a few seconds.**

USE OF VEGETABLE & FRUIT PEELINGS

• Vegetable or fruit peelings stored in the freezer are useful while making stock.

MEASUREMENTS

LIQUID MEASURE

1 tsp (level measure)	=	5ml
1 Tbsp (level measure)	=	15ml
1 ltr	=	1000ml

SOLID MEASURE

1 tsp	=	5gms
1 Tbsp	=	15gms
1 kg	=	1000gms

ABBREVIATIONS

gm	=	grams
Kg	=	Kilogram
ml	=	millilitre
ltr	=	litre
tsp	=	teaspoon
Tbsp	=	Tablespoon

VEGETABLES

1 medium sized beetroot	=	100 g
1 medium sized bitter gourd	=	75 g
1 medium sized brinjal	=	60 g
1 small sized carrot	=	50 g
1 small sized capsicum	=	100 g
1 small sized chow-chow	=	200 g
1 bunch coriander leaves	=	30 g
1 small cucumber	=	125 g
1 medium sized gooseberry	=	10 g
1 medium sized lime	=	40 g
1 medium sized mango	=	250 g
1 small sized onion	=	50 g
1 small sized potato	=	30 g
1 small sized radish	=	50 g
1 medium sized tomato	=	50 g

Pickling Techniques

- PREPARATION BASICS
- PICKLING BASICS
- STERLISING AND STORING

More than any other food, vegetables inspire cooks with their endless variety. In most parts of Asia, vegetables are prized as highly as meats and are treated as carefully. But in most western cooking they are literally pushed aside and are served as mere accompaniments to meat. More often than not such lack-lustre treatment stems from lack of knowledge, both of the different vegetables themselves and of the many cooking techniques that can be applied to them.

When it comes to pickling, vegetables are endearing subjects as they are truly versatile. All the same, one has take great care while pickling so that they are stored hygienically.

Of course, the following hints do not cover every possibility. But they will teach you the rules – and the reasons behind the rules – that govern the preparation of most any vegetable. After that the way is clear to your own improvisation and invention. The creative possibilities are limitless.

PREPARATION BASICS

USING YOUNG FRESH VEGETABLES
- Use young fresh vegetables, wash and drain well, removing any damaged portions or tough stalks. Chop, shred or leave whole according to the recipe. They are then ready for brining or dry salting - processes which extract some of the water from the vegetables.

SELECTING SEASONAL VEGETABLES
- Select fresh vegetables and fruits for pickling during the season when they are tasty, relatively cheap and available in abundant quantities.

IMPORTANCE OF FRESHNESS
- Freshness of vegetables and fruits for pickling is important as it improves the taste and also keeps for a long time.

BUYING UNBLEMISHED VEGETABLES
- Any vegetable or fruit that you buy for pickling should be unblemished. Never try to chop off the unblemished portion and use.

SCRUBBING VEGETABLES
- Vegetables for pickling should be thoroughly scrubbed and dried to prevent the setting in of bacterial activity later.

VEGETABLES WITH MOISTURE CONTENT
- For vegetables with a lot of moisture content like beetroot, cucumber, onion, cabbage, cauliflower and beans, cut and immerse completely in a solution of brine (1/2kg coarse salt in 4 ltrs of water) for 24 hours. Rinse in cold water, drain and dry thoroughly. Now use these for pickling.

CRUNCHY MIXED VEGETABLE PICKLE
- While pickling mixed vegetables - do not blanch or cook if you want a crunchy pickle.

FRESHENING STALE VEGETABLES
- Soak stale vegetables in water to which the juice of one lime has been added to freshen them.

PRICKING WHOLE FRUIT
- When making pickles with whole fruit, prick each with a fork.

MAKING VEGETABLES CRISP
- To make vegetables crisp, cut vegetables and fruits in desired shapes and soak in lime juice & water for 2 hours.

REMOVING MOISTURE
- Soaking vegetables in salt overnight brings out the extra moisture in them (however mangoes and limes soaked overnight, must be wiped dry before use).

USING BOILING WATER
- Always use boiling water to cook vegetables instead of cold water.

WHEN TO ADD FAT OR SPICES
- Always add melted butter, cream or spices to boiled vegetables only when all the water (even the last drop) is drained away.

GRATING CARROT AND RADISH
- Wash carrot and radish very well before grating. Wash once before peeling and then again after peeling, before you grate them. This way you ensure that there is no grit left whatsoever.

USE OF WATER
- Never drown out vegetables while cooking. Use enough water to keep the pan from burning. Less salt will be needed.

COOKING APRICOT OR RHUBARB
- Add a piece of fresh lime rind to dried apricot or rhubarb when cooking. Less sugar will be required and the flavour of the fruit will improve.

WASHING ARTICHOKES
- Wash artichokes well under the cold tap to flush out any grit. An artichoke will stand upright best, if you trim the bottom with a sharp knife, rubbing the stalk with lime juice, to prevent discolouration. Cutting the tips of the inner circle of leaves, is to make the artichoke easier to eat. Unlike most other vegetables, artichokes are cooked in water, enough to well cover them, for anything from 20 to 45 minutes, according to the variety, size, recipe or personal preference. A draining spoon is handy to lift them carefully out of the pan, before turning them upside down to drain.

CLEANING ASPARAGUS ROOTS
- Soak the asparagus roots in water for a day. Remove from the water, skin the asparagus roots and immerse in rice-washed water. Cut each piece into 1cm thick rounds after removing the central stem and return to the same water to prevent discolouration.

PREPARING BAMBOO SHOOTS
- Remove the outer leaves of the bamboo shoots and soak them overnight in water to which four teaspoons (20g) salt has been added. Cut them into 1" pieces and rinse in 3 changes of water for 3 days. Alternatively it may be cooked in 3 changes of water the same day.

SLICING BANANAS
- While slicing bananas, dip the knife in lime juice between each cut, to prevent the bananas from turning brown.

COOKING BEANS
- Add a little baking soda while cooking beans to retain its natural green colour.

SOFTER CLUSTER BEANS
- Fry cluster beans in oil before cooking in water, to make them softer.

BEETROOT – PREVENTING LOSS OF COLOUR
- Before boiling beetroot with damaged skin, hold the broken spot over a gas flame and seal it. This facilitates the prevention of "bleeding" and loss of colour of the beetroot.

- Bake rather than boil beetroot to prevent discolouration. Wash the beetroot, place in an aluminium pan and cook in a baking oven. They will remain tender yet crunchy.

CUTTING CELERY
- Celery should have the root left on because this is one of the best parts : remove the coarse outer stems, and the leaves of all but the smallest heart stems, and turn the root to a slight point. Now cut the head into quarters, right down through the root. However celery is to be cooked, most varieties need blanching about 10 minutes first, to mellow their strong flavour.

CUTTING DRUMSTICK
- Cut the drumsticks into 4" lengths. Cook till partly tender in sufficient water to which a teaspoon (5 g) salt has been added. Cool and remove the inner pith of the drumstick with a thin sharp spoon.

SOAKING DRIED CEREAL
- To soak dried cereal or gram at short notice, use warm water instead of cold water.

GRINDING CHILLI POWDER
- Grind chilli powder in the mincer for a lovely texture although it is simpler to grind it in a local mill.

GRATING COCONUT
- To grate coconut into a coarse powder, keep the coconut in the deep-freezer for at least 5 hours before grating.

- To get uniformly small coconut gratings, break the coconut and keep it in the fridge the previous day.

COOKING CORN KERNEL
- Remember to take off the corn kernel as sook as they are tender. If cooked longer they tend to toughen again.

PREPARING CUCUMBER
- Soak cucumber in salt water for about an hour before using, to make them more digestible.

PEELING GARLIC
- To peel garlic easily, use any of the following methods :
  a) heat in a dry pan
  b) rub oil & place in the sun
  c) keep in the fridge, remove & peel
  d) place on a chopping board and press its flat side firmly with the palm of your hand.

- Alternatively apply a little oil to the pods, rub them on a rough surface, such as a piece of jute sacking and blow immediately. The remaining scales left on the pods can be easily removed with the fingers.

Pickling Techniques

REMOVING GINGER SKINS
- To remove ginger skins, if used in large quantities during pickle preparation, first wash them thoroughly, to remove the mud and rub them on a rough surface. The skin at the knots and knobs can be removed with a spoon.

SKINNING GRAPES
- To skin grapes, dip them in boiling water for 2 minutes. Remove and immediately pour cold water over the grapes. The skin will now peel off without any difficulty.

SEEDING GRAPES
- To seed grapes sterilize a two pronged fork by dipping it in boiling water for a few moments. Then push one end of the fork into the grape from the stalk end and gently ease out the seed.

COOKING GREENS FASTER
- To cook greens faster, add a pinch of cooking soda to them while boiling, to speed-up the cooking process.

FOR BETTER HERBAL FLAVOUR
- Soak dried herbs in hot water for a few minutes, then in cold water to bring out their flavour.

REMOVING STICKINESS FROM LADY'S FINGER
- Cook lady's finger in tamarind water to remove its stickiness.

- While making curry or any dish with lady's finger, place a slice of lime in the cooking pan. This will keep the stickiness away.

PREPARING LETTUCE LEAVES
- Always tear lettuce leaves. Never cut them.

- To make lettuce leaves crisp and crunchy immerse them in a bowl of cold water with raw potato slices or just stand it in water overnight.

BLEMISHLESS LIMES
- For pickling, choose ripe yellow limes with thin smooth skins, free from blemishes.

CUTTING MAHANI ROOTS
- Soak the mahani roots in water for a day. Remove from the water, skin the mahani roots and immerse in rice-washed water. Cut each piece into 1cm thick rounds after removing the central stem and return to the same water to prevent discolouration.

SELECTING SALTED TENDER MANGO
- Soak tender mangoes in brine. Select only the firm ones and discard the soft ones.

PEELING & CUTTING ONION THE TEARLESS WAY

- Prevent tears when cutting onion by keeping the cut side of the onion towards the board, while you lean back and cut.

- Another good way of cutting onion is to peel them and after cutting them in half, soak in a pan of water for a few minutes, before proceeding to cut them fine.

- You will shed fewer tears if you cut the root end of the onion last.

- If onions are soaked in water before chopping, the eyes will not water.

- If you chew a gum while peeling onions, while chopping them your eyes will not water.

- Skins of small onion can be removed easily, if they are soaked in warm water for half an hour.

NON-POISONOUS MUSHROOMS
- To check whether mushrooms are poisonous or not, boil the mushrooms in water with a few flakes of garlic. If the mushrooms are poisonous, the water will turn black. If they don't, then the mushrooms are safe for consumption.

PEELING ORANGES
- Before peeling oranges, run boiling water over them. The rind and the pith will come off easily.

- Oranges will peel more easily if you pop them into boiling water for 3 minutes first.

CHOPPING PAPAYA
- Prick the papaya all over with a fork. Set aside for a few hours for the milky juice to drain out. Wash thoroughly, seed and cut as desired.

CUTTING PINEAPPLE
- Wash the pineapples well. Hold the fruit by its crown and remove the eyes with the help of a sharp, stainless steel knife, by making diagonal incisions. Slice, cube or chop as desired.

GRINDING & CHOPPING RAISIN
- Adding in a little lime juice while grinding sticky fruits like raisin, makes for easier grinding and better flavour.

- It is easier to chop raisin, if a thin film of butter is put on both sides of the knife.

CHOPPING GREEN HERBS
- Salad leaves, coriander and mint etc., should preferably be plucked leaf by leaf rather than cut with a knife, in order to preserve their juices.

FIRMING-UP TOMATOES
- To firm up soft tomatoes, put in cold water to which a little salt is added. The tomatoes will become hard within 10 minutes.

DRYING SPICES
- Dry whole spices in the sun for at least 3 days before use, powder if desired, cool and store.

CLEANING SPINACH & MUSTARD GREENS
- Spinach and mustard greens are usually full of mud and grit; so they have to be washed very well. The best way is to cut off the stems, roots and wash them. Then put them into a colander and immerse in a pail of water. Lift in and out of the water, half a dozen times and all the dirt will fall away from the leaves. Rinse once more under the tap, cut and cook.

HULLING STRAWBERRY
- Fresh strawberry should always be hulled i.e. the stalks to be removed, after washing. If done before, they absorb too much water through the open end and soon turn soft & mushy. Green chillies are to be treated similarly.

POWDERING NUTS
- To get a finer powder of nuts such as walnuts, cashewnuts, etc, keep them in the fridge for a few hours before powdering.

PICKLING BASICS

HANDLING PICKLES
- Avoid use of wet hands or spoons, while transferring pickles into small containers, as moisture leads to fungal growth.
- Always use a clean, dry spoon for taking out pickles from the jar. Replace the cap immediately to prevent fungus spores from falling in. These are always present in the atmosphere, especially during wet weather.

PREVENTING FUNGAL FORMATION
- Rub clove oil on the lid to prevent fungus from the pickles, otherwise cap with a wax paper rubbed with clove oil.
- Wipe bottles from the inside with a cloth dipped in hot salted oil preferably before storing pickles to keep the pickle fungus-free.
- After refilling a pickle container, rub salt on the mouth of the container to prevent it from spoiling.
- Oil-based pickles tend to become dry and gather white fungus on top after a period of time. This can be prevented by placing two small round pebbles collected from the river side, on the top. With that little weight, oil will float on top keeping the pickle fresh for a long time.
- Place kitchen foil before screwing-on the lid of the pickle container to prevent fungus formation.
- To prevent fungus formation, add 2 teaspoons of vinegar into the bottle and shake well before bottling a pickle.
- Keep an eye on the pickles after you have stored them and check for any bubbles. If they appear over the surface, it is a signal that fermentation has started. Add more salt on the top surface and sun for a few more days.

FUNGAL TREATMENT
- Pickles which develop mildew or fungus on top, can usually be saved by carefully removing the spoiled bit with a clean, dry spoon and storing in the refrigerator.
- However, if it develops fungus again, you should remove the top bit again and heat the rest quite thoroughly to kill any fungus spores. Then pour into another freshly sterilized jar. If it tastes at all bad or gets mildewed again, it should be thrown out.
- Remove fungus which forms on the top of pickles with a spoon, heat the rest of the pickle, pour a little mustard oil over it and store.
- Remove fungus from pickles, add 10 to 12 drops of acetic acid and transfer the pickle into a clean, new jar. The pickle will be good as new.
- For mango pickle that begins to mildew, don't throw away the pickle but remove the layer of mildew properly, add some oil and keep in the sun. The pickle will taste as good as ever.
- If lime pickle has turned sour and stale, add a pinch of sugar, 2 teaspoons vinegar and keep it in the sun for 2-3 days. The pickle will taste better.
- Pickles go bad quickly if there is not enough salt, oil or vinegar used for pickling or if the fruit or vegetable still retains water. Also, they need daily shaking and putting in the sun before they are ready for use.

MAINTAINING PICKLE TEXTURE
- Pickle pieces will not lose their shape if a little vinegar is added to the pickle.

- **Wherever oil is mentioned use gingelly oil unless specifically stated. Refined oil is more suitable if the pickle has to be preserved for longer periods. If gingelly oil is kept for too long it tends to get a rancid smell and taste.**
- **When oil is mentioned for heating and cooling, heating is always to smoking point.**

OIL FOR GARLIC PICKLE
- A lot more oil is required for pickles with garlic as an ingredient in it, for it is highly susceptible to bacterial activity. The extra oil on top will inhibit the growth of bacteria.

SUNNING PICKLES
- While sunning turn now and then to make for even drying.

Pickling Techniques

CHOICE OF OIL
- Except Avakkai pickle (mango or other vegetables) where traditionally pure raw gingelly oil is used, use sunflower oil or refined oil if desired.

WATER FOR PICKLING
- Whenever water is mentioned, it is boiled and cooled water.
- For pickles that require water preferably use soft water. Clear rain water, is however the best.
- The fact that sometimes pickles become dark in colour is due to the water used, which may have contained iron or sulphur compounds.
- In all water based or liquid based pickles, the spicy liquid should stand a clear 1" above the pickle.

SUGAR – SALT QUANTITIES
- Where sugar, salt and turmeric powder are used quantities may be varied a little to suit the individual palate. However, with salt go slow in changing, as the pickle tends to spoil. Refrigerate in that case although it is no guarantee. Besides taste is altered by storing in the refrigerator.

PRESERVING SPICE POWDERS
- Powders used for preparing pickles can be preserved for a longer time if they are roasted thoroughly before being ground.

QUALITY PICKLING
- The success of pickles depends upon the quality of the ingredients used. Oil, condiments and even salt should be of the best quality.

VINEGAR IN PICKLING
- All types of pickle, whether raw or cooked, sweetened or unsweetened can be preserved by the action of the acetic acid in vinegar. It is important that good vinegar is used for pickling, with an acetic acid content of at least 5 per cent. This is not always stated on the bottle, so, if you have any doubts, always enquire.

THE TURMERIC ADVANTAGE
- Turmeric is added to pickles because it not only adds colour to it, but because it is a remarkable preservative too.

TAMARIND BASED PICKLES
- As regards all tamarind based pickles - if the salt is high and oil the stands a clear 2" above pickle - the pickle will last for as long as 6 months to a year.

STERILISING AND STORING

JAR STERLISING
- Clean, wash and dry pickle jars in the sunlight before storing pickles.
- To sterilise bottles meant for pickles invert the bottle over the whistle of the pressure cooker and let the steam off. The bottles will be fully sterilised.
- To clean used and empty pickle bottles put warm water in them. Add three tablespoons synthetic vinegar, a tablespoon of washing powder and shake at intervals. Leave overnight and rinse in the morning. They will be odour-free.

STORING PICKLES
- Pickles should be mixed and prepared only in stainless steel bowls. Do not use brass or iron utensils.
- The jars in which the pickles are stored should preferably be covered with a screw-type lid.

CHOICE OF JARS
- Check all jars against chipping or cracking before filling them up.
- Do not use metal jars for storing pickles or metal spoons for stirring, cooling and mixing the pickles as their acid content will erode the metal. Always use wooden spoons for this purpose.
- Bottle pickles only when the contents are quite cold and pour over sufficient oil to cover.

STORAGE TEMPERATURE
- Store pickle jars in a cool, dry and dark place. Storage temperature between 45° - 60°C helps maintain good colour and a longer life.
- All pickles, properly sealed, should be stored in a dry, cool and dark place. Most pickles benefit by being left to mature for 6-8 weeks.

SALT IN PICKLING
- Use pure salt, free from additives, otherwise the pickle gets cloudy.
- There is no hard and fast rule regarding the amount of salt to be used in pickle-making and the amounts used are a matter of tolerance and taste. This can be resolved by sound judgement and successive sampling of the pickle.
- For all acidic fruits like lime and raw mango, the proportion of salt to fruit should be 1:4 in volume.
- As firmness in pickles contributes to its keeping and to its eating qualities, never be miserly with salt or vinegar.

Base Preparations

Pickles are vegetables, fruits, sprouts or grains blended with whole or ground spices mostly in a spicy or saucy base. They may be based in curd, tamarind, lime juice, vinegar or sugar syrup. Though these may be familiar to many, their subtle impact and nuances may be lost to most.

Find below practical guidance on how to prepare these basic sauces, syrups and powders. These can be prepared in the average kitchen with minimum of equipment. They can easily be purchased from local stores although they may not be as good and fresh as their home-made counterparts.

Curd, tamarind, lime juice and vinegar go well with hot and spicy pickles. Sugar syrup, as obvious, is used in sweet pickling. Vinegar may be used in both types of pickling to advantage being a natural preservative.

CURD SETTING
TAMARIND PULP
LIME JUICE
VINEGAR
SUGAR SYRUP
SPICE POWDERS
SPROUTING

CURD SETTING

- Bring milk to a boil. Keep on stirring. When it starts rising remove from fire. While still lukewarm add 1 teaspoon of curd or thick butter-milk to the milk (for about 1 litre milk) and leave undistrubed in a warm place. Curd will be ready in about 8 hours. In winter or the rainy season, more curd ie. about 1 tablespoon should be added to the milk and it will take a longer time to set. A pinch of sugar may be added to the milk to give a little sweetness to the curd.

- Curd made in an earthern pot is thicker and more delicious, as the excess water which is often left after curd formation, is absorbed by the earthern pot. However, except aluminium, any other kind of vessel may be used for the purpose of setting curd.

- By adding more curd when setting, you get a more sour product.

- To keep curd fresh for a longer time, fill the vessel containing curd with water to the brim and refrigerate. Change the water everyday. The curd will neither become rancid not turn yellow and will remain fresh for about a week.

- Pushing aside the cream and scum which collects on the top, pour lukewarm milk into a bowl. Stir one teaspoon curd gently and leave undisturbed for 8 hours or overnight. While lukewarm milk enhances its taste, removal of cream and scum from the milk ensures lump-free curd.

> - To make thick curd, mix warm milk and curd in a mixer for a few seconds and then pour in the bowl and cover for setting as usual.

- It is better to use separate small bowls for setting curd for the family instead of a big bowl, because scooping out spoonfuls of it mars its appearance.

- Curd is firmer and better tasting if set the night before - even in summer - and put into the refrigerator in the morning. However, if you do not have a refrigerator or icebox, it might be better to set it in the mornings in summer, otherwise it may become too sour by lunch time.

> - As weather affects its taste and quality, the amount of curd used should be varied accordingly.

- In winter, placing the curd bowl inside full rice or pulse tins hastens the fermentation process.

- To check excessive acid development in curd, the bowl should be covered with a wet cloth.

- When setting curd in cool weather, the bowl is usually wrapped with a thick cloth to maintain its warmth.

- To prepare curd faster, put the milk with a spoon of curd in a casserole. The curd will be ready within four hours even in hilly areas.

- Curd sets faster if dry red chilli halves are added to the milk.

- If you run short of curd and want it immediately, add a little citric acid to warm milk.

- To prevent curd from becoming sour in the hot season, add 1 teaspoon sugar to hot milk and allow to cool. When still lukewarm, add a spoon of curd and set in a warm place. The curd will not become sour quickly.

- To prevent curd from becoming sour, add few pieces of chopped coconut. It will remain fresh longer.

- To prevent the souring of curds in raitas, add a few curry leaves.

- When buttermilk gets sour, add enough water. After an hour take out the water collected on top of the buttermilk. You can use this water for making gravy and save on the use of lime.

- If you find that the curd has not set properly, gently heat the container by immersing it in hot water. The curd that will form will be of 'rock' consistency.

- If curd is made from full cream milk instead of skimmed one, it is nutritionally better and tastes better.

TAMARIND PULP

- To obtain thick tamarind extract, soak it in warm water to cover, for about 30 minutes. Gently run in the mixer, so as not to crush the seeds or alternatively squeeze with the hand. Strain and use.

> - Tamarind comes in several varieties but it will be better to use the fleshier ones as though expensive, is economical in the long run.

- New tamarind is more acidic and lighter in colour than old tamarind which is rather sweet and less sour. A combination of these two varieties will give best results, both in terms of colour and taste.

- It will be interesting to note that new tamarind requires lots of oil and spices compared to old tamarind. A judicious use of the two will be cost effective.

LIME JUICE

- It is an important souring agent used in pickling to give a mild gentle taste. It is mostly used in mixed vegetable pickling in conjunction with vinegar.

> - Lime juice does numerous other things besides giving flavour :
> it can replace vinegar;
> by counteracting the richness of foods, lime juice helps digestion and
> it delays the discolouration of certain fruits and vegetables like apples.

- If you squeeze a refrigerated lime you won't get much juice out of it - better to let it reach room temperature first.

- Add a dash of salt to squeezed lime juice, to prevent it getting bitter. Stored in the fridge, it lasts for a month or two.

VINEGAR

- For most purposes wine vinegar is better than malt vinegar or cider vinegar. The difference in the flavour, quality, colour, price and most importantly in its use, naturally depends upon what vinegar is made of. Cheap vinegars taste harsh and spoil good pickles; but a selection of good ones can bring new life to them.

- Bulk vinegars, sold loose, are of a lower strength generally, and are not suitable for pickling.

- Malt vinegar can be bought in its natural brown colour and also as white distilled vinegar. Either can be used but white is normally used where a pale-coloured pickle is required.

- White wine and cider vinegar are suitable for pickling but they are more expensive and their more delicate flavours can be overwhelmed in a strong pickle.

- Spiced vinegars can be bought but they are easily made and offer opportunities for individual tastes and ideas. They are at their best if the spices are allowed to steep in the unheated vinegar for 6-8 weeks before the vinegar is used. The vinegar must be tightly covered during the steeping process. Strain when required for use.

- If spiced vinegar is required for use at short notice, the vinegar and spices should be put in a heatproof basin, and the basin stood over a saucepan of water. The basin must be covered with a plate, otherwise much of the flavour will be lost. Bring the water in the saucepan to the boil, then remove it from the heat. Allow the spices to steep in the warm vinegar for 2-3 hours. Strain and cool.

- Use whole rather than ground spices when spicing vinegar and tie them in a muslin bag before immersing in the vinegar. Ground spices tend to produce a cloudy vinegar, even with careful straining .

- Generally speaking, cold vinegar gives better results when pickling vegetables that should be served crisp, such as onions or cabbage and hot vinegar is better with softer pickles, such as plums or walnuts.

CHOICE PICKLING – THE VINEGAR WAY

- **Cold Pickling :** Pack the prepared (brined and rinsed) vegetables, such as cauliflower, cabbage, cucumber, beans or onion into clean jars. Leave a headspace of roughly 1". Tip the jar and drain off any water that may have collected at the bottom. Fill with spiced vinegar, covering the contents with at least 1/2" of vinegar. Cover with airtight, vinegar-proof lids.

- **Hot Pickling :** Cook the vegetables and while still hot pack them into hot jars. Cover with the spiced vinegar to a depth of at least 1/2". Cover with airtight, vinegar-proof lids.

Fruit Pickling : Put the sweetened spiced vinegar in a saucepan and add the fruit. Simmer until tender. Remove the fruit with a perforated spoon and pack into hot, clean jars, leaving about 1" headspace. Boil the vinegar rapidly, uncovered, until it is reduced by one-third. Fill the jars with the hot, syrupy vinegar, covering the fruit by at least 1/2". Cover with airtight, vinegar-proof lids.

Any surplus vinegar should be kept in a covered jar, because some pickled fruits - pears, for example – will absorb more vinegar than others and the jars may require topping up.

- Fruits for pickling do not require brining or salting. Use only fresh, sound fruit that is just ripe.

- If pickling whole fruits such as plums, prick all over with a silver or stainless steel fork, to prevent them shrivelling during the pickling process.

SUGAR SYRUP

Mix just enough water to cover the sugar.

Heat it to dissolve slowly, stirring in between. Do not allow it to boil until completely dissolved.

Once the sugar is boiling resist the temptation of stirring. If there are any crystals on the sides of the pan, wipe with a cloth dipped in hot water.

Boil the syrup in steady temperature.

'Over stirring' will affect the 'correct consistency' of the syrup when it is boiling.

- **One-String Consistency :** Thin long string is formed upto 2 - 3 inches when tested between the thumb and forefinger.

- **Two-String Consistency :** When tested between the fingers, two string is formed.

SPICE POWDERS

GARAM MASALA POWDER

Wherever garam masala powder appears in a recipe, choose any one of the following varieties, as desired.

VARIETY 1 : PUNGENT

400 g	coriander seeds
100 g	black pepper
20 g	cloves
20 g	black cardamoms
75 g	cummin seeds
10 g	cinnamon
15 g	bay leaves
40 g	dried ginger powder

Roast all the ingredients (except dried ginger powder) separately and then powder together fine. Sieve and store in an airtight jar.

VARIETY 2 : KASHMIRI

10 g	black cummin seeds
25 g	black cardamoms
10 g	black pepper
15 g	cinnamon
10 g	cloves
2	blades mace
3 g	nutmeg, grate

Powder together as such without roasting and bottle.

VARIETY 3 : MILD

30 g	cummin seeds
15 g	peppercorns
15	cloves
5	cardamoms

Powder finely and store in an airtight jar.

VARIETY 4 : SWEET

25 g	green cardamom
25 g	black cummin seeds
4-1"	sticks of cinnamon
12	cloves
3 g	allspice

Grind together, sieve and bottle. Best as a garnish.

VARIETY 5 : HOT

25 g	black cummin seeds
12 g	cardamom
10 g	black peppercorns
5 g	cloves
5 g	blades of mace
3 g	nutmeg, grate
3	bay leaves
2-1"	sticks of cinnamon

Sun-dry all the ingredients, powder, sieve and store in an airtight jar.

PANCH PHORAN POWDER

- Panch phoran is a powdered combination of the following 5 different aromatic spices — black mustard seeds, black cummin seeds, black onion seeds, fenugreek seeds, and fennel seeds — used to flavour legumes and vegetable dishes.

SPROUTING

Sprouts are the cheapest and the most nutritious form of available food. Sprouts are an excellent substitute for expensive fruits. Sprouting is a process of germination where many remarkable changes take place. The seed is already a treasure-house of proteins, fats, carbohydrates, vitamins and minerals.

During sprouting the dormant enzymes become active. The starch stored in the seeds are converted into sugars like glucose, fructose etc. Proteins are broken down into their constituent amino acids. Saturated fat is converted into fatty acids. The body's capacity to assimilate vitamins dramatically increases. The stored minerals are set free so that they can be absorbed easily. Side by side some important nutrients also start forming. These are mostly water soluble vitamins like vitamin B complex and vitamin C. There is a significant rise in the content of vitamin A and vitamin E. Sprouts developed in light also show increase in vitamin K.

Sprouting is very easy. Wash and rinse good variety seeds to remove any toxic chemicals. Soak in clean water in a bowl, big enough to allow space for the sprouts to grow. Cover in a manner to allow enough air to enter and set in a slightly warm place. Drain the water after 24 hours. Wash the seeds 2-3 times a day and each time drain off the water completely.

Alternatively the drained grains may be tied in a loosely woven, cotton cloth and hung in the kitchen. In winter you may need to sprinkle water over it 2-3 times a day and in summer about 5-6 times. The best place for hanging sprouts is by the side of the kitchen tap.

After a day some of the seeds might not have germinated. Discard these as they will rot and affect the healthy seeds.

The time of sprouting differs for different grains. Some like peas take 2-3 days to sprout fully after soaking in the water, while the rest like groundnut, green gram etc. may take just a day.

In summer sprouting time is much less than in winter. In winter if the grains are soaked in slightly lukewarm water, the germination time can be reduced. However, ensure that the water is not hot. It should be below tepid temperature, ie. just slightly warmer than tap water.

Do not allow the sprouts to soak in the water as they will begin to rot. The seeds should sprout at least half an inch before being used. Generally sprouting takes 2-3 days depending upon the seed temperature and humidity for eg. green gram sprouts in a short time whereas alfalfa takes longer. Water, air, heat and light control the process of sprouting. For maximum nutritive value sprouts are best eaten raw. Sprouts can safely be stored in the refrigerator.

All edible grains, seeds and legumes are suitable for sprouting.

GRAINS

- Wheat, maize, ragi, bajra, barley etc.

SEEDS

- Alfalfa, radish, fenugreek, carrot, coriander, pumpkin, musk melon, watercress etc.,

LEGUMES

- Green gram, bengal gram, moth, groundnut, peas, soyabean etc.

HOW TO SPROUT FENUGREEK

- Soak the fenugreek seeds in sufficient water overnight. Drain away the water the following day and tie the soaked seeds in a clean cloth. Hang the bundle in a warm place for a day or two keeping it moist. Ensure that the sprouts are medium in size. Longer sprouting tends to make the pickle bitter.

One particular sprout can be taken alone or several different sprouts can be mixed and eaten together. The latter way is more beneficial as they provide all the amino acids.

Sprouted grains or sprouts can compete with fruits in nutritional properties. The sprouts not only become easily digestible and nutritious but the change in their food substances and texture makes them delicious.

KING OF SPROUTS

- Alfalfa has been rightly named the "king of all sprouts" as it is rich in minerals, vitamins A, B, C, E, K and amino acids.

GROUNDNUT

- Groundnut is a very rich source of protein. It contains more protein than meat and far more than any other vegetable food except soyabean and yeast. It is best eaten after soaking overnight.

SOYABEAN

- Soyabean is the most complete protein food and can completely repalce animal protein. It is a rich source of lecithin.

SPROUT CHART

Seed type	Quantity of dried seeds in Tablespoon	Soaking time in hours	Room temp. in degrees celsius	Watering time daily	Sprouting time in days	Yield in cups*	Length of shoot in centimetres
Alfalfa	1½	6 hrs.	25°C	Once	5	3	3 cm
Whole Bengal Gram (Brown)	1½	18 hrs.	25°C	Twice	4	1	2.5 cm
Whole Bengal Gram (white)	1½	10 hrs	25°C	Thrice	3	1	2.5 cm
Fenugreek	1½	8 hrs.	25°C	Twice	3	1	1 cm
Whole Green Gram	1½	12 hrs.	25°C	Twice	1	1½	1.5 cm
Lentils	1½	12 hrs.	25°C	Twice	4	2	2.5 cm
Moth	1½	12 hrs	25°C	Twice	5	1½	3 cm
Mustard	1½	No Soaking Needed	25°C	Once	5	1½	2.5 cm
Radish	1½	-do-	25°C	Once	3	½	2.5 cm
Soyabean	1½	20 hrs.	25°C	Thrice	4	2½	3.5 cm
Sunflower	1½	4 hrs.	25°C	Once	2	½	*
Whole Wheat	1½	12 hrs.	25°C	Twice	3	½	Same length as the grain

*NOTE : 1 standard cup holds 250 ml.

Home Guides

Buying Guide

Of all foods, vegetables and fruits — the produce of fields and gardens - constitute by far the most varied and abundant source of nourishment. Buying fruits and vegetables truly is an art — which vegetables to pick up, which ones to avoid, when to buy so that they are most economical and add to taste.

Vegetables and fruits because of their great variety, offer the widest scope for pickling. There are no cast-iron rules on how to buy them. The best guides are, as always, common sense, based on familarity with each vegetable / fruit and its special characteristics — and the picklers' own imagination.

However, find below simple instructions that will be a great boon not only to picklers but to every householder.

TASTY ASH GOURD AND BITTER GOURD
- Fully matured ash gourd and bitter gourd are better tasting and have more medicinal value.

RIPENING BANANAS
- Green bananas need ripening for a few days but speckled or yellow ones are ready for eating. Refrigerate if not likely to be consumed soon.

ALL ABOUT BEANS
- Beans come in several varieties. They should look bright green, be tender, firm, crisp and should snap readily when broken, with immature seeds. A dull colour indicates dryness. A watery and mouldy condition can be spotted out easily. Beans tend to toughen in cold storage.

- Good quality beans are easy to spot. Avoid buying the bruised, patched, spotted or shrivelled ones. The pods shouldn't be flabby. Hard and tough skin is not good.

- Before cooking, you need to top and tail them as well as remove the thread that runs along the edges. Don't neglect to do this; coarse threads coming into your mouth are unpleasant. Store in a plastic bag in the refrigerator till use. Ensure that they are not wet when you put them in or they will blacken and rot very quickly.

TENDER CLUSTER BEANS
- These shoud be a tender green colour, should bend easily. Avoid the mature ones with hard skins and pronounced seeds.

SELECTING BEETROOT
- Choose beetroots with deeper colour as it is richer in vitamin A.

- Beetroots should be smooth, free from blemish, may have some soil on them and preferably medium-sized.

- The green leaves at the top do not always indicate the condition of the beets. And they are mostly removed much before we come to see them. Avoid slimy tops and the ones with deep cracks, flabby flesh, shrivelled skins or with deep scars on top.

HOW TO PICK BITTER GOURD
- Green colour in bitter gourd indicates more bitterness than in the white variety.

- While buying bitter gourd, check that its rough, scaly skin is unmarred by yellow patches. The pieces should feel firm to the touch. Avoid buying overripe, oversized ones.

CHOOSING BRINJALS
- To select brinjals with minimum seeds, buy the ones with a round scar at the tip. If the scar is oval in shape, the brinjal will have lots of seeds, which will add to its bitterness. Heaviness is also indicative of more seeds.

- When you buy brinjals, choose firm, unshrivelled, unscarred, shiny ones and don't store too long. Look carefully for any holes, for these warn you against worms, to which brinjals are very susceptible. Wrap in cling-film and refrigerate as this vegetable tends to absorb all the flavours around it.

- They should be firm, free from blemishes and of a uniform dark

---

BUYING CAULIFLOWER

- **Cauliflowers should be round, white and compact with closely knit flowerets.**

- **When buying cauliflower, remember that the quality is indicated by white, clean, heavy, firm and compact heads, with outer leaves fresh, turgid and green. Avoid plants where the flower clusters have developed enough to cause the separation of the clusters. Yellowing leaves may indicate age. Avoid spotted, speckled, or bruised heads as wasteful. Smugly or spotted appearance indicates plant lice.**

colour. Dark brown spots on the surface indicate decay.

GOOD BOTTLE GOURD
- Bottle gourd should be light green; the skin should not be very thick and hard. The gourd should be heavy.

SOLID CABBAGES
- Cabbage heads should be solid, hard and heavy for their size. Avoid heads which are badly affected by worm injury and decay, with yellow leaves or burst heads. Soft heads indicate poor quality. Yellow leaves indicate the age. Those with burst heads, should be avoided. Holes indicate worms.

BRUSSELS SPROUTS
- There are miniature cabbages, called Brussels sprouts. These should be hard, firm, and of a bright green colour. Puffy cabbages are wasteful as they tend to be watery and shrink a lot on cooking.

SELECTING CARROT
- Carrots should be firm, smooth, fresh in appearance, well-shaped, clean and of good colour.

GOOD QUALITY CELERY
- Good quality celery is medium sized with thick and solid stems, But it should be brittle. Stringy celery is not good. Rotting and insects can be easily spotted on the celery.

COCONUT SMART
- Coconuts can stay fresh and good for eating for a month or two. However ensure that they are fresh before buying them. Shake the coconut, and if you can hear the water splashing around inside, it is fresh and worth buying. The older the coconuts get, the less water there is and the more chances of them going bad soon.

HEALTHY TENDER CORN
- Corncobs should be filled with firm bright, plump, milky kernels covered with fresh green husks.

- When you buy corn, open up the husks a little to check that the kernels are plump, juicy and soft. Immature kernels lack flavour and are small in size. Look for fresh, greenish husks. Avoid the straw coloured, unhealthy looking pieces. Never buy husked ears. Store the ears in the refrigerator till use.

- Corns lose flavour very fast; the taste depends on the freshness.

TASTY CUCUMBER
- Cucumbers should be firm, bright, well-shaped and of good colour. Avoid withered cucumbers which are tough, rubbery and bitter. Puffy cucumbers should be avoided. Sunken areas are a sign of decay.

- Care should be taken while buying cucumber and ridge gourd as some of them may turn out to be bitter. Taste a small piece in each before buying.

- But cucumbers have a delicious taste when tender and a different but good taste when fully matured.

DRY FRUITS ARE NEVER DRY
- Dry fruits that you buy should be moist, sticky and never dry. If they are dry, they are stocks of the last season.

SELECTING GARLIC
- A garlic bulb has a number of cloves, each in its own skin and all enclosed in an outer skin. It should be dry, clean, with big cloves, not soft, with the outer skin intact.

- Its decay is indiacted by mould or rot, which is black in colour. Avoid the yellow and the shrivelled ones.

SWEET GRAPES
- Green grapes with a slight yellow tinge are sweetest. Purple grapes look luscious but are usually sour, so it is best to buy them after tasting.

GREENS CHOICE
- Greens should be clean, fresh, green and tender. The stalks should be tender too. Stems indicate the age. The leaves may be small or big but they should not be wilted or sagging.

- The watery ones are wasteful. Yellow leaves should be avoided. The greens attacked by worms are full of holes.

- Only in certain varieties, the stems can be used. The presence of soil does not matter though it has to be washed off thoroughly before cutting. Mustard greens should be tender, crisp, fresh and of a nice green colour.

HOT GREEN CHILLIS
- The small ones tend to be very hot, the medium sized are moderately hot and the large ones are usually not hot at all.

GOOD CAPSICUM
- Simla mirchi or capsicum should be firm, bright green and shining, without soft tops. Avoid the dull and dry ones.

TENDER LADY'S FINGER
- Lady's finger should be green and tender. Avoid the ones, with their seeds visible outside. The hexagonal lines should not be pronounced as such ones tend to be overmature. The thorny ones might not be good.

- Make sure the tail ends snap easily. Those that don't are tough.

Buying Guide

JUICY LIMES
- Limes with the smoothest skins have the most juice and flavour. Their peels are also best for making into lime pickle.
- If limes are soaked in water every day for 1 hour, then they will last longer and will not spoil easily.

BUYING LOTUS ROOTS
- When you buy lotus roots be sure you buy firm pieces which snap easily.

IDEAL MANGOES
- Select mangoes for pickles that are healthy, unripe fully developed and preferably of the tart variety.

MORE ABOUT MUSHROOMS

- **Buy mushrooms preferably only when you intend to use them. They do not keep well. If they turn black and mushy, throw away; bad mushrooms can be dangerous.**
- **As regards mushrooms the ideal specimens are plump, fair, with an unblemished complexion. Check for stems turning limp or brown; cut them off before using.**

ONIONS FOREVER
- Buy onions with pointed ends, as they are never spoilt and can be easily chopped. Their bulbs should be bright, clean, dry well-shaped and hard. Rot can attack the outer or the inner scales. This can be spotted out.
- The ones, with woody stems in centre, should be avoided. Moisture at the neck indicates decay. Onions, split in two, are wasteful.

GOOD QUALITY ORANGES
- When buying oranges do not go by the look alone. Feel each one and discard any that seem soft, light or spongy. Go in for those that feel compact, heavy and have a nice, orange colour.
- Brown spots on the skin indicate a good quality orange.

BUYING PEAS
- Bright green pods, velvety to touch, puffed up, fresh and tender-looking are the best. The flat or the dark green ones are mostly empty. Overmature pods look puffed up and yellowish in colour. Such peas have no flavour or taste. The water-soaked ones are not to be bought.
- Store in the refrigerator in their pods till use - shelled peas tend to dry out faster.
- Dried peas and beans should be washed and soaked overnight with a teaspoon of bicarbonate of soda to every 500g of pulses. Drain well and use fresh water for cooking. Salt should be added when the pulses are done. Adding it before inhibits cooking.

POTATO CARE
- Old potatoes can be stored but the new ones will perish fast. The new ones are covered with peeling skin. Soil on the potatoes do not affect their taste.
- When you buy potatoes, avoid pieces which are scarred, cut, or patched (black or green). Most of their goodness lies just under the skin, so peel as thinly as possible. If the potatoes are new, just scrub, don't scrape. Never store potatoes in polythene bags; as the resultant condensation makes them rot.
- Leathery, soft, discoloured potatoes should be avoided. The green colour on the skin indicates that the potato is sunburnt. They are usually not tasty to eat. The rotted portion can be cut away but is a waste.
- The medium-sized ones, in a uniform golden brown colour, are the best. Of course, the size we choose depends on what use we want to put the potatoes to. The misshapen ones are okay. The inner rot can't be detected on the outside.

HEALTHY SPINACH
- When you buy spinach, look for fresh green leaves that are neither wilted, black or bruised. Before using wash well in 3-4 changes of water. It is best to cut off the hard, usually muddy stems, chop the rest of the leaves and immerse in a large bowl of water to dislodge grit, insects and soil.

APPEARANCE OF TOMATO
- Tomatoes should be firm, red, not overripe, smooth and free from blemishes. The soft ones tend to be watery. Avoid those with cracks.

BETTER TURNIPS
- Turnips should be smooth and firm, with a few scars around the top. Yellow wilted tops indicate age. Coarse and large turnips which are light, for their size, might be woody, pithy, or too pungent in flavour.

GREEN VEGETABLES
- Green vegetables should be fresh, crisp and green – not yellow.

VEGETABLE PREPARATION
- All vegetables should be prepared as near to the cooking time as possible, to retain their flavour and vitamin content.

FIRM ROOTS AND TUBERS
- Roots and tubers should feel firm.

FRESH LEAFY VEGETABLES
- Green leafy vegetables tend to decay and lose their freshness if kept for long. Buy them only when required. They may sometimes be restored by trimming and placing in water.

Storage Guide

As the name indicates, this guide spells out how each and every vegetable, herb, spice, green or oil is to be stored without losing its freshness & flavour and sometimes for how long. Some of the hints listed out may be known to many but they nevertheless are useful to keep in sight.

Nothing can match garden-fresh vegetables but as these are not practically possible to procure, they may be successfully stored without much loss of flavour and nutrients. Most vegetables do not take kindly to exposure to light.

As for spices and grains, it's altogether a different story. They are generally sunned for a few days in sharp sunlight to keep them vermin-free.

VEGETABLE STORAGE

- All kinds of vegetables and fruits should be put in either plastic or paper bags and then placed in the fridge. This helps in reducing the evaporation of moisture. If stored uncovered the crispness and flavour of both vegetables and fruits will deteriorate rapidly as water will evaporate form the vegetable and fruit tissues. Outside a fridge, preserve them by putting them in polythene bags in which holes have been punched all over about 1" apart. When the bags are full, secure the top tightly with a rubber band or a piece of wire.

- Vegetables will remain fresh for a longer time in the refrigerator if you wrap them in a newspaper.

- Certain vegetables must not be stored together : few people are aware that onions tend to hasten the spoilage of potatoes. Thick-skinned root vegetables like yam, potatoes and colocasia (arbi) should be stored in a cool dry place.

- To keep vegetables fresh for a longer period in the fridge, line the bottom of the vegetable tray with a small towel and place another towel on top of the vegetables. The towels will absorb all the excess moisture.

- Alternatively keep a medium sized sponge in the vegetable tray of the refrigerator. When the sponge becomes wet, squeeze out the water and reuse.

- To keep perishable vegetables like carrot, lady's finger, french beans, brinjal, curry leaves and coriander leaves, fresh for about a week, wash, wipe-dry, wrap them in a clean cloth and refrigerate.

BLEMISHLESS BANANAS

- To keep bananas fresh and blemishless for many days, wrap them in a damp muslin cloth and store in the refrigerator.

LEAFLESS CARROTS

- When storing carrots, before refrigerating, remove the thick stalks and leaves if any. They absorb moisture from the roots, causing them to lose freshness faster.

COCONUTS GO A LONG WAY

- To keep coconut kernels fresh, put some salt water in them.
- If broken coconuts are immersed in water it will not spoil for 4 days. Change the water daily. Wash thoroughly before use.

FRESH CORIANDER & MINT

- Coriander and mint leaves stay fresh for a few days in the refrigerator if washed, dried, put into polythene bags and secured with rubber bands.

- Coriander and mint leaves can also be kept fresh for a few days without a refrigerator, if kept with their roots in water. Arrange in a jar or glass half-filled with water.

- Keep green coriander fresh, by immersing the roots in a glass of water, to which a pinch of salt is added.

- Store coriander leaves and mint leaves separately in airtight containers in the refrigerator, along with a whole raw egg, kept under or over the leaves. The heat emnating from egg dries up the moisture, keeping the leaves fresh and dry for more than a fortnight.

- Coriander leaves will stay fresh for 2 to 3 weeks, if stored inside a banana leaf in the fridge or wrapped in a thin cloth placed in a stainless steel container in the fridge.

- Mint will keep fresh longer if a dash of soda bicarbonate is added to the washing water.

CRISP CURRY LEAVES

- Store curry leaves in a stainless steel box in the refrigerator. They will stay fresh for over a month. Alternatively wrap them in a damp cloth.

- You may also fry curry leaves in oil and then store in an air-tight container. They can be used straight-away while preparing any dish.

- Select curry leaves which are dark & oily, as they have more flavour.

FRUGAL FENUGREEK
- Fenugreek leaves can be dried when they are freely and cheaply available. Store in airtight tins or jars. Soak in water for about 15 minutes, drain and use like fresh fenugreek leaves. However, dry the leaves in the shade to preserve their flavour.

FRESH GINGER
- Fresh ginger wrapped in a damp cloth and set over a water pot will remain fresh for 10 days.

PRESERVED GINGER-GARLIC PASTE
- Ginger-garlic paste can be preserved for months together in the refrigerator if you add a little vinegar.

FRESH GREENS
- To keep greens fresh, immerse the roots in water and wrap the green portion with a wet cloth.

FRESH GREEN CHILLIES
- Green chillies will stay fresh for long if kept in an airtight bottle with a dash of turmeric powder added to the chillies. Keep the bottle in a cool place.

- To prevent green chillies from losing their freshness, remove their stems before storing.

- Wrap green chillies, lime and ginger in aluminium foil and refrigerate. They will remain fresh.

PRESERVING LEAFY VEGETABLES
- To preserve leafy vegetables like spinach, coriander, etc. do not cut their roots or stems. Dry indoors and store in a covered container, not an airtight container.

CRISP LETTUCE & CUCUMBER
- To keep lettuce and cucumber fresh and crisp, place them on a stone brick floor and cover with a pudding bowl. They will remain good for several days.

FRESH LIMES
- If cut limes are stored in the salt water, they will remain fresh for a week.

ONIONS WITHOUT TEARS
- Onions should be placed in plastic bags and stored in the vegetable bin. Onions will then not cause you to shed tears when you are peeling them. Outside a fridge, onions should be stored in a loosely woven bag with good circulation of air. High temperature and humidity cause sprouting and decay of dry onions.

- Store onions in the fridge. It reduces your tears while cutting them.

PREVENT ONION SPROUTING
- To prevent onions from sprouting, singe the roots with a redhot poker.

RIPENING IN RAW PLANTAIN
- To prevent raw plantain from ripening, immerse them in water.

SPROUTING & GREENING IN POTATOES
- To prevent potatoes from sprouting when stored in bulk, keep two apples with them.

- Store potatoes in a cool, dark and dry place with good air circulation. Light causes greening. Potatoes which have turned sweet because of storage in the fridge, will improve in flavour if kept at room temperature for about a week or so.

FIRM TOMATOES
- Tomatoes which have gone soft will become firm if soaked in cold water for half an hour before use.

- To ripen tomatoes quickly, put solid tomatoes together in a brown paper bag; leave for 3-4 days where it is dark but not damp. Do not put in the hot sun, as this softens them.

DRY SALT
- Salt keeps dry in moist weather if a pinch of arrowroot powder is added to it.

- To prevent salt going damp, keep a few grains of rice in the jar.

FRIDGE - FRESH
- To prevent the mixing of smells, wrap fruits in plastic bags before being stored in the refrigerator.

LONG LASTING APPLES
- Apples keep longer if they do not touch each other. Outside the refrigerator they stay best wrapped separately in a newspaper and kept in a basket.

RIPENING IN BANANAS
- Green bananas ripen faster if placed near an overripe one! However, they will ripen fast in any warm place.

- Ripe bananas can be kept in the refrigerator to slow down further ripening. However, they should be wrapped well in paper. The cold turn the skins dark brown but the inside is fine if consumed within a few days.

RIPENING OF MANGOES
- If unripe mangoes are immersed in a tin of wheat flour, they will ripen quicker than when kept exposed.

RIPENING OF PEACHES / APRICOTS
- Peaches or apricots can be ripened quickly if kept in a cardboard or wooden box covered with layers of newspaper. Check daily for any which have ripened enough to be eaten.

- Never wash or wipe peaches before storing because removal of fuzz hastens their spoiling.

STORING STRAWBERRIES
- Strawberries may be stored in the refrigerator for a few days, provided you arrange them in a colander carefully so that they are not crushed together and the cold air circulates around them.

PRESERVING DRY FRUITS
- Preserve dry fruits like almonds and cashewnuts using cloves as the preserving agent.
- Almonds will remain fresh for years if three to four tablespoons of sugar is added to the container in which they are stored.
- Store raisins, cashewnuts and grated coconut in the fridge to keep them fresh and to avoid weevils.
- Store raisins, sultanas etc. in bottles with holes punched on the lids to prevent them from becoming mouldy.

STORING LENTILS, PULSES & GRAMS
- Clean lentils and pulses. Put out in the sun for 2 days Store in dry tins. Buy in small quantities to avoid vermin setting in.
- Red gram, when stored with dried coconut halves, lasts longer and remains free from spoilage.

KEEPING SPICE POWDERS FRESH
- To keep spice powders, rice, flour, bengal gram powder fresh for months, store in dry polythene bags in the fridge.

KEEPING ASAFOETIDA SOFT
- If two chillies are placed along with raw asafoetida, they will continue to remain soft. Change the chillies every week.

STORING CHILLI POWDER
- To prevent chilli powder from getting rancid, smear a little groundnut oil on the inside of the jar before storing the chilli powder.

SALTED TAMARIND
- To preserve tamarind, add salt to it, mix well and store in an air-tight bottle.

REFINING COOKING OILS
- To refine filtered cooking oil or groundnut oil at home, add a pinch of alum and 10g cooking soda to a 5kg oil tin. In a couple of days you will see a black sediment settled at the bottom.
- To keep sesame oil fresh for a few months without being spoilt, add a lump of jaggery to the oil.

SAFE & CLEAN HONEY
- In order to keep honey both safe and clean, store it in a bottle and add two or three cloves to it.

Nutrient Saver Guide

There is nothing nutritionally wrong with a vegetarian diet. Infact, the healthy diet recommended by nutritionists is the kind of diet vegetarians already eat - containing less fat, more fruit, more vegetables and more dietary fibre.

Although basically a healthy diet, it would be worth remembering that much loss takes place during the various stages of vegetable preparation, from washing to peeling, from soaking to cutting and boiling.

An useful canon to be observed in vegetable preparation is to always wash vegetables before peeling and cutting. As it is, there is enormous time gap between delivery from the grower to the buyer and much more from the buyer to the table. It is therefore appropriate that great care is taken to keep the nutrient loss at a minimum, wherever possible.

THROUGH PEELING & CUTTING

- As most of the vitamins and minerals of green vegetables lie generally close to the skin, peel vegetables thinly to avoid loss of vitamins.
- Cut vegetables should be used immediately as exposure destroys vitamin C. Therefore, wrap tightly on cutting.

THROUGH SALTING

- Add salt to vegetables at the end of cooking to prevent draining of nutrients from the vegetables by the process of reverse osmosis.

THROUGH WASHING & SOAKING

- To prevent loss of nutrients all vegetables should be washed before they are cut.

- To preserve the natural flavour and texture of green vegetables, ensure that they are washed only just before cooking, preferably under running water as soaking tends to leech away the water-soluble vitamins.

- Use shallow well-salted water to retain and preserve nutrients, because there is a heavy loss of mineral salts with deep water.

> - In making vegetables go cold, instead of letting them do so by running cold water through them or by plunging them straight into deep cold water for 2 or 3 minutes – or long enough to cool them – after they have been blanched (or boiled) and drained. This abruptly halts their cooking, consequently they dont lose any of their colour, flavour, texture or nutrients, as they do if just left around simply to cool.

- Do not soak vegetables too long in buttermilk or water as it drains away the nutrients.

- Vegetables that are to be eaten raw should be immersed in an equal quantity of vinegar and water for quarter of an hour. This will help kill any bacteria they might contain.

- Pre-soak the lentils, pulses and rice, not only to reduce cooking time, but also bring out the flavour and preserve the nutrients.

THROUGH COOKING

- If you choose vegetables of the same size or cut them into equal-sized pieces they will cook quickly, and will be ready at the same time. The fewer outer green leaves removed the better because that's where most of the goodness is.

- Put vegetables into fast boiling water over maximum heat so that the water can quickly come back to the boil– when cooking time starts. Only then should you lower the heat, allowing a vegetable to boil slowly for its alloted time. The shorter the cooking time, the greater the food value and the better the flavour, colour and texture.

- Cook vegetables as far as possible in their skins to preserve their vitamin content.

- Prolonged cooking of vegetables by any method also destroys a number of vitamins.

- Vegetables keep their goodness and cook best in a covered pan large enough for the vegetable to be in one layer, not piled up in a small pan.

> - Do not throw away the water used for cooking vegetables as it contains valuable minerals, salts and vitamins. Preferably cook in just enough water.

- Vegetable should always be cooked until barely tender, because then they have a better appearance, flavour and retain more food value than when cooked longer.

- Whenever you cook any vegetable which has to be mashed after cooking, cut it into big pieces as it can then be mashed well. It will also cook faster and lesser nutrients are lost.

- A few drops of coconut oil added to the water when boiling gram, dried peas or vegetables, saves time and preserves vitamins.

- Green leafy vegetables should be cooked without much stirring as the atmospheric oxygen will enter the vegetables and destroy the vitamins.

- Boil peas in their pods and then shell them to retain all their food value. However, wash the pods well before boiling.

Vegetable are 'protective foods', protecting the body from illness, so of course they're best when eaten fresh and raw, nothing lost by cooking. Next best is to prepare and cook them perfectly. Most of us know the smell and flavour of a freshly picked tomato or grape, but many people don't seem to realize that the flavour of a freshly picked green vegetable is no less rewarding, although there's no glorious smell to advertise it.

You can't see vitamins disappearing any more than you can see an egg going bad, but this is just what begins to happen when you pick or dig up a vegetable, especially greens. The longer they are stored, the greater the loss, and the sooner they are prepared before a meal and the more they are cut up, the faster that loss accelerates.

Microwave Oven Guide

Cooking vegetables and fruits in Microwave Ovens is ideal because microwave cooking helps retain the nutrients, flavour, colour and texture of the fruit or vegetable. On account of its speed in cooking and less loss of flavour & nutrients, it is an ideal alternative cooking method.

Exact timing of any recipe depends on many variables : the size and shape of the food to be cooked; the temperature; the amount of fat and sugar in it; and how moist it is. Different ovens, with slightly different power outputs, will also affect the length of cooking time. When in doubt, always undercook, then allow standing time before cooking to see if the dish is ready. If it is not, place it back into the oven.

If food comes straight from the fridge into the microwave, it's going to take a minute or two longer to cook than food at room temperature : the exact time will depend on the quantity of food.

Find below instructions on how to cook in a microwave oven, what dishes to use and their shape, the sizes of food and the placement of food in the oven.

GENERAL FEATURES

- Cooking vegetables in microwave is ideal because microwave cooking retains the nutrients, flavour, colour and texture of fruits and vegetables.

- Because microwaves only penetrate about 5 cms into the food, for even cooking it is necessary either to stir foods or turn foods which cannot be stirred. Alternatively it may be raised on a rack.

- Foods will cook faster in the microwave oven if they are cut into smaller pieces.

- Microwaves can penetrate light, porous food more easily than dense, heavy, fibrous food. Hence **pumpkin** cooks faster in microwave than carrot or potato.

- By elevating the cooking dish off the floor of the oven and keeping the food moving through the pattern of microwaves, the turntable ensures even cooking, helping to eliminate cold spots.

- Foods cook fastest in microwave-safe plastic containers as opposed to glass containers.

- Microwave-safe plastic spoons can be left in the sauce during cooking for easy stirring.

- You can stir-fry in the microwave in a browning dish or frying skillet using less oil than in a conventional stove.

COOKING INSTRUCTIONS

- Evaporate excess moisture from a hot blanched vegetable by returning it to the empty pan, and tossing over moderate heat for a minute or two uncovered. If you don't do this, it will splutter and make the fat watery. Otherwise refresh the vegetables, after blanching, if for some reason you are not going to saute it straightaway. If watery, like courgettes cover in a colander with a weighted plate until required.

> **● Toast almonds by placing in a shallow dish and microwaving on HIGH : 50g will take 4 minutes. Stir several times until light brown.**

- Peel and place **apples** in the microwave and heat on HIGH for 3 minutes, then stand for 5 minutes covered. Cool and remove the skin.

- Soak **artichokes** in water for 15 minutes to soften. Remove the coarse, outer leaves, trim the remaining leaves and the base. Rinse, drain and apply lime juice. Wrap in an oven bag, secure and microwave each artichoke for 7 minutes on HIGH. Allow to stand for 5 more minutes.

- Trim **asparagus** and peel the base of the stalks. Place on a plate with tips facing the centre. Sprinkle a little water, cover with cling film and cook on HIGH for 8 minutes. Stand for 3 minutes. Peel the thicker stalks of asparagus with a potato peeler to ensure proper cooking.

- Cook a firm **banana** in its skin on high for 1 minute. Stand for 2 minutes.

- To cook fresh **broad beans** place in a small covered dish with 2 tablespoons of water. Cook on HIGH : 250g will take 8 minutes.

- Certain types of beans, e.g. **red kidney beans (rajma)**, must be boiled for 10 minutes to destroy the toxins.

- To cook 500g **beetroot**, prick well with a fork on all sides and place in a plastic bag. Cook on HIGH for 12 minutes. Rearrange halfway through. Stand for 5 minutes.

- To cook **brinjal** slice, rinse and put in an oven bag and secure. Cook on HIGH for 8 minutes.

- To cook 500g **brussels sprouts**, trim, rinse and make a slit in each base. Place in an oven bag, secure and cook on HIGH for 8 minutes. Stand for 3 minutes.

> - The colder the food is when you put it in the microwave oven, the longer it will take to cook. Always allow for this in timing.

- To cook 500g **cabbage**, shred, rinse and put in a plastic freezer bag. Microwave on HIGH for 6 minutes. Stand for 4 minutes.

- To cook **capsicum**, chop, rinse, place in an oven bag and secure. Cook on HIGH : 2 capsicums will take 6 minutes.

- To cook 500g **carrot**, clean, chop, put in a oven bag and secure. Cook on HIGH for 8 minutes and stand for 3 minutes. Cook **baby carrots** unpeeled to retain all its goodness and flavour.

- To cook 500g **cauliflower**, separate into florets, rinse, place in an oven bag and secure. Cook on HIGH for 10 minutes and stand for 3 minutes.

- Cook **cauliflower, broccoli** and **asparagus** with the stems placed towards the outside of the dish.

- To cook **celery** slice thinly, place in a small covered dish and cook on HIGH for 6 minutes per 250g. Stand for 3 minutes.

- Cook **cereals** in a large dish as they tend to boil over. To distribute the heat evenly stir several time during cooking. During standing time leave the cereals covered.

- To eliminate fat, enhance aroma and colour microwave 15g of **chilli powder** in a small covered glass container on HIGH for 1½ minutes, shaking several times during cooking.

- Warm **citrus fruits** in the microwave for 30 seconds on HIGH before squeezing to obtain more juice.

- To toast **coconut**, place 100g in a microwave - safe plate and cook on HIGH for 6 minutes. Stir several times during cooking to ensure that it does not burn.

- To cook whole **courgettes**, prick with a fork, add 2 tablespoons of water, cover and cook on HIGH for 8 minutes per 500g. Stir halfway through the cooking time.

- To peel **garlic** cloves, place on a rack and heat for 30 seconds per clove on HIGH. The garlic will then slip out of the skin.

- Trim, cut and rinse **kohlrabi**, place in an oven bag and secure. Cook on HIGH for 8 minutes per 250g and stand for 3 minutes.

- To cook a small **marrow**, rinse, prick and place in an oven bag. Secure and cook on HIGH for 7 minutes per 500g.

- To cook fresh **mushrooms**, wash, slice, place in an oven bag and secure. Cook on HIGH for 5 minutes per 250g.

- To peel **onions** easily, place in a covered container and heat on HIGH for 2 minutes.

- To cook whole **onions**, peel, place in an oven bag and secure. Cook on HIGH : 3 onions will take 5 minutes, stand for 3 minutes.

- To peel **peaches**, prick the skin with a fork, place on a microwave rack and heat for 40 seconds per peach (the timing will vary with the ripeness, size and firmness of the fruit). Thereafter use a knife to remove the skin.

- To speed up the cooking of **dried peas** and **other pulses**, instead of soaking in water overnight, cover with cold water and bring to the boil on HIGH for 10 minutes, then simmer on DEFROST for 30 minutes.

- To cook **fresh peas**, shell, rinse, put in an oven bag and secure. Cook on HIGH : 500g will take 9 minutes.

- To peel **plums** easily heat on HIGH for 1 minute and then allow to stand for 2 minutes.

> - Always cook potatoes in their jackets after piercing the skin to prevent them from bursting. Arrange around the rim of the turntable and cook on HIGH : 1 medium potato will take 4 minutes.
>
> - To cook peeled potatoes, wash, cut, put in an oven bag and cook on HIGH : 500g will take 10 minutes.

- **Sesame seeds** and **poppy seeds** can be toasted easily in the microwave oven. Cook on HIGH on a plate, without butter or oil, but keep turning them about.

- Heat **pumpkin** in the microwave on HIGH for 2 minutes. It softens and makes it easier to chop.

- To cook **pumpkin**, peel, chop, place in an oven bag and secure. Cook on HIGH : 500g will take 9 minutes.

- To make **old spices** fresh place them in the microwave and heat for 45 seconds on HIGH before using.

- Sweetcorn tastes well if cooked on the cob in the microwave. Wrap individually in cling film. If the leaves are present, cook them as they are. Cook on HIGH : 1 cob will take 4 minutes.

- When cooking sweetcorn in its leaves, you can pull them back before cooking and rub the corn with garlic or herbs.

- To cook fresh **spinach**, chop, rinse and put in an oven bag. Cook on HIGH : 250g will take 4 minutes.

- Scrub, pierce the skin of **sweet potato** and place around the turntable on a piece of kitchen paper. Sweet potatoes should be uniform in size and shape for even cooking. Microwave on HIGH : 500g will take 10 minutes. Turn sweet potatoes over halfway through cooking.

- To peel a **tomato**, prick the skin lightly with a fork, place on a roasting rack and heat for 45 seconds on HIGH. Stand for 5 minutes, then peel.

- Place whole **tomatoes** on a small plate, prick and cook uncovered on HIGH : 1 tomato will take 2 minutes.

- To cook **turnip**, peel, chop, place in an oven bag and secure. Cook on HIGH : 500g will take 9 minutes.

DISHES

- Shapes of dishes are important in the microwave : choose dishes with rounded corners; ring moulds are the best shape for microwave penetration; a large, flat and shallow dish will cook the same amount of food faster than a deep dish.

- Shapes of food are equally important: aim for uniform pieces of food. Cut vegetables to uniform size or you will find some pieces are cooked while others are not. If the food can't be made into an even shape, put the thick part towards the edge of the turntable and shield the thinner end with foil if necessary.

SPECIAL FEATURES

- For tender, even cooking cut vegetables into small uniform pieces.

- Always undercook vegetables so that they are still crisp and crunchy at the end of the standing time. This is because vegetables continue to cook during standing time also.

- Stir or shake vegetables at least once during cooking.

- Since only very small amounts of water are used to cook vegetables in a microwave oven, it is not necessary to drain them before serving. Water-soluble vitamins and minerals are retained and quick cooking means less of the other nutrients are lost.

- Cook vegetables in a dish that fits them exactly. Half-filled dishes take longer to cook.

- Overcooked vegetables can be pureed and used in soups.

- Garden-fresh vegetables cook more quickly than those bought at the supermarket because of their slightly higher water content.

- To steam vegetables, cover them with a lid or microwave-safe cling film and cook on HIGH for the required time.

- Small quantities of vegetables can be blanched in the microwave before freezing. Place the vegetable in a dish with 600ml water, cover and heat on HIGH for one-third of the usual cooking time for the vegetable. After cooking, drain and immerse the vegetables in ice-cold water to cool them quickly, then package in the usual way for freezing.

- While cooking soft-fibred vegetables like mushrooms add a little water, butter or stock.

- Slice thinly and use more water while cooking beans and carrots. Being densely fibred they can become tough during cooking.

- Frozen vegetables can be cooked straight from the freezer, on HIGH without defrosting and without addition of water.

- Always prick the skins of vegetables such as **tomatoes** and **potatoes**, otherwise they may burst.

- Some vegetables like **cabbage, brussels sprouts** and **broccoli** can only be cooked once. They get soggy if reheated.

- If cooking vegetables covered with a sauce made with cream or sour cream, cook on MEDIUM-LOW or MEDIUM to prevent curdling.

Classique

*pickles are
the traditional
favourites,
commonly
prepared in
every Indian home
whenever quality
vegetables and fruits
are plentifully
and
cheaply available.*

Recipes : Classique

001. Spiced mango : hot
002. Spiced lime : hot
003. Spiced kalakkai : hot
004. Pounded gooseberry : hot
005. Sour mango ginger – garlic : hot
006. Kidarangai : hot
007. Drumstick pith : hot
008. Elephant yam in tamarind sauce : hot
009. Sweet & sour garlic : hot
010. Spicy ginger in tamarind sauce : hot
011. Gonkura – green chilli : instant
012. Spiced brinjal in tamarind sauce : hot
013. Fried star gooseberry : instant
014. Sweet & sour green chilli : hot
015. Green pepper in lime juice : watery
016. Sweet & sour cauliflower : instant
017. Sour colocasia : hot
018. Mango avakkai – garlic (old method) : hot
019. Mango avakkai – garlic (new method) : hot
020. Green coriander – green chilli : hot
021. Spicy grated mango : instant
022. Mango avakkai (old method) : hot
023. Mango ginger – green spices : salty
024. Curry leaf in tamarind sauce : hot
025. Mint – dried red chilli - tamarind : hot
026. Spiced carrot – peas in lime juice : watery
027. Small red onion in tamarind sauce : hot
028. Spring onion – green chilli : hot
029. Onion – green spices : hot
030. Sweet & sour orange peel : hot
031. Tomato – tamarind : hot
032. Plantain flower : hot
033. Spiced green tamarind : tender
034. Mahani in buttermilk : watery

Before venturing into pickling, it will be worthwhile to get acquainted with the introductory part of the book which carries detailed information on pickling. These are spelt out as **Kitchen Fundamentals.**

A reading of the **Home Guides** is recommended for successful pickling. They contain valuable information on buying, storing, nutrient saving and microwave oven cooking. The **Appendix & Glossary** will clear any further doubts.

Kitchen Spices are indispensible to pickling. The use of spices, their effectiveness and impact are spelt out in three parts in the ensuing pages.

001 Spiced Mango : Hot

1 kg	cut mango, size into small pieces
50 g	chilli powder
20 g	mustard seeds, sun-dry & powder
5 g	turmeric powder
5 g	fenugreek seeds &
5 g	asafoetida, roast both in oil & powder
120 g	salt
500 ml	oil

1. Combine the spice powders and salt with a little oil to a paste.
2. Stir in the mango pieces and set aside for 2 days.
3. Pour over the reserved oil to cover the pickle.
4. The pickle is ready for use after 2 weeks. It lasts for 1 year.

002 Spiced Lime : Hot

1 kg	lime, cut into small pieces & seed
100 g	chilli powder
10 g	asafoetida &
5 g	fenugreek seeds, roast both in oil & powder
5 g	turmeric powder
20 g	jaggery, grate
20 g	mustard seeds : for seasoning
200 g	salt
400 ml	oil

1. Marinate the lime pieces in the salt for 7 days till it reaches a honeyed consistency.
2. Sprinkle the spice powders and jaggery over the lime pieces.
3. Heat the oil, add mustard seeds and allow to crackle.
4. Pour the seasoning over the lime pieces and stir thoroughly.
5. The pickle is ready for use. It lasts for 1 year.

003 Spiced Kalakkai : Hot

500 g	kalakkai, split vertically without severing & seed
5 g	mustard seeds : for seasoning
60 g	chilli powder;
5 g	turmeric powder;
5 g	asafoetida, roast in oil & powder;
2 g	fenugreek seeds, roast in oil & powder;
15 g	jaggery, grate &
110 g	salt, combine all evenly
125 ml	oil

> Kalakkai is a very sour berry and hence requires more chilli powder and jaggery than usual. Else the pickle will be very sour. Remove the seeds and immediately salt to prevent discolouration.

1. Heat the oil, add mustard seeds and allow to crackle.
2. Add in the kalakkai pieces, jaggery and fry for a few minutes till partly tender.
3. Blend in the spice mixture and remove.
4. The pickle is ready for use. It lasts for 2 months. Sun occasionally.

004 Pounded Gooseberry : Hot

500 g	gooseberry, pound coarsely & seed
50 g	chilli powder
25 g	jaggery, grate
5 g	turmeric powder
5 g	asafoetida, roast in oil & powder
5 g	mustard seeds : for seasoning
110 g	salt
200 ml	oil

1. Combine the jaggery, salt and turmeric powder with the pounded gooseberry in a jar. Cover and set aside for 7 days.
2. Heat a little oil, add mustard seeds and allow to crackle.
3. Add in the pounded gooseberry and stir-fry for a few minutes.
4. Stir in the chilli, asafoetida powders, the remaining oil and heat until dry.
5. The pickle is now ready for use. It lasts for 3 months. Sun occasionally.

Salting the pickle

Salting is very crucial to pickling. In general when sour vegetables or fruits are pickled, the proportion of salt to the pickled vegetable will be in the ratio of 1:5. If the pickled vegetable is very sour, it may even be increased to 1:4.

005 Sour Mango Ginger – Garlic : Hot

500 g	peeled mango ginger, chop
100 g	peeled garlic, chop
175 g	cleaned tamarind, obtain thick extract using water
75 g	jaggery, grate
50 g	chilli powder
5 g	turmeric powder
5 g	fenugreek seeds &
5 g	asafoetida, roast both in oil & powder
5 g	mustard seeds : for seasoning
90 g	salt
250 ml	oil

1. Heat a little oil, add mustard seeds and allow to crackle.
2. Add in the chopped mango ginger, garlic and fry for a few minutes. Set aside.
3. In the same pan heat some more oil, stir in the tamarind extract, jaggery, turmeric powder, salt and bring to the boil.
4. Allow to thicken over a high flame.
5. Lower the heat, add in the fried ingredients, chilli, fenugreek and asafoetida powders.
6. Continue cooking for about 30 minutes, adding the remaining oil little by little.
7. Remove when the mixture becomes jam-like and the oil separates.
8. The pickle is ready for use. It lasts for 2 months.

006 Kidarangai : Hot

1 kg	kidarangai, cut into small pieces & seed
125 g	chilli powder
10 g	turmeric powder
10 g	fenugreek seeds &
10 g	asafoetida, roast both in oil & powder
30 g	jaggery, grate
30 g	mustard seeds : for seasoning
250 g	salt
400 ml	oil

1. Marinate the kidarangai pieces in the salt for 7 days till it reaches a honeyed consistency.
2. Sprinkle the spice powders and jaggery over the kidarangai.
3. Heat the oil, add mustard seeds and allow to crackle.
4. Pour the seasoning over the kidarangai and stir thoroughly.
5. The pickle is ready for use. It lasts for 1 year.

007 Drumstick Pith : Hot

500 g	cooked drumstick inner pith,
5 g	salt : for boiling drumsticks
125 g	cleaned tamarind, obtain thick extract using water
25 g	jaggery, grate
5 g	mustard seeds : for seasoning
50 g	chilli powder
5 g	turmeric powder
3 g	fenugreek seeds &
3 g	asafoetida, roast both in oil & powder
50 g	salt : for pickle
250 ml	oil

1. Cut the drumsticks into 4" lengths. Cook till partly tender in sufficient water to which a teaspoon (5g) salt has been added.
2. Cool and remove the inner pith of the drumsticks, fry in a little oil and set aside.
3. In the same pan heat some more oil, add mustard seeds and allow to crackle.
4. Follow with the tamarind extract, jaggery, salt and bring to the boil. Allow to thicken over a high flame.
5. Lower the heat, stir in the chilli, turmeric, fenugreek, asafoetida powders and the fried drumstick pith.
6. Continue cooking for about 30 minutes, adding the remaining oil little by little.
7. Remove when the mixture becomes jam-like and the oil seperates.
8. The pickle is ready for use. It lasts for 2 months.

- To recognise a tender drumstick, twist with both the hands. If soft to the touch and flexible they are tender. Very thin drumsticks will hardly contain any flesh and are therefore uneconomical.
- Drumstick pickles should generally be prepared while they are in season as sometimes they are slightly bitter & less fleshy. Use the seeds also when pickling.
- Take care not to overcook the drumsticks as the pickle tends to get mushy. Also gently & carefully remove the pith without the stringy portions atttached to the skin.

008 Elephant Yam in Tamarind Sauce : Hot

500 g	chopped elephant yam, peel & soak in thin tamarind water
60 g	cleaned tamarind, obtain thin extract using water
70 g	jaggery, grate
60 g	dried red chillies &
5 g	asafoetida, roast both in oil & powder
5 g	turmeric powder
5 g	mustard seeds : for seasoning
75 g	salt
250 ml	oil

Note : Choose the pink coloured elephant yam — and not the cream variety — as these cause less irritation.

1. Cook the chopped yam in the thin tamarind water, to which a teaspoon (5g) salt has been added, till partly tender.
2. Deep-fry the cooked yam in a little oil and allow to cool.
3. Heat some more oil, add mustard seeds and allow to crackle.
4. Stir in the tamarind extract, jaggery, turmeric powder and the salt.
5. Bring to the boil and allow to thicken over a high flame.
6. Lower the heat, add in the fried yam, chilli, asafoetida powders and the remaining oil.
7. Continue cooking for about 30 minutes until the mixture becomes jam-like and the oil separates.
8. The pickle is ready for use. It lasts for 2 months.

009 Sweet & Sour Garlic : Hot

500 g	peeled garlic
10 g	mustard seeds : for seasoning
125 g	cleaned tamarind, obtain thick extract using water
100 g	jaggery, grate
60 g	chilli powder
5 g	turmeric powder
3 g	asafoetida, roast in oil & powder
2 g	fenugreek seeds, roast in oil & pound
100 g	salt
200 ml	oil

1. Stir-fry the garlic in a little oil till almost tender. Set aside.
2. In the same pan heat some more oil, add mustard seeds and allow to crackle.
3. Stir in the tamarind extract, jaggery, salt and bring to the boil. Allow to thicken over a high flame.
4. Lower the heat, stir in the chilli, turmeric, fenugreek, asafoetida powders and the fried garlic.
5. Continue cooking for about 30 minutes, adding the remaining oil little by little.
6. Remove when the mixture becomes jam-like and the oil separates.
7. The pickle is ready for use. It lasts for 2 months.

010 Spicy Ginger in Tamarind Sauce : Hot

500 g	fresh ginger, scrape, chop & grind
15 g	mustard seeds : for seasoning
250 g	cleaned tamarind, obtain thick extract using water
75 g	jaggery, grate
70 g	chilli powder
15 g	asafoetida &
5 g	fenugreek seeds, roast both in oil & powder
5 g	turmeric powder
140 g	salt
250 ml	oil

1. Stir-fry the ginger paste in a little oil and set aside.
2. In the same pan heat some more oil, add mustard seeds and allow to crackle.
3. Follow with the tamarind extract, jaggery, salt and bring to the boil. Allow to thicken over a high flame.
4. Lower the heat, stir in the chilli, turmeric, fenugreek, asafoetida powders and the fried ginger.
5. Continue cooking for about 30 minutes, adding the remaining oil, little by little.
6. Remove when the mixture becomes jam-like and the oil separates.
7. The pickle is ready for use. It lasts for 2 months.

011 Gonkura – Green Chilli : Instant

500 g	tender gonkura, wash, air-dry & chop
60 g	green chillies, chop
15 g	cleaned tamarind, dry-roast
40 g	jaggery, grate
25 g	chilli powder
25 g	mustard seeds &
12 g	cummin seeds, sun-dry both & powder
12 g	turmeric powder
12 g	fenugreek seeds &
12 g	asafoetida, roast both in oil & powder
115 g	salt
250 ml	oil

1. Stir-fry the chopped gonkura, the chopped green chillies separately in a little oil and set aside.
2. Grind all the ingredients to a coarse paste.
3. In the same pan, heat the remaining oil and stir-fry the ground mixture for about 20 minutes.
4. Remove when the mixture leaves the sides of the pan.
5. The pickle is ready for use. It lasts for 2 months and is best refrigerated.

012 Spiced Brinjal in Tamarind Sauce : Hot

500 g	tender brinjal, size into small pieces
40 g	green chillies, chop fine
25 g	peeled garlic, chop
100 g	cleaned tamarind, obtain thick extract using water
100 g	jaggery, grate
25 g	chilli powder
10 g	turmeric powder
10 g	cummin seeds, dry roast & powder
20 g	mustard seeds;
20 g	split husked black gram;
20 g	split husked bengal gram &
a few	sprigs curry leaves : all for seasoning
50 g	salt
200 ml	oil

1. Heat a little oil, add mustard seeds and allow to crackle.
2. Add in the black gram, bengal gram and fry till golden brown.
3. Stir in the curry leaves, cut brinjal, green chillies, garlic, stir-fry over low heat till tender and set aside.
4. In the same pan heat some more oil, add the tamarind extract, jaggery, turmeric powder, salt and bring to the boil. Allow to thicken over a high flame.
5. Lower the heat, stir in the fried ingredients, chilli and cummin powders.
6. Continue cooking for about 30 minutes, adding the remaining oil, little by little.
7. Remove when the mixture becomes jam-like and the oil separates.
8. The pickle is ready for use. It lasts for 2 months.

013 Fried Star Gooseberry : Instant

125 g	star gooseberry, keep whole
3 g	mustard seeds : for seasoning
10 g	chilli powder;
2 g	turmeric powder &
2 g	asafoetida, roast in oil & powder, combine all evenly
8 g	jaggery, grate
25 g	salt
40 ml	oil

1. Heat the oil, add mustard seeds and allow to crackle.
2. Add in the whole gooseberry and stir-fry till partly tender.
3. Stir in the spice mixture, jaggery, salt and fry for a few more minutes.
4. Remove when the gooseberries are fully cooked and the mixture is well blended.
5. The pickle is ready for use. It keeps for 2 weeks.

> **Note :** **Star gooseberry** requires at least 200 grams salt for every kilogram of it, as it is very sour. Because of its high water content, it does not last too long. Hence prepare in smaller quantities.

014 Sweet & Sour Green Chilli : Hot

500 g	green chillies, wash, wipe & grind coarsely
25 g	mustard seeds : for seasoning
250 g	cleaned tamarind, obtain thick extract using water
125 g	jaggery, grate
25 g	chilli powder
5 g	turmeric powder
5 g	asafoetida &
2 g	fenugreek seeds, roast both in oil & powder
200 g	salt
250 ml	oil

1. Heat a little oil, add mustard seeds and allow to crackle.
2. Add in the green chillies and fry for 2 minutes.
3. Follow with the tamarind extract, jaggery, salt and bring to the boil. Allow to thicken over a high flame.
4. Lower the heat, stir in the chilli, turmeric, fenugreek and asafoetida powders.
5. Continue cooking for about 30 minutes, adding the remaining oil, little by little.
6. Remove when the mixture becomes jam-like and the oil separates.
7. The pickle is ready for use. It lasts for 2 months.

015 Green pepper in Lime Juice : Watery

1 kg	green pepper with string, cut into 1" lengths
400 g	salt
400 ml	lime juice
water	sufficient to cover

1. Boil the salt and water till crystals appear at the edge of the pan. Cool and strain.
2. Stir in the lime juice and green pepper into the strained salt water.
3. The pickle is ready for use after 1 week. It lasts for 1 year.

016 Sweet & Sour Cauliflower : Instant

500 g	cauliflower florets
10 g	salt : for marinating
10 g	mustard seeds : for seasoning
80 g	cleaned tamarind, obtain thick extract using water
25 g	jaggery, grate
30 g	chilli powder
10 g	turmeric powder
5 g	fenugreek seeds &
5 g	asafoetida, roast both in oil & powder
70 g	salt : for pickle
250 ml	oil

> Cauliflower may be used raw after rinsing in warm salt water. Blanching, i.e. soaking in hot water for 2 minutes – is permitted as crunchiness is very vital to this pickle. It will be useful to observe this rule in all mixed vegetable pickling.

1. Soak the cauliflower florets for an hour in warm water (sufficient to cover) to which two teaspoons (10g) salt has been added. Rinse well, drain and air-dry.
2. Heat a little oil, add mustard seeds and allow to crackle.
3. Add in the dried florets, stir-fry for a few minutes and set aside.
4. In the same pan heat some more oil, stir in the tamarind extract, jaggery and bring to the boil.
5. Add in the chilli, turmeric, fenugreek, asafoetida powders, salt and allow to thicken over a high flame.
6. Stir in the dried florets and continue cooking for about 30 minutes.
7. Remove when the mixture becomes jam-like and the oil separates.
8. The pickle is ready for use. It lasts for 2 months.

017 Sour Colocasia : Hot

500 g	colocasia, parboil, peel & chop
10 g	coriander seeds &
50 g	green coriander, wash, air-dry & chop, grind both to a paste
a few	sprigs curry leaves : both for seasoning
10 g	mustard seeds &
85 g	cleaned tamarind, obtain thick extract using water
85 g	jaggery, grate
60 g	chilli powder
10 g	turmeric powder
85 g	salt
375 ml	oil

1. Steam the colocasia till partly tender after adding a teaspoon (5g) salt. Allow to cool, peel and chop.
2. Deep-fry the chopped colocasia in a little oil and set aside.
3. Heat a little oil, add mustard seeds and allow to crackle.
4. Add in the curry leaves and allow to turn crisp.
5. Stir in the tamarind extract, jaggery, turmeric powder, the remaining salt and bring to the boil. Allow to thicken over a high flame.
6. Lower the heat, add in the fried colocasia, the spice paste, chilli powder and the remaining oil little by little.
7. Continue cooking for about 30 minutes until the mixture becomes jam-like and the oil separates.
8. The pickle is ready for use. It lasts for 2 months.

018 Mango Avakkai – Garlic : Hot

Old Method

1kg	mango pieces, cut with shell into 8 pieces each & seed
150g	chilli powder
100g	peeled garlic
150g	mustard seeds, sun-dry & powder
10g	fenugreek seeds, roast in oil & powder
200g	salt
600ml	raw gingelly oil

1. Combine the spice powders (except garlic) with the salt evenly.
2. Dip the mango pieces in the oil and squeeze out the excess oil.
3. Thereafter roll the mango pieces in the spice mixture and arrange in a jar.
4. Sprinkle a little spice mixture, add in a few garlic cloves and pour a little oil over the mangoes.
5. Repeat this process until all the mango pieces are layered.
6. Sprinkle any left over spice mixture over the pickle and set aside for 3 days. Do not stir.
7. On the 4th day, stir well and pour over the reserved oil to cover the pickle. Mix thoroughly.
8. The pickle is ready for use after 2 weeks. It lasts for 1 year.

Avakkai Mango

Choose medium sour raw mangoes which are hard, dark green with smooth skins, free from blemishes. They should be slightly fibrous to retain a crunchy texture.

While cutting the mango, remove the seed and cut with the shell. Discard the thin inner sheath sticking to the shell, wipe with a thin cloth and air-dry indoors. It is important that the shell is retained. Though the pickle therefore consumes more oil and chilly powder, it helps to keep the pickle crisp and crunchy for upto a year. Traditionally gingelly oil is preferred, although some use mustard oil.

019 New Method

6	measures mango pieces, cut with shell into 12 pieces each & seed
1	measure salt
1	measure chilli powder
1/8th	measure powdered raw mustard seeds
1/16th	measure powdered roasted fenugreek seeds
100 g	peeled garlic
5 g	fenugreek seeds, keep whole
300 ml	raw gingelly oil

1. Measure the mango pieces in any measure of your choice. For every 6 measures of mango add 1 measure of chilli powder, 1 measure of salt, 1/8th measure of mustard powder, 1/16th measure of fenugreek powder and 1 tsp of fenugreek seeds.
2. Combine the spice powders with the salt.
3. Sprinkle a layer of the spice mixture in a jar.
4. Dip the mango pieces in the oil and squeeze out the excess oil.
5. Thereafter roll the mango pieces in the spice mixture and arrange in the jar.
6. Sprinkle over a little spice mixture, fenugreek seeds, peeled garlic and pour over a little oil.
7. Repeat this process till all the mango pieces are layered. Stir in the remaining spice mixture and garlic.
8. Cover the pickle and set aside for 3 days. On the 4th day stir well and pour over the remaining oil to cover the pickle. Stir well.
9. The pickle is ready for use after 2 weeks. It lasts for 1 year.

020 Green Coriander – Green Chilli : Hot

500 g	green coriander, wash, air-dry & grind fine
100 g	green chillies, coarsely grind
20 g	mustard seeds : for seasoning
200 g	cleaned tamarind, obtain thick extract using water
150 g	jaggery, grate
50 g	chilli powder
10 g	turmeric powder
5 g	asafoetida &
5 g	fenugreek seeds, roast both in oil & powder
150 g	salt
300 ml	oil

1. Stir-fry the ground coriander and the green chilli in a little oil. Set aside.
2. In the same pan heat some more oil, add mustard seeds and allow to crackle.

3. Follow with the tamarind extract, jaggery, salt and bring to the boil. Allow to thicken over a high flame.
4. Lower the heat, stir in the fried ingredients, chilli, turmeric, fenugreek and asafoetida powders.
5. Continue cooking for about 30 minutes, adding the remaining oil, little by little.
6. Remove when the mixture becomes jam-like and the oil separates.
7. The pickle is ready for use. It lasts for 2 months.

021 Spicy Grated Mango : Instant

500 g	seeded mango, peel & grate
10 g	mustard seeds : for seasoning
30 g	chilli powder;
5 g	asafoetida, roast in oil & powder;
3 g	turmeric powder &
3 g	fenugreek seeds, roast in oil & powder, combine all evenly
10 g	jaggery, grate
60 g	salt
200 ml	oil

1. Marinate the grated mango in the salt and set aside for 3 hours.
2. Heat a little oil, add mustard seeds and allow to crackle.
3. Add in the grated mango and cook over low heat till transluscent.
4. Stir in the spice mixture, jaggery, the remaining oil and continue cooking till well blended.
5. Remove when the mixture becomes jam-like and the oil separates.
6. The pickle is ready for use. It lasts for 6 months.

022 Mango Avakkai : Hot (Old Method)

1 kg	cut mango, with shell, size medium & air-dry
150 g	chilli powder;
40 g	raw mustard seeds, sun-dry & powder;
20 g	fenugreek seeds, dry-roast & powder;
10 g	turmeric powder &
250 g	salt, combine all evenly
600 ml	raw gingelly oil

1. Dip the mango pieces in the oil and squeeze out the excess oil.
2. Thereafter roll the mango pieces in the spice mixture and arrange in a jar.
3. Sprinkle over a little spice mixture and pour over a little oil.
4. Repeat this process until all the mango pieces are layered.
5. Cover and set aside for 3 days. On the 4th day pour over the remaining oil to cover the mixture. Stir well.
6. The pickle is ready for use after 2 weeks. It lasts for 1 year.

023 Mango Ginger – Green Spices : Salty

125 g	peeled mango ginger, cut into rings
5 g	tender green chillies, chop
8 g	tender green pepper, string
35 ml	lime juice
20 g	salt

1. Combine the sliced mango ginger with the other ingredients thoroughly.
2. The pickle is ready for use. It keeps for 10 days and longer in the refrigerator. Toss daily.

024 Curry Leaf in Tamarind Sauce : Hot

500 g	curry leaves, wash, air-dry & devein
20 g	mustard seeds : for seasoning
250 g	cleaned tamarind, obtain thick extract using water
100 g	jaggery, grate
110 g	chilli powder
10 g	turmeric powder
10 g	fenugreek seeds &
5 g	asafoetida, roast both in oil & powder
130 g	salt
400 ml	oil

1. Stir-fry the curry leaves in a little oil. Allow to cool, grind and set aside.
2. In the same pan heat some more oil, add mustard seeds and allow to crackle.
3. Follow with the tamarind extract, jaggery, salt and bring to the boil. Allow to thicken over a high flame.
4. Lower the heat, stir in the chilli, turmeric, fenugreek, asafoetida powders and the curry leaf paste.
5. Continue cooking for about 30 minutes, adding the remaining oil, little by little.
6. Remove when the mixture becomes jam-like and the oil separates.
7. The pickle is ready for use. It lasts for 2 months.

025 Mint – Dried Red Chilli – Tamarind : Hot

- 500 g mint leaves, wash & air-dry
- 20 g mustard seeds : for seasoning
- 250 g cleaned tamarind, obtain thick extract using water
- 75 g jaggery, grate
- 140 g dried red chillies, roast in oil & powder
- 20 g turmeric powder
- 20 g fenugreek seeds &
- 20 g asafoetida, roast both in oil & powder
- 150 g salt
- 250 ml oil

1. Stir-fry the mint leaves in a little oil. Allow to cool, grind fine and set aside.
2. In the same pan heat some more oil, add mustard seeds and allow to crackle.
3. Follow with the tamarind extract, jaggery, salt and bring to the boil. Allow to thicken over a high flame.
4. Lower the heat, stir in the chilli, turmeric, fenugreek, asafoetida powders and the mint paste.
5. Continue cooking for about 20 minutes, adding the remaining oil, little by little.
6. Remove when the mixture thickens and the oil separates.
7. The pickle is ready for use. It lasts for 2 months.

026 Spiced Carrot – Peas in Lime Juice : Watery

- 125 g carrot, peel & chop
- 60 g capsicum, chop
- 60 g shelled peas, steam
- 15 g green chillies, chop fine
- 15 g chilli powder
- 85 ml lime juice
- 30 g salt

1. Combine all the ingredients thoroughly.
2. The pickle is ready for use. It keeps for 10 days and is best refrigerated.

027 Small Red Onion in Tamarind Sauce : Hot

- 500 g small red onion, peel, chop & grind
- 5 g mustard seeds : for seasoning
- 30 g cleaned tamarind, obtain thick extract using water
- 40 g chilli powder
- 3 g turmeric powder
- 3 g fenugreek seeds &
- 5 g asafoetida, roast both in oil & powder
- 12 g jaggery, grate
- 40 g salt
- 250 ml oil

1. Stir-fry the onion paste in a little oil and set aside.
2. In the same pan heat some more oil, add mustard seeds and allow to crackle.
3. Follow with the tamarind extract, jaggery, salt and bring to the boil. Allow to thicken over a high flame.
4. Lower the heat, stir in the chilli, turmeric, fenugreek, asafoetida powders and the fried onion paste.
5. Continue cooking for about 30 minutes, adding the remaining oil, little by little.
6. Remove when the mixture becomes jam-like and the oil separates.
7. The pickle is ready for use. It lasts for 2 months.

028 Spring Onion – Green Chilli : Hot

- 500 g spring onion bulbs, chop
- 140 g green chillies, chop
- 10 g mustard seeds &
- a few sprigs curry leaves : both for seasoning
- 10 g turmeric powder
- 8 g chilli powder
- 50 g cleaned tamarind, obtain thick extract using water
- 50 g jaggery, grate
- 8 g sugar
- 120 g salt
- 100 ml oil

1. Heat half the oil, add mustard seeds and allow to crackle.
2. Follow with the curry leaves, chopped green chillies, chopped onion and fry for a few minutes.
3. Stir in the tamarind extract, jaggery, sugar, salt and bring to the boil. Allow to thicken over a high flame.
4. Lower the heat, add in the chilli and turmeric powders.
5. Continue cooking for about 30 minutes, adding the remaining oil, little by little.
6. Remove when the mixture becomes jam-like and the oil separates.
5. The pickle is ready for use. It lasts for 2 months and is best refrigerated.

029 Onion – Green Spices : Hot

500 g	onion, peel, chop & grind coarsely
60 g	green coriander, wash, air-dry, chop & grind fine
165 g	green chillies, chop & grind
40 g	cleaned tamarind, obtain thick extract using water
25 g	jaggery, grate
5 g	split husked black gram, roast in a little oil & powder
5 g	mustard seeds &
a few	sprigs curry leaves : both for seasoning
45 g	salt
350 ml	oil

1. Stir-fry the onion, coriander and the green chilli paste in a little oil. Set aside.
2. In the same pan heat some more oil, add the mustard seeds, curry leaves and fry till done.
3. Follow with the tamarind extract, jaggery, salt and bring to the boil. Allow to thicken over a high flame.
4. Lower the heat, stir in the chilli, turmeric, fenugreek, asafoetida, gram powders and the fried green spice paste.
5. Continue cooking for about 30 minutes, adding the remaining oil, little by little.
6. Remove when the mixture becomes jam-like and the oil separates.
7. The pickle is ready for use. It lasts for 2 months.

030 Sweet & Sour Orange Peel : Hot

500 g	orange peel, scrape slightly, remove strings & chop fine
20 g	mustard seeds &
a few	sprigs curry leaves : both for seasoning
25 g	dried red chillies, break into bits
25 g	green chillies, chop
170 g	cleaned tamarind, obtain thick extract using water
70 g	jaggery, grate
15 g	chilli powder
10 g	turmeric powder
5 g	fenugreek seeds &
5 g	asafoetida, roast both in oil & powder
60 g	salt
250 ml	oil

1. Stir-fry the chopped orange peel, green chillies, red chillies in a little oil and set aside.
2. In the same pan heat some more oil, add the mustard seeds, curry leaves and allow to crackle.
3. Follow with the tamarind extract, jaggery, salt and bring to the boil. Allow to thicken over a high flame.
4. Lower the heat, stir in the chilli, turmeric, fenugreek, asafoetida powders and the fried ingredients.
5. Continue cooking for about 20 minutes, adding the remaining oil, little by little.
6. Remove when the mixture becomes jam-like and the oil separates.
7. The pickle is ready for use. It lasts for 2 months and is best refrigerated.

031 Tomato – Tamarind : Hot

1 kg	sour tomato, chop
200 g	peeled garlic
200 g	cleaned tamarind
225 g	chilli powder
50 g	mustard seeds, sun-dry & powder
50 g	fenugreek seeds, roast in oil & powder
5 g	turmeric powder
10 g	mustard seeds;
10 g	dried red chillies, break into bits;
10 g	split husked bengal gram &
a few	sprigs curry leaves : all for seasoning
250 g	salt
500 ml	oil

1. Marinate the tomato pieces in the salt and turmeric powder for 3 days.
2. On the 4th day squeeze out the tomato from the salt water.
3. Dry the squeezed tomato pieces for 2 days in sharp sunlight. Turn over the pieces once or twice for even drying.
4. Simultaneously soak the tamarind in the salt water of the tomato for those 2 days.
5. Sun the soaked tamarind with the juice for 2 more days after thorough cleaning.
6. Grind the soaked tamarind to a coarse paste.
7. Add in the tomato, grind a little coarsely and remove.
8. Blend in the spice powders and set aside.
9. Heat the oil, add mustard seeds and allow to crackle.
10. Add in the bengal gram, curry leaves, garlic, red chillies and fry till the garlic becomes tender.
11. Pour the seasoning over the pickle, stir well and set aside.
12. The pickle is ready for use. It lasts for 1 year.

032 Plantain Flower : Hot

- 500 g chopped plantain flower, remove stamen & immerse in thin buttermilk
- 5 g cleaned tamarind, obtain thin extract using water
- 20 g mustard seeds : for seasoning
- 10 g split husked black gram
- 60 g cleaned tamarind, obtain thick extract using water
- 30 g jaggery, grate
- 40 g chilli powder
- 5 g turmeric powder
- 5 g asafoetida &
- 5 g fenugreek seeds, roast both in oil & powder
- 40 g salt
- 200 ml oil

Plantain Flower

Removing the stamens from the plantain flower is truly an art. Remove the petals, hold the bunch of flowers with the blunt edge of a knife, tug at the stamens altogether and they will come of at one go.

1. Cook the chopped plantain flower in the thin tamarind extract and sufficient water to which a teaspoon (5g) salt has been added. Drain and set aside.
2. Heat a little oil, add the mustard seeds, black gram and fry till done.
3. Stir in the cooked plantain flower, fry for a few minutes and set aside.
4. In the same pan, heat some more oil, stir in the tamarind extract, jaggery, salt and bring to the boil. Allow to thicken over a high flame.
5. Lower the heat, stir in the chilli, turmeric, fenugreek and asafoetida powders.
6. Add in the fried plantain flower and continue cooking for about 20 minutes, adding the remaining oil little by little.
7. Remove when the mixture thickens and the oil separates.
8. The pickle is ready for use. It lasts for 2 months.

033 Spiced Green Tamarind : Tender

- 125 g tender green tamarind
- 2 g turmeric powder
- 10 g jaggery, grate
- 15 g dried red chillies
- 3 g mustard seeds
- 2 cloves garlic, peel & chop
- 5 g split husked black gram
- 2 g asafoetida, roast in oil & powder
- 30 g salt
- 10 ml oil

1. Pound the tamarind with the salt and turmeric powder. Set aside for 3 days.
2. On the 4th day pound again for proper blending and store.
3. This basic pickle lasts for 2 years.
4. Whenever required, take the desired quantity of the prepared tamarind.
5. Fry the mustard seeds, black gram, red chillies, garlic and asafoetida powder in the oil till done.
6. Remove and allow to cool. Grind the fried ingredients and jaggery with the prepared tamarind very coarsely.
7. The pickle is ready for use. It keeps for 15 days.

034 Mahani in Buttermilk : Watery

- 1 kg mahani root pieces
- 800 ml sour curd,* whip with 1200ml water & remove cream
- 70 g chilli powder;
- 20 g raw mustard seeds, sun-dry & powder;
- 5 g turmeric powder &
- 150 g salt, combine all evenly

1. Drop the mahani root pieces in the rice-washed water.
2. Cut each piece into small 2cm thick rounds after removing the central stem and immerse in the same water to prevent discolouration.
3. Combine the spice mixture with the water and whipped curd thoroughly.
4. Drop in the mahani pieces, mix well and set aside for 15 days.
5. Stir twice daily.
6. The pickle is ready for use. It lasts for several years.

* Refer **Base Preparations** for setting curd of rock-thick consistency.

KITCHEN SPICES

[PART – I]

ALLSPICE
It is available whole or ground and is used to flavour vegetables, curry powder blends, pickles and sweetmeats. A combination of clove, cinnamon, nutmeg and black pepper, allspice is used in *Ayurveda* medicine to aid digestion.

ANISEEDS
Highly aromatic, and has excellent digestive properties. In many parts of India, it is chewed after meals to aid digestion and to act as a breath-freshener. Due to its digestive properties, aniseeds are very good for children and nursing mothers.

Consumed in the form of tea with warm milk and honey at bedtime aniseeds relieves colic in babies and indigestion & hearthburn in adults. Small additions of aniseeds powder helps the very young digest their first solid foods.

ASAFOETIDA
A strong spice, it is the resin of a plant and is used in its root form and as a powder. Asafoetida has a distinctive pungent flavour & aroma, largely due to the presence of the sulphur compound and so is used in very small amounts. Its strong digestive properties like thymol seeds, help to counteract flatulence.

BAY LEAVES
Widely used as a flavouring agent in the seasoning of vegetables, bay leaves stimulate digestion. It is also a necessary ingredient in the preparation of boquet garni, a classic seasoning mixture, in stocks and in casseroles. The oil from the leaves is useful in the treatment of rheumatism, hysteria and flatulence. Externally, it is also used for treating sprains and bruises.

BLACK PEPPER
Comes in the form of whole dried peppercorns and ground pepper powder. Pepper stimulates the taste buds and helps to promote gastric secretions, thereby aiding digestion. It is also said to cure a host of other problems like cough due to congestion of phlegm, dandruff, chronic diarrhoea, blisters on the body, gastric catarrh, rheumatism, nausea, anorexia, piles, epilepsy, gonorrhoea, paralysis, pain in the ear, indigestion, jaundice, toothache, piles, disturbing dreams, venereal diseases, eye troubles and heart weakness.

CARDAMOM
Two types of cardamom - the small and large - are utilized for culinary purposes. The small ones are found in two varieties, namely the strong flavoured, green cardamom and the mild flavoured, bleached white cardamom. This highly aromatic spice stimulates the digestion, easing bowel spasms and flatulence.

Cardamom is often combined with bitter remedies to prevent gripping effect of taxatives. It is also useful in treating intestinal colic, excessive headache, dryness of the mouth, cough & dyspepsia. It is often brewed along with other spices in teas and is used to clear sore throats & cold. It is also chewed as a mouth freshener and digestive.

KITCHEN SPICES	
Part - II	Page 72
Part - III	Page 96

CHILLIES – GREEN & RED
This familiar condiment is a powerful local stimulant, producing burning sensation on contact with the skin.

Fresh green chillies are an important ingredient and is used in almost all dishes. In cooking, although the seeds of the chillies may be discarded before using the meat of the chilli, they add an enormous amount of flavour as well as bite to dishes.

Dried red chillies enhance the flavour of vegetable dishes and pickles. They are used whole as well as in crushed and powdered forms. Handle chillies cautiously, as they can burn your skin as well as your mouth.

Externally, it is used in ointments, liniments and plasters as a counter-irritant to treat muscular pains, arthritis, neuralgia, lumbago & unbroken chilblains, itching, swelling on the hands & legs due to exposure to cold and poor blood circulation.

Internally, chillies are a major circulatory stimulant. It is the most powerful and persistent heart stimulant known. Its influence reaches every organ.

It is also an excellent remedy to ward off chills, and is useful at the onset of colds. It supports the body's defense system and causes sweating. It is rich in vitamin C and is antibacterial. Small amounts of chillies stimulate a debilitated appetite too.

Unique Flavours

are

the popular

and typical

preparations of

different regions,

presenting varied styles,

delighting

the palate

with

the masterful

use of spices.

Recipes : Unique Flavours

035. Cucumber avakkai (dosakkai) : hot [Andhra Pradesh]
036. Fenugreek sorrel leaves (gonkura) : hot [Andhra Pradesh]
037. Peeled spiced mango (Maagaya) : hot [Andhra Pradesh]
038. Spicy mango (avakkai) : hot [Andhra Pradesh]
039. Spiced bamboo shoot in vinegar : sweet [North Eastern]
040. Sour noga tenga : sweet [Assamese]
041. Spiced elephant apple (Tekheda) : salty [Assamese]
042. Spicy tamarind – jaggery (tetuler achar) : sweet [Bengali]
043. Green chilli in mustard sauce : hot [Delhi]
044. Sour mango – green chilli : instant [Goan]
045. Spiced lime (metha nimbu) : sweet [Gujarathi]
046. Spiced grated mango (chhundo) : sweet [Gujarathi]
047. Mustard cauliflower – lime : watery [Kanarese]
048. Gunda : hot [Gujarathi]
049. Green walnuts in spiced vinegar : watery [Kashmiri]
050. Mango (kadu manga) : tender [Kerala]
051. Spiced ada manga : hot [Kerala]
052. Ginger in tamarind (puli inji) : sweet [Kerala]
053. Mustard mango (kadugu manga) : tender [Palakkad, Kerala]
054. Raw mango in oil (mangai curry) : hot [Palakkad, Kerala]
055. Stuffed fenugreek lime : hot [Marathi]
056. Sour garlic – coconut : salty [Mangalore, Kanarese]
057. Spiced tamarind (imli chutney) : sweet [Mathura, Uttar Pradesh]
058. Boiled sweet potato – mango : instant [Mysore, Kanarese]
059. Whole ripe mango (buffena) : sweet [Parsi]
060. Mustard mixed vegetable – onion - ginger : hot [Punjabi]
061. Stuffed fresh red chilli (burvan lal mirch) : hot [Punjabi]
062. Aniseed mango : hot [Rajasthani]
063. Grated spiced mango : watery [Sindhi]
064. Sour spiced grated mango (kadukash) : salty [Sindhi]
065. Spicy mango in oil (ennai mangai) : hot [Tamilnadu]
066. Fenugreek mango (vendhaya mangai) : hot [Tamilnadu]

The recipes in *Unique Flavours* being regional specialities may be too hot, too sweet, too pungent or too sour for the unacquainted. The quantities of spices used, especially chilli powder, salt, tamarind, sugar etc. may be altered to suit the individual palate.

035 Cucumber Avakkai (Dosakkai) : Hot
[Andhra Pradesh]

500 g	cucumber, scrape, cut into chunks & air-dry
40 g	dried red chillies, sun-dry & powder;
5 g	turmeric powder &
50 g	mustard seeds, sun-dry & powder, combine all three evenly
300 ml	raw gingelly oil
50 g	salt

1. Sprinkle some spice mixture at the bottom of a jar.
2. Dip the cucumber chunks in the oil, then in the spice mixture and arrange in the jar.
3. Sprinkle some spice mixture and pour over a little oil.
4. Repeat this process until all the cucumber pieces are exhausted.
5. Sprinkle over the remaining spice mixture and oil, if any.
6. Set the pickle aside for 3 days. Do not stir.
7. On the 4th day stir the pickle thoroughly and add more oil if required, to cover.
8. The pickle is ready for use.
It lasts for 6 months.

036 Fenugreek – Sorrel Leaves (Gonkura) : Hot
[Andhra Pradesh]

500 g	tender sorrel leaves, remove stems, wash, air-dry & chop fine
30 g	cleaned tamarind, dry-roast
80 g	dried red chillies;
20 g	fenugreek seeds &
5 g	mustard seeds, roast all three in oil
40 g	split husked bengal gram;
10 g	asafoetida, roast in oil & powder;
a few	sprigs curry leaves &
5 g	mustard seeds : all for seasoning
100 g	salt
200 ml	oil

Sorrel Leaves
Commonly known as 'Gonkura' comes in 2 varieties - green & red. The green is preferable, as it is tastier and less pungent. They are sour tasting and can be used as such, although a dash of tamarind will enhance the taste. Wash & dry the leaves before cutting, to prevent stickiness.

1. Stir-fry the sorrel leaves in very little oil, a few at a time and set aside. The leaves will take about 10 minutes to get cooked.
2. Transfer the fried leaves to a jar, add the salt and set aside for 3 days
3. On the 4th day remove the salted leaves, pound together and store.
4. As and when required, take the desired quantity of the pounded sorrel leaves.
5. Grind together with the tamarind, red chillies, mustard and fenugreek seeds.
6. Heat the oil, add the mustard seeds, black gram, curry leaves and fry till the gram becomes golden.
8. Blend the seasoning into the ground mixture.
9. The pickle is ready for use after 3 days. It lasts for 1 month.

037 Peeled Spiced Mango (Maagaya) : Hot [Andhra Pradesh]

500 g	seeded mango, peel & size into thick boat shaped pieces
35 g	chilli powder
5 g	fenugreek seeds &
5 g	asafoetida, roast both in oil & powder
5 g	turmeric powder &
75 g	salt, combine both evenly
200 ml	oil : heat & cool

1. Add the salt-turmeric mixture to the mango pieces and set aside for 3 days.
2. On the 4th day, squeeze the mango pieces and sun again for 2 days. Sun the salt water also for 2 days.
3. Blend the chilli, fenugreek and asafoetida powders into the salt water.
4. Stir in the mango pieces and mix well.
5. Pour the cooled oil over the pickle to cover and stir thoroughly.
6. The pickle is ready for use after 2 days.
It lasts for 6 months.

038 Spicy Mango (Avakkai) : Hot [Andhra Pradesh]

1 kg	cut mango, size medium with shell
250 g	chilli powder
250 g	mustard seeds, sun-dry & powder
50 g	fenugreek seeds, roast in oil & powder
20 g	turmeric powder
100 g	bengal gram whole
300 g	salt
500 ml	oil

1. Combine the spice powders with the salt evenly.
2. Dip the mango pieces in the oil and squeeze out the excess oil.
3. Thereafter roll the mango pieces in the spice mixture and arrange in a jar.
4. Sprinkle a little spice mixture and pour a little oil over the mangoes.
5. Repeat this process until all the mango pieces are layered.
6. Sprinkle any left over spice mixture over the pickle and set aside for 3 days. Do not stir.
7. On the 4th day, stir well and pour over the remaining oil to cover the pickle. Stir well.
8. The pickle is ready for use after 2 weeks. It lasts for 1 year.

039 Spiced Bamboo Shoot in Vinegar : Sweet [Arunachal Pradesh]

250 g	fresh bamboo shoot, cook & mince
200 g	sugar
30 g	onion, peel & chop
10 g	chilli powder
5	cloves garlic, peel
5 g	onion seeds;
5 g	cummin seeds;
1-1"	stick of cinnamon &
5	cardamoms, shell & crush, tie all in a spice bag
75 ml	vinegar
35 g	salt

Bamboo Shoot
Generally bamboo shoots are strong and pungent. To reduce their pungency, remove the outer leaves of the bamboo shoots and soak them overnight in water to which four teaspoons (20g) salt has been added. Cut them into 1" pieces and rinse in 3 changes of water for 3 days. Alternatively, boil thrice, each time in fresh water.

1. Combine all the ingredients (except the spice bag & vinegar) with 200ml water and heat until the sugar dissolves.
2. Drop the spice bag into the bamboo shoot mixture. Simmer until thick and syrupy.
3. Remove the spice bag after squeezing and discard.
4. Add in the vinegar, heat till well blended and remove.
5. The pickle is ready for use. It keeps for 2 weeks and is best refrigerated.

040 Sour Noga Tenga : Sweet [Assamese]

500 g	noga tenga
400 g	sugar
20 g	peppercorns, dry-roast & powder
10 g	aniseeds, dry-roast & powder
2	cloves;
2	cardamoms &
1-1"	stick of cinnamon, keep all three whole
30 ml	lime juice
20 ml	vinegar, heat & cool
40 g	salt
100 ml	oil

1. Stir-fry the noga tenga in a little oil for a few minutes.
2. Add in sufficient water, salt and continue cooking until tender.
3. Stir in the sugar and heat till the mixture becomes syrupy.
4. Blend in the spice powders, whole spices and remove.
5. Pour over the lime juice, cooled vinegar, the remaining oil and stir well.
5. The pickle is ready for use. It lasts for 6 months.

> **Preparing pickles seasonally is wise on two counts:**
>
> **economy and taste.**

041 Spiced Elephant Apple (Tekheda) : Salty
[Assamese]

500 g	big green elephant apple, boil, cool, chop & seed
10 g	panch phoran powder
5 g	turmeric powder
5 g	white mustard seeds;
5 g	aniseeds &
3 g	fenugreek seeds, sun-dry all three & powder
25 g	sugar
25 ml	vinegar
75 g	salt
150 ml	oil

1. Combine the cooked elephant apple with the salt and sugar.
2. Allow to remain in the bowl until all the juice given out by the elephant apple has evaporated.
3. Add the spice mixture into the dry elephant apple and stir well.
4. Transfer to a jar and sun the mixture for 8 days.
5. Heat the oil, add the panch phoran, turmeric powders and fry for a second.
6. Stir in the spiced elephant apple, vinegar, blend well and remove.
7. The pickle is ready for use. It lasts for 6 months.

042 Spicy Tamarind – Jaggery (Tetuler Achar) : Sweet
[Bengali]

500 g	cleaned tamarind
300 g	jaggery, grate;
5 g	turmeric powder &
5 g	salt, combine
5 g	panch phoran powder
5 g	mustard seeds, sun-dry & powder;
5 g	chilli powder &
100 ml	oil, combine all to a paste

1. Combine the tamarind with the salt-turmeric mixture and sun for 4 days.
2. Blend the spice paste into the salted tamarind and again sun the mixture for 1 day.
3. Stir in the panch phoran powder and mix thoroughly.
4. The pickle is ready for use. It lasts for 2 months. Sun frequently.

> **Tamarind extract**
> To obtain tamarind extract soak the tamarind in warm water for 30 minutes. Squeeze well with the fingers and strain through a big wire sieve. Alternatively run the soaked tamarind in the mixer, taking care to seed completely (as seeds impart a granular texture & a bitter taste).

043 Green Chilli in Mustard Sauce : Hot [Delhi]

> **Mustard sauce**
> Sun-dry mustard seeds. Allow to cool and powder in the mixer without adding water. Remove, add water and whisk thoroughly until a fine aroma emanates.

500 g	green chillies
50 g	mustard seeds, soak in water for 1 hour &
40 g	onion, peel, chop & grind both to a paste with 2 chillies
50 g	dried mango powder
5 g	turmeric powder
5 g	black cummin seeds, dry-roast & powder
50 ml	lime juice
125 g	salt
150 ml	mustard oil
50 ml	oil

1. Stuff a pinch of mango powder into each chilli.
2. Add 200ml water to the mustard mixture, whisk well and strain. Retain the liquid.
3. Heat the oil, add the stuffed chillies and stir-fry for a few minutes.
4. Add in the strained mustard water, cummin, turmeric powders, salt and cook over low heat until the chillies soften.
5. Blend in the lime juice and serve.
6. The pickle is ready for use. It lasts for 2 months.

044 Sour Mango – Green Chilli : Instant [Goan]

250 g	seeded green mango, size medium
5	green chillies, slit & seed
20 g	salt
30 ml	water

1. Add salt to the mango pieces and mix thoroughly.
2. Stir in the green chillies, water and set aside for 2 hours.
3. The pickle is ready for use. It keeps for a week in the refrigerator.

045 Spiced Lime (Metha Nimbu) : Sweet [Gujarathi]

500 g	lime, cut into 8 pieces each & seed
125 g	sugar / 200g jaggery
25 g	chilli powder;
5 g	turmeric powder &
5 g	asafoetida, roast in oil & powder, combine all three evenly
50 g	salt

1. Combine the lime pieces with the salt-turmeric mixture and set aside for 1 month.
2. Add in the spice powders and sugar / jaggery into the softened salted lime.
3. The pickle is ready for use after 3 days. It lasts for 6 months.

046 Spiced Grated Mango (Chhundo) : Sweet [Gujarathi]

1 kg	seeded fibrous mango, peel & shred
600 g	sugar
10 g	chilli powder;
10 g	turmeric powder &
10 g	cummin seeds, roast in oil & powder, combine all evenly
25 g	salt

1. Combine the shredded mango with all the ingredients evenly.
2. Spread the mixture in a shallow wide-mouthed jar and cover with a thin cloth.
3. Sun the mixture for 5 days till the syrup attains a single-thread consistency, stirring 3 times daily.
4. The pickle lasts for 1 year.

> **Grating mango**
>
> Always soak mangoes in water for a few hours so that the milky substance is completely washed off. Wipe-dry and grate without peeling if the skins are thin. Otherwise peel slightly and grate. Soak the grated mango in salt (100 grams to every kilogram of mango) to get a crunchier pickle.

047 Mustard Cauliflower – Lime : Watery [Kanarese]

250 g	cauliflower florets
100 g	lime, cut into small pieces & seed
40 g	salt, combine with 200ml water
30 g	dried red chillies
10 g	mustard seeds, sun-dry & powder
5 g	turmeric powder
5 g	mustard seeds &
3 g	asafoetida, roast in oil & powder : both for seasoning
15 ml	oil

1. Bring the salt solution to boiling. Continue heating until it gets reduced by one-third.
2. Pack the cauliflower florets and lime pieces in a jar.
3. Pour over the cooled salt water (reserving 50ml) and set aside for a day.
4. Next day grind the chillies and mustard separately into a paste with 50ml salt water.
5. Blend the spice paste into the pickle mixture.
6. Heat oil, add mustard seeds, turmeric, asafoetida powders and fry till done.
7. Pour the seasoning over the pickle mixture and set aside for 2 days.
8. The pickle lasts for 1 month.

048 Gunda : Hot [Gujarathi]

- 500 g   gunda, cut & scrape seeds with a salted knife
- 150 g   mango pieces &
- 35 g   salt, combine & retain the sour salt water of mangoes
- 5 g   turmeric powder
- 20 g   salt : for pickle

1. Add salt and turmeric powder to the gundas.
2. Immerse in the sour salt water of the mangoes for 20 days.
3. The pickle is ready for use when the gundas cease to be sticky.
4. It lasts for 3 months.

049 Green Walnuts in Spiced Vinegar : Watery [Kashmiri]

- 500 g   green walnuts, prick with a needle
- 60 g   salt, make a solution with 500ml water
- 250 ml   vinegar;
- 2   dried red chillies;
- 1   clove;
- 1-1"   stick of cinnamon &
- 1   cardamom, tie all in a spice bag

1. Soak the pricked walnuts in the salt solution for 4 days.
2. Drain and soak in fresh salt solution of the same strength for 7 more days.
3. Bring to the boil with the spice bag and simmer for 20 minutes. Remove and allow to cool.
4. Drain thoroughly and spread to dry indoors on a tray for 2 days.
5. Pack in a jar, cover with the cold spiced vinegar and set aside for 6 weeks.
6. The pickle lasts for 2 months.

050 Mango (Kadu Manga) : Tender [Kerala]

- 1 kg   fresh tender mango, with stem, keep whole
- 250 g   salt

1. In a jar sprinkle a layer of salt and follow with a layer of mango.
2. Repeat this process till all the mangoes are layered. Make sure that the final layer is that of salt.
3. Shake the jar twice daily for 3 days.
4. Seal the mouth of the jar with an oven-toasted oiled banana leaf and store the jar underground for 6 months.
5. This may be consumed as such or spiced with chilli and mustard powders for a variation.
6. The pickle lasts for more than a year.

051 Spiced Ada Manga : Hot [Kerala]

- 500 g   seeded mango, split without severing
- 30 g   green chillies, slit without removing stem
- 10   cloves garlic, peel & chop
- 1/2"   piece of fresh ginger, scrape & slice thinly
- 15 g   chilli powder
- 5 g   mustard seeds;
- 3 g   fenugreek seeds;
- 3 g   cummin seeds;
- 5 g   asafoetida &
- 2 g   peppercorns, roast all in oil & powder together
- 5 g   turmeric powder
- 5 g   mustard seeds;
- 3 g   fenugreek seeds &
- a few   sprigs curry leaves : all for seasoning
- 50 g   jaggery, grate
- 25 ml   vinegar
- 60 g   salt
- 50 ml   oil

1. Apply the salt on the inside of the mango slices and set aside for a day.
2. Remove the mango slices from the salt water given out by the mangoes and sun for a day.
3. Return to the salt water in the evening and again sun-dry the next day.
4. Repeat this process till the mangoes are dried yet soft.
5. Heat a little oil, fry the ginger, garlic, green chillies and set aside.
6. In the same pan heat the remaining oil, add in the mustard seeds, fenugreek seeds, curry leaves and allow to crackle.
7. Lower the heat and blend in the spice powders. Remove and allow to cool.
8. Stuff the spice mixture into the mango slices.
9. In a jar sprinkle a little of the ginger mixture and follow with a layer of the stuffed mangoes.
10. Repeat this process till all the stuffed mangoes are layered.
11. Combine the jaggery with the vinegar and pour the mixture over the mangoes.
12. Set aside for 2 days. Shake the jar well twice daily.
13. The pickle is ready for use after 2 weeks. It lasts for 6 months.

052 Ginger in Tamarind (Puli Inji) : Sweet [Kerala]

250 g	fresh ginger, scrape & chop fine
250 g	green chilli, chop fine
40 g	cleaned tamarind, obtain thick extract using 250ml water
100 g	jaggery, grate
2	dried red chillies, break into bits
5 g	mustard seeds
a few	sprigs curry leaves
125 g	salt
50 ml	oil

1. Stir-fry the chopped ginger and green chillies in half the oil till partly tender. Set aside.
2. Bring the tamarind extract, jaggery and salt to the boil.
3. Add in the sauted ginger, green chillies and cook until the mixture thickens.
4. Heat the remaining oil, add mustard seeds, broken chillies, curry leaves and fry till done.
5. Pour the seasoning over the ginger mixture and remove.
6. The pickle is ready for use. It lasts for 3 months.

053 Mustard Mango (Kadugu Manga) : Tender [Palakkad, Kerala]

1 kg	tender mango with stems, keep whole
60 g	dried red chillies &
50 g	mustard seeds, sun-dry both & powder coarsely
5 g	asafoetida, roast in oil & powder
300 g	salt

1. Bring the water to boiling with the salt. Remove the scum that forms on the surface of the water.
2. Strain the boiled salt water and allow to cool.
3. Blend the spice powders into the cooled salt water.
4. Add the mangoes into the spicy sauce, mix thoroughly and set aside for 10 days.
5. The pickle lasts for 1 year. Stir and sun occasionally.

Fresh ginger
Ginger with a pink hue is tender, therefore less stringy and less pungent. Buy in the season when they are at their cheapest and tenderest.

054 Raw Mango in Oil (Mangai Curry) : Hot [Palakkad, Kerala]

125 g	cubed mango
5 g	chilli powder
2 g	asafoetida, roast in oil & powder
2 g	mustard seeds &
a few	sprigs curry leaves : both for seasoning
12 g	salt
20 ml	oil

1. Add the salt and chilli powder to the cubed mango and toss well.
2. Heat the oil, add mustard seeds and allow to crackle.
3. Add in the curry leaves, asafoetida powder and fry till done. Remove and allow to cool.
4. Pour the seasoning over the mango mixture and blend well.
5. The pickle is ready for use after 1 week. It keeps for 5 days and longer in the refrigerator.

055 Stuffed Fenugreek Lime : Hot [Marathi]

1 kg	lime, keep whole
100 g	salt
50 g	chilli powder
30 g	fenugreek seeds, roast in oil & powder
300 ml	oil

1. Bring the water to the boil and remove.
2. Add in the whole limes, cover and let stand for 3 minutes. Uncover and let stand for 30 minutes. Remove the limes and wipe dry.
3. Heat the oil to smoking point, add the limes and fry till light brown.
4. Slit each lime into 2 without severing and fill in the spice mixture.
5. Pack the stuffed lime into a jar and pour over the pre-heated oil.
6. The pickle is ready for use after 10 days. It lasts for 2 months. Sun occasionally.

056 Sour Garlic – Coconut : Salty
[Mangalore, Kanarese]

50 g	peeled garlic, chop
20 g	dried red chillies, break into bits
25 g	cleaned tamarind, dry-roast
200 g	grated coconut, dry-roast
20 g	salt

Peeling Garlic
A painless way of peeling garlic is to either store in the refrigerator for a few hours, or roast over low heat in a dry pan for a few minutes, or toast in the oven for a few seconds. When cool, the peels will come off in a jiffy.

1. Combine all the ingredients and grind to a coarse paste. Add no water.
2. The pickle is ready for use. It keeps for 1 week in the refrigerator.

057 Spiced Tamarind (Imli Chutney) : Sweet
[Mathura, UP]

250 g	cleaned tamarind, obtain thick extract using water
200 g	jaggery, grate
15 g	cummin seeds, dry-roast & powder
5 g	chilli powder
1-1"	piece of fresh ginger, scrape & chop
2	green chillies, chop
3 g	black salt
15 g	salt

1. Blend the grated jaggery into the tamarind extract.
2. Stir in the remaining ingredients and mix thoroughly.
3. The pickle is ready for use. It keeps for 10 days in the refrigerator.

058 Boiled Sweet Potato – Mango : Instant
[Mysore, Kanarese]

125 g	sweet potato, half-boil, peel & crumble
60 g	seeded raw mango, peel & chop fine
8 g	green chillies, chop
8 g	split husked black gram, dry-roast
5 g	dried red chillies, break into bits
3 g	cummin seeds;
5 g	mustard seeds &
a few	sprigs curry leaves : all three for seasoning
10 g	salt
50 ml	oil

1. Stir-fry the crumbled sweet potato and the chopped mango separately in a little oil. Set aside.
2. Grind together the fried sweet potato, mango, gram, red chillies to a paste along with the curry leaves and green chillies. Add no water.
3. In the same pan heat the remaining oil, add the mustard seeds, cummin seeds and allow to crackle.
4. Blend the seasoning into the mixture.
5. The pickle is ready for use. It keeps for 1 week in the refrigerator.

059 Whole Ripe Mango (Buffena) : Sweet *[Parsi]*

500 g	large ripe mango, keep whole
20 g	mustard seeds, sun-dry & powder
5 g	chilli powder
5	cloves garlic, peel & chop;
1-1"	stick of cinnamon;
2	cardamoms &
2	cloves, grind all to a paste using vinegar
2 g	turmeric powder
100 g	jaggery, grate
150 ml	vinegar
60 g	salt
125 ml	oil

1. Heat a little oil to smoking point. Reduce the heat, add the mangoes and cook till tender. Remove and drain the oil.
2. Combine the spice powders, spice paste, jaggery, salt with the vinegar and the drained oil.
3. Spread the spice paste over the cooked mangoes uniformly and arrange in a wide-mouthed jar.
4. Mix the remaining oil (after heating and cooling) into the mangoes thoroughly.
5. Cover and allow the pickle to mature for 10 days before use. It lasts for 6 months.

060 Mustard Mixed Vegetable – Onion-Ginger : Hot [Punjabi]

175 g	turnip, peel & julienne
175 g	carrot, peel & julienne
150 g	cauliflower florets
25 g	fresh ginger, scrape & chop;
10 g	garlic, peel &
25 g	onion, peel & chop, grind all three to a paste using vinegar
25 g	chilli powder
15 g	jaggery, grate
10 g	mustard seeds, sun-dry & powder
3 g	garam masala powder
125 ml	vinegar
60 g	salt
250 ml	oil

1. Tie the vegetables in a thin cloth. Bring sufficient water to the boil.
2. Dip in the vegetable bag for 2 minutes and remove.
3. Spread the blanched vegetables to dry on a clean cloth.
4. Stir-fry the ginger-garlic-onion paste in a little oil till the oil separates and remove.
5. Combine the fried paste, chilli, mustard and garam masala powders with the salt evenly.
6. Stir in the dried vegetables and add a little oil.
7. Transfer to a jar, mix thoroughly and sun for 3 hours every day, for 5 days.
8. Boil together the vinegar and jaggery until the syrup reaches a single-thread consistency. Remove and allow to cool.
9. Pour the sweetened vinegar over the pickle mixture along with the remaining oil.
10. The pickle is ready for use after 3 days. It lasts for 1 month. Sun and stir occasionally.

061 Stuffed Fresh Red Chilli (Burvan Lal Mirch) : Hot [Punjabi]

Stuffing the Chilli

For preparaing stuffed chilli pickles, cut both ends of the chilli a little with a sharp scissor. Run the sharp edge of a thin pointed knife to remove the seeds and fibres inside the chilli. Pound the seeds and fibres with the other spices and stuff back the mixture into the chillies.

500 g	fresh red chillies
150 g	dried mango powder
100 g	mustard seeds;
100 g	onion seeds;
40 g	cummin seeds;
50 g	aniseeds;
50 g	fenugreek seeds;
50 g	chilli powder;
25 g	turmeric powder &
5	cardamoms, dry-roast all & powder
20 g	asafoetida, roast in oil & powder
250 g	salt
20 ml	lime juice
1000 ml	oil ; heat & cool

1. Make a hole at the rear end of each chilli and seed.
2. Combine the spice powders with a little oil and lime juice to a paste.
3. Stuff the spice paste into the chillies with the help of a toothpick and arrange in a jar.
4. Pour over the remaining oil and leave indoors for 1 month. Shake every 2 days.
5. The pickle is ready for use. It lasts for 4 months. Sun occasionally.

062 Aniseed Mango : Hot [Rajasthani]

1 kg	seeded mango, size medium
15 g	split husked mustard seeds
40 g	dried red chillies, sun-dry &
40 g	aniseeds, dry-roast, powder both coarsely
5 g	turmeric powder
5 g	asafoetida, roast in oil & powder
70 g	salt
350 ml	mustard oil

1. Combine all the ingredients with the mango pieces and oil.
2. The pickle is ready for use after 3 weeks.
3. It lasts for 1 year.

Asafoetida

Break the asafoetida lump into smaller bits. Deep-fry the bits in oil till done - this makes for complete frying. Drain, cool and grind. Store in an airtight spice jar to retain their full aroma and flavour.

063 Grated Spiced Mango: Watery [Sindhi]

500 g	seeded mango, peel & grate
50 g	chilli powder;
10 g	mustard seeds, sun-dry & powder;
10 g	fenugreek seeds, roast in oil & powder;
5 g	turmeric powder &
10 g	asafoetida, roast in oil & powder, combine all evenly
5	cloves garlic, peel & chop
5 ml	acetic acid
100 g	salt
40 ml	oil : heat & cool
water	sufficient to soak : boil & cool small pieces of muslin

1. Combine the grated mango, spice mixture, garlic, salt and 20ml oil.
2. Tie small portions of the pickle mixture in each piece of cloth.
3. Add the acetic acid and 20ml oil to the cooled water in a jar.
4. Drop the pickle packs into the jar and store.
5. To ensure that the packs stay immersed in the water, press down the packs every 5 days.
6. The pickle is ready for use after 15 days. It lasts for 2 months.

064 Sour Spiced Grated Mango (Kadukash) : Salty [Sindhi]

1 kg	seeded mango, peel & grate
10 g	kashmiri chilli powder
10 g	fenugreek seeds;
10 g	aniseeds;
5 g	peppercorns;
5 g	onion seeds &
3 g	cummin seeds, dry-roast & pound
3 g	turmeric powder
1 g	grated nutmeg
1	blade of mace &
1-1"	stick of cinnamon, grind both coarsely
50 g	salt
200 ml	vinegar
200 ml	oil

1. Mix all the ingredients with the grated mango (except mace, nutmeg, cinnamon, vinegar & oil) and set aside overnight.
2. Next day add the remaining ingredients and mix well. Top up with oil.
3. The pickle is ready for use after a week. It lasts for 3 months.

065 Spicy Mango in Oil (Ennai Mangai) : Hot [Tamilnadu]

500 g	cut mango, size into small pieces
50 g	mustard seeds &
25 g	fenugreek seeds, dry-roast both & powder
25 g	chilli powder
25 g	aniseeds &
12 g	peppercorns, dry-roast both & powder
12 g	turmeric powder
75 g	salt
250 ml	oil

1. Combine the spice powders with the salt evenly.
2. Stir the mango pieces into the spice mixture along with the oil and transfer to a jar.
3. The pickle is ready for use after 10 days. It lasts for 6 months. Stir occasionally.

066 Fenugreek Mango (Vendhaya Mangai) : Hot [Tamilnadu]

1 kg	cut large mango, size medium
60 g	chilli powder
30 g	fenugreek seeds, dry-roast &
20 g	mustard seeds, sun-dry & powder together
10 g	turmeric powder
10 g	asafoetida, roast in oil & powder
120 g	salt
300 ml	oil

1. Combine the chilli, fenugreek, mustard, turmeric powders with the salt and a little oil to a paste.
2. Stir the mango pieces into the spice paste and set aside for 3 days.
3. Sun the spiced mango for 2 days. Also sun the reserved sauce for 2 days.
4. Blend the sauce into the sunned mango.
5. Add in the asafoetida powder and the remaining oil to cover. Stir thoroughly.
6. The pickle is ready for use after 2 weeks. It lasts for 1 year.

Fenugreek

Always roast fenugreek seeds with or without oil, till they turn a shade darker and a good aroma emnates. Remove, cool, grind and store in airtight spice jars.

Exclusive

recipes are

unusual creations

from

successful efforts

to

stimulate

the

appetite transforming

the simplest pickle

into

a delectable delicacy.

Recipes : Exclusive

067. Artichoke – Capsicum - Tomato : Watery
068. Asparagus in buttermilk : watery
069. Bamboo shoot in curd : hot
070. Bitter gourd – bean sprouts - onion : hot
071. Sprout stuffed bitter gourd : hot
072. Bitter gourd – mango - raisin : sweet
073. Sour capsicum – bean sprout : hot
074. Stuffed kalakkai chain : oilless
075. Sour chambakai : hot
076. Sour spiced sprouted bengal gram : salty
077. Corn – ginger : hot
078. Sour cucumber – spring onion : hot
079. Spicy curd – mango : oilless
080. Curry leaf seed : hot
081. Drumstick pith – green chilli : hot
082. Sprouted fenugreek in tamarind sauce : hot
083. Green garlic in lime juice : hot
084. Star gooseberry : sweet
085. Sprouted green gram : hot
086. Spicy irumban puli : watery
087. Raw jackfruit in lime juice : hot
088. Spiced kumquat – mango ginger : hot
089. Sweet & sour kumquat : hot
090. Sambaara lime : hot
091. Sambaara mango : hot
092. Lime leaf – curry leaves : instant
093. Mango ginger in tamarind sauce : hot
094. Sour sprouted moth – thymol seeds : hot
095. Mudukottan leaf in tamarind sauce : hot
096. Mulberry : hot
097. Mustard mushroom in vinegar : instant
098. Sour mushroom – spring onion : salty
099. Mushroom – bamboo shoot - water chestnut : sweet
100. Spicy mushroom : hot
101. Sour naravallikai : hot
102. Sweet spiced nutmeg : hot
103. Aromatic omavalli : hot
104. Sour & spicy green peas : hot
105. Sour pineapple – fruit & nut : sweet
106. Sour & spicy plantain flower : hot
107. Plantain stem : hot
108. Potato – green coriander in lime juice : hot
109. Sour red pumpkin : sweet
110. Spiced round gourd : instant
111. Star fruit in tamarind sauce : hot
112. Spiced spinach : hot
113. Tudhuvelai berry / leaf – tamarind : instant
114. Tulsi – gram – green chilli : instant
115. Wheat sprout – bengal gram sprout : hot

067 Artichoke – Capsicum - Tomato : Watery

500 g	artichoke, cook
100 g	capsicum, chop fine
100 g	tomato, blanch, seed & chop
20 g	small red onion, peel & chop fine
20 g	dried red chillies, break into bits
5	cloves garlic, peel & chop fine
3	green chillies, chop
3 g	fresh thyme, chop
10 ml	soya sauce
100 ml	vinegar
100 ml	lime juice
60 g	salt
100 ml	olive oil

1. Stir-fry the chopped onion and garlic in a little oil till tender.
2. Add in the chillies and fry for a minute.
3. Follow with the artichoke, capsicum and fry for a while over low heat till partly tender.
4. Add in the chopped tomato, soya sauce, chopped thyme, salt, the remaining oil and cook till well blended.
5. Stir in the lime juice, vinegar and remove when the mixture begins to bubble.
6. The pickle is ready for use. It lasts for 1 month and is best refrigerated.

Artichoke : Wash well under the cold tap to flush out any grit. An artichoke will stand upright best if you trim the bottom with a sharp knife, rubbing the stalk with lime juice to prevent discolouration. Cutting the tips of the inner circle of leaves is to make the artichoke easier to eat. Unlike most other vegetables, artichokes are cooked in water enough to well cover them, for anything from 20-45 minutes, according to the variety, size, recipe or personal preference. A draining spoon is handy to lift them carefully out of the pan, before turning them upside down to drain.

068 Asparagus in Buttermilk : Watery

1 kg	asparagus root pieces
800 ml	curd, whip with 1500ml water & remove cream
20 g	mustard seeds, sun-dry & powder;
50 g	chilli powder &
200 g	salt, combine all three evenly

Asparagus
Soak the asparagus roots in water for a day. Remove from the water, skin the asparagus roots and immerse in rice-washed water. Cut each root into 1cm thick rounds after removing the central stem and return to the same water to prevent discolouration.

1. Blend the spice powders into the whipped buttermilk.
2. Remove the asparagus root pieces from the rice-washed water.
3. Drop the root pieces into the spiced buttermilk.
4. Mix well and set aside for 15 days.
5. Stir twice daily.
6. The pickle lasts for 1 year.

069 Bamboo Shoot in Curd : Hot

250 g	small bamboo shoots
200 ml	slightly sour whipped curd
5 g	chilli powder
25 g	green chillies, coarsely pound
50 g	onion, peel & chop
25 g	green coriander, clean, air-dry & chop
5 g	mustard seeds &
50 ml	oil : both for seasoning
60 g	salt
200 ml	oil : for deep-frying

1. Deep-fry the bamboo shoot pieces in oil, over a medium flame till crisp.
2. Sprinkle with a little salt, chilli powder, mix well and set aside.
3. Coarsely pound the green chillies with the remaining salt.
4. Heat the oil, add mustard seeds and allow to crackle.
5. Add in the pounded green chillies, chopped coriander and stir-fry for a while.
6. Pour the seasoning over the whipped curd and blend well.
7. Stir in the fried bamboo shoot pieces and mix well.
8. The pickle is ready for use. It keeps for 1 week in the refrigerator.

070 Bitter gourd – Bean Sprouts - Onion : Hot

500 g	seeded bitter gourd, cut into small pieces
5 g	salt : for marinating bitter gourd
100 g	red kidney bean sprouts, soak overnight, drain & sprout
100 g	onion, peel
100 g	tomato, blanch, peel & puree
50 g	cleaned tamarind, obtain thick extract using water
50 g	jaggery, grate
50 g	chilli powder
20 g	peeled garlic, chop
30 g	green coriander, clean, air-dry & chop
5 g	coriander seeds, sun-dry & powder
3 g	fenugreek seeds, roast in oil & powder
5 g	mustard seeds
5 g	split husked black gram : both for seasoning
125 g	salt
200 ml	oil
a few	sprigs curry leaves

1. Cook the bean sprouts in sufficient water till tender. Remove the water and reserve.
2. Marinate the bitter gourd pieces in a teaspoon (5g) salt for half an hour. Squeeze out the water and pat-dry.
3. Heat oil, add mustard seeds, black gram and fry till done.
4. Stir in the chopped onion, garlic and cook till light brown.
5. Add in the tomato puree, tamarind extract, jaggery, salt and the reserved water. Allow to thicken over a high flame.
6. Follow with the spice powders, the bean sprouts, the salted bitter gourd, chopped coriander, curry leaves and remove when the mixture becomes jam-like.
7. The pickle is ready for use. It lasts for 1 month.

071 Sprout Stuffed Bitter gourd : Hot

500 g	bitter gourd, scrape lightly, seed & cut into thin rings
5 g	salt : for marinating bitter gourd
200 g	whole green gram sprouts
50 g	onion, peel & chop;
3	dried red chillies &
3	cloves garlic, peel, grind all three to a paste
3 g	coriander seeds, dry-roast & powder
2 g	turmeric powder
50 g	tomato, blanch, peel & puree
75 ml	lime juice
75 g	salt
200 ml	oil

1. Soak the bitter gourd rings for 1 hour in water to which a teaspoon (5g) salt has been added.
2. Remove from the salt water and wipe-dry.
3. Heat a little oil, add in the spice paste and fry for a few minutes.
4. Follow with the salted bitter gourd and fry for a while till partly tender.
5. Add in the tomato puree, the gram sprouts and cook till tender.
6. Stir in the lime juice and remove when the mixture begins to bubble.
7. The pickle is ready for use. It keeps for 2 weeks in the refrigerator.

072 Bitter gourd – Mango - Raisin : Sweet

250 g	small tender bitter gourd, slit
100 g	seeded raw mango, peel & grate
50 g	seedless raisin, chop fine
25 g	chilli powder
3 g	coriander seeds &
3 g	aniseeds, dry-roast both & powder
2 g	turmeric powder
5 g	sugar
20 ml	lime juice
50 g	salt
125 ml	oil

1. Add salt to the slit bitter gourd and set aside for 3 hours.
2. Wash the salted bitter gourd in running water and pat-dry.
3. Combine all the spices and salt with the mango, raisin and lime juice.
4. Fill the spice mixture into the slit bitter gourd and tie each with a thread.
5. Heat a little oil, stir in the spiced bitter gourd, a few at a time and fry over low heat till tender.
6. The pickle is ready for use. It lasts for 1 month. Stir frequently and sun occasionally.

073 Sour Capsicum – Bean Sprout : Hot

250 g	capsicum, slice
150 g	bean sprouts
100 g	spring onion, chop
50 ml	vinegar
30 ml	ginger juice
20 g	chopped celery
15 ml	tomato puree
10 g	dried red chillies, grind fine using vinegar
3 g	peppercorns, dry-roast & powder
50 g	salt
50 ml	oil

1. Heat a little oil, add the sliced capsicum, chopped celery, spring onion and fry till partly tender.
2. Add in the ginger juice, heat for a while and remove.
3. In the same pan heat the remaining oil, stir in the tomato puree, salt and bring to the boil.
4. Follow with the chilli paste, pepper powder and again bring to the boil.
5. Continue cooking over low heat until the oil separates.
6. Stir in the fried vegetables, the bean sprouts and the vinegar. Cook till well blended and remove.
7. The pickle is ready for use. It keeps for 10 days and longer in the refrigerator.

074 Stuffed Kalakkai Chain : Oilless

500 g	kalakkai, split & seed
60 g	chilli powder;
10 g	asafoetida, roast in oil & powder;
10 g	turmeric powder &
110 g	salt, combine all evenly

1. Split the kalakkai vertically without severing and seed.
2. Stuff the spice mixture into the split kalakkai on the two inner sides. Close and set aside.
3. Prick the kalakkai with a needle and make a chain using a clean thread. Hang the pickle chain in an airy place.
4. The pickle is ready for use. It lasts for 1 month. Sun covered, occasionally.

075 Sour Chambakai : Hot

500 g	half-ripe chambakai, keep whole, wash, wipe & remove stalks
30 g	chilli powder
5 g	mustard seeds;
1 g	fenugreek seeds &
5 g	asafoetida, roast all three in oil & powder
10 g	jaggery, grate
10 g	mustard seeds
100 g	salt
200 ml	oil

1. Marinate the chambakai in salt for 2 days. Toss daily.
2. Add the spice powders into the salted chambakai and mix well.
3. Heat oil, add mustard seeds and allow to crackle.
4. Pour the seasoning over the spiced chambakai and stir thoroughly.
5. The pickle is ready for use after a day. It lasts for 6 months.

076 Sour Spiced Sprouted Bengal Gram : Salty

125 g	bengal gram sprouts
50 g	onion, peel & chop fine
15 g	green coriander, clean, air-dry & chop fine
15 g	chilli powder
3 g	turmeric powder
3	cloves garlic, peel & chop fine
50 ml	lime juice
35 g	salt
50 ml	oil

1. Heat a little oil, stir-fry the sprouted bengal gram for a while and set aside.
2. In the same pan heat the remaining oil, add the chopped onion, garlic, coriander and fry for a few minutes.
3. Follow with the gram sprouts, chilli, turmeric powders, and the salt.
4. Cook till well blended, add in the lime juice and remove when the mixture begins to bubble.
5. The pickle is ready for use. It keeps for 1 month and is best refrigerated. Sun occasionally.

077 Corn – Ginger : Hot

250 g	stripped corn (from 4 corncobs)
15 ml	vinegar
1-1"	piece of fresh ginger, scrape & grind fine
10 g	white peppercorns
20 g	salt
25 ml	oil

1. Cook the corn cobs in a pressure cooker in enough water till done.
2. Strip the corn off the cob while still hot and allow to cool.
3. Heat the oil in a pan, stir in the ginger paste and fry till the oil separates.
4. Stir in the stripped corn and cook till done.
5. Add in the pepper powder, vinegar, salt and simmer till well blended.
6. The pickle is ready for use. It keeps for 2 weeks and is best refrigerated.

078 Sour Cucumber – Spring Onion : Hot

250 g	cucumber, cut into squares
50 g	salt : for marinating cucumber
100 g	spring onion, chop
30 ml	oil
45 ml	tomato puree
150 ml	vinegar
20 g	chopped bamboo shoot
5	dried red chillies
1-1"	piece of fresh ginger, scrape & slice thinly
5 g	sugar
20 g	salt : for pickle

1. Stir-fry the marinated cucumber, chopped spring onion, the chopped bamboo shoot in a little oil till partly tender and set aside.
2. In the same pan heat the remaining oil, add the tomato puree and bring to the boil.
3. Lower the heat and cook till the oil separates.
4. Add in the vinegar and cook over a high flame.
5. Allow the mixture to thicken again.
6. Stir in the fried vegetables, sliced ginger, chilli powder, sugar and salt.
7. Cook till the mixture thickens again and remove.
8. The pickle is ready for use. It lasts for 2 months and is best refrigerated.

079 Spicy Curd – Mango : Oilless

125 ml	slightly sour curd, whip with 25ml water
50 g	seeded raw mango, chop fine
2	green chillies, chop
3 g	dried ginger powder
1	lime leaf &
2	curry leaves, wash both, air-dry & devein
1 g	asafoetida, roast in oil & powder
5 g	salt

1. Combine all the ingredients except the whipped curd.
2. Stir the mixture into the whipped curd.
3. The pickle is ready for use. It keeps for 2 days and longer in the refrigerator.

080 Curry Leaf Seed : Hot

500 g	tender curry leaf seeds, wash, slit & air-dry
75 g	chilli powder
75 g	jaggery, grate
5 g	turmeric powder
10 g	mustard seeds : for seasoning
150 g	salt
250 ml	oil

1. Stir-fry the curry leaf seeds in a little oil and set aside.
2. Heat some more oil, add mustard seeds and allow to crackle. Add in the jaggery, turmeric powder and salt.
3. Bring to the boil and allow to thicken over a high flame.
4. Lower the heat, stir in the fried seeds and the remaining spice powders.
5. Continue cooking over low heat until the mixture becomes jam-like and the oil separates.
6. The pickle is ready for use. It lasts for 2 months.

Curry leaf seeds

Tender curry leaf seeds are highly aromatic as they contain volatile oils. They should be picked before they turn a deep purplish maroon, at which stage they are very tough, with seeds and inedible.

081 Drumstick Pith – Green Chilli : Hot

500 g	cooked drumstick inner pith
75 g	green chillies, chop fine
25 g	fresh ginger, scrape & shred
5 g	cummin seeds
3 g	turmeric powder
40 g	cleaned tamarind, obtain thick extract using water
50 ml	lime juice
5 g	sugar
3 g	black salt
60 g	salt
200 ml	oil

Note: To obtain the inner pith of **drumsticks**, cut them into 4" lengths. Cook till partly tender in lightly salted water. Cool and remove the inner pith with a thin sharp spoon.

1. Heat a little oil, add cummin seeds and fry till done.
2. Stir in the chopped green chillies, shredded ginger and fry for a few minutes.
3. Follow with the cooked drumstick pith, stir-fry for a while and set aside.
4. In the same pan heat the remaining oil, stir in the tamarind extract, sugar, salts, turmeric powder and bring to the boil. Allow to thicken.
5. Add in the fried drumstick pith, continue cooking over low heat until the mixture becomes jam-like and the oil separates.
6. Pour in the lime juice and remove when the mixture begins to bubble.
7. The pickle is ready for use. It lasts for 3 month.

082 Sprouted Fenugreek in Tamarind Sauce : Hot

1,500 g	fenugreek sprouts (obtained from 500g seeds)
25 g	mustard seeds : for seasoning
750 g	cleaned tamarind, obtain thick extract using water
125 g	jaggery, grate
400 g	chilli powder
25 g	turmeric powder
10 g	asafoetida, roast in oil & powder
500 g	salt
750 ml	oil

How to sprout fenugreek

Soak the fenugreek seeds in sufficient water overnight. Drain away the water the following day and tie the soaked seeds in a clean cloth. Hang the bundle in a warm place for a day or two, keeping it moist. Ensure that the sprouts are medium in size. Longer sprouting tends to make the pickle bitter.

1. Stir-fry the fenugreek sprouts over low heat for exactly 2 minutes and set aside. Longer frying makes the sprouts bitter.
2. In the same pan heat some more oil, add mustard seeds and allow to crackle.
3. Stir in the tamarind extract, jaggery, salt and bring to the boil. Allow to thicken over a high flame.
4. Lower the heat, stir in the chilli, turmeric, asafoetida powders, the remaining oil and continue cooking for about 45 minutes until the mixture thickens.
5. Add in the fried sprouts and cook for 15 minutes until the mixture becomes jam-like and the oil separates.
6. The pickle is ready for use. It lasts for 6 months.

083 Green Garlic in Lime Juice : Hot

50g	green garlic, chop
20	green chillies, chop
15g	green coriander, clean, air-dry & chop
10g	peppercorns, sun-dry & powder
5g	sugar
75ml	lime juice
30g	salt

1. Combine the sugar and salt with the lime juice.
2. Stir in the chopped vegetable and set aside for 1 hour.
3. Blend in the pepper powder.
4. The pickle is ready for use. It keeps for 2 days in the refrigerator.

084 Star Gooseberry : Sweet

1 kg	tender star gooseberry, prick all over with fork
1 kg	sugar
400 ml	water
10	cardamoms, crush
5 g	edible camphor
5 g	saffron, dissolve in a little milk

1. Heat together the sugar and water till the syrup reaches a single-thread consistency.
2. Remove the scum by adding a little milk when the syrup boils.
3. Drop the pricked star gooseberry into the boiling syrup.
4. Add in the honey, saffron, cardamom, mix well and remove.
5. Stir in the camphor and mix thoroughly.
6. The pickle is ready for use after 1 month. It lasts for 1 year.

085 Sprouted Green Gram : Hot

125 g	whole green gram sprouts
50 g	green coriander, clean, air-dry & chop
50 g	onion, peel & chop
30 g	green chillies;
5	cloves garlic, peel &
2-1"	pieces of fresh ginger, scrape & chop, grind all three to a paste
5 g	dried mango powder
5 g	chilli powder
3 g	cummin seeds, dry-roast & powder
10 ml	lime juice
10 g	cleaned tamarind, obtain thick extract using water
30 g	salt
30 ml	oil

1. Heat a little oil, add mustard seeds and allow to crackle.
2. Add in the sprouted gram, the spice paste, fry for a few minutes till partly tender and set aside.
3. In the same pan heat some more oil, stir in the chopped onion and fry till transluscent.
4. Stir in the tamarind extract and bring to the boil. Allow to thicken over a high flame.
5. Stir in the chopped coriander, cummin and the dried mango powders.
6. Continue cooking until the mixture becomes jam-like and the oil separates.
7. Add in the fried sprouts, the lime juice and remove when the mixture begins to bubble.
8. The pickle is ready for use. It lasts for 1 month.

086 Spicy Irumban Puli : Watery

500 g	irumban puli
40 g	salt : for marinating
200 ml	water : boil & cool
40 g	dried red chillies;
25 g	peeled garlic;
1-1"	piece of fresh ginger, scrape & chop;
10 g	fenugreek seeds &
5 g	asafoetida, roast in oil & powder, grind all to a paste using water
12 g	split husked mustard seeds
5	cloves garlic, peel & chop
1-1"	piece of fresh ginger, scrape & julienne
5 g	mustard seeds &
5 g	fenugreek seeds : both for seasoning
5 g	turmeric powder
5 g	sugar
40 ml	vinegar
100 g	salt : for pickle
100 ml	oil

1. Marinate the irumban puli in salt and turmeric powder for a day. Sun-dry for 4 days.
2. Heat a little oil, add the mustard seeds, fenugreek seeds and allow to crackle.
3. Add in the chopped garlic, ginger and fry for a few minutes till tender.
4. Stir in the spice paste and fry for a few minutes.
5. Pour in the cooled water and bring to the boil.
6. When the water begins to bubble, stir in the vinegar, sugar, salt and continue cooking over a high flame. Allow to thicken and remove.
7. Add in the salted irumban puli, husked mustard seeds and stir well.
8. The pickle is ready for use after 2 days. Stir daily. It lasts for 4 months.

Note : Tamarind is widely used as a souring agent in pickling in India. Other similar souring agents are kodam puli, bilimbi puli, irumban puli and kokum. These are mostly found in the south and north east parts of India.

087 Raw Jackfruit in Lime Juice : Hot

125 g	cubed raw tender jackfruit
50 g	green coriander, clean, air-dry & chop
20 g	green chillies &
50g	salt, grind both to a paste
5g	mustard seeds
3g	cummin seeds
50ml	lime juice
50ml	vinegar
50ml	oil

1. Steam the cubed jackfruit gently till done but not mushy. Bruise till lightly shredded.
2. Heat a little oil, add mustard, cummin seeds and fry till done.
3. Stir in the chopped coriander, the green chilli paste and fry for a few minutes.
3. Add in the steamed jackfruit and cook till well blended.
4. Stir in the lime juice, vinegar and remove when the mixture begins to bubble.
5. The pickle is ready for use. It lasts for 2 months. Sun occasionally.

088 Spiced Kumquat – Mango Ginger : Hot

500g	kumquat, chop fine & seed
125g	peeled mango ginger, chop fine
40g	green chillies, chop fine
12g	jaggery, grate
25g	chilli powder;
5g	fenugreek seeds, roast in oil & powder;
5g	turmeric powder &
5g	asafoetida, roast in oil & powder, combine all evenly
5g	mustard seeds &
a few	sprigs curry leaves : both for seasoning
150g	salt
250ml	oil

1. Marinate the chopped kumquat in salt for 5 days. Blend in the spice mixture.
2. Heat a little oil, add mustard seeds and allow to crackle. Drop in the curry leaves and fry till crisp.
3. Stir in the mango ginger pieces, chopped green chilli and fry for a few minutes over low heat.
4. Add in the jaggery and stir well till the jaggery melts.
5. Pour the seasoning and the remaining oil (after heating & cooling) over the spiced kumquat. Stir thoroughly.
6. The pickle is ready for use. It lasts for 2 months in the refrigerator.

089 Sweet & Sour Kumquat : Hot

500 g	kumquat, chop fine & seed
60 g	jaggery, grate
25 g	green chillies, chop fine
25 g	dried red chillies, seed & break into bits
12 g	chilli powder;
3 g	fenugreek seeds, roast in oil & powder;
3 g	turmeric powder &
3 g	asafoetida, roast in oil & powder, combine
125 g	salt
200 ml	oil
5 g	mustard seeds;
3 g	split husked bengal gram &
a few	sprigs curry leaves : all three for seasoning

1. Heat a little oil, add mustard seeds and allow to crackle.
2. Drop in the curry leaves & bengal gram and fry till done.
3. Add in the green and red chillies and fry a while.
4. Stir in the kumquat pieces, some more oil and cook covered, over low heat for a few minutes.
5. Uncover, add in the spice mixture, salt, jaggery and cook till well blended, adding the remaining oil, little by little.
6. The pickle is ready for use. It lasts for 1 month and longer in the refrigerator.

The Kumquat orange is a member of the citrus family, botanically known as *fortunella japonica*. Though an orange, it has a hint of narthangai in taste. It is a versatile fruit and apart from being pickled, is used for making jams, jellies and squashes.

090 Sambara Lime : Hot

1 kg	lime, slit into 4 without severing
100 g	chilli powder
20 g	asafoetida;
10 g	cummin seeds &
10 g	fenugreek seeds, roast all three in oil & powder
10 g	turmeric powder &
200 g	salt, combine both evenly
400 ml	oil

1. Stuff each lime with the salt-turmeric mixture.
2. Sprinkle a little salt-turmeric mixture at the base of a jar.
3. Pack in the stuffed limes, sprinkle over the remaining salt-turmeric mixture and cap tight.
4. Shake the jar daily for 45 days by which time the limes will be ready for pickling.
5. Cut the salted limes into small pieces. Combine the chilli, cummin, fenugreek and asafoetida powders.
6. Stir the spice mixture into the lime pieces, pour over the oil and set aside for 2 days.
7. The pickle is ready for use after 1 week. It lasts for 1 year.

091 Sambara Mango : Hot

500 g	cut mango, size into small pieces
35 g	chilli powder
10 g	fenugreek seeds;
10 g	cummin seeds &
5 g	asafoetida, roast all three in oil & powder
75 g	salt
200 ml	oil
5 g	mustard seeds &
a few	sprigs curry leaves : both for seasoning

1. Marinate the mango pieces in salt for a day.
2. Next day remove the mango pieces from the salt water. Strain and store the salt water.
3. Sun-dry the salted mango for 4 days till the pieces are three-fourths' dry.
4. Combine the mango pieces with the spice powders evenly.
5. Heat the oil, add the mustard seeds, curry leaves and allow to crackle.
6. Pour in the salt water and an equal amount of water.
7. When the water begins to boil, stir in the mango mixture and remove after one boil.
8. The pickle is ready for use after 5 days. It lasts for 6 months.

092 Lime Leaf – Curry Leaves : Instant

1 kg	lime leaves &
200 g	curry leaves, devein, wash & air-dry
400 g	chilli powder
240 g	cleaned tamarind, dry-roast
25 g	asafoetida, roast in oil & powder
240 g	salt
800 ml	oil

1. Grind together all the ingredients coarsely and roll into small balls.
2. This dry pickle is ready for use. It lasts for 2 years.
3. Serve each time after adding a little water or oil or both, if desired.

093 Mango Ginger in Tamarind Sauce : Hot

500 g	peeled mango ginger, chop & grind
5 g	mustard seeds : for seasoning
150 g	cleaned tamarind, obtain thick extract
75 g	jaggery, grate
50 g	chilli powder
5 g	turmeric powder
5 g	fenugreek seeds &
5 g	asafoetida, roast both in oil & powder
75 g	salt
250 ml	oil

1. Fry the mango ginger paste in some oil. Set aside.
2. In the same pan heat some more oil, add mustard seeds and allow to crackle.
3. Follow with the tamarind extract, jaggery, salt and bring to the boil. Allow to thicken over a high flame.
4. Lower the heat, stir in the chilli, turmeric, fenugreek, asafoetida powders, the fried mango ginger and the remaining oil.
5. Cook until the oil separates.
6. The pickle is ready for use. It lasts for 6 months.

094 Sour Sprouted Moth – Thymol seeds : Hot

250 g	moth sprouts
5 g	turmeric powder
5 g	thymol seeds
30 g	cleaned tamarind, obtain extract using water
30 g	green chillies &
15 g	green coriander, clean, air-dry & grind both fine
30 g	salt
75 ml	oil

1. Heat a little oil, add the sprouted moth, turmeric powder, salt and cook till almost tender. Set aside.
2. Heat the remaining oil and fry the thymol seeds till done. Follow with the chilli-coriander paste and cook for a few minutes.
3. Stir in the tamarind extract and bring to the boil. Allow to thicken.
4. Add in the moth mixture and continue cooking over low heat.
5. Remove when the mixture becomes jam-like and the oil separates.
6. The pickle is ready for use. It lasts for 1 month and is best refrigerated.

095 Mudukottan Leaf in Tamarind Sauce : Hot

500 g	mudukottan leaves, wash, air-dry & chop
60 g	dried red chillies, dry-roast & powder
40 g	cleaned tamarind, obtain thick extract using water
20 g	jaggery, grate
10 g	asafoetida, roast in oil & powder
10 g	turmeric powder
10 g	mustard seeds : for seasoning
80 g	salt
100 ml	oil

1. Stir-fry the mudukottan leaves in a little oil. Allow to cool and grind coarsely.
2. Heat the oil, add mustard seeds and allow to crackle.
3. Pour in the tamarind extract, jaggery and allow to thicken over a high flame.
4. Stir in the ground mudukottan leaves, chilli, turmeric, asafoetida powders and the salt.
5. Continue cooking over low heat until the mixture becomes jam-like and the oil separates.
6. The pickle is ready for use. It lasts for 2 months.

096 Mulberry : Hot

500 g	half-ripe mulberry, halve
25 g	dried red chillies, roast in oil & powder
25 g	jaggery, grate
10 g	mustard seeds, sun-dry & powder
5 g	fenugreek seeds &
5 g	asafoetida, roast both in oil & powder
5 g	turmeric powder
75 g	salt
175 ml	oil

1. Heat a little oil, add in the mulberry pieces and stir-fry for a few minutes till partly tender.
2. Stir in the spice powders, jaggery and the remaining oil.
3. Continue cooking until the mulberry pieces soften and the oil separates.
4. The pickle is ready for use. It lasts for 2 months.

097 Mustard Mushroom in Vinegar : Instant

250 g	mushroom, wash, air-dry & slice
20 g	green chillies, chop
10 g	white mustard seeds, sun-dry & powder
5 g	dried ginger powder
100 ml	vinegar
35 g	salt
25 ml	oil

1. Heat oil, add chopped green chillies and stir-fry for a few minutes.
2. Follow with the sliced mushroom and cook for 5 minutes over low heat until partly tender.
3. Stir in the spice powders, salt, vinegar and simmer till well blended.
4. The pickle is ready for use. It lasts for 1 month and is best refrigerated.

098 Sour Mushroom – Spring Onion : Salty

250 g	fresh mushroom or 100g tinned mushroom
125 g	spring onion, chop fine
150 ml	oil
75 g	bamboo shoot pieces
75 ml	vinegar

100 g	tomato, blanch, peel & obtain puree
5 g	white peppercorns, dry-roast & powder
50 g	salt

1. Boil the fresh mushroom in 300ml water for about 10 minutes.
2. Drain out the water, discard the stems and chop the caps into square pieces.
3. Heat a little oil, add the chopped spring onion, the chopped mushroom and the bamboo shoots pieces.
4. Stir-fry for a few minutes till almost tender and set aside.
5. In the same pan cook the tomato puree in a little oil until the oil separates.
6. Add in the salt, pepper, chilli powders and heat for a while.
7. Stir in the fried vegetable, vinegar and continue cooking till well blended.
8. The pickle is ready for use. It keeps for 1 week and is best refrigerated.

099 Mushroom – Bamboo Shoot – Water Chestnut : Sweet

150 g	mushroom, wash, pat-dry & halve
125 g	sliced bamboo shoot
125 g	water chestnut, slice
1-1"	piece of fresh ginger, pound;
2-1"	sticks of cinnamon &
5	cardamoms, tie all three in a spice bag
175 ml	vinegar
125 g	sugar
50 g	salt
50 ml	oil

1. Stir-fry the halved mushroom, the sliced bamboo shoot, the sliced chestnut in the oil for a few minutes.
2. Add in the vinegar, sugar, salt, the spice bag and bring to the boil.
3. Cook for 10 minutes and remove.
4. Squeeze out and discard the spice bag.
5. The pickle is ready for use. It lasts for 2 months and is best refrigerated.

100 Spicy Mushroom : Hot

125 g	fresh mushroom, wash, pat-dry & chop fine	2-1"	pieces of fresh ginger, scrape & chop
75 g	onion, keep whole	5	cloves garlic
30 g	green coriander, clean, air-dry & chop	10	almonds
		10	peppercorns
5	dried red chillies	1 g	grated nutmeg
3 g	sugar	20 ml	lime juice
3 g	cummin seeds	20 ml	vinegar
2 g	coriander seeds	10 g	cleaned tamarind, obtain thick extract using water
2 g	black cummin seeds		
2 g	aniseeds		
2 g	poppy seeds		
2	cloves	20 g	salt
1	blade of mace	50 ml	oil

1. Dry-roast the spices, chilli and powder together.
2. Pound the onions and toast over the fire. Peel and grind to a paste along with the chopped coriander, ginger and garlic.
3. Stir-fry the ground mixture in a little oil and set aside.
4. In the same pan heat some more oil, pour in the tamarind extract, sugar, salt and bring to the boil.
5. Stir in the chopped mushroom and allow to thicken.
6. Add in the fried spice paste, the spice mixture and combine thoroughly.
7. Blend in the lime juice, vinegar and remove when the mixture begins to bubble.
8. The pickle is ready for use. It lasts for 1 month and is best refrigerated.

101 Sour Naravallikai : Hot

500g	naravallikai
40g	chilli powder
10g	mustard seeds, sun-dry & powder
8g	fenugreek seeds &
5g	asafoetida, roast both in oil & powder
5g	turmeric powder
150ml	lime juice
125g	salt
200ml	oil : heat & cool

1. Pound the naravallikai, remove the cap and seed.
2. Combine the spice powders with the salt evenly.
3. Stuff the spice mixture into the naravallikai.
4. Pour the lime juice and the pre-heated oil over the mixture to cover. Set aside for 2 days and stir thoroughly.
5. The pickle is ready for use after 10 days. It lasts for 6 months.

Use fresh vegetables, wash throughly to free them from mud and grit. Cook them until almost tender. Longer cooking destroys crispness, freshness as well as food value, flavour, texture and colour.

102 Sweet Spiced Nutmeg : Hot

500 g	fresh nutmeg skin, chop fine
125 g	cleaned tamarind, obtain thick extract using water
125 g	jaggery, grate
40 g	chilli powder
3 g	mustard seeds, sun-dry & powder
3 g	turmeric powder
5 g	peppercorns;
2 g	fenugreek seeds &
2 g	asafoetida, roast all three in oil & powder
120 g	salt
200 ml	oil

1. Stir-fry the chopped nutmeg skin in a little oil and set aside.
2. In the same pan, heat some more oil, pour in the tamarind extract, jaggery, turmeric powder and salt. Allow to thicken over a high flame.
3. Stir in the chilli, mustard, fenugreek, pepper and asafoetida powders.
4. Continue cooking over low heat adding the fried nutmeg and the remaining oil little by little.
5. Remove when the mixture becomes jam-like and the oil separates.
6. The pickle is ready for use. It lasts for 2 months.

103 Aromatic Omavalli : Hot

125 g	omavalli leaves, wash, air-dry & chop fine
100 g	dried red chillies, grind to a paste using water
100 g	cleaned tamarind, obtain thick extract using water
100 g	split husked black gram
20 g	mustard seeds, sun-dry & powder
10 g	jaggery, grate
5 g	turmeric powder
75 g	salt
175 ml	oil

1. Stir-fry the chilli paste in a little oil.
2. When the oil separates, add the chopped omavalli, stir-fry for a few minutes and set aside.
3. In the same pan heat the remaining oil, add in the tamarind extract, jaggery and bring to the boil. Allow to thicken over a high flame.
4. Stir in the mustard, turmeric powders, the fried omavalli-chilli mixture and the salt.
5. Continue cooking over low heat until the mixture becomes jam-like and the oil separates.
6. The pickle is ready for use. It lasts for 1 month.

104 Sour & Spicy Green Peas : Hot

250 g	shelled green peas
75 g	onion, peel & chop
20 g	green chillies, chop
15 g	coriander seeds &
5 g	cummin seeds, dry-roast both & powder
5 g	chilli powder
3 g	tumeric powder
1 g	garam masala powder
1-1"	piece of fresh ginger, scrape & grind fine
5	cloves garlic, peel & grind fine
5	peppercorns
2	cardamoms
2	cloves
1-1"	stick of cinnamon
1	bay leaf
50 g	tomato puree
20 g	cleaned tamarind, obtain thick extract using water
25 ml	lime juice
50 g	salt
75 ml	oil

1. Stir-fry the shelled peas in a little oil over low heat till almost cooked. Set aside.
2. In the same pan, heat some more oil, add the whole spices and fry for a minute.
3. Stir in the chopped green chilli, ginger-garlic paste, the spice powders, fry for a while and set aside.
4. Heat the remaining oil, add the chopped onion and fry till translucent.
5. Pour in the tomato puree, tamarind extract and allow to thicken over a high flame.
6. Add in the fried peas, continue cooking until the mixture becomes jam-like and the oil separates.
7. Stir in the spice mixture, the lime juice and remove when the mixture begins to bubble.
8. The pickle is ready for use. It lasts for 1 month.

105 Sour Pineapple – Fruit & Nut : Sweet

250 g	grated pineapple
300 g	sugar
125 g	cored apple, peel & grate
25 g	seeded raw mango, peel & grate
25 g	shelled pistachio, sliver;
25 g	almond, blanch, peel & sliver;
25 g	shelled walnut &
25 g	cashewnut, halve, combine all
25 g	seedless raisin, chop
25 g	date, stone & chop
3 g	cardamom powder
25 ml	vinegar
30 g	salt

Always buy half-ripe pineapples for pickling to get a sweet and sour taste. Cut off the heads, peel thickly, remove the eyes and cut into chunks or finely chop as desired.

1. Cook the grated pineapple in sufficient water till partly tender.
2. Add in the grated apple, mango, chopped raisin, date and cook till partly done.
3. Follow with the sugar, salt and stir to dissolve.
4. Add in the cardamom powder, vinegar, the nut mixture and cook till thick.
5. The pickle is ready for use. It lasts for 2 months and is best refrigerated.

106 Sour & Spicy Plantain Flower : Hot

500 g	chopped plantain flower, deep-fry & drain
200 g	tomato puree
75 g	onion, peel & chop
2-1"	pieces of fresh ginger, scrape & chop
20 g	peeled garlic, chop
5 g	cummin seeds
3 g	coriander seeds
3 g	turmeric powder
3 g	garam masala powder
15 g	cleaned tamarind, obtain thick extract
40 g	chilli powder
50 g	salt
200 ml	oil

1. Stir-fry the ginger-garlic paste in a little oil and set aside.
2. Fry the chopped onion till transluscent in the remaining oil.
3. Stir in the tomato puree, the tamarind extract and bring to the boil. Allow to thicken.
4. Add in the fried plantain flower, the fried spice paste and the spice powders.
5. Continue cooking over low heat until the mixture becomes jam-like and the oil separates.
6. The pickle is ready for use. It lasts for 2 months.

107 Plantain Stem : Hot

125 g	chopped plantain stem
5 g	salt : for marinating
10 g	green coriander, clean, air-dry & chop;
3	green chillies;
1-1"	piece of fresh ginger, scrape & chop;
3 g	coriander seeds;
3 g	cummin seeds &
2	cloves garlic, peel & chop, grind all to a paste
3 g	turmeric powder
3 g	garam masala powder
50 ml	lime juice
20 g	salt : for pickle
50 ml	oil

1. Salt the plantain stem pieces for 1 hour. Drain and dry on a clean cloth.
2. Add in the lime juice and salt.
3. Heat the oil and stir-fry the spice paste.
4. Stir in the spice powders, the dried plantain stem and cook till well blended.
5. The pickle is ready for use. It keeps for 1 week and is best refrigerated.

108 Potato – Green Coriander in Lime Juice : Hot

250 g	potato, peel, cube & deep-fry
50 g	green chillies, chop
15 g	green coriander, clean, air-dry & chop
2-1"	pieces of fresh ginger, scrape &
3	cloves garlic, peel & grind both to a paste
5 g	sugar
100 ml	lime juice
60 g	salt
125 ml	oil

1. Stir-fry the ginger-garlic paste in the oil remaining after deep-frying the potato.
2. Add in the coriander-green chilli paste and fry till the oil separates.
3. Follow with the sugar, salt, lime juice and mix well.
4. Stir in the fried potato, heat for a while and remove when well blended.
5. The pickle is ready for use. It keeps for 15 days and is best refrigerated.

109 Sour Red Pumpkin : Sweet

250 g	tender red pumpkin, cube with skin & deep-fry
20 g	jaggery, grate
10 g	chilli powder
10 g	cleaned tamarind, obtain thick extract using water
5 g	dried mango powder
5 g	turmeric powder
5 g	coriander seeds, sun-dry & powder
3 g	fenugreek seeds
2	dried red chillies, break into bits
2	cloves
1-1"	stick of cinnamon
35 g	salt
100 ml	oil

1. Heat a little oil, add the cloves, cinnamon, fenugreek seeds, dried red chillies and fry for a minute. Set aside.
2. In the same pan heat the remaining oil, stir in the tamarind extract, jaggery, salt and bring to the boil. Allow to thicken over a high flame.
3. Stir in the chilli, turmeric, coriander and the dried mango powders. Continue cooking until the mixture becomes jam-like and the oil separates.
4. Add in the fried spices, fried pumpkin and remove when well blended.
5. The pickle is ready for use. It lasts for 1 month.

110 Spiced Round gourd : Instant

125 g	tender round gourd, peel & make deep cross cuts
	water sufficient to immerse
5 g	aniseeds &
5 g	mustard seeds, sun-dry both & powder
5 g	chilli powder
5 g	fenugreek seeds;
3 g	onion seeds &
3 g	asafoetida, roast all three in oil & powder
3 g	turmeric powder
10 g	salt
50 ml	oil

1. Bring the water to boiling.
2. Drop the tindas into the boiling water and let stand for 2 minutes. Remove and sun-dry for half an hour.
3. Combine the spice powders and salt with a little oil to a paste.
4. Stuff the spice paste into the gourds and pack in a jar.
5. Pour over the remaining oil (after heating & cooling) and sun the mixture for 3 days.
6. The pickle keeps for 1 week and longer in the refrigerator.

111 Star Fruit in Tamarind Sauce : Hot

1 kg	star fruit, remove ridges, innerstem, seeds & chop
40 g	cleaned tamarind, obtain thick extract using water
50 g	sugar
50 g	chilli powder
15 g	green chillies, chop
10 g	turmeric powder
10 g	fenugreek seeds &
10 g	asafoetida, roast both in oil & powder
10 g	mustard seeds : for seasoning
90 g	salt
250 ml	oil

1. Heat a little oil, add mustard seeds and allow to crackle.
2. Stir-fry the green chillies for a few minutes.
3. Add in the chopped star fruit and stir-fry till tender.
4. Pour in the tamarind extract, chilli, turmeric powders, sugar, salt and the remaining oil.
5. Bring to the boil and allow to thicken over a high flame.
6. Continue cooking over low heat until the mixture becomes jam-like and the oil separates.
7. Blend in the fenugreek, asafoetida powders and remove.
8. The pickle is ready for use. It lasts for 1 year.

112 Spiced Spinach : Hot

125 g	spinach, wash, pat-dry & remove hard stems
10 g	chilli powder
2	green cardamoms
1 g	garam masala powder
1	clove
1	blade of mace
1/2"	stick of cinnamon
10 ml	lime juice
5 ml	vinegar
15 g	salt
50 ml	oil

1. Boil the spinach for a few minutes in just enough water until tender. Cool and chop fine.
2. Heat the oil and fry the spices.
3. Add in the chopped spinach, the spice powders and cook till the oil separates.
4. Pour in the vinegar, lime juice and remove when the mixture begins to bubble.
5. The pickle is ready for use. It keeps for 15 days and is best refrigerated.

113 Tudhuvelai Berry / Leaf – Tamarind : Instant

500 g	thuduvelai berries / leaves
100 g	cleaned tamarind, obtain thick extract using water
40 g	jaggery, grate
40 g	chilli powder
5 g	turmeric powder
5 g	asafoetida, roast in oil & powder
10 g	mustard seeds : for seasoning
50 g	salt
200 ml	oil

1. Stir-fry the leaves / berries in a little oil and set aside.
2. Heat half the remaining oil, add mustard seeds and allow to crackle.
3. Add in the tamarind extract, jaggery and bring to the boil. Allow to thicken over a high flame.
4. Stir in the fried leaves / berries, chilli, turmeric, asafoetida powders, salt and the remaining oil.
5. Continue cooking over low heat until the mixture becomes jam-like and the oil separates.
6. The pickle is ready for use. It lasts for 1 month.

114 Tulsi – Gram-Green Chilli : Instant

125 g	tulsi, wash, air-dry & chop fine
100 g	dried red chillies, chop & grind
100 g	cleaned tamarind, obtain thick extract using water
100 g	split husked black gram
20 g	mustard seeds, sun-dry & powder
75 g	salt
125 ml	oil

1. Stir-fry the chilli paste in a little oil.
2. When the oil separates, add in the chopped tulsi, stir-fry for a few minutes and set aside.
3. In the same pan heat the remaining oil, add in the tamarind extract and bring to the boil. Allow to thicken over a high flame.
4. Stir in the mustard, turmeric powders, the spiced tulsi and the salt.
5. Continue cooking over low heat until the mixture becomes jam-like and the oil separates.
6. The pickle is ready for use. It lasts for 1 month.

115 Wheat Sprout – Bengal Gram Sprout : Hot

125 g	wheat sprouts
75 g	whole bengal gram sprouts
100 g	capsicum, chop
100 g	spring onion, chop
30 g	green coriander, clean, air-dry & chop
30 g	green chillies, chop
25 g	cleaned tamarind, obtain thick extract using water
5 g	turmeric powder
5 g	sugar
30 g	salt
30 ml	oil

1. Stir-fry the wheat sprouts, bengal gram sprouts and the chopped coriander in a little oil for a few minutes over low heat. Set aside.
2. Stir-fry the chopped capsicum, spring onion and green chillies in some more oil. Set aside.
3. Heat the tamarind extract with the turmeric powder, sugar, salt and bring to the boil. Allow to thicken over a high flame.
4. Add in the fried sprouts, vegetables and continue cooking.
5. Remove when the mixture becomes jam-like and the oil separates.
6. The pickle is ready for use. It lasts for 1 month and is best refrigerated. Sun occasionally.

KITCHEN SPICES

[PART – II]

KITCHEN SPICES	
Part - I	Page 42
Part - III	Page 96

CINNAMON

Cinnamon is the aromatic bark of the cinnamon tree. In fact, the bark of the cassia tree is also sold as cinnamon, due to its similar taste, but that is not the true cinnamon. Besides its high value as an aromatic spice since ancient times, it is also used as a medicine to treat colds, to warm the digestion and to ease flatulence. Also used to ease menstrual cramps, its astringency makes it valuable for controlling diarrhoea.

Cinnamon is said to cure anorexia, aid mucous formation, chronic sinusitis, cold and bronchitis. Also distilled water of cinnamon relieves abdominal colic, nausea and vomitting. One of grandma's treatments for easing nervous tension, brain fag and poor memory is to mix cinnamon powder with honey and eat it every night. It has an expectorant action in asthma and controls frequency of urination in old age due to weakness of the sphincter muscles.

CLOVES

Cloves are the highly aromatic dried flower buds of the clove tree. It removes the the hoarseness of voice if chewed with or without sugar candy. Heaviness of the head and catarrh in the nose can be corrected by applying a paste of clove to the forehead and nose. It binds the bowels, stimulates appetite and aids digestion. Clove oil has analgesic qualities and is well-known remedy for toothaches. For severe earaches, fumes of cloves roasted over a hot griddle, when taken by a cloth puff over the ear, gives relief. In some cases, it even cures them.

CORIANDER LEAVES

The fresh green leaves of the coriander plant also known as the chinese parsley, is highly nutritious. It is a rich source of iron, calcium, beta-carotene (precursor of vitamin A) and vitamin C. It is good for the digestive system, reducing flatulence.

It stimulates the appetite, aiding the secretion of gastric juices. These leaves are useful in treating dyspepsia and billiousness. Coriander soaked in water for a short time is a cure for persistent vomiting. A few drops of coriander juice put in the eyes cools them, relieving tiredness. It is also said to lower the eye power.

CORIANDER SEEDS

The dried seeds like fresh coriander also has digestive properties, which are best brought out with carbohydrates.

CUMMIN SEEDS

Cummin seeds comes in two varieties - black cummin and white cummin. Both are used in daily cuisine. Its flavour comes out best on roasting it or adding it to hot oil.

Half a teaspoon of tamarind pulp and honey, taken before breakfast is recommended for morning sickness, nausea and vomiting, billiousness and jaundice.

CURRY LEAVES

It is mainly used as a seasoning in vegetable dishes, curries, soups, raitas, salads, snacks etc. as a flavouring agent.

DILL SEEDS

It is a culinary herb which improves the digestion and appetite. Its seeds are said to be useful in curing headaches, head colds and paralysis. It also stimulates and strengthens the liver, lungs and stomach.

FENUGREEK LEAVES

Fenugreek leaves are useful in relieving flatulence, indigestion, bronchitis, distaste for food, rheumatic pain and lumbago. Its paste is used as a poultice in burns, scalds and swellings. Its seeds are highly recommended in cases of diarrhoea, dysentery and cough. It is a useful source of vitamins and minerals, particularly calcium.

GARLIC

Garlic, according to Ayurvedic texts, is a rejuvenator, a stimulant that renews the tissues and enriches the blood. It is hot in action, induces urination and controls flatulence.

Eating garlic can significantly lower blood cholesterol and other fats as well as blood sugar. It can reduce arterial blood clotting and blood pressure.

It has also been used successfully to control diarrhoea, dysentery, pulmonary tuberculosis, diphtheria, whooping cough, typhoid and hepatitis, and is also effective against many fungal skin infections.

Exotic

pickles

are

the rare collections

for

the adventurous

ranging from

the LOVE - LOVI

to

the OLIVE ;

truly

a bonanza

Recipes : Exotic

116.	Mustard anbazhanga : hot		143.	Green chilli in curd : salty
117.	Artichoke in vinegar : watery		144.	Sprouted green gram – cocum : hot
118.	Sour apricot – dry fruits: sweet		145.	Sour & spicy sprouted green gram : hot
119.	Garlic, ginger – bamboo shoot : hot		146.	Roasted groundnut – chilli - garlic : hot
120.	Four angled beans in lime juice : hot		147.	Sour guava : hot
121.	Spicy bean sprouts – onion : hot		148.	Spiced horsegram – onion : hot
122.	Berginger : sweet		149.	Tender raw jackfruit – mango powder : hot
123.	Bel murabba : sweet		150.	Kovakkai – onion - gram : hot
124.	Fried bilimbi – gram : hot		151.	Spice stuffed lady's finger in lime juice : hot
125.	Sour, ripe bitter gourd : hot		152.	Spiced lime – fresh red chillies : watery
126.	Bitter gourd – onion : hot		153.	Spice ball – coconut : instant
127.	Small bitter gourd – green spices : hot		154.	Steamed lotus stem : hot
128.	Sour, oven toasted brinjal : hot		155.	Stuffed lotus stem : hot
129.	Capsicum – bitter gourd - mango stuffing : hot		156.	Spiced love-lovi : hot
130.	Capsicum – green spices : hot		157.	Dry fruit in tamarind sauce : sweet
131.	Cabbage strips – stuffed lime : oilless		158.	Mango – brinjal : instant
132.	Cauliflower – date - onion : hot		159.	Mango – gooseberry - onion : hot
133.	Mustard carrot – garlic : hot		160.	Mango – tamarind avakkai : hot
134.	Spiced baby carrot : watery		161.	Mango avakkai – mustard - sesame : hot
135.	Mixed gram sprouts : hot		162.	Spicy mango – garlic : tender
136.	Sour cherry in tamarind sauce : hot		163.	Mango – green chilli : tender
137.	Chow chow – green spices : hot		164.	Mango avakkai – ginger : tender
138.	Spicy corn – onion - sprouts : hot		165.	Spicy cooked mango : watery
139.	Sour & spicy date: sweet		166.	Mixed vegetable – garlic in lime juice : hot
140.	Sour fenugreek leaf – green spices : hot			
141.	Spicy stuffed fresh red chilli : hot			
142.	Perky gherkin : oilless			

167. Mixed vegetable in vinegar : sweet
168. Mixed vegetable – green spices : watery
169. Mushroom in tamarind sauce : hot
170. Button mushroom – ginger - onion : oilless
171. Spicy nutrinuggets – capsicum : hot
172. Ripe olive – fenugreek - onion seeds : hot
173. Papaya preserve : sweet
174. Small white onion in mustard oil : hot
175. Green peas in tamarind sauce : hot
176. Sour pineapple : sweet
177. Plantain flower in tamarind sauce : hot
178. Raw plantain – gram - green chilli : hot
179. Potato avakkai : hot
180. Sweet & sour raisin : hot
181. Lotus stem – mustard - aniseed : hot
182. Green tamarind – gram - red chilli : hot
183. Sweet & sour pidikarnai : instant
184. Wild mustard – grated coconut : instant
185. Green turmeric in lime juice : oilless
186. Wheat – coconut : instant
187. Sour & spicy green tomato : hot
188. Woodapple – ginger : sweet
189. Tudhuvelai berry – lime juice : hot

SUN DRIED VEGETABLES

Fenugreek leaves : Smear fenugreek leaves with salt and dry in the sun thoroughly. Store in a tin and cook in water whenever needed.

Potato : Parboil potatoes in salted water to taste. Remove from fire and drain the excess water. When cool, cut the potatoes into thin slices. Spread on a cloth in the sunlight and dry thoroughly. Store in an airtight tin. Deep-fry the chips, a few at a time, till crisp. Serve as a snack.

Cauliflower : From the whole cauliflower, take out the single buds. Tie these separately with a thread and hang in the sunlight. Dry thoroughly for a few days. Store in an airtight tin. Soak the dried buds in water when needed and use.

Onion : Take the desired quantity of medium-sized onions. Peel and cut into long thin strips. Spread on a paper or cloth and dry thoroughly. Store in a airtight tin. Fry in fat and use in soups, pulaos and other dishes.

Brinjal : Take the desired quantity of medium sized brinjals. Dice into small bits. Smear with salt and dry thoroughly in the hot sun on a cloth for a couple of days. Store in an airtight tin. Soak in water and use in curries and gravies.

Lady's fingers : Sun-dry sliced lady's fingers for a day. Soak them overnight in sufficient salted sour curd. The following day, dry the vegetables pieces till the curd has been absorbed by the vegetable. Dry for a couple of days till these are free from moisture and completely dry. Store in an airtight tin. Deep-fry and serve with rice.

For two cups of vegetable slices, use three cups of curd. Bitter gourd can be similarly prepared.

Beans : Take the desired quantity of beans, top and tail them. Parboil in water with salt and turmeric powder to taste. Remove from fire. Drain the excess water and dry thoroughly in the sunlight on a cloth for a few days. Store in an airtight tin. Before using deep-fry in fat and serve with rice.

Gooseberry : Gooseberries after being parboiled in salted water can be dried in the hot sun till they shrivel. Store in a tin and use as a pickle or for making fresh hot pickles and for pachadi (raita).

Peas : Parboil shelled peas in salted water. Take out, drain the water and dry in the sunlight till they shrivel up. Store in a tin and cook in boiling water whenever needed.

116 Mustard Anbazhanga : Hot

- 500 g anbazhanga, make 2 slits over each
- 30 g chilli powder
- 15 g mustard seeds, sun-dry & powder
- 5 g asafoetida, roast in oil & powder
- 125 g salt
- 200 ml oil

1. Marinate the anbazhanga in salt for 2 days. Shake the jar twice daily.
2. On the 3rd day stir in the chilli, mustard, asafoetida powders and oil. Spread a piece of cloth dipped in oil and cover.
3. The pickle is ready for use after 15 days. It lasts for 4 months.

117 Artichoke in Vinegar : Watery

- 500 g artichoke, wash & scrape
- 60 g salt, combine with 1000ml water
- 20 g chilli powder;
- 10 g peppercorns;
- 5 cardamoms;
- 2-1" sticks of cinnamon &
- 5 cloves, tie all in a spice bag
- 400 ml vinegar

1. Drop the artichoke into the salt water and bring to the boil.
2. Lower the heat and cook till tender. Do not discard the salt water.
3. Bring the vinegar to boiling with the spice bag. Remove the spice bag after squeezing and allow to cool.
4. Pour the cold spiced vinegar over the cooked artichoke to cover and set aside for 8 weeks.
5. The pickle lasts for 6 months.

Artichoke
Wash well under a cold tap to flush out any grit. An artichoke will stand upright best if you trim the bottom with a sharp knife, rubbing the stalk with lemon juice to prevent discolouration. Cutting the tips of the inner circle of leaves is to make the artichoke easier to eat.

118 Sour Apricot – Dry Fruits : Sweet

- 500 g dried apricot
- 500 g sugar
- 500 ml lime juice
- 150 g almond, blanch & sliver
- 150 g dried date, stone & pound
- 30 g peppercorns;
- 30 g black cummin seeds &
- 15 g cardamoms, crush all three coarsely
- 100 ml vinegar
- 150 g salt

1. Soak the apricot in lime juice for 24 hours. Crush and pass the soaked apricot through a wire sieve.
2. Add in all the remaining ingredients except vinegar to the apricot pulp and mix thoroughly.
3. Sun the mixture for a week.
4. Blend in the vinegar and sun the pickle for 10 more days.
5. The pickle lasts for 3 months. Sun occasionally.

119 Garlic, Ginger – Bamboo Shoot : Hot

- 500 g fresh peeled tender bamboo shoot, chop fine
- 25 g peeled garlic, peel & halve
- 25 g fresh ginger, scrape & chop
- 12 g chilli powder;
- 12 g peppercorns;
- 5 g fenugreek seeds, roast in oil;
- 5 g asafoetida, roast in oil &
- 5 g mustard seeds, sun-dry, combine all & powder
- 100 ml vinegar, heat & cool
- 100 g salt
- 100 ml oil

1. Cook the bamboo shoot pieces in sufficient water till tender. Cool and chop fine.
2. Marinate the chopped bamboo shoot in salt.
3. Stir-fry the ginger and garlic for a few minutes in a little oil.
4. Blend in the salted bamboo shoot and the spice powders.
5. Pour over the vinegar and stir thoroughly.
6. The pickle is ready for use. It lasts for 4 months.

120 Four Angled Beans in Lime Juice : Hot

- 125 g tender four angled beans, cut into 1/2" pieces
- 12 g chilli powder
- 3 g asafoetida, roast in oil & powder
- 3 g mustard seeds
- 40 ml lime juice
- 15 g salt
- 15 ml oil

1. Blend together the chilli, asafoetida powders and the salt in the lime juice.
2. Stir in the four angled beans and mix well.
3. Heat the oil, add mustard seeds and allow to crackle. Pour the seasoning over the pickle.
4. The pickle is ready for use after 2 days. It keeps for 15 days.

121 Spicy Bean Sprouts – Onion : Hot

125 g	bean sprouts	3 g	turmeric powder
30 g	onion, peel & chop fine	2	cloves & asafoetida, roast both in oil & powder
10 g	green coriander, clean, air-dry & chop	2 g	
20 g	cleaned tamarind, obtain thick extract using water	2 g	garam masala powder
		3 g	mustard seeds
5 g	chilli powder	2 g	cummin seeds
3 g	peppercorns, roast in oil & powder	3 g	sugar
		35 g	salt
		50 ml	oil

1. Heat a little oil, pour in the tamarind extract and bring to the boil. Allow to thicken over a high flame and set aside.
2. In the same pan heat some more oil, add the mustard seeds, cummin seeds and fry till done.
3. Add in the chopped onion and fry till transluscent.
4. Follow with the bean sprouts and stir-fry over low heat till tender.
5. Stir in the chopped coriander, the thickened tamarind extract, spice powders, salt and the sugar.
6. Continue cooking until the mixture becomes jam-like and the oil separates.
7. The pickle is ready for use. It lasts for 2 months.

122 Ber Ginger : Sweet

500 g	ripe ber, remove stems	3 g	black cummin seeds, sun-dry all three & powder
50 g	dried red chillies, pound		
2-1"	pieces of fresh ginger, scrape & thinly slice	5 g	turmeric powder
		250 g	sugar, prepare thick syrup with 100ml water
10 g	mustard seeds;		
3 g	aniseeds &	100 g	salt

1. Sun the bers for 2 days. Slit and seed carefully so as not to tear them.
2. Combine the pounded chillies and spice powders with the salt evenly.
3. Stuff the spice mixture into the slit bers.
4. Add the stuffed bers and sliced ginger into the hot sugar syrup and remove from the fire.
5. The pickle is ready for use after 2 days. It lasts for 3 months. Stir frequently.

123 Bel Murubba : Sweet

500 g	tender raw bel, peel, cut into small pieces & remove pips	300 ml	oil
		5	cardamoms, peel & crush
		a few	drops of kewra essence
400 g	sugar		

1. Soak the bel pieces in water for 4 hours. Drain out the water and dry for 2 hours.
2. Prepare a syrup with the sugar using 50ml water.
3. Drop the crushed cardamom and bel pieces into the syrup.
4. Cook over low heat till they turn brown and remove.
5. Cool, add the kewra essence, cover the bel pieces with the oil and set aside.
6. The pickle is ready for use after 2 weeks. It lasts for 2 months. Sun occasionally.

124 Fried Bilimbi – Gram : Hot

500 g	bilimbi	5	cloves garlic, peel & chop
40 g	split husked bengal gram, dry-roast & powder	5 g	mustard seeds;
		3 g	fenugreek seeds &
12 g	chilli powder	a few	sprigs curry leaves : all three for seasoning
5 g	green chillies, chop		
3 g	fenugreek seeds &		
3 g	asafoetida, roast both in oil & powder	40 ml	vinegar
		50 g	salt : for pickle
		100 ml	oil

1. Add salt and 50ml oil to the bilimbis. Set aside for 6 days.
2. Heat the remaining oil, add the mustard seeds, fenugreek seeds, curry leaves and allow to crackle.
3. Add in the green chillies, garlic and fry for a few minutes.
4. Follow with the chilli, asafoetida and bengal gram powders. Stir-fry for a few seconds and set aside.

5. Heat together the vinegar and salt water from the bilimbis.
6. When it begins to boil, stir in the salted bilimbi, fenugreek powder, seasoning and remove.
7. The pickle is ready for use after 15 days. It lasts for 6 months.

125 Sour, Ripe Bitter gourd : Hot

500 g	ripe bitter gourd, slit & seed	20 g	split husked black gram, fry both in oil till golden
10 g	salt : for marinating		
50 g	green coriander, wash, air-dry & chop	10 g	dried mango powder
50 g	cleaned tamarind, obtain thick extract using water	5 g	mustard seeds, sun-dry & powder
50 g	jaggery, grate	5 g	turmeric powder
70 g	chilli powder		
20 g	split husked bengal gram &	125 g	salt : for pickle
		200 ml	oil

1. Marinate the bitter gourd in salt for one hour.
2. Stir-fry the chopped coriander in a little oil and grind with the roasted gram.
3. Combine the chilli, mustard, turmeric, mango powders, the coriander mixture and the salt with a little oil to a paste.
4. Squeeze-out the marinated bitter gourd and stuff in the spice paste. Coat a little spice paste on the outside of the bitter gourd as well.
5. Stir-fry the stuffed bitter gourd in a little oil, cover and cook over medium heat till partly tender, stirring frequently.
6. Add in the tamarind extract, jaggery, the remaining oil and continue cooking until the oil separates.
7. The pickle is ready for use. It lasts for 2 months.

126 Bitter gourd – Onion : Hot

500 g	bitter gourd, scrape lightly & cut into thin rings		all three in oil & powder
5 g	salt : for marinating	5	cloves garlic, peel &
500 g	onion, peel & chop	1-1"	piece of fresh ginger, scrape, grind both to a paste
20 g	green coriander, clean, air-dry & chop		
3 g	mustard seeds	5 g	turmeric powder
2 g	fenugreek seeds	a pinch	sugar
5 g	coriander seeds;	75 ml	lime juice
5 g	cummin seeds &	50 ml	vinegar
2 g	asafoetida, roast	100 g	salt
		500 ml	oil

1. Boil the bitter gourd pieces in sufficient water to which a teaspoon (5g) salt has been added.
2. Remove, squeeze and set aside.
3. Heat a little oil, add mustard seeds and allow to crackle.
4. Follow with the fenugreek seeds, asafoetida powder and fry till done.
5. Add in the chopped onion and fry till translucent.
6. Stir in the ginger-garlic paste, a little oil and fry for a few more minutes till done.
7. Add in the parboiled bittergourd, the chopped coriander, spice powders, the remaining oil and continue cooking over low heat.
8. Stir in the lime juice, vinegar, sugar and remove when well blended.
9. The pickle is ready for use. It lasts for 1 month and is best refrigerated.

127 Small Bitter gourd – Green Spices : Hot

500 g	small sized bitter gourd, scrape, slit, remove pulp & seeds	1-1"	piece of fresh ginger, scrape & chop, grind all to a paste
15 g	salt &	10 g	chilli powder
5 g	turmeric powder, combine	3 g	coriander seeds;
50 g	onion, peel & chop;	3 g	cummin seeds &
20 g	peeled garlic, chop;	3 g	asafoetida, roast all three in oil & powder
50 g	green chillies &	60 g	salt
		150 ml	oil

1. Rub the salt-turmeric mixture on the inside and outside of the bitter gorud. Set aside for 5 hours.
2. Heat a little oil, add the spice paste and fry till done.
3. Follow with the remaining spice powders, salt and remove when well blended. Allow to cool.
4. Stuff the cooked spice mixture into the bitter gourd and secure with a thread.
5. Heat the remaining oil, add the tamarind extract, jaggery and bring to the boil. Allow to thicken over a high flame.
6. Stir in the stuffed bitter gourd and cook covered, stirring gently occasionally.
7. Remove when the bitter gourd is cooked and the oil separates.
8. The pickle is ready for use. It lasts for 1 month.

128 Sour, Oven Toasted Brinjal : Hot

500 g	seedless brinjal, keep whole
100 g	cleaned tamarind, obtain thick extract using water
100 g	jaggery, grate
40 g	green chillies, chop
20 g	chilli powder
5 g	cummin seeds : for seasoning
5	cloves garlic, peel & chop
5 g	turmeric powder
40 ml	lime juice
75 g	salt
200 ml	oil

1. Smear the brinjal with a little oil and toast over the fire till done. Cool, peel and crumble.
2. Heat the remaining oil, add in the cummin seeds, green chillies and fry for a few minutes.
3. Stir in the tamarind extract, jaggery, chilli, turmeric powders, garlic, the salt and cook till thick.
4. Lower the heat and stir in the crumbled brinjal.
5. Continue cooking until the mixture becomes jam-like and the oil separates.
6. Stir in the lime juice and remove when the mixture begins to bubble.
7. The pickle is ready for use. It lasts for 2 months.

129 Capsicum – Bitter gourd – Mango Stuffing : Hot

500 g	capsicum, split in middle, seed & retain seeds
150 g	grated bitter gourd, scrape
150 g	seeded raw mango, peel & grate
20 g	salt : for marinating
20 g	chilli powder
5 g	turmeric powder
3 g	asafoetida;
2 g	fenugreek seeds &
2 g	aniseeds, roast all three in oil & powder
150 ml	vinegar
75 g	salt : for pickle
150 ml	oil

1. Marinate the bitter gourd in 20g salt for one hour. Rinse in water, squeeze well and air dry.
2. Combine the spices, grated bitter gourd, grated mango, capsicum seeds with the salt and oil to a paste.
3. Stuff the vegetable-spice paste into the split capsicum, join and pack in a jar.
4. Gently pour over the vinegar and set aside for a week. Sun occasionally.
5. The pickle lasts for 3 months.

Capsicum should be glossy, firm and free of wrinkles. Blanching them 3 minutes before cooking makes them more digestible and takes the edge off their very strong flavour.

130 Capsicum – Green Spices : Hot

500 g	capsicum, size into small pieces
100 g	onion, peel & chop
50 g	tomato, chop
50 g	roasted groundnuts, peel & pound coarsely
40 g	green chillies, chop fine
15 g	green coriander, clean, air-dry & chop
1-1"	piece of fresh ginger, scrape & chop fine
3	cloves garlic, peel & chop
5 g	cummin seeds
3 g	garam masala powder
3 g	turmeric powder
5 g	sugar
75 g	salt
100 ml	oil

1. Heat a little oil, add cummin seeds and allow to crackle. Add in the chopped onion and fry till translucent.
2. Stir in the chopped green chillies, ginger, and the garlic. Fry till done and set aside.
3. In the same pan heat some more oil, pour in the tamarind extract and bring to the boil. Allow to thicken and set aside.
4. Heat the remaining oil, add in the capsicum pieces and cook till tender.
5. Follow with the chopped tomato, coriander and continue cooking.
6. Stir in the cooked tamarind extract, pounded groundnuts, garam masala powder, turmeric powder, sugar and salt.
7. Continue cooking until the mixture becomes jam-like and the oil separates.
8. The pickle is ready for use. It lasts for 2 months.

131 Cabbage Strips – Stuffed Lime : Oilless

500 g	cabbage, remove outer leaves & cut into thin strips
500 g	lime, split into 8 pieces each without severing & seed
20 g	seedless raisin, chop
5 g	coriander seeds &
5 g	mustard seeds, sun-dry both & powder
10 g	turmeric powder
50 ml	lime juice
125 g	salt

1. Combine the spice powders evenly and stuff the spice mixture into the limes.
2. Mix the stuffed limes and the shredded cabbage thoroughly in a jar.
3. Sun the mixture for 3 days.
4. Blend in the lime juice and the chopped raisin.
5. The pickle is ready for use after 3 days. It lasts for 1 month and is best refrigerated.

132 Cauliflower – Date - Onion : Hot

500 g	cauliflower florets	2-1"	pieces of fresh ginger, scrape & chop, grind all three to a paste
10 g	salt : for marinating		
25 g	seedless date, chop fine	25 g	jaggery, grate
50 g	small red onion, peel & chop;	25 g	chilli powder
		200 ml	lime juice
75 g	green chillies, chop &	75 g	salt : for pickle
		300 ml	oil

1. Marinate the florets in two teaspoons (5g) salt for 8 hours. Drain, rinse and sun-dry for a day.
2. Heat a little oil, stir-fry the spice paste until the oil separates.
3. Add in the jaggery and the remaining oil.
4. After the jaggery melts drop in the salted florets, chopped date, chilli powder and the salt.
5. Cook for a while, blend in the lime juice and remove.
6. Sun the mixture for 4 days before use.
7. The pickle lasts for 1 month and longer in the refrigerator. Stir once daily.

133 Mustard Carrot – Garlic : Hot

500 g	carrot, peel & julienne
25 g	peeled garlic, chop fine
50 g	chilli powder
10 g	mustard seeds, sun-dry & powder
5 g	turmeric powder
5 g	rock salt
60 g	salt
150 ml	mustard oil

1. Combine the spice mixture with the julienned carrots.
2. Blend in the mustard oil and sun for a day.
3. The pickle is ready for use after 3 days. It lasts for 4 months.

To grate, wash **carrots** once before and after peeling. This helps remove all the grit whatsoever.
To refrigerate **carrots** remove the thick stalks, if any, as they absorb moisture from the roots, causing them to lose their freshness.

134 Spiced Baby carrot : Watery

125 g	baby carrot, peel & split into 4 lengthwise
10 g	green chillies, chop
1/2"	piece of fresh ginger, scrape & chop fine
3 g	chilli powder
3 g	turmeric powder
3 g	split husked mustard seeds;
2 g	fenugreek seeds &
1 g	aniseeds, dry-roast all three & powder
100 ml	water
25 g	salt

1. Blend the spice powders in the water.
2. Add in the chopped ginger, green chillies, carrot pieces and stir thoroughly.
3. Sun the mixture for 3 days. Ensure that water covers the mixture.
4. The pickle keeps for 2 weeks. Sun occasionally.

2–3" long **Baby carrots** are delicious. Carrots toughen with age and develop woody cores that should be removed before cooking. Even cored, they should be cooked for 30 minutes to soften.

135 Mixed Gram Sprouts : Hot

50 g	alfalfa sprouts
50 g	green gram whole, sprouts
50 g	red gram whole, sprouts
50 g	black gram whole, sprouts
50 g	bengal gram whole, sprouts
25 g	fenugreek seeds, sprouts
30 g	cleaned tamarind, obtain thick extract using water
15 g	jaggery, grate
30 g	green chillies, chop
5 g	chilli powder
5 g	turmeric powder
3 g	asafoetida, roast in oil & powder
3 g	mustard seeds
40 g	salt
50 ml	oil

1. Heat a little oil, add mustard seeds and allow to crackle.
2. Add in the chopped green chilli, the mixed sprouts, fry for a few minutes till partly tender and set aside.
3. In the same pan heat some more oil, add in the tamarind extract, jaggery, salt and bring to the boil. Allow to thicken over a high flame.
4. Stir in the spice powders and the fried sprouts.
5. Continue cooking over low heat until the mixture becomes jam-like and the oil separates.
6. The pickle is ready for use. It lasts for 2 months.

136 Sour Cherry in Tamarind Sauce : Hot

500 g	sour cherry, stone
5 g	salt : for marinating
30 g	cleaned tamarind, obtain thick extract using water
40 g	jaggery, grate
30 g	chilli powder
5 g	fenugreek seeds &
5 g	asafoetida, roast both in oil & powder
5 g	turmeric powder
5 g	mustard seeds : for seasoning
50 g	salt
150 ml	oil

1. Marinate the cherries in a teaspoon (5g) salt for a day.
2. Stir-fry the cherries in a little oil till tender and set aside.
3. In the same pan heat some more oil, add mustard seeds and allow to crackle.
4. Pour in the tamarind extract and bring to the boil along with the jaggery. Allow to thicken over a high flame.
5. Add in the cherries and continue cooking over low heat for a few minutes till well blended.
6. Stir in the salt, chilli, turmeric powders, the remaining oil and cook till the oil separates.
7. Blend in the fenugreek, asafoetida powders and remove.
8. The pickle is ready for use. It lasts for 2 months.

137 Chow Chow – Green Spices : Hot

500 g	chopped chow chow, peel & seed
10 g	salt : for marinating
100 g	sour tomato, chop;
20 g	green coriander, wash, air-dry, chop;
30 g	green chillies, chop &
30 g	salt : for pickle, grind all to a paste
10 g	dried red chillies, break into bits
20 g	split husked red gram
20 g	split husked black gram
5 g	asafoetida &
3 g	fenugreek seeds, roast both in oil & powder
3 g	turmeric powder
20 g	jaggery, grate
20 ml	lime juice
200 ml	oil

1. Marinate the chopped chow chow in a teaspoon (5g) salt for half a day.
2. Drain and sun-dry for a day. Turn over a few times for even drying.
3. Heat a little oil, add mustard seeds and allow to crackle. Add in the gram and fry till golden brown.
4. Drop in the chillies, fry for a minute, follow with the spice paste and stir-fry until the oil separates.
5. Add in the chow chow and cook till partly tender.
6. Stir in the chilli, turmeric powders, jaggery, salt, the remaining oil and continue cooking till the oil separates.
7. Pour over the lime juice and heat for a few minutes.
8. Blend in the fenugreek, asafoetida powders and remove.
9. The pickle is ready for use. It lasts for 2 months.

138 Spicy Corn – Onion - Sprouts : Hot

200 g	steamed corn kernels	1-1"	piece of fresh ginger, scrape & chop, grind all three to a paste	3 g	cummin seeds &
100 g	onion, peel & grate			3 g	garam masala powder
75 g	bengal gram whole, sprouts			2 g	asafoetida, roast all three in oil & powder
75 g	seedless raisin, chop	30 g	fresh fennel leaves &	2 g	turmeric powder
10 g	dried mango powder	10 g	green coriander, clean, air-dry & chop both	150 ml	lime juice
40 g	green chillies;	5 g	chilli powder	75 g	salt
5	cloves garlic, peel &	3 g	coriander seeds;	150 ml	oil

1. Stir-fry the grated onion and the chilli-ginger-garlic paste in a little oil. Set aside.
2. In the same pan heat some more oil, add the cooked corn, bengal gram sprouts and cook over low heat till tender.
3. Add in the chopped fenugreek, coriander, the spice powders, salt, the remaining oil and continue cooking.
4. Add in the chopped raisin, lime juice and remove when the mixture begins to bubble.
5. The pickle is ready for use. It keeps for 5 days in the refrigerator.

> **Sweet corn** grown as a vegetable contains both sugar and starch. Just turning yellow and eaten within an hour of being picked, sweet corn is a magically different vegetable from the beautiful looking golden but over-ripe corn cobs sold across the counter. The tiny end-of-the season ones are sometimes the best of all.

139 Sour & Spicy Date : Sweet

500 g	date, slit & stone
500 g	seedless raisin, chop
100 g	dried mango powder;
75 g	peppercorns, sun-dry & powder;
75 g	dried ginger powder &
150 g	salt, combine all evenly
500 g	sugar, combine with 1000 ml vinegar to dissolve

1. Drop the date into boiling water and set aside for 10 minutes. Drain and allow to dry.
2. Stuff the spice mixture into the dates and sprinkle over a little of the spice mixture.
3. Pour the sweetened vinegar over the dates and sun for 10 days.
4. The pickle is ready for use. It lasts for 6 months.

140 Sour Fenugreek Leaf – Green Spices : Hot

125 g	fresh fenugreek leaves	25 ml	lime juice	
15 g	green coriander, clean, air-dry & chop fine	25 g	salt	
		75 ml	oil	
10 g	cleaned tamarind, obtain thick extract using water	a pinch sugar		
20	green chillies;			
2	cloves garlic, peel;			
1-1"	piece of fresh ginger, scrape & chop;			
1	cardamom &			
5	peppercorns, grind all to a paste			
2 g	cummin seeds			
2 g	turmeric powder			

1. Heat a little oil, add cummin seeds and fry till done.
2. Add in the spice paste and stir-fry until the oil separates.
3. Follow with the chopped fenugreek, coriander, cook till tender and set aside.
4. In the same pan heat some more oil, stir in the tamarind extract, tomato puree, sugar and bring to the boil.
5. Allow to thicken over a high flame.
6. Continue cooking until the mixture becomes jam-like and the oil separates.
7. Stir in the fried fenugreek mixture, the remaining oil and cook till well blended.
8. Pour over the lime juice and remove when the mixture begins to bubble.
9. The pickle is ready for use. It lasts for 1 month in the refrigerator.

141 Spicy Stuffed Fresh Red Chilli : Hot

1 kg	fresh red chillies, slit, remove & retain seeds
350 g	dried mango powder;
50 g	aniseeds &
50 g	split mustard seeds, dry-roast both & powder
50 g	split fenugreek seeds &
50 g	coriander seeds, roast both in oil & powder
400 g	salt 400 ml oil

1. Combine the powdered spices, chilli seeds and the salt with the oil to a paste.
2. Stuff the spice blend into the chillies and pack in a jar in an upright position.
3. Pour over the oil and set aside for 2 weeks.
4. The pickle is ready for use. It lasts for 1 year. Sun occasionally.

142 Perky Gherkin : Oilless

125 g	gherkins, peel & cut into chunks
5 g	green chillies, chop
3 g	peppercorns, crush
3	cloves garlic, peel & chop
8 g	salt

1. Pack the gherkins in a jar and add all the remaining ingredients.
2. Store in an airy place.
3. The pickle is ready for use after 4 days. It keeps for 15 days and is best refrigerated.

143 Green Chilli in Curd : Salty

500 g	tender green chillies, chop
400 ml	curd, whip with 80 g salt & remove cream

1. Blend the chopped green chillies with the whipped curd and salt. Set aside for 2 days.
2. The pickle lasts for 2 months and is best refrigerated. Shake daily.

144 Sprouted Green Gram – Cocum : Hot

125 g	green gram whole, sprouts
50 g	green coriander, clean, air-dry & chop
50 g	onion &
5	cloves garlic, peel, chop both & grind together
10 g	dried cocum, chop
5 g	chilli powder
3	green chillies, mince
3 g	turmeric powder
3 g	cummin seeds
20 g	salt
30 ml	oil

1. Stir-fry the sprouts in a little oil till partly tender and set aside.
2. In the same pan heat the remaining oil, add the cummin seeds and fry till done.
3. Stir in the onion-garlic-chilli paste and heat till the raw smell disappears.
4. Add in the fried sprouts, turmeric, chilli powders, salt, chopped cocum, coriander, cook till well blended and remove.
5. The pickle is now ready for use. It keeps for 15 days in the refrigerator.

145 Sour & Spicy Sprouted Green Gram : Hot

125 g	green gram whole, sprouts
100 g	cabbage, shred thickly
25 g	spring onion, chop fine
2-1"	pieces of fresh ginger, scrape & chop;
30 g	green coriander, clean, air-dry, chop &
20 g	green chillies, grind all three to a paste
2 g	sugar
20 ml	vinegar
20 ml	lime juice
25 g	salt
75 ml	oil

a pinch asafoetida, roast in oil & powder

1. Stir-fry the spice paste and asafoetida powder in a little oil till done.
2. Add in the green gram sprouts, shredded cabbage, chopped spring onion, the remaining oil and cook till partly tender.
3. Stir in the lime juice, vinegar, sugar, salt and remove when the mixture begins to bubble.
4. The pickle is ready for use. It lasts for 1 month in the refrigerator.

146 Roasted Groundnut – Chilli - Garlic : Hot

500 g	shelled fried groundnut, peel
60 g	cleaned tamarind
60 g	green chillies, chop
40 g	dried red chillies, break into bits
10 g	turmeric powder
10	cloves garlic, peel
100 g	salt
100 ml	oil

1. Stir-fry the chopped green chillies, peeled garlic, broken red chillies and tamarind in the oil. Set aside.
2. Grind together all the ingredients with the groundnuts, salt and turmeric powder to a coarse paste. Set aside for 3 days.
3. The pickle lasts for 1 month and longer in the refrigerator.

147 Sour Guava : Hot

125 g	guava, chop fine & seed	3 g	peppercorns, dry-roast both & powder
10 g	seedless raisin, chop	3 g	chilli powder
3	green chillies, chop	3 g	mustard seeds : for seasoning
8 g	cleaned tamarind, obtain thick extract using water	1	cardamom
		50 g	sugar
		10 ml	rose water
		10 ml	lime juice
5 g	jaggery, grate	12 g	salt
3 g	cummin seeds &	10 ml	oil

1. Heat the oil, add mustard seeds and allow to crackle.
2. Immediately add in the cummin, chilli, pepper powders and cardamom.
3. Follow with the cut guava, green chillies and fry for a few minutes over low heat.
4. Add in the tamarind extract and bring to the boil. Allow to thicken over a high flame.
5. Stir in the sugar, jaggery and the salt.
6. Continue cooking for a few minutes over low heat and remove.
7. When cool, add in the rose water, lime juice and the chopped raisin.
8. The pickle is ready for use. It keeps for 1 week and is best refrigerated.

148 Spiced Horsegram – Onion : Hot

125 g	horsegram, soak in water for 1 hour
125 g	onion, peel &
10 g	green chillies, chop both & grind together
12 g	cleaned tamarind, obtain thick extract using water
3	cloves garlic, peel & chop
3 g	dried red chillies, roast in oil & powder
3 g	chilli powder
15 g	jaggery, grate
15 g	salt
25 ml	oil

1. Cook the horsegram in a little water. Drain and allow to dry.
2. Stir-fry the chopped garlic in a little oil for a minute.
3. In the same pan heat the remaining oil, add in the onion-chilli paste and cook until the oil separates.
4. Add in the cooked horsegram and stir-fry for a minute.
5. Pour in the tamarind extract, jaggery, salt and bring to the boil. Allow to thicken over a high flame.
6. Stir in the chilli powder and continue cooking over low heat.
7. Remove when the mixture becomes jam-like and the oil separates.
8. The pickle is ready for use. It keeps for 1 week and is best refrigerated.

149 Tender Raw Jackfruit – Mango Powder : Hot

500 g	tender raw jackfruit, peel outer skin & chop
30 g	dried mango powder
20 g	chilli powder
15 g	mustard seeds &
10 g	coriander seeds, dry-roast both & powder
10 g	turmeric powder
10 g	cummin seeds ;
10 g	onion seeds &
5 g	aniseeds, sun-dry all three & powder
10 g	salt, for steaming jackfruit
60 g	salt
75 ml	oil

1. Steam the chopped jackfruit with the salt till almost tender.
2. Combine the spice powders and salt with a little oil to a paste.
3. Add in the dried jackfruit pieces and blend well.
4. Pour over the remaining oil to cover and set aside for 15 days. Stir daily.
5. The pickle lasts for 3 months.

150 Kovakkai – Onion – Gram : Hot

500 g	kovakkai, chop
300 g	onion, peel & chop
100 g	green chillies, chop
40 g	fresh ginger, scrape, chop & grind
100 g	cleaned tamarind, obtain thick extract using water
100 g	jaggery, grate
50 g	chilli powder
25 g	split husked black gram, roast in oil & pound
5 g	fenugreek seeds &
5 g	asafoetida, roast both in oil & powder
5 g	turmeric powder
5 g	mustard seeds : for seasoning
60 g	salt
250 ml	oil

1. Stir-fry the ginger paste in a little oil and set aside.
2. Heat some more oil, add mustard seeds and allow to crackle.
3. Add in the fried ginger, onion, chopped kovakkai, green chillies and fry for a few minutes over low heat.
4. Follow with the pounded gram, fry for a while and set aside.
5. In the same pan heat the remaining oil, pour in the tamarind extract, turmeric powder, jaggery and salt.
6. Bring to the boil and allow to thicken over a high flame.
7. Add in the kovakkai mixture and the spice powders.
8. Continue cooking over low heat until the mixture becomes jam-like and the oil separates.
9. The pickle is ready for use. It lasts for 2 months.

151 Spice Stuffed Lady's Finger in Lime Juice : Hot

500 g	lady's finger, cut both ends & slit
2-1"	pieces of fresh ginger, scrape & chop
25 g	chilli powder
10 g	mustard seeds, sun-dry & powder
10 g	fenugreek seeds;
10 g	cummin seeds &
5 g	asafoetida, roast all three in oil & powder
5 g	turmeric powder
a few	sprigs curry leaves : for seasoning
20 g	sugar
200 ml	lime juice
60 g	salt
100 ml	oil

Note : While buying **Lady's finger** make sure the tail ends snap easily. Those that don't are tough. When used whole, trim the pods carefully to retain the liquid; otherwise they will lose their shape during pickling.

1. Combine all the spice powders with a little oil and lime juice to a paste.
2. Stuff the spice paste into the lady's finger.
3. Heat the remaining oil, add the chopped ginger and stir-fry for a few minutes.
4. Add in the curry leaves and fry till crisp.
4. Stir in the stuffed lady's finger, sugar, the remaining lime juice and salt.
5. Cook for a few minutes and remove when the lime juice begins to bubble.
6. The pickle is now ready for use. It lasts for 2 months.

152 Spiced Lime – Fresh Red Chillies : Watery

1 kg	lime, keep whole
100 g	salt, make a solution with 1200ml water
250 g	fresh red chillies, cut into large pieces
30 g	coriander seeds ;
30 g	cummin seeds ;
30 g	mustard seeds &
20 g	onion seeds, dry-roast all & powder
20 g	garam masala powder
20 g	fenugreek seeds &
10 g	asafoetida, roast both in oil & powder
200 g	salt
500 ml	oil

1. Soak the limes in the salt solution overnight.
2. Next day wipe-dry, cut into 8 pieces each and seed.
3. Combine the salt, chillies with the lime pieces and sun-dry for 4 days.
4. Stir in the spice powders, oil and sun again for a week.
5. The pickle is ready for use. It lasts for 1 year.

153 Spice Ball – Coconut : Instant

125 g	spice balls, roast in oil
10 g	dried red chillies, roast in oil
50 g	grated coconut, dry-roast
15 g	cleaned tamarind, dry-roast
20 g	salt
25 ml	oil

1. Grind together all the ingredients using a little water.
2. The pickle is ready for use. It keeps for 1 week in the refrigerator.

154 Steamed Lotus Stem : Hot

500 g	lotus stem, clean, cut into 1" wafers and pressure cook till tender
10 g	green coriander, clean, air-dry & chop
5 g	garam masala powder
5 g	chilli powder
5 g	cummin seeds;
5 g	coriander seeds &
10 g	peppercorns, dry-roast all three & powder
3	green chillies, chop fine
50 ml	lime juice
20 ml	vinegar
10 g	cleaned tamarind, obtain thick extract using water
50 g	salt
200 ml	oil

1. Stir-fry the cooked lotus stem slices in a little oil.
2. Follow with the chopped green chillies, the chopped coriander and fry for a while. Set aside.
3. In the same pan heat the remaining oil, stir in the tamarind extract, the remaining oil, spice powders, salt and bring to the boil. Allow to thicken.
4. Pour in the vinegar, lime juice and remove when the mixture begins to bubble.
5. The pickle is ready for use. It lasts for 1 month and is best refrigerated.

Lotus Stem

Buy lotus stems that are firm and snap easily. Peel and slice them. Soak them in water for about 10 minutes to remove the iron taste. Dip the soaked slices in boiling water and remove to cold water again.

155 Stuffed Lotus Stem : Hot

500 g	thick white lotus stem, wash, scrape & cut into 5cm pieces
10 g	salt : for cooking lotus stem
25 g	cleaned tamarind, obtain thick extract using water
10 g	jaggery, grate
25	green chillies;
2	cloves garlic, peel;
1-1"	piece of fresh ginger, scrape & chop;
5 g	dried pomegranate seeds;
5 g	chilli powder;
5 g	dried mango powder;
5 g	cummin seeds, dry-roast;
5 g	coriander seeds, dry-roast;
3 g	turmeric powder &
3 g	thymol seeds, grind all to a paste with half the salt
50 g	salt
200 ml	oil

1. Pressure cook the lotus stem pieces with a little salt and 5ml oil till tender. Allow to cool.
2. Stir-fry the spice paste in a little oil, remove and allow to cool.
3. Slit the cooked lotus stems and pack in the spice paste.
4. Heat a little oil, pour in the tamarind extract, jaggery, the remaining salt and the remaining spice paste, if any.
5. Cook till the mixture becomes jam-like and the oil separates.
6. Add in the stuffed lotus stem, stir-fry gently until well blended and remove.
7. The pickle is ready for use. It lasts for 1 month and is best refrigerated.

156 Spiced Love-Lovi : Hot

500 g	ripe love-lovi, halve
50 g	small onion, peel & slice
25 g	peeled garlic, chop
1-1"	piece of fresh ginger, scrape & slice
25 g	chilli powder;
10 g	fenugreek seeds, sun-dry & powder;
5 g	turmeric powder &
5 g	asafoetida, roast in oil & powder, combine all evenly
25 g	dried red chillies, break into bits;
10 g	peppercorns;
5 g	mustard seeds;
5 g	fenugreek seeds;
5 g	cummin seeds &
a few	sprigs curry leaves : all for seasoning
60 ml	vinegar
60 g	salt
100 ml	oil

1. Add the spice mixture into the love lovi and set aside for 2 days. Shake well twice daily.
2. Stir-fry the onion, ginger, garlic in a little oil and set aside.
3. Heat some more oil, add the mustard, fenugreek, cummin seeds, peppercorns, red chillies, curry leaves and fry for a while.
4. Stir in the salt, vinegar and heat well. Remove and allow to cool.
5. Combine the fried ingredients with the spiced love-lovi.
6. Pour over the spiced vinegar, the remaining oil and mix thoroughly.
7. The pickle is ready for use after 15 days. It lasts for 6 months.

157 Dry Fruit in Tamarind Sauce : Sweet

150 g	cubed mango preserve	5 g	panch phoran powder
150 g	date, stone & chop	150 g	sugar
100 g	dried apricot, soak, stone & chop	60 g	salt
100 g	seedless raisin, chop	30 ml	oil
100 g	cleaned tamarind, obtain thick extract using water		

1. Heat the oil to smoking point. Lower the heat and fry the panch phoran powder for a few seconds.
2. Add in the chopped mango preserve, date, apricot along with the water in which they were soaked.
3. Stir in the tamarind extract, sugar, salt, raisin and simmer till the mixture thickens.
4. The pickle is ready for use after 2 days. It lasts for 2 months.

158 Mango – Brinjal : Instant

125 g	seeded mango, peel & chop	2 g	asafoetida, roast in oil & powder : all for seasoning
60 g	brinjal, keep whole		
8 g	salt		
2	dried red chillies, break into bits;	2 g	turmeric powder
2 g	mustard seeds;		
2 g	fenugreek seeds &	20 ml	oil

1. Smear the brinjal with a little oil and toast over the fire. Allow to cool and peel.
2. Grind the chopped mango and the toasted brinjal with the salt coarsely.
3. Heat the remaining oil, add mustard seeds and allow to crackle.
4. Add in the fenugreek seeds, broken chillies, asafoetida, turmeric powders and fry till done.
5. Pour the seasoning over the ground mixture and stir thoroughly.
6. The pickle is ready for use. It keeps for 1 week and is best refrigerated.

159 Mango – Gooseberry – Onion : Hot

350 g	seeded mango, peel & chop	5 g	turmeric powder
80 g	stoned gooseberry, chop	5 g	onion seeds;
		5 g	peppercorns;
70 g	small red onion, peel & keep whole	3 g	aniseeds &
		3 g	fenugreek seeds, sun-dry all & crush together
30 g	fresh ginger, scrape & slice thin		
		2 g	asafoetida, roast in oil & powder
20 g	chilli powder		
15 g	dried red chillies, break into bits	80 g	salt
		350 ml	oil

1. Heat the oil and remove. When the oil is still lukewarm, add in the broken red chillies, the spice powders, salt and blend well.
2. Stir in the prepared vegetables and mix thoroughly.
3. The pickle is ready for use after 7 days. It lasts for 6 months.

Note : The fleshy, fibrous pulp of the **tamarind fruit** is acidic. It does not lose its vitamin C content on drying.

160 Mango – Tamarind Avakkai : Hot

500 g	seeded mango, peel & size into medium thick flakes
60 g	chilli powder
60 g	mustard seeds, sun-dry & powder
125 ml	water : boil & cool
25 g	split husked bengal gram;
5	dried red chillies, break into bits;
5 g	mustard seeds;
5 g	fenugreek seeds &
a few	sprigs curry leaves : all for seasoning
125 g	salt
375 ml	raw gingelly oil

1. Soak the mustard powder in water for 10 minutes. Blend in the chilli powder and salt.
2. Stir in the mango pieces and a little oil. Mix well and set aside for 2 days.
3. Thereafter sun the mixture for 3 days.
4. Heat a little oil, add mustard seeds and allow to crackle.
5. Add in the bengal gram, fenugreek seeds, red chillies, curry leaves and fry for awhile.
6. Pour the seasoning and the remaining oil over the mixture. Stir thoroughly and cover.
7. The pickle is ready for use after 2 days. It lasts for 4 months.

161 Mango Avakkai – Mustard - Sesame : Hot

1 kg	cut mango, with shell, size into small pieces & air-dry
100 g	mustard seeds, sun-dry & powder
100 g	white sesame seeds, dry-roast & powder
100 g	chilli powder
200 g	salt
400 ml	raw gingelly oil

1. Combine the chilli, mustard, sesame powders and the salt with a little oil.
2. Stir in the mango pieces and pour over the remaining oil to cover.
3. Set the mixture aside for 15 days. Stir thoroughly.
4. The pickle lasts for 1 year.

162 Spicy Mango – Garlic : Tender

1 kg	tender mango with soft seeds, keep whole
10	cloves garlic, peel
60 g	dried red chillies;
25 g	mustard seeds &
10 g	peppercorns, sun-dry all three & powder
10 g	turmeric powder
5 g	asafoetida, roast in oil & powder
275 g	salt
10 ml	castor oil : for coating mangoes
5 g	turmeric powder &
10 ml	oil : for capping

1. Smear the castor oil over the mangoes.
2. Combine the oiled mangoes with the salt in a jar and set aside for 5 days. Stir daily.
3. Drain out and strain the salt water given out by the mangoes.
4. Boil the salt water and allow to cool.
5. Grind the chilli, pepper, mustard, turmeric and asafoetida powders with the cooled salt water.
6. Add the salted mangoes along with the garlic into the spicy liquid and set aside for 5 more days.
7. Place a thin cloth dipped in oil and turmeric powder over the mouth of the jar before placing the lid over it.
8. The pickle lasts for 1 year. Stir occasionally.

163 Mango – Green Chilli : Tender

1 kg	tender mango with soft seeds, keep whole
10	green chillies, chop
250 g	salt

1. In a jar sprinkle a layer of salt, a little chopped green chilli and follow with a layer of mango.
2. Repeat this process till all the mangoes are exhausted. Make sure that the final layer is that of salt.
3. Cap tight, tie with a clean cloth and set the pickle aside for 10 days. Shake daily.
4. The pickle lasts for 1 year. Stir occasionally.

164 Mango Avakkai – Ginger : Tender

Mango
Termed the "the king of Asiatic fruits", it comes in various shades of green, yellow and red. The best ones are juicy, sweet, with very little fibre and a deliciously piquant flavour. The worst type of mangoes are very fibrous with a turpentine flavour. Its sourness is due to the presence of oxalic, citric, malic and succinic acids.

5 measures	tender mango, keep whole
1 measure	salt
1/2 measure	fresh ginger, scrape & chop fine
1/2 measure	chilli powder
20 g	fenugreek seeds, roast in oil & powder
10 g	mustard seeds, sun-dry & powder
5 g	turmeric powder
1500 ml	raw gingelly oil

1. Soak the mangoes in water, remove, wash thoroughly and air-dry. Cut the mango into small pieces.
2. Combine the spice powders with the salt evenly.
3. Sprinkle some spice mixture into a jar and pour over a little oil.
4. Dip a few mango pieces in the oil, roll in the spice mixture and arrange in the jar.
5. Sprinkle a little chopped ginger.
6. Follow with a layer of the spice mixture and pour over a little oil.
7. Repeat this process until the mango and ginger are completely layered.
8. Sprinkle the remaining spice mixture over the mango mixture and set aside for 3 days.
9. On the 4th day stir the pickle thoroughly and pour over the remaining oil to cover.
10. The pickle is ready for use. It lasts for 6 months. Sun and stir occasionally.

165 Spicy Cooked Mango: Watery

500 g	cut mango, size into small pieces water sufficient to cover
30 g	dried red chillies;
5 g	cummin seeds &
5 g	mustard seeds, sun-dry all three & powder
a few	sprigs curry leaves : for seasoning
3 g	turmeric powder
60 g	salt
50 ml	oil

1. Add 25g salt to the mango pieces and set aside overnight.
2. Next morning drain and discard the salt water.
3. Squeeze out the mango pieces and air-dry for 4 hours.
4. Boil together the water with 35g salt and remove when crystals appear at the edge of the water.
5. Heat the oil to smoking point, add in the curry leaves and allow to turn crisp.
6. Lower the flame, stir in the ground spices, turmeric powder and fry for a few seconds.
7. Pour in the salted boiling water and boil for a few minutes. Stir in the mangoes and remove.
8. The pickle is ready for use after 4 days. It lasts for 1 month.

166 Mixed Vegetable – Garlic in Lime Juice: Hot

500 g	mixed vegetables : choice – peas, carrot, cauliflower, brinjal, mango, bitter gourd, ginger, green chillies, singly or combined, peel, shell, scrape, cut, separate into florets, chop as required
15 g	salt : for blanching
200 g	peeled garlic, chop
50 g	chilli powder
5 g	mustard seeds, sun-dry & powder
5 g	turmeric powder
5 g	fenugreek seeds &
3 g	asafoetida, roast both in oil & powder
5 g	mustard seeds : for seasoning
175 ml	lime juice
50 ml	vinegar
50 g	salt
500 ml	oil

1. Blanch the prepared vegetables in lightly salted boiling water for 2 minutes. Drain and dry on a clean cloth.
2. Add the salt and turmeric powder to the lime juice. Stir in the dried vegetables and set aside for 30 minutes.
3. Heat a little oil, add mustard seeds and allow to crackle. Add in the dried vegetables, garlic and stir-fry for a few minutes over low heat.
4. Add in the spice powders and keep frying until the vegetables are partly tender. Remove and allow to cool.
5. Pour over the vinegar, the remaining oil and stir thoroughly.
6. The pickle is ready for use after 2 days. It lasts for 2 months.

167 Mixed Vegetable in Vinegar: Sweet

500 g	cauliflower florets		
500 g	turnip, peel & julienne	2-1"	pieces of fresh ginger, scrape, grind both to a paste
500 g	carrot, peel & julienne	75 g	chilli powder
250 g	shelled green peas, parboil	20 g	mustard seeds, sun-dry & powder
10 g	salt : for blanching		
500 g	jaggery, grate	10 g	turmeric powder
15 g	garam masala powder	800 ml	vinegar
		250 g	salt
20 g	peeled garlic &	200 ml	oil

1. Tie the prepared vegetables in a thin cloth. Blanch the vegetable bag in lightly salted boiling water for 2 minutes. Transfer to cold water and remove.
2. Untie the vegetables and sun-dry for an hour.
2. Stir-fry the ginger-garlic paste in a little oil and remove.
3. Blend in the spice powders and salt.
4. Stir in the dried vegetables and set aside for 4 days.
5. Bring the vinegar and jaggery to the boil. Allow to cool.
6. Pour the cooled sweetened vinegar into the vegetable mixture and sun for 3 more days.
7. The pickle is ready for use. It lasts for 1 month. Shake daily.

168 Mixed Vegetable – Green Spices: Watery

500 g	carrot, peel & chop
500 g	cauliflower florets
250 g	sugar, make a sugar syrup of thin consistency with 100ml water
50 g	fresh ginger, scrape & chop fine
100 g	green chillies, chop fine
5 g	turmeric powder

5 g	fenugreek seeds, soak in 5ml vinegar & grind to a paste
2 g	onion seeds
2 g	asafoetida, roast in oil & powder
75 g	salt
250 ml	vinegar

1. Combine the prepared vegetables with the chopped ginger and green chillies.
2. Add in the onion seeds, spice powders, salt, the fenugreek paste, vinegar and the sugar.
3. Stir thoroughly and sun the mixture for a day.
4. The pickle is ready for use. It keeps for 10 days and is best refrigerated.

169 Mushroom in Tamarind Suace : Hot

125 g	mushroom, wash, air-dry & chop
5 g	chilli powder
5	cloves garlic, peel;
2	green chillies &
1-1"	piece of fresh ginger, scrape & chop, grind all three to a paste
10 ml	lime juice
5 g	cleaned tamarind, obtain thick extract using water
5 g	tomato puree
12 g	salt
50 ml	oil

1. Marinate the chopped mushroom in the spice paste and set aside.
2. Heat a little oil, add mustard seeds and allow to crackle.
3. Stir in the marinated mushroom and continue cooking till partly tender and set aside.
4. In the same pan heat the remaining oil, pour in the tamarind extract, tomato puree, turmeric powder, jaggery, salt and bring to the boil. Allow to thicken over a high flame.
5. Add in the lime juice and remove when the mixture begins to bubble.
6. The pickle is ready for use. It lasts for 1 month.

170 Button Mushroom – Ginger - Onion : Oilless

500 g	button mushroom, wash, air-dry & halve
40 g	chopped onion, peel
20 ml	lime juice
150 ml	vinegar
2-1"	pieces of fresh ginger, scrape & grind
20 g	peppercorns, sun-dry & powder
1	blade of mace
50 g	salt

1. Heat together the mushroom, onion, spice powders, salt and vinegar.
2. Cook covered over low heat until the mushroom shrivels.
3. Remove the mushroom and onion with a perforated spoon and trasfer to a jar.
4. Pour over the hot vinegar and cap tight.
6. The pickle is ready for use. It lasts for 1 month and is best refrigerated.

Mushrooms
The youngest of these fungi, button mushrooms have the mildest flavour. They are neat in shape and size. When mature, their caps partially open and are known as cup mushrooms. When fully mature, they become flatter. To cook them, cut off the earthy base of the stalk and wipe the caps with a damp cloth. If dirty, wash them quickly and dry thoroughly before pickling.

171 Spicy Nutrinuggets – Capsicum : Hot

125 g	nutrinuggets kima
10 g	salt : for cooking nutrinuggets
110 g	capsicum, cut into chunks
100 g	mushroom, soak in 60ml vinegar
2	small red onion, peel & chop
1/2"	piece of fresh ginger, scrape & chop
4	green chillies, chop
10 g	mustard seeds, sun-dry & powder
10 g	chilli powder
5 g	turmeric powder
3 g	fenugreek seeds, roast in oil & powder
100 ml	vinegar : heat & cool
40 g	salt
50 ml	oil

Prepared from the highly nutrition packed soyabean, **nutrinuggets** are the richest source of protein in the vegetable kingdom and also superior to animal protein.

1. Boil the nutrinuggets in one litre water to which 20g salt has been added. Drain, chop and air-dry.
2. Stir-fry the chopped onion, ginger and green chillies in a little oil till golden brown.
3. Stir in the chopped nutrinuggets, capsicum, mushroom and fry for a few minutes.
4. Remove, blend in the spice powders, vinegar, salt and the remaining oil (after heating & cooling).
5. The pickle is ready for use. It keeps for 5 days and is best refrigerated.

172 Ripe Olive – Fenugreek – Onion Seeds : Hot

500 g	ripe olive
75 g	onion seeds
75 g	fenugreek seeds
50 g	chilli powder;
5 g	fenugreek seeds, roast in oil & powder;
25 g	sugar &
5 g	aniseeds, roast in oil & powder, combine all evenly
150 ml	vinegar : beat & cool
50 g	salt
50 ml	mustard oil

> Generally speaking green **olives** are the unripe fruit, black the ripened, but there are emerald olives, purple olives, thick black juicy olives – some very small, others lush as plums. The large varieties are used in pickling and the smaller ones for oil extraction. Olives keep best in a jar, covered with olive oil.

1. Soak the whole olives in hot water overnight. Remove from the water and dry thoroughly the following day.
2. Make cross slits, apply salt all over and sun-dry thoroughly.
3. Remove the seeds from the dried salted olives, roll into the spice mixture and sun-dry for 7 days.
4. Heat the oil, add the onion seeds, fenugreek seeds and allow to crackle.
5. Pour in the vinegar and blend the seasoning into the spiced olives.
6. The pickle is ready for use. It lasts for 2 months.

173 Papaya Preserve : Sweet

500 g	peeled half-ripe papaya, chop fine & parboil	water	sufficient to cover
400 g	sugar	15 ml	citric acid
		2 g	salt

1. Combine the salt, sugar, sufficient water and heat till the sugar dissolves.
2. Add in the citric acid, boil for 3 minutes, remove and strain.
3. Reheat the sugar syrup and stir in the papaya pieces.
4. Continue cooking over low heat till the syrup reaches a single-thread consistency and remove.
5. The pickle is ready for use after 4 days. It lasts for 3 months and is best refrigerated.

174 Small White Onion in Mustard Oil : Hot

125 g	small white onion, peel & slit
10 g	chilli powder;
15 g	salt &
5 g	mustard seeds, sun-dry & powder, combine with oil to a paste
125 ml	mustard oil

> There are several varieties of **onion**, varying in water content and in sweetness. The less water and sugar, the stronger the flavour. Purple, violet-tinged and white onions are the mildest. Yellow ones the most pungent.

1. Slit the onions and pack in the spice mixture.
2. Pour over the remaining oil and sun the spiced onion for 3 days.
3. The pickle is ready for use. It keeps for 5 days in the refrigerator.

175 Green Peas in Tamarind Sauce : Hot

250 g	shelled green peas, parboil
25 g	green coriander, clean, air-dry & chop
1-1"	piece of fresh ginger, scrape & chop
20 g	cleaned tamarind, obtain thick extract using water
3 g	cummin seeds
3 g	garam masala powder
2 g	asafoetida, roast in oil & powder
2 g	sugar
10 ml	lime juice
50 g	salt
75 ml	oil

1. Heat a little oil, pour in the tamarind extract and cook till syrupy. Set aside.
2. Heat some more oil, add cummin seeds and allow to crackle.
3. Add in the chopped ginger, the parboiled peas and stir-fry for a few minutes.
4. Follow with the chopped coriander, salt, asafoetida, garam masala powders and fry till done.
5. Stir in the tamarind syrup. Continue cooking until the mixture becomes jam-like and the oil separates.
6. Blend in the lime juice.
7. Remove when the mixture begins to bubble.
8. The pickle is ready for use. It lasts for 2 months.

176 Sour Pineapple : Sweet

500 g	ripe pineapple pieces	2	cloves garlic, peel &
600 g	sugar	50 ml	vinegar, grind all to a paste
2	dried red chillies;		
2-1"	pieces of fresh ginger, scrape & chop;	25 g	salt

1. Combine all the ingredients and cook over medium heat for a few minutes.
2. Lower the heat and continue cooking till the pineapple pieces become tender.
3. Stir continuously and remove when jam-like.
4. The pickle is ready for use. It lasts for 2 months.

177 Plantain Flower in Tamarind Sauce : Hot

500 g	chopped plantain flower, cook in 5g thin tamarind extract
50 g	onion, peel & chop fine
50 g	green chillies, chop fine
25 ml	tomato puree
50 g	cleaned tamarind, obtain thick extract using water
30 g	jaggery, grate
30g	green coriander, clean, air-dry & chop
5 g	chilli powder
40g	salt
200ml	oil
a pinch turmeric powder	

1. Heat a little oil, add cummin seeds and allow to crackle.
2. Add in the chopped onion and fry till transluscent.
3. Follow with the cooked plantain flower, stir-fry for a few minutes and set aside.
4. In the same pan heat some more oil, stir in the chopped green chillies, coriander and fry for a while.
5. Follow with the tomato puree, tamarind extract, jaggery, turmeric powder, salt and bring to the boil. Allow to thicken over a high flame.
6. Add in the spiced fried plantain flower, cook until the mixture becomes jam-like and the oil separates.
7. The pickle is ready for use. It lasts for 2 months.

178 Raw Plantain – Gram – Green Chilli : Hot

500 g	peeled, mature raw plantain, grate	10 g	turmeric powder
150 g	cleaned tamarind, obtain thick extract using water	30 g	mustard seeds;
		20 g	split husked black gram;
60 g	jaggery, grate	20 g	split husked bengal gram &
50 g	green chillies, chop fine	a few	sprigs curry leaves : all for seasoning
30 g	peeled garlic, chop	60 g	salt
20 g	chilli powder	150 ml	oil

1. Heat a little oil, add mustard seeds and allow to crackle.
2. Add in the black gram, bengal gram and fry till golden.
3. Stir-fry the curry leaves and green chillies.
4. Add in the garlic, grated plantain and fry till tender. Set aside.
5. In the same pan heat some more oil, pour in the tamarind extract, jaggery, turmeric powder and the salt.
6. Bring to the boil and allow to thicken over a high flame.
8. Add in the fried ingredients, chilli powder and the remaining oil.
9. Continue cooking over low heat until the mixture becomes jam-like and the oil separates.
10. The pickle is ready for use. It lasts for 1 month and is best refrigerated.

179 Potato Avakkai : Hot

500 g	potato, peel & julienne	3 g	asafoetida, roast both in oil & powder
3	cloves garlic, peel & chop	3 g	garam masala powder
125 g	mustard seeds, sun-dry & powder	3 g	turmeric powder
115 g	chilli powder	3 g	mustard seeds: for seasoning
250 ml	lime juice	125 g	salt
25 g	fenugreek seeds &	250 ml	raw gingelly oil

1. Combine the chilli, mustard, fenugreek powders with the salt and half the oil. Set aside for 15 minutes.
2. Heat and cool the remaining oil (reserving 2 teaspoon for seasoning). Stir in the potato pieces and set aside for 15 minutes.
3. Stir-fry the asafoetida, mustard seeds, turmeric, garam masala powders, chopped garlic in a little oil and remove.
4. Add the spice paste and fried ingredients into the potato mixture. Stir well and set aside for 3 more days.
5. Blend in the lime juice.
6. The pickle is ready for use after 15 days. It lasts for 2 months. Sun occasionally.

180 Sweet & Sour Raisin : Hot

500 g	seedless raisin, chop
100 g	dried red chillies, seed, roast in oil & powder
50 g	sugar
300 ml	lime juice
50 g	salt
80 ml	oil

1. Blend the salt and chilli powder with the lime juice.
2. Drop in the chopped raisin and stir thoroughly.
3. Place a piece of cloth over the pickle, pour over a little oil and close the jar.
4. Uncover the jar after 7 days, add in the remaining oil, sugar and stir thoroughly.
5. The pickle is ready for use. It lasts for 2 months. Stir occasionally.

181 Lotus Stem – Mustard – Aniseed : Hot

500 g	lotus stem, peel outer skin & cut into ½ cm thick pieces
25 g	chilli powder
20 g	aniseeds &
20 g	mustard seeds, sun-dry both & powder
5 g	turmeric powder
50 g	salt
200 ml	oil

1. Heat the oil to smoking point and remove. When the oil is still lukewarm, blend in the spice powders and salt.
2. Immediately add in the lotus stem pieces and stir well.
3. Transfer the pickle to a wide-mouthed jar and sun for 7 days.
4. The pickle is ready for use after a week. It lasts for 2 months. Sun and stir occasionally.

182 Green Tamarind – Gram - Red Chilli : Hot

1 kg	tender green tamarind, size into small pieces
100 g	dried red chillies, break into bits
25 g	split husked black gram
10 g	asafoetida
5 g	mustard seeds &
a few	sprigs curry leaves: both for seasoning
200 g	salt
250 ml	oil

1. Fry the red chillies, black gram and asafoetida in a little oil.
2. Stir in the tamarind pieces and fry for a few minutes.
3. Cool and grind along with the salt to a coarse paste.
4. Heat the oil, add mustard seeds and allow to crackle.
5. Add in the curry leaves, fry till crisp and remove.
6. Pour the seasoning over the tamarind mixture and blend well.
7. The pickle is ready for use. It lasts for 1 year.

183 Sweet & Sour Pidikarnai : Instant

500 g	pidikarnai, cut & boil, peel & crumble
60 g	cleaned tamarind, obtain thick extract using water
70 g	jaggery, grate
60 g	chilli powder
10 g	asafoetida, roast in oil & powder
80 g	salt
80 ml	oil

1. Stir-fry the crumbled pidikarnai in a little oil and set aside.
2. In the same pan heat some more oil, add in the tamarind extract, jaggery and bring to the boil. Allow to thicken over a high flame.
3. Stir in the chilli, asafoetida powders, salt, the remaining oil and the fried pidikarnai.
4. Continue cooking over low heat until the mixture becomes jam-like and the oil separates.
5. The pickle is ready for use. It lasts for 2 months.

184 Wild Mustard – Grated Coconut : Instant

125 g	wild mustard;
50 g	grated coconut &
20 g	dried red chillies, dry-roast all three
20 g	cleaned tamarind
30 g	salt
100 ml	oil

1. Grind together all the roasted ingredients with the tamarind and salt using a little water.
2. Heat the oil and stir-fry the ground ingredients for a while.
3. The pickle is ready for use. It keeps for 10 days in the refrigerator.

185 Green Turmeric in Lime Juice : Oilless

500 g	fresh green turmeric, scrape & slice into thin rounds	50 g	green chillies, chop
		250 ml	lime juice
		75 g	salt

1. Combine the turmeric slices with the green chillies.
2. Add in the salt, lime juice and transfer to a jar.
3. Sun the mixture for 5 days.
4. The pickle lasts for 1 month and longer in the refrigerator.
5. Stir frequently and sun occasionally.

186 Wheat – Coconut : Instant

125 g	wheat, dry-roast	10 g	green coriander, wash, air-dry & chop
50 g	grated coconut, dry-roast		
30 g	dried red chillies, break into bits	5 g	mustard seeds; sprigs curry leaves & oil : all three for seasoning
10 g	cleaned tamarind	15 ml	
5 g	split husked black gram	10 g	salt

1. Grind the roasted wheat, grated coconut, broken chillies and tamarind with the salt to a smooth paste.
2. Heat the oil, add mustard seeds and allow to crackle.
3. Add in the black gram, curry leaves, chopped coriander, fry for a few minutes and remove.
4. Pour the seasoning over the wheat mixture and blend well.
5. The pickle is now ready for use. It keeps for 1 week in the refrigerator.

187 Sour & Spicy Green Tomato : Hot

1 kg	green tomato, chop	5 g	garam masala powder
100 g	green chillies, chop fine	5 g	turmeric powder
40 g	fresh ginger, scrape & grate	20 g	sugar
		120 ml	vinegar
15 g	cummin seeds	350 ml	water
5 g	asafoetida, roast in oil & powder	100 g	salt
		60 ml	oil

1. Fry the cummin seeds and asafoetida powder in a little oil.
2. Add in the ginger, green chillies and stir-fry for a few minutes over low heat.
3. Stir in the tomatoes, cook until the skins begin to peel, adding the oil little by little and set aside.
4. Combine the vinegar, turmeric, garam masala powders, water, sugar, salt and bring to the boil.
5. Add in the fried spiced tomato and continue cooking. Remove when the mixture becomes thick and jam-like.
6. The pickle is ready for use. It lasts for 1 year.

188 Woodapple – Ginger : Sweet

500 g	woodapple kernel, chop	5	cloves garlic, peel &
500 g	sugar	40 g	fresh ginger, scrape & chop, grind all three fine using vinegar
125 g	seedless raisin, chop		
50 g	dried red chillies;		
400 ml	vinegar	50 g	salt

1. Soak the woodapple in 300ml vinegar, squeeze out the fruit and strain the juice.
2. Combine the sugar, the spice paste, salt, the remaining vinegar and bring to the boil.
3. Stir in the woodapple juice and continue cooking for a few minutes until the mixture becomes jam-like.
4. Add in the chopped raisin and remove.
5. The pickle is ready for use after 4 days. It lasts for 3 months and is best refrigerated.

189 Tudhuvelai Berry in Lime Juice : Hot

125 g	tudhuvelai berry, prick with fork or halve	2 g	asafoetida, roast in oil & powder
50 g	green chillies, chop	2 g	mustard seeds: for seasoning
		15 g	salt
15 ml	lime juice	20 ml	oil

1. Drop the berries in rice-washed water for a day.
2. Drain out the water and add fresh rice-washed water.
3. Repeat this process three times totally to remove the bitterness from the berries.
4. Drain, add the salt, lime juice, asafoetida powder and set aside.
5. Heat the oil, add mustard seeds and allow to crackle.
6. Add in the chopped green chillies and fry for a minute.
7. Pour the seasoning over the berries. Shake daily.
8. The pickle is ready for use after 2 days. It keeps for 3 weeks in the refrigerator.

KITCHEN SPICES

[PART – III]

KITCHEN SPICES	
Part - I	Page 42
Part - II	Page 72

GINGELLY SEEDS
It is an excellent cure for all types of skin diseases, urine troubles, piles, leprosy, rheumatism, wounds and worm troubles. It improves blood and is said to increase vitality.

GINGER
Ginger is used in its fresh and dried forms. It is warming and stimulating, promotes gastric secretion and aids the absorption of food. It is an excellent remedy for easing indigestion, colic, flatulence and travelling sickness. It also has a stimulating effect on the heart and circulation. Ginger has a warming expectorant action on the lungs, dispelling mucous and phlegm; its tea is good for colds and flu. Ginger juice or tea massaged into the scalp is said to stimulate hair growth. In Chinese herbal medicine, fresh ginger root is good for cold and dried ginger suitable for treating respiratory and digestive disorders.

JAGGERY
Jaggery enjoys the pride of occasions in India, as it is used in all auspicious functions as a shagun – a good omen. Besides giving good strength to the body, if taken in limits, it is also capable of helping to cure a good number ailments and give great energy. Newly prepared jaggery is supposed to increase phlegm, cough and worm troubles. One-year-old jaggery is however, supposed to be very good. Again, after 3 years, its beneficial properties are said to diminish.

MUSTARD
Mustard is another ancient cure for head colds; a poultice and plaster made from the powdered seeds is applied to the forehead. Mustard oil helps cure leprosy.

NEEM LEAVES
The entire neem tree – root, stem, bark, leaves, blossom, seeds and flowers – everything has some medicinal purpose. The decoction prepared from the leaves works as an antiseptic lotion and is used for dressing wounds and ulcers. Those suffering from blood impurities can have a bath with this decoction where soap is to be avoided. Poultices prepared from boiled leaves can be apllied on swellings.

NUTMEG
The seeds and covering of this plant are generally used. Nutmeg helps to relieve flatulence, vomiting and nausea. Excess of nutmeg consumption is considered toxic and leads to disorientation, double-vision, hallucination and convulsions. The outer skin of the nutmeg yields another spice called mace or javitri, which is stronger than nutmeg.

ONION
Raw onion is a natural stimulant and digestive. It is especially rich in organic silicon, which keeps the blood at normal temperature. A silicon deficiency would result in undernourished hair and dandruff, as well as unhealthy colouring of nails. Onion is responsible for normalising the percentage of blood cholesterol by oxidising the excess of it.

It also exerts a specific action on arteriosclerosis and is considered useful as a preventive medicine in cardiovascular disorders. A spoonful of onion juice with a spoonful of honey is said to be a powerful aphrodisiac. Onions are also good for nerves, anaemia and insomnia. Cooked or fried onions are difficult to digest and highly gas forming.

PARSLEY
Parsley helps in maintaining normal action of the adrenal and thyroid glands. It is a strong diuretic for treating urinary infections, kidney stones as well as fluid retention. As it encourages uric acid elimination it is good for gout. It is said to increase the amount of mother's milk and tones the uterine muscles. It is a rich source of vitamin C and iron. Parsley also acts as a detoxicant, a good laxative and is also good for blood and digestion. Parsley leaves are a well-known breath freshner, the traditional antidote for the pungent garlic and onion. The seeds or leaves of parsley steeped in water can be used as a hair-rinse.

POPPY SEEDS
Medicinally, morphine and codeine that are vital constituents of unripe poppy seeds are used to relieve pain and induce sleep. It is the ripe seeds of poppy that are used in cooking.

RAISINS
Highly alkaline in nature, raisins are very effective for relieving acidosis. Because of its pure fructose content, it is also considered a quick energy food.

Quick Serve

are

the instant,

no-nonsense

recipes.

Turn out

time-saving,

tongue-tickling

temptations

in

a

jiffy.

Recipes : Quick Serve

190. Amaranth leaves in tamarind sauce : hot
191. Amaranth leaves peppered : hot
192. Black gram – tamarind : hot
193. Cabbage in lime juice : salty
194. Cabbage in vinegar : watery
195. Capsicum – green chilli in tamarind sauce : hot
196. Carrot in tamarind sauce : sweet
197. Carrot – green chilli in lime juice : hot
198. Red carrot in vinegar : watery
199. Sour carrot – onion : hot
200. Sour & spicy carrot – peas : sweet
201. Cauliflower in tamarind sauce : tender
202. Cauliflower – lime strips : tender
203. Cauliflower – gram in lime juice : hot
204. Mixed gram in tamarind : salty
205. Celery in vinegar : salty
206. Gram, groundnut in tamarind : hot
207. Sour & spiced cereal – mango : hot
208. Sour gram : hot
209. Spicy kichilikai : hot
210. Fried narthangai : hot
211. Sour narthangai : sweet
212. Kidarangai – ginger : hot
213. Boiled kidarangai : salty
214. Spicy cereal – green coriander : tender
215. Coconut - tamarind : hot
216. Spicy coconut – mango : hot
217. Flavoury coconut – mango : salty
218. Sour cocum : sweet
219. Coconut – mango - green spices : tender
220. Green coriander – sesame : hot
221. Garlic – cucumber in vinegar : watery
222. Ginger – cucumber in vinegar : salty
223. Cucumber in lime juice : watery
224. Spicy curd : watery
225. Curry leaf – coconut : hot
226. Spiced date : sweet
227. Dried red chilli in lime juice : hot
228. Fenugreek greens – tamarind : tender
229. Fresh red chilli – tamarind - garlic : hot
230. Sour fresh red chilli : hot
231. Fried gram – mango : hot
232. Steamed spicy garlic in lime juice : watery
233. Ginger in lime juice : watery
234. Ginger in raw tamarind sauce : salty
235. Sesame green chilli – tamarind : hot
236. Green chilli – ginger - garlic vinegared : hot
237. Sour ground raw gooseberry : hot
238. Unripe grape – coconut - green coriander : salty
239. Green grape : hot
240. Mint, green coriander – onion - mango powder : tender
241. Raw groundnut – cummin : hot

242. Roasted groundnut – tamarind : hot
243. Sour raw groundnut – green coriander : tender
244. Roasted groundnut – ginger : salty
245. Guava – tomato : watery
246. Sour & spiced ripe jackfruit : sweet
247. Jaggery – black gram : sweet
248. Small kalakkai – cummin seed : hot
249. Fried lime : hot
250. Lime – green coriander - coconut : tender
251. Spiced stuffed boiled lime : watery
252. Lime – ginger - green chilli : hot
253. Mango pachadi : hot
254. Cooked mango preserve : sweet
255. Cooked mango : hot
256. Mango – green coriander : tender
257. Mango – mint : tender
258. Mango – curry leaf : tender
259. Mango – cabbage : hot
260. Mango – green gram : hot
261. Mango – bengal gram : hot
262. Grated mango pachadi : hot
263. Mango – groundnut pachadi : hot
264. Spiced ripe mango : sweet
265. Spiced ripe mango in vinegar : hot
266. Half-ripe mango – onion : hot
267. Half-ripe mango – coconut : hot
268. Mild mango : salty
269. Spiced sliced mango : sweet
270. Mango ginger – lime : hot
271. Mango ginger in lime juice : hot
272. Mint – onion - mango : tender
273. Raisin – almond - pistachio : sweet
274. Button mushroom : watery
275. Spiced mixed vegetable – ginger : hot
276. Mixed vegetable in lime juice : watery
277. Sour mixed vegetable – garlic : watery
278. Button mushroom – green spices : tender
279. Sour spiced button mushroom : watery
280. Mixed vegetable in tamarind sauce : hot
281. Sour spring onion – honey - green chilli : sweet
282. Pear – tomato - onion : sweet
283. Perky pineapple : sweet
284. Pirandai – gram : hot
285. Sour spiced raw plantain : sweet
286. Sweet & sour poppy seeds in curd : watery
287. Poppy seed – garlic - green chilli : hot
288. Radish – lentils : hot
289. Black raisin in lime juice : sweet
290. Raisin – green spices : tender
291. Spiced red gram – tamarind : hot
292. Rhubarb – date - onion : watery
293. Spicy ridge gourd – lentils : hot
294. Spiced ridge gourd – gram : hot
295. Carrot in spicy mahani liquid : watery
296. Sesame – gram - green chilli : hot
297. Sesame – groundnut - green spices : tender

298. Spinach – green spices : tender
299. Spicy sprouted pulses – onion : tender
300. Spicy sugarcane juice – dry fruits : sweet
301. Raw sweet potato – mango : hot
302. Green tamarind – green chilli : hot
303. Spicy tamarind : sweet
304. Tamarind – ginger - green chilli : hot
305. Sweet tamarind – ginger - garlic : hot
306. Tamarind – green chilli : salty
307. Spicy tamarind – green chilli : hot
308. Ugadi tamarind – neem - mango : sweet
309. Peppered tamarind – cucumber seeds : sweet
310. Spicy tamarind – cummin - jaggery : sweet
311. Tamarind – mint - dried ginger : sweet
312. Salted tamarind : hot
313. Tamarind – ginger - garlic - date : hot
314. Spicy tamarind – raisin : sweet
315. Sunned spiced tamarind : sweet
316. Sesame green tomato : hot
317. Sour tomato – green coriander : tender
318. Tomato – green spices : tender
319. Spiced ripe tomato : sweet
320. Tomato – onion - green chilli : hot
321. Ripe tomato – ginger - garlic : sweet
322. Tomato – raisin : sweet
323. Ground tomato – aniseed : hot
324. Sour tomato – onion : watery
325. Green tomato – jaggery : sweet
326. Spicy tomato – dry fruit : sweet
327. Sour tomato – gram - garlic : hot
328. Sour tomato – raisin - apricot : sweet
329. Turnip in mustard sauce: watery
330. Sour grated elephant yam – tamarind : hot
331. Sour elephant yam – garlic : hot
332. Spicy elephant yam – mustard : hot
333. Woodapple – tamarind : hot

VEGETABLE SMART

- Once the vegetables are washed, do not let them stand in the water as this causes leeching of valuable nutrients.
- Scrape the outer skin of carrots, radish etc instead of peeling.
- Use the green leaves of radish and onions.
- Cook vegetables in as little water as possible
- Cook vegetables like potatoes with their skin and brinjals with their calyx. Ofcourse wash well before cooking.
- Do not drop the vegetables into the water until the water has begun to boil.
- Remove vegetables as soon as they are tender otherwise they tend to get mushy.
- Green vegetables retain their colour better if cooked uncovered for the first few minutes.
- Stir vegetables only when you must, as every time you stir, some of the vitamins are destroyed.

190 Amaranth Leaves in Tamarind Sauce : Hot

500 g	amaranth leaves, wash, air-dry & chop
10	cloves garlic, peel & chop
40 g	dried red chillies;
3 g	cummin seeds;
3 g	fenugreek seeds &
3 g	asafoetida, roast all in oil & powder
3 g	turmeric powder
100 g	cleaned tamarind, obtain thick extract using water
30 g	jaggery, grate
50 g	salt
250 ml	oil

1. Stir-fry the amaranth leaves in a little oil till tender. Cool, chop fine and set aside.
2. In the same pan heat some more oil, add the garlic and fry for a few minutes.
3. Pour over the tamarind extract, jaggery, turmeric powder and the salt.
4. Bring to the boil and allow to thicken over a high flame.
5. Stir in the chopped amaranth, the spice powders, the remaining oil and continue cooking over low heat.
6. Remove when the mixture becomes jam-like and the oil separates.
7. The pickle is ready for use. It lasts for 2 months.

191 Amaranth Leaves Peppered : Hot

125 g	amaranth leaves, wash, air-dry & chop
25 g	cleaned tamarind,
10 g	peppercorns &
5 g	split husked black gram, dry roast
12 g	salt

1. Add a little water and grind all the ingredients to a coarse or fine paste as desired.
2. The pickle keeps for 5 days and is best refrigerated.

192 Black Gram – Tamarind : Hot

125 g	split husked black gram, roast in oil
50 g	cleaned tamarind, dry-roast
10 g	dried red chillies, break into bits
3 g	mustard seeds &
3 g	fenugreek seeds : both for seasoning
3 g	asafoetida, roast in oil & powder
15 g	salt
10 ml	oil

1. Heat the oil, add mustard seeds and allow to crackle.
2. Follow with the fenugreek seeds, chillies, asafoetida powder and stir-fry for a few minutes.
3. Cool and grind the roasted ingredients with the salt using a little water.
4. The pickle is ready for use. It keeps for 1 week and is best refrigerated.

193 Cabbage in Lime Juice : Salty

125 g	cabbage leaves, inner portion to be used, shred thickly
5 g	grated coconut, dry-roast;
1-1"	piece of fresh ginger, scrape & chop;
5 g	green chillies &
10 g	salt, grind all to a paste
50 ml	lime juice
3 g	mustard seeds : for seasoning
10 ml	oil

1. Combine the shredded cabbage with the spice paste and lime juice.
2. Stir in the oil and blend well.
3. Heat the oil, add mustard seeds and allow to crackle.
4. Pour the seasoning over the cabbage mixture and blend well.
5. The pickle is ready for use. It keeps for 1 week and is best refrigerated.

194 Cabbage in Vinegar : Watery

500 g	cabbage, shred thickly
10 g	peppercorns, sun-dry & powder
3	cloves
1-1"	stick of cinnamon
300 ml	vinegar
50 g	salt

1. Combine all the ingredients and bring to the boil.
2. Lower the heat and continue cooking till the cabbage becomes tender. Remove and cool.
3. The pickle lasts for 1 month and is best refrigerated.

Note : Bulk **vinegar**, sold loose, are of a lower strength generally, and are not suitable for pickling.
Malt vinegar can be bought in its natural brown colour and also as white distilled vinegar. Either can be used, but white is normally used where a pale-coloured pickle is required.

195 Capsicum – Green Chilli in Tamarind Sauce : Hot

125 g	capsicum, chop & seed
10 g	green chillies, chop
15 g	cleaned tamarind, obtain thick extract using water
15 g	salt
25 ml	oil

1. Stir-fry the chopped capsicum and green chillies in a little oil.
2. Allow to cool, grind to a paste with the salt and set aside.
3. In the same pan heat some more oil, add in the tamarind extract and bring to the boil.
4. Allow to thicken over a high flame.
5. Lower the heat and stir in the ground paste.
6. Continue cooking until the mixture becomes jam-like and the oil separates.
7. The pickle is ready for use. It keeps for 2 weeks.

196 Carrot in Tamarind Sauce : Sweet

500 g	carrot, peel & chop
50 g	cleaned tamarind, obtain thick extract using water
75 g	jaggery, grate
15 g	chilli powder
5 g	turmeric powder
5 g	asafoetida &
3 g	fenugreek seeds, roast in oil & powder
5 g	mustard seeds : for seasoning
40 g	salt
250 ml	oil

1. Heat the oil, add mustard seeds and allow to crackle.
2. Add in the chopped carrot, turmeric powder, salt and fry over low heat till tender.
3. Stir in the tamarind extract, jaggery and bring to the boil. Allow to thicken over a high flame.
4. Blend in the spice powders.
5. Continue cooking over low heat until the mixture becomes jam-like and the oil separates.
6. The pickle is ready for use. It lasts for 2 months.

Note : Internally **chillies** are a major circulatory stimulant. It is the most powerful and persistent heart stimulant known. It is also an excellent remedy to ward off chills and is useful at the onset of colds. It supports the body's defence system and causes sweating.

197 Carrot – Green Chilli in Lime Juice : Hot

125 g	carrot, peel & chop
15 g	green chillies, chop
3 g	turmeric powder
50 ml	lime juice
20 g	salt
3 g	mustard seeds;
3 g	asafoetida &
10 ml	oil : all three for seasoning

1. Combine all the ingredients and mix thoroughly.
2. Heat the oil, add mustard seeds and allow to crackle.
3. Add in the asaofetida powder and pour the seasoning over the carrot mixture.
4. Set the pickle aside for 2 hours before serving. It keeps for 3 days.

198 Red Carrot in Vinegar : Watery

125 g	red carrot, peel & grate
10 g	dried red chillies &
2	cloves garlic, peel, grind both to a paste using vinegar
50 ml	vinegar
10 g	salt
20 ml	oil

1. Combine all the ingredients in a glass jar thoroughly.
2. Pour over the oil to cover the mixture and stir well.
3. The pickle keeps for 1 week in the refrigerator.

199 Sour Carrot – Onion : Hot

500 g	carrot, peel & thickly grate
400 g	onion, peel &
80 g	green chillies, chop both & grind together
100 g	fresh ginger, scrape &
10	cloves garlic, peel, grind both to a paste
50 g	cleaned tamarind, obtain thick extract using water
50 g	jaggery, grate
15 g	chilli powder
10 g	split husked black gram, dry-roast & powder
10 g	asafoetida, roast in oil & powder
10 g	turmeric powder
10 g	mustard seeds : for seasoning
60 g	salt
200 ml	oil

1. Heat a little oil in a pan, stir-fry the ginger-garlic paste for a few minutes and set aside.
2. In the same pan heat the remaining oil, add mustard seeds and allow to crackle.
3. Stir in the onion-chilli paste and fry for a few minutes.
3. Pour in the tamarind extract, jaggery, turmeric powder, salt and bring to the boil. Allow to thicken over a high flame.
4. Add in the grated carrot, fried ginger-garlic paste, chilli, black gram and asafoetida powders.
5. Continue cooking over low heat until the mixture becomes jam-like and the oil separates.
6. The pickle is ready for use. It lasts for 2 months.

200 Sour & Spicy Carrot – Peas : Sweet

500g	***carrot, peel & chop***
500g	***shelled peas***
80g	***cleaned tamarind, obtain thick extract using vinegar***
125g	***jaggery, grate***
80g	***green chillies, chop;***
10g	***mustard seeds &***
30g	***fresh ginger, scrape & chop, grind all three to a paste***
10g	***turmeric powder***
5g	***garam masala powder***
1	***bay leaf***
200ml	***vinegar***
100g	***salt***
400ml	***oil***

Peas

Really fresh peas will be crisp, bright green and smooth, one kilogram yielding about 500 grams of shelled tender peas. Don't overcook else they lose their flavour, texture and brilliant green colour.

1. Heat a little oil in a pan, drop in the bay leaf and fry for a minute.
2. Add in the vegetables, stir-fry for a few minutes and set aside.
3. Heat some more oil, fry the spice paste till the oil separates and set aside.
4. In the same pan heat the remaining oil, add in the tamarind extract, turmeric, garam masala powders, jaggery and the salt.
5. Bring to the boil and allow to thicken over a high flame.
6. Lower the heat, add in the fried vegetables and the spice paste.
7. Continue cooking until the mixture becomes jam-like and the oil separates.
8. The pickle is ready for use. It lasts for 2 months.

201 Cauliflower in Tamarind Sauce : Tender

500 g	***cauliflower florets***
5 g	***salt : for marinating***
75 g	***cleaned tamarind, obtain thick extract using water***
30 g	***jaggery, grate***
30 g	***chilli powder***
5 g	***turmeric powder***
3 g	***fenugreek &***
3 g	***asafoetida, roast both in oil & powder***
5 g	***mustard seeds : for seasoning***
75 g	***salt : for pickle***
250 ml	***oil***

1. Marinate the florets in one teaspoon (5g) salt for 8 hours. Drain, rinse and sun-dry for a day.
2. Heat a little oil, add mustard seeds and allow to crackle.
3. Follow with the dried florets, stir-fry for a few minutes and set aside.
4. In the same pan heat the remaining oil, add in the tamarind extract, jaggery and bring to the boil. Allow to thicken over a high flame.
5. Stir in the chilli, turmeric, fenugreek, asafoetida powders, salt and the fried florets.
6. Continue cooking over low heat until the mixture becomes jam-like and the oil separates.
7. The pickle is ready for use. It lasts for 2 months.

202 Cauliflower – Lime Strips : Tender

125 g	***cauliflower florets***
40 g	***lime, cut into thin strips & seed***
1-1"	***piece of fresh ginger, scrape & chop***
5 g	***dried red chillies, break into bits***
3 g	***mustard seeds***
3 g	***turmeric powder***
3 g	***asafoetida, roast in oil & powder***
30 ml	***lime juice***
25 g	***salt***

1. Boil 400ml water with the salt, remove and allow to cool.
2. Add the cauliflower florets and chopped lime into the cooled salt water.
3. Stir in the lime juice and set aside overnight.
4. Remove the florets and lime from the salt water the following day. Retain the water.
5. Grind the chopped ginger, dried red chillies, asafoetida, turmeric powder and mustard seeds with the reserved water to a paste.

6. Combine the florets and lime pieces with the spice paste thoroughly.
7. The pickle is ready for use. It keeps for 10 days and longer in the refrigerator. Stir frequently.

203 Cauliflower – Gram in Lime Juice : Hot

500 g	cauliflower florets
30 g	chilli powder
5 g	turmeric powder
2 g	fenugreek seeds, roast in oil & powder
2	cloves garlic, peel & chop
5 g	mustard seeds
5 g	split husked black gram
5 g	split husked bengal gram
3	dried red chillies, break into bits
a few	sprigs curry leaves
150 ml	lime juice
60 g	salt
25 ml	oil

1. Combine the lime juice with the turmeric powder and salt. Set aside for half an hour.
2. Blend in the florets, garlic, chilli and fenugreek powders.
3. Heat the oil, add mustard seeds and allow to crackle.
4. Follow with the bengal gram, black gram, chillies, curry leaves and the asafoetida powder. Fry till the grams turn golden.
5. Pour the seasoning over the cauliflower mixture and stir thoroughly.
6. The pickle is ready for use. It lasts for 1 month and longer in the refrigerator.

204 Mixed Gram in Tamarind : Salty

125 g	green gram, dried whole
75 g	bengal gram, dried whole
75 g	cow peas, dried whole
30 g	green chillies, chop
25 g	curry leaves, wash, air-dry & devein
5 g	mustard seeds
5 g	fenugreek seeds &
5 g	asafoetida, roast both in oil & powder
5 g	chilli powder
5 g	turmeric powder
25 g	cleaned tamarind, obtain thick extract using water
30 ml	lime juice
30 g	salt
30 ml	oil

1. Heat a little oil, add mustard seeds and allow to crackle.
2. Stir in the curry leaves, green chillies, asafoetida, fenugreek powders and fry for a few seconds.
3. Add in the gram and stir-fry for a few minutes till done. Set aside.
4. In the same pan heat the remaining oil, stir in the tamarind extract, chilli, turmeric powders and salt.
5. Bring to the boil and allow to thicken over a high flame.
6. Add in the gram mixture and continue cooking over low heat.
7. Remove when the mixture becomes jam-like and the oil separates.
8. The pickle is ready for use. It keeps for 10 days and is best refrigerated.

205 Celery in Vinegar : Salty

500 g	celery chunks
30 ml	soya sauce
150 ml	vinegar
40 g	salt
40 ml	oil

Celery
Celery should have the root left on because this is one of the best parts ; remove the coarse outer stems, and the leaves of all but the smallest heart stems, and turn the root to a slight point. Now cut the head into quarters, right down through the root. However celery is to be cooked, most varieties need blanching about 10 minutes first, to mellow their strong flavour.

1. Remove the fibrous portions of the celery and cut into chunks.
2. Blanch the celery chunks for 2 minutes in boiling water to which a teaspoon (5g) salt has been added for 2 minutes. Drain and dry immediately.
3. Blend the vinegar, soya sauce and oil into the salted celery while it is still hot.
4. The pickle is ready for use. It lasts for 1 month in the refrigerator.

206 Gram, Groundnut in Tamarind : Hot

40 g	bengal gram, dried whole;
40 g	green gram, dried whole &
40 g	groundnut, partly dried whole, soak all three overnight & cook till tender
5 g	cleaned tamarind, obtain thick extract using water
5 g	jaggery, grate
10 g	chilli powder
2 g	fenugreek seeds &
2 g	asafoetida, roast both in oil & powder
5 g	mustard seeds &
a few	sprigs curry leaves : both for seasoning
15 g	salt
25 ml	oil

1. Drain away the water from the cooked cereal and allow to dry indoors for 3 hours.
2. Heat a little oil, add mustard seeds and allow to crackle.
3. Add in the curry leaves, dried cereal, fry over low heat for a while and set aside.
4. In the same pan heat the remaining oil, pour in the tamarind extract along with the jaggery, turmeric powder and salt.
5. Bring to the boil and allow to thicken over a high flame.
6. Stir in the fried cereal, chilli, fenugreek, asafoetida powders and continue cooking until the mixture becomes jam-like.
7. The pickle is ready for use. It keeps for 15 days in the refrigerator. Sun occasionally.

207 Sour & Spiced Cereal – Mango : Hot

40 g	green gram, dried whole;
40 g	cow peas, dried whole &
40 g	groundnut, partly dried whole, soak all three overnight & cook till tender
20 g	seeded raw mango, peel, chop & soak in 5g salt for 1 hour
5 g	chilli powder
2 g	fenugreek seeds &
2 g	asafoetida, roast both in oil & powder
5 g	turmeric powder
5 g	mustard seeds;
10 g	green chillies, chop &
a few	sprigs curry leaves : all three for seasoning
20 g	salt
25 ml	oil

1. Drain out the water from the cooked cereal and allow to dry indoors for 3 hours.
2. Heat the oil, add mustard seeds and allow to crackle.
3. Add in the chillies, curry leaves, dried cereal and stir-fry for a while.
4. Blend in the chilli, fenugreek, asafoetida, turmeric powders, chopped mango and salt.
5. The pickle is ready for use. It keeps for 15 days in the refrigerator. Sun occasionally.

208 Sour Gram : Hot

40 g	bengal gram, dried whole;
40 g	field beans, dried whole &
40 g	groundnut, partly dried whole, soak all three overnight & cook till tender
12 g	chilli powder
3 g	fenugreek seeds &
3 g	asafoetida, roast both in oil & powder
2 g	turmeric powder
5 g	cleaned tamarind, obtain thick extract using water
5 g	jaggery, grate
5 g	mustard seeds &
a few	sprigs curry leaves : both for seasoning
5 ml	lime juice
5 ml	vinegar
20 g	salt
25 ml	oil

1. Drain out the water from the cooked cereal and allow to dry indoors for 3 hours.
2. Heat a little oil, add mustard seeds and allow to crackle.
3. Add in the curry leaves, dried cereal, stir-fry for a while and set aside.
4. In the same pan heat the remaining oil, pour in the tamarind extract along with the jaggery, turmeric powder and salt.
5. Bring to the boil and allow to thicken over a high flame.
6. Stir in the fried cereal, chilli, fenugreek, asafoetida powders and vinegar.
7. Continue cooking over low heat until the mixture becomes jam-like.
8. Pour in the lime juice, allow the mixture to bubble and remove.
9. The pickle is ready for use. It keeps for 15 days in the refrigerator. Sun occasionally.

209 Spicy Kichilikai : Hot

500 g	kichilikai, scrape lightly, chop & seed
50 g	chilli powder;
10 g	asafoetida, roast in oil & powder;
5 g	turmeric powder &
120 g	salt, combine all evenly
10 g	mustard seeds : for seasoning
200 ml	gingelly oil

1. Heat a little oil, add mustard seeds and allow to crackle.
2. Add in the chopped kichilikai and stir-fry for a few minutes till tender.
3. Stir in the spice mixture, the remaining oil, blend well for a few minutes and remove.
4. The pickle is ready for use. It lasts for 2 months.

210 Fried Narthangai : Hot

125 g	narthangai, scrape lightly, chop & seed
12 g	chilli powder
3 g	turmeric powder
3 g	mustard seeds : for seasoning
20 g	salt
50 ml	oil

1. Heat the oil, add mustard seeds and allow to crackle.
2. Add in the chopped narthangai and stir-fry till tender.
3. Blend in the chilli, turmeric powders, salt and remove.
4. The pickle is ready for use. It keeps for 1 week.

211 Sour Narthangai : Sweet

125 g	narthangai, scrape lightly, chop & seed
40 g	cleaned tamarind, obtain thick extract using water
20 g	jaggery, grate
20 g	green chillies, chop
5 g	turmeric powder
5 g	mustard seeds : for seasoning
25 g	salt
50 ml	oil

1. Heat the oil, add mustard seeds and allow to crackle.
2. Add in the chopped narthangai, green chilli and stir-fry till partly tender.
3. Pour in the tamarind extract, jaggery, turmeric powder, salt and bring to the boil.
4. Allow to thicken and remove.
5. The pickle is ready for use. It keeps for 15 days and is best refrigerated.

212 Kidrangai – Ginger : Hot

500 g	kidarangai, scrape lightly, chop & seed
20 g	green chillies, chop
2-1"	pieces of fresh ginger, scrape & chop
50 g	chilli powder;
5 g	turmeric powder;
5 g	fenugreek seeds, roast in oil & powder;
5 g	asafoetida, roast in oil & powder, combine all evenly
5 g	mustard seeds : for seasoning
120 g	salt
200 ml	gingelly oil

1. Heat a little oil, add mustard seeds and allow to crackle.
2. Add in the ginger, green chillies, the chopped kidarangai and stir-fry for a few minutes till almost tender.
3. Stir in the spice mixture, salt, the remaining oil, blend well for a few minutes and remove.
4. The pickle is ready for use. It lasts for 2 months.

> Elumichai, Kidarangai, Nathangai, Kolumichangai, Kichilikai, Kamala Orange, Kumquat Orange – all belong to citrus fruit category. Some are very sour, some have a hint of bitterness and some are bitter-sweet tasting.

213 Boiled Kidarangai : Salty

500 g	kidarangai, keep whole
60 g	chilli powder;
8 g	fenugreek seeds, roast in oil & powder;
8 g	asafoetida, roast in oil & powder;
8 g	turmeric powder &
120 g	salt, combine all evenly
10 g	mustard seeds : for seasoning
200 ml	gingelly oil

1. Drop the whole kidarangai into boiling water and set aside for 3 hours.
2. Wipe, cool, chop fine and seed.
3. Heat a little oil, add mustard seeds and allow to crackle.
4. Add in the chopped kidarangai, the remaining oil and fry for a few minutes till partly tender.
5. Stir in the spice mixture and remove when the kidarangai becomes tender.
6. The pickle is ready for use after 3 days. It lasts for 4 months.

214 Spicy Cereal – Green Coriander : Tender

40 g	field beans, dried whole;
40 g	cow peas, dried whole &
40 g	groundnut, partly dried whole, soak all three overnight & cook till tender
30 g	green coriander, wash, air-dry & chop
15 g	green chillies, chop
5 g	chilli powder
5 g	dried mango powder
1 g	garam masala powder
2 g	turmeric powder
5 g	mustard seeds : for seasoning
2 g	sugar
10 ml	vinegar
15 g	salt
25 ml	oil

1. Drain out the water from the cooked cereal and allow to dry indoors for 3 hours.
2. Heat a little oil, add mustard seeds and allow to crackle.
3. Follow with the chillies, chopped coriander, dried cereal and stir-fry till dry.
4. Pour in the vinegar, sugar and stir to dissolve.
5. Add in the chilli, garam masala, turmeric powders, dried mango powder, salt and the remaining oil.
6. Continue cooking over low heat until the mixture thickens.
7. The pickle is ready for use.
8. It keeps for 15 days in the refrigerator. Sun occasionally.

215 Coconut – Tamarind : Hot

125 g	grated coconut, dry-roast
10 g	cleaned tamarind, dry-roast
5 g	mustard seeds
5 g	split husked black gram
3 g	asafoetida, roast in oil & powder
2 g	turmeric powder
3	green chillies, chop
2	dried red chillies, break into bits
8 g	salt
10 ml	oil

1. Heat the oil, fry the mustard seeds, black gram, asafoetida powder, red and green chillies for a few minutes till done.
2. Remove, cool, grind the fried gram and spices with the remaining ingredients to a fine paste using a little water.
3. The pickle is ready for use. It keeps for 1 week in the refrigerator.

216 Spicy Coconut – Mango : Hot

125 g	grated coconut, dry-roast
150 g	seeded raw mango, peel & grate
30 g	green chillies, chop
5 g	mustard seeds;
5 g	split husked black gram;
5 g	split husked bengal gram &
a few	sprigs curry leaves: all for seasoning
2 g	asafoetida, roast in oil & powder
25 g	salt
25 ml	oil

1. Stir-fry the green chillies and the grated mango in a little oil for a few minutes.
2. Grind together all the ingredients coarsely except the seasoning using a little water.
3. Heat the remaining oil, add mustard seeds and allow to crackle.
4. Stir in the black gram, bengal gram, curry leaves and fry till done.
5. Pour the seasoning over the pickle and mix thoroughly.
6. The pickle is ready for use. It keeps only for 2 days but longer in the refrigerator.

217 Flavoury Coconut – Mango : Salty

125 g	grated coconut, dry roast
60 g	seeded raw mango, peel & chop
30 g	green chillies, chop;
1-1"	piece of fresh ginger, scrape;
2	cloves garlic, peel &
5 g	thymol seeds, dry-roast, grind all to a paste
25 g	salt

1. Grind all the ingredients together to a coarse paste using a little water.
2. The pickle keeps for 2 days and longer in the refrigerator.

218 Sour Cocum : Sweet

500 g	cocum, wash in hot water	250 ml	vinegar
2-1"	pieces of fresh ginger, scrape & slice fine	80 g	salt
8	dried red chillies, break into bits		
10	cloves garlic, peel & chop		
150 g	jaggery, grate		
150 g	sugar		

1. Grind the cocum with the chillies.
2. Combine the cocum paste with the ginger, garlic, vinegar, jaggery, salt and sugar in a pan.
3. Cook over low heat and remove when the mixture thickens.
4. The pickle is ready for use. It lasts for 1 month.

219 Coconut – Mango – Green Spices : Tender

100 g	grated coconut, dry-roast	30 g	green chillies, chop
100 g	seeded raw mango, peel & chop	8	cloves garlic, peel & chop
30 g	green coriander &	3 g	cummin seeds
10 g	mint leaves, wash, air-dry & chop both	3 g	turmeric powder
		5 g	sugar
		25 g	salt

1. Grind together all the ingredients to a coarse paste. Add no water.
2. The pickle is ready for use. It keeps for 1 week in the refrigerator.

220 Green Coriander – Sesame : Hot

125 g	green coriander, wash, air-dry & chop	50 ml	lime juice
35 g	green chillies, chop	35 g	salt
2-1"	pieces of fresh ginger, scrape & chop	15 ml	oil
10 g	white sesame seeds;		
5 g	cummin seeds &		
5 g	pomegranate seeds, dry-roast all three & powder		
15 g	jaggery, grate		

1. Grind together all the ingredients with the salt to a smooth paste.
2. The pickle keeps only for 2 days but longer if refrigerated.

> **Coriander leaves**
> Coriander leaves are highly nutritious, being a rich source of iron, calcium, beta-carotene (precursor of vitamin A) and vitamin C. It is good for the digestive system and reduces flatulence. It stimulates the appetite, aiding the secretion of gastric juices.

221 Garlic – Cucumber in Vinegar : Watery

125 g	cucumber, scrub & slice
2	cloves garlic, crush
50 ml	vinegar
12 g	salt
15 ml	oil
a pinch of sugar	

1. Combine all the ingredients, adding oil at the end.
2. The pickle is ready for use. It keeps for 10 days.

222 Ginger – Cucumber in Vinegar : Salty

125 g	cucumber, scrub & slice
1-1"	piece of fresh ginger, scrape & chop fine
25 g	sugar
50 ml	vinegar
12 g	salt

1. Combine the vinegar, sugar, salt, ginger and bring to the boil.
2. Pour the spiced vinegar over the cucumber slices and allow to cool.
3. The pickle is ready for use. It keeps for 20 days.

223 Cucumber in Lime Juice : Watery

125 g	cucumber, scrub & chop
5 g	mustard seeds;
2 g	asafoetida, roast in oil & powder;
a few	sprigs curry leaves &
25 ml	oil : all for seasoning
30 ml	lime juice
12 g	salt

1. Marinate the chopped cucumber in the salt.
2. Heat the oil, add mustard seeds and allow to crackle.
3. Stir in the asafoetida powder, curry leaves and fry for a minute.
4. Blend the seasoning and the lime juice into the salted cucumber.
5. The pickle is ready for use. It keeps for 5 days and longer in the refrigerator. Stir daily.

Variation :
A variety of vegetables may be similarly pickled, such as carrot, cabbage, capsicum, cauliflower and tomato.

224 Spicy Curd : Watery

125 g	sour curd, whip & remove cream
5 ml	lime juice
10 g	green chillies, chop;
1-1"	piece of fresh ginger, scrape &
a few	sprigs curry leaves, wash, air-dry, devein & chop, grind all three to a paste
3 g	split husked black gram;
3 g	mustard seeds &
5 ml	oil : all three for seasoning
20 g	salt

1. Blend the lime juice and the spice paste into the sour curd.
2. Heat the oil, add mustard seeds and allow to crackle. Add in the black gram and fry till golden.
3. Pour the seasoning over the curd mixture, stir well and allow to stand for a day.
4. The pickle is ready for use. It keeps for 2 weeks and is best refrigerated.

225 Curry Leaf – Coconut : Hot

125 g	curry leaves, wash, air-dry, devein & chop
125 g	grated coconut, dry-roast
40 g	onion, peel & chop
30 g	green chillies, chop
2-1"	pieces of fresh ginger, scrape & chop
25 g	dried red chillies, break into bits &
5 g	mustard seeds : both for seasoning
50 g	salt
125 ml	oil

1. Stir-fry the curry leaves, green chillies, ginger, onion in a little oil and set aside.
2. Grind all the ingredients to a smooth paste using a little water.
3. Heat some more oil, add mustard seeds and allow to crackle.
4. Add in the chillies, fry for a while and remove.
5. Pour the seasoning along with the remaining oil (after heating) over the mixture and stir well.
6. The pickle is ready for use. It keeps only for 2 days but longer if refrigerated.

226 Spiced Date : Sweet

125 g	date, slit, stone & soak in boiling water
25 g	cleaned tamarind
30 g	jaggery, grate
5 g	chilli powder
5 g	coriander seeds &
5 g	cummin seeds, dry-roast both & powder
10 g	salt

1. Grind the tamarind and date using a little water.
2. Add in the grated jaggery, spice powders, salt and blend well.
3. The pickle is ready for use. It keeps for 1 week if refrigerated.

227 Dried Red Chilli in Lime Juice : Hot

125 g	dried red chillies, remove stem &
50 g	fresh ginger, scrape & chop, grind both to a paste
40 g	peeled garlic, chop fine
10 g	sugar
125 ml	lime juice
60 g	salt
100 ml	oil

1. Heat a little oil, add the chilli-ginger paste and cook till the oil separates.
2. Add in the chopped garlic, sugar, salt, the remaining oil and continue cooking for a few minutes.
3. Stir in the lime juice and remove when the mixture begins to bubble.
4. The pickle is ready for use. It keeps for 5 days in the refrigerator.

228 Fenugreek Greens – Tamarind : Tender

125 g	fenugreek greens, wash, air-dry & chop
4	dried red chillies, break into bits
25 g	cleaned tamarind
15 g	jaggery, grate
15 g	salt
75 ml	oil

1. Fry the red chillies in a little oil and set aside.
2. Stir-fry the chopped fenugreek in the remaining oil.
3. Grind together all the ingredients to a fine paste.
4. The pickle is ready for use. It keeps only for 2 days but longer if refrigerated.

Fenugreek leaves
Fenugreek leaves are useful in relieving flatulence, indigestion and bronchitis. Its seeds are highly recommended in cases of diarrhoea and cough.

Tamarind
Tamarind acts as a laxative and has anti-billious properties. Both the flower and fruit stimulate the bowel movements.

229 Fresh Red Chilli – Tamarind - Garlic : Hot

500 g	fresh red chillies
200 g	cleaned tamarind
100 g	peeled garlic
15 g	cummin seeds &
5 g	fenugreek seeds, dry-roast both & powder
5 g	mustard seeds;
2	dried red chillies, break into bits &
a few	sprigs curry leaves : all three for seasoning
200 g	salt
50 ml	oil

1. Grind together the fresh red chillies, tamarind and salt very coarsely. Set aside for 3 days.
2. On the 4th day, grind together the roasted spices and garlic.
3. Grind the fresh red chilli mixture with the spice mixture.
4. Whenever required take the desired quantity of the prepared fresh red chillies.
5. Heat a little oil, fry the mustard seeds, dried red chillies, curry leaves and remove.
6. Cool and pour the seasoning over the prepared fresh red chillies.
7. The pickle is ready for use. It lasts for 6 months.

230 Sour Fresh Red Chilli : Hot

500 g	fresh red chillies, cut into small pieces
125 g	cleaned tamarind
75 g	jaggery, grate
10 g	asafoetida
10 g	mustard seeds : for seasoning
125 g	salt
125 ml	oil

1. Stir-fry the chillies, asafoetida and tamarind in a little oil. Allow to cool.
2. Grind all the ingredients together coarsely.
3. Heat the remaining oil, add mustard seeds and allow to crackle.
4. Blend the seasoning into the pickle.
5. The pickle is ready for use. It lasts for 2 months. Sun occasionally.

231 Fried Gram – Mango : Hot

125 g	fried gram
450 g	seeded raw mango, peel & chop
20 g	dried red chillies, break into bits
10 g	mustard seeds
10 g	fenugreek seeds
5 g	asafoetida, roast in oil & powder
40 g	salt
50 ml	oil

1. Heat the oil, add mustard seeds and allow to crackle.
2. Add in the fenugreek seeds, red chillies, asafoetida powder and fry for a few minutes.
3. Cool and grind coarsely with the chopped mango, fried gram and the salt.
4. The pickle is ready for use. It keeps for 1 week and longer in the refrigerator.

232 Steamed Spicy Garlic in Lime Juice : Watery

500 g	peeled garlic
60 g	jaggery, grate
25 g	chilli powder
10 g	coriander seeds;
5 g	cummin seeds;
5 g	asafoetida &
5 g	fenugreek seeds, roast all in oil & powder
5 g	turmeric powder
5 g	mustard seeds : for seasoning
150 ml	lime juice
20 ml	vinegar
50 g	salt
250 ml	oil

1. Steam the peeled garlic for 5 minutes till very soft. Allow to cool.
2. Heat a little oil, add mustard seeds and allow to crackle.
3. Add in the steamed garlic and stir-fry for a few minutes.
4. Stir in the lime juice and vinegar.
5. Heat gently along with the jaggery, salt and the spice powders.
6. Cook along with the remaining oil until the jaggery dissolves and the spice powders blend into the mixture.
7. The pickle is ready for use. It lasts for 2 months.

233 Ginger in Lime Juice : Watery

125 g	fresh ginger, scrape & chop
30 ml	lime juice
3 g	turmeric powder
5 g	mustard seeds : for seasoning
20 g	salt
20 ml	oil

1. Combine the lime juice, turmeric powder and salt with the chopped ginger.
2. Heat the oil, add mustard seeds and allow to crackle.
3. Pour the seasoning over the ginger mixture and stir thoroughly.
4. The pickle is ready for use. It keeps for 1 week and longer in the refrigerator.

234 Ginger in Raw Tamarind Sauce : Salty

125 g	fresh ginger, scrape & chop
15 g	cleaned tamarind, obtain thick extract using water
5 g	turmeric powder
5 g	mustard seeds : for seasoning
20 g	salt
20 ml	oil

1. Combine the chopped ginger with the tamarind extract, turmeric powder and salt.
2. Heat the oil, add mustard seeds and allow to crackle.
3. Pour the seasoning over the ginger mixture and stir thoroughly.
4. The pickle is ready for use. It keeps for 1 week and longer in the refrigerator.

Ginger is used worldwide in its fresh and dried form in medicinal and food preparations. Ginger is warming and stimulating, promotes gastric secretion and aids the absorption of food. It is an excellent remedy for easing indigestion and flatulence. It also has a stimulating effect on the heart and circulation. Ginger has a warming expectorant action on the lungs, dispelling mucous and phlegm. Dried ginger is thought to be more suitable for treating respiratory and digestive disorders.

235 Sesame Green Chilli – Tamarind : Hot

500 g	green chillies, chop
250 g	cleaned tamarind
50 g	sesame seeds;
15 g	mustard seeds &
15 g	cummin seeds, dry-roast all three & powder
10 g	fenugreek seeds, roast in oil & powder
10 g	turmeric powder
200 g	salt
200 ml	oil

1. Grind the green chilli, tamarind and the salt coarsely.
2. Add in the roasted powders and grind again fine.
3. Heat the oil, stir in the ground mixture and stir-fry until the mixture leaves the sides of the pan.
4. The pickle is ready for use. It lasts for 2 months.

236 Green Chilli – Ginger-Garlic Vinegared : Hot

1 kg	green chillies, chop
300 g	fresh ginger, scrape &
200 g	peeled garlic, chop both & grind fine
40 g	cummin seeds, sun-dry & powder coarsely
40 g	chilli powder
a few	sprigs curry leaves
700 g	sugar, soak in 700ml vinegar
400 g	salt
800 ml	oil

1. Heat the oil and stir-fry the ginger-garlic paste.
2. Add in the chopped green chilli and fry for a few minutes.
3. Stir in the remaining ingredients except cummin powder. Cook over low heat until the contents are reduced to half.
4. Blend in the cummin powder and remove.
5. The pickle is ready for use.
   It lasts for 1 year.

237 Sour Ground Raw Gooseberry : Hot

125 g	seeded gooseberry, chop
25 g	cleaned tamarind
30 g	dried red chillies;
15 g	black gram &
3 g	asafoetida, roast all three in oil
3 g	turmeric powder
5 g	mustard seeds : for seasoning
55 g	salt
15 ml	oil

1. Grind together the gooseberry with the tamarind, turmeric powder, salt, roasted chilli and asafoetida coarsely using a little water.
2. Add in the roasted gram and grind again coarsely.
3. Heat the oil, add mustard seeds and allow to crackle.
4. Pour the seasoning over the gooseberry mixture and stir well.
5. The pickle is ready for use. It keeps for 1 week and longer in the refrigerator.

238 Unripe Grape – Coconut – Green Coriander : Salty

125 g	unripe grapes, remove seeds & crush
15 g	grated coconut, dry-roast
15 g	green coriander, wash, air-dry & chop
7	green chillies, chop
5 g	cummin seeds
5 g	sugar
25 g	salt

1. Grind together all the ingredients coarsely except the grapes and green coriander.
2. Add in the grapes, green coriander and grind fine. Add no water.
3. The pickle is ready for use. It keeps for 5 days in the refrigerator.

239 Green Grape : Hot

500 g	green grapes, wash, slit & seed
60 g	chilli powder
10 g	fenugreek seeds &
10 g	asafoetida, roast both in oil & powder
15 g	mustard seeds : for seasoning
100 g	salt
100 ml	oil

1. Heat a little oil, add mustard seeds and allow to crackle.
2. Add in the slit green grapes, chilli, fenugreek, asafoetida powders and the salt.
3. Stir-fry for a few minutes and remove.
4. The pickle is ready for use. It lasts for 1 month.

Grapes : Basically of four main types, each one being superior to the other for the purposes for which they are grown; wine, dried fruits (raisins etc), the table and fresh grape juice.
Grapes revitalise and rejuvenate the whole system, according to Ayurveds. Basically grapes are rich in sugar, vitamins, minerals and assimilable iron.
Due to its tartaric acid content grapes act as a laxative, while also stimulating the liver, kidneys and eliminating toxins from the body.

240 Mint, Green Coriander – Onion - Mango Powder : Tender

125 g	mint leaves &
125 g	green coriander, wash, air-dry & chop
40 g	onion, peel & chop
30 g	green chillies, chop
5	cloves garlic, peel & chop
10 g	dried mango powder
20 g	sugar
20 g	salt

1. Grind together all the ingredients to a fine paste.
2. The pickle is now ready for use. It keeps for 1 week and is best refrigerated.

241 Raw Groundnut – Cummin : Hot

125 g	shelled raw groundnut
15 g	dried red chillies, break into bits
10 g	cummin seeds, dry-roast
10 g	cleaned tamarind
5 g	asafoetida, roast in oil & powder
20 g	salt
20 ml	oil

1. Stir-fry the groundnut in a little oil and set aside.
2. In the same pan fry the red chillies and set aside.
3. Grind together the groundnut, red chillies, roasted cummin, asafoetida powder, salt and the tamarind coarsely with a little water.
4. The pickle is ready for use. It keeps for 5 days and is best refrigerated.

242 Roasted Groundnut – Tamarind : Hot

125 g	shelled roasted groundnut, husk
10 g	cleaned tamarind
15 g	dried red chillies;
2 g	asafoetida &
2 g	split husked black gram, roast all three in oil & powder
2 g	mustard seeds : for seasoning
20 g	salt
20 ml	oil

1. Grind together the groundnut, tamarind, roasted powders and salt to a fine paste with a little water.
2. Heat the oil, add mustard seeds and allow to crackle.
3. Pour the seasoning over the ground mixture and stir thoroughly.
4. The pickle is ready for use. It keeps for 3 weeks and longer in the refrigerator.

Groundnuts
Nutritional as they are, and used raw or roasted, they have a rather dominant flavour which limits their use in pickling.

243 Sour Raw Groundnut – Green Coriander : Tender

125 g	shelled raw groundnut, peel & soak in water for 2 hrs
75 g	seeded raw mango, peel & chop;
50 g	green coriander, wash, air-dry & chop;
40 g	green chillies, chop;
10 g	sugar &
25 g	salt, grind all fine with the soaked groundnut
5 g	turmeric powder;
5 g	mustard seeds;
5 g	asafoetida &
20 ml	oil : all for seasoning

1. Heat the oil, add mustard seeds and allow to crackle. Add in the asafoetida, turmeric powders and remove.
2. Pour the seasoning over the groundnut mixture and blend well.
3. The pickle is ready for use. It keeps for 5 days in the refrigerator.

244 Roasted Groundnut – Ginger : Salty

125 g	shelled roasted groundnut, husk
15 g	green chillies, chop
1-1"	piece of fresh ginger, scrape & chop
10 ml	lime juice
10 g	salt

1. Grind together all the ingredients to a fine paste.
2. Blend in the lime juice.
3. The pickle is ready for use. It keeps for 1 week in the refrigerator.

245 Guava – Tomato : Watery

125 g	guava, chop fine & seed
25 g	tomato, chop & seed
5 g	chilli powder
3 g	green chillies, chop
3 g	jaggery, grate
3 g	mustard seeds, sun-dry & powder
3 g	garam masala powder
1	clove garlic, peel & grind to a paste
40 ml	vinegar
150 ml	water
15 g	salt

1. Grind all the ingredients (except the chopped guava) with 300ml water and filter.
2. Cook the mixture along with the chopped guava for 10 minutes till thick.
3. Pour into bottles while still hot. Cork when cool.
4. The pickle is ready for use. It keeps for 10 days in the refrigerator.

246 Sour Spiced Ripe Jackfruit : Sweet

500 g	ripe jackfruit, segment, seed & chop
20 g	onion &
7	cloves garlic, peel & chop both
500 ml	water
10 g	chilli powder;
5 g	peppercorns;
5	cardamoms;
2-1"	sticks of cinnamon &
2	blades of mace, tie all in a spice bag
2 g	citric acid crystals, dissolve in a little water
175 g	sugar
100 ml	vinegar
30 g	salt

1. Combine the water, dissolved citric acid with the jackfruit pieces and bring to the boil.
2. Drop in the spice bag and allow the mixture to thicken.
3. Add in the the sugar, salt and cook till the mixture thickens again.
4. When the mixture reaches a single-thread consistency, add in the vinegar, cook for a few minutes and remove.
5. The pickle is ready for use. It lasts for 6 months.

247 Jaggery – Black Gram : Sweet

Jaggery
Besides giving good strength to the body, if taken in limits, it is also capable of helping to cure a good number of ailments and give great energy. However, newly prepared jaggery increases phlegm. One year old jaggery is supposed to be very good. Again after 3 years, its beneficial properties are said to diminish.

500 g	jaggery, grate
200 g	split husked black gram
150 g	dried red chillies, break into bits
100 g	green coriander, wash, air-dry & chop
100 g	cleaned tamarind
10 g	mustard seeds : for seasoning
a few	sprigs curry leaves
100 g	salt
100 ml	oil

1. Heat a little oil, add mustard seeds and allow to crackle. Add in the black gram and fry till golden.
2. Follow with the dried red chillies, curry leaves, chopped green coriander and fry for a few minutes over low heat till done. Allow to cool.
3. Grind together the roasted ingredients, jaggery, tamarind and salt using a little water.
4. The pickle is ready for use. It lasts for 1 month.

248 Small Kalakkai – Cummin Seeds : Hot

500 g	small kalakkai, remove stems
75 g	chilli powder
10 g	cummin seeds;
5 g	fenugreek seeds &
5 g	asafoetida, roast all three in oil & powder
20 g	jaggery, grate
125 g	salt
200 ml	oil : heat and cool

1. Combine the spice powders, jaggery and salt evenly.
2. Stir in the kalakkai and mix well.
3. Pour over the oil and stir thoroughly.
4. The pickle is ready for use after 4 days. It lasts for 1 month.

249 Fried Lime : Hot

500 g	lime, scrape lightly & keep whole
50 g	chilli powder
10 g	mustard seeds : for seasoning
5 g	asafoetida, roast in oil & powder
100 g	salt
200 ml	oil

1. Stir-fry the limes in a little oil, a few at a time, till light brown.
2. Remove, allow to cool, cut into small pieces and seed.
3. Sprinkle the chilli, asafoetida powders and salt over the lime pieces.
4. Heat the oil, add mustard seeds and allow to crackle.
5. Pour the seasoning over the lime pieces and mix thoroughly.
6. The pickle is ready for use. It lasts for 1 month.

Variation
You may instead cut the lime into small pieces straightaway and fry them in oil. Otherwise the preparation is identical.

250 Lime – Green Coriander-Coconut : Tender

125 g	lime, peel, segment & seed thoroughly
30 g	grated coconut, dry-roast
20 g	green coriander, wash, air-dry & chop
15 g	green chillies, chop
2 g	chilli powder
2 g	sugar
2 g	mustard seeds &
10 ml	oil : both for seasoning
25 g	salt

1. Peel the limes, remove the thin inner skin, seed and separate the fruit.
2. Grind the fruit with the other ingredients (except the sugar) to a smooth paste without water. Blend in the sugar.
3. Heat the oil, add mustard seeds and allow to crackle.
4. Stir in the spice paste, fry for a few minutes and remove.
5. The pickle is ready for use. It keeps only for 2 days but longer if refrigerated.

251 Spiced Stuffed Boiled Lime : Watery

125 g	lime, scrape lightly & keep whole
	water sufficient to cover
30 ml	lime juice
2	cloves garlic, peel & chop
20 g	chilli powder
2 g	turmeric powder
2 g	onion seeds;
2 g	mustard seeds;
2 g	cummin seeds &
2 g	fenugreek seeds, sun-dry all & powder
40 g	salt
50 ml	oil : heat & cool

1. Drop the limes into the boiling water along with the turmeric powder.
2. Remove the limes from the water after 2 minutes, wipe and allow to cool. Cut into 4 without severing.
3. Combine the powdered spices, chilli powder, garlic and salt with a little oil to a paste.
4. Stuff the spice paste into the limes, sprinkle over the remaining spice paste and pack in a jar.
6. Stir in the remaining oil and the lime juice.
7. The pickle is ready for use. It keeps for 15 days.

Variation
Similar pickle may be prepared without the addition of cummin and mustard powder.

> **Lime**
> It may be called "nature's cure-all" as it improves the functioning of the liver. The citric acid in lime has wonderful curative powders in all kinds of digestive troubles. It can be used both externally and internally for sore-throat, cough and diptheria.

252 Lime – Ginger-Green Chilli : Hot

125 g	lime, chop & seed
15 g	green chillies, chop fine
1-1"	piece of fresh ginger, scrape & chop
3 g	mustard seeds, sun-dry & powder
20 g	salt
5 ml	oil

1. Combine all the ingredients and set aside for 3 days.
2. The pickle is ready for use. It keeps for 10 days and longer in the refrigerator. Stir daily.

253 Mango Pachadi : Hot

- 500 g   seeded mango, peel & slice
- 25 g   dried red chillies &
- 5   cloves garlic, peel, grind both fine
- 50 g   salt
- 100 ml   oil

1. Marinate the mango slices in one teaspoon (5g) salt and set aside for 2 hours. Squeeze out the salt water.
2. Stir-fry the chilli-garlic paste in a little oil for a few minutes. Remove and set aside.
3. In the same pan heat some more oil, add in the mango slices and the remaining salt.
4. Cook over low heat for 20 minutes until the mango slices become transluscent and dry.
5. Stir in the chilli-garlic paste and the remaining oil.
6. Continue cooking over low heat until the mixture becomes jam-like and leaves the sides of the pan.
7. The pickle is ready for use. It lasts for 1 month in the refrigerator.

254 Cooked Mango Preserve : Sweet

- 1 kg   seeded mango, peel & grate
- 500 g   jaggery, grate
- 50 g   chilli powder
- 10 g   mustard seeds : for seasoning
- 5 g   asafoetida, roast in oil & powder
- 50 g   salt
- 250 ml   oil

1. Marinate the grated mango in the salt. Cover and set aside for 2 hours.
2. Heat a little oil, add mustard seeds and allow to crackle.
3. Add in the asafoetida powder, the grated mango and stir-fry for a few minutes.
4. When the mango is partly tender, add in the chilli powder, jaggery and the remaining oil.
5. Continue cooking over low heat until the mixture reaches a jam-like consistency and immediately transfer to a jar.
6. The pickle is ready for use. It lasts for 1 year.

255 Cooked Mango : Hot

- 125 g   cut mango, size into 2" lengths
- 40 g   jaggery, grate
- 100 ml   water
- 5 g   chilli powder
- 2 g   asafoetida, roast in oil & powder
- 2 g   turmeric powder
- 2 g   mustard seeds &
- a few   sprigs curry leaves : both for seasoning
- 12 g   salt
- 20 ml   oil

1. Heat the oil, add the mustard seeds, curry leaves and allow to crackle.
2. Pour over 100ml water and bring to the boil.
3. Stir in the mango pieces, spice powders, jaggery and the salt.
4. Continue cooking until the mango pieces become partly tender.
5. The pickle is ready for use. It keeps for 10 days and longer if refrigerated.

Mangoes

Romani and Malgova mangoes which are thick, large, fleshy and not very sour-tasting are ideal for preparing grated mango pickle.
Mangoes with a little fibre, of slightly sour taste are best suited for cut mango pickle.
Very sour and fibrous mangoes are generally unsuited for pickle-making.
Select mangoes for pickles that are healthy, unripe, fully developed and preferably of the tart variety.

---

256 Mango – Green Coriander : Tender

- 500 g   seeded sour mango, peel & grate
- 40 g   chilli powder
- 25 g   green coriander, wash, air-dry & grind fine
- 25 g   jaggery, grate
- 5 g   fenugreek seeds, roast in oil & powder
- 3 g   mustard seeds;
- 2   dried red chillies, break into bits &
- a few   sprigs curry leaves : all for seasoning
- 50 g   salt
- 200 ml   oil

1. Heat a little oil, add the mustard seeds, curry leaves and allow to crackle.
2. Add in the dried red chillies and fry for a minute.
3. Stir in the coriander paste and fry for a while.
4. Follow with the grated mango and continue cooking for a few minutes.
5. Pour in the remaining oil, jaggery, salt and allow to thicken.
6. Stir in the chilli and fenugreek powders.
7. Remove when the mixture becomes jam-like and the oil separates.
8. The pickle is ready for use. It lasts for 2 months.

257 Mango – Mint : Tender

500 g	seeded sour mango, peel & grate
25 g	mint leaves, wash, air-dry & grind fine
35 g	jaggery, grate
30 g	chilli powder
15 g	green chillies, chop
5 g	fenugreek seeds, roast in oil & powder
2 g	mustard seeds;
2 g	cummin seeds &
2	dried red chillies, break into bits : all for seasoning
60 g	salt
200 ml	oil

1. Heat a little oil, add the mustard seeds, cummin seeds and allow to crackle.
2. Add in the dried red chillies and fry for a minute.
3. Stir in the mint paste and fry for a while.
4. Follow with the grated mango, chopped green chillies and continue cooking for a few minutes.
5. Pour in the remaining oil, jaggery, salt and allow to thicken.
6. Add in the chilli and fenugreek powders.
7. Remove when the mixture becomes jam-like and the oil separates.
8. The pickle is ready for use. It lasts for 2 months.

> **Mint**
> This herb stimulates the digestive tract and reduces nausea & vomiting. It is also well known for the treatment of colds. It is also an effective remedy for flatulence. It stimulates the liver and gall bladder thus increasing bile secretion.

258 Mango – Curry Leaf : Tender

500 g	seeded mango, peel & grate
25 g	curry leaves, clean, devein & grind fine
40 g	jaggery, grate
35 g	chilli powder
5 g	fenugreek seeds, roast in oil & powder
3 g	mustard seeds &
2	dried red chillies, break into bits: both for seasoning
60 g	salt
200 ml	oil

1. Heat a little oil, add mustard seeds and allow to crackle.
2. Add in the dried red chillies and fry for a minute.
3. Stir in the curry leaf paste and fry for a while.
4. Follow with the grated mango and continue cooking for a few minutes.
5. Pour in the remaining oil, jaggery, salt and allow to thicken.
6. Add in the chilli and fenugreek powders.
7. Remove when the mixture becomes jam-like and the oil separates.
8. The pickle is ready for use. It lasts for 2 months.

259 Mango – Cabbage : Hot

125 g	seeded sour mango, peel & grate
60 g	shredded cabbage
5 g	salt : for marinating
5 g	chilli powder
3 g	fenugreek seeds &
3 g	asafoetida, roast both in oil & powder
3 g	mustard seeds;
2	green chillies, chop &
a few	sprigs curry leaves : all for seasoning
10 g	salt : for pickle
25 ml	oil

1. Marinate the shredded cabbage in a teaspoon (5g) salt for one hour.
2. Combine the grated mango and the salted cabbage with the chilli powder and salt.
3. Sprinkle over the fenugreek and asafoetida powders.
4. Heat the oil, add mustard seeds and allow to crackle.
5. Add in the green chillies, curry leaves and fry for a minute.
6. Pour the seasoning over the cabbage-mango mixture and blend well.
7. The pickle is ready for use.
8. Place in the sun for a day. The pickle will keep for a week.

260 Mango – Green Gram : Hot

125 g	seeded mango, peel & chop
60 g	split husked green gram, soak in water for 1 hour
3	dried red chillies, break into bits;
3 g	mustard seeds;
3 g	fenugreek seeds &
2 g	asafoetida, roast in oil : all for seasoning
12 g	salt
20 ml	oil

1. Grind together the soaked green gram and the chopped mango with the salt coarsely.
2. Heat the oil, add mustard seeds and allow to crackle.
3. Add in the fenugreek seeds, dried red chillies, asafoetida and fry till done.
4. Pour the seasoning over the mango-green gram mixture and grind again coarsely.
5. The pickle is ready for use. It keeps for 1 week and is best refrigerated.

261 Mango – Bengal Gram : Hot

125 g	seeded mango, peel & chop
60 g	split husked bengal gram, soak for 1 hour & drain
3	dried red chillies, break into bits;
3 g	mustard seeds;
2 g	fenugreek seeds &
2 g	asafoetida, roast in oil : all for seasoning
12 g	salt
20 ml	oil

1. Grind together the soaked bengal gram and the chopped mango with the salt coarsely.
2. Heat the oil, add mustard seeds and allow to crackle.
3. Add in the fenugreek seeds, dried red chillies, asafoetida and fry till done.
4. Pour the seasoning over the mango-bengal gram mixture and grind again coarsely.
5. The pickle is ready for use. It keeps for 1 week and is best refrigerated.

262 Grated Mango Pachadi : Hot

125 g	seeded mature mango, peel & grate
5 g	chilli powder
2 g	turmeric powder
2 g	asafoetida, roast in oil & powder
3 g	mustard seeds : for seasoning
10 g	salt
10 ml	oil

1. Marinate the grated mango with the salt for 4 hours. Squeeze out the salt water.
2. Add the spice powders to the grated mango and mix thoroughly.
3. Heat the oil in a pan, add mustard seeds and allow to crackle.
4. Remove and allow to cool. Pour the seasoning over the mango mixture and stir well.
5. The pickle is ready for use. It keeps for 5 days.

263 Mango – Groundnut Pachadi : Hot

125 g	seeded mango, peel & chop
60 g	shelled groundnut, roast & husk
2	dried red chillies, break into bits;
3 g	mustard seeds;
3 g	fenugreek seeds &
2 g	asafoetida, roast in oil : all for seasoning
10 g	salt
20 ml	oil

1. Grind together the husked groundnut and the chopped mango with the salt coarsely.
2. Heat the oil, add mustard seeds and allow to crackle.
3. Add in the fenugreek seeds, broken chillies, asafoetida powder and fry till done.
4. Pour the seasoning over the groundnut-mango mixture and grind again coarsely.
5. The pickle is ready for use. It keeps only for 2 days but longer if refrigerated.

> **Mango** contains soluble fibre which is noted for its cholesterol - lowering capacity.

264 Spiced Ripe Mango : Sweet

125 g	cubed ripe mango
3 g	chilli powder
2 g	garam masala powder
2 g	asafoetida, roast in oil & powder
2 g	fenugreek seeds : for seasoning
5 g	sugar
10 g	salt
15 ml	oil

1. Heat the oil, add fenugreek seeds and allow to crackle.
2. Add in the asafoetida powder and the cubed mango.
3. Lower the heat, cover and cook until the mango pieces soften.
4. Uncover, add in the chilli, garam masala powders, sugar, salt and continue cooking for a few minutes.
5. Blend well and remove.
6. The pickle is ready for use. It keeps for 1 week and is best refrigerated.

265 Spiced Ripe Mango in Vinegar : Hot

500 g	seeded ripe mango, peel & slice thin lengthwise	3 g	fenugreek seeds &	
1-1"	piece of fresh ginger, scrape & chop	2 g	cummin seeds, dry-roast all & powder	
2	cloves garlic, peel & chop fine	50 ml	vinegar	
2	green chillies, keep whole	40 g	salt	
5 g	chilli powder	40 ml	oil : heat & cool	
5 g	mustard seeds;			
3 g	coriander seeds;			

1. Combine the mango slices, whole green chillies with the vinegar and salt. Set aside.
2. Stir-fry the chopped ginger, garlic in a little oil for a few minutes and remove.
3. Blend in the powdered spices and allow to cool.
4. Add the spice mixture and the remaining oil to the mango mixture.
5. Mix thoroughly and cap tight.
6. The pickle is ready for use. It lasts for 2 months.

266 Half-Ripe Mango – Onion : Hot

125 g	seeded half-ripe mango, peel & cube
10 g	onion, peel & chop fine
5 g	green chillies, chop fine
2 g	mustard seeds : for seasoning
5 g	sugar
5 g	salt
20 ml	oil

1. Heat the oil, add mustard seeds and allow to crackle.
2. Add in the chopped onion and fry till crisp.
3. Stir in the other ingredients, fry for a few seconds and remove.
4. The pickle is ready for use. It keeps for 5 days and is best refrigerated.

267 Half-Ripe Mango – Coconut : Hot

125 g	cut half-ripe mango, size into small pieces
50 g	grated coconut, dry-roast;
6	green chillies, chop;
1/2"	piece of fresh ginger, scrape &
6 g	salt, grind all to a paste
2 ml	raw mustard oil

1. Combine the mango pieces with the green spice paste.
2. Blend in the mustard oil.
3. The pickle is ready for use. It keeps for 5 days in the refrigerator.

268 Mild Mango : Salty

125 g	seeded mango, peel & chop fine
10 g	green chillies, chop fine
2 g	mustard seeds &
2 g	asafoetida, roast in oil & powder: both for seasoning
10 g	salt
20 ml	oil

1. Combine the chopped mango and green chillies with the salt evenly.
2. Heat the oil, add mustard seeds and allow to crackle.
3. Add in the asafoetida powder and fry for a second.
4. Pour the seasoning over the mango mixture and blend well.
5. The pickle is now ready for use. It keeps for 15 days and is best refrigerated.

269 Spiced Sliced Mango : Sweet

500 g	sliced mango, size lengthwise
350 g	sugar
75 ml	water
10 g	chilli powder
3 g	dried ginger powder
2 g	cummin seeds;
2 g	onion seeds &
2 g	peppercorns, dry-roast all three & powder coarsely
70 ml	vinegar
20 g	salt

1. Marinate the mango slices in the salt and sun for 3 hours. Discard the salt water given out by the mangoes.
2. Dissolve the sugar and water over low heat. Add the mango slices, spice powders and continue heating.

3. When almost dry add in the vinegar and stir continuously, ensuring the slices remain intact.
4. Remove when soft but dry.
5. The pickle is ready for use after 4 days. It lasts for 4 months if refrigerated.

270 Mango Ginger – Lime : Hot

125 g	peeled mango ginger, chop
125 g	lime, chop fine & seed
25 g	tender green chillies, chop fine
10 g	mustard seeds
5 g	turmeric powder
3 g	asafoetida, roast in oil & powder
40 g	salt
75 ml	oil

1. Combine the chopped mango-ginger and green chilli with the chopped lime.
2. Add in the salt, turmeric powder and toss well.
3. Heat the oil, add mustard seeds and allow to crackle. Stir in the asafoetida powder.
4. Pour the seasoning over the mango-ginger mixture and blend well.
5. The pickle is ready for use after 1 hour. It keeps for 1 week and longer in the refrigerator.

271 Mango Ginger in Lime Juice : Hot

500 g	mango ginger, scrape & chop
25 g	chilli powder
10 g	mustard seeds
5 g	asafoetida, roast in oil & powder
125 ml	lime juice
75 g	salt
75 ml	oil

1. Heat a little oil, add mustard seeds and allow to crackle.
2. Stir in the chopped mango ginger and stir-fry till partly tender.
3. Add in the chilli, asafoetida powders, lime juice, salt and the remaining oil.
4. Continue cooking over low heat until the mango-ginger becomes tender.
5. The pickle is ready for use. It lasts for 1 month.

272 Mint – Onion - Mango : Tender

125 g	mint leaves, wash, air-dry & chop fine
50 g	onion, peel & chop
30 g	seeded raw mango, peel & chop
30 g	green chillies, chop
10 g	chilli powder
5 g	mustard seeds : for seasoning
25 g	salt
25 ml	oil

1. Grind together all the ingredients to a smooth paste except the seasoning.
2. Heat the oil, add mustard seeds and allow to crackle.
3. Pour the seasoning over the mint-onion mixture and blend well.
4. The pickle is ready for use. It keeps only for 2 days but longer in the refrigerator.

273 Raisin – Almond - Pistachio : Sweet

250 g	seedless raisin, chop
60 g	almond &
60 g	pistachio, blanch both & sliver
100 g	sugar
20	strands of saffron, soak in warm water
10 g	peppercorns
5 g	chilli powder
175 ml	lime juice
50 g	salt

1. Grind the chopped raisin with the peppercorns, chilli powder, sugar, saffron and salt to a fine paste.
2. Stir in the dried fruits, lime juice and blend well.
3. The pickle is ready for use. It keeps for 1 week in the refrigerator.

274 Button Mushroom : Watery

125 g	button mushroom, chop fine
15 g	green chillies, chop
15 g	green coriander, clean, air-dry & chop
5 g	mint, clean, air-dry & chop
2 g	cummin seeds, dry-roast & pound
2 g	chat masala powder
50 ml	vinegar
12 g	salt
50 ml	oil

1. Cook the mushroom in sufficient water till tender yet chrunchy. Remove and discard the water.
2. Heat the oil, stir in the chopped green chilli, coriander, mint and the spice powders.
3. Add in the cooked mushroom, vinegar, salt and allow to thicken.
4. The pickle is ready for use. It keeps for 2 weeks and is best refrigerated.

275 Spiced Mixed Vegetable – Ginger : Hot

100 g	cauliflower florets
100 g	carrot;
100 g	turnip;
75 g	beetroot;
75 g	potato &
25 g	onion, peel all & chop
50 g	shelled peas
50 g	fresh ginger, scrape & slice
25 g	dried red chillies, break into bits
15 g	date, stone & chop
10 g	tender green chillies, chop
5 g	garlic, peel
20 g	cleaned tamarind, obtain thick extract using water
25 g	jaggery, grate
10 g	mustard seeds &
5 g	peppercorns, sun-dry both & powder
5 g	turmeric powder
1-1"	stick of cinnamon, keep whole
100 ml	vinegar
60 g	salt
250 ml	oil

1. Stir-fry the onion in a little oil till golden brown and set aside.
2. In the same pan heat some more oil, fry the ginger, garlic, green and red chillies for a few minutes.
3. Add in the prepared vegetables, date, fried onion and cook till partly tender.
4. Stir in the tamarind extract, jaggery, salt and cook till the mixture thickens.
5. Blend in the spice powders, vinegar and remove.
6. Pour the oil over the vegetable mixture to cover and sun for a week.
7. The pickle lasts for 3 months.

276 Mixed Vegetable in Lime Juice : Watery

150 g	potato, peel & chop
150 g	beetroot, peel & chop
150 g	carrot, peel & chop
20 g	chilli powder
5 g	asafoetida, roast in oil & powder
5 g	turmeric powder
175 ml	lime juice
60 g	salt
75 ml	oil

1. Combine the turmeric powder with the lime juice and oil. Set aside for half an hour.
2. Blend in the salt and chilli powder.
3. Follow with the cut vegetables and mix thoroughly.
4. Shake well, cover and set aside.
5. The pickle is ready for use. It lasts for 1 month if refrigerated.

277 Sour Mixed Vegetable – Garlic : Watery

1 kg	mixed vegetables, choice — snakegourd, brinjal, kovakkai, stem greens, cowpeas, pumpkin or papaya
100 g	peeled garlic, chop
2-1"	pieces of fresh ginger, scrape & chop
100 g	fresh red chillies, chop
400 ml	water : boil & cool
50 ml	vinegar
5 g	turmeric powder
10 g	mustard seeds
100 ml	lime juice
150 g	salt
25 ml	oil

1. Pressure cook all the prepared vegetables till half tender.
2. Steam the garlic and chillies till half tender.
3. Combine the water, vinegar, salt, turmeric powder and bring to the boil. Allow to thicken and remove.
4. Stir in the cooked vegetables.
5. Heat the oil, add mustard seeds and allow to crackle. Add in the ginger and fry for a few minutes.
6. Cool and pour the seasoning over the vegetable mixture. Stir well.
7. Add in the lime juice and mix thoroughly.
8. The pickle is ready for use. It lasts for 1 month.

Mixed Vegetable Pickling

While pickling mixed vegetables do not blanch or cook too long to retain their crunchiness.

To freshen up stale vegetables before pickling, soak them for 2 hours in water, to which the juice of a lime has been added.

The danger with mixed vegetables pickles is that, the extra moisture in them tends to increase bacterial activity. To bring out the excess water out, soak the vegetables in salt overnight.

To boil vegetables, always use boiling water instead of cold water. Never drown out the vegetables while cooking. Use enough water to keep the pan from burning.

278 Button Mushroom – Green Spices : Tender

125 g	button mushroom, wash & air-dry
12 g	small red onion, peel & chop
1	clove bill garlic, peel & chop
1/2"	piece of fresh ginger, scrape & chop fine
8 g	chilli powder;
2 g	thymol seeds &
2 g	cummin seeds, sun-dry & powder, combine all three evenly
5 ml	lime juice
40 ml	vinegar, combine with 2ml citric acid
20 g	salt
75 ml	oil

1. Stir-fry the mushroom, ginger, garlic and onion in a little oil.
2. Add in the powdered spices, transfer to a jar and mix thoroughly.
3. Pour over the lime juice, the vinegar mixture, salt and the remaining oil to cover. Sun for 7 days.
4. The pickle is ready for use. It keeps for 2 weeks.

279 Sour Spiced Button Mushroom : Watery

125 g	button mushroom, wash & air-dry
8 g	dried red chillies;
3 g	mustard seeds;
3 g	coriander seeds;
2 g	fenugreek seeds &
2 g	cummin seeds, sun-dry all & powder together
40 ml	vinegar
5 ml	lime juice
12 g	salt
50 ml	oil

> To check whether mushrooms are poisonous or not, boil them in water, with a few flakes of garlic. If the mushrooms are poisonous, the water will turn black. If it doesn't, they are then safe for consumption.

1. Cook the mushroom in sufficient water till tender yet chrunchy. Remove and discard the water.
2. Heat the oil, stir in the spice mixture, salt, cooked mushroom and the vinegar.
3. Cook over low heat and allow to thicken.
4. Blend in the lime juice and remove when the mixture begins to bubble.
4. The pickle is ready for use. It keeps for 2 weeks and is best refrigerated.

280 Mixed Vegetable in Tamarind Sauce : Hot

125 g	brinjal, cube
125 g	radish, peel & cube
125 g	sweet potato, peel & cube
125 g	red pumpkin, peel & cube
50 g	cleaned tamarind, obtain thick extract using water
50 g	jaggery, grate
30 g	dried red chillies, break into bits
5 g	turmeric powder
3 g	panch phoran powder
40 g	salt
100 ml	oil

1. Heat the oil, fry the panch phoran powder and the broken red chillies for a minute.
2. Add in the vegetables, stir-fry for a few minutes and set aside.
3. In the same pan add the tamarind extract, jaggery, turmeric powder, salt and bring to the boil. Allow to thicken over a high flame.
4. Stir in the fried vegetables and continue cooking over low heat.
5. Remove when the mixture turns jam-like and the oil separates.
6. The pickle is ready for use. It lasts for 2 months.

281 Sour Spring Onion – Honey - Green Chillies : Sweet

500 g	spring onion bulbs, chop
60 g	green coriander, wash, air-dry & chop
30 g	green chillies, chop fine
2-1"	pieces of fresh ginger, scrape & chop
2	cloves garlic, peel & chop
1	star anise, keep whole
5 g	asafoetida, roast in oil & powder
300 ml	vinegar
100 ml	honey
5 ml	soya sauce
80 g	salt
a pinch of ajinomoto	

1. Combine the vinegar, honey, soya sauce and ajinomoto till well blended.
2. Add in the chopped vegetables, star anise, asafoetida powder, salt and stir thoroughly.
3. The pickle is ready for use. It lasts for 1 month and is best refrigerated.

282 Pear – Tomato - Onion : Sweet

500 g	cored pear, peel & chop
250 g	jaggery, grate
150 g	onion, peel & chop
150 g	tomato, slice
120 g	chopped celery
75 g	seedless raisin, chop
5 g	chilli powder
5 g	dried ginger powder
300 ml	vinegar
5 g	salt

1. Combine all the ingredients in a pan and bring to the boil.
2. Lower the heat, cook till the fruits and vegetables soften.
3. Add in the jaggery, salt and continue cooking until the mixture thickens.
4. The pickle is ready for use. It lasts for 3 months.

283 Perky Pineapple : Sweet

125 g	half-ripe pineapple chunks
70 g	jaggery, grate
2	dried red chillies, break into bits
2	green chillies, chop;
2	peppercorns;
2 g	fenugreek seeds &
2 g	cummin seeds, grind all to a paste
2 g	mustard seeds : for seasoning
8 g	salt
50 ml	oil

1. Cook the pineapple chunks in sufficient water till almost tender.
2. Heat the oil, add mustard seeds and allow to crackle.
3. Add in the dried red chillies and fry for a minute.
4. Stir in the jaggery, salt and the spice paste.
5. Continue cooking over low heat until the mixture thickens and remove.
6. The pickle is ready for use. It keeps for 15 days and is best refrigerated.

284 Pirandai – Gram : Hot

500 g	tender pirandai, string & chop
30 g	dried red chillies &
50 g	split husked black gram, dry-roast each separately
60 g	cleaned tamarind
10 g	mustard seeds : for seasoning
10 g	turmeric powder
60 g	salt
150 ml	oil

1. Stir-fry the chopped pirandai in a little oil till the moisture evaporates.
2. Grind together the chopped pirandai, roasted chilli, roasted black gram, turmeric powder and tamarind with the salt.
3. Heat the remaining oil, add mustard seeds and allow to crackle.
4. Blend in the pickle mixture and stir-fry until it leaves the sides of the pan.
5. The pickle is ready for use. It lasts for 1 month.

Note : The tender leaves & shoots of **pirandai** are a real delicacy and used in pickling. Pirandai is rich in calcium, carotene and vitamin C. It is useful for treating asthma, scurvy and digestive troubles.

285 Sour Spiced Raw Plantain : Sweet

125 g	peeled raw plantain, chop fine
30 g	sugar
5 g	seedless raisin, chop
8 g	dried red chillies, break into bits;
2 g	cummin seeds &
2	cloves garlic, peel & chop, grind all fine using vinegar
25 ml	vinegar
3 ml	lime juice
5 g	salt

1. Combine the spice paste, sugar, vinegar and bring to the boil, stirring all the time.
2. Add in the raisin, lime juice and remove when the mixture begins to bubble.
3. The pickle is ready for use. It keeps for 15 days in the refrigerator.

Note : While slicing **raw plantain**, dip the knife in lime juice between each cut, to prevent them from turning brown.

286 Sweet & Sour Poppy Seeds in Curd : Watery

125 g	poppy seeds, soak in water & grind to a paste
100 ml	yogurt, whip & remove cream
15 g	cleaned tamarind, obtain thick extract using water
15 g	dried red chillies, break into bits
5 g	turmeric powder
5 g	mustard seeds : for seasoning
15 g	sugar
15 g	salt
20 ml	oil

1. Combine the poppy seed paste, tamarind extract, sugar and the salt. Set aside.
2. Heat the oil, add mustard seeds and allow to crackle.
3. Add in the dried red chillies and fry for a minute.
4. Stir in the poppy seed mixture, turmeric powder and cook for a few minutes. Allow to thicken.
5. Pour in the yogurt, blend well and remove.
6. The pickle is ready for use. It keeps for 5 days in the refrigerator.

Poppy seeds
Known to the Egyptians more than 35 centuries ago, poppy seed is usually a 'health food buy'. Medicinally morphine and codeine that are the vital constituents of the unripe poppy seeds are used to relieve pain and induce sleep. It is the ripe seeds of the poppy that are used for pickling.

287 Poppy Seed – Garlic – Green Chilli : Hot

125 g	poppy seeds
15 g	green chillies &
3	cloves garlic, peel, chop both & grind to a paste
20 ml	lime juice
15 g	salt
20 ml	raw mustard oil

1. Wash and soak the poppy seeds in sufficient water for 3 hours.
2. Drain and grind to a paste.
3. Stir in the chilli-garlic paste. Blend in the lime juice, salt and the oil.
4. The pickle is ready for use. It keeps for 1 week in the refrigerator.

288 Radish – Lentils : Hot

500 g	white radish, scrape, top, tail & chop fine
40 g	dried red chillies, break into bits;
30 g	split husked blackgram;
5 g	split husked bengal gram &
5 g	asafoetida, roast all in oil & powder
75 g	cleaned tamarind, obtain thick extract using water
10 g	jaggery, grate
25 g	salt
50 ml	oil

1. Stir-fry the radish pieces in a little oil and set aside.
2. Heat the remaining oil, add the tamarind extract, jaggery and the salt.
3. Bring to the boil and allow to thicken over a high flame.
4. Add in the powdered spices, fried radish and continue cooking over low heat.
5. Remove when the mixture becomes jam-like and the oil separates.
6. The pickle is ready for use. It lasts for 2 months.

Note : Lentils don't need soaking if they are cooked in simmering water for about 20 minutes.

289 Black Raisin in Lime Juice : Sweet

125 g	black raisin, clean & seed
125 g	sugar
25 g	seedless raisin, clean & chop
5 g	mint leaves, wash, air-dry & chop
5 g	chilli powder
3 g	cummin seeds
75 ml	lime juice
15 g	salt

1. Soak the black raisin in sufficient lukewarm water for half an hour.
2. Grind the soaked black raisin with all the ingredients except the chopped seedless raisin and lime juice.
3. Add in the lime juice, the chopped seedless raisin and set aside for half an hour.
4. The pickle is ready for use. It keeps only for 3 days but longer if refrigerated.

290 Raisin – Green Spices : Tender

125 g	seedless raisin, chop
15 g	green coriander &
a few	mint leaves, wash, air-dry & chop both
3	green chillies, chop
10 ml	lime juice
5 g	salt

1. Grind all the ingredients to a fine paste.
2. Stir in the lime juice and blend well.
3. The pickle is ready for use. It keeps for 5 days and is best refrigerated.

Note : When sticky fruits like raisins have to be ground, add in little lime juice for easier grinding and better flavour.

291 Spiced Red Gram – Tamarind : Hot

125 g	split husked red gram, roast in oil till golden
20 g	cleaned tamarind
20 g	jaggery, grate
20 g	dried red chillies &
2	green chillies, roast both in oil
5 g	cummin seeds
5	cloves garlic, peel & chop
5 g	mustard seeds &
5 g	asafoetida, roast in oil & powder : both for seasoning
20 g	salt
20 ml	oil

1. Grind all the ingredients (except the cummin & garlic) coarsely.
2. Add in the garlic, cummin seeds and grind well using a little water.
3. Heat the oil, add mustard seeds, allow to crackle and remove. Blend in the asafoetida powder.
4. Pour the seasoning over the gram mixture and stir thoroughly.
5. The pickle is ready for use. It keeps for 5 days and longer in the refrigerator.

292 Rhubarb – Date - Onion : Watery

500 g	rhubarb, chop
300 g	sugar
125 g	onion, peel & chop
75 g	date, stone & chop
5 g	garam masala powder
5 g	dried ginger powder
5 g	chilli powder
200 ml	vinegar
15 g	salt

Rhubarb

Though regarded and used as a fruit, rhubarb is really a vegetable. It's leaves contain a toxic element, making them unsafe to eat. But it has long been used medicinally for its purgative qualities.

1. Cook the rhubarb, onion and date in half the vinegar till tender.
2. Stir in the remaining vinegar, spice powders, sugar and salt.
3. Continue cooking over low heat till the mixture becomes jam-like.
4. The pickle is ready for use. It lasts for 2 months.

293 Spicy Ridge Gourd – Lentils : Hot

125 g	peeled tender ridge gourd, chop
15 g	green chillies, chop fine
10 g	cleaned tamarind
3 g	jaggery, grate
3 g	split husked bengal gram &
3 g	split husked black gram, fry both in oil till golden
3	cloves garlic, peel & chop
3 g	cummin seeds, dry-roast
3 g	mustard seeds: for seasoning
10 g	salt
10 ml	oil

1. Stir-fry the green chillies in a little oil for a few minutes and set aside.
2. In the same pan heat some more oil, fry the chopped ridge gourd for a few minutes and set aside.
3. Grind together the green chillies, tamarind, jaggery, salt and the fried gram coarsely.
4. Add in the fried ridge gourd, grind again coarsely and remove.
5. Separately grind the garlic, cummin seeds and blend into the coarsely ground mixture.
6. Heat the remaining oil, add mustard seeds and allow to crackle.
7. Pour the seasoning over the pickle mixture and stir thoroughly.
8. The pickle is ready for use. It keeps only for 2 days but longer if refrigerated.

294 Spiced Ridge Gourd – Gram : Hot

125 g	*peeled tender ridge gourd, chop;*
25 g	*split husked red gram;*
15 g	*split husked bengal gram &*
10 g	*dried red chillies, roast each separately in oil*
10 g	*cleaned tamarind*
5 g	*mustard seeds;*
3 g	*asafoetida, roast in oil & powder;*
a few	*sprigs curry leaves &*
50 ml	*oil : all for seasoning*
15 g	*salt*

1. Grind together coarsely all the ingredients except the seasoning using a little water.
2. Heat the oil, add mustard seeds and allow to crackle. Add in the curry leaves and fry till crisp.
3. Pour the seasoning and asafoetida powder over the ground mixture. Blend well.
4. The pickle is ready for use. It keeps only for 2 days and longer if refrigerated.

295 Carrot in Spicy Mahani Liquid : Watery

125 ml	*spicy mahani liquid*
60 g	*carrot, peel & chop*
2 g	*chilli powder*
6 g	*salt*

1. Pack the carrot, chilli powder and salt in a jar.
2. Pour over the mahani liquid and blend well.
3. The pickle is ready for use. It keeps for 10 days and longer in the refrigerator.

> **Mahani Juice** is referred to as **'Oota'** in pickling parlance. It is a blend of mustard powder, chilli powder, turmeric powder and salt in buttermilk in which the mahani pieces are soaked. Not prepared specially for the pickle. On the contrary, the mahani pickle is prepared with more than the required quantity of juice, for use in pickling other vegetables. However, a little extra salt and chilli powder have to be added due to the addition of the vegetables.

Variation : A variety of vegetables may be similarly pickled. These include carrot, cabbage, capsicum, cauliflower, thammatangai, chathuranchikdikai, mukkura kandakaya, tender bel, tender small kalakkai, star gooseberry, tender drumstick (thread like), tender ahathikai (thread like), tender bitter berries, tender green chilli, cluster beans, dhadi avarakkai (winged beans), gor chikdikai, kudhina kommulu and thethankottai .

296 Sesame – Gram - Green Chilli : Hot

500 g	*sesame seeds, dry-roast & powder*
80 g	*cleaned tamarind, obtain thick extract using water*
60 g	*jaggery, grate*
40 g	*dried red chillies, roast in oil & powder*
40 g	*green chillies, chop*
10 g	*turmeric powder*
10 g	*mustard seeds;*
10 g	*split husked bengal gram &*
10 g	*split husked black gram : all three for seasoning*
80 g	*salt*
300 ml	*oil*

1. Heat the oil, add mustard seeds and allow to crackle. Add in the gram and fry till golden brown.
2. Follow with the green chillies and fry for a few minutes.
3. Pour in the tamarind extract, jaggery, turmeric powder and salt.
4. Bring to the boil and allow to thicken over a high flame.
5. Stir in the chilli, sesame powders and continue cooking over low heat.
6. Remove when the mixture becomes jam-like and the oil separates.
7. The pickle is ready for use. It lasts for 1 month.

> **Note : Sesame seeds** also known as gingelly seeds are very nutritious and therfore useful in the treatment of anaemia. It also helps in the cure of piles and ulcers.

297 Sesame – Groundnut – Green Spices : Tender

125 g	sesame seeds, dry-roast
90 g	roasted groundnut, husk
60 g	onion, peel & chop
35 g	green chillies, chop
30 g	green coriander, wash, air-dry & chop
20 g	cleaned tamarind
20 g	jaggery, grate
15	cloves garlic, peel & chop
30 g	salt
75 ml	oil : heat & cool

1. Grind together all the ingredients to a smooth paste using a little water.
2. Pour the pre-heated oil over the ground mixture and blend well.
3. The pickle is ready for use. It keeps for 10 days and longer in the refrigerator.

298 Spinach – Green Spices : Tender

125 g	spinach;
125 g	mint leaves &
125 g	green coriander, wash, air-dry & chop all three
40 g	green chillies, chop
25 g	salt
20 ml	oil

1. Stir-fry the chopped spinach, mint and coriander in a little oil till tender.
2. Grind together all the ingredients to a coarse paste.
3. The pickle is ready for use. It keeps for 1 week in the refrigerator.

299 Spicy Sprouted Pulses – Onion : Tender

125 g	sprouted pulses : choice – whole bengal gram, horse gram, black gram, green gram
50 g	onion &
3	cloves garlic, peel & chop both
1-1"	piece of fresh ginger, scrape & chop
10 g	green chillies, chop
5 g	chilli powder
5 g	turmeric powder
2 g	garam masala powder
30 ml	lime juice
15 g	salt

1. Stir-fry the chillies, onion, garlic and ginger in a little oil. Cool and grind to a coarse paste.
2. Heat the oil, fry the sprouted pulses for a few minutes along with the spice paste, lime juice, chilli, turmeric, garam masala powders and the salt.
3. The pickle is ready for use. It keeps for 1 week in the refrigerator.

300 Spicy Sugarcane Juice – Dry Fruits : Sweet

500 ml	sugarcane juice, strain
150 g	peeled banana, chop
25 g	seedless raisin, halve
25 g	dried date, stone & grate
10	cashewnuts, chop
1-1"	piece of fresh ginger, scrape, chop & grind
10 g	chilli powder
10 g	cummin seeds;
5 g	fenugreek seeds;
5 g	peppercorns &
5 g	coriander seeds, dry-roast all & powder
5 g	dried mango powder
20 g	salt

1. Boil the sugarcane juice and remove the scum as it forms.
2. Add in the dried mango powder and allow to thicken.
3. Stir in the remaining ingredients and blend well.
4. The pickle is ready for use. It keeps for 2 weeks in the refrigerator.

301 Raw Sweet Potato – Mango : Hot

125 g	sweet potato, peel & grate
125 g	seeded raw mango, peel & grate
20 g	dried red chillies;
10 g	mustard seeds &
5 g	fenugreek seeds : all three for seasoning
5 g	asafoetida, roast in oil & powder
5 g	turmeric powder
20 g	salt
60 ml	oil

1. Heat a little oil, add mustard seeds and allow to crackle. Follow with the fenugreek seeds, red chillies, asafoetida powder, fry till done and remove.
2. In the same pan heat the remaining oil, separately stir-fry the grated sweet potato and mango.
3. Grind the fried ingredients with the salt and turmeric powder coarsely.
4. The pickle is ready for use. It keeps for 1 week in the refrigerator.

302 Green Tamarind – Green Chilli : Hot

500 g	tender green tamarind, size into small pieces
100 g	green chillies, chop
10 g	turmeric powder
5 g	fenugreek seeds &
5 g	asafoetida, roast both in oil & powder
100 g	salt 20ml oil

1. Grind together all the ingredients (except fenugreek & asafoetida) coarsely. This basic tamarind pickle lasts for months together.
2. As and when required, heat the oil, add 100g of the prepared tamarind along with the powdered spices. Blend well and remove.
3. The pickle lasts for 2 months.

303 Spicy Tamarind : Sweet

125 g	cleaned tamarind, obtain thick extract using water
250 g	jaggery, grate
15 g	dried ginger powder
15 g	peppercorns;
5 g	aniseeds;
5 g	cummin seeds &
5 g	coriander seeds, sun-dry all & powder
5 g	chilli powder
5 g	rock salt
25 g	salt
75 ml	oil

1. Heat the oil, add the tamarind extract, jaggery, salt and bring to the boil.
2. Allow to thicken over a high flame and stir in the spice powders.
3. Continue cooking over low heat until the mixture becomes jam-like and the oil separates.
4. The pickle is ready for use. It keeps for 15 days in the refrigerator.

304 Tamarind – Ginger – Green Chilli : Hot

500 g	cleaned tamarind, obtain thick extract using water
500 g	fresh ginger, scrape & chop fine
240 g	jaggery, grate
100 g	green chillies, chop fine
40 g	chilli powder
10 g	mustard seeds &
a few	sprigs curry leaves : both for seasoning
200 g	salt
600 ml	oil

1. Heat the oil, add mustard seeds and allow to crackle.
2. Stir-fry the chopped green chillies, ginger and the curry leaves.
3. Pour in the tamarind extract, jaggery, chilli powder and salt.
4. Bring to the boil and allow to thicken over a high flame.
5. Continue cooking over low heat until the mixture becomes jam-like and the oil separates.
6. The pickle is ready for use. It lasts for 3 months.

305 Sweet Tamarind – Ginger – Garlic : Hot

500 g	cleaned tamarind, soak in vinegar for 30 minutes & obtain thick extract
500 g	green chillies, chop
500 g	peeled garlic, chop
500 g	fresh ginger, scrape & chop
400 g	sugar
50 g	cummin seeds, sun-dry & powder
20 g	turmeric powder
1500 ml	vinegar
300 g	salt
600 ml	oil

1. Stir-fry the chopped ginger, garlic in a little oil and set aside.
2. Heat a little oil, add mustard seeds and allow to crackle.
3. Add in the chopped green chillies and fry for a few minutes.
4. Pour in the tamarind extract, sugar, turmeric, cummin powders, vinegar, salt and the remaining oil.
5. Bring to the boil and allow to thicken over a high flame.
6. Continue cooking over low heat until the mixture becomes jam-like and the oil separates.
7. The pickle is ready for use. It lasts for 6 months.

306 Tamarind – Green Chilli : Salty

500 g	cleaned tamarind
40 g	green chillies, chop
15 g	turmeric powder
100 g	salt

1. Grind together the tamarind and green chillies without adding water.
2. Add in the salt, turmeric powder and mix thoroughly.
3. This basic tamarind pickle lasts for years.
4. As and when required take 100g of the prepared tamarind mixture.
5. Heat 50ml oil, add 5g mustard seeds and allow to crackle. Blend in 2g asafoetida powder.
6. Pour the seasoning over the prepared tamarind and mix thoroughly. It lasts for 2 months.

307 Spicy Tamarind – Green Chilli : Hot

1 kg	cleaned tamarind
50 g	dried red chillies, break into bits
50 g	green chillies, chop
10 g	turmeric powder
10 g	asafoetida, roast in oil & powder
10 g	mustard seeds &
10 g	fenugreek seeds : both for seasoning
250 g	salt
20 ml	oil

1. Grind the tamarind with the salt and turmeric powder coarsely. Store in a covered jar.
2. Heat the oil, add mustard seeds and allow to crackle.
3. Add in the fenugreek seeds, asafoetida powder, chopped green chillies, broken red chillies and fry for a few minutes. Cool and grind coarsely.
4. Blend the tamarind mixture in the spice mixture.
5. The pickle is ready for use. It lasts for 1 year.

308 Ugadi Tamarind – Neem - Mango : Sweet

125 g	cleaned tamarind, obtain thin extract using water
125 g	jaggery, grate
75 g	seeded raw mango, peel & chop fine
10 g	neem flower
5	green chillies, chop fine
3	dried red chillies, break into bits
3 g	split husked bengal gram
3 g	split husked black gram
15 g	salt
10 ml	oil

1. Combine all the ingredients evenly and serve.
2. This raw pickle keeps for 1 week and longer in the refrigerator.

309 Peppered Tamarind – Cucumber Seeds : Sweet

125 g	cleaned tamarind, obtain thick extract using water
125 g	jaggery, grate
50 g	cucumber seeds, peel & pound coarsely
20 g	peppercorns &
10 g	dried red chillies, sun-dry both & powder
5 g	turmeric powder
5 g	mustard seeds : for seasoning
40 g	salt
35 ml	oil

1. Combine all the ingredients, except seasoning, evenly.
2. Heat the oil, add mustard seeds and allow to crackle.
3. Pour the seasoning over the mixture and stir thoroughly.
4. The pickle is ready for use. It keeps for 1 week and longer in the refrigerator.

> To preserve **tamarind**, add salt to it, mix well and store in an air-tight container.

310 Spicy Tamarind – Cummin - Jaggery : Sweet

125 g	cleaned tamarind, obtain thick extract using water
300 g	jaggery, grate
60 g	dried red chillies, break into bits
5	cloves garlic, peel
5 g	cummin seeds, dry-roast
60 g	salt

1. Grind the dried red chillies, cummin seeds, garlic and jaggery with the salt to a fine paste.
2. Pour in the tamarind extract and blend well.
3. The pickle is ready for use. It keeps for 1 week and longer in the refrigerator.

––––––– Variation –––––––
Grind all the ingredients together with the tamarind (without soaking in water) to a fine paste and refrigerate.

311 Tamarind – Mint – Dried Ginger : Sweet

500 g	cleaned tamarind, obtain thick extract using water
250 g	jaggery, grate
25 g	mint leaves, wash, air-dry, chop & grind fine
25 g	chilli powder
25 g	dried ginger powder
150 g	salt

1. Combine the tamarind extract, jaggery, dried ginger powder and chilli powder with the salt.
2. Bring to the boil and allow to thicken over a high flame.
3. Stir in the mint paste and continue cooking over low heat until the mixture becomes jam-like.
4. The pickle is ready for use. It lasts for 1 month.

Variation
Grind all the ingredients together with the tamarind (without soaking in water) to a fine paste and refrigerate.

312 Salted Tamarind : Hot

500 g	cleaned tamarind
5 g	turmeric powder
125 g	salt
5 g	dried red chillies, break into bits;
5 g	green chillies, chop;
3 g	mustard seeds;
3 g	asafoetida, roast in oil & powder;
3 g	fenugreek seeds &
50 ml	oil : all for seasoning

1. Grind together the tamarind, turmeric powder and salt coarsely. Set aside.
2. This basic pickle remains fresh for a whole year.
3. As and when required take 100g of the prepared tamarind and set aside.
4. Heat the oil, add the mustard seeds, fenugreek seeds and allow to crackle.
5. Add in the green chillies, red chillies, asafoetida powder and fry for a few minutes.
6. Blend the seasoning into the tamarind mixture.
7. The pickle is ready for use. It lasts for 2 months.

313 Tamarind – Ginger – Garlic – Date : Hot

125 g	cleaned tamarind, obtain thick extract using vinegar	125 g	green chillies, chop
		15 g	cummin seeds
		10 g	turmeric powder
125 g	peeled garlic, chop	90 g	sugar
125 g	fresh ginger, scrape & chop	150 ml	vinegar
		10 g	salt
125 g	date, stone & chop	30 ml	oil

1. Grind together all the ingredients (except tamarind) using vinegar.
2. Stir-fry the spice paste in the oil till done.
3. Pour in the tamarind extract and bring to the boil. Allow to thicken over a high flame.
4. The pickle is ready for use. It keeps for 1 week and is best refrigerated.

314 Spicy Tamarind – Raisin : Sweet

125 g	cleaned tamarind, obtain thick extract using water	1-1"	piece of fresh ginger, scrape & chop
5	dried dates, soak in water, cut lengthwise & stone	3 g	cummin seeds & peppercorns, sun-dry both & powder
		3 g	
25 g	seedless raisin, chop	3 g	chilli powder
		1 g	garam masala powder
12 g	jaggery, grate	2 g	rock salt
12 g	sugar	25 g	salt

1. Combine all the ingredients and bring to the boil.
2. Allow to thicken and remove.
3. The pickle is ready for use. It keeps for 15 days and is best refrigerated.

315 Sunned Spiced Tamarind : Sweet

500 g	cleaned tamarind
250 g	jaggery, grate, make a syrup of one-string consistency with 200 ml water
30 g	chilli powder
10 g	fenugreek seeds;
10 g	cummin seeds &
10 g	aniseeds, dry-roast all three & powder
50 g	salt

1. Combine the powdered spices with the chilli powder and salt evenly.
2. Blend the spice mixture with the tamarind pieces thoroughly.
3. Pour the jaggery syrup into the spiced tamarind mixture and heat till well blended.
4. Sun the pickle for 2 days.
5. The pickle lasts for 2 months.

316 Sesame Green Tomato : Hot

125 g	green tomato, chop fine
20 g	green chillies, chop
10 g	jaggery, grate
10 g	sesame seeds &
3 g	asafoetida, roast both in oil & powder
3 g	turmeric powder
3 g	mustard seeds &
3 g	cummin seeds : both for seasoning
10 g	salt
5 ml	oil

1. Heat the oil, add mustard seeds and allow to crackle.
2. Add in the cummin seeds, green chillies and stir-fry for a minute.
3. Stir in the chopped tomato, turmeric powder, salt and cook for a few minutes.
4. Add in the sesame, asafoetida powders, jaggery and remove when well blended.
5. The pickle is ready for use. It keeps for 5 days in the refrigerator.

317 Sour Tomato – Green Coriander : Tender

125 g	sour tomato, chop
10 g	green chillies, chop
12 g	green coriander, wash, air-dry & chop
1-1"	piece of fresh ginger, scrape & chop
2	cloves garlic, peel & chop
2 g	aniseeds, roast in a little oil
10 g	salt
25 ml	oil

1. Stir-fry the chopped tomato in a little oil and set aside.
2. In the same pan heat the remaining oil, add the chopped coriander, green chillies, ginger, garlic and fry for a few minutes.
3. Add in the fried tomato and stir-fry for a few minutes till the oil separates.
4. Blend in the salt and roasted aniseeds.
5. The pickle is ready for use. It keeps for 15 days and is best refrigerated.

318 Tomato – Green Spices : Tender

125 g	ripe tomato, chop;
50 g	onion, peel & chop;
25 g	green chillies, chop &
10 g	salt, grind all to a paste
5 g	green coriander, wash, air-dry & chop
1-1"	piece of fresh ginger, scrape & chop fine
3 g	asafoetida, roast in oil & powder
5	peppercorns, dry-roast & powder
1 g	garam masala powder
75 ml	oil

1. Stir-fry the chopped coriander, ginger for a few minutes in a little oil and set aside.
2. Heat the remaining oil, add the ground tomato mixture and allow to thicken over a high flame.
3. Stir in the fried ingredients, pepper, asafoetida, garam masala powders and salt.
4. Continue cooking over low heat until the mixture becomes jam-like and the oil separates.
5. The pickle is ready for use. It keeps for 2 weeks and is best refrigerated.

319 Spiced Ripe Tomato : Sweet

125 g	ripe tomato, chop
5 g	green chillies, chop & grind
2 g	onion seeds;
2 g	fenugreek seeds &
2 g	peppercorns, dry-roast all three & powder
2 g	chilli powder
1-1"	stick of cinnamon;
1	clove &
1	cardamom, keep all three whole
12 g	sugar
15 ml	vinegar
10 g	salt
15 ml	oil

1. Fry the cinnamon, clove and cardamom in a little oil for a few minutes.
2. Add in the green chilli paste, onion seeds, chilli, fenugreek, pepper powders and fry for a few more minutes.
3. Stir in the tomato, sugar, salt, the remaining oil and continue cooking for a while.
4. Blend in the vinegar, heat well and remove.
5. The pickle is ready for use. It keeps for 2 weeks and is best refrigerated.

320　Tomato – Onion - Green Chilli : Hot

125 g	ripe tomato, peel & chop;	3 g	turmeric powder
50 g	onion, peel & chop &	15 g	salt
30 g	green chillies, chop, grind all three to a paste	60 ml	oil
10 g	tamarind, obtain thick extract using water		
3 g	mustard seeds, sun-dry & powder		

1. Stir-fry the tomato-onion-chilli paste in a little oil.
2. Add in the tamarind extract, turmeric powder and the salt.
3. Bring to the boil and allow to thicken over a high flame.
4. Stir in the mustard powder, the remaining oil and continue cooking over low heat.
5. Remove when the mixture becomes jam-like and the oil separates.
6. The pickle is ready for use. It keeps for 2 weeks and is best refrigerated.

More about tomatoes

Enthusiastic cultivation has furnished a wide range of tomatoes, including low-acid yellow types. Red tomatoes are the most common ones: some varieties are smooth and round, while other Mediteranean-type tomatoes are flattened and ridged. Plum tomatoes, despite their name, are pear-shaped; with relatively small seed clusters.

Tomatoes should be firm-fleshed, with unwrinkled skins. The best fruits are those that have ripened in the sun on the plant; tomatoes ripened artificially have much less flavour. A sign of a naturally ripened tomato is a faint flush of green at the stem end. Tomatoes keep fresh longer, look more cheerful and are easier to eat if the stalks are left on.

Tomatoes are a rich source of vitamin A, C and K, a tonic for the nervous system, a blood purifier and also serves as a skin-toner. Besides it removes constipation and strengthens the teeth. This cholesterol-free fruit is easily digestible. It is a versatile fruit and its proper use enhances health and vigour. A spot of sugar reduces the bitterness of tomatoes' seeds.

321　Ripe Tomato – Ginger - Garlic : Sweet

500 g	ripe tomato, chop	50 ml	vinegar
5 g	seeded dried red chillies	15 g	salt
2-1"	pieces of fresh ginger, scrape & chop		
10	cloves garlic, peel & chop		
5 g	seedless raisin, chop		
2	cloves &		
1-1"	stick of cinnamon, keep both whole		
35 g	sugar		

1. Boil the chopped tomato, salt, cinnamon and cloves in 25ml vinegar till soft.
2. Rub the cooked tomato through a wire-sieve and set aside the tomato extract.
3. Heat the sugar and the remaining vinegar until the sugar dissolves.
4. Stir in the ground spices, the tomato extract and continue cooking over a high flame until the mixture thickens.
5. The pickle is ready for use. It keeps for 1 week and is best refrigerated.

322　Tomato – Raisin : Sweet

125 g	ripe tomato, blanch, peel, chop & puree	3 g	salt
60 g	sugar	40 ml	oil
15 g	seedless raisin, chop		
3 g	dried ginger powder		
3 g	garam masala powder		
2 g	chilli powder		
8 ml	lime juice		

1. Heat a little oil to smoking point. Reduce the heat, fry the garam masala powder for a few seconds and set aside.
2. In the same pan heat more oil, add the remaining ingredients except the lime juice.
3. Allow the mixture to thicken over a high flame.
4. Blend in the lime juice and remove when the mixture begins to bubble.
5. The pickle is ready for use. It keeps for 5 days and longer in the refrigerator.

323 Ground Tomato – Aniseed : Hot

500 g	sour tomato, chop
50 g	chilli powder
40 g	cleaned tamarind
15 g	aniseeds &
10 g	asafoetida, roast both in oil & powder
10 g	mustard seeds : for seasoning
5 g	turmeric powder
50 ml	vinegar
50 g	salt
200 ml	groundnut oil

1. Heat a little oil, add mustard seeds and allow to crackle.
2. Add in the tomato pieces, stir-fry for a few minutes and set aside.
3. In the same pan heat some more oil, pour in the tamarind extract and bring to the boil.
4. Allow to thicken over a high flame.
5. Stir in the powdered spices, chilli, turmeric powders, salt and the remaining oil.
6. Lower the heat, add in the tomato mixture and vinegar.
7. Continue cooking for a few minutes until the mixture becomes jam-like and the oil separates.
8. The pickle is ready for use. It lasts for 3 months.

324 Sour Tomato – Onion : Watery

500 g	sour tomato, keep whole water sufficient to immerse
100 g	onion, peel & chop
40 g	green chillies, chop
5 g	cummin seeds, dry-roast & powder
1-1"	piece of fresh ginger, scrape & chop
20 ml	vinegar
40 g	salt
75 ml	oil

1. Bring the water to boiling. Blanch the tomato in the boiling water for 3 minutes. Peel and chop.
2. Stir-fry the chopped onion and green chillies in a little oil.
3. Add in the cummin powder, ginger, salt and fry for a few more minutes.
4. Follow with the tomato, vinegar and continue cooking until the mixture thickens.
5. The pickle is ready for use. It lasts for 1 month and is best refrigerated.

325 Green Tomato – Jaggery : Sweet

500 g	green tomato, chop
50 g	jaggery, grate
5	cloves garlic, peel &
10 g	fresh ginger, scrape, chop both & grind to a paste
10 g	chilli powder
50 ml	vinegar
40 g	salt
375 ml	oil

1. Cook the chopped tomato in a pan till partly tender.
2. In the same pan heat the oil, add the cooked tomato and fry till translucent.
3. Add in the chilli powder, jaggery, salt, vinegar, the remaining oil and bring to the boil. Allow to thicken over a high flame.
4. Continue cooking over low heat until the mixture becomes jam-like and the oil separates.
5. The pickle is ready for use. It lasts for 1 month and is best refrigerated.

326 Spicy Tomato – Dry Fruit : Sweet

125 g	ripe tomato, chop
25 g	jaggery, grate
15 g	sugar
5	dried dates, stone & chop
5	cloves garlic, peel & chop
1-1"	piece of fresh ginger, scrape & chop
10 g	seedless raisin, chop
2 g	chilli powder
2 g	coriander seeds, sun-dry & powder
1	cardamom;
1	clove &
1-1"	stick of cinnamon, keep all three whole
20 ml	vinegar
5 g	salt

1. Cook the chopped tomato till tender. Pass through a wire sieve and obtain a thick puree.
2. Combine the vinegar with the sugar and jaggery.
3. Bring to the boil and remove when well blended.
4. Strain and stir in all the remaining ingredients except the tomato puree.
5. Bring the mixture to the boil, add in the tomato puree, cook till thick and dry. The pickle is ready for use.
6. It keeps for 10 days and is best refrigerated.

327 Sour Tomato – Gram – Garlic : Hot

500 g	sour tomato, chop
50 g	peeled garlic, chop
150 g	cleaned tamarind
50 g	chilli powder
30 g	split husked bengal gram
30 g	split husked black gram
10 g	mustard seeds : for seasoning
40 g	salt
200 ml	oil

1. Arrange a layer of the chopped tomato. Follow with a layer of the tamarind.
2. Repeat this process till the tomato and tamarind are exhausted.
3. Heat the oil, add mustard seeds and allow to crackle.
4. Add in the bengal gram, black gram and fry till golden.
5. Follow with the chopped garlic and fry for a few minutes.
6. Pour the seasoning over the tomato-tamarind mixture and bring to the boil.
7. Continue cooking over low heat till the oil separates.
8. Stir in the chilli powder and remove when well blended.
9. The pickle is ready for use. It lasts for 6 months.

328 Sour Tomato – Raisin – Apricot : Sweet

500 g	sour tomato, keep whole
	water sufficient to immerse
75 g	jaggery, grate
50 g	seedless raisin, chop
50 g	dried apricot, soak in water & chop
30 g	chilli powder
10 g	turmeric powder
5 g	cummin seeds;
5 g	mustard seeds &
a few	sprigs curry leaves : all three for seasoning
100 ml	vinegar
40 g	salt
100 ml	oil

1. Bring the water to boiling. Blanch the tomato in the boiling water for 3 minutes. Peel off the skins and chop.
2. Heat a little oil, add mustard seeds and allow to crackle.
3. Follow with the cummin seeds, curry leaves and fry for a few seconds.
4. Add in the tomato, raisin, apricot and continue cooking over a medium flame until all the moisture evaporates.
5. Stir in the chilli, turmeric powders, jaggery, salt and the remaining oil.
6. Continue cooking over low heat until the mixture thickens and the oil separates.
7. Blend in the vinegar and remove.
8. The pickle is ready for use. It lasts for 1 month.

329 Turnip in Mustard Sauce : Watery

500 g	turnip, scrape & slice
	water sufficient to immerse
30 g	chilli powder
10 g	mustard seeds, sun-dry & powder
40 g	salt

1. Boil the turnip slices in sufficient water for 2 minutes, remove and allow to cool. Do not discard the water.
2. Stir in the salt, chilli, mustard powders and transfer to a jar. Sun the mixture for a week.
3. The pickle lasts for 2 months. Sun occasionally.

330 Sour Grated Elephant Yam – Tamarind : Hot

125 g	elephant yam, peel & grate
25 g	dried red chillies, remove stems
25 g	cleaned tamarind
5 g	jaggery, grate
2 g	asafoetida
5 g	mustard seeds;
5 g	split husked black gram;
5 g	cummin seeds &
25 ml	oil : all for seasoning
25 g	salt

1. Stir-fry the grated yam in a little oil. Allow to cool.
2. Grind together the fried yam with the tamarind, chillies, salt and asafoetida.
3. Heat the oil, add the mustard seeds, cummin seeds, black gram dal and fry till done.
4. Combine the seasoning and jaggery with the spicy yam paste. Grind coarsely.
5. The pickle is ready for use. It keeps for 1 week and is best refrigerated.

331 Sour Elephant Yam – Garlic : Hot

500 g	elephant yam, peel, chop & steam
100 g	peeled garlic
75 g	cleaned tamarind
50 g	chilli powder
15 g	turmeric powder
15 g	fenugreek seeds &
5 g	asafoetida, roast both in oil & powder
20 g	split husked bengal gram;
15 g	mustard seeds &
a few	sprigs curry leaves : both for seasoning
50 ml	vinegar : heat & cool
40 g	salt
375 ml	oil

1. Grind the chopped elephant yam with the tamarind, turmeric powder and the salt very coarsely. Set aside for a day.
2. Next day grind the yam mixture with the garlic coarsely. Blend in the chilli and fenugreek powders.
3. Heat a little oil, add the bengal gram, mustard seeds, curry leaves, asafoetida powder and fry till done. Allow to cool.
4. Pour the seasoning and the remaining oil over the prepared yam.
5. Blend in the pre-heated vinegar.
6. The pickle is ready for use after a week. It lasts for 3 months.

332 Spicy Elephant Yam – Mustard : Hot

500 g	elephant yam, peel & chop
60 g	cleaned tamarind, obtain thin extract using water
60 g	chilli powder
10 g	mustard seeds, sun-dry & powder
3	cloves, keep whole
50 g	sugar
80 g	salt
150 ml	oil

1. Cook the chopped yam in thin tamarind water to which a teaspoon (5g) salt has been added till tender.
2. Allow to cool and grind to a fine paste.
3. Fry the cloves in a little oil. Stir in the yam paste, fry a while and set aside.
4. In the same pan heat some more oil, add in the tamarind extract, sugar and salt.
5. Bring to the boil and allow to thicken over a high flame.
6. Lower the heat, add in the fried yam, chilli, mustard powders and the remaining oil.
7. Continue cooking until the mixture becomes jam-like and the oil separates.
8. The pickle is ready for use. It lasts for 2 months.

It is impossible to overstate the importance of freshness in vegetables. They are more tender, juicy and full of flavour just before they are quite full grown. If kept too long after picking they not only become deficient in flavour and texture, but their nutrional value also diminishes.

---

333 Wood Apple – Tamarind : Hot

Wood apple is a whitish spherical fruit with a hard woody pericarp and aromatic pulp. The pulp of the raw fruit arrests secretion or bleeding. The ripe fruit is refreshing, aromatic, digestive and a tonic. It prevents scurvy and relieves flatulence. It is rich in vitamins and minerals.

500 g	wood apple kernel, chop
40 g	dried red chillies, roast in oil & powder
20 g	cleaned tamarind, obtain thick extract using water
5 g	turmeric powder
5 g	asafoetida, roast in oil & powder
5 g	mustard seeds : for seasoning
30 g	salt
100 ml	oil

1. Stir-fry the chopped woodapple kernels in a little oil and set aside.
2. In the same pan heat some more oil, add mustard seeds and allow to crackle.
3. Pour in the tamarind extract and bring to the boil. Allow to thicken over a high flame.
4. Add in the chilli, turmeric, asafoetida powders, salt along with the fried woodapple and the remaining oil.
5. Continue cooking over low heat until the mixture becomes jam-like and the oil separates.
6. The pickle is ready for use. It lasts for 1 month.

Assorted

pickles

are

a wide range of

hot, sweet and tart

recipes of

familiar and unfamiliar vegetables

pickled in

exciting and imaginative ways

to tempt

even

the uninitiated.

Recipes : Assorted

334. Mustard anbazhanga in vinegar : hot
335. Garlic, ginger – spicy anbazhanga : hot
336. Spiced anbazhanga : hot
337. Salted anbazhanga : watery
338. Apple : sweet
339. Apple – date & raisin : sweet
340. Sour & spiced apple : sweet
341. Sour apple – dry fruit : sweet
342. Apricot in spiced vinegar : sweet
343. Spicy asparagus : hot
344. Cummin, bamboo shoot – onion : hot
345. Sour & spiced bean : sweet
346. Bean in tamarind sauce : hot
347. Sweet & sour bamboo shoot : hot
348. Spiced broad bean : hot
349. Cluster bean in tamarind sauce : hot
350. Beetroot – ginger : hot
351. Beetroot – onion - tomato in tamarind sauce : hot
352. Lime, beetroot – tomato - onion : hot
353. Spicy beetroot in vinegar : hot
354. Beetroot – gram : hot
355. Sour & spiced bengal gram : hot
356. Bengal gram – mango : hot
357. Sweet & sour ber : hot
358. Bilimbi : hot
359. Dried bilimbi – raisin : hot
360. Bitter gourd in lime juice : hot
361. Bitter gourd in vinegar : hot
362. Spicy bitter gourd in tamarind sauce : hot
363. Sour bitter gourd : hot
364. Bitter gourd in ground spices : hot
365. Spicy bitter gourd in lime juice : hot
366. Sour bitter gourd – ginger : hot
367. Bottle gourd – raw mango : hot
368. Sour & spicy brinjal : hot
369. Brinjal – mango : hot
370. Spiced brinjal in vinegar : hot
371. Sour, toasted brinjal : hot
372. Brinjal – lime strips : hot
373. Stuffed brinjal : hot
374. Sweet & sour brinjal - raisin : hot
375. Fried spiced brinjal : hot
376. Brinjal – green spices : hot
377. Spicy brinjal – fresh red chillies : hot
378. Brinjal – green coriander - onion - tomato : hot
379. Spicy brinjal in tamarind sauce : hot
380. Pounded brinjal – tamarind : hot
381. Sour brinjal – green spices : hot
382. Spicy brinjal : hot

383. Mustard brinjal : watery
384. Brinjal – onion - tomato : hot
385. Sour brinjal – cashew : sweet
386. Cabbage in tamarind sauce : hot
387. Capsicum in vinegar : watery
388. Cabbage – lime : hot
389. Cabbage – onion - tomato : hot
390. Cabbage – carrot - green spices : hot
391. Sour cabbage – ground spices : hot
392. Sour & spicy capsicum : hot
393. Capsicum in tamarind sauce : hot
394. Sour capsicum – brinjal : sweet
395. Spiced capsicum – onion in vinegar : sweet
396. Sweet & sour carrot : hot
397. Ginger, garlic carrot : hot
398. Aniseed, mustard – carrot : hot
399. Spicy carrot – date : sweet
400. Carrot – walnut : sweet
401. Sour carrot – raisin : sweet
402. Spicy carrot – dry fruit : sweet
403. Cauliflower in lime juice : hot
404. Sour cauliflower – mango : hot
405. Cauliflower – almond - date : hot
406. Spicy cauliflower – carrot : hot
407. Cauliflower – cummin - mango : hot
408. Cauliflower – spring onion : hot
409. Mustard cauliflower : watery
410. Spicy cauliflower : watery
411. Sour cherry in lime juice : hot
412. Cherry in vinegar : sweet
413. Chow chow in tamarind sauce : hot
414. Chow chow in lime juice : hot
415. Spiced kolumichai : salty
416. Spiced narthangai : hot
417. Spiced narthangai in tamarind : hot
418. Fried kidarangai : hot
419. Kidarangai in tamarind sauce : hot
420. Spiced narthangai in tomato juice : hot
421. Flavoury kumquat : hot
422. Coconut – green coriander : hot
423. Spiced colocasia : hot
424. Sour & spiced colocasia : hot
425. Coriander seeds – grated coconut : hot
426. Green coriander – ginger - garlic : hot
427. Sour green coriander – dried red chilli : hot
428. Baby corn in vinegar : hot
429. Spiced green coriander – onion : hot
430. Sweet & sour green coriander – ginger : hot
431. Pounded cucumber – green coriander : hot
432. Toasted cucumber in tamarind sauce : hot
433. Ginger, garlic – cucumber : hot

Assorted

434. Grated cucumber – poppy seeds : hot
435. Cucumber – dill : salty
436. Spicy cucumber – onion : hot
437. Cucumber in tamarind sauce : hot
438. Sour & spicy cucumber : hot
439. Sweet & sour cucumber : watery
440. Cucumber in spiced vinegar : watery
441. Cucumber – celery - onion in vinegar : sweet
442. Cucumber in vinegar : sweet
443. Spiced curd – tamarind : sweet
444. Spiced curry leaf – green chilli : hot
445. Curry leaf – green coriander : hot
446. Spicy date in vinegar : sweet
447. Sour & spicy curry lime – garlic : hot
448. Spicy curry lime : hot
449. Date in tamarind sauce : sweet
450. Spicy curry lime – onion : hot
451. Date – raisin in lime juice: sweet
452. Drumstick avakkai : hot
453. Drumstick – green spices : hot
454. Spiced fresh red chilli – tamarind : hot
455. Spiced fresh red chilli – grated mango : hot
456. Stuffed kashmiri red chilli : hot
457. Fresh red chilli in tomato sauce : hot
458. Fresh red chilli – fenugreek ; hot
459. Sour spiced garlic : hot
460. Spicy hill garlic in lime juice : hot
461. Garlic – pepper - tamarind: hot
462. Peppered sour garlic : hot
463. Spiced garlic : hot
464. Sour & spicy garlic : watery
465. Gherkin in mustard oil : hot
466. Sour ginger : hot
467. Ginger – green chilli in lime juice : hot
468. Sweet & sour ginger : hot
469. Sweet & sour ginger – garlic : hot
470. Sour cut ginger – green spices : hot
471. Ginger in sweet vinegar : watery
472. Ginger preserve : sweet
473. Spiced gonkura : hot
474. Gonkura – onion : hot
475. Gonkura – coriander seeds : hot
476. Gonkura – garlic - green chilli : hot
477. Cut gooseberry avakkai : hot
478. Gooseberry - tamarind : hot
479. Spicy fried gooseberry : hot
480. Cooked gooseberry in lime juice : hot
481. Ground gooseberry : hot
482. Gooseberry avakkai in tamarind sauce : hot
483. Sour cut gooseberry : hot
484. Steamed gooseberry – garlic : hot
485. Sour gooseberry : hot
486. Fried gooseberry whole in oil : hot
487. Star gooseberry sauce : hot

488.	Gooseberry – ginger - garlic : hot	511.	Green chilli spice stuffed : hot
489.	Gooseberry whole: watery	512.	Large green chilli in mustard oil : hot
490.	Curd gooseberry – green chilli : watery	513.	Green chilli – garlic : hot
491.	Gooseberry preserve : sweet	514.	Large green chilli – mango - green coriander stuffed : hot
492.	Fried gooseberry in spicy sauce : watery	515.	Sour green chilli – ginger : sweet
493.	Spicy steamed gooseberry in curd : hot	516.	Sweet & sour green chilli – tamarind : hot
494.	Spiced gooseberry : sweet	517.	Garlic, mustard – green chilli : hot
495.	Grated gooseberry : sweet	518.	Sour green chilli – green spices : hot
496.	Honeyed gooseberry : sweet	519.	Spicy green chilli – mint : hot
497.	Sour gooseberry – onion - raisin : sweet	520.	Green chilli – mustard - mango stuffed : hot
498.	Sour gooseberry – onion : sweet	521.	Green chilli – ginger blend : hot
499.	Ground star gooseberry : hot	522.	Tanjore green chilli in tamarind sauce : hot
500.	Star gooseberry – green chilli : hot	523.	Sour & spicy green chilli - tamarind : hot
501.	Sour & spicy green chilli : hot	524.	Stuffed spicy green chilli : hot
502.	Fried green chilli in vinegar : hot	525.	Stuffed mustard – green chilli : hot
503.	Green chilli in tamarind sauce : hot	526.	Green chilli – tamarind : sweet
504.	Sweet & sour green chilli – green coriander : hot	527.	Green gram – mango : hot
505.	Ground green chilli : hot	528.	Ripe black grape : sweet
506.	Green chilli – onion : hot	529.	Raw groundnut – coconut - mango : hot
507.	Green chilli – mango - mustard : hot	530.	Spiced raw groundnut – mango : hot
508.	Green chilli – mango - thymol seeds : hot	531.	Guava in tamarind sauce : hot
509.	Sweet & sour mustard green chilli : hot	532.	Ripe jackfruit – mustard - aniseed : hot
		533.	Mustard jackfruit : hot
510.	Sweet & sour green chilli – sesame : hot	534.	Steamed raw jackfruit : hot

535. Spicy jackfruit : sweet
536. Spicy kalakkai : sweet
537. Spicy small kalakkai : hot
538. Salted small kalakkai : watery
539. Salted small kalakkai : salty
540. Small kalakkai : hot
541. Small kalakkai in buttermilk : watery
542. Khol rabi – aniseed – mustard : hot
543. Khol rabi – capsicum : hot
544. Spicy kovakkai – green chilli : hot
545. Kovakkai in buttermilk : watery
546. Lady's finger in lime juice : hot
547. Sour lime – thymol seeds : sweet
548. Stuffed lady's finger – ginger : hot
549. Spiced lady's finger – raw mango : hot
550. Economical dried lime : hot
551. Lime – fenugreek – mustard : hot
552. Spiced lime – fresh red chilli – ginger : hot
553. Lime – green chilli paste : hot
554. Spicy lime – date : hot
555. Spicy lime in groundnut oil : hot
556. Spice stuffed lime : hot
557. Economical spiced lime : hot
558. Lime in vinegar : hot
559. Spiced lime whole : hot
560. Stuffed lime – green chilli : hot
561. Spiced lime – ginger – garlic : hot
562. Lime – ginger : hot
563. Steamed lime : hot
564. Lime – green pepper – garlic : hot
565. Steamed lime in spicy vinegar : hot
566. Lime – ginger – green chilli stuffed : hot
567. Lime – ginger – green chilli in vinegar : hot
568. Malta lime – mustard – garlic : hot
569. Sweet & sour lime : watery
570. Lime whole : salty
571. Aromatic lime whole : salty
572. Aromatic lime – lime juice : salty
573. Stuffed lime : salty
574. Sweet & sour lime whole – thymol seeds : watery
575. Lime in spicy sauce : watery
576. Lime – ginger – green chilli : watery
577. Lime in spiced vinegar : watery
578. Lime in oil : sweet
579. Sliced lime : sweet
580. Peppered lime – ginger : sweet
581. Lime : sweet
582. Stuffed lime : sweet
583. Lime – date – jaggery : sweet
584. Peeled lime – raisin : sweet
585. Spiced lime – vinegar : sweet
586. Lime – coriander seeds : sweet
587. Sour lime – raisin : sweet
588. Spicy lime – fenugreek : sweet

589.	Lime preserve – jaggery : sweet
590.	Spiced lime – jaggery : sweet
591.	Ground lime peel : hot
592.	Spiced lime strips : sweet
593.	Sour peeled lime : sweet
594.	Spiced loquat – jaggery : sweet
595.	Loquat preserve : sweet
596.	Cooked lotus stem : hot
597.	Love-lovi – mustard - ginger spiced : hot
598.	Dried love-lovi in vinegar : sweet
599.	Dried love-lovi – garlic - ginger : sweet
600.	Sour makoy leaves : hot
601.	Sour cut mango : hot
602.	Cut mango : hot
603.	Mango avakkai – bengal gram : hot
604.	Spicy mango – mustard : hot
605.	Sweet & sour spiced mango : hot
606.	Sour mango : hot
607.	Aromatic mango : hot
608.	Mango – mustard - garlic : hot
609.	Split mango in mustard oil : hot
610.	Spiced peeled mango : hot
611.	Spicy stuffed mango : hot
612.	Mango – green spices : hot
613.	Juicy mango : hot
614.	Sliced tender spicy mango : hot
615.	Spicy tender mango : hot
616.	Mango – bengal gram - fenugreek : hot
617.	Treated mango : hot
618.	Small mango avakkai : tender
619.	Pounded mango : hot
620.	Salted baby mango : tender
621.	Tender mango – ginger - green chilli : hot
622.	Mango – lime juice : hot
623.	Spice stuffed mango : hot
624.	Spicy mango – coriander seeds : hot
625.	Peppered mango : hot
626.	Dried mango – onion - garlic : hot
627.	Seasoned spiced tender mango : hot
628.	Vinegared tender mango : hot
629.	Spiced tender cut mango : hot
630.	Tender mango : hot
631.	Plain tender mango : watery
632.	Spicy slit mango : watery
633.	Dried raw mango : salty
634.	Spiced dried mango : sweet
635.	Peppered mango – ginger: sweet
636.	Preserved mango – lime juice : sweet
637.	Mango preserve : sweet
638.	Spiced mango : sweet
639.	Dried mango – date - raisin : sweet
640.	Mango – fig - cashew : sweet
641.	Mango murabba : sweet
642.	Sour spiced mango – dry fruit : sweet
643.	Spicy shredded mango : sweet

644. Mango avakkai – jaggery : sweet
645. Mango ginger – garlic : hot
646. Mango ginger in lime juice : watery
647. Mango ginger : hot
648. Mango ginger – green chilli in tamarind sauce : hot
649. Mango ginger – green pepper in lime juice : hot
650. Sour mango ginger : hot
651. Mango ginger avakkai : hot
652. Mint – ginger - onion : hot
653. Mint – onion in tamarind sauce : hot
654. Mint – garlic in tamarind sauce : hot
655. Mint in tamarind sauce : hot
656. Mixed fruit in spiced vinegar : sweet
657. Mixed fruit in lime – pineapple juice : sweet
658. Sour mint – raisin : sweet
659. Spicy mixed fruit – jaggery in vinegar : sweet
660. Mustard mixed fruit : sweet
661. Sour apple – pineapple : sweet
662. Apple – fig in vinegar : sweet
663. Banana – date - raisin : sweet
664. Mixed cauliflower – potato - peas : hot
665. Vinegared mixed vegetable in lime juice : hot
666. Mixed cauliflower – carrot - peas in lime juice : hot
667. Sour lady's finger – snake gourd : hot
668. Mixed vegetable – date - green spices : hot
669. Mixed vegetable – mango - lime : hot
670. Radish – brinjal : hot
671. Mango – lime - kalakkai : hot
672. Colocasia – brinjal : hot
673. Brinjal – potato : hot
674. Spiced mixed vegetable – lime strips : hot
675. Assorted vegetables : hot
676. Sour & spiced mixed vegetable : hot
677. Spicy mixed vegetable : hot
678. Sour mixed vegetable in mustard sauce : hot
679. Mixed vegetable – mustard - garlic : hot
680. Fried mixed vegetable in vinegar : hot
681. Spiced cauliflower – carrot : hot
682. Mixed vegetable in tamarind – vinegar : hot
683. Mango – lime : hot
684. Mixed vegetable in mustard sauce : hot
685. Cauliflower – broccoli : hot
686. Cauliflower – carrot - turnip : hot
687. Salted mango – loquat : hot
688. Mixed vegetable green chilli in lime juice : hot
689. Sour mixed vegetable : hot
690. Carrot – peas - beans in lime juice : hot

691. Cauliflower – carrot - peas in vinegar : watery
692. Mixed vegetable : hot
693. Spiced vegetable in vinegar : watery
694. Mixed vegetable in vinegar : watery
695. Mixed vegetable : sweet
696. Mixed vegetable in oil : sweet
697. Mustard mixed vegetable : sweet
698. Spicy mixed vegetable – date : sweet
699. Sour small red onion : hot
700. Small red onion – green chilli in lime juice : hot
701. Spicy small red onion : hot
702. Mustard onion : hot
703. Salted Mustard : watery
704. Onion in spiced vinegar : watery
705. Baby onion in spiced vinegar : hot
706. White onion in mustard sauce : watery
707. Mustard white onion : watery
708. Sour button onion : sweet
709. Sour onion – aniseed : hot
710. Stuffed small red onion :hot
711. Onion – tamarind : hot
712. Spicy onion : hot
713. Spiced onion – green chilli : hot
714. Spiced onion in tamarind sauce : hot
715. Small white onion – beetroot : hot
716. Sour papaya – onion : hot
717. Papaya – ginger - garlic : hot
718. Mustard papaya : hot
719. Sour & spicy papaya : hot
720. Papaya – raisin - lime juice : sweet
721. Spiced pear – tamarind : hot
722. Pear – tamarind : hot
723. Spiced pear : sweet
724. Sour & spiced pear : sweet
725. Sour pear : sweet
726. Pineapple : sweet
727. Pineapple preserve : sweet
728. Sour pineapple – green chilli : sweet
729. Pineapple – mint - mango : sweet
730. Sour pineapple – dry fruits : sweet
731. Pineapple – onion : sweet
732. Raw plantain – tamarind : hot
733. Plantain flower – green chilli - green coriander : hot
734. Spicy plantain flower – onion - brinjal : hot
735. Dried plum – raisin - mango : hot
736. Plum – date in vinegar : sweet
737. Sour plum – dried ginger : sweet
738. Spiced ripe plum in vinegar : sweet
739. Plum – apple - date in spiced vinegar : sweet
740. Ripe plum – jaggery : sweet
741. Spicy potato in lime juice : hot
742. Spicy potato – peas - coconut : hot

Assorted

743. Sour spiced potato – mustard : sweet
744. Sweet & sour pumpkin – green coriander : hot
745. Sour pumpkin – raisin : sweet
746. Pumpkin – raisin in vinegar : sweet
747. Spicy white pumpkin – onion - tomato : hot
748. White pumpkin – dry fruits : sweet
749. Mustard radish : hot
750. Radish – ginger in lime juice : hot
751. Spicy mustard white radish : hot
752. White radish preserve : sweet
753. Sour raisin – date : sweet
754. Ridge gourd – onion : hot
755. Peppered mahani in lime juice : hot
756. Mahani in lime juice : watery
757. Mahani – green chilli in buttermilk : watery
758. Sesame seed in tamarind sauce : hot
759. Spicy snake gourd – tamarind : hot
760. Sour bitterberry : salty
761. Snake gourd : sweet
762. Spicy star fruit : hot
763. Sweet & sour bitterberry : hot
764. Spiced bitterberry : hot
765. Snake gourd – onion - green spices : hot
766. Spiced tamarind – garlic : hot
767. Tamarind – gram - green chilli : hot
768. Tamarind – garlic - green coriander : hot
769. Spicy tamarind – cummin seeds : sweet
770. Sour tamarind – raisin : sweet
771. Tamarind – green coriander - jaggery : sweet
772. Tamarind – jaggery : sweet
773. Tapioca in lime juice : hot
774. Thammatangai in lime juice : hot
775. Thummutikai in whipped curd : watery
776. Steamed green tomato : hot
777. Green tomato – tamarind : hot
778. Sour green tomato : sweet
779. Green tomato : sweet
780. Sour green tomato – mustard : sweet
781. Green tomato in vinegar : sweet
782. Green tomato – sesame - coconut : sweet
783. Spicy tomato : hot
784. Tomato – asafoetida - garlic : hot
785. Spiced tomato : hot
786. Spiced tomato – tamarind : hot
787. Sour & spicy tomato - green spices : hot
788. Tomato – onion - ginger : hot
789. Sour & spicy tomato : sweet
790. Tomato – ginger in mustard sauce : hot

791. Sour & spicy traditional ground tomato : hot
792. Traditional ground tomato : hot
793. Ground tomato : hot
794. Sour tomato – raisin : sweet
795. Mustard tomato in groundnut oil. : hot
796. Sour tomato – green spices : hot
797. Traditional tomato : hot
798. Tomato – gram - garlic : hot
799. Tomato – onion - raisin - plum : hot
800. Sour ground tomato : hot
801. Tomato – fenugreek - mustard : hot
802. Sour tomato – garlic : hot
803. Tomato paste – tamarind : hot
804. Sour tomato – onion - ginger : sweet
805. Tomato – raisin - almond in vinegar : sweet
806. Sour & spiced tomato – onion - capsicum : sweet
807. Tudhuvelai berry in curd : watery
808. Spicy turnip – onion : hot
809. Sour turnip – mustard : sweet
810. Turnip – onion - apple : sweet
811. Spiced turnip – ginger - garlic : sweet
812. Sweet & sour elephant yam – green coriander : hot
813. Spiced elephant yam – onion - ginger : hot
814. Spiced sour elephant yam – garlic : hot

THE LEAFY WAY

Leaf vegetables range in flavour from the near sweetness of some varieties of lettuce to the refreshing bitterness of fenugreek leaves and the pronounced tartness of sorrel. All are rich in vitamins A & C, as well as in iron and other minerals essential to health.

All leaves should be cooked as soon as possible after they are picked: both flavour and food value suffer if the leaves are stored too long.

Leaves are always best when they are young and tender, but small size is not always an index of age. Each vegetable is available in many varieties, and the young leaves of one variety may be larger than the fully grown leaves of another. There are, however, a few basic tips: young leaves are glossy, so avoid vegetables that have developed the dull surface of maturity; and, of course, reject specimens that are discoloured or limp.

If you must store leaves for a few days, keep them cool and moist. Sealed air-proof wrappings will prevent the still-living leaves from breathing and cause them to rot; always make sure that air can circulate around the leaves.

Before storing, rinse the leaves in cold water and shake off the excess. Place the leaves inside a loose-fitting, open bag or wrap them in a damp cloth, and keep them in the salad drawer of a refrigerator: the moist atmosphere slows down the rate at which their cells lose water and they will retain their crispness longer.

Low-growing leaves, particularly spinach, require a thorough washing before storing to remove grit and, possibly, insects. With spinach and sorrel, the tough stems should be removed first and discarded. However you cook sorrel, do not use iron or aluminium pans; it reacts with these metals and becomes acrid.

334 Mustard Anbazhanga in Vinegar : Hot

1 kg	tender anbazhanga, make 2 slits over each
10	cloves garlic, peel & chop
60 g	chilli powder
30 g	split husked mustard seeds, sun-dry & powder
10 g	turmeric powder
10 g	asafoetida, roast in oil & powder
5 g	fenugreek seeds : for seasoning
400 ml	vinegar
250 g	salt
300 ml	oil

1. Marinate the anbazhanga in salt for 3 days. Shake the jar twice daily.
2. On the 3rd day stir in the chilli, mustard and turmeric powders.
3. Uncover and sun for a day, turning them over once or twice.
4. Blend in the vinegar when cool.
5. Heat oil, add fenugreek seeds and allow to crackle.
6. Add in the chopped garlic, asafoetida powder and stir-fry for a few minutes.
7. Pour the seasoning over the spiced anbazhanga and mix thoroughly.
8. The pickle is ready for use after 15 days. It lasts for 1 year.

335 Garlic, Ginger – Spicy Anbazhanga : Hot

500 g	tender anbazhanga, make 2 slits over each
30 g	green chillies, chop
25 g	peeled garlic, peel & chop
30 g	fresh ginger, scrape & chop
a few	sprigs curry leaves
15 g	chilli powder
10 g	mustard seeds, sun-dry & powder
5 g	fenugreek seeds;
5 g	red gram &
5 g	asafoetida, roast all three in oil & powder
125 g	salt
200 ml	oil

1. Marinate the anbazhanga in salt for a day. Shake the jar twice daily.
2. Remove them from the salt water and sun-dry for a day. Put back into the salt water in the evening.
3. Fry the garlic, green chilli, ginger, curry leaves in a little oil till done and remove.
4. Stir in the salted anbazhanga, chilli, mustard, spice powders and the remaining oil.
5. Blend well and set aside for 3 hours.
6. The pickle is ready for use after 15 days. It lasts for 6 months.

336 Spiced Anbazhanga : Hot

500 g	tender anbazhanga
40 g	salt : for marinating
200 ml	water, boil & cool
40 g	dried red chillies;
25 g	peeled garlic;
10 g	fenugreek seeds;
5 g	cummin seeds &
1-1"	piece of fresh ginger, scrape & chop, grind all to a paste using water
12 g	split husked mustard seeds
5	cloves garlic, peel & chop
1-1"	piece of fresh ginger, scrape & julienne
5 g	mustard seeds &
5 g	fenugreek seeds : for seasoning
5 g	turmeric powder
5 g	sugar
40 ml	vinegar
100 g	salt : for pickle
200 ml	oil

1. Marinate the anbazhanga in salt and turmeric powder for a day. Sun-dry for 4 days.
2. Heat the oil, add the mustard seeds, fenugreek seeds and allow to crackle.
3. Add in the chopped garlic and ginger. Stir-fry for a few minutes till tender.
4. Blend in the ground paste and fry for a while.
5. Pour in the cooled water and bring to the boil.
6. Lower the heat, allow the water to simmer, add in the vinegar, sugar and salt.
7. Allow to thicken over a high flame and remove.
8. Stir in the salted anbazhanga and husked mustard seeds thoroughly.
9. The pickle is ready for use after 2 days. Stir daily. It lasts for 4 months.

337 Salted Anbazhanga : Watery

1 kg	tender anbazhanga
300 g	salt

water sufficient to cover, boil & cool

1. Marinate the anbazhanga in the salt for a week.
2. Drain out the salt water.
3. Pour the boiled and cooled water over the pickle.
4. As and when required take out the anbazhanga pieces, wipe and sun-dry for 2 days.
5. The pickle will last for over a year.

338 Apple : Sweet

500 g	cooking apple, halve	5 g	turmeric powder
250 g	sugar	5 g	peppercorns;
2-1"	pieces of fresh ginger, scrape & grate	5	cardamoms &
		4	cloves garlic, peel, grind all three fine
5 g	chilli powder		
50 ml	vinegar	20 g	salt

1. Steam the halved apple, cool, peel, core and crumble.
2. Cook together the crumbled apple, ginger pieces and ground spices. Stir frequently.
3. Lower the heat, add in the chilli, turmeric powders, vinegar, sugar and salt.
4. Allow to thicken and remove when the mixture reaches a jam-like consistency.
5. The pickle is ready for use. It lasts for 1 month and is best refrigerated.

339 Apple – Date & Raisin : Sweet

500 g	sliced cooking apple, peel & core
50 g	date, stone & dice
20 g	seedless raisin, chop
20 g	chilli powder
5	cloves garlic, peel & crush
1-1"	piece of fresh ginger, scrape & grate
3 g	cummin seeds, dry roast & powder
3 g	garam masala powder
100 g	sugar
75 ml	vinegar
20 g	salt

1. Combine all the ingredients (save raisin, date & sugar) and cook over low heat until the apples soften.
2. Continue cooking adding the remaining ingredients until the sugar dissolves and the mixture thickens.
3. The pickle is ready for use. It lasts for 1 month and is best refrigerated.

340 Sour & Spiced Apple : Sweet

500 g	chopped cooking apple, peel & core
100 g	seedless raisin, chop
25 g	onion, peel & chop fine
30 g	fresh ginger, scrape & grate
5 g	chilli powder
5 g	coriander seeds;
5 g	cummin seeds &
5 g	mustard seeds, dry roast all three & powder
3 g	turmeric powder
100 g	jaggery, grate
100 ml	vinegar
40 g	salt

1. Combine the raisin, onion, ginger, vinegar, jaggery, salt and cook over low heat.
2. When the onion becomes tender, add in the chopped apple and continue cooking till the apple becomes tender.
3. Stir in the remaining spice powders. Cook until the mixture is browned and done.
4. The pickle is ready for use. It lasts for 2 months and is best refrigerated.

Apple
An apple is a food, medicine, tonic, cosmetic and bowel regulator, all rolled in one. Cooking apples are best suited for pickling due to their sour taste as opposed to sweet apples. Add lime juice to chopped apple to prevent discolouration. Apples keep longer if they do not touch each other.

341 Sour Apple – Dry Fruit : Sweet

500 g	chopped cooking apple, peel & core		
500 g	sugar		
300 g	seedless raisin, chop		
250 g	dried apricot, stone & chop		
5	cardamoms;		
2	cloves &		
1-1"	stick of cinnamon, tie all three in a spice bag	600 ml	vinegar
		20 ml	lime juice
water sufficient to soak		25 g	salt

1. Soak the chopped apricot in water overnight. Drain and set aside.
2. Combine the chopped apple, apricot, raisin, salt and half the vinegar in a pan.
3. Drop the spice bag into the pan and cook the mixture gently until the apples become tender, pressing the spice bag occasionally with a wooden spoon.
4. Stir in the sugar, the remaining vinegar and continue cooking until thick.
5. Add in the lime juice, allow to bubble and remove the spice bag after squeezing.
6. The pickle is ready for use. It lasts for 1 month and is best refrigerated.

342 Apricot in Spiced Vinegar : Sweet

500 g	fresh apricot, halve & stone	1 g	dried ginger powder &
300 ml	vinegar	1 g	mustard seeds, sun-dry & powder, tie all in a spice bag
300 g	sugar		
1	clove;		
1-1"	stick of cinnamon;		
1 g	coriander seeds;	30 g	salt

1. Heat together the vinegar and sugar in a pan. Drop in the spice bag and allow to simmer for 20 minutes. Remove the spice bag after squeezing.
2. Add in the apricot, salt and simmer until tender.
3. Remove the cooked apricot and heat the vinegar alone rapidly for 10 minutes to reduce.
4. Pour the reduced vinegar over the cooked fruit.
5. Cap immediately and set the pickle aside for 4 weeks.
6. The pickle lasts for 2 months. However, refrigerate the pickle on opening.

343 Spicy Asparagus : Hot

500 g	asparagus root pieces
100 g	small onion, peel & chop
60 g	green chillies, chop
5	cloves garlic, peel
45 g	dried red chillies;
5 g	turmeric powder &
5 g	husked mustard seeds, sun-dry, grind all three using vinegar
25 g	husked mustard seeds: for seasoning
35 g	sugar
300 ml	vinegar
110 g	salt, combine with 50ml water
150 ml	oil

Asparagus is the undoubted aristocrat of stalk vegetables. It may range in colour from green to white, often with violet tinges. The whole asparagus stalk is edible; but the tough skin must be peeled from the lower part of the stem.

1. Drop the asaparagus root into rice-washed water. Remove, chop and put back into the same water to prevent discolouration.
2. Heat the oil, add mustard seeds and allow to crackle. Add in the chillies, garlic, onion, spice paste and fry a while.
3. Stir in the vinegar and the salt solution.
4. Drop in the asparagus root pieces, bring to the boil and remove.
5. The pickle is ready for use after 15 days. It lasts for 6 months.

344 Cummin, Bamboo Shoot – Onion : Hot

500 g	fresh tender bamboo shoot pieces, peel	5	cardamoms, shell & crush, tie all in a spice bag
250 g	onion, peel & chop;	40 g	chilli powder
40 g	cummin seeds, crush;	5	cloves garlic, peel & chop
1-1"	stick of cinnamon, pound &	150 g	sugar
		125 ml	vinegar
		75 g	salt

1. Cook the bamboo shoot pieces over high heat in 3 changes of water till tender. Cool and chop fine.
2. Combine the chopped bamboo shoot with the remaining ingredients (except the spice bag) in a pan and cook over low heat until the sugar dissolves.
3. Drop in the spice bag and continue cooking till the mixture becomes syrupy.
4. Squeeze the spice bag well and discard.
5. Pour in the vinegar and cook for a few more minutes till the mixture thickens again.
6. The pickle is ready for use. It lasts for 2 months.

345 Sour & Spiced Bean : Sweet

500 g	tender beans, top, tail & julienne
10 g	salt, combine with 300ml water
20 g	chilli powder
15 g	thymol seeds
10 g	mustard seeds, grind to a paste using vinegar
10 g	flour
5 g	turmeric powder
250 g	sugar
300 ml	vinegar
60 g	salt : for pickle

1. Cook the beans in 300ml salted boiling water till tender yet crunchy. Drain and transfer to a jar.
2. Combine the mustard paste, thymol seeds, chilli, turmeric powders, sugar and salt in vinegar.
3. Bring to the boil, add in the flour and keep stirring till the sugar dissolves.
4. Boil the mixture for 3 minutes, pour over the beans and set the pickle aside for 6 weeks.
5. The pickle lasts for 2 months. However, refrigerate on opening.

346 Bean in Tamarind Sauce : Hot

500 g	tender beans, top, tail & chop	
50 g	cleaned tamarind, obtain thick extract using water	
50 g	jaggery, grate	
10 g	mustard seeds: for seasoning	
15 g	chilli powder	
5 g	fenugreek seeds &	
5 g	asafoetida, roast both in oil & powder	
5 g	turmeric powder	
60 g	salt	
250 ml	oil	

1. Stir-fry the chopped beans in a little oil and set aside.
2. In the same pan heat some more oil, add mustard seeds and allow to crackle.
3. Pour in the tamarind extract, jaggery, salt and bring to the boil. Allow to thicken over a high flame.
4. Lower the heat, add in the fried beans, chilli, turmeric, fenugreek, asafoetida powders, salt and the remaining oil.
5. Continue cooking for a few minutes and remove when the oil separates.
6. The pickle is ready for use. It lasts for 2 months.

347 Sweet & Sour Bamboo Shoot : Hot

500 g	fresh tender bamboo shoot pieces, peel		25 g	fenugreek seeds &
125 g	cubed jaggery, grate		5 g	asafoetida, roast both in oil & powder
75 g	chilli powder		3 g	turmeric powder
125 g	mustard seeds, sun-dry & powder		3	cloves garlic, peel & chop
125 ml	lime juice		5 g	mustard seeds: for seasoning
3 g	garam masala powder		200 g	salt
			250 ml	oil

1. Cook the bamboo shoot pieces in sufficient water till tender. Cool and chop fine.
2. Stir-fry the chopped bamboo shoots in half the oil.
3. Add in the jaggery and stir to dissolve. Blend in the chilli, fenugreek, mustard, turmeric powders and salt.
4. Remove and set aside for 3 days. Shake at least twice daily.
5. Pour over the lime juice and stir well.
6. Heat some more oil, add mustard seeds and allow to crackle. Follow with the chopped garlic, asafoetida powder and remove.
7. When the oil is still luke warm, add in the garam masala powder and blend well.
8. Pour the spicy oil over the mixture along with the remaining oil to cover. Sun for a week.
9. The pickle is ready for use after 1 month. It lasts for 6 months. Sun occasionally.

348 Spiced Broad Bean : Hot

500 g	tender broad beans, top, tail & julienne	5 g	black cummin seeds, sun-dry all three & powder
10 g	chilli powder	300 ml	vinegar
5 g	turmeric powder	200 ml	water
5 g	mustard seeds;	100 g	salt : for pickle
5 g	aniseeds &	100 ml	oil

1. Cook the beans in lightly salted boiling water till tender yet crunchy and sun-dry for 3 hours.
2. Combine the spice powders and salt with the oil to a paste.
3. Coat the beans with the spice paste and sun again for 3 hours. Turn once or twice during sunning.
4. The pickle is ready for use after a day. It lasts for 3 months.
5. Sun occasionally.

349 Cluster Bean in Tamarind Sauce : Hot

500 g	cluster beans, top, tail & chop
50 g	cleaned tamarind, obtain thick extract using water
50 g	jaggery, grate
15 g	chilli powder
5 g	turmeric powder
5 g	fenugreek seeds &
5 g	asafoetida, roast both in oil & powder
5 g	mustard seeds : for seasoning
50 g	salt
100 ml	oil

1. Stir-fry the chopped cluster beans in a little oil and set aside.
2. In the same pan heat some more oil, add mustard seeds and allow to crackle.
3. Pour in the tamarind extract, jaggery, salt and bring to the boil. Allow to thicken over a high flame.
4. Add in the chilli, turmeric, fenugreek, asafoetida powders, salt and the fried cluster beans.
5. Continue cooking for a few minutes over low heat, adding the remaining oil little by little.
6. Remove when the mixture becomes jam-like and the oil separates.
7. The pickle is ready for use. It lasts for 2 months.

350 Beetroot – Ginger : Hot

500 g	beetroot, steam, peel & chop	3 g	asafoetida, roast both in oil & powder
80 g	fresh ginger, scrape & chop	3 g	turmeric powder
20 g	chilli powder	200 ml	vinegar
10 g	jaggery, grate	50 g	salt
3 g	fenugreek seeds &	75 ml	oil

1. Stir-fry the chopped ginger in a little oil.
2. Stir in the chopped beetroot and fry over low heat till tender.
3. Add in all the remaining ingredients including the vinegar, bring to the boil and remove when well blended.
4. The pickle is ready for use. It lasts for 1 month and is best refrigerated.

351 Beetroot – Onion - Tomato in Tamarind Sauce : Hot

500 g	parboiled beetroot, peel & chop	50 g	cleaned tamarind, obtain thick extract using water
15 g	salt : for marinating		
200 g	tomato, chop;	50 g	jaggery, grate
150 g	onion, peel & chop;	5 g	fenugreek seeds &
35 g	dried red chillies, break into bits &	3 g	asafoetida, roast both in oil & powder
15 g	green chillies, chop, grind all together fine	3 g	turmeric powder
30 g	peeled garlic, peel & chop	60 g	salt
		250 ml	oil

1. Heat the oil, add mustard seeds and allow to crackle. Fry the chopped garlic.
2. Stir in the spice paste and fry for a few minutes.
3. Add in the chopped beetroot and fry for a while.
4. Pour in the tamarind extract, jaggery, turmeric powder, salt and bring to the boil.
5. When the mixture thickens, stir in the asafoetida, fenugreek powders and cook till well blended.
6. Remove when the mixture reaches a jam-like consistency and the oil separates.
7. The pickle is ready for use. It lasts for 2 months.

352 Lime, Beetroot – Tomato - Onion : Hot

500 g	beetroot, boil, peel & chop	5 g	asafoetida, roast both in oil & powder
75 g	tomato, chop &		
100 g	onion, peel & chop, grind both to a paste	5 g	mustard seeds : for seasoning
3 g	turmeric powder	5 g	sugar
		200 ml	lime juice
50 g	dried red chillies &	60 g	salt
		200 ml	oil

1. Heat the oil, add mustard seeds and allow to crackle.
2. Follow with the ground paste, chopped beetroot and fry for a few minutes.
3. Add in the chilli, asafoetida, turmeric powders, sugar and salt.
4. Continue cooking over low heat until the mixture becomes jam-like and the oil separates.
5. Stir in the lime juice and remove when the mixture begins to bubble.
6. The pickle is ready for use. It lasts for 2 months.

353 Spicy Beetroot in Vinegar : Hot

500 g	beetroot, boil, peel & cube fine	2-1"	pieces of fresh ginger, scrape &
10 g	chilli powder		
30 g	coriander seeds;	5 g	grated nutmeg, tie all in a spice bag
20 g	cummin seeds;		
20 g	peppercorns;	5 g	mustard seeds : for seasoning
15 g	garlic, peel;		
12	cardamoms;		
6	cloves;	300 ml	vinegar
2-1"	sticks of cinnamon;	60 g	salt
		200 ml	oil

1. Drop the spice bag into the vinegar and boil together over low heat for one hour. Remove the spice bag after squeezing and set aside.
2. Heat the oil, add mustard seeds and pour the seasoning over the cubed beetroot.
3. Stir in the spiced vinegar, chilli powder, salt, cover and set aside for 2 days.
4. The pickle lasts for 2 months.

Beetroot with its crimson flesh, is usually cooked and served without embellishment. Whether it is young or old, boil beetroot whole, with its skin intact, to hold in all its colour and flavour. The cooked skin peels off easily. Beetroot contains a lot of fibre and potassium which helps lower blood pressure.

354 Beetroot – Gram : Hot

500 g	beetroot, peel & grate fine
40 g	green coriander, wash, air-dry & chop
60 g	cleaned tamarind, obtain thick extract using water
60 g	dried red chillies
40 g	split husked black gram
40 g	split husked bengal gram
20 g	mustard seeds
10 g	asafoetida
60 g	salt
200 ml	oil

1. Roast the mustard seeds, gram, asafoetida and dried red chillies in a little oil. Remove when the gram turns golden and set aside.
2. In the same pan stir-fry the grated beetroot for a few minutes and set aside.
3. Grind the fried ingredients with the chopped coriander and salt to a smooth paste.
4. Heat the oil, add in the tamarind extract and cook till jam-like.
5. Add in the ground paste, remaining oil and continue cooking until the oil separates.
6. The pickle is ready for use. It lasts for 1 month.

355 Sour & Spiced Bengal Gram : Hot

125 g	split husked bengal gram, roast & powder	25 g	cleaned tamarind, obtain thick extract using water
50 g	green chillies, chop		
25 g	green coriander, wash, air-dry & chop	3 g	asafoetida, roast in oil & powder
		2 g	turmeric powder
3 g	mustard seeds: for seasoning	25 g	salt
		75 ml	oil

1. Heat the oil, add mustard seeds and allow to crackle. Add in the chopped green chillies and fry for a minute.
2. Stir in the tamarind extract, turmeric powder, salt and bring to the boil.
3. Lower the heat, add in the roasted bengal gram powder, asafoetida powder and cook for a few minutes.
4. Sprinkle the chopped coriander and remove when the mixture leaves the sides of the pan.
5. The pickle is ready for use. It keeps for 1 week and is best refrigerated.

356 Sweet & Sour Ber : Hot

500 g	ripe ber, seed
120 g	cleaned tamarind, obtain thick extract using water
80 g	jaggery, grate
50 g	chilli powder
5 g	turmeric powder
5 g	asafoetida &
3 g	fenugreek seeds, roast both in oil & powder
5 g	mustard seeds &
a few	sprigs curry leaves : both for seasoning
100 g	salt
150 ml	oil

1. Stir-fry the ber in a little oil and set aside.
2. Heat the oil, add the mustard seeds, curry leaves and allow to crackle.
3. Pour in the tamarind extract, jaggery and bring to the boil. Allow to thicken over a high flame.
4. Lower the heat, stir in the chilli, turmeric, fenugreek, asafoetida powders, salt and the fried ber.
5. Remove when the mixture thickens and the oil separates.
6. The pickle is ready for use. It lasts for 2 months.

357 Bengal Gram – Mango : Hot

125 g	split husked bengal gram		
300 g	chopped unripe mango, peel		
20 g	dried red chillies, break into bits;		
5 g	mustard seeds;		
3 g	fenugreek seeds &		
3 g	asafoetida, all for seasoning	35 g	salt
		50 ml	oil

1. Soak the bengal gram in water for an hour and drain.
2. Coarsely grind the soaked gram and the chopped mango separately.
3. Heat the oil, add the mustard seeds, fenugreek seeds, dried red chillies, asafoetida and fry for a few minutes.
4. Pour the seasoning over the mango-bengal gram mixture and grind again coarsely with the salt.
5. The pickle is ready for use. It keeps for 1 week and is best refrigerated.

358 Bilimbi : Hot

500 g	bilimbi
20 g	salt : for marinating
25 g	chilli powder
5 g	split husked mustard seeds
3 g	turmeric powder
5 g	peppercorns &
3 g	cummin seeds, dry roast both & powder coarsely
3 g	asafoetida &
3 g	fenugreek seeds, roast both in oil & powder
20 g	sugar
40 ml	vinegar
40 g	salt : for pickle
125 ml	oil

1. Marinate the bilimbi in salt for 2 days and set aside. Discard the salt water.
2. Add all the ingredients to the salted bilimbi and sun-dry for a day.
3. Mix thoroughly and sun for 7 more days.
4. The pickle is ready for use after 1 week. It lasts for 6 months.

> **Bilimbi**, also called 'bilimbi puli'/ star fruit, is a sour fruit sometimes used as a substitute for lime. It is best when green with tinges of yellow - mature but not yet tough.

359 Dried Bilimbi – Raisin : Hot

500 g	dried bilimbi
25 g	salt : for marinating
100 g	seedless raisin, chop
5	cloves garlic, peel & chop
2-1"	pieces of fresh ginger, scrape & chop
a few	sprigs curry leaves : for seasoning
25 g	chilli powder;
5 g	husked mustard seeds;
5 g	fenugreek seeds;
5 g	asafoetida &
5 g	cummin seeds, roast all separately & powder
5 g	turmeric powder
12 g	sugar
50 g	salt
50 ml	vinegar

1. Marinate the bilimbi in salt overnight. Remove from the salt water and sun for 2 days till dry but soft.
2. Stif-fry the ginger and garlic in a little oil till brown and set aside.
3. In the same pan, add some more oil and drop in the curry leaves.
4. Fry all the other ingredients (except bilimbi and raisin) for 2 minutes and remove.
5. Add in the salted bilimbi, raisin, the fried ginger - garlic and stir well.
6. Set the pickle aside for 5 days. Stir daily.
7. The pickle lasts for 6 months.

360 Bitter gourd in Lime Juice : Hot

500 g	bitter gourd, scrape lightly, seed & cut into rings
5 g	salt : for marinating
50 g	chilli powder;
5 g	turmeric powder &
10 g	mustard seeds, sun-dry & powder, combine all three
100 ml	lime juice
50 g	salt : for pickle
50 ml	oil, heat & cool

1. Marinate the bitter gourd pieces in salt and sun-dry for 2 hours.
2. Rinse in water, drain, add a portion of the salt and cook the bitter gourd pieces for 5 minutes.
3. Pat-dry the bitter gourd pieces on a kitchen towel.
4. Coat the spice powders and the remaining salt over the bitter gourd pieces.
5. Pour over the oil and the lime juice.
6. Mix thoroughly and set aside for a week.
7. The pickle is ready for use after 3 days. It lasts for 2 months.

361 Bitter gourd in Vinegar : Hot

500 g	bitter gourd, scrape lightly, seed & julienne
20 g	mustard seeds, grind all fine using vinegar
2-1"	pieces of fresh ginger, scrape & chop;
5	cloves garlic, peel & chop;
50 g	dried red chillies &
5 g	turmeric powder
400 ml	vinegar
20 g	sugar
125 g	salt

1. Cook the bitter gourd in sufficient vinegar.
2. Add in all the remaining ingredients, continue cooking till well blended and remove.
3. Pour in the remaining pre-heated vinegar, stir well and set aside.
4. The pickle is ready for use when the vinegar soaks into the bitter gourd. It lasts for 2 months.

> **Bitter gourd** might be bitter but it certainly has excellent medicinal virtues. It is antidotal, antipyretic tonic, appetising, stomachic, antibilious and laxative. It contains an 'insulin like principle' desingated as "plant insulin" wich has been found highly beneficial in lowering the blood and urine sugar levels.

362 Spicy Bitter gourd in Tamarind Sauce : Hot

500 g	bitter gourd slices, scrape lightly & seed	80 g	cleaned tamarind, obtain thick extract using vinegar	3 g	coriander seeds;
80 g	salt : for marinating			3 g	fenugreek seeds &
100 g	onion, peel & slice thinly	80 g	chilli powder;	5 g	turmeric powder, grind all to a paste using vinegar
60 g	seedless raisin, chop	25 g	peeled garlic, chop;	150 ml	vinegar
80 ml	oil : for frying	3 g	cummin seeds, dry roast & powder;	100 g	salt : for pickle
80 g	jaggery, grate			100 ml	oil

1. Marinate the bitter gourd in salt for 2 hours. Squeeze out the salt water and sun-dry for 2 hours.
2. Fry the bitter gourd and onion slices separately in a little oil till crisp.
3. Stir-fry the raisin separately, ensuring it retains its softness and set aside.
4. In the same pan heat some more oil, stir in the tamarind extract, jaggery, vinegar, turmeric powder, salt and bring to the boil. Allow to thicken.
5. Lower the heat, add in the fried ingredients, spice paste and the remaining oil.
6. Continue cooking until the mixture becomes jam-like and the oil separates.
7. The pickle is ready for use. It lasts for 2 months.

363 Sour Bitter gourd : Hot

500 g	bitter gourd, scrape lightly, split, seed & cut into pieces
80 g	salt : for marinating
80 g	chilli powder
80 g	cleaned tamarind, obtain thick extract using water
80 g	jaggery, grate
5 g	mustard seeds &
5 g	cummin seeds, sun-dry both & powder
5 g	turmeric powder
5 g	asafoetida, roast in oil & powder
80 ml	vinegar, heat & cool
80 ml	lime juice
80 g	salt : for pickle
400 ml	oil

1. Marinate the bitter gourd pieces in salt for 2 hours and sun-dry for half an hour.
2. Remove the bitter gourd from the salt water and stir-fry for a few minutes.
3. Pour in the tamarind extract, jaggery and bring to the boil. Allow to thicken.
4. Lower the heat and add in the remaining oil.
5. Stir in all the other ingredients (except vinegar & lime juice) and again bring to the boil.
6. When the mixture thickens again, add in the vinegar, salt and heat a while.
7. Follow with the lime juice and remove when the mixture begins to bubble.
8. The pickle is ready for use after 3 days. It lasts for 2 months.

364 Bitter gourd in Ground Spices : Hot

500 g	bitter gourd, scrape lightly, thinly slice & seed
150 g	small onion, peel & chop;
100 g	green chillies, chop;
30 g	dried red chillies &
20 g	thymol seeds, grind all together fine
5 g	turmeric powder
50 g	cleaned tamarind, obtain thick extract using water
50 g	sugar
50 ml	lime juice
125 g	salt
200 ml	oil

1. Marinate the bitter gourd pieces with the salt and turmeric powder for 2 hours.
2. Combine the oil with the ground spice mixture to a paste.
3. Apply the spice paste over the salted bitter gourd.
4. Pour over the remaining oil and sun the spiced bitter gourd for 5 days in mild sunlight.
5. The pickle is ready for use. It lasts for 2 months.
6. Sun occasionally.

> Select bitter gourds that are light green or white rather than dark green in colour, as they will otherwise be bitter and contain more seeds. Avoid yellow-tinged bitter gourds.

365 Spicy Bitter gourd in Lime Juice : Hot

500 g	bitter gourd, scrape lightly, thinly slice & seed
100 g	green chillies, chop fine
2-1"	pieces of fresh ginger, scrape & chop
15 g	cummin seeds;
15 g	coriander seeds &
10 g	mustard seeds, dry roast all three & powder
100 ml	lime juice
100 g	salt
200 ml	oil

1. Combine all the spice powders, salt, ginger, green chillies with the lime juice in a jar.
2. Add in the bitter gourd pieces and stir thoroughly.
3. Pour over the oil to cover the pickle and sun for 4 days.
4. The pickle lasts for 3 months.
5. Sun occasionally.

> To reduce the bitterness in **bitter gourd** marinate them in salt for 30 minutes and squeeze-dry before use. Additionally cook in dilute tamarind water before pickling. A dash of lime juice and/or a generous amount of jaggery are helpful.

366 Sour Bitter gourd – Ginger : Hot

500 g	bitter gourd, scrape lightly, halve & seed
80 g	green chillies, chop
30 g	fresh ginger, scrape & chop
10	cloves garlic, peel & chop
10 g	mustard seeds &
10 g	fenugreek seeds : both for seasoning
300 ml	vinegar
120 g	salt
120 ml	oil

1. Marinate the halved bitter gourd in salt for half an hour.
2. Heat the oil, add the mustard seeds, fenugreek seeds and allow to crackle.
3. Stir in the ginger, garlic, green chillies and stir-fry for a few minutes.
4. Add in the salted bitter gourd and fry for 30 minutes over gentle heat until tender.
5. Pour over the vinegar, the remaining salt and bring to the boil. Remove and cool.
6. The pickle is ready for use. It lasts for 3 months.

367 Bottle gourd – Raw Mango : Hot

125 g	bottle gourd, peel & chop
125 g	chopped raw mango, peel
50 g	grated coconut, dry roast
25 g	green coriander, wash, air-dry & chop
25 g	green chillies, chop
5 g	mustard seeds : for seasoning
25 g	salt
25 ml	oil

1. Stir-fry the bottle gourd in a little oil till tender. Allow to cool.
2. Grind together all the ingredients with the fried gourd to a smooth paste. Add no water.
3. Heat the oil, add mustard seeds and allow to crackle.
4. Pour the seasoning over the gourd paste and blend well.
5. The pickle is ready for use. It keeps for 1 week in the refrigerator.

368 Sour & Spicy Brinjal : Hot

500 g	seedless brinjal, size into small pieces
50 g	dried red chillies, roast in oil & powder
10	cloves garlic, peel &
2-1"	pieces of fresh ginger, scrape, chop & grind both to a paste
10 g	cummin seeds;
10 g	mustard seeds &
10 g	fenugreek seeds, roast all three in oil & powder
5 g	turmeric powder
250 ml	vinegar
60 g	salt
400 ml	oil

1. Fry the spice paste in a little oil and set aside.
2. In the same pan stir-fry the brinjal pieces till they shrink to half their size.
3. Add in the spice powders, vinegar, salt and the spice paste.
4. Continue cooking until the mixture is well blended and the oil separates.
5. The pickle is ready for use. It lasts for 2 months.

369 Brinjal – Mango : Hot

125 g	seedless brinjal, keep whole
250 g	seeded raw mango, peel & chop
25 g	dried red chillies, powder coarsely
5 g	turmeric powder
3 g	asafoetida, roast in oil & powder
3 g	fenugreek seeds &
3 g	mustard seeds : both for seasoning
30 g	salt
40 ml	oil

1. Stir-fry the chopped mango in a little oil and set aside.
2. Coat the brinjals with oil and toast over the fire. Cool, peel and crumble.
3. Grind the crumbled brinjal and the chopped mango with the salt coarsely.
4. Heat the oil, add the mustard seeds, fenugreek seeds, allow to crackle and remove.
5. Blend in the chilli, turmeric and asafoetida powders.
6. Pour the seasoning over the brinjal-mango mixture and mix thoroughly.
7. The pickle is ready for use. It keeps for 1 week and is best refrigerated.

370 Spiced Brinjal in Vinegar : Hot

500 g	seedless brinjal, cube
20 g	salt : for marinating
30 g	kashmiri chilli powder;
10 g	turmeric powder &
20 g	peppercorns, sun-dry & powder, combine all three evenly
2-1"	pieces of fresh ginger, scrape;
10 g	mustard seeds;
5	cloves garlic, peel &
5 g	cummin seeds, grind all together
150 ml	vinegar
60 g	salt : for pickle
200 ml	oil

1. Sprinkle salt over the cubed brinjal and sun for 2 hours.
2. Combine the spice powders and the spice paste with the vinegar.
3. Spread the blend over the brinjal and let stand for one hour.
4. Transfer the spiced brinjal to a jar, pour over the oil and sun for 2 weeks.
5. The pickle lasts for 2 months.

371 Sour, Toasted Brinjal : Hot

500 g	seedless brinjal, toast over the fire		
70 g	green chillies, chop		
20 g	green coriander, wash, air-dry & chop		
5 g	asafoetida, roast in oil & powder		
10 g	mustard seeds &	75 ml	lime juice
a few	sprigs curry leaves: both for seasoning	60 g	salt
		200 ml	oil

1. Skin and chop the toasted brinjal.
2. Stir-fry the chillies, coriander and brinjal in a little oil.
3. Grind the fried brinjal mixture with the salt and asafoetida powder coarsely. Add no water.
4. Heat the oil, add mustard seeds and allow to crackle. Follow with the curry leaves and allow to turn crisp.
5. Add in the brinjal paste and stir-fry until the mixture leaves the sides of the pan.
6. Blend in the lime juice and remove when the mixture begins to bubble.
7. The pickle is ready for use. It lasts for 1 month.

372 Brinjal – Lime Strips : Hot

500 g	sour country brinjal, split into 2 without severing	40 g	dried red chillies;
		5 g	fenugreek seeds &
300 g	lime, cut into thin strips	5 g	asafoetida, roast all three in oil & powder
10 g	salt : for marinating lime		
		10 g	mustard seeds: for seasoning
15 g	mustard seeds, sun dry & powder	75 g	salt
5 g	turmeric powder	200 ml	oil

1. Marinate the lime pieces in salt and set aside.
2. Combine all the spice powders with the salt.
3. Dip the brinjal pieces in a little oil, squeeze a little and roll in the spice mixture.
4. Add in the salted lime pieces, mix thoroughly and allow to soak for 2 days.
5. Sun the mixture for 5 days.
6. Season the mustard seeds in the remaining oil, pour over the mixture and stir thoroughly.
7. The pickle is ready for use. It lasts for 6 months.
8. Sun occasionally.

373 Stuffed Brinjal : Hot

125 g	seedless brinjal, split into 4 without severing	3 g	turmeric powder
		3 g	mustard seeds: for seasoning
10 g	chilli powder	15 g	salt
5 g	jaggery, grate	25 ml	oil

1. Cook the brinjal in sufficient water to which a teaspoon (5g) salt has been added.
2. Combine all the spice powders with the remaining salt.
3. Fill the spice mixture into the split brinjal, join and arrange in a dish.
4. Heat the oil, add mustard seeds and allow to crackle.
5. Pour the seasoning over the spiced brinjal.
6. Cover and set aside for 4 days. Stir once daily.
7. The pickle keeps for 3 weeks.
8. Sun occasionally.

374 Sweet & Sour Brinjal – Raisin : Hot

Brinjals should be heavy, firm, free from blemishes and of a uniform dark colour.

500 g	seedless brinjal, cube
10 g	salt : for marinating
100 g	seedless raisin, grind
75 g	cleaned tamarind, obtain thick extract using water
50 g	jaggery, grate
25 g	dried red chillies, break into bits
5 g	mustard seeds
5 g	turmeric powder
40 g	salt : for pickle
200 ml	oil

1. Marinate the cubed brinjal in salt for half an hour and remove.
2. Stir-fry the salted brinjal in a little oil for a while and set aside.
3. Heat some more oil, add mustard seeds and allow to crackle.
4. Add in the broken chillies and fry for a minute.
5. In the same pan heat the remaining oil, add in the tamarind extract, jaggery and bring to the boil. Allow to thicken over a high flame.
6. Stir in the fried brinjal, raisin, turmeric powder and salt.
7. Continue cooking over low heat until the mixture becomes jam-like and the oil separates.
8. The pickle is ready for use. It lasts for 2 months.

375 Fried Spiced Brinjal : Hot

500 g	brinjal, cube
30 g	peeled garlic;
2-1"	pieces of fresh ginger, scrape & chop;
5	dried red chillies &
100 g	salt, grind all to a paste using vinegar
3 g	turmeric powder
3	green chillies, chop
5 g	mustard seeds,
3 g	fenugreek seeds & a few sprigs curry leaves : all three for seasoning
175 ml	vinegar
100 ml	oil

1. Heat the oil, add mustard seeds and allow to crackle.
2. Add in the fenugreek seeds, curry leaves and fry for a minute.
3. Stir in the spice paste, turmeric powder and fry for a few minutes.
4. Lower the heat, add in the vinegar, brinjal, green chillies and continue cooking until the oil separates.
5. The pickle is ready for use. It lasts for 2 months.

376 Brinjal – Green Spices : Hot

500 g	seedless brinjal, cube
25 g	salt : for marinating
50 g	cleaned tamarind, obtain thick extract using water
200 g	onion, peel;
20 g	garlic, peel &
40 g	green chillies, chop all three & grind to a paste
3 g	aniseeds
40 g	salt : for pickle
250 ml	oil

1. Marinate the cubed brinjal in (25g) salt for half an hour and remove.
2. Stir-fry the salted brinjal in a little oil for a while and set aside.
3. In the same pan heat the remaining oil, fry the aniseeds till done.
4. Add in the tamarind extract and bring to the boil. Allow to thicken over a high flame.
5. Stir in the fried brinjal, the spice paste and salt.
6. Continue cooking over low heat until the mixture becomes jam-like and the oil separates.
7. The pickle is ready for use. It lasts for 2 months.

377 Spicy Brinjal – Fresh Red Chillies : Hot

500 g	seedless tiny brinjal, cut into 4 pieces each
200 g	large fresh red chillies, split into 4
30 g	fresh ginger, scrape &
30 g	peeled garlic, chop & grind both to a paste
15 g	dried mango powder
5 g	turmeric powder
3 g	cummin seeds &
3 g	mustard seeds, dry-roast both & powder
3 g	onion seeds
150 g	jaggery, grate
300 ml	vinegar
175 g	salt
300 ml	oil

1. Dry the brinjal and chillies in the sun for two hours.
2. Heat a little oil to smoking point. Fry the onion seeds over low heat for a few seconds.
3. Follow with the ginger-garlic paste and fry for a minute.
4. Add in the jaggery, salt, vinegar and stir to dissolve.
5. Drop in the brinjal, chillies and continue cooking, adding the remaining oil, a little at a time.
6. Blend in the spice powders.
7. Remove when the mixture becomes dry and the oil separates.
8. The pickle is ready for use. It lasts for 2 months.

Brinjal
Brinjals are glossy and colourful, most run the spectrum of purples from mauve to near near-black, but white and green varieties also exist. Some types are round, some elongated, all have the same mildly sweet flavour; the best are young and firm, with unblemished skins.

378 Brinjal – Green Coriander-Onion-Tomato : Hot

500 g	seedless brinjal, cube
20 g	salt : for marinating
100 g	onion, peel & chop
75 g	tomato, chop
75 g	green chillies, chop
20 g	green coriander, wash, air-dry & chop
5	cloves garlic, peel & grind
5 g	mustard seeds;
5 g	cummin seeds & a few sprigs curry leaves : all three for seasoning
175 ml	lime juice
60 g	salt : for pickle
75 ml	oil

1. Marinate the cubed brinjal in salt for 4 hours and remove.
2. Stir-fry the salted brinjal in a little oil for a few minutes and set aside.
3. Heat some more oil, add mustard seeds and allow to crackle.
4. Follow with the cummin seeds, curry leaves, coriander and fry for a while.
5. Add in the chopped onion, tomato, green chillies, fried brinjal, garlic paste, salt and stir-fry for a few minutes.
6. Pour in the lime juice, stir thoroughly and remove when the mixture begins to bubble.
7. The pickle is ready for use. It lasts for 1 month.

379 Spicy Brinjal in Tamarind Sauce : Hot

500 g	seedless brinjal, cube
20 g	salt : for marinating
50 g	peeled garlic &
40 g	fresh ginger, scrape & chop, grind both to a paste
25 g	cleaned tamarind, obtain thick extract using water
50 g	jaggery, grate
20 g	chilli powder
5 g	peppercorns;
5 g	mustard seeds &
3 g	fenugreek seeds, dry-roast all three & powder
2	cardamoms;
1-1"	stick of cinnamon &
2	cloves, powder all three together
50 ml	vinegar
40 g	salt : for pickle
150 ml	oil

1. Marinate the cubed brinjal in salt for 4 hours. Squeeze out and set aside.
2. Stir-fry the salted brinjal in a little oil till tender and set aside.
3. Heat a little oil, add mustard seeds and allow to crackle.
4. Add in the ginger-garlic paste, stir-fry for a few minutes and set aside.
5. In the same pan heat some more oil, pour in the tamarind extract, vinegar, jaggery and salt.
6. Bring to the boil and allow to thicken over a high flame.
7. Add in the ginger-garlic paste, fried brinjal, the remaining oil, cook till blended and stir in the spice powders.
8. Remove when the mixture becomes dry and the oil separates.
9. The pickle is ready for use. It lasts for 2 months.

380 Pounded Brinjal – Tamarind : Hot

500 g	brinjal, cube
300 g	cleaned tamarind
200 g	dried red chillies;
5 g	fenugreek seeds &
5 g	asafoetida, roast all three in oil & powder
10 g	mustard seeds : for seasoning
175 g	salt
500 ml	oil

1. Marinate the cubed brinjal in salt and sun-dry for 3 days.
2. Pound the dried brinjal with the tamarind, chilli, fenugreek and asafoetida powders.
3. Heat the oil, add mustard seeds and allow to crackle.
4. Add in the brinjal mixture and stir-fry for a while until the mixture leaves the sides of the pan.
5. The pickle is ready for use. It lasts for 6 months.

381 Sour Brinjal – Green Spices : Hot

500 g	seedless brinjal, cut into thin lengthy pieces
25 g	green chillies, chop
10 g	dried red chillies;
10 g	mustard seeds;
5 g	coriander seeds;
5 g	cummin seeds &
5 g	aniseeds, grind all fine using vinegar
5 g	turmeric powder
5	cloves garlic, peel & chop;
2-1"	pieces of fresh ginger, scrape & chop;
a few	sprigs curry leaves;
1-1"	stick of cinnamon & a few bay leaves, pound all together lightly
150 ml	vinegar
50 g	salt
100 ml	oil

1. Scrape each brinjal piece with a sharp knife. Cook in sufficient vinegar and cool.
2. Smear the brinjal pieces with the salt and turmeric powder.
3. Fry the salted brinjal in oil till golden brown. Drain and set aside.
4. Combine all the ingredients with the fried brinjal.
5. Pour over the reserved vinegar, oil (after heating and cooling) and stir thoroughly.
6. The pickle is ready for use when the vinegar soaks into the brinjal pieces. It lasts for 2 months.

382 Spicy Brinjal : Hot

500 g	brinjal, cut into lengthwise pieces
80 g	green chillies, chop
15 g	mustard seeds;
10 g	coriander seeds;
3	dried red chillies;
1-1"	piece of fresh ginger, scrape & chop;
2	cloves garlic, peel & chop;
5 g	cummin seeds, grind all to a paste using vinegar
5 g	turmeric powder
1-1"	stick of cinnamon
a few	sprigs curry leaves
300 ml	vinegar : heat & cool
75 g	salt
100 ml	oil

1. Rub the tumeric powder and salt over the brinjal pieces and set aside.
2. Stir-fry the brinjal, green chillies and curry leaves in a little oil.
3. Add in the spice paste and stir-fry for 2 minutes.
4. Stir in the vinegar, salt, cinnamon, heat well and remove.
5. The pickle is ready for use. It lasts for 2 months.

383 Mustard Brinjal : Watery

125 g	seedless brinjal, split into 4 without severing
15 g	salt, combine with 100ml water
10 g	chilli powder;
4 g	split husked mustard seeds &
3 g	turmeric powder, mix all three evenly
10 ml	oil

1. Bring the salt water to boiling.
2. Blanch the brinjal in the salted boiling water for 5 minutes and remove when soft.
3. When cool stuff the spice mixture into the brinjal and pack in a jar.
4. Pour over water sufficient to cover the pickle. Sun the jar with contents for 3 days.
5. The pickle keeps for 3 weeks.
6. Sun frequently.

Note : Select **brinjals** without any holes, for these indicate worms, to which they are very susceptible. Wrap in cling-film and refrigerate, as brinjals tend to absorb all the flavours around them.
To prevent cut brinjals from discolouring, soak them in plain water, salt water or dilute tamarind water.

384 Brinjal – Onion – Tomato : Hot

500 g	tender brinjal	40 g	peeled garlic;	1-1"	piece of fresh ginger, scrape & chop
15 g	salt : for cooking brinjal	5 g	mustard seeds;		
100 g	onion, peel & chop fine	5 g	cummin seeds &	5 g	turmeric powder
100 g	tomato, chop	3 g	fenugreek seeds, grind all to a paste using vinegar	5 g	sugar
60 g	chilli powder;			400 ml	vinegar
2-1"	pieces of fresh ginger, scrape;	10 g	mustard seeds	150 g	salt
		10	cloves garlic, peel & chop	200 ml	oil

1. Pressure cook the brinjal pieces with the salt and turmeric powder.
2. Heat 100ml oil and fry the cooked brinjals.
3. Heat a part of the remaining oil, add mustard seeds and allow to crackle.
4. Lower the heat, add in the turmeric powder, chopped onion and fry till transluscent.
5. Follow with the ginger, garlic and stir-fry for a while.
6. Stir in the ground paste and fry for a few more minutes.
7. Add in the tomato pieces and cook until the oil separates.
8. Follow with the fried brinjal, sugar, salt and continue cooking.
9. Pour over the vinegar and stir well till the sugar dissolves.
10. The pickle is ready for use. It lasts for 3 months.

385 Sour Brinjal – Cashew : Sweet

500 g	seedless brinjal, cube	2-1"	pieces of fresh ginger, scrape & chop;	5 g	cummin seeds, grind all to a paste with vinegar
20 g	salt : for marinating	3	cloves garlic, peel & chop;	150 ml	vinegar
250 g	sugar	5 g	mustard seeds &	40 g	salt : for pickle
75 g	cashewnuts, halve	5 g	turmeric powder	150 ml	oil
25 g	chilli powder				

1. Marinate the cubed brinjal in (20g) salt for half an hour. Squeeze out and set aside.
2. Stir-fry the salted brinjal and the spice paste separately in a little oil for a few minutes and set aside.
3. Lower the heat and continue frying adding the vinegar a little by little, until the oil separates.
4. Add in the halved cashews and fry for a few minutes.
5. Stir in the fried brinjal, sugar, salt and continue cooking until the mixture becomes syrupy.
6. Blend in the chilli, turmeric powders for a few minutes and remove.
7. The pickle is ready for use. It lasts for 2 months.

386 Cabbage in Tamarind Sauce : Hot

250 g	cabbage, shred thickly
25 g	cleaned tamarind, obtain thick extract using water
25 g	jaggery, grate
10 g	chilli powder
5 g	turmeric powder
2 g	fenugreek seeds &
2 g	asafoetida, roast both in oil & powder
5 g	mustard seeds : for seasoning
15 g	salt
125 ml	oil

1. Stir-fry the shredded cabbage in a little oil and set aside.
2. In the same pan heat some more oil, add mustard seeds and allow to crackle.
3. Pour in the tamarind extract, jaggery, salt and bring to the boil. Allow to thicken over a high flame.
4. Add in the chilli, turmeric, fenugreek, asafoetida powders, salt, fried cabbage and the remaining oil.
5. Continue cooking over low heat until the mixture thickens and the oil separates.
6. The pickle is ready for use. It lasts for 2 months.

387 Capsicum in Vinegar : Watery

500 g	capsicum, quarter & seed
5 g	mustard seeds
5 g	allspice
400 ml	water
60 g	sugar
100 ml	vinegar
10 g	salt

1. Combine the vinegar, water, sugar, mustard seeds, allspice and heat to boiling.
2. Add in the capsicum pieces and heat gently until partly tender.
3. Transfer to hot jars and seal.
4. The pickle is ready for use. It lasts for 2 months.

388 Cabbage – Lime : Hot

500 g	cabbage, shred thickly	5 g	cummin seeds, sun-dry & powder, combine all three evenly
250 g	lime, chop fine & seed		
20 g	chilli powder;	100 ml	lime juice
5 g	turmeric powder &	60 g	salt

1. Combine the shredded cabbage with the lime pieces in a jar.
2. Add in the lime juice, spice powders, salt, toss well and sun for 2 days.
3. The pickle is ready for use after 3 days. It lasts for 1 month and is best refrigerated.

389 Cabbage – Onion - Tomato : Hot

- 500 g cabbage, shred thickly
- 400 g tomato, chop;
- 400 g onion, peel & chop;
- 150 g green chillies, chop;
- 20 g split husked blackgram &
- 20 g split husked bengal gram, grind all together fine
- 2-1" pieces of fresh ginger, scrape &
- 5 cloves garlic, peel, grind both to a paste
- 75 g cleaned tamarind, obtain thick extract using water
- 150 g salt
- 500 ml oil

1. Soak the shredded cabbage in water to which a teaspoon (5g) salt has been added for an hour.
2. Drain and sun-dry the cabbage for an hour.
3. Stir-fry the dried cabbage in a little oil till the moisture evaporates.
4. Allow to cool and grind to a coarse paste.
5. Fry the tomato mixture in a little oil for a while.
6. Pour in the tamarind extract, salt and continue cooking for a few more minutes.
7. Add in the ground cabbage, fry a while and follow with the ginger-garlic paste.
8. Remove when the mixture becomes jam-like and the oil separates.
9. The pickle is ready for use. It lasts for 2 months.

> **Cabbage** - red, white or green - is a versatile vegetable. Cabbages are at their best when tightly formed with unblemished outer leaves. To pickle blanch for 2 minutes in lightly salted water or marinate in salt. Thereafter air-dry and pickle. If blanched for too long, it may result in a pickle that smells and tastes sulphurous.

390 Cabbage – Carrot - Green Spices : Hot

- 500 g cabbage, shred thickly
- 500 g carrot, peel & grate thickly
- 100 g onion, peel & chop;
- 30 g green chillies, chop;
- 5 cloves garlic, peel &
- 2-1" pieces of fresh ginger, scrape, grind all together fine
- 20 g chilli powder
- 10 g mustard seeds &
- 5 g fenugreek seeds : both for seasoning
- 500 ml vinegar
- 100 g salt
- 100 ml oil

1. Blanch the vegetables in boiling water for 3 minutes and drain.
2. Combine the drained vegetables with the salt and the green spice paste. Set aside for 2 hours.
3. Heat the oil, add the mustard seeds, fenugreek seeds and allow to crackle.
4. Remove from the fire. Add in the chilli powder, vinegar, spiced vegetables and mix thoroughly.
5. The pickle is ready for use after 3 days. It lasts for 1 month and is best refrigerated.

391 Sour Cabbage – Ground Spices : Hot

- 500 g cabbage, shred thickly
- 40 g salt, combine with 100ml water
- 15 g dried red chillies;
- 10 g mustard seeds;
- 5 cloves garlic, peel &
- 1-1" piece of fresh ginger, scrape & chop, grind all to a paste using vinegar
- 2 g turmeric powder
- 350 ml vinegar
- 30 g salt : for pickle

1. Soak the shredded cabbage in the salt solution for 8 hours.
2. Add the salt, turmeric powder and vinegar to the spice paste.
3. Squeeze out the cabbage from the salt solution and add to the above mixture.
4. Mix thoroughly, transfer to a jar and cap tight.
5. The pickle is ready for use when the vinegar soaks into the cabbage.
6. It lasts for 1 month and is best refrigerated.

392 Sour & Spicy Capsicum : Hot

500 g	capsicum, chop
100 g	fresh ginger, scrape & chop;
30 g	dried red chillies, break into bits;
5	cloves garlic, peel & chop;
25 g	green chillies, chop &
5 g	mustard seeds, grind all to a paste using vinegar
120 g	cleaned tamarind, obtain thick extract using vinegar
150 g	jaggery, grate
40 ml	vinegar
75 g	salt
200 ml	oil

1. Heat a little oil in a pan, stir-fry the chopped capsicum till partly tender and set aside.
2. In the same pan heat a part of the remaining oil, add in the tamarind extract and jaggery.
3. Bring to the boil and allow to thicken over a high flame.
4. Stir in the chopped capsicum, ground paste, vinegar and the remaining oil.
5. Continue cooking over low heat until the mixture becomes jam-like and the oil separates.
6. The pickle is ready for use. It lasts for 2 months.

393 Capsicum in Tamarind Sauce : Hot

500 g	capsicum, chop & seed
100 g	cleaned tamarind, obtain thick extract using water
25 g	jaggery, grate
15 g	chilli powder
3 g	fenugreek seeds &
3 g	asafoetida, roast both in oil & powder
3 g	turmeric powder
5 g	mustard seeds : for seasoning
40 g	salt
250 ml	oil

1. Stir-fry the chopped capsicum in a little oil and set aside.
2. In the same pan heat some more oil, add mustard seeds and allow to crackle.
3. Pour in the tamarind extract, jaggery, salt and bring to the boil. Allow to thicken over a high flame.
4. Add in the chilli, turmeric, fenugreek, asafoetida powders, salt, fried capsicum and the remaining oil.
5. Continue cooking over low heat until the mixture thickens and the oil separates.
6. The pickle is ready for use. It lasts for 2 months.

Capsicum also called sweet peppers is surprisingly light for its size. It consists of a firm case of flesh surrounding only a cluster of flat seeds and a few ribs or whitish pith. As sweet peppers ripen, their colour changes from green to yellow or red; the riper the fruit, the sweeter the flavour. The seeds and pith are discarded to get a less spicier pickle. Additionally, it helps preserve the pickle for longer periods.

---

394 Sour Capsicum – Brinjal : Sweet

500 g	capsicum, slice	10 g	cummin seeds, dry-roast & powder
500 g	brinjal, chop		
400 g	cooking apple, peel, core & chop	10 g	turmeric powder
400 g	seedless raisin, chop		a few sprigs curry leaves
200 g	fresh ginger, scrape & grate	400 g	jaggery, grate
		800 ml	vinegar
20 g	chilli powder	125 g	salt
10 g	coriander seeds &		

1. Cook the chopped vegetables till partly tender.
2. Add in the raisin, salt, the powdered spices, curry leaves, ginger, jaggery and the vinegar.
3. Bring to the boil until the mixture thickens.
4. Lower the heat and cook till syrupy, stirring continuously.
5. The pickle is ready for use. It lasts for 3 months.

395 Spiced Capsicum – Onion in Vinegar : Sweet

500 g	capsicum, chop
200 g	onion, peel & chop
2 g	dried tarragon
2 g	cloves
2 g	thymol seeds
350 g	sugar
550 ml	vinegar
8 g	salt

1. Heat together in a pan the chopped onion, tarragon, cloves, thymol seeds, sugar, salt and vinegar until the sugar dissolves, stirring continously.
2. Add in the choppped capsicum, boil rapidly for half an hour and remove.
3. The pickle is ready for use. It lasts for 3 months.

396 Sweet & Sour Carrot : Hot

500 g	carrot, peel & quarter
50 g	cleaned tamarind, soak in 50ml vinegar & obtain thick extract
50 g	jaggery, grate
2-1"	pieces of fresh ginger, scrape & chop;
30 g	green chillies, chop &
5 g	mustard seeds, grind all three fine
5 g	turmeric powder
2	bay leaves
40 g	salt
200 ml	oil

1. Stir-fry the ginger-chilli-mustard paste in a little oil.
2. Lower the heat, add in the bay leaves and fry for a minute.
3. Blend in the turmeric powder, salt and jaggery.
4. Add in the carrot and continue to cook over low heat.
5. Pour in the tamarind-vinegar extract, heat for a few minutes and remove.
6. Cool and transfer the contents to a jar. Sun the mixture for 20 days. Shake daily.
7. The pickle lasts for 2 months.

397 Ginger, Garlic – Carrot : Hot

500 g	carrot, scrape & julienne
40 g	dried red chillies, break into bits;
2-1"	pieces of fresh ginger, scrape;
10	cloves garlic, peel;
5 g	cummin seeds;
5 g	mustard seeds &
3 g	fenugreek seeds, soak in vinegar, grind all to a paste using vinegar
40 g	sugar
125 ml	vinegar
60 g	salt
250 ml	oil

1. Sun-dry the carrot for 3 days and turn them over frequently.
2. Heat a little oil in a pan, fry the spice paste until the oil separates and set aside.
3. Combine the carrot with the sugar, salt, vinegar and cook until partly tender.
4. Stir in the spice paste, continue cooking until the mixture becomes jam-like and the oil separates.
5. The pickle is ready for use. It lasts for 1 month.

398 Aniseed, Mustard – Carrot : Hot

500 g	carrot, peel & julienne
50 g	dried red chillies;
30 g	mustard seeds &
15 g	aniseeds, pound all three coarsely
70 g	salt
200 ml	oil

1. Marinate the carrot with two teaspoons (10g) salt.
2. Combine the spice mixture and the remaining salt with a little oil to a paste. Stir in the salted carrot.
3. Pour over the remaining oil and blend well. Sun for 4 days.
4. The pickle lasts for 1 month.

399 Spicy Carrot – Date : Sweet

500 g	carrot, peel & chop
500 g	date, stone & chop
100 g	seedless raisin, chop
10	figs, chop
30 g	chilli powder
5 g	mustard seeds, crush;
5 g	cummin seeds, pound;
3	cloves;
3	cardamoms &
1-1"	stick of cinnamon, tie all in a spice bag

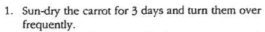

There are many varieties of carrot. Broadly, they can be classified into two groups, namely, Asiatic types and European types. The former are marked by their larger size, darker colour and sweet taste. However, the latter are preferred due to their smooth surface, thin core, better shape and less fibrous nature..

150 g	jaggery, grate
300 ml	vinegar
75 g	salt

1. Bring 150ml vinegar to the boiling along with the spice bag. Simmer for 30 minutes and remove.
2. Discard the spice bag after squeezing, allow the vinegar to cool and set aside.
3. Heat together the remaining ingredients along with the remaining vinegar over a gentle flame till soft and well blended.
4. Stir in the spiced vinegar and mix well.
5. The pickle is ready for use. It lasts for 2 months and is best refrigerated.

400 Carrot – Walnut : Sweet

500 g	carrot, peel & julienne
100 g	slivered walnut, blanch & peel
5 g	dried ginger powder
2 g	grated nutmeg
1	clove
200 g	sugar
200 ml	vinegar
35 g	salt

1. Blanch the chopped carrot in lightly salted boiling water for 5 minutes until the carrot is cooked yet crunchy. Drain and reserve the water.
2. Pour the reserved water in a pan, stir in the vinegar, sugar, ginger powder, grated nutmeg, clove and bring rapidly to the boil.
3. Boil until the water is reduced by a quarter.
4. Add in the chopped carrot, walnuts and continue cooking for 10 minutes until the carrots become translucent.
5. The pickle is ready for use after a day. It lasts for 1 month and is best refrigerated.

401 Sour Carrot – Raisin : Sweet

500 g	carrot, peel & grate
400 g	sugar
60 g	seedless raisin, chop
10	almonds, peel, blanch & cut into slivers
20 g	chilli powder
2-1"	pieces of fresh ginger, scrape & slice
2	cloves garlic, peel & chop
5	cardamoms, crush
300 ml	vinegar
100 ml	water
30 g	salt

1. Cook the carrot, garlic and ginger in the water over low heat until the water is reduced to half.
2. Stir in the chilli powder, vinegar, sugar, salt, raisin, almond and cardamom.
3. Continue cooking until the mixture becomes thick and jam-like.
4. The pickle is ready for use after 2 days. It lasts for 1 month.

402 Spicy Carrot – Dry Fruit : Sweet

500 g	carrot, peel & julienne	2-1"	pieces of fresh ginger, scrape & chop
10 g	salt : for marinating	25 g	peeled garlic, chop
500 g	jaggery, grate	15 g	mustard seeds, grind to a paste using vinegar
50 g	dried apricot &		
50 g	dried date, stone & chop		
50 g	seedless raisin, chop	5 g	turmeric powder
12 g	chilli powder	125 ml	vinegar
5 g	peppercorns	50 g	salt : for pickle

1. Marinate the carrot pieces with the salt and turmeric powder.
2. Squeeze out the salt water from the carrot and sun-dry for 3 days.
3. Soak the chopped apricot and date in a little vinegar.
4. Heat the remaining vinegar with the jaggery for a few minutes. Strain and allow to cool.
5. Combine all the ingredients thoroughly with the salt.
6. The pickle is ready for use after 7 days. It lasts for 2 months.

403 Cauliflower in Lime Juice : Hot

500 g	cauliflower florets	150 ml	lime juice
10 g	salt : for marinating	10 g	mustard seeds: for seasoning
25 g	chilli powder;		
2 g	turmeric powder &	3 g	asafoetida, roast in oil & powder
50 g	salt : for pickle, combine all three evenly		
		75 ml	oil

1. Marinate the florets in two teaspoons (10g) salt for 8 hours. Drain, rinse and sun-dry for a day.
2. Add the spice mixture, salt, lime juice into the dried salted florets and stir thoroughly.
3. Heat the oil, add mustard seeds and allow to crackle.
4. Add in the asafoetida powder and pour the seasoning over the cauliflower mixture. Blend well.
5. Sun the mixture for 2 days before use.
6. The pickle lasts for 1 month and longer in the refrigerator. Stir once daily.

404 Sour Cauliflower – Mango : Hot

500 g	cauliflower, separate into florets	5	dried red chillies, break into bits & seed: both for seasoning
10 g	salt : for marinating		
100 g	seeded raw mango, peel & chop;		
75 g	green chillies, chop fine &	10 g	chilli powder
		5 g	turmeric powder
2-1"	pieces of fresh ginger, scrape & chop, grind all three to a paste	100 ml	lime juice
		75 g	salt : for pickle
3 g	cummin seeds &	250 ml	oil

1. Marinate the florets in two teaspoons (10g) salt for 8 hours. Drain, rinse and sun-dry for a day.
2. Fry the cummin seeds and dried red chillies in a little oil.
3. Stir in the spice paste and continue cooking until the oil separates.
4. Follow with the spice powders, lime juice, salt and remove after a minute.
5. Add in the cauliflower florets and mix thoroughly.
6. Sun the mixture for 4 days before use.
7. The pickle lasts for 1 month and longer in the refrigerator. Stir once daily.

405 Cauliflower – Almond - Date : Hot

500 g	cauliflower, separate into florets	5 g	mustard seeds, sun-dry & powder
10 g	salt : for marinating	3 g	turmeric powder
100 g	seedless date, chop fine	3 g	dried ginger powder
25	almonds, blanch, peel, air-dry & cut into slivers	3 1-1"	cloves stick of cinnamon
25 g	chilli powder	50 g	salt : for pickle
150 ml	lime juice	200 ml	oil

1. Marinate the florets in two teaspoons (10g) salt for 8 hours. Drain, rinse and sun-dry for a day.
2. Fry the clove and cinnamon in oil and remove.
3. When the heat has reduced a little, stir in the lime juice, spice mixture and blend well.
4. Add in the chopped date, slivered almond, florets and stir thoroughly.
5. Sun the mixture for 4 days before use.
6. The pickle lasts for 1 month and longer in the refrigerator. Stir once daily.

406 Spicy Cauliflower – Carrot : Hot

500 g	cauliflower, separate into florets;	10 g	seedless raisin, chop
25 g	shelled peas &	3 g	black cummin seeds;
125 g	carrot, peel & chop, combine all three	3 g 3 g	aniseeds & fenugreek seeds, dry-roast all three & powder
30 g 1-1"	chilli powder piece of fresh ginger, scrape & slice	3 g	turmeric powder
1	clove garlic, peel & chop	225 ml 50 g	lime juice salt
15 g	sugar	150 ml	oil

1. Soak the vegetables in water to which a teaspoon (5g) salt has been added overnight.
2. Add in the chilli, turmeric powders and salt to the prepared vegetables. Sun-dry till the cauliflower mixture gives out water and shrinks.
3. Transfer to a jar. Sun the jar with contents for 2 days.
4. Stir in the roasted spice powders, ginger, raisin into the vegetables and sun-dry for 2 more days.
5. Heat the oil, add mustard seeds and allow to crackle. Follow with the garlic, sugar and remove when the sugar dissolves.
6. Blend the seasoning and lime juice into the spiced vegetables.
7. The pickle is ready for use after 5 days. It lasts for 2 months. Sun occasionally.

Note : Cauliflower may be used raw after rinsing in warm salt water. Blanching, i.e., soaking in hot water for 2 minutes, is permitted as crunchiness is very vital to this pickle. It will be useful to observe this rule in all mixed vegetable pickling.

407 Cauliflower – Cummin - Mango : Hot

500 g	cauliflower, separate into florets	5 g	green chillies, slit
150 g	seeded raw mango, peel & chop	100 ml 10 ml	vinegar lime juice
10 g	salt : for marinating	50 g	salt : for pickle
15 g	cummin seeds	75 ml	oil
10 g	dried red chillies, roast in oil & powder		
2-1"	pieces of fresh ginger, scrape & chop		

1. Marinate the florets and mango pieces in 2 teaspoons (10g) salt for 4 hours.
2. Discard the salt water and allow to dry overnight on a clean cloth.
3. Heat a little oil and add cummin seeds. Follow with the ginger, green chillies and stir-fry for a few minutes.
4. Add in the vinegar, the remaining oil, cook for a few minutes and remove.
5. When the oil is still lukewarm stir in the chilli powder, florets, mango, salt and the lime juice.
6. Combine well and sun the mixture for 5 days.
7. The pickle lasts for 1 month.

408 Cauliflower – Spring Onion : Hot

500 g	cauliflower, separate into florets
100 g	spring onion, peel & chop
25 g	green chillies, chop
200 ml	vinegar
35 g	salt
50 ml	oil

1. Soak the florets overnight in water to which a teaspoon (5g) salt has been added.
2. Remove, air-dry and set aside.
3. Stir-fry the spring onion and green chillies in the oil.
4. Add in the dried cauliflower, salt and the vinegar. Mix thoroughly.
5. Sun the mixture for 4 days.
6. The pickle lasts for 1 month.

409 Mustard Cauliflower : Watery

500 g	cauliflower, separate into florets
10 g	salt : for marinating
40 g	chilli powder
5 g	mustard seeds, sun-dry & powder
3 g	asafoetida, roast in oil & powder
3 g	turmeric powder
375 ml	water
50 ml	lime juice
65 g	salt : for pickle
5 g	mustard seeds &
50 ml	oil : both for seasoning

1. Marinate the florets in two teaspoons (10g) salt for 8 hours. Drain, rinse and sun-dry for a day.
2. Add the spice powders, salt, lime juice, water into the dried salted florets and stir thoroughly.
3. Heat the oil, add mustard seeds and allow to crackle.
4. Blend the seasoning into the cauliflower mixture and mix well.
5. Sun the mixture for 4 days before use.
6. The pickle lasts for 1 month and longer in the refrigerator.
7. Stir once daily and ensure that the florets are immersed in the spicy liquid.

410 Spicy Cauliflower : Watery

500 g	cauliflower, separate into florets
10 g	salt : for marinating
2-1"	pieces of fresh ginger, scrape, chop & grind fine
25 g	chilli powder;
10 g	mustard seeds, sun-dry & powder;
5 g	garam masala powder;
5 g	turmeric powder &
50 g	salt : for pickle, combine all evenly
125 ml	lime juice
50 ml	vinegar : heat & cool
50 ml	oil

1. Marinate the florets in two teaspoons (10g) salt for 8 hours. Drain, rinse and sun-dry for a day.
2. Stir-fry the ginger paste in a little oil until the oil separates and remove.
3. Blend in the spice mixture, cooled vinegar and the lime juice.
4. Add in the dried florets and mix thoroughly.
5. Sun the mixture for 4 days before use.
6. The pickle lasts for 1 month and longer in the refrigerator. Stir once daily.

Vegetables
Cook vegetables in as little water as possible. Stir only when you must, else valuable vitamins will be destroyed.

411 Sour Cherry in Lime Juice : Hot

Prick **cherries** before pickling in order to retain their shape. Otherwise they will shrink during cooking due to their high water content.

500 g	sour cherry, stone
5 g	salt : for marinating
20 g	jaggery, grate
20 g	chilli powder
3 g	turmeric powder
3 g	fenugreek seeds &
3 g	asafoetida, roast both in oil & powder
5 g	mustard seeds : for seasoning
40 ml	lime juice
40 g	salt : for pickle
150 ml	oil

1. Marinate the cherries in a teaspoon (5g) salt for a day.
2. Heat a little oil, add mustard seeds and allow to crackle.
3. Stir in the cherries, jaggery and turmeric powder.
4. Stir-fry for a few minutes over low heat until the cherries become partly tender.
5. Add in the salt, chilli, fenugreek, asafoetida powders, the remaining oil and continue cooking till the oil separates.
6. Blend in the lime juice and remove when the mixture begins to bubble.
7. The pickle is ready for use. It lasts for 2 months.

412 Cherry in Vinegar : Sweet

500 g	sweet cherry, stone	1-1"	stick of cinnamon, tie both in a spice bag
200 g	jaggery, grate		
2	cloves &		
150 ml	vinegar	5 g	salt

1. Combine the vinegar and jaggery, drop in the spice bag and heat the mixture.
2. Stir the mixture until the jaggery dissolves.
3. Lower the heat, add in the cherries and cook until they soften.
4. Remove the cherries with a perforated spoon and arrange in a jar.
5. Bring the remaining liquid alone to rapid boil for 5 minutes until the liquid is reduced by half.
6. Squeeze out and discard the spice bag.
7. Pour the spiced liquid over the cherries. Cover, seal and set aside for 2 months.
8. The pickle lasts for 4 months.

413 Chow Chow in Tamarind Sauce : Hot

500 g	chopped chow chow, peel & seed		
5 g	salt : for marinating		
20 g	chilli powder		
20 g	cleaned tamarind, obtain thick extract using water		
20 g	jaggery, grate		
10 g	mustard seeds: for seasoning	3 g	turmeric powder
3 g	fenugreek seeds &	40 g	salt : for pickle
3 g	asafoetida, roast both in oil & powder	150 ml	oil

1. Marinate the chow chow in a teaspoon (5g) salt for a day.
2. Drain and sun-dry for a day. Turn over a few times for even drying.
3. Stir-fry the chow chow in a little oil till tender and set aside.
4. In the same pan heat some more oil, add mustard seeds and allow to crackle.
5. Pour in the tamarind extract and bring to the boil along with the jaggery. Allow to thicken over a high flame.
6. Add in the chow chow and continue cooking over low heat till well blended.
7. Stir in the salt, chilli, turmeric powders, the remaining oil and cook till the oil separates.
8. Blend in the fenugreek, asafoetida powders and remove.
9. The pickle is ready for use. It lasts for 2 months.

414 Chow Chow in Lime Juice : Hot

500 g	chopped chow chow, peel & seed	3 g	fenugreek seeds, roast both in oil & powder
5 g	salt : for marinating	3 g	turmeric powder
25 g	chilli powder		
20 g	jaggery, grate	40 ml	lime juice
10 g	mustard seeds: for seasoning	35 g	salt : for pickle
5 g	asafoetida &	150 ml	oil

1. Marinate the chopped chow chow in a teaspoon (5g) salt for half a day.
2. Drain and sun-dry for a day. Turn over a few times for even drying.
3. Heat a little oil, add mustard seeds and allow to crackle.
4. Stir in the chow chow, jaggery and turmeric powder.
5. Stir-fry for a few minutes till the chow chow becomes partly tender.
6. Add in the salt, chilli, fenugreek, asafoetida powders, the remaining oil and continue cooking till the oil separates.
7. Blend in the lime juice and remove when the mixture begins to bubble.
8. The pickle is ready for use. It lasts for 2 months.

415 Spiced Kolumichai : Salty

1 kg	kolumichai, chop & seed
75 g	chilli powder
10 g	turmeric powder
250 g	salt

1. Pack the chopped kolumichai in a jar. Add the salt, chilli powder and toss well. Cover and set aside for 10 days. Stir twice daily.
2. Remove the kolumichai from the salt water and sun-dry.
3. Return to the salt water every night.
4. Repeat this procedure till the entire salt water is absorbed by the chopped kolumichai.
5. The pickle is ready for use when the chopped kolumichai is soft yet dry. It lasts for several years.

416 Spiced Narthangai : Hot

1 kg	narthangai, scrape lightly, chop & seed
150 g	dried red chillies, roast in oil & powder coarsely
5 g	asafoetida &
5 g	fenugreek seeds, roast both in oil & powder
5 g	turmeric powder
10 g	mustard seeds : for seasoning
20 ml	vinegar
300 g	salt
300 ml	gingelly oil

1. Marinate the narthangai pieces in salt for a week. Stir daily.
2. Sprinkle the spice mixture over the salted narthangai pieces.
3. Heat a little oil, add mustard seeds and allow to crackle.
4. Pour the vinegar, seasoning and the remaining oil (after heating) over the pickle. Mix thoroughly.
5. The pickle is ready for use after 2 days. It lasts for 1 year.

417 Spiced Narthangai in Tamarind : Hot

500 g	narthangai, scrape lightly, chop & seed
150 g	cleaned tamarind, obtain thick extract using water
75 g	jaggery, grate
20 g	green chillies, chop
25 g	dried red chillies, break into bits
15 g	chilli powder
5 g	fenugreek seeds &
5 g	asafoetida, roast both in oil & powder
5 g	turmeric powder
5 g	mustard seeds &
a few	sprigs curry leaves : both for seasoning
100 g	salt
200 ml	oil

1. Stir-fry the chopped narthangai in a little oil and set aside.
2. In the same pan, heat some more oil, add mustard seeds and allow to crackle.
3. Add in the curry leaves, green chillies, red chillies and fry for a while.
4. Pour in the tamarind extract, jaggery, the salt and bring to the boil. Allow to thicken over a high flame.
5. Blend in the chilli, turmeric, fenugreek and asafoetida powders.
6. Lower the heat, add in the fried narthangai and the remaining oil.
7. Continue cooking until the mixture thickens and the oil separates.
8. The pickle is ready for use. It lasts for 1 month.

418 Fried Kidarangai : Hot

1 kg	kidarangai, keep whole
120 g	chilli powder;
5 g	turmeric powder;
5 g	fenugreek seeds, roast in oil & powder &
5 g	asafoetida, roast in oil & powder, combine all evenly
240 g	salt
10 g	mustard seeds : for seasoning
400 ml	gingelly oil

1. Heat a little oil. Drop in the kidarangai and cook by turning it all around over low heat.
2. When cool, cut the kidarangai into small pieces and seed.
3. Sprinkle the spice mixture over the kidarangai pieces.
4. Heat the remaining oil, add mustard seeds and allow to crackle.
5. Pour the seasoning over the kidarangai pieces and stir thoroughly.
6. The pickle is ready for use after 2 days. It lasts for 1 year.

Variation : Alternatively the kidarangai pieces may be chopped and directly fried for a different flavour.

419 Kidarangai in Tamarind Sauce : Hot

500 g	kidarangai, chop & seed water sufficient to cover
60 g	chilli powder
25 g	cleaned tamarind, obtain thick extract using water
40 g	jaggery, grate
5 g	fenugreek seeds &
5 g	asafoetida, roast both in oil & powder
5 g	tumeric powder
150 g	salt

1. Cook the chopped kidarangai in the tamarind extract and water sufficient to cover the pieces.
2. Stir in the chilli, turmeric powders, jaggery, salt and heat the mixture.
3. Cover and continue cooking for a few minutes without stirring until tender.
4. Remove, add in the asafoetida, fenugreek powders, cover and set aside.
5. The pickle is ready for use. It lasts for 4 months. Sun occasionally.

420 Spiced Narthangai in Tomato Juice : Hot

500 g	*narthangai, scrape lightly, chop & seed*
20 g	*green chillies, chop*
30 g	*cleaned tamarind, obtain thick extract using water*
20 g	*jaggery, grate*
10 g	*mustard seeds : for seasoning*
2 g	*turmeric powder*
40 ml	*thick tomato juice*
100 g	*salt*
200 ml	*gingelly oil*

1. Steam the narthangai pieces with the salt and turmeric powder till partly tender.
2. Stir-fry the steamed narthangai for a few minutes in a little oil and set aside.
3. Heat some more oil, add mustard seeds and allow to crackle.
4. Add in the green chillies and stir-fry for a few minutes.
5. Pour in the tamarind extract, jaggery, tomato juice and the remaining oil. Cook over high heat till the mixture thickens, stirring continuously.
6. Add in the fried narthangai and continue cooking over low heat.
7. Remove when the mixture becomes jam-like and the oil separates.
8. The pickle is ready for use. It lasts for 2 months.

421 Flavoury Kumquat : Hot

500 g	*kumquat, chop & seed*
50 g	*chilli powder*
25 g	*jaggery, grate*
5 g	*asafoetida, roast in oil & powder*
5 g	*mustard seeds &*
a few	*sprigs curry leaves : both for seasoning*
125 g	*salt*
250 ml	*oil*

1. Marinate the kumquat pieces in the salt for one week.
2. Blend in the chilli, asafoetida powders and jaggery.
3. Heat the oil, add mustard seeds and allow to crackle. Add in the curry leaves and fry till crisp.
4. Pour the seasoning over the pickle and stir well till the jaggery dissolves.
5. The pickle is ready for use. It lasts for 6 months if steeped in oil.

422 Coconut – Green Coriander : Hot

125 g	*grated coconut, dry-roast*
30 g	*green coriander, wash, air-dry & chop*
20 g	*green chillies, chop*
5 g	*dried red chillies, break into bits*
5 g	*cleaned tamarind, obtain thick extract using water*
5 g	*jaggery, grate*
25 g	*salt*
20 ml	*oil*

1. Stir-fry the green chillies and chopped coriander in little oil and set aside.
2. Cool and grind with the roasted coconut to a coarse paste.
3. Heat the oil, add the red chillies and fry for a few minutes.
4. Stir in the tamarind extract, jaggery, salt and bring to the boil. Allow to thicken over a high flame.
5. Lower the heat, add in the ground paste and blend well.
6. Remove when the mixture thickens and the oil separates.
7. The pickle is ready for use. It keeps for 10 days if refrigerated.

423 Spiced Colocasia : Hot

500 g	*colocasia*
20 g	*chilli powder*
10	*cloves garlic, peel &*
3 g	*thymol seeds, grind both to a paste*
75 ml	*vinegar*
40 g	*salt*
250 ml	*oil*

1. Boil the colocasia in water to which a teaspoon (5g) salt has been added. Cool, peel and cut into rounds.
2. Combine the garlic-thymol paste, chilli powder and salt.
3. Apply the spice mixture over the colocasia rounds.
4. Heat the oil, add the spiced colocasia and fry for a few minutes.
5. Pour over the vinegar, heat well and remove.
6. The pickle is ready for use. It lasts for 3 months.

> Rather than pressure-cook, boil **colocasia** in a pan of water to prevent it from getting overcooked and mushy. Since it has a slimy texture, deep-fry before pickling to retain its shape and crispness.

424 Sour & Spiced Colocasia : Hot

500 g	colocasia	2 g	fenugreek seeds, roast in oil & powder
25 g	chilli powder		
2 g	panch phoran powder	20 ml	lime juice
2 g	aniseeds, dry-roast & powder	80 ml	vinegar
		40 g	salt
3 g	grated nutmeg	150 ml	oil

1. Boil the colocasia till tender in water to which a teaspoon (5g) salt has been added until tender.
2. Peel, flatten and fry in very hot oil till golden brown.
3. Stir in the panch phoran, aniseeds, chilli, fenugreek powders, grated nutmeg, lime juice, vinegar and the salt.
4. Continue cooking over low heat until the oil separates. Set aside for 2 days.
5. The pickle lasts for 2 months.

Note : Always cut **green coriander** with the scissor directly into the pan rather than chop, to avoid wastage. **Coriander paste** should never be over fried. Longer frying takes away its colour and flavour.

425 Coriander Seeds – Grated Coconut : Hot

125 g	coriander seeds &	25 g	cleaned tamarind, obtain thick extract using water
3	dried red chillies, roast both in oil & powder		
		5 g	mustard seeds &
30 g	grated coconut, dry-roast & grind coarsely	a few	sprigs curry leaves : both for seasoning
3 g	turmeric powder	20 g	salt
		25 ml	oil

1. Heat the oil, add mustard seeds and allow to crackle. Add in the curry leaves and fry till crisp.
2. Pour in the tamarind extract, bring to the boil and allow to thicken over a high flame.
3. Stir in the chilli, coriander, turmeric powders, coconut paste and the salt.
4. Continue cooking over low heat until the mixture becomes jam-like and the oil separates.
5. The pickle is ready for use. It keeps for 2 weeks and longer in the refrigerator.

426 Green Coriander – Ginger-Garlic : Hot

500 g	green coriander, wash, air-dry, chop &
240 g	green chillies, grind both to a paste
150 g	cleaned tamarind, obtain thick extract using water
60 g	jaggery, grate
2-1"	pieces of fresh ginger, scrape &
3	cloves garlic, peel, chop both & grind to a paste
3 g	fenugreek seeds &
5 g	asafoetida, roast both in oil & powder
3 g	turmeric powder
5 g	mustard seeds &
5 g	cummin seeds : both for seasoning
140 g	salt
300 ml	oil

1. Heat a little oil, add the mustard seeds, cummin seeds and allow to crackle.
2. Follow with the ginger-garlic paste, fry for a few minutes and set aside.
3. In the same pan heat the remaining oil, add in the tamarind extract, jaggery, turmeric powder, salt and bring to the boil. Allow to thicken over a high flame.
4. Add in the coriander-chilli paste and cook over low heat till well blended.
5. Stir in the ginger-garlic paste, asafoetida and fenugreek powders.
6. Remove when the mixture becomes jam-like and the oil separates.
7. The pickle is ready for use. It lasts for 2 months.

427 Sour Green Coriander – Dried Red Chilli : Hot

500 g	green coriander, wash, air-dry & grind
160 g	cleaned tamarind, obtain thick extract using water
70 g	jaggery, grate
80 g	dried red chillies;
5 g	asafoetida &
5 g	fenugreek seeds, roast all three in oil & powder
5 g	turmeric powder
5 g	mustard seeds : for seasoning
130 g	salt
250 ml	oil

1. Heat a little oil, add mustard seeds and allow to crackle. Stir in the coriander paste, fry for a few minutes and set aside.

2. In the same pan heat some more oil, add in the tamarind extract, jaggery and bring to the boil. Allow to thicken over a high flame.
3. Stir in the coriander paste, chilli, asafoetida, fenugreek, turmeric powders, salt and the remaining oil.
4. Continue cooking over low heat until the mixture becomes jam-like and the oil separates.
5. The pickle is ready for use. It lasts for 6 months.

428 Baby Corn in Vinegar : Hot

500 g	small baby corn	2	pieces of star anise
15 g	dried red chillies		
3-1"	pieces of fresh ginger, scrape & cut into thin strips	120 g	sugar
		200 ml	vinegar
		15 ml	soya sauce
		40 g	salt

1. Parboil the baby corn in boiling water to which a teaspoon (5g) salt has been added.
2. Drain, pat-dry and pack into jars.
3. Combine the remaining ingredients with the vinegar and bring to the boil till the sugar dissolves.
4. Pour the spiced vinegar over the baby corn and seal.
5. The pickle is ready for use after 1 week. It lasts for 3 months. Stir occasionally.

429 Spiced Green Coriander – Onion : Hot

500 g	green corainder, wash, air-dry &
300 g	onion, peel, chop both & grind to a paste
100 g	chilli powder
50 g	dried mango powder
5 g	fenugreek seeds &
5 g	asafoetida, roast both in oil & powder
5 g	turmeric powder
10 g	mustard seeds : for seasoning
100 g	salt
400 ml	oil

1. Heat a little oil, add mustard seeds and allow to crackle.
2. Stir in the coriander-onion paste, fry for a few minutes till transluscent.
3. Blend in the chilli, dried mango, fenugreek, asafoetida, turmeric powders, salt and the remaining oil.
4. Remove when the mixture becomes jam-like and the oil separates.
5. The pickle is now ready for use. It lasts for 6 months.

430 Sweet & Sour Green Coriander – Ginger : Hot

500 g	green coriander, wash, air-dry & chop;		
250 g	green chillies, chop &		
50 g	fresh ginger, scrape & chop, grind all three to a paste		
150 g	cleaned tamarind, obtain thick extract using water		
100 g	jaggery, grate	5 g	mustard seeds: for seasoning
5 g	asafoetida, roast in oil & powder	100 g	salt
5 g	turmeric powder	300 ml	oil

1. Heat a little oil, add mustard seeds and allow to crackle. Stir in the coriander-chilli-ginger paste, fry for a few minutes and set aside.
2. In the same pan heat some more oil, add in the tamarind extract, jaggery and bring to the boil. Allow to thicken over a high flame.
3. Stir in the ground paste, asafoetida, turmeric powders, salt and the remaining oil.
4. Continue cooking over low heat until the mixture becomes jam-like and the oil separates.
5. The pickle is ready for use. It lasts for 6 months.

431 Pounded Cucumber – Green Coriander : Hot

125 g	cucumber, scrub & chop
5 g	salt : for marinating
12	green chillies, chop fine
10 g	green coriander, wash, air-dry & chop
10 g	cleaned tamarind
5 g	split husked black gram
2 g	cummin seeds, sun-dry & powder
2 g	mustard seeds &
a few	sprigs curry leaves : both for seasoning
15 g	salt
50 ml	oil

1. Stir-fry the chopped green chillies in a little oil. Grind coarsely with the tamarind and salt.
2. Add in the chopped cucumber and pound again coarsely. Blend in the powdered cummin.
3. Heat the remaining oil, add mustard seeds and allow to crackle.
4. Follow with the black gram, curry leaves, chopped coriander and fry for a few minutes.
5. Pour the seasoning over the ground mixture and stir well.
6. The pickle is ready for use. It keeps for 2 days and longer in the refrigerator.

432 Toasted Cucumber in Tamarind Sauce : Hot

500 g	cucumber, scrub
40 g	green chillies, chop
70 g	cleaned tamarind, obtain thick extract using water
20 g	jaggery, grate
10	cloves garlic, peel & chop
5 g	cummin seeds : for seasoning
5 g	chilli powder
3 g	turmeric powder
60 g	salt
200 ml	oil

1. Brush the cucumber with a little oil and toast over the fire till done. Cool, peel and crumble.
2. Heat the remaining oil, add the cummin seeds, green chillies and fry for a few minutes.
3. Stir in the tamarind extract, jaggery, turmeric powder, salt and bring to the boil. Allow to thicken over a high flame.
4. Add in the crumbled cucumber, chopped garlic and chilli powder.
5. Continue cooking over low heat until the mixture becomes jam-like and the oil separates.
6. The pickle is ready for use. It lasts for 2 months.

433 Ginger, Garlic – Cucumber : Hot

500 g	cucumber, scrub & julienne
40 g	dried red chillies;
30 g	fresh ginger, scrape & chop;
5	cloves garlic, peel &
5 g	mustard seeds, grind all to a paste using vinegar
5 g	turmeric powder
200 ml	vinegar
75 g	salt

1. Marinate the cucumber pieces in salt for 6 hours.
2. Combine the vinegar, turmeric powder, salt with the spice paste and mix thoroughly.
3. Stir in the salted cucumber pieces, press well and cap tight.
4. The pickle is ready for use when the vinegar soaks in. It lasts for 2 months.

434 Grated Cucumber – Poppy Seeds : Hot

500 g	cucumber, scrub & grate
5 g	salt : for marinating
60 g	green chillies;
20 g	poppy seeds, soak in water for 2 hours &
10 g	green coriander, wash, air-dry & chop, grind all three to a paste
40 g	cleaned tamarind, obtain thick extract using water
10 g	mustard seeds: for seasoning
30 g	jaggery, grate
10 g	chilli powder
3 g	turmeric powder
3 g	fenugreek seeds &
3 g	asafoetida, roast both in oil & powder
60 g	salt : for pickle
200 ml	oil

1. Marinate the grated cucumber with a teaspoon (5g) salt and set aside for half a day.
2. Squeeze and sun-dry for a day. Turn over a few times for even drying.
3. Heat oil, stir-fry the salted cucumber till partly tender and set aside.
4. In the same pan heat some more oil, add mustard seeds and allow to crackle.
5. Stir in the spice paste and fry for a few minutes.
6. Pour in the tamarind extract and bring to the boil along with the jaggery. Allow to thicken over a high flame.
7. Add in the fried cucumber, salt, chilli, fenugreek, asafoetida, turmeric powders and the remaining oil.
8. Continue cooking over low heat until the mixture becomes jam-like and the oil separates.
9. The pickle is ready for use. It lasts for 2 months.

435 Cucumber – Dill : Salty

500 g	cucumber, scrub & keep whole
5 g	dill seeds
5 g	alum
400 ml	water
5 g	mustard seeds
200 ml	vinegar
60 g	salt

1. Pack the whole cucumbers, dill, alum and mustard seeds in a jar.
2. Combine the water, vinegar, salt and bring to the boil.
3. Pour the boiling liquid over the cucumbers. Stir well and cap tight.
4. The pickle is ready for use after 2 days. It lasts for 1 month in the refrigerator.

436 Spicy Cucumber – Onion : Hot

500 g	cucumber, scrub & slice	5 g	mustard seeds;
120 g	onion, peel & chop	2	cloves &
40 g	green chillies, chop	1-1"	stick of cinnamon, tie all in a spice bag
60 g	salt, combine with		
400 ml	water &	3 g	turmeric powder
5 g	alum powder: for brine	3 g	thymol seeds
		20 g	sugar
10 g	dried red chillies;	250 ml	vinegar
10 g	dried ginger powder;	30 g	salt : for pickle

1. Soak the cucumber, onion, chillies in the brine overnight. Drain out the following day.
2. Combine the vinegar, sugar, turmeric powder, thymol seeds and bring to the boil along with the spice bag.
3. Drop in the drained vegetables, salt and boil exactly for 2 minutes. Allow to cool.
4. Squeeze out the spice bag from the mixture and transfer to a jar.
5. The pickle is ready for use after 2 days. It lasts for 1 month.

437 Cucumber in Tamarind Sauce : Hot

125 g	cucumber, scrub & chop	2 g	fenugreek seeds &
5 g	salt : for marinating	2 g	asafoetida, roast all in oil & powder
5 g	cleaned tamarind, obtain thick extract using water		
		2 g	turmeric powder
5 g	jaggery, grate	12 g	salt
5 g	dried red chillies;	10 ml	oil1. Marinate the chopped cucumber in a teaspoon (5g) salt for 15 minutes.
2 g	green chillies, chop;		
3 g	split husked black gram;		
3 g	mustard seeds;		

1. Squeeze out the excess water.
2. Stir-fry the marinated cucumber in a little oil till partly tender and set aside.
3. In the same pan heat some more oil, pour in the tamarind extract, jaggery and bring to the boil. Allow to thicken over a high flame.
4. Stir in the fried cucumber, spice powders and salt.
5. Continue cooking over low heat until the mixture reaches a jam-like consistency.
6. The pickle is ready for use. It keeps for 3 days and longer in the refrigerator.

438 Sour & Spicy Cucumber : Hot

500 g	cucumber, scrub & cube	3 g	fenugreek seeds &
5 g	salt : for marinating	3 g	asafoetida, roast both in oil & powder
20 g	chilli powder		
40 g	green chillies, chop;	400 ml	water
1-1"	piece of fresh ginger, scrape & chop;	120 ml	vinegar
		70 g	salt : for pickle
5	cloves garlic, peel &	100 ml	oil
a few	sprigs dill leaves, grind all to a paste		
3 g	turmeric powder		

1. Marinate the cubed cucumber with a teaspoon (5g) salt and set aside for half a day.
2. Squeeze and sun-dry for a day. Turn over a few times for even drying.
3. Heat a little oil, stir-fry the salted cucumber till partly tender and set aside.
4. In the same pan heat some more oil, add mustard seeds and allow to crackle.
5. Stir in the spice paste and fry for a while.
6. Pour in the vinegar and bring to the boil. Allow to thicken over a high flame.
7. Add in the fried cucumber, salt, chilli, fenugreek, asafoetida, turmeric powders and the remaining oil.
8. Continue cooking over low heat until the mixture becomes jam-like and the oil separates.
9. The pickle is ready for use. It lasts for 2 months.

Cucumber comes in whitish green or dark green colour and turns orange, yellow or brownish yellow when it matures. Their sizes range from 8 to 30 cms. Fresh, firm, smooth beetroots, regular in shape and dark green in colour are the best variety for pickling.

---

439 Sweet & Sour Cucumber : Watery

500g	cucumber, scrub & cut into 1/2" slices
5 g	peppercorns
50 g	sugar
200 ml	vinegar
400 ml	water
60 g	salt

1. Combine the vinegar, water, sugar, salt and boil for 20 minutes.
2. Stir in the sliced cucumber, peppercorns and continue cooking over low heat until partly tender.
3. The pickle is ready for use. It lasts for 2 months in the refrigerator.

440 Cucumber in Spiced Vinegar : Watery

500 g	cucumber, scrub & cut into chunks
20	peppercorns;
2	blades of mace;
5	dried red chillies;
5	cloves;
2-1"	pieces of fresh ginger, pound;
1-1"	stick of cinnamon &
10 g	sugar, tie all in a spice bag
600 ml	vinegar
75 g	salt

1. Bring the vinegar and the spice bag to the boil. Simmer for 30 minutes.
2. Remove and allow to cool. Squeeze out and discard the spice bag.
3. In a jar arrange a layer of cucumber pieces and dust with the salt.
4. Repeat this process until all the cucumber pieces are layered. However, finish with a layer of salt.
5. Set aside for 24 hours, then rinse thoroughly in cold water and drain well.
6. Pack into jars, cover with the cold spiced vinegar, cap tight and set aside for a month.
7. The pickle is ready for use after 1 month. It lasts for 2 months.

441 Cucumber – Celery - Onion in Vinegar : Sweet

500 g	small cucumber, scrub & keep whole
250 g	celery, chop
250 g	small onion, peel
5 g	turmeric powder
5 g	salt : for marinating
5	dried red chillies;
5	cloves garlic, peel & crush;
2-1"	pieces of fresh ginger, pound;
1	bay leaf &
1 g	grated nutmeg, tie all in a spice bag
10 g	mustard seeds, sun-dry & powder
250 g	sugar
400 ml	vinegar
75 g	salt

1. Marinate the cucumber, onion, celery in two teaspoons (10g) salt overnight. Drain and set aside.
2. Bring the mustard, turmeric powders, vinegar, sugar and the spice bag to the boil.
3. Remove and squeeze out the spice bag.
4. Add in the prepared vegetables, the remaining salt and cook over low heat until partly tender. Allow to thicken.
5. Transfer to a jar and cap tight.
6. The pickle is ready for use. It lasts for 2 months in the refrigerator.

442 Cucumber in Vinegar : Sweet

500 g	cucumber, scrub & keep whole
4 kg	salt, combine with
9000 ml	water : for brine
400 ml	vinegar
800 ml	water
1 kg	sugar
250 ml	vinegar
4 g	alum

1. Soak the whole cucumbers in brine for 3 days.
2. Rinse and soak them in fresh water for 3 more days, changing the water everyday.
3. Wash them thoroughly and cut into 1" squares.
4. Combine 800ml water and 400ml vinegar. Drop in the cucumber pieces and cook over low heat.
5. Take off the fire when the mixture begins to boil and remove the cucumber pieces from the liquid.
6. Add the alum to the cucumber pieces.
7. Pour over the liquid and allow to soak for 1½ days.
8. Rinse the cucumber pieces and boil in a mixture of 1kg sugar and 250ml vinegar.
9. Continue cooking over low heat until the mixture becomes thick and syrupy.
10. Transfer to a jar and cap tight.
11. The pickle is ready for use after 2 days. It lasts for 6 months.

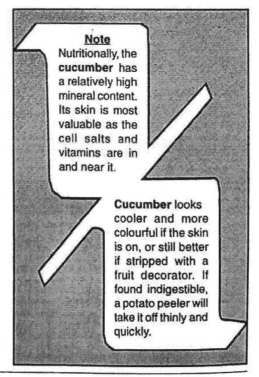

Note
Nutritionally, the **cucumber** has a relatively high mineral content. Its skin is most valuable as the cell salts and vitamins are in and near it.

Cucumber looks cooler and more colourful if the skin is on, or still better if stripped with a fruit decorator. If found indigestible, a potato peeler will take it off thinly and quickly.

443 Spiced Curd – Tamarind : Sweet

125 g	sour curd, whip & remove cream	3 g	mustard seeds;	
3 g	whole panch phoran &	a few	sprigs curry leaves &	
1	green cardamom, dry-roast both & powder	10 ml	oil : all for seasoning	
10 g	cleaned tamarind, obtain thick extract using water	12 g	salt	
50 g	jaggery, grate			
3	dried red chillies, break into bits;			

1. Heat the oil, add mustard seeds and allow to crackle.
2. Follow with the dried red chillies, curry leaves and fry for a minute.
3. Stir in the tamarind extract, salt, jaggery and bring to the boil. Allow to thicken.
4. Lower the heat, add in the powdered spices, blend well and remove.
5. When cool, stir in the whipped curd.
6. The pickle is ready for use. It keeps for 1 week and is best refrigerated.

444 Spiced Curry Leaf – Green Chilli : Hot

500 g	curry leaves, wash, air-dry, devein & grind	80 g	jaggery, grate
100 g	green chillies, chop &	20 g	chilli powder
10	cloves garlic, peel, grind both to a paste	10 g	turmeric powder
240 g	cleaned tamarind, obtain thick extract using water	5 g	cummin seeds, dry-roast & powder
		120 g	salt
		250 ml	oil

1. Stir-fry the curry leaf paste in a little oil and set aside.
2. In the same pan fry the chilli-garlic paste for a few minutes.
3. Stir in the tamarind extract, jaggery, turmeric powder and the salt.
4. Bring to the boil and allow to thicken over a high flame.
5. Add in the fried curry leaf paste, the cummin and chilli powders.
6. Continue cooking over low heat until the mixture becomes jam-like and the oil separates.
7. The pickle is ready for use. It lasts for 2 months.

445 Curry Leaf – Green Coriander : Hot

500 g	curry leaves &	5 g	mustard seeds, sun-dry & powder
100 g	green coriander, wash, airdry, chop both & grind to a paste	5 g	asafoetida &
		5 g	fenugreek seeds, roast both in oil & powder
250 g	cleaned tamarind, obtain thick extract using water	10 g	mustard seeds: for seasoning
125 g	chilli powder	125 g	salt
100 g	jaggery, grate	250 ml	oil

1. Heat a little oil, add mustard seeds and allow to crackle.
2. Stir-fry the curry leaf-coriander paste for a few minutes and set aside.
3. In the same pan heat some more oil, add in the tamarind extract, jaggery and bring to the boil. Allow to thicken over a high flame.
4. Stir in the fried paste, chilli, asafoetida, fenugreek, mustard, turmeric powders, salt and the remaining oil.
5. Continue cooking over low heat until the mixture becomes jam-like and the oil separates.
6. The pickle is ready for use. It lasts for 6 months.

446 Spicy Date in Vinegar : Sweet

500 g	date, slit, stone, chop & grind fine		
5	cloves garlic, peel ;		
2	dried red chillies &		
2-1"	pieces of fresh ginger, scrape & chop, grind all three to a paste using vinegar		
200 g	sugar	200 ml	vinegar
2	cloves	20 g	salt
2	cardamoms	50 ml	oil

1. Stir-fry the date paste in a little oil and set aside.
2. Bring the remaining vinegar to the boil with the sugar till syrupy.
3. Stir in the chilli-ginger-garlic paste, whole spices, salt and cook till the sugar syrup thickens.
4. Add in the fried date paste, the remaining oil and cook till well blended.
5. The pickle is ready for use. It lasts for 1 month.

447 Sour & Spicy Curry Lime – Garlic : Hot

1 kg	chopped curry lime, scrape lightly & seed	30 g	turmeric powder
180 g	chilli powder	30 g	fenugreek seeds
150 g	peeled garlic	20 g	cummin seeds &
120 g	split husked mustard seeds	20 g	asafoetida, roast all three in oil & powder
100 g	green chillies, slit	a few	sprigs curry leaves
70 g	fresh ginger, scrape & slice	600 ml	vinegar
		300 g	salt
150 g	sugar	300 ml	oil

1. Combine the chopped lime and half the garlic with the salt and green chillies in a wide-mouthed jar. Set aside overnight.
2. Next day sun the jar with contents. Turn over the limes occasionally until the water evaporates, to ensure even drying.
3. Heat a little oil, add in the curry leaves, remaining garlic, ginger, the spiced lime pieces and fry for a while.
4. Lower the heat and stir in the spice powders.
5. Follow with the remaining oil, the spiced vinegar, blend well and remove.
6. The pickle is ready for use after 1 week. It lasts for 1 year.

448 Spicy Curry Lime : Hot

1 kg	chopped curry lime, scrape lightly & seed	5 g	fenugreek seeds, roast in oil & powder
150 g	peeled garlic	5 g	mustard seeds;
100 g	chilli powder	5 g	fenugreek seeds &
50 g	green chillies, slit	a few	sprigs curry leaves : all three for seasoning
40 g	seedless raisin, chop		
2-1"	pieces of fresh ginger, scrape & chop	50 g	sugar
		400 ml	vinegar
		250 g	salt
5 g	turmeric powder	150 ml	oil

1. Marinate the chopped lime in salt and set aside for a day.
2. Grind together the chilli, fenugreek and turmeric powders with the raisin to a paste using a little vinegar.
3. Heat a little oil, add the mustard seeds, fenugreek seeds and allow to crackle.
4. Drop in the curry leaves and fry till crisp.
5. Add in the green chillies, ginger, garlic and stir-fry for a while.
6. Stir in the spice paste and fry for a few minutes.
7. Add in the salted lime, vinegar, sugar and cook for a few minutes.
8. Pour in the remaining oil and simmer for 15 minutes, stirring occasionally and remove.
9. The pickle is ready for use after 1 month. It lasts for 1 year.

449 Date in Tamarind Sauce : Sweet

500 g	date, slit, stone & chop fine	
100 g	cleaned tamarind, obtain thick extract using water	
125 g	jaggery, grate	
10 g	cummin seeds	
15 g	chilli powder	
40 g	salt	

1. Heat the oil and fry in the cummin seeds.
2. In the same pan add in the tamarind extract, jaggery, salt and bring to the boil. Allow to thicken over a high flame.
3. Lower the heat, stir in the date and chilli powder.
4. Continue cooking until the mixture becomes jam-like and the oil separates.
5. The pickle is now ready for use. It lasts for 1 month.

Note : Tamarind extract from new tamarind is more sour, absorbs more oil and chilli powder. Therefore, to prepare tamarind extract economically, combine equal quantities of old and new tamarind.

450 Spicy Curry Lime – Onion : Hot

1 kg	chopped curry lime, scrape lightly, chop & seed	20 g	cummin seeds, roast, grind all to a paste
		5 g	turmeric powder
		5 g	fenugreek seeds &
50 g	chilli powder	5 g	asafoetida, roast both in oil & powder
150 ml	vinegar		
100 g	small onion, peel & chop;	20 g	peppercorns;
50 g	peeled garlic, chop;	5 g	fenugreek seeds &
40 g	fresh ginger, scrape & chop;	a few	sprigs curry leaves : all three for seasoning
		80 g	sugar
40 g	green chillies, chop &	225 g	salt
		400 ml	oil

> Always buy dried red chillies in season when they are of good colour, pungent and inexpensive. Sun-dry, powder and store to retain their colour.

1. Add the chilli, turmeric, fenugreek, asafoetida powders, salt, 50ml oil to the lime pieces and set aside for a week.
2. Heat the remaining oil, add in the fenugreek seeds, peppercorns and curry leaves.
3. After they crackle stir in the spice paste and fry for a while.
4. Drop in the spiced curry lime and stir-fry for a few minutes. Stir in the vinegar and sugar.
5. Continue cooking over low heat until the mixture becomes jam-like and the oil seperates.
6. The pickle is ready for use after 1 week. It lasts for 1 year.

451 Date – Raisin in Lime Juice : Sweet

500 g	date, slit, stone & chop fine	20	limes, extract juice & retain skins
750 g	sugar	10 g	chilli powder
75 g	seedless raisin, chop	5 g	garam masala powder
		10 g	salt

1. Cut the lime skins into small pieces and steam for 5 minutes.
2. Combine the sugar, lime juice and stir to dissolve.
3. Add in the chopped date, raisin, cooked lime pieces, chilli, garam masala powders and salt.
4. Cook over low heat till the mixture thickens.
5. The pickle is ready for use after 2 days. It lasts for 6 months.

452 Drumstick Avakkai : Hot

500 g	tender drumstick, scrape skin slightly & cut into 2" long pieces
50 g	chilli powder
25 g	peeled garlic, chop
25 g	cleaned tamarind, obtain thick extract using water
25 g	jaggery, grate
25 g	mustard seeds, sun-dry & powder
2	dried red chillies, break into bits
5 g	turmeric powder
5 g	fenugreek seeds &
5 g	asafoetida, roast both in oil & powder
50 g	salt
150 ml	raw gingelly oil

> Drumstick should be pickled in season when it is sweet, with no hint of bitterness. Choose tender drumsticks with less fibre. The seeds also may be used in pickling. Where drumstick inner pith is required, parboil them so that the final texture of the pickle is coarse and crunchy.

1. Stir-fry the dried red chillies and garlic in a little oil.
2. Add in the tamarind extract, jaggery, bring to the boil and remove.
3. Combine the spice powders, salt, drumstick pieces and the remaining oil evenly.
4. Stir in the tamarind mixture and blend well.
5. Sun the pickle every third day for 15 days.
6. The pickle lasts for 3 months.

453 Drumstick – Green Spices : Hot

500g	drumstick pith, scrape & cut into 4" lengths
75g	green chillies, chop;
25g	cleaned tamarind;
5	cloves garlic, peel &
1-1"	piece of fresh ginger, scrape & chop, grind all together to a paste
10g	jaggery, grate
5g	turmeric powder
10g	mustard seeds : for seasoning
40g	salt
200ml	oil

1. Cook the drumstick pieces in sufficient water to which a teaspoon (5g) salt has been added till partly tender.
2. Cool and remove the inner pith of the drumsticks. Stir-fry the pith in a little oil and set aside.
3. In the same pan heat some more oil, add mustard seeds and allow to crackle.
4. Add in the spice paste and fry for a few minutes.
5. Stir in the fried drumstick pith, turmeric powder and the salt.
6. Continue cooking until the mixture leaves the sides of the pan.
7. The pickle is ready for use. It lasts for 2 months.

454 Spiced Fresh Red Chilli – Tamarind : Hot

1 kg	fresh red chillies
250 g	cleaned tamarind
75 g	fenugreek seeds &
75 g	cummin seeds, roast both in oil & powder
75 g	mustard seeds &
75 g	sesame seeds, dry-roast both & powder
10 g	turmeric powder
400 g	salt
400 ml	oil

1. Grind together the red chillies, salt, tamarind and turmeric powder to a coarse paste.
2. Store the paste for 3 days in a jar with its mouth covered with a thin cloth.
3. Heat the oil in a pan and remove. When the oil is still lukewarm blend in the ground paste, powdered spices and mix thoroughly. Store when cool.
4. The pickle is ready for use. It lasts for 1 year.

455 Spiced Fresh Red Chilli – Grated Mango : Hot

500 g	fresh red chillies
50 g	seeded raw mango, peel & grate
50 g	aniseeds;
50 g	fenugreek seeds;
50 g	coriander seeds;
50 g	onion seeds &
50 g	black cummin seeds, dry-roast all & powder
5 g	asafoetida, roast in oil & powder
250 g	salt
250 ml	oil

1. Make a hole at the rear end of each chilli and seed.
2. Combine the grated mango, chilli seeds and roasted powders with the salt.
3. Stuff the spice mixture through the rear end of the chilli and pack tight in a jar.
4. Sprinkle over the remaining spice mixture and the oil. Set aside for 4 days.
5. The pickle is ready for use after a week. It lasts for 1 month. Sun occasionally.

456 Stuffed Kashmiri Red Chilli : Hot

500 g	kashmiri red chillies
500 g	dried mango powder
100 g	mustard seeds;
100 g	onion seeds;
50 g	coriander seeds;
50 g	aniseeds;
50 g	fenugreek seeds;
25 g	turmeric powder &
5	cardamoms, dry-roast all & powder
20 g	asafoetida, roast in oil & powder
500 g	salt
1000 ml	oil

1. Make a hole at the rear end of each chilli and seed.
2. Combine the spice powders with a little oil to a paste.
3. Stuff the spice paste into the chillies with the help of a toothpick.
4. Sun the chillies for 4 days.
5. Transfer to a jar and cover with oil.
6. The pickle is ready for use. It lasts for 2 months. Sun occasionally.

457 Fresh Red Chilli in Tomato Sauce : Hot

500 g	fresh red chillies, keep whole
200 g	salt, combine with 1000ml water
50 g	white mustard seeds, sun-dry & powder
5 g	chilli powder
25 g	salt : for pickle
150 ml	lime juice
20 ml	tomato sauce
100 ml	oil

1. Drop the chillies into the salt solution. Cover and set aside for 15 days.
2. Remove and sun-dry till the water completely evaporates.
3. Cut into pieces, transfer to a jar and sun for 4 days.
4. Heat the oil and remove. Blend in the chilli, mustard powders, salt and the tomato sauce.
5. Add in the dried salted chillies and mix thoroughly.
6. Stir in the lime juice and cook the mixture over low heat.
7. Remove when the mixture begins to bubble.
8. The pickle is ready for use. It lasts for 6 months. Sun occasionally.

458 Fresh Red Chilli – Fenugreek : Hot

1 kg	fresh red chillies
250 g	cleaned tamarind
50 g	fenugreek seeds &
15 g	asafoetida, roast both in oil & powder
400 g	salt
400 ml	oil

1. Grind together the red chillies, salt and tamarind coarsely. Set aside for 2 days.
2. On the 3rd day remove the twigs from the ground mixture and pound again.
3. Add in the fenugreek, asafoetida powders and grind once more. Blend in the oil.
4. The pickle is ready for use after a week. It lasts for 1 year.

459 Sour Spiced Garlic : Hot

500 g	peeled garlic	60 g	jaggery, grate
25 g	chilli powder	5 g	mustard seeds: for seasoning
5 g	cummin seeds;		
5 g	fenugreek seeds &	200 ml	lime juice
5 g	mustard seeds, dry-roast all three & powder	50 g	salt
		200 ml	oil

1. Heat a little oil, add mustard seeds and allow to crackle.
2. Add in the peeled garlic and cook over low heat till tender.
3. Stir in all the spice powders, jaggery, salt, the remaining oil and blend well.
4. Pour in the lime juice after the jaggery has melted.
5. Remove when the mixture begins to bubble.
6. The pickle is ready for use after 3 days. It lasts for 1 month. Sun occasionally.

460 Spicy Hill Garlic in Lime Juice : Hot

500 g	peeled hill garlic, chop & dry in mild sun	15 g	fenugreek seeds, roast in oil & powder;
800 ml	lime juice	300 g	salt &
100 g	chilli powder;	200 ml	oil, combine all evenly

1. Combine the garlic and lime juice in a wide mouthed container. Sun for 3 days.
2. Add in the spice mixture, mix thoroughly and sun for 7 days.
3. The pickle is ready for use. It lasts for 1 month.

461 Garlic – Pepper – Tamarind : Hot

500 g	peeled garlic, chop	10 g	split husked blackgram, roast in oil till golden
150 g	cleaned tamarind, obtain thick extract using water		
		5 g	mustard seeds &
		a few	sprigs curry leaves : both for seasoning
60 g	jaggery, grate		
30 g	peppercorns, powder coarsely	50 g	salt
10 g	turmeric powder	200 ml	oil

1. Stir-fry the chopped garlic, pepper powder in a little oil and set aside.
2. In the same pan heat some more oil, add mustard seeds and allow to crackle.
3. Stir in the curry leaves, roasted gram, tamarind extract, jaggery, turmeric powder, salt and bring to the boil. Allow to thicken over a high flame.
4. Add in the fried garlic-pepper mixture and cook over low heat.
5. Remove when the mixture becomes jam-like and the oil separates.
6. The pickle is ready for use. It lasts for 1 month.

462 Peppered Sour Garlic : Hot

500 g	peeled garlic, chop
15 g	dried red chillies, roast;
15 g	peppercorns &
15 g	green coriander, wash, air-dry & chop, grind all to a paste
10 g	turmeric powder
125 g	cleaned tamarind, obtain thick extract using water
60 g	jaggery, grate
60 g	salt
200 ml	oil

1. Stir-fry the spice paste in a little oil and set aside.
2. In the same pan heat some more oil, add in the tamarind extract, turmeric powder, jaggery, salt and bring to the boil. Allow to thicken over a high flame.
3. Stir in the fried spice paste and cook over low heat.
4. Remove when the mixture becomes jam-like and the oil separates.
5. The pickle is ready for use. It lasts for 1 month.

463 Spiced Garlic : Hot

500 g	peeled garlic
50 g	jaggery, grate
30 g	cleaned tamarind, obtain thick extract using water
25 g	chilli powder
15 g	fenugreek seeds
50 ml	vinegar, heat & cool
50 g	salt
200 ml	oil

1. Heat a little oil, add fenugreek seeds and allow to crackle.
2. Follow with the peeled garlic, stir-fry till tender and set aside.
3. In the same pan heat some more oil, add in the tamarind extract and bring to the boil. Allow to thicken over a high flame.
4. Lower the heat, add in the fried garlic, chilli powder, jaggery, salt and the remaining oil.
5. Continue cooking until the mixture becomes jam-like and the oil separates.
6. Stir in the cooled vinegar and remove.
7. The pickle is ready for use. It lasts for 3 months.

> To peel Garlic easily: a) heat in a dry pan; b) rub oil & place in the sun; c) keep in the fridge, remove & peel; d) place on a chopping board and press its flat side firmly with the palm of the hand or e) apply oil, rub on a rough surface like jute sacking and blow immediately.

464 Sour & Spicy Garlic : Watery

500 g	peeled garlic	5 g	fenugeek seeds : both for seasoning
100 g	dried red chillies;		
10 g	turmeric powder;	40 g	sugar
5 g	fenugreek seeds &	200 ml	vinegar : heat & cool
5 g	cummin seeds, grind all fine		
400 ml	water : boil & cool	150 g	salt
5 g	mustard seeds &	200 ml	oil

1. Steam the peeled garlic till tender, wipe and air-dry.
2. Stir-fry the dried garlic for a few minutes in a little oil and set aside.
3. In the same pan heat some more oil, add the mustard seeds, fenugreek seeds and allow to crackle.
4. Lower the heat and fry the spice paste for a few minutes.
5. Pour in the cooled water and bring to the boil.
6. When the water begins to bubble, stir in the vinegar, sugar, salt and the fried garlic.
7. Continue cooking over a high flame until the mixture thickens and remove.
8. The pickle is ready for use. It lasts for 4 months.

465 Gherkin in Mustard Oil : Hot

500 g	gherkins, make a slit lengthwise
30 g	chilli powder
5 g	asafoetida, roast in oil & powder
5 g	turmeric powder
60 g	salt
30 g	mustard oil

1. Heat a little oil to smoking point. When the oil is still lukewarm blend in the spice powders and salt.
2. Stuff the spice mixture into the gherkins and set aside for 3 days.
3. Pour over the remaining oil and store.
4. The pickle is ready for use after 2 weeks. It lasts for 6 months.

466 Sour Ginger : Hot

500 g	fresh ginger, scrape & chop;
50 g	green chillies;
10 g	dried red chillies &
10	cloves garlic, peel & chop, grind all together fine
120 g	cleaned tamarind, obtain thick extract using water
25 g	jaggery, grate
5 g	mustard seeds, sun-dry & powder
5 g	fenugreek seeds, roast in oil & powder
5 g	turmeric powder
5 g	mustard seeds &
a few	sprigs curry leaves : both for seasoning
120 g	salt
250 ml	oil

1. Stir-fry the ginger-chilli-garlic paste in a little oil and set aside.
2. In the same pan heat some more oil, add mustard seeds and allow to crackle.
3. Add in the curry leaves, tamarind extract, jaggery, turmeric powder, salt and bring to the boil. Allow to thicken over a high flame.
4. Lower the heat, stir in the spice paste and the remaining oil.
5. Continue cooking until the mixture becomes jam-like and the oil separates.
6. Blend in the mustard, fenugreek powders and remove.
7. The pickle is ready for use. It lasts for 2 months.

467 Ginger – Green Chilli in Lime Juice : Hot

125 g	fresh ginger, scrape & grate
25 g	green chillies, chop fine
5 g	mustard seeds, sun-dry & powder
5 g	asafoetida, roast in oil & powder
5 g	turmeric powder
50 ml	lime juice
25 g	salt
50 ml	oil

1. Stir-fry the green chillies and ginger in a little oil till tender.
2. Lower the heat, add in the remaining oil, turmeric powder, salt, lime juice, the remaining oil and blend well.
3. Stir in the mustard, asafoetida powders and remove when the mixture begins to bubble.
4. The pickle is ready for use: It keeps for 15 days and longer in the refrigerator.

468 Sweet & Sour Ginger : Hot

125 g	fresh ginger, scrape & grind
50 g	cleaned tamarind
10 g	jaggery, grate
10 g	dried red chillies, break into bits
5 g	mustard seeds;
a few	sprigs curry leaves &
50 ml	oil : all three for seasoning
40 g	salt

1. Grind the ginger pieces with the red chillies, tamarind and salt very coarsely. Set aside for 3 days.
2. On the 4th day grind the ginger mixture with the jaggery and set aside.
3. This basic pickle lasts for 6 months.
4. Whenever required take the desired quantity of the prepared ginger.
5. Heat a little oil, stir-fry the mustard seeds, curry leaves and remove.
6. Cool and pour the seasoning over the prepared ginger.
7. The pickle is ready for use. It keeps for 15 days.

469 Sweet & Sour Ginge – Garlic : Hot

125 g	fresh ginger, scrape &
125 g	peeled garlic, chop both & grind to a paste
175 g	cleaned tamarind
100 g	jaggery, grate
5 g	fenugreek seeds, roast in oil & powder;
50 g	chilli powder &
5 g	mustard seeds, sun-dry & powder, combine all three evenly
10 g	split husked bengal gram;
10 g	dried red chillies, break into bits;
10 g	mustard seeds &
5 g	fenugreek seeds : all for seasoning
90 g	salt
150 ml	oil : heat & cool

1. Grind the tamarind with the spice mixture.
2. Add in the jaggery, salt, the ginger-garlic paste and grind well.
3. Pour the oil over the mixture and blend well.
4. This basic pickle lasts for 1 year.
5. Heat the oil, add the mustard seeds, fenugreek seeds and allow to crackle. Add in the chillies, gram and fry for a while.
6. Pour the seasoning over the pickle and mix thoroughly.
7. The pickle is ready for use. It keeps for 15 days.

470 Sour Cut Ginger – Green Spices : Hot

500 g	fresh ginger, scrape & chop
250 g	cleaned tamarind, obtain thick extract using water
100 g	jaggery, grate
40 g	green coriander, wash, air-dry & chop
30 g	green chillies, chop
20 g	dried red chillies, break into bits
10 g	turmeric powder
a few	sprigs curry leaves, chop
250 g	salt
300 ml	oil

1. Stir-fry the chopped ginger in a little oil and set aside.
2. In the same pan heat some more oil, add in the red chillies, green chillies, curry leaves and fry for a while.
3. Remove, allow to cool and grind fine with the salt.
4. Heat the remaining oil, pour in the tamarind extract and bring to the boil. Allow to thicken over a high flame.
5. Add in the spice paste, the fried ginger, jaggery and turmeric powder.
6. Continue cooking over low heat until the mixture becomes jam-like and the oil separates.
7. The pickle is ready for use. It lasts for 2 months.

Ginger
Ginger is the pungent rhizome of the ginger plant. Avoid old, withered pieces and buy plump, fair-skinned ones. If fresh and young, the skin can be scraped off with a teaspoon, otherwise peel thinly. Store in a dry, airy basket. It can also be frozen.

471 Ginger in Sweet Vinegar : Watery

500 g	fresh ginger, scrape & slice
100 g	sugar
200 ml	vinegar
30 g	salt

1. Bring the vinegar to boiling. Add in the sugar, salt and stir to dissolve. Remove and allow to cool.
2. Pour the cooled spiced vinegar over the sliced ginger and set aside for 3 days.
3. The pickle lasts for 3 months.

472 Ginger Preserve : Sweet

Preserves are whole small fruit or fruit pieces cooked in sugar syrup until clear and thick.

500 g	ginger preserve, to be fresh & syrupy
400 g	sugar
30 g	peeled garlic, chop;
20 g	seeded dried red chillies &
2-1"	pieces of fresh ginger, scrape & chop, grind all three fine using vinegar
400 ml	vinegar
20 g	salt

1. Cook together the vinegar and sugar till syrupy.
2. Add in the spice paste, salt and simmer for a few minutes.
3. Stir in the ginger preserve (pieces with its syrup) and continue cooking over low heat.
4. Remove when the mixture thickens and reaches a jam-like consistency.
5. The pickle is ready for use. It lasts for 2 months.

473 Spiced Gonkura : Hot

500 g	tender gonkura, remove stems, wash, air-dry & chop
60 g	chilli powder
20 g	coriander seeds &
20 g	cummin seeds, sun-dry both & powder
20 g	cleaned tamarind, obtain thick extract using water
40 g	jaggery, grate
5 g	asafoetida, roast in oil & powder
10 g	turmeric powder
110 g	salt
200 ml	oil

1. Stir-fry the gonkura in very little oil, a few at a time and set aside. The leaves will take about 10 minutes to get cooked.
2. In the same pan heat some more oil, add in the tamarind extract, jaggery, turmeric powder, salt and bring to the boil. Allow to thicken over a high flame.
3. Stir in the fried gonkura and roasted powders.
4. Continue cooking over low heat until the mixture becomes jam-like and the oil separates.
5. The pickle is ready for use. It lasts for 2 months.

474 Gonkura – Onion : Hot

500 g	tender gonkura, remove stems, wash, air-dry & chop
100 g	onion, peel & chop fine
25 g	cleaned tamarind, obtain thick extract using water
50 g	jaggery, grate
75 g	dried red chillies;
5 g	fenugreek seeds &
5 g	asafoetida, roast all three in oil & powder
5 g	turmeric powder
115 g	salt
200 ml	oil

1. Stir-fry the gonkura in very little oil, a few at a time and set aside. The leaves will take about 10 minutes to get cooked.
2. Add in the chopped onion and fry for a few minutes till translucent.
3. Pour in the tamarind extract, jaggery and bring to the boil. Allow to thicken over a high flame.
4. Add in the fried gonkura, powdered spices, turmeric powder and salt.
5. Continue cooking over low heat until the mixture becomes jam-like and the oil separates.
6. The pickle is ready for use. It lasts for 1 month.

475 Gonkura – Coriander Seeds : Hot

500 g	gonkura, remove stems, wash, air-dry & chop fine
50 g	dried red chillies &
15 g	coriander seeds, roast both separately
10 g	cleaned tamarind, obtain thick extract using water
10 g	jaggery, grate
100 g	salt
5 g	mustard seeds &
200 ml	oil : for seasoning

1. Stir-fry the gonkura in very little oil, a few at a time and set aside. The leaves will take about 10 minutes to get cooked.
2. In the same pan heat the remaining oil, add mustard seeds and allow to crackle.
3. Pour in the tamarind extract, jaggery, turmeric powder, salt and bring to the boil. Allow to thicken over a high flame.
4. Add in the fried leaves and the roasted powders.
5. Continue cooking over low heat until the mixture becomes jam-like and the oil separates.
6. The pickle is ready for use. It lasts for 1 month.

476 Gonkura – Garlic - Green Chillies : Hot

500 g	gonkura, remove stems, wash, air-dry & chop fine
125 g	green chillies &
25 g	peeled garlic, chop both & grind together
40 g	split husked black gram
15 g	mustard seeds
a few	sprigs curry leaves
100 g	salt
200 ml	oil

Green and red sorrel leaves are 2 varieties of gonkura, the green being popular due to its pungent taste. Being sticky wash amd air-dry before chopping.

1. Stir-fry the gonkura in very little oil, a few at a time and set aside. The leaves will take about 10 minutes to get cooked.
2. Transfer the fried leaves to a jar, add the salt and set aside for 3 days
3. On the 4th day remove the salted leaves, pound together and store.
4. As and when required, take the desired quantity of the pounded gonkura and grind with the chilli-garlic paste.
5. Heat the oil, add mustard seeds and allow to crackle. Add in the black gram, curry leaves and fry till the gram becomes golden.
6. Blend the seasoning into the ground mixture.
7. The pickle is ready for use after 3 days. It lasts for 1 month.

477 Cut Gooseberry Avakkai : Hot

1 kg	gooseberry, cut & seed
400 g	chilli powder;
100 g	mustard seeds, sun-dry & powder;
25 g	turmeric powder &
25 g	fenugreek seeds, dry-roast & powder, combine all evenly
250 g	salt
1000 ml	raw gingelly oil

1. Combine the spice powders with the salt evenly.
2. Dip the cut gooseberry in the oil, roll in the spice mixture and arrange in a jar.
3. Sprinkle a little spice mixture and pour a little oil over the gooseberry.
4. Repeat this process until all the gooseberry pieces are exhausted.
5. Sprinkle any left over spice mixture over the pickle and set aside for 3 days. Do not stir.
6. On the 4th day, stir well and add the reserved oil to cover the pickle.
7. The pickle is ready for use after 3 weeks. It lasts for 1 year.

478 Gooseberry – Tamarind : Hot

500 g	gooseberry, chop fine & seed
60 g	dried red chillies, roast & powder
50 g	cleaned tamarind, obtain thick extract using water
5 g	asafoetida, roast in oil & powder
5 g	turmeric powder
10 g	mustard seeds : for seasoning
110 g	salt
200 ml	oil

1. Stir-fry the chopped gooseberry in a little oil and set aside.
2. Heat the remaining oil, add mustard seeds and allow to crackle.
3. Stir in the tamarind extract and bring to the boil. Allow to thicken over a high flame.
4. Lower the heat, add the fried gooseberry, turmeric, chilli, asafoetida powders and salt.
5. Continue cooking until the mixture becomes jam-like and the oil separates.
6. The pickle is ready for use. It lasts for 2 months.

479 Spicy Fried Gooseberry : Hot

1 kg	gooseberry, keep whole
400 ml	water
100 g	chilli powder
10 g	asafoetida, roast in oil & powder
10 g	turmeric powder
10 g	mustard seeds : for seasoning
220 g	salt
50 ml	oil

1. Heat the oil, add mustard seeds and allow to crackle. Add in the gooseberries and fry for a few minutes.
2. Stir in the spice powders, salt and fry for a few seconds.
3. Immediately add 400ml water and bring to the boil.
4. Continue cooking until the gooseberries are cooked and all the water has evaporated. Ensure that the gooseberries are dry but not fried.
5. The pickle is ready for use after 10 days. It lasts for 1 year.

480 Cooked Gooseberry in Lime Juice : Hot

500 g	gooseberry, steam, cut & seed		
50 g	chilli powder		
5 g	fenugreek seeds &		
5 g	asafoetida, roast both in oil & powder		
5 g	mustard seeds : for seasoning		
60 ml	lime juice	120 g	salt
10 ml	vinegar	200 ml	oil

1. Heat a little oil, add mustard seeds and allow to crackle.
2. Add in the cooked gooseberry and stir-fry for 2 minutes.
3. Stir in the salt and the spice powders.
4. Blend in the remaining oil (after heating), lime juice and vinegar.
5. Remove the mixture when it begins to bubble.
6. The pickle is ready for use after a day. It lasts for 1 month.

481 Ground Gooseberry : Hot

1 kg	gooseberry pulp
150 g	chilli powder
20 g	asafoetida &
10 g	fenugreek seeds, roast both in oil & powder
10 g	turmeric powder
10 g	mustard seeds : for seasoning
2000 ml	water, make a solution with 4g alum
100 ml	vinegar
300 g	salt
400 ml	oil

1. Cook the gooseberry in the alum solution till tender. Wash thoroughly, stone and mash well.
2. Heat a little oil, add mustard seeds and allow to crackle.
3. Add in the mashed gooseberry and cook for a few minutes over low heat.
4. Stir in the spice powders, salt, the remaining oil and continue cooking for a few more minutes.
5. Pour over the vinegar, heat well and remove.
6. The pickle is ready for use after 10 days. It lasts for 1 year.

> Gooseberry being hard in texture and having a slightly bitter taste is generally half-boiled before pickling. They can however be marinated in salt or steamed or sauted in oil before being pickled. For gooseberry preserve (murabba) the Himalayan variety is best suited.

482 Gooseberry Avakkai in Tamarind Sauce : Hot

1 kg	gooseberry, keep whole
150 g	cleaned tamarind, obtain thick extract using water
150 g	chilli powder
50 g	mustard seeds, sun-dry & powder
300 g	salt
600 ml	raw gingelly oil

1. Stir-fry the whole gooseberry in a little oil over low heat, a few at a time and allow to cool.
2. Heat the tamarind extract till bubbles appear and allow to cool. Stir in the fried gooseberry.
3. Add in the chilli, mustard powders, salt, the remaining oil (after heating) and mix thoroughly.
4. The pickle is ready for use after 3 days. It lasts for 1 year.

483 Sour Cut Gooseberry : Hot

500 g	gooseberry, chop fine & seed	5 g	asafoetida, roast in oil & powder
50 g	chilli powder		
25 g	cleaned new tamarind, obtain thick extract using water	5 g	mustard seeds &
		20 ml	oil : both for seasoning
10 g	mustard seeds, sun-dry & powder	125 ml	oil : heat to smoking point & cool
25 ml	lime juice	110 g	salt

1. Heat the tamarind extract to boiling and allow to cool.
2. Combine all the ingredients with the pre-heated oil and the cooked tamarind.
3. Heat 20ml oil, add mustard seeds and allow to crackle. Add in the asafoetida powder and remove.
4. Cool and pour the seasoning over the pickle.
5. The pickle is ready for use after 15 days. It lasts for 6 months.

> Dried red chilies come in several varieties of pungency and colour. To prepare chilli powder of optimum colour and hotness, combine 1kg Tanjore chillies, 1kg Mangalore chillies and 3kgs thin long chillies and powder.

484 Steamed Gooseberry – Garlic : Hot

500 g	gooseberry, keep whole
50 g	peeled garlic, chop
40 g	chilli powder
10 g	mustard seeds;
5 g	cummin seeds &
5 g	split husked black gram, dry-roast all three & powder
5 g	asafoetida, roast in oil & powder
20 g	mustard seeds : for seasoning
200 ml	vinegar
120 g	salt
150 ml	oil

1. Steam the gooseberries till almost tender. Add the salt and sun-dry for 3 days.
2. Stir-fry the garlic in a little oil and set aside.
3. Heat a little oil, add mustard seeds and allow to crackle.
4. Stir in the dry gooseberries and fry for a few minutes.
5. Lower the heat, add in the spice powders, fried garlic, vinegar, the remaining oil, blend well and remove.
6. The pickle is ready for use. It lasts for 6 months.

485 Sour Gooseberry : Hot

500 g	gooseberry
	water sufficient to cover
40 g	chilli powder
5 g	turmeric powder
5 g	asafoetida &
5 g	fenugreek seeds, roast both in oil & powder
10 g	mustard seeds : for seasoning
40 ml	lime juice
125 g	salt
200 ml	oil

1. Bring the water to the boil.
2. Drop the gooseberry into the boiling water for a few minutes, remove and cool.
3. Remove the sections from each gooseberry and deseed.
4. Marinate the cooked gooseberry pieces in the salt and lime juice. Sun-dry for a week.
5. Sprinkle the spice mixture over the dried gooseberries and blend well.
6. Heat the oil, add mustard seeds and allow to crackle.
7. Pour the seasoning over the pickle mixture and stir thoroughly.
8. The pickle is ready for use. It lasts for 2 months.

486 Fried Gooseberry Whole in Oil : Hot

1 kg	gooseberry, keep whole
	water sufficient to cover
60 g	chilli powder
10 g	turmeric powder
225 g	salt
400 ml	oil

1. Bring the water to the boil.
2. Drop the gooseberries into the boiling water and set aside for 10 minutes to soften.
3. Remove the gooseberries from the water with a perforated spoon and allow to dry on a thick cloth.
4. Stir-fry the cooked gooseberry in a little oil. Stir in the chilli, turmeric powders, salt and remove.
5. Use the pickle after 4 days when it turns less thick. It lasts for 1 year.

487 Star Gooseberry Sauce : Hot

500 g	gooseberry
200 ml	water
15 g	chilli powder;
5 g	turmeric powder &
5 g	asafoetida, roast in oil & powder, combine all three evenly
3	dried red chillies, slit & seed
7 g	peppercorns, pound
5 g	mustard seeds &
5 g	fenugreek seeds : both for seasoning
5 g	sugar
135 g	salt
25 ml	oil

1. Bring the water to the boil with the salt, remove and allow to cool.
2. Drop in the gooseberry and transfer to a wide-mouthed vessel.
3. Tie the mouth of the vessel with steamed banana leaves and cook covered until 3/4ths part of the water evaporates.
4. Remove the banana leaves and continue cooking until all the water evaporates. Remove and set aside.
5. Heat the oil, add the mustard seeds, fenugreek seeds and allow to crackle.
6. Add in the dried red chillies, pounded peppercorns, fry for a minute and remove.
7. Blend in the spice mixture and the sugar.
8. Pour the spice mixture over the gooseberry and mix thoroughly.
9. The pickle is ready for use. It lasts for 2 months.

488 Gooseberry – Ginger - Garlic : Hot

1¼ kg	gooseberry	5 g	fenugreek seeds &	10 g	mustard seeds &
40 g	salt : for cooking gooseberry	3 g	cummin seeds, grind all to a paste	5 g	fenugreek seeds : both for seasoning
100 ml	water	15 g	split husked mustard seeds	5 g	turmeric powder
30 g	chilli powder;			5 g	sugar
25 g	peeled garlic;	50 g	peeled garlic, chop	100 ml	vinegar
1-1"	piece of fresh ginger, scrape & chop;	1-1"	piece of fresh ginger, scrape & chop	100 g	salt : for pickle
				100 ml	oil

1. Bring sufficient water to the boil with 75g salt and turmeric powder.
2. Drop in the fresh gooseberry and cook till tender. Wipe and sun-dry for 3 hours till the water evaporates.
3. Heat a little oil, add the mustard seeds, fenugreek seeds and allow to crackle.
4. Add in the garlic, ginger and cook over low heat till partly tender.
5. Follow with the turmeric powder, spice paste, the remaining oil and fry for a few minutes.
6. Pour over the cooled water and bring to the boil.
7. When the water begins to bubble, stir in the vinegar, sugar and salt.
8. Continue cooking, allow to thicken, remove and cool.
9. Drop in the salted gooseberry and stir well. Follow with the husked mustard seeds and mix thoroughly.
10. The pickle is ready for use. It lasts for 4 months. Stir frequently. Sun occasionally.

489 Gooseberry Whole : Watery

500 g	gooseberry, keep whole
2000 ml	water : boil & cool
50 g	chilli powder
5 g	asafoetida, roast in oil & powder
5 g	turmeric powder
5 g	mustard seeds &
20 ml	oil : both for seasoning
150 g	salt

1. Arrange the gooseberries in a jar.
2. Blend the turmeric, asafoetida powders and salt into the cooled water.
3. Pour the spiced water over the gooseberries to cover.
4. Heat the oil, add mustard seeds and allow to crackle.
5. Pour the seasoning over the gooseberry mixture and cap tight.
6. The pickle is ready for use after 2 days. It lasts for 4 months.
7. If at any time the water level goes down, pour over some water (after heating & cooling), to cover the gooseberries. Sun and stir frequently.

490 Curd Gooseberry – Green Chilli : Watery

500 g	gooseberry, steam, cool & seed
500 ml	slightly sour curd, whip with 400ml water & remove cream
60 g	green chillies, chop fine
20 g	chilli powder
5 g	asafoetida, roast in oil & powder
5 g	turmeric powder
5 g	mustard seeds &
a few	sprigs curry leaves : both for seasoning
125 g	salt
50 ml	oil

1. Drop the steamed gooseberry into the whipped curd.
2. Heat the oil, add mustard seeds and allow to crackle.
3. Stir in the green chillies, curry leaves, chilli, turmeric, asafoetida powders and saute for a few minutes.
4. Pour the seasoning over the gooseberry mixture and blend well.
5. The pickle is ready for use after 4 days. It lasts for 1 month and longer in the refrigerator.

491 Gooseberry Preserve : Sweet

1 kg	gooseberry, prick all over with a fork
2 kgs	sugar
30 g	big cardamoms, peel & crush
10 g	lime (pan-ka-chuna)
5 g	saffron strands, soak in warm water
a few	drops saffron essence
40 g	salt

1. Dissolve the lime in water. Drop in the gooseberry and set aside for an hour.
2. Drain out the lime water and wash the gooseberry in 3 to 4 changes of water.
3. Cook in water with salt till tender. Drain and set aside.
4. Boil the sugar in 400ml water to form a thick syrup.
5. Add in the boiled gooseberry, cardamom and cook over low heat till the syrup thickens again.
6. Remove, cool and add the saffron essence.
7. The pickle is ready for use after 15 days. It lasts for 2 years.

492 Fried Gooseberry in Spicy Sauce : Watery

500 g	gooseberry, keep whole	10 g	cummin seeds &
50 g	salt, make a solution with 200ml water	10 g	sesame seeds, sun-dry both & powder
60 g	dried red chillies, roast in oil & powder	10 g	turmeric powder
		80 g	salt : for pickle
		200 ml	oil

1. Fry the whole gooseberries in a little oil till tender. Seed and segment.
2. Marinate the cooked gooseberry pieces in the salt solution for 8 hours.
3. Combine the salt, turmeric powder and powdered spices with water to make a paste.
4. Stir in the salted gooseberry.
5. Add the required measure of salt water of the gooseberry pieces to obtain the necessary semi-thick consistency.
6. The pickle is ready after 10 days. It lasts for 6 months.

493 Spicy Steamed Gooseberry in Curd : Hot

500 g	gooseberry, steam, remove sections & air-dry	5 g	asafoetida, roast in oil &
250 ml	sour curd, whip with 125ml water & remove cream	125 g	salt, grind all three fine
50 g	green chillies;	5 g	mustard seeds &
		a few	sprigs curry leaves : both for seasoning
		5 g	turmeric powder

1. Marinate the steamed gooseberry with the salt and turmeric powder for 2 days.
2. Heat the oil, add mustard seeds and allow to crackle.
3. Add in the curry leaves, spice paste and fry for a few minutes.
4. Stir in the marinated gooseberry and fry for a while.
5. Follow with the whipped curd and remove when the mixture begins to bubble.
6. Ensure that the pan is not too hot, or else the pickle will curdle.
7. The pickle is ready for use. It lasts for 2 months in the refrigerator.

Gooseberry is well known for its high vitamin C content & revitalising effects. However, every kg of whole gooseberry yields only 800g of pieces after seeding.

494 Spiced Gooseberry : Sweet

1 kg	gooseberry, keep whole	2-1"	sticks of cinnamon
500 g	sugar	5	cardamoms
10 g	aniseeds, dry-roast & powder	20 ml	lime juice
5	cloves	80 g	salt

1. Add the salt to the gooseberry, so that it is submerged in it. Set aside for a month.
2. Remove the gooseberry and rub off its papery skin under ordinary water.
3. Sun-dry the gooseberry for 2 days.
4. Lightly heat the sugar in a pan. Pour in the lime juice and blend well over very low heat.
5. Stir in the aniseed powder, gooseberry and continue cooking till well blended.
6. Add in the whole spices and remove.
7. The pickle is ready for use. It lasts for 2 years.

495 Grated Gooseberry : Sweet

1 kg	gooseberry, grate & seed	3 kgs	sugar
		5 g	salt

1. Marinate the grated gooseberry in the salt for a few minutes. Discard the water and air-dry.
2. Heat the gooseberry and the sugar in a pan, stirring continuously. Add no water as the mixture itself will give out water.
3. Simmer gently and stir continuously. Remove when the mixture becomes thick and sticky.
4. The pickle is ready for use after 1 month. It lasts for 2 years.

496 Honeyed Gooseberry : Sweet

1 kg	ripe gooseberry, prick all over with a fork	10 g	edible camphor
1 kg	sugar	5 g	saffron, dissolve in a little milk
800 ml	water	120 ml	honey

1. Heat together the sugar and water till the syrup reaches a single-thread consistency.
2. Remove the dirt by adding a little milk when the syrup boils.
3. Add the pricked gooseberries into the boiling syrup.
4. Stir in the saffron, honey and remove.
5. Add camphor and mix thoroughly.
6. The pickle is ready for use after 1 month. It lasts for 2 years. Stir frequently.

497 Sour Gooseberry – Onion - Raisin : Sweet

1 kg	gooseberry, keep whole	40 g	dried ginger powder
600 g	sugar	5	cardamoms
500 g	seedless raisin, chop	5	cloves
150 g	onion, peel & chop	2-1"	sticks of cinnamon
	water sufficient to cover	400 ml	vinegar
		50 g	salt

1. Cook together the gooseberry and onion in sufficient water till tender.
2. Add in the raisin, salt, dried ginger powder, whole spices, half the vinegar and continue cooking until the mixture thickens.
3. Stir in the sugar, the remaining vinegar and simmer until the mixture reaches a jam-like consistency.
4. The pickle is ready for use after 4 weeks. It lasts for 1 year.

498 Sour Gooseberry – Onion : Sweet

1 kg	gooseberry, halve & seed		
800 g	sugar		
150 g	onion &		
5	cloves garlic, peel & chop both		
5 g	garam masala powder		
400 ml	vinegar		
40 g	salt		

1. Cook the gooseberry with the sugar, onion and garlic.
2. Add in the vinegar and continue cooking.
3. Stir in the salt, garam masala powder and cook till the mixture becomes jam-like.
4. The pickle is ready for use. It lasts for 1 year.

499 Ground Star Gooseberry : Hot

500 g	star gooseberry, cut & seed
45 g	chilli powder
25 g	split husked blackgram
30 g	jaggery, grate
10 g	asafoetida, roast in oil & powder
5 g	mustard seeds : for seasoning
100 g	salt
200 ml	oil

1. Grind together coarsely all the ingredients except mustard seeds.
2. Heat a little oil, add mustard seeds and allow to crackle.
3. Stir in the asafoetida, fenugreek powders, the remaining oil and remove.
4. The pickle is ready for use. It lasts for 2 months.

500 Star Gooseberry – Green Chilli : Hot

1 kg	star gooseberry, chop & seed	10 g	fenugreek seeds, roast both in oil & powder
200 g	green chillies, chop	60 ml	vinegar : heat & cool
20 g	mustard seeds: for seasoning	200 g	salt
10 g	asafoetida &	400 ml	oil

1. Marinate the chopped star gooseberry in salt for a while.
2. Heat the oil, add mustard seeds and allow to crackle.
3. Add in the chopped green chillies, salted star gooseberry along with the salt water and fry for a few minutes.
4. Stir in the asafoetida, fenugreek powders and remove.
5. When cool, pour over the pre-heated vinegar and mix thoroughly.
6. The pickle is ready for use after a day. It lasts for 1 year.

501 Sour & Spicy Green Chilli : Hot

500g	green chillies, slit
15g	mustard seeds &
10g	peppercorns, sun-dry both & powder
10g	fenugreek seeds &
5g	asafoetida, roast both in oil & powder
125ml	lime juice
125g	salt
300ml	oil

1. Stir-fry the green chillies in a little oil till tender.
2. Add in the roasted spice powders, salt and mix thoroughly.
3. When the mixture has cooled, add in the lime juice, the remaining oil (after heating) and stir well.
4. Cap tight and set aside for 6 weeks.
5. The pickle is ready for use. It lasts for 3 months.

502 Fried Green Chilli in Vinegar : Hot

500 g	green chillies, slit		
20 g	peeled garlic, chop;		
30 g	fresh ginger, scrape & chop;		
20 g	cummin seeds;		
5 g	mustard seeds &		
5 g	fenugreek seeds, grind all to a paste		
20 g	sugar	200 g	salt
250 ml	vinegar	200 ml	oil

1. Sprinkle the salt over the chillies, cover and set aside overnight.
2. The following day rinse the chillies in water and shake dry.
3. Stir-fry the spice paste in a little oil for a few minutes.
4. Add in the slit chillies, salt, sugar and vinegar, a little by little.
5. Continue cooking over a high flame adding the remaining oil till the chillies are cooked.
6. The pickle is ready for use. It lasts for 6 months.

503 Green Chilli in Tamarind Sauce : Hot

500 g	green chillies, slit
250 g	cleaned tamarind, obtain thick extract using water
130 g	jaggery, grate
40 g	fresh ginger, scrape & chop fine
20 g	chilli powder
5 g	asafoetida, roast in oil & powder
5 g	turmeric powder
5 g	mustard seeds : for seasoning
40 ml	lime juice
200 g	salt
200 ml	oil

1. Heat a little oil, add mustard seeds and allow to crackle.
2. Add in the cut green chillies, chilli, asafoetida powders, ginger and fry for a while.
3. Stir in the tamarind extract, jaggery, turmeric powder, salt, the remaining oil and allow to thicken over a high flame.
4. Continue cooking over low heat until the mixture becomes jam-like and the oil seperates.
5. Pour in the lime juice and remove when the mixture begins to bubble.
6. The pickle is ready for use the next day. It lasts for 2 months.

504 Sweet & Sour Green Chilli – Green Coriander : Hot

500 g	green chillies, chop
200 g	green coriander, wash, air-dry & chop
250 g	cleaned tamarind
130 g	jaggery, grate
20 g	chilli powder
10 g	asafoetida, roast in oil & powder
10 g	split husked black gram, dry-roast & powder
5 g	mustard seeds, sun-dry & powder
5 g	turmeric powder
200 g	salt
200 ml	oil

1. Stir-fry the chopped green chillies, coriander in a little oil and set aside.
2. Grind the tamarind with the salt coarsely.
3. Add in the fried green chillies, coriander and grind fine.
4. Blend in the spice powders, jaggery and the remaining oil (after heating & cooling).
5. The pickle is ready for use after 2 days. It lasts for 6 months.

505 Ground Green Chilli : Hot

500 g	green chillies, chop & grind coarsely
250 g	cleaned tamarind, obtain thick extract using water
130 g	jaggery, grate
40 g	mustard seeds : for seasoning
20 g	chilli powder
10 g	turmeric powder
5 g	fenugreek seeds &
5 g	asafoetida, roast in oil & powder
200 g	salt
200 ml	oil

1. Stir-fry the green chilli paste in a little oil till the moisture evaporates and set aside.
2. In the same pan heat some more oil, add mustard seeds and allow to crackle.
3. Pour in the tamarind extract, jaggery, turmeric powder, salt and bring to the boil. Allow to thicken over a high flame.
4. Lower the heat, add in the fried green chillies, chilli powder, asafoetida, fenugreek powders and the remaining oil.
5. Continue cooking over low heat until the mixture becomes jam-like and the oil separates.
6. The pickle is ready for use. It lasts for 3 months.

506 Green Chilli – Onion : Hot

500 g	green chillies &	10 g	mustard seeds;
300 g	onion, peel, chop both & grind together	10 g	split husked black gram &
		a few	sprigs curry leaves : all three for seasoning
250 g	cleaned tamarind, obtain thick extract using water		
		40 g	sugar
20 g	chilli powder	200 g	salt
10 g	turmeric powder	200 ml	oil

1. Heat a little oil, add mustard seeds and allow to crackle. Add in the curry leaves, black gram and fry till the gram turns golden.
2. Add in the spice paste and fry for a few minutes.
3. Stir in the tamarind extract, sugar, salt, chilli, turmeric powders and bring to the boil.
4. Allow to thicken over a high flame and add in the remaining oil.
5. Continue cooking over low heat until the mixture becomes jam-like and the oil separates.
6. The pickle is ready for use. It lasts for 1 month.

507 Green Chilli – Mango – Mustard : Hot

500 g	green chillies, slit	10 g	turmeric powder &
50 g	dried mango powder	10 g	asafoetida, roast in oil & powder, combine evenly
50 g	mustard seeds, sun-dry & powder;		
10 g	fenugreek seeds, roast in oil & powder;	175 g	salt
		200 ml	oil : heat & cool

1. Combine the green chillies and the spice mixture thoroughly.
2. Sprinkle the salt, the dried mango powder and stir well.
3. Pour over the pre-heated oil to cover the pickle. Sun and stir the pickle for 5 days.
4. The pickle lasts for 4 months.

508 Green Chilli – Mango – Thymol Seeds : Hot

500 g	long fat green chillies	40 g	jaggery, grate
		20 g	chilli powder
500 g	seeded raw mango, peel & grate	10 g	turmeric powder
		250 g	salt
60 g	thymol seeds	250 ml	oil

1. Stir-fry the thymol seeds in a little oil till done.
2. Add in the cut green chillies, grated mango, jaggery and fry for a few minutes.
3. Stir in the salt, chilli, turmeric powders and remove when the mixture leaves the sides of the pan.
4. The pickle is ready for use after a day. It lasts for 1 month.

509 Sweet & Sour Mustard Green Chilli : Hot

500 g	green chillies, retain stem & slit	5 g	fenugreek seeds &
10 g	mint leaves, wash, air-dry & chop	5 g	asafoetida, roast both in oil & powder
5	cloves garlic, peel & chop	5 g	poppy seeds, grind
60 g	chilli powder		
20 g	mustard seeds &	150 g	jaggery, grate
5 g	cummin seeds, sun-dry both & powder	250 ml	vinegar
		200 g	salt
5 g	turmeric powder	100 ml	oil

1. Fry the green chillies in a little oil over low heat till they turn pale and white.
2. Add in the chopped garlic, mint, ground poppy seeds and fry for a minute.
3. Stir in the spice powders and stir-fry for a few seconds.
4. Add in the vinegar, jaggery, salt, the remaining oil and remove after the jaggery melts.
5. The pickle is ready for use after 2 days. It lasts for 2 months.

510 Sweet & Sour Green Chilli – Sesame : Hot

500 g	green chillies, slit	20 g	fenugreek seeds, roast both in oil & powder
250 g	cleaned tamarind, obtain thick extract using water		
		200 g	salt
125 g	jaggery, grate	200 ml	groundnut oil: heat & cool
50 g	sesame seeds &		

1. Stir-fry the chillies in a part of the oil till they change colour.
2. Add in the tamarind extract, jaggery and bring to the boil. Allow to thicken over a high flame.
3. Stir in the spice powders, salt and the remaining oil.
4. Continue cooking over low heat until the mixture becomes jam-like and the oil separates.
5. The pickle is ready for use. It lasts for 6 months.
6. Sun and stir occasionally.

511 Green Chilli Spice Stuffed: Hot

500 g	green chillies, slit
50 g	dried mango powder;
50 g	mustard seeds, sun-dry & powder;
15 g	aniseeds, sun-dry & powder;
15 g	fenugreek seeds, roast in oil & powder;
15 g	turmeric powder;
a few	sprigs curry leaves &
125 g	salt, combine all evenly
250 ml	groundnut oil: heat & cool

1. Stuff the spice mixture into the chillies.
2. Sprinkle the remaining spice mixture over the chillies and stir thoroughly.
3. Pour the pre-heated oil over the pickle and sun the pickle for 7 days.
4. The pickle is ready for use. It lasts for 2 months. Sun occasionally.

512 Large Green Chilli in Mustard Oil: Hot

500 g	large green chillies, slit
15 g	mustard seeds, sun-dry & powder
a few	sprigs curry leaves
20 g	sugar
150 ml	lime juice
125 g	salt
200 ml	mustard oil: heat & cool

1. Combine the green chillies with the salt and lime juice. Sun the mixture for 3 days.
2. Combine the spiced chillies with the mustard powder, sugar, curry leaves, the cooled oil and sun for 7 days.
3. The pickle is ready for use. It lasts for 3 months. Sun occasionally.

513 Green Chilli – Garlic: Hot

125 g	green chillies, slit & keep stem end intact	30 g	salt, pound both together
25 g	peeled garlic &	25 ml	coconut oil

1. Stuff the pounded garlic mixture into the slit chillies and stir-fry in the oil.
2. Cool and pack in a jar. Pour over the remaining oil and blend well.
3. The pickle is ready for use. It keeps for 15 days.

514 Large Green Chilli – Mango – Green Coriander Stuffed: Hot

500 g	large green chillies, large sized		
250 g	seeded raw mango, peel & grate		
250 g	green coriander, wash, air-dry & chop		
1-1"	piece of fresh ginger, scrape & grind		
2	cloves garlic, peel & grind		
5 g	mustard seeds, sun-dry & powder		
5 g	turmeric powder		
5 g	cummin seeds: for seasoning	200 g	salt
		200 ml	oil

1. Remove the stalks off the chillies. Make a slit in the middle of each.
2. Fry the cummin seeds in half the oil. Follow with the ginger-garlic paste, chopped coriander, fry for a few minutes and remove.
3. Stir in the mustard, turmeric powders, grated mango, salt and blend well.
4. Stuff the spice mixture into the chillies and pack tight in a jar. Pour over the reserved oil.
5. Sun the pickle for 2 days with the mouth of the jar tied with a thin cloth.
6. The pickle is ready for use after 4 days. It lasts for 6 months. Sun occasionally.

515 Sour Green Chilli – Ginger: Sweet

500 g	green chillies, slit & keep stem end intact		
125 g	cleaned tamarind, obtain thick extract with 600ml vinegar		
400 g	sugar		
100 g	fresh ginger, scrape &		
25 g	peeled garlic, chop both & grind to a paste		
50 g	dried red chillies, roast in oil & powder		
25 g	mustard seeds, sun-dry & powder;		
25 g	cummin seeds &		
10 g	fenugreek seeds, dry-roast both & powder, combine all three	5 g	garam masala powder
		250 g	salt
		350 ml	oil

1. Stir-fry the ginger-garlic paste in a little oil for a few minutes and set aside.
2. In the same pan heat some more oil, add in the green chillies and fry for a few minutes.
3. Pour in the tamarind extract, sugar, salt and bring to the boil. Allow to thicken over a high flame.
4. Stir in the fried paste, powdered spices and the remaining oil.
5. Continue cooking over low heat until the mixture becomes jam-like and the oil separates.
6. The pickle is ready for use. It lasts for 2 months.

516 Sweet & Sour Green Chilli – Tamarind : Hot

- 500 g green chillies, slit;
- 250 g cleaned tamarind;
- 125 g jaggery, grate;
- 5 g asafoetida, roast in oil;
- 5 g turmeric powder &
- 200 g salt, grind all together coarsely
- 50 ml oil
- 30 g roasted groundnut, skin & powder
- 30 g sesame seeds, dry-roast & crush
- 25 g dried red chillies, roast in oil
- 10 g mustard seeds: for seasoning

1. Add the roasted powders to the green chilli mixture and grind fine.
2. Heat a little oil, add mustard seeds and allow to crackle.
3. Stir in the ground mixture and fry until the mixture leaves the sides of the pan.
4. The pickle is ready for use. It lasts for 2 months.

517 Garlic Mustard – Green Chilli : Hot

- 500 g green chillies, remove stem & slit
- 60 g peeled garlic, chop;
- 20 g mustard seeds, sun-dry;
- 125 g salt &
- 10 g turmeric powder, grind all to a paste
- 5 g fenugreek seeds : for seasoning
- 125 ml lime juice
- 20 ml water
- 150 ml oil

1. Heat a little oil, add fenugreek seeds and allow to crackle.
2. Stir-fry the green chillies for a few minutes till soft.
3. Add in the spice paste, 20ml water, lime juice and the remaining oil.
4. Continue cooking over low heat until the mixture leaves the sides of the pan.
5. The pickle is ready for use. It lasts for 3 months and is best refrigerated.

518 Sour Green Chilli – Green Spices : Hot

- 500 g green chillies, chop
- 100 g fresh ginger, scrape &
- 50 g peeled garlic, grind both together
- 25 g coriander seeds, sun-dry & powder
- 200 ml lime juice
- 150 g salt
- 75 ml oil

1. Heat a little oil, add mustard seeds and allow to crackle.
2. Add in the ginger-garlic paste and stir-fry for a few minutes.
3. Follow with the chopped green chillies, salt, the remaining oil and continue cooking till well blended.
4. Pour over the lime juice and stir thoroughly.
5. Remove when the mixture begins to bubble and sun-dry for an hour.
6. The pickle is ready for use after a day. It lasts for 6 months.

519 Spicy Green Chilli – Mint : Hot

- 500 g green chillies, slit
- 15 g mint leaves, wash, air-dry & chop
- 15 g jaggery, grate
- 5 cloves garlic, peel & chop
- 12 g chilli powder
- 10 g mustard seeds;
- 5 g cummin seeds;
- 3 g aniseeds &
- 3 g thymol seeds, dry-roast all & powder
- 5 g turmeric powder
- 5 g fenugreek seeds, roast in oil & powder
- 150 ml vinegar
- 150 g salt
- 25 ml oil

1. Fry the slit green chillies in the oil till they turn white in colour.
2. Stir in the chopped mint, garlic and fry for a few minutes.
3. Add in the spice powders, jaggery, salt and the vinegar.
4. Continue cooking over low heat for a few minutes and remove.
5. The pickle is ready for use after 2 days. It lasts for 1 month. Sun occasionally.

> Green Chillies come in several grades of pungency but the very small ones called *Usi Milagai* are sheer dynamite. However, for chilli pickles, less spicy chillies are the most suitable. Chillies are rich in vitamin C and have anti-bacterial properties. Small amounts of chillies stimulate a debilitated appetite too.

520 Green Chilli – Mustard - Mango Stuffed : Hot

- 500 g green chillies, slit into 2
- 50 g dried mango powder
- 50 g mustard seeds &
- 8 g aniseeds, sun-dry both & powder
- 5 g fenugreek seeds, roast in oil & powder
- 5 g turmeric powder
- 125 g salt
- 200 ml oil : heat & cool

1. Combine the spice powders (except the dried mango powder & salt) evenly.
2. Stuff the spice powders into the green chillies and set aside.
3. Sprinkle the dried mango powder, salt over the stuffed green chillies and shake well.
4. Pour the pre-heated oil over the mixture to cover.
5. The pickle is ready for use after 5 days. It lasts for 3 months. Sun occasionally.

521 Green Chilli – Ginger Blend : Hot

- 500 g green chillies &
- 125 g salt, grind both together
- 100 g fresh ginger, scrape & grind
- 125 g cleaned tamarind, obtain thick extract using water
- 100 g jaggery, grate
- 10 g mustard seeds &
- a few sprigs curry leaves: both for seasoning
- 5 g asafoetida &
- 5 g fenugreek seeds, roast both in oil & powder
- 5 g turmeric powder
- 200 ml oil

1. Stir-fry the ginger paste in a little oil and set aside.
2. Heat the remaining oil, add mustard seeds and allow to crackle. Add in the curry leaves, green chilli paste and fry for a few minutes.
3. Pour in the tamarind extract, jaggery, turmeric powder and bring to the boil. Allow to thicken over a high flame.
4. Add in the ginger paste, fenugreek and asafoetida powders.
5. Continue cooking over low heat until the mixture becomes jam-like and the oil separates.
6. The pickle is ready for use. It lasts for 2 months.

522 Tanjore Green Chilli in Tamarind Sauce : Hot

- 500 g green chillies, wash, wipe, air-dry, remove stems & slit
- 250 g cleaned tamarind, obtain thick extract using water
- 50 g mustard seeds, sun-dry;
- 50 g cummin seeds, dry-roast;
- 35 g fenugreek seeds, roast in oil &
- 10 g asafoetida, roast in oil & powder all together
- 10 g mustard seeds
- 175 g salt
- 200 ml oil

1. Measure the volume of roasted spices and take an equal measure of salt.
2. Bring the tamarind extract to the boil, allow to thicken and remove.
3. Combine with the spice powders and the salt to a paste.
4. Stuff the spice paste into the slit green chillies.
5. Heat a little oil, add mustard seeds and allow to crackle.
6. Stir in the stuffed green chillies, the remaining oil and the spice paste, if any.
7. Cook covered over low heat until the chillies become tender and the oil separates.
8. Cool and pack tight in a jar and sun occasionally.
9. The pickle is ready for use. It lasts for 2 months.

523 Sour & Spicy Green Chilli – Tamarind : Hot

- 500 g green chillies, slit
- 250 g cleaned tamarind, obtain thick extract using water
- 50 g sesame seeds, pound coarsely
- 10 g fenugreek seeds, roast in oil & powder
- 5 g mustard seeds, sun-dry & powder
- 5 g mustard seeds
- 15 ml vinegar
- 200 g salt
- 250 ml oil

1. Heat a little oil, pour in the tamarind extract and bring to the boil. Allow to thicken and remove.
2. In the same pan, heat some more oil, add the mustard seeds, pounded sesame seeds and allow to crackle.
3. Add in the slit green chillies and fry for a few minutes until brown in colour.
4. Stir in the fenugreek, mustard powders, tamarind extract and vinegar.
5. Continue cooking until the mixture is well blended and the oil separates.
6. The pickle is ready for use. It lasts for 2 months.

524 Stuffed Spicy Green Chilli : Hot

500 g	green chillies, slit
15 g	aniseeds &
15 g	onion seeds, dry-roast both & powder
150 ml	lime juice
10 g	mustard seeds, sun-dry & powder
5 g	asafoetida, roast in oil & powder
175 g	salt
200 ml	oil

1. Combine the powdered ingredients with the salt evenly.
2. Stuff the spice into the slit mixture green chillies and transfer to a jar.
3. Pour over the oil and the lime juice. Blend well and sun for 10 days.
4. The pickle is ready for use. It lasts for two months. Sun occasionally.

525 Stuffed Mustard – Green Chilli : Hot

500 g	green chillies, slit
15 g	mustard seeds, sun-dry & powder
5 g	turmeric powder
125 ml	lime juice
125 g	salt
25 ml	oil

1. Combine the mustard, turmeric powders with the salt and oil to a paste.
2. Stuff the spice paste into the slit green chillies.
3. Pour over the lime juice and blend well.
4. The pickle is ready for use after 1 week. It lasts for 2 months. Sun occasionally.

526 Green Chilli – Tamarind : Sweet

500 g	green chillies, cut into large pieces
150 g	cleaned tamarind, soak in vinegar for 3 hrs & obtain thick extract
200 ml	vinegar
5	cloves garlic, peel &
2-1"	pieces of fresh ginger, scrape, chop both & grind to a paste
15 g	cummin seeds &
15 g	fenugreek seeds, roast both in oil & powder
250 g	sugar
200 g	salt
200 ml	oil

1. Stir-fry the ginger-garlic paste in a little oil for a few minutes.
2. Pour in the tamarind extract, sugar, vinegar, the remaining oil and cook for a few minutes.
3. Add in the cut green chillies, spice powders and cook till the mixture thickens.
4. Remove when the mixture reaches a jam-like consistency and the oil separates.
5. The pickle is ready for use. It lasts for 6 months.

527 Green Gram – Mango : Hot

125 g	split green gram, dry-roast & powder coarsely
125 g	seeded raw mango, peel & chop fine
40 g	chilli powder
20 g	mustard seeds, sun-dry & powder
5 g	fenugreek seeds, roast in oil & powder
60 g	salt
300 ml	oil : heat & cool

1. Combine the spice powders, gram powder with the salt and oil.
2. Sprinkle some spice mixture in a jar and pour over a little oil.
3. Dip a few mango pieces in the oil, roll in the spice mixture and arrange in the jar.
4. Follow with a layer of the spice mixture and pour over a little oil.
5. Repeat this process until the mango pieces are exhausted.
6. Sprinkle the remaining spice mixture over the pickle and set aside for 3 days.
7. On the 4th day stir the pickle thoroughly and pour over the remaining oil to cover.
8. The pickle is ready for use after 15 days. It lasts for 1 year.

Note: Green Gram is one of the several varieties of legumes or dals, very nutritive and rich in protein and potassium. Wash several times under cold running water before cooking and soak overnight to save cooking time.

528 Ripe Black Grape : Sweet

125 g	ripe black grape, slit & seed
75 g	jaggery, grate
1-1"	piece of fresh ginger, scrape & chop;
8 g	chilli powder;
5 g	turmeric powder &
15 g	salt, grind all together fine
3 g	fenugreek seeds &
3 g	asafoetida, roast both in oil & powder
25 ml	oil

1. Sun-dry the black grapes for an hour.
2. Heat oil and melt the jaggery over low heat.
3. Add in the grapes, the spice paste and the powdered spices. Blend well over low heat and remove.
4. The pickle is ready for use. It keeps for 10 days and is best refrigerated.

529 Raw Groundnut – Coconut Mango : Hot

500 g	shelled raw groundnut, mince
200 g	seeded raw mango, peel & chop
100 g	grated coconut
50 g	green chillies, chop
20 g	mustard seeds, sun-dry & powder;
10 g	chilli powder &
80 g	salt, combine all three evenly
5 g	mustard seeds : for seasoning
5 g	asafoetida, roast in oil & powder
200 ml	oil

1. Combine the minced groundnuts, chopped mango and the grated coconut.
2. Blend in the spice mixture, transfer to a wide-mouthed jar and sun for 3 days.
3. Heat a little oil, add mustard seeds and allow to crackle. Stir in the asafoetida powder, green chillies and fry for a while.
4. Pour the seasoning over the pickle along with the remaining oil and mix thoroughly.
5. The pickle is ready for use after 7 days. It lasts for 1 month in the refrigerator.

530 Spiced Raw Groundnut – Mango : Hot

500 g	raw groundnut, peel
400 g	seeded raw mango, peel & chop fine
50 g	dried red chillies &
10 g	mustard seeds, sun-dry both & powder coarsely
10 g	aniseeds;
10 g	onion seeds &
10 g	cummin seeds, dry-roast all three & powder
10 g	fenugreek seeds &
10 g	asafoetida, roast both in oil & powder
10 g	turmeric powder
100 g	salt
300 ml	oil

1. Marinate the chopped mango and groundnut in a little salt for a whole day.
2. Next day drain the salt water and sun-dry the groundnut and the mango pieces.
3. Heat the oil to smoking point. When the oil is still lukewarm, blend in the spice powders and the powdered spices.
4. Add in the salted groundnut, mango and mix well.
5. Pour over the salt water and top up with the remaining oil.
6. The pickle is ready for use. It lasts for 2 months. Sun frequently.

531 Guava in Tamarind Sauce : Hot

500 g	guava, half ripe
40 g	cleaned tamarind, obtain thick extract using water
20 g	jaggery, grate
20 g	dried red chillies;
10 g	fenugreek seeds &
10 g	asafoetida, roast all three in oil & powder
10 g	turmeric powder
10 g	mustard seeds : for seasoning
30 g	salt
20 ml	oil

1. Cut the guavas into half. Scoop out the seed portion and grate thickly.
2. Stir-fry the grated guava in a little oil till almost tender and set aside.
3. In the same pan heat the remaining oil, add mustard seeds and allow to crackle.
4. Pour in the tamarind extract, jaggery, turmeric powder and bring to the boil. Allow to thicken over a high flame.
5. Stir in the chilli, fenugreek, asafoetida powders, salt and the fried guava.
6. Continue cooking over low heat until the mixture becomes jam-like and the oil separates.
7. The pickle is ready for use. It lasts for 1 month and is best refrigerated.

532 Ripe Jackfruit – Mustard - Aniseed : Hot

500 g	ripe jackfruit segments
15 g	mustard seeds &
10 g	aniseeds, sun-dry both & powder
10 g	chilli powder
5 g	turmeric powder
25 g	salt
50 ml	oil : heat & cool

1. Soak the jackfruit segments in water for one hour.
2. Remove and steam till tender. Pat-dry on a thick towel and sun-dry for 3 days.
3. Combine the remaining ingredients with the dried jackfruit and sun the mixture for 2 more days.
4. Pour the pre-heated oil over the mixture to cover and again sun the mixture for 7 days.
5. The pickle lasts for 2 months.

> These are two varieties of **jackfruit** the thin, smaller sweeter variety and the fleshier, less sweet variety. The larger ones are more suitable for pickling, as they are thicker and firmer.

533 Musard jackfruit : Hot

500 g	mature raw jackfruit, peel & cut into big pieces
20 g	chilli powder
20 g	mustard seeds, sun-dry & powder
10 g	turmeric powder
5 g	garam masala powder
50 g	salt
125 ml	oil : heat & cool

1. Marinate the jackfruit pieces in the salt, turmeric powder and sun for 2 days.
2. Combine the mustard, chilli, garam masala powders with a little oil to a paste.
3. Stir in the salted jackfruit pieces, the remaining oil and transfer to a jar.
4. Sun and stir the mixture for 7 days.
5. Use the pickle after 3 days. It lasts for 3 months.

534 Steamed Raw Jackfruit : Hot

125 g	mature raw jackfruit segments, seed & chop	3 g	asafoetida, roast in oil & powder
10 g	chilli powder	5 g	mustard seeds : for seasoning
3 g	turmeric powder	12 g	salt
		25 ml	oil

1. Steam the chopped jackfruit with a teaspoon (5g) salt till tender. Remove and allow to cool.
2. Heat the oil, add mustard seeds and allow to crackle. Add in the chopped jackfruit and fry for a few minutes over low heat.
3. Blend in the spice powders, salt and set aside for a day.
4. The pickle keeps for 2 weeks and is best refrigerated.

535 Spicy Jackfruit : Sweet

500 g	salted ripe jackfruit
7 g	onion &
3	cloves garlic, peel & chop both
1-1"	piece of fresh ginger, scrape & chop
20 g	chilli powder
3 g	mustard seeds
3 g	cummin seeds
3	cloves
3	cardamoms
1-1"	stick of cinnamon
50 g	sugar
50 ml	vinegar
50 g	salt
125 ml	oil

1. Heat the oil, add mustard seeds and allow to crackle.
2. Add in the ginger, garlic, onion and fry for a few minutes till the onion becomes translucent.
3. Stir in the chilli powder, cummin seeds, salt, whole spices, salted jackfruit and transfer to a jar.
4. Sun the mixture for 4 days and stir occasionally.
5. Blend in the sugar, vinegar and again sun the mixture for 4 days.
6. Pour the remaining oil over the mixture after heating and cooling.
7. The pickle is ready for use. It lasts for 3 months.

Preparation of salted jackfruit

a. Marinate the jackfruit pieces with 8% salt water. Ensure that the pieces are immersed in the salt water.
b. Add 1% salt daily, till the salt level reaches 15%. This will take 7 days.
c. Set the pieces aside for 10 days.

536 Spicy Kalakkai : Sweet

500 g	kalakkai, remove stems	5 g	mustard seeds;
250 g	jaggery, grate	3 g	fenugreek seeds & aniseeds, dry-roast all together & powder
50 g	chilli powder	3 g	
10 g	turmeric powder		
5 g	cummin seeds;	50 g	salt
5 g	onion seeds;	200 ml	oil

1. Coat the kalakkai with the mixture comprising chilli, turmeric powders and half the salt.
2. Sun the spiced kalakkai for 4 hours.
3. Melt the jaggery over low heat. Add in the kalakkai, the remaining salt, stir well and remove.
4. Immediately add in the remaining spice powders, the remaining oil (after heating & cooling) and mix thoroughly.
5. Keep the pickle for 5 days in the sun and for a further 5 days indoors.
6. The pickle lasts for 2 months.

537 Spicy Small Kalakkai: Hot

500 g	small kalakkai, remove stems, cut lengthwise & seed
60 g	chilli powder
10 g	mustard seeds, sun-dry & powder
5 g	fenugreek seeds &
5 g	asafoetida, roast both in oil & powder
5 g	turmeric powder
125 g	salt
200 ml	oil

1. Stir-fry the kalakkai in a little oil over low heat till almost tender.
2. Heat the remaining oil to smoking point. When the oil is still lukewarm, blend in the spice powders and the salt.
3. The pickle is ready for use after 2 days. It lasts for 2 months. Sun and stir occasionally.

538 Salted Small Kalakkai: Watery

125 g	small kalakkai, remove stems
30 g	salt
100 ml	water

1. Pack the kalakkai in a jar.
2. Boil 100ml water with 30g salt and allow to cool.
3. Pour the cooled salt water over the kalakkai and set aside for 2 days.
4. The pickle keeps for 15 days.

539 Salted Small Kalakkai: Salty

125 g	small kalakkai, remove stems
25 g	salt

1. Mix together and shake daily.
2. The pickle is ready for use after 2 days. It keeps for 1 week.

540 Small Kalakkai: Hot

500 g	small kalakkai, remove stems
60 g	chilli powder
5 g	turmeric powder
5 g	asafoetida, roast in oil & powder
125 g	salt
200 ml	oil

1. Stir-fry the kalakkai in a little oil over low heat for a few minutes till tender and remove.
2. When the oil is still lukewarm, add in all the spice powders, salt and stir well.
3. Pour over the reserved oil (after heating) and mix thoroughly.
4. The pickle is ready for use. It lasts for 4 months.

541 Small Kalakkai in Buttermilk: Watery

500 g	small kalakkai, remove stems
400 ml	curd, whip with 200ml water & remove cream
120 g	salt

1. Blend the kalakkai with the whipped curd and the salt. Set aside for 2 days.
2. The pickle lasts for 1 month and longer in the refrigerator. Shake daily.

542 Khol Rabi – Aniseed – Mustard: Hot

500 g	khol rabi with its leaves, cube
25 g	chilli powder;
15 g	mustard seeds, sun-dry & powder;
10 g	dried ginger powder &
15 g	aniseeds, sun-dry & powder, combine all evenly
10 g	jaggery, grate
3	cloves
100 ml	vinegar
25 g	salt
150 ml	oil

1. Tear each leaf into 2 bits, cube the khol rabi without peeling and sun till dry.
2. Dip the cubed khol rabi in oil and roll in the spice mixture.
3. Add in the remaining oil, the remaining spice mixture, stir well and set aside for a week.
4. The pickle lasts for 2 months. Sun occasionally.

543 Khol Rabi – Capsicum : Hot

500 g	khol rabi with its leaves
200 g	capsicum, cut into chunks
30 g	chilli powder;
15 g	mustard seeds, sun-dry & powder;
10 g	dried ginger powder &
5 g	cummin seeds, sun-dry & powder, combine all evenly
10 g	sugar
75 ml	lime juice
30 g	salt
75 ml	oil

1. Tear each leaf into 2 bits, cube the khol rabi without peeling.
2. Allow the vegetable pieces to dry indoors overnight.
3. Dip the pieces in the oil and roll in the spice mixture.
4. Add in the remaining oil, the spice mixture and stir well.
5. Pack the pickle mixture tightly in a jar and sun for 10 days.
6. The pickle lasts for 6 months.

544 Spicy Kovakkai – Green Chilli : Hot

125 g	kovakkai, chop	3 g	split husked black gram;
25 g	green chillies, chop		
40 g	cleaned tamarind	3 g	split husked bengal gram &
3	cloves garlic, peel & chop	a few	sprigs curry leaves : all for seasoning
6 g	chilli powder		
3 g	fenugreek seeds, roast in oil & powder	12 ml	lime juice
		12 g	sugar
3 g	cummin seeds	40 g	salt
3 g	mustard seeds;	25 ml	oil

1. Stir-fry the chopped green chillies in a little oil for a few minutes. Remove and allow to cool.
2. Grind the fried chillies coarsely with the tamarind and the salt.
3. Stir the spice paste into the kovakkai pieces and grind coarsely. Set aside.
4. Separately grind the garlic, cummin seeds, chilli, fenugreek powders and blend into the coarsely ground mixture.
5. Heat the remaining oil, add mustard seeds and allow to crackle.
6. Add in the black gram, bengal gram, curry leaves and fry well.
7. Pour the seasoning over the kovakkai mixture and mix thoroughly.
8. The pickle is ready for use. It keeps for 1 week and longer in the refrigerator.

546 Lady's Finger in Lime Juice : Hot

125 g	tender lady's finger, cut both ends & slit lengthwise
6 g	chilli powder
3 g	mustard seeds, sun-dry & powder
3 g	turmeric powder
40 ml	lime juice
10 g	salt
25 ml	oil

1. Combine the spices and salt with a little oil to a paste.
2. Stuff the spice paste into the slit lady's finger and pack in a jar.
3. Pour over the lime juice, the remaining oil and blend well. Set aside for 2 days.
4. The pickle keeps for 5 days.

545 Kovakkai in Buttermilk : Watery

500 g	kovakkai (cut into thin half rounds)
400 ml	curd, whip with 200ml water & remove cream
80 g	salt

1. Blend the kovakkai pieces with the whipped curd and salt. Set aside for 2 days.
2. The pickle is ready for use. It lasts for 2 months and is best refrigerated. Shake daily.

547 Sour Lime – Thymol Seeds : Sweet

500 g	lime, cut into 8 pieces each & seed
250 g	sugar
25 g	chilli powder
10 g	thymol seeds, sun-dry & powder
5 g	turmeric powder
5 g	asafoetida, roast in oil & powder
40 g	salt

1. Extract half the juice of the limes and cut the peels into thin strips.
2. Steam the lime pieces till soft and allow to cool.
3. Combine the lime peels and lime juice with the remaining ingredients. Sun the mixture for 5 days.
4. The pickle lasts for 3 months.

548 Stuffed Lady's Finger – Ginger : Hot

500 g	tender lady's finger
40 g	green chillies, slit
40 g	fresh ginger, scrape & chop
5 g	asafoetida, roast in oil & powder;
10 g	turmeric powder &
60 g	salt, combine all three evenly
200 ml	lime juice
5 g	lime (pan-ka-chuna), dissolve in water

1. Soak the lady's finger in lime water, wash thoroughly, remove and air-dry.
2. Cut both the ends, slit the dried lady's finger.
3. Fill in the spice mixture and closely pack the stuffed lady's finger in a wide-mouthed jar closely.
4. Add in the slit green chillies, chopped ginger and set aside for a day.
5. Next day, pour over the lime juice and set aside for 2 more days. Shake daily.
6. The pickle is ready for use after a week. It lasts for 1 month. Sun occasionally.

549 Spiced Lady's Finger – Raw Mango : Hot

125 g	tender lady's finger, cut both ends
50 g	seeded raw mango, peel & chop
6 g	chilli powder
5 g	jaggery, grate
3 g	mustard seeds &
3 g	cummin seeds, sun-dry both & powder
3 g	turmeric powder
3 g	asafoetida, roast in oil & powder
1	bay leaf
10 g	salt
25 ml	oil

1. Combine the powdered spices, jaggery with the salt and oil evenly.
2. Stir-fry the lady's finger in a little oil till partly tender. Remove and retain the seeds.
3. In the same pan heat some more oil, add in the bay leaf and fry for a minute.
4. Follow with the chopped mango and fry till tender.
5. Stir in the spice mixture and blend well.
6. When cool, stuff a little of the spice mixture into each lady's finger.
7. Sprinkle the remaining spice mixture over the lady's finger and set aside for 3 days.
8. The pickle keeps for 1 week and longer if sunned occasionally.

550 Economical Dried Lime : Hot

500 g	salted dried lime pieces
150 ml	water
50 g	chilli powder
5 g	fenugreek seeds &
5 g	asafoetida, roast both in oil & powder
5 g	mustard seeds &
200 ml	oil : both for seasoning
25 g	salt

1. Wash the salted lime pieces in water. Bring 150ml water to the boil.
2. Cook the lime pieces in the boiling water for a few minutes and remove.
3. Stir in the chilli, fenugreek, asafoetida powders and the salt.
4. Heat oil, add mustard seeds and allow to crackle.
5. Pour the seasoning over the pickle and blend well.
6. The pickle is ready for use. It lasts for 6 weeks.

> The sour and sweet taste of limes is due to the presence of acids and sugar. If the fruits are sour they contain more acid. Conversely, if they are sweet, they contain more sugar. Generally when the fruit ripens, the concentration of acids diminishes and that of sugar increases.

551 Lime – Fenugreek – Mustard : Hot

500 g	lime, scrape lightly & keep whole water sufficient to immerse
60 g	chilli powder;
50 g	split husked mustard seeds, sun-dry & pound;
25 g	fenugreek seeds, roast in oil & powder;
5 g	asafoetida, roast in oil & powder;
5 g	turmeric powder &
125 g	salt, combine all evenly
200 ml	groundnut oil : heat & cool

1. Blanch the limes for 10 minutes in hot water. Drain, allow to cool and dry. Cut into 8 pieces each and seed.
2. Combine the spice mixture with the lime pieces and mix thoroughly.
3. Pour over the pre-heated oil, stir well and set aside for 7 days.
4. The pickle lasts for 6 months.

552 Spiced Lime – Fresh Red Chilli – Ginger : Hot

500 g	lime, slit into 4 without severing
50 g	fresh red chillies, chop
40 g	fresh ginger, scrape & slice thinly
12 g	chilli powder
5 g	mustard seeds : for seasoning
5 g	fenugreek seeds &
2 g	asafoetida, roast both in oil & powder
100 ml	lime juice, blend with 5g salt
125 g	salt
200 ml	oil

1. Stuff most of the salt inside the limes and rub a little on the outside.
2. Arrange in a jar and set aside for 15 days. Shake daily.
3. Heat the oil, add mustard seeds and allow to crackle.
4. Stir in the limes, ginger, chillies and cook till partly tender.
5. Lower the heat, add in the chilli, asafoetida powders and stir-fry for a while.
6. Stir in the fenugreek powder, salted lime juice, cook for 2 minutes and remove.
7. The pickle is ready for use after 15 days. It lasts for 6 months.

553 Lime – Green Chilli Paste : Hot

1 kg	lime pieces, cut into 8 pieces each & seed thoroughly
200 g	green chillies, chop
240 g	salt &
10 g	turmeric powder, combine both evenly
10 g	chilli powder
10 g	asafoetida, roast in oil & powder
20 g	mustard seeds : for seasoning
400 ml	oil

1. Marinate the lime pieces in the salt-turmeric mixture for 2 days.
2. Grind the salted lime and green chillies to a coarse paste.
3. Heat the oil, add mustard seeds and allow to crackle.
4. Add in the lime paste and stir-fry for a few minutes over low heat.
5. Stir in the chilli, asafoetida powders and remove when the mixture leaves the sides of the pan.
6. The pickle is ready for use. It lasts for 1 year.

554 Spicy Lime – Date : Hot

1 kg	lime pieces, cut into 8 pieces each & seed
250 g	date, keep whole
100 g	sugar
80 g	chilli powder
60 g	green chillies, chop
50 g	peeled garlic, grind
300 ml	vinegar: heat & cool
275 g	salt
300 ml	oil

1. Boil the date till tender, cool, stone and slice.
2. Stir-fry the garlic paste in a little oil.
3. Add in the lime slices, the reamining oil and continue cooking over low heat for a few minutes.
4. Stir in the sliced date, chopped green chillies, chilli powder, sugar, salt and stir-fry for a minute.
5. Pour in the pre-heated vinegar, stir well and remove.
6. The pickle is ready for use after 15 days. It lasts for 1 year.

555 Spicy Lime in Groundnut Oil : Hot

500 g	lime, scrape slightly, keep whole
50 ml	water
65 g	chilli powder
10 g	fenugreek seeds &
5 g	cummin seeds, roast both in oil & powder
5 g	turmeric powder
5 g	garlic, peel & crush
5 g	mustard seeds : for seasoning
1	bay leaf
5 ml	acetic acid
120 g	salt
175 ml	groundnut oil

1. Heat water, add the limes and bring to the boil. Remove when the limes begin to burst.
2. Take out the limes with a perforated spoon, cool, cut into 8 pieces each and seed. Add salt, mix well and pack in a jar.
3. Sun the pickle for 8 days. Stir daily.
4. Heat a little oil, add mustard seeds and allow to crackle.
5. Stir in the crushed garlic, bay leaves and fry for a few minutes over low heat.
6. Drop in the lime pieces, the remaining oil and stir-fry for 15 minutes.
7. Add in the chilli, fenugreek, cummin, turmeric powders and fry for a few seconds over low heat.
8. Pour 50ml hot water over the lime mixture and cook for 20 minutes thoroughly. Stir frequently. Remove, cool, add acetic acid and mix well.
9. The pickle is ready for use. It lasts for 1 month.

556 Spice Stuffed Lime : Hot

500 g	lime, extract juice & retain cups	
60 g	chilli powder	
5 g	turmeric powder	
5 g	coriander seeds;	
5 g	aniseeds;	
3 g	fenugreek seeds;	
3 g	cummin seeds &	
3 g	thymol seeds, powder all together	
100 g	salt	
200 ml	oil : heat & cool	

1. Combine the spice powders with the salt evenly.
2. Pour the lime juice into a jar. Fill the spice mixture into the lime cups and arrange in the jar.
3. Add the pre-heated oil to cover the mixture.
4. Sun the mixture for 7 days.
5. The pickle lasts for 3 months. Sun occasionally.

557 Economical Spiced Lime : Hot

500 g	lime, cut into 8 pieces each & seed
50 g	chilli powder
5 g	mustard seeds, sun-dry & powder
3 g	garlic powder
3 g	asafoetida, roast in oil & powder
5 g	mustard seeds : for seasoning
100 g	salt
200 ml	oil

1. Extract a third of the juice from the limes. Reserve the juice for other recipes. Cut the lime peels into small pieces.
2. Steam the lime pieces with the garlic powder and salt. Remove, cool and set aside for 4 days.
3. Heat the oil, add mustard seeds, allow to crackle and remove.
4. Stir in the chilli, mustard and asafoetida powders.
5. Pour the seasoning over the lime pieces and mix thoroughly.
6. The pickle is ready for use after 4 days. It lasts for 4 months.

558 Lime in Vinegar : Hot

500 g	lime, cut into 8 pieces each & seed
50 g	chilli powder;
15 g	mustard seeds, sun-dry & powder;
15 g	coriander seeds, sun-dry & powder;
5 g	turmeric powder &
4	sprigs curry leaves, grind all to a paste using vinegar
50 g	sugar
200 ml	vinegar
125 g	salt 150ml oil

1. Marinate the lime pieces in the salt and set aside for one month. Stir daily.
2. Wash the dried salted lime and sun-dry for 8 hours.
3. Stir-fry the spice paste in oil for a few minutes.
4. Add in the prepared limes and cook for 30 minutes.
5. Pour in the vinegar, sugar and cook for 15 more minutes.
6. The pickle is ready for use after 7 days. It lasts for 6 months.

559 Spiced Lime Whole : Hot

500 g	lime, scrape slightly, keep whole	2	cloves garlic, peel &
		50 ml	vinegar, grind all to a paste
50 g	dried red chillies;		
15 g	mustard seeds;	2	cloves garlic, peel
15 g	cummin seeds;		
1-1"	piece of fresh ginger, scrape & chop;	5 g	onion seeds
		125 g	salt
		200 ml	oil

1. Heat half of the oil in a pan, saute the limes till slightly brown and set aside.
2. Allow to cool, make criss-cross slits over the limes and set aside.
3. In the same pan heat a portion of the remaining oil, add the onion seeds, peeled garlic and the spice paste. Stir-fry over low heat for a few minutes.
4. Add in the slit limes, salt and the remaining oil.
5. Continue cooking for a few minutes till tender and remove.
6. The pickle is ready for use after 5 days. It lasts for 6 months.

560 Stuffed Lime – Green Chilli : Hot

500 g	lime, slit into 4 without severing		
15 g	green chillies, slit & fry in oil		
50 g	dried red chillies;		
15 g	mustard seeds, sun-dry;		
10 g	fenugreek seeds, dry-roast;		
5	cloves garlic, peel;		
5 g	turmeric powder &	20 ml	vinegar
120 g	salt, grind all fine	200 ml	oil

1. Stuff the spice mixture into the limes and transfer to a jar.
2. Stir in the green chillies, vinegar, oil and set aside for 3 days.
3. Thereafter sun the mixture for 2 days.
4. The pickle is ready for use after 15 days. It lasts for 6 months.

561 Spiced Lime – Ginger - Garlic : Hot

500 g	lime, keep whole
100 g	salt &
5 g	turmeric powder, combine evenly
2-1"	pieces of fresh ginger, scrape & slice
5	cloves garlic, peel & crush
50 g	dried red chillies;
10 g	mustard seeds;
5 g	fenugreek seeds &
5 g	aniseeds, dry-roast all & powder
200 ml	oil

1. Soak the limes overnight in sufficient water to which two teaspoons (10g) salt has been added. Wipe-dry, cut into 8 pieces each and seed.
2. Rub the salt-turmeric mixture over the lime pieces and set aside.
3. Stir-fry the ginger and garlic in a little oil over low heat for a few minutes.
4. Blend in the spice powders for a few seconds and remove.
5. Stir in the lime pieces and the remaining oil.
6. Sun the pickle for a week. Stir daily.
7. The pickle lasts for 3 months.

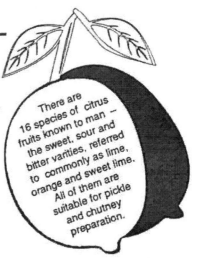

There are 16 species of citrus fruits known to man – the sweet, sour and bitter varities, referred to commonly as lime, orange and sweet lime. All of them are suitable for pickle and chutney preparation.

562 Lime – Ginger : Hot

1 kg	lime, cut into 8 pieces each & seed	20 g	turmeric powder
40 g	dried red chillies, grind to a paste using water	15 g	asafoetida, roast in oil & powder
		20 g	mustard seeds: for seasoning
30 g	fresh ginger, scrape & slice	200 g	salt
		400 ml	oil

1. Add the salt, turmeric powder to the lime pieces and set aside for 5 days.
2. Heat the oil, add mustard seeds and allow to crackle.
3. Stir in the chilli paste, ginger, asafoetida powder and stir-fry for a few minutes.
4. Pour the seasoning over the lime mixture.
5. The pickle is ready for use after 15 days. It lasts for 2 years.

563 Steamed Lime : Hot

500 g	lime, cut into small pieces & seed	5 g	fenugreek seeds;
		5 g	asafoetida & roast both in oil & powder
50 g	dried red chillies (or) green chillies, grind fine		
		5 g	turmeric powder
5 g	mustard seeds &	5 g	mustard seeds: for seasoning
5 g	cummin seeds, sun-dry both & powder	100 g	salt
		200 ml	oil

1. Squeeze out one-third of the juice from the lime pieces. (This lime juice may be used in other recipes.)
2. Add the salt, ground chilli to the lime pieces and sun for 5 days till completely dry.
3. As and when required steam the lime pieces.
4. Sprinkle the spice powders over the lime pieces.
5. Heat the oil, add mustard seeds and allow to crackle.
6. Pour the seasoning over the spiced lime pieces and stir thoroughly.
7. The pickle is ready for use. It lasts for 2 months.

564 Lime – Green Pepper - Garlic : Hot

500 g	lime, keep whole	3 g	fenugreek seeds: both for seasoning
100 g	peeled garlic		
30 g	green pepper	100 ml	water
20 g	fresh red chillies, slit	15 ml	vinegar
2-1"	pieces of fresh ginger, scrape & chop	5 g	sugar
		125 g	salt
10 g	mustard seeds &	150 ml	oil

1. Pressure cook the limes, drain out the water, wipe and air dry. Cut the limes into 8 pieces each without severing.
2. Pressure cook the green pepper, chillies, discard the water and air-dry.
3. Heat the oil, add the mustard seeds, fenugreek seeds and allow to crackle.
4. Add in the ginger, garlic and fry for a few minutes.
5. Stir in the vinegar, water, sugar, salt and bring to the boil. Allow to thicken.
6. Follow with the cut lime, green pepper, chillies, heat a while and remove.
7. The pickle is ready for use. It lasts for 1 month in the refrigerator.

565 Steamed Lime in Spicy Vinegar : Hot

500 g	lime, scrape slightly, keep whole	15 g	mustard seeds, sun-dry & powder
50 g	chilli powder or 75g green chillies, chop	10 g	fenugreek seeds &
50 g	fresh ginger, scrape & chop	5 g	asafoetida, roast both in oil & powder
10	cloves garlic, peel & chop	100 ml	vinegar, boil with 200ml water & cool
15 g	green chillies, chop	150 g	salt
		150 ml	oil

1. Steam the whole limes for 20 minutes, cool, cut into small pieces and seed.
2. Add the salt to the lime pieces, cover and set aside for a week.
3. Heat a little oil, stir-fry the chopped ginger-garlic and green chillies till brown.
4. Combine all the spice powders, lime pieces, fried green spices with the cooled vinegar mixture.
5. Heat the remaining oil, cool and pour over the pickle.
6. The pickle is ready for use. It lasts for 3 months.

566 Lime – Ginger - Green Chilli Stuffed : Hot

1 kg	lime, scrape lightly & keep whole
200 ml	water
100 g	green chillies, chop
50 g	chilli powder
40 g	fresh ginger, scrape & slice thinly
200 g	salt
400 ml	oil

1. Deep-fry the limes till soft and golden brown. Remove and allow to cool. Cut into four without severing.
2. Boil the water with the salt till crystals begin to form at the edge of the water and remove.
3. Stuff each lime with one chilli and a slice of ginger. Pack in a jar.
4. Sprinkle over the chilli powder and pour over the salt water.
5. Cover and set aside for 15 days. Shake twice daily.
6. The pickle lasts for 1 year.

567 Lime – Ginger - Green Chilli in Vinegar : Hot

500 g	lime, cut into small pieces & seed	125 g	salt
60 g	green chillies, chop	175 ml	oil
50 g	fresh ginger, scrape & chop		
5 g	chilli powder		
5 g	turmeric powder		
5 g	mustard seeds, sun-dry & powder		
5 g	asafoetida &		
5 g	fenugreek seeds, roast both in oil & powder		
100 ml	vinegar : heat & cool		

1. Marinate the lime pieces in the salt and sun for 15 days. Shake daily.
2. Heat the oil to smoking point. Lower the heat, add the mustard seeds, fenugreek seeds and allow to crackle.
3. Stir in the green chillies, ginger and saute for a few minutes.
4. Remove and stir in the chilli, asafoetida and turmeric powders. Blend in the pre-heated vinegar.
5. Add the spice mixture to the limes and stir well.
6. Sun the mixture for 15 days. The pickle lasts for 3 months.

568 Malta Lime – Mustard - Garlic : Hot

1 kg	sliced malta lime, skin thinly & slice lengthwise	5 g	asafoetida, roast both in oil & powder
90 g	chilli powder	150 g	sugar
80 g	green chillies, slit	250 ml	vinegar
50 g	peeled garlic, chop	300 g	salt
60 g	fresh ginger, scrape & thinly slice	400 ml	oil
30 g	split husked mustard seeds		
10 g	turmeric powder		
a few	sprigs curry leaves		
10 g	fenugreek seeds &		

1. Marinate the lime slices in salt for 2 days. Sun-dry the salted lime for 2 days.
2. Stir-fry the green chillies, ginger and garlic in a little oil and set aside.
3. In the same pan heat some more oil, add in the curry leaves and allow to turn crisp.
4. Add the lime pieces and stir-fry till half done.
5. Follow with the chilli powder, mustard seeds, turmeric, fenugreek, asafoetida powders and fry for a minute.
6. Stir in the vinegar, green chilli mixture, sugar, salt and the remaining oil.
7. Cook over low heat for a few minutes and remove.
8. The pickle is ready for use after 1 month. It lasts for 1 year.

569 Sweet & Sour Lime : Watery

500 g	lime, scrape slightly, keep whole	50 g	chilli powder &
600 ml	water	60 g	salt, combine both evenly
250 g	jaggery, grate	300 ml	vinegar

1. Bring the water to boil, drop in the limes, wait for one boil, remove from the fire and allow to cool.
2. Remove the limes from the water, wipe and cut each into 4 without severing.
3. Stuff the chilli-salt mixture into the limes. Pack in a jar and set aside for 15 days.
4. Heat together the vinegar and jaggery till syrupy. Cool and pour the sweetened vinegar over the limes.
5. The pickle is ready for use after 4 days. It lasts for 6 months.

570 Lime Whole : Salty

1 kg	lime, keep whole
water	sufficient to immerse
500 g	salt

1. Soak the limes in water for 4 days. Change the water every day. Wipe and dry.
2. Place some salt at the bottom of a jar, arrange a layer of the limes and sprinkle over some salt.
3. Repeat this process until all the limes are packed and salted. Make sure the top layer is that of salt.
4. Cap tight and leave in a sunny location to mature for 2 months. Do not shake the jar.
5. The pickle is ready for use when the lime skins become soft. It lasts for 2 years.

571 Aromatic Whole Lime : Salty

1 kg	lime, scrape lightly & prick each with a fork, keep whole	50 ml	lime juice
		5	cloves
		10 g	black salt
10 g	thymol seeds, crush	225 g	salt

1. Combine the whole limes, cloves and thymol seeds with the salts.
2. Pack in a jar and pour over the lime juice.
3. Sun the pickle till the limes become brown and tender.
4. The pickle is ready for use. It lasts for 1 year.

Lime Value
Limes are rich in vitamin C, provitamin A, vitamin B and also in minerals. Limes are used in treating defects of the liver. They retard excessive production of bile, besides improving blood circulation.

572 Aromatic Lime – Lime Juice : Salty

500 g	lime, slit into 4 without severing
2-1"	pieces of fresh ginger, scrape & slice fine
5 g	whole panch phoran
60 ml	lime juice
100 g	salt

1. Stuff most of the salt into the slit limes and rub a little on the outside.
2. Pack the stuffed limes in a jar and sun for 4 days.
3. On the 4th day, pour over the lime juice and turn over the limes.
4. Stir in the panch phoran, ginger and mix thoroughly.
5. Sun the pickle for a month.
6. The pickle is ready for use. It lasts for 6 months.

573 Stuffed Lime : Salty

1 kg lime, slit each into 4 without severing
150 g salt

1. Stuff the limes with the salt and sun for 6 days. Shake daily.
2. The pickle is ready for use after 15 days. It lasts for 1 year.

574 Sweet & Sour Whole Lime – Thymol Seeds : Watery

1 kg	lime, keep whole	250 g	sugar
200 ml	water	400 ml	vinegar
80 g	thymol seeds	275 g	salt
		200 ml	oil

1. Prick the limes several times with a fork and pack in a jar.
2. Boil together the remaining ingredients for a few minutes.
3. Pour the hot spicy liquid over the limes and allow to cool.
4. Cap tight and keep in a sunny location for 2 months. Shake occasionally.
5. The pickle is ready for use after 1 month. It lasts for 1 year.

575 Lime in Spicy Sauce : Watery

500 g	lime, scrape lightly & keep whole
	water sufficient to immerse
150 g	chilli powder
20 g	mustard seeds &
20 g	cummin seeds, sun-dry both & powder
1-1"	piece of fresh ginger, scrape &
20 g	peeled garlic, chop both & grind to a paste
5	green chillies, slit
10 g	turmeric powder
120 ml	lime juice
100 ml	vinegar : heat & cool
250 g	salt

1. Boil the limes in the water till they change colour.
2. Drain, allow to cool, dry for a day, cut into 8 pieces each and seed.
3. Stir-fry the garlic-ginger paste, green chillies in a little oil and set aside. Add in the spice powders and salt.
4. Stir in the lime pieces and mix thoroughly. Blend in the lime juice and vinegar.
5. Sun the pickle mixture for 2 days.
6. The pickle is ready for use after 4 days. It lasts for 6 months.

576 Lime – Ginger – Green Chilli : Watery

500 g	lime, cut into large pieces & seed		
50 g	fresh ginger, scrape & slice thinly		
50 g	green chillies, slit	750 ml	water
15 g	chilli powder	150 g	salt

1. Boil together the limes with the water and salt until the water is reduced to half.
2. Drop in the lime pieces, green chillies and ginger. Stir well, cover and set aside.
3. When cool, store in a jar for 10 days. Stir daily.
4. Blend in the chilli powder.
5. The pickle is ready for use after 2 days. It lasts for 4 months.

577 Lime in Spiced Vinegar : Watery

1 kg	lime, keep whole water sufficient to immerse
10 g	black cummin seeds &
300 g	salt, combine evenly
300 ml	vinegar

1. Bring the water to boiling. Drop the limes and allow to stand for a minute uncovered.
2. Remove from the fire, strain in a colander and allow to cool.
3. Wipe and cut each lime into 4 without severing.
4. Stuff the salt-cummin seed mixture into the limes.
5. Pack tight in a jar and set aside for a week. Shake daily.
6. Pour over the vinegar to cover.
7. The pickle is ready for use after 15 days. It lasts for 1 year.

578 Lime in Oil : Sweet

500 g	lime, cut into small pieces & seed
20 g	chilli powder
5 g	fenugreek seeds &
5 g	asafoetida, roast both in oil & powder
10 g	mustard seeds:
	for seasoning
5 g	turmeric powder
150 g	sugar
100 g	salt
200 ml	oil

1. Combine the lime pieces with the chilli, turmeric powders and salt. Set aside for a week. Shake daily.
2. Stir in the fenugreek, asafoetida powders and sugar over the salted lime pieces.
3. Heat the oil, add mustard seeds and allow to crackle.
4. Pour the seasoning over the lime pieces and mix thoroughly. Set aside for a week and stir daily.
5. The pickle lasts for 6 months. Sun the pickle occasionally.

——— Variation ———

The lime pieces may be steamed before the spice mixture added.

579 Sliced Lime : Sweet

500 g	lime, cut into ¾ cm thick round slices & seed
300 g	sugar / 500g jaggery, grate
10 g	chilli powder
40 g	salt

1. Sprinkle the salt over the lime slices and set aside.
2. Pack the lime slices in a jar and sun for 4 days. Stir daily.
3. On the 5th day, add the sugar and chilli powder to the lime slices. Alternatively the mixture may be heated till a thick sugar syrup is formed.
4. Sun the pickle mixture for a week till the limes soften.
5. The pickle lasts for 6 months.

580 Peppered Lime – Ginger : Sweet

1 kg	lime, scrape lightly, keep whole	10 g	asafoetida, roast in oil & powder	
500 g	jaggery, grate / 500 g sugar	90 g	salt	
water	sufficient to immerse	10 g	black salt	
100 g	fresh ginger, scrape & slice			
30 g	peppercorns;			
20 g	cummin seeds;			
10 g	aniseeds;			
10 g	cloves &			
10 g	cinnamon, sun-dry all & powder together			

1. Soak the limes in water for 24 hours. Remove, wipe-dry, cut into 8 pieces each and seed.
2. Marinate the lime pieces in salt for 10 days. Shake daily.
3. Combine all the ingredients except jaggery with the lime pieces. Stir thoroughly.
4. Heat the jaggery and water to make a syrup of single-thread consistency.
5. Cool and pour the jaggery syrup over the lime pieces.
6. The pickle is ready for use after a week. It lasts for 1 year.

581 Lime : Sweet

500 g	lime, cut into thin strips & seed
100 ml	water
1 kg	sugar
60 g	kashmiri chilli powder
5 g	asafoetida, roast in oil & powder
5 g	turmeric powder
125 g	salt

1. Combine all the ingredients except sugar evenly.
2. Boil the sugar and water to make a syrup of two-thread consistency. Allow to cool.
3. Stir in the spicy lime mixture into the sugar syrup.
4. The pickle is ready for use after 1 week. It lasts for 2 months.

582 Stuffed Lime : Sweet

1 kg	lime, slit into 4 without severing
500 g	sugar
20 g	chilli powder
10 g	asafoetida, roast in oil & powder
10 g	turmeric powder &
75 g	salt, combine both evenly

1. Stuff the limes with the salt-turmeric mixture and pack in an air-tight jar for a month. Set aside.
2. Drain out the salt water and cut into small pieces.
3. Stir in the chilli, asafoetida powders and sugar into the salt water.
4. Blend the lime pieces into the spiced salt water.
5. The pickle is ready for use after 10 days. It lasts for 1 year.

583 Lime – Date - Jaggery : Sweet

1 kg	lime, cut into 8 pieces each & seed	50 g	chilli powder
1 kg	jaggery, grate	30 g	cleaned tamarind
500 g	date, stone & chop	50 ml	vinegar
		200 g	salt

1. Marinate the limes in the salt and set aside for 3 days, uncovered. Shake daily.
2. Spread on a cloth to dry in the sun for 2 days.
3. Coarsely pound the lime, jaggery and date using the vinegar.
4. Stir in the chilli powder, tamarind and pound again coarsely.
5. The pickle is ready for use after a week. It lasts for 1 year.

584 Peeled Lime – Raisin : Sweet

500 g	lime, peel, segment & seed
80 g	seedless raisin, chop
300 g	powdered sugar
10 g	chilli powder;
10 g	peppercorns &
3 g	cummin seeds, dry-roast all three & powder
2 g	asafoetida, roast in oil & powder
40 g	salt

1. Combine the lime segments, raisins and sugar evenly.
2. Blend in the spice powders and the salt.
3. Arrange in a wide-mouthed jar and sun the pickle for 10 days.
4. The pickle lasts for 6 months.

585 Spiced Lime – Vinegar : Sweet

1 kg	lime, slice fine & seed
20 g	chilli powder
10 g	cummin seeds, sun-dry & powder
10 g	garam masala powder
400 g	sugar
200 ml	vinegar
150 g	salt

1. Add the salt to the lime slices and sun for 4 days.
2. Combine all the spice powders, sugar and vinegar. Stir well and sun for 4 more days.
3. The pickle lasts for 1 year.

586 Lime – Coriander Seeds : Sweet

1 kg	lime, cut into 4 without severing
2 kgs	sugar, make a syrup of single-thread consistency with 400ml water
80 g	chilli powder
30 g	coriander seeds, sun-dry & powder
10 g	turmeric powder
80 g	salt

1. Stuff the salt and turmeric powder into the limes and set aside for 15 days. Shake twice daily.
2. Remove the limes from the brine and sun dry.
3. Stir in the sugar syrup, chilli, coriander powders and the brine.
4. When cool stir in the dried lime pieces.
5. The pickle is ready for use after 5 days. It lasts for 1 year.

587 Sour Lime – Raisin : Sweet

1 kg	lime, slit into 4 without severing
2 kgs	seedless raisin, chop
400 g	dried red chillies, soak in little vinegar
200 g	peeled garlic
200 g	fresh ginger, scrape
600 g	sugar
800 ml	vinegar
500 g	salt

1. Stuff the salt into the limes and set aside for 6 days.
2. On the 7th day remove the limes from the salt water and cut into small pieces.
3. Chop half the garlic and ginger. Grind the remaining garlic and ginger with the chillies using a little vinegar.
4. Stir all the remaining ingredients except the lime pieces into the remaining vinegar.
5. Finally add in the lime pieces and set aside for 10 days.
6. The pickle lasts for 1 year.

588 Spicy Lime – Fenugreek : Sweet

1 kg	lime, slit into 4 without severing
80 g	salt &
20 g	turmeric powder, combine both
60 g	split husked fenugreek seeds
50 g	chilli powder
40 g	split husked mustard seeds
20 g	split husked coriander seeds
20 g	aniseeds, pound coarsely
20 g	asafoetida, roast in oil & powder
1200 g	sugar

1. Stuff the salt-turmeric mixture into the limes.
2. Arrange in a jar and stir daily for a month.
3. Sever the limes into 4 pieces and dry indoors.
4. Stir in the remaining ingredients the same evening.
5. The pickle is ready for use after a week. It lasts for 2 years.

589 Lime Preserve – Jaggery : Sweet

1 kg	lime, scrape slightly, keep whole & prick with a fork
400 g	jaggery, grate
20 g	dried ginger powder
20 g	cummin seeds;
10 g	peppercorns &
5 g	thymol seeds, dry-roast all three & powder
5 g	garlic powder
5 g	asafoetida, roast in oil & powder
5 g	grated nutmeg
60 ml	honey
10 g	sugar
80 g	salt

1. Coat the limes with the salt and sun for 5 days.
2. Smear the lime pieces with the honey. Then smear with the jaggery and sun for 10 days.
3. Add the spice powders, grated nutmeg and sugar to the spiced limes. Stir thoroughly.
4. The pickle is now ready for use. It lasts for several years.

590 Spiced Lime – Jaggery : Sweet

1 kg	lime, cut into 8 pieces each & seed
600 g	jaggery, grate
300 ml	water
20 g	chilli powder
10 g	garam masala powder
10 g	aniseeds;
5 g	coriander seeds &
5 g	onion seeds, sun-dry all three & pound coarsely
80 g	salt

1. Heat together the jaggery and water till the jaggery dissolves.
2. Stir in all the spice powders, salt, heat for 15 minutes and remove.
3. Pour the hot spicy liquid over the lime pieces and stir well.
4. Sun the mixture for a week.
5. The pickle lasts for 1 year.

591 Ground Lime Peel : Hot

125 g	peeled lime, extract juice & retain peels
15 g	dried red chillies;
2 g	split husked black gram;
2 g	fenugreek seeds &
2 g	mustard seeds, roast all in oil & powder coarsely
15 g	sugar
15 ml	lime juice
5 ml	vinegar : heat & cool
30 g	salt
40 ml	oil : heat & cool

1. Grind the spice powders, sugar, salt and the peeled limes to a smooth paste.
2. Blend in the pre-heated oil, vinegar and the lime juice.
3. The pickle is ready for use. It keeps for 2 weeks and is best refrigerated.

592 Spiced Lime Strips : Sweet

1 kg	lime, extract juice & retain peels
500 g	sugar
20 g	chilli powder
10	cardamoms
5	cloves
75 g	salt

1. Cut the lime peels into thin long strips and soak in the lime juice.
2. Add in the salt and sun the soaked peels for 6 days till tender. Shake daily.
3. Stir in the chilli powder, whole spices and sugar.
4. Sun the mixture for 5 more days till the sugar dissolves.
5. The pickle lasts for 1 year.

593 Sour Peeled Lime : Sweet

500 g	lime, peel, dice & seed
1 kg	sugar
300 ml	water
10 g	chilli powder
3	cloves &
1"	stick of cinnamon, powder both
25 g	salt

1. Sprinkle the salt over the lime pieces and set aside.
2. Boil the sugar and water to make a syrup of single-thread consistency.
3. Stir in all the other ingredients, cook till the mixture boils and remove.
4. The pickle is ready for use after a week. It lasts for 6 months.

594 Spiced Loquat – Jaggery : Sweet

500 g	half-ripe loquat, slit	5	cardamoms
500 g	jaggery, grate	2-1"	sticks of cinnamon
20 g	aniseeds, dry-roast & powder	40 ml	lime juice
5 g	chilli powder	50 g	salt

1. Marinate the slit loquat in the salt. Cover and set aside for 4 days till it gives out water.
2. Bring water to the boil and remove. Add in the salted loquat.
3. When the water has cooled, remove the salted loquat with a perforated spoon and sun-dry for 2 days.
4. Blend the aniseed, chilli powders with the dried loquat and sun for 5 days.
5. Melt the jaggery over low heat and blend in the lime juice.
6. Add in the spiced dried loquat, mix thoroughly and remove.
7. Stir in the whole spices and sun for 10 days.
8. The pickle lasts for 6 months.

595 Loquat Preserve : Sweet

500 g	loquat, peel, seed & bruise
500 g	sugar
400 ml	water
10 g	salt

> Loquats for pickling should be fleshy, sour and half-ripe. The mature ones are rather bland and insipid.

1. Heat together the sugar, water till the sugar dissolves and strain.
2. Cook the bruised loquat in the sugar syrup over low heat until the mixture becomes thick and jam-like.
3. The pickle is ready for use after 3 days. It lasts for 6 months.

596 Cooked Lotus Stem : Hot

500 g	lotus stem, peel & cut into round slices
30 g	mustard seeds, sun-dry & powder;
25 g	chilli powder &
5 g	turmeric powder, combine all three evenly
50 g	salt
200 ml	oil

1. Steam the lotus stem pieces till partly tender.
2. Remove and allow to dry on a clean cloth.
3. Dip the lotus stem pieces in a little oil, roll in the spice mixture and transfer to a jar.
4. Blend in the remaining oil, the spice mixture and set aside for 4 days.
5. The pickle lasts for 2 months. Sun occasionally.

597 Love-Lovi – Mustard – Ginger Spiced : Hot

500 g	ripe love-lovi
50 g	chilli powder
25 g	dried ginger powder
20 g	split husked mustard seeds, pound
10 g	turmeric powder
10 g	asafoetida, roast in oil & powder
5	cloves garlic, peel & chop fine
5 g	fenugreek seeds &
a few	sprigs curry leaves : both for seasoning
50 g	salt
200 ml	oil

1. Stir-fry the chopped garlic in a little oil and set aside.
2. In the same pan heat some more oil, add in the love-lovi and sti-fry till tender. Remove and mash with a wooden spoon.
3. Stir in the chilli, ginger, mustard, turmeric, asafoetida powders, salt and set aside.
4. Heat the remaining oil, add the fenugreek seeds, curry leaves and allow to crackle.
5. Add in the mashed spiced love-lovi, fried garlic and cook till the moisture evaporates.
6. The pickle is ready for use after 4 days. It lasts for 6 months.

598 Dried Love-Lovi in Vinegar : Sweet

500 g	cut dried love-lovi
150 g	seedless raisin, grind using vinegar
60 g	peeled garlic, chop
60 g	fresh ginger, scrape & slice
25 g	green chillies, slit
80 g	dried red chillies;
10 g	fenugreek seeds &
5 g	turmeric powder, grind all three to a paste using vinegar
300 ml	vinegar
200 g	sugar
200 g	salt
200 ml	oil

1. Soak the love-lovi in 100g salt for 5 hours. Remove from the salt water and sun-dry for a day.
2. Stir-fry the ginger, garlic and green chillies in a little oil.
3. Add in the chilli paste and fry for a while.
4. Stir in the ground raisins, sugar, vinegar, the remaining salt, oil, bring to the boil and remove.
5. Add in the dried love-lovi and mix thoroughly.
6. The pickle is ready for use after 15 days. It lasts for 6 months.

599 Dried Love-Lovi – Garlic – Ginger : Sweet

1 kg	dried powdered love-lovi		
1 kg	sugar		
80 g	chilli powder;		
80 g	fresh ginger, scrape & chop;		
60 g	peeled garlic, chop &	300 ml	vinegar
40 g	mustard seeds, grind all to a paste using vinegar	80 g	salt

1. Cook the love-lovi till tender with just enough water to cover. Drain, pass through a wire sieve and take out the puree.
2. Heat the vinegar with sugar and stir to dissolve.
3. Add in the spice paste, love-lovi puree, salt, bring to the boil and remove. Use after 15 days.
4. The pickle lasts for 1 year.

600 Sour Makoy Leaves : Hot

500 g	makoy leaves, wash, air-dry & chop
300 g	onion, peel & chop;
300 g	tomato, chop &
100 g	green chillies, chop, grind all three to a paste
30 g	fresh ginger, scrape &
5	cloves garlic, peel, chop both & grind to a paste
75 g	tamarind, obtain thick extract using water
75 g	jaggery, grate
125 g	salt
250 ml	oil

1. Stir-fry the ginger-garlic paste in a little oil for a few minutes.
2. Stir in the makoy leaves, fry till tender and set aside.
3. In the same pan heat the remaining oil, add in the onion mixture and fry till the mixture becomes transluscent.
4. Pour in the tamarind extract, jaggery, salt and bring to the boil over a high flame.
5. Add in the fried ingredients and continue cooking over low heat.
6. Remove when the mixture becomes jam-like and the oil separates.
7. The pickle is ready for use. It lasts for 2 months.

601 Sour Cut Mango : Hot

1 kg	cut mango, size into 1" pieces
10 g	salt : for marinating
50 g	chilli powder
10 g	turmeric powder
10 g	asafoetida &
5 g	fenugreek seeds, roast both in oil & powder
50 ml	vinegar
120 g	salt, make a solution with 200ml water
600 ml	oil : heat & cool

1. Marinate the mango pieces in salt for 3 days.
2. Drain and discard the salt water given out by the mango pieces.
3. Sun-dry the salted mango pieces for 4 hours.
4. Blend in the spice powders, vinegar and the pre-heated oil.
5. Pour the spiced liquid over the cut mango.
6. Cool and pour the salt solution over the mango pieces.
7. The pickle is ready for use. It lasts for 1 year.

Mango: This golden fruit is a great nourisher of the body. It contains plenty of minerals and vitamins like A and C. Mangoes are considered to be good laxatives. It contains soluble fibre noted for its cholesterol-lowering capacity.

602 Cut Mango : Hot

500 g	cut fibrous mango, size into 1" pieces
30 g	chilli powder
10 g	mustard seeds &
5 g	aniseeds, sun-dry both & powder
5 g	fenugreek seeds, roast in oil & powder
5 g	turmeric powder
200 ml	water : boil & cool
65 g	salt
150 ml	oil

1. Combine the spice powders with the salt evenly.
2. Blend in the water with half the oil.
3. Stir in the mango pieces and pour over the remaining oil to cover.
4. Sun the mixture for 2 days. Shake daily.
5. The pickle is ready for use when the mango pieces become soft. It lasts for 2 months.
6. Sun and stir the pickle frequently.

603 Mango Avakkai – Bengal Gram : Hot

1 kg	cut mango, size into 1" pieces
50 g	chilli powder
150 g	mustard seeds, sun-dry & powder
150 g	whole unhusked bengal gram
30 g	fenugreek seeds, roast in oil & powder
30 g	fenugreek seeds, keep whole
20 g	turmeric powder
200 g	salt
800 ml	raw gingelly oil

1. Combine the spice powders with the salt evenly.
2. Dip the mango pieces in oil, roll in the spice mixture and arrange in a jar.
3. Sprinkle a little spice mixture, throw in a few fenugreek seeds and whole bengal gram.
4. Pour a little oil over the mango pieces.
5. Repeat this process until all the mango pieces are layered.
6. Sprinkle the remaining spice mixture, if any, over the mango mixture and set aside for 3 days. Do not stir.
7. On the 4th day, stir well and add the reserved oil to cover the pickle.
8. The pickle is ready for use after 2 weeks. It lasts for 1 year.

604 Spicy Mango – Mustard : Hot

500 g	cut mango, size into small pieces
300 g	jaggery, grate
25 g	chilli powder
20 g	split husked mustard seeds
10 g	split husked coriander seeds
10 g	split husked fenugreek seeds
3	dried red chillies, break into bits
3 g	asafoetida, roast in oil & powder
2-1"	sticks of cinnamon, powder
50 g	salt
25 ml	oil

1. Add two teaspoons (10g) salt to the mango pieces and set aside for 2 days. Shake twice daily.
2. Spread to dry in the shade for 2 days.
3. Heat the oil, add in the chillies and fry for a minute. Stir in the remaining salt, spices and jaggery.
4. Blend over low heat for a few minutes and remove after the jaggery has melted.
5. Cool and add the mango pieces.
6. The pickle is ready for use after 7 days. It lasts for 6 months.

605 Sweet & Sour Spiced Mango : Hot

500 g	cut mango, size medium
25 g	dried red chillies;
5 g	mustard seeds;
5 g	cummin seeds;
3 g	coriander seeds;
3 g	fenugreek seeds &
2-1"	pieces of fresh ginger, scrape & chop, grind all to a paste using vinegar
5	cloves garlic, peel
12 g	green chillies, slit
3 g	turmeric powder
a few	sprigs curry leaves
125 g	sugar
250 ml	vinegar
75 g	salt
150 ml	oil

1. Apply the salt and turmeric powder to the mango pieces. Set aside overnight.
2. Next morning drain out all the salt water.
3. Fry the curry leaves, whole garlic and green chillies in a little oil.
4. Stir in the ground spices and fry for a few minutes.
5. Add in the mango pieces, vinegar, sugar, the remaining oil and cook over low heat.
6. Remove when the mango pieces become tender.
7. The pickle is ready for use after 4 days. It lasts for 4 months.

606 Sour Mango : Hot

125 g	cut mango, size medium
2	dried red chillies;
2 g	cummin seeds;
1/2"	piece of fresh ginger, scrape & chop;
2	cloves garlic, peel &
5 ml	vinegar, grind all to a paste
15 g	salt
75 ml	oil

1. Marinate the mango pieces in salt for 1 hour. Squeeze out the salt water and set aside.
2. Stir-fry the spice paste in a little oil till dry.
3. Add in the cut mango, the remaining oil and cook over low heat till transluscent.
4. Pour over the vinegar, cook for a few minutes and remove.
5. The pickle is ready for use after 2 days. It keeps for 15 days and longer in the refrigerator.

607 Aromatic Mango : Hot

1 kg	cut mango, with shell, size into 1" pieces
100 g	mustard seeds, sun-dry & powder;
80 g	chilli powder;
5 g	turmeric powder &
150 g	salt, combine all evenly
80 g	split husked bengal gram;
50 g	dried red chillies;
5 g	fenugreek seeds;
5 g	asafoetida, roast in oil & powder;
5 g	mustard seeds &
a few	sprigs curry leaves : all for seasoning
400 ml	oil

1. Fry the fenugreek seeds, mustard seeds, bengal gram, chillies, curry leaves and asafoetida powder in a little oil till done.
2. Remove and allow to cool. Pour the seasoning over the spice mixture and blend well.
3. Stir in the mango pieces, the remaining oil and mix thoroughly.
4. The pickle is ready for use after 15 days. It lasts for 1 year.

608 Mango – Mustard - Garlic : Hot

1 kg	cut mango, size into small pieces	10 g	mustard seeds, sun-dry & powder
150 g	peeled garlic, chop	10 g	coriander seeds &
150 g	dried red chillies;	10 g	peppercorns, roast both in oil & powder
50 g	mustard seeds;		
10 g	asafoetida, roast in oil &	a few	sprigs curry leaves
10 g	turmeric powder, grind all with salt water of mangoes	300 g	salt
		600 ml	oil

1. Marinate the mango pieces in salt and set aside for 5 days. Stir daily.
2. Drain the mango pieces from the salt water and reserve the same.
3. Blend in the roasted powdered spices with the chilli paste.
4. Fry the drained mango pieces in a little oil, a few at a time and set aside.
5. Stir-fry the chopped garlic and curry leaves in a little oil.
6. Combine the chilli paste, garlic mixture and the remaining oil with the mango pieces thoroughly.
7. Cool and transfer the pickle mixture to a jar.
8. Place a thin cloth dipped in a little oil and turmeric powder over the mouth of the jar and cap tight.
9. The pickle is ready for use after 4 days. It lasts for 1 year.

609 Split Mango in Mustard Oil : Hot

500 g	seeded split mango, without severing	15 g	chilli powder
40 g	salt &	2 g	mustard seeds &
3 g	turmeric powder, combine both evenly	2 g	cummin seeds, sun-dry both & powder
		125 ml	mustard oil

1. Coat the mangoes with the salt-turmeric mixture and sun for 4 days.
2. Combine the spice powders with a little oil to a paste.
3. Stuff the spice paste into the mangoes and arrange in a jar.
4. Pour over the reserved oil and sun the pickle for a month.
5. The pickle lasts for 3 months. Sun frequently.

610 Spiced Peeled Mango : Hot

1 kg	seeded large fleshy mango, peel & slice into finger lengths	5 g	turmeric powder
		3 g	fenugreek seeds, roast in oil & powder
50 g	dried red chillies, roast in oil & powder	3 g	fenugreek seeds;
		3 g	mustard seeds &
5	cloves garlic, peel & halve	10 ml	oil : all three for seasoning
2-1"	pieces of fresh ginger, scrape & slice	10 g	sugar
		60 ml	vinegar
10 g	split husked mustard seeds, pound	100 g	salt
		250 ml	oil : heat & cool

1. Marinate the mango slices in salt for 2 days. Drain out the salt water and sun-dry for a day. Drop again into the salt water.
2. Heat oil, add the mustard, fenugreek seeds and allow to crackle.
3. Add in the ginger, garlic, turmeric powder and fry over low heat for a few minutes.
4. Pour over the vinegar and bring to the boil. Add in the sugar and stir to dissolve.
5. Blend in the mustard seeds, chilli, fenugreek powders and remove. Allow to cool.
6. Stir in the mango pieces and the pre-heated oil into the spiced vinegar. Mix thoroughly.
7. The pickle is ready for use after 1 week. It lasts for 1 year.

611 Spicy Stuffed Mango : Hot

1 kg	seeded mango, split into 4 without severing	10 g	thymol seeds, dry-roast all three & powder
60 g	salt : for marinating	10 g	fenugreek seeds &
50 g	chilli powder	5 g	asafoetida, roast both in oil & powder
20 g	mustard seeds, sun-dry & powder	5 g	turmeric powder
20 g	aniseeds;	60 g	salt : for pickle
10 g	onion seeds &	350 ml	oil

1. Marinate the split mango in salt and set aside for a day.
2. Combine the spice powders with the salt evenly.
3. Heat the oil to smoking point and allow to cool. Blend in the spice mixture to a paste.
4. Stuff the spice paste into the salted mangoes.
5. Sprinkle the remaining spice paste, pour over the remaining oil, pack tight in a jar and sun for 3 days.
6. Remove and keep the pickle mixture indoors for 3 days. Lid tight and set aside for 15 days. Shake daily.
7. The pickle lasts for 1 year.

612 Mango – Green Spices : Hot

1 kg	cut mango, size into small pieces
60 g	chilli powder
60 g	green chillies, slit
60 g	peeled garlic, pound
40 g	fresh ginger, scrape & slice
5 g	turmeric powder
5 g	fenugreek seeds &
5 g	asafoetida, roast both in oil & powder
5 g	split husked bengal gram &
5 g	sesame seeds, dry-roast both & powder
150 ml	vinegar : heat & cool
150 g	salt
300 ml	oil

1. Stir-fry the garlic, ginger and green chillies in a little oil for a few minutes.
2. Lower the flame, add in the chilli, turmeric, fenugreek, asafoetida powders, the remaining oil and fry for a few seconds.
3. Remove from the fire, stir in the mango pieces, the remaining powders, vinegar, salt and mix thoroughly.
4. The pickle is ready for use after 15 days. It lasts for 1 year.

613 Juicy Mango : Hot

1 kg	cut mango, peel & size medium lengthwise
40 g	dried red chillies;
10 g	asafoetida &
10 g	fenugreek seeds, roast all three in oil & powder together
10 g	turmeric powder
10 g	mustard seeds;
10 g	split husked bengal gram;
8	dried red chillies &
a few	sprigs curry leaves : all for seasoning
150 g	salt
400 ml	oil

1. Combine the salt and turmeric powder with the mango pieces. Set aside for 3 days.
2. On the 4th day squeeze out the salt water given out by the mango pieces and sun the pieces for 2 days.
3. Simultaneously sun the salt water of the mangoes after straining.
4. Blend in the chilli, fenugreek and asafoetida powders along with the mango pieces into the salt water.
5. Heat a little oil, fry the bengal gram, mustard seeds, red chillies and the curry leaves.
6. Pour the seasoning over the mango mixture.
7. Add in the remaining oil after heating and cooling. Stir the pickle the following day.
8. The pickle is ready for use. It lasts for 1 year.

614 Sliced Tender Spicy Mango : Hot

500 g	tender mango, seeds unformed, split
20 g	chilli powder;
5 g	aniseeds;
3 g	turmeric powder &
60 g	salt, combine all evenly
15 g	fenugreek seeds;
15 g	black cummin seeds &
15 g	mustard seeds, dry-roast all three, powder & sieve
10 g	sugar
10 g	panch phoran powder
5 g	lime (pan-ka-chuna), make a solution with 600ml water
40 ml	vinegar
100 ml	oil

1. Drop the mango pieces in the lime solution for one hour and remove.
2. Marinate the mango pieces in salt for 4 days.
3. On the 5th day remove the mango pieces from the salt water and wash thoroughly.
4. Roll the mango pieces in the chilli mixture and allow to dry indoors.
5. When dry, roll the mango pieces in the roasted spice powders and sugar.
6. Transfer to a jar and sun the mixture for 7 days.
7. Heat the oil, add in the panch phoran powder and vinegar. Remove and allow to cool.
8. Pour the seasoning over the pickle mixture and stir thoroughly.
9. Sun the pickle for 7 more days.
10. The pickle lasts for 6 months.

615 Spicy Tender Mango : Hot

1 kg	tender mango with soft seeds, keep whole
100 g	chilli powder
25 g	coriander seeds;
25 g	cummin seeds &
25 g	fenugreek seeds, roast all three in oil & powder
10 g	mustard seeds: for seasoning
175 g	salt
400 ml	oil

1. Combine the powdered spices with the salt evenly.
2. Arrange a layer of mango in a wide-mouthed shallow jar.
3. Sprinkle over a layer of the spice mixture. Follow with a layer of mango.
4. Repeat this process until all the mangoes and the spice mixture are layered.
5. Heat the oil, add mustard seeds and allow to crackle.
6. Cool and pour the seasoning over the mango mixture. Stir after 2 days.
7. The pickle is ready for use after 2 months. It lasts for 1 year.
8. However ensure that the pickle is steeped in oil.

MANGOES

Mango is a luscious, slightly acidic fruit that is much prized as a dessert.

The soluble mineral salts present in mangoes contain necessary amounts of potassium, tartaric acid and citric acid.

There are sour as well as sweet mangoes. Unripe mangoes are generally sour but some of them tend to be sweetish.

Ripe mangoes are sweet and are abundant from July and September.

Mangoes are chiefly divided into two categories:

★ The fruits whose juice are sucked and

★ The fruits that can be cut into slices. They are called Kalmi mangoes.

616 Mango – Bengal Gram – Fenugreek : Hot

500 g	cut sour mango, size into small pieces;
125 g	whole bengal gram &
75 g	salt, combine all three & set aside for 2 days
50 g	chilli powder
25 g	mustard seeds, sun-dry & powder
15 g	fenugreek seeds, roast in oil & powder
3 g	mustard seeds &
a few	sprigs curry leaves: both for seasoning
200 ml	oil

1. Combine the spice powders with the salt-soaked mango mixture and stir well.
2. Heat a little oil, add the mustard seeds, curry leaves and fry till done.
3. Pour the seasoning and the remaining oil (after heating & cooling) into the mango mixture. Stir thoroughly.
4. The pickle is ready for use after 10 days. It lasts for 2 months.

617 Treated Mango : Hot

500 g	sliced mango, peel & size lengthwise
30 g	chilli powder
5 g	turmeric powder
5 g	asafoetida, roast in oil & powder
5 g	dried red chillies, break into bits;
5 g	split husked black gram;
5 g	mustard seeds;
5 g	fenugreek seeds &
a few	sprigs curry leaves : all for seasoning
75 g	salt
250 ml	oil : heat & cool

1. Marinate the mango slices in the salt-turmeric mixture for 3 days.
2. Squeeze out the mango slices from the salt water and sun for 2 days.
3. Separately sun the salt water also for 2 days.
4. Strain the salt water, blend in the chilli and asafoetida powders.
5. Pour the spicy liquid over the mango pieces and stir well.
6. Heat a little oil, add the mustard seeds, fenugreek seeds and allow to crackle.
7. Follow with the dried red chillies, black gram, curry leaves and fry till golden.
8. Pour the seasoning and the remaining oil over the mango mixture. Do not stir.
9. Stir the mango mixture the following day.
10. The pickle is ready for use. It lasts for 6 months.

618 Small Mango Avakkai : Tender

500 g	tender mango with soft centres, keep whole
40 g	chilli powder
25 g	mustard seeds, grind to a paste with 25ml water
5 g	turmeric powder
50 g	salt
200 ml	raw gingelly oil

1. Combine the mustard paste and salt with the chilli and turmeric powders.
2. Add in the mangoes and pour over the oil to cover.
3. The pickle is ready for use after 2 weeks. It lasts for 1 month. Stir occasionally.

619 Pounded Mango : Hot

1 kg	cut mango, size into small pieces
60 g	chilli powder;
50 g	mustard seeds, sun-dry & powder;
5 g	turmeric powder &
5 g	asafoetida, roast in oil & powder, combine all evenly
120 g	salt
400 ml	oil : heat & cool

1. Marinate the mango pieces with the salt-turmeric mixture in the evening and set aside.
2. The following morning remove the mango pieces from the salt water and sun for a day.
3. Reserve the salt water.
4. The same evening pound the pieces coarsely and drop back into the salt water.
5. Blend the spice mixture with the mango mixture.
6. Pour the pre-heated oil over the pickle to cover.
7. The pickle is ready for use after 2 weeks. It lasts for 1 year.

Variation
Instead of mustard powder and asafoetida powder, addition of fenugreek seeds, coriander seeds, cummin seeds, onion seeds, aniseeds, peppercorns, cinnamon and cloves will make for the totally different flavour. Spices may be added to taste.

Tender Mangoes
Its selection is very important. Avoid the soft, yellow, scarred ones. The firm, bright green, unblemished ones are ideal. The round variety is tastier than the long variety. Slightly larger mangoes are preferred because of their slight sour taste. After salting for ten days discard the soft mangoes.

620   Salted Baby Mango : Tender

1 kg	small sour tender mango, keep whole	250 g	salt
		10 ml	castor oil

1. Smear the mangoes with the castor oil and toss well.
2. Combine the salt and the oiled mangoes in a jar.
3. Cover and set aside for 10 days until all the salt has dissolved. Shake the jar twice daily.
4. Drain and strain the salt water. Bring to the boil and allow to cool.
5. Pour back the cooled salt water over the mangoes and stir occasionally.
6. The pickle is ready for use after 5 days. It lasts for 1 year.

621   Tender Mango – Ginger – Green Chilli : Hot

500 g	tender mango with soft seeds, size into thin slices
125 g	fresh ginger, scrape & thinly slice
125 g	green chillies, slit
100 g	salted dried lime pieces
40 ml	lime juice;
40 ml	vinegar &
150 ml	oil, combine all three evenly
5 g	turmeric powder
5 g	aniseeds;
5 g	fenugreek seeds;
3 g	asafoetida &
3 g	onion seeds, roast all in oil & powder together
3 g	chilli powder
75 g	salt

1. Combine the spice powders and salt with the vinegar mixture.
2. Combine the ginger, green chilli and lime pieces with the mango slices.
3. Sprinkle some spice mixture at the base of a jar.
4. Dip the mango mixture in the spice mixture and arrange in the jar.
5. Sprinkle some spice mixture and pour over a little oil.
6. Repeat this process until the mango mixture is exhausted.
7. Add in any remaining spice mixture and oil over the pickle.
8. Sun the pickle for a week or until the mango skins lighten.
9. Pack in jars and cover with the remaining oil.
10. The pickle is ready for use. It lasts for 6 months.

622   Mango – Lime Juice : Hot

500 g	chopped mango, peel	2 g	asafoetida, roast both in oil & powder
30 g	chilli powder	2 g	mustard seeds : for seasoning
50 ml	lime juice		
2 g	turmeric powder	60 g	salt
2 g	fenugreek seeds &	125 ml	oil

1. Marinate the chopped mango with the salt in a jar and sun for 2 days.
2. Thereafter, combine the spice mixture with the salted mangoes.
3. Pour over the lime juice and blend well.
4. Heat the oil, add mustard seeds and allow to crackle. Remove and allow to cool.
5. Pour the seasoning over the mango mixture and stir thoroughly.
6. The pickle is ready for use. It lasts for 2 months. Sun occasionally.

623   Spice Stuffed Mango : Hot

500 g	seeded mango, split into 4 without severing
30 g	chilli powder;
10 g	split husked mustard seeds;
10 g	aniseeds, roast in oil & powder;
10 g	fenugreek seeds, roast both in oil & powder;
10 g	dried ginger powder &
5 g	asafoetida, roast in oil & powder, combine all evenly
60 g	salt
200 ml	oil

1. Blend all the spice powders with a little oil to a paste.
2. Stuff the spice paste into the split mango and pack tight in a jar. Set aside for 3 days.
3. Pour over the remaining oil to cover.
4. The pickle is ready for use. It lasts for 6 months. Stir occasionally.

624   Spicy Mango – Coriander Seeds : Hot

500 g	seeded mango, peel & grate
30 g	chilli powder
15 g	coriander seeds;
8 g	onion seeds &
3 g	cummin seeds, dry-roast all three & powder
3 g	asafoetida, roast in oil & powder
3 g	turmeric powder
60 g	sugar
60 g	salt
200 ml	oil

1. Combine the spice powders with the salt evenly.
2. Squeeze out the water from the grated mango.
3. Stir the squeezed mango into the spice mixture along with the oil, transfer to a jar and sun for a month.
4. The pickle lasts for 3 months. Sun occasionally.

625 Peppered Mango: Hot

500 g	cut mango, size into small pieces
25 g	black pepper;
10 g	aniseeds;
10 g	fenugreek seeds;
10 g	onion seeds &
5 g	mustard seeds, dry-roast all & powder
5 g	turmeric powder
60 g	salt
200 ml	oil

1. Arrange a layer of the mango in a wide-mouthed shallow jar.
2. Sprinkle over a layer of the spice mixture and follow with a layer of the mango.
3. Repeat this process until all the mango pieces are layered.
4. Sprinkle the remaining spice mixture over the mango mixture and set aside.
5. Pour the oil over the mango mixture and stir every day for 10 days.
6. The pickle is ready for use after 5 days. It lasts for 1 year.

626 Dried Mango – Onion - Garlic: Hot

500 g	dried unsalted mango
20 g	onion, peel & slice
20 g	peeled garlic, chop
50 g	green chillies, pound
2-1"	pieces of fresh ginger, scrape & chop
10 g	seedless raisin, chop
20 g	sugar
150 ml	vinegar
75 g	salt

1. Soak the dried mango in sufficient hot water to soften.
2. Combine all the ingredients with the salt evenly.
3. Stir in the soaked mango and transfer to a jar.
4. Heat the vinegar to boiling and pour over the mango mixture. Sun for a month.
5. The pickle lasts for 6 months. Sun occasionally.

627 Seasoned Spiced Tender Mango: Hot

1 kg	tender mango with soft seeds, keep whole	10 g	mustard seeds: for seasoning
100 g	dried red chillies;	325 g	salt
10 g	fenugreek seeds;	20 ml	castor oil: for coating mangoes
10 g	asafoetida powder &	75 ml	oil
10 g	turmeric powder, roast all in oil & powder coarsely	5 g	turmeric powder &
		10 ml	oil: for capping

1. Smear the castor oil over the mangoes. Add the salt and set aside for 5 days.
2. Drain out and strain the salt water given out by the mangoes.
3. Boil the salt water and allow to cool.
4. Grind the spice powders with the cooled salt water.
5. Add the salted mangoes into the spicy liquid.
6. Heat the oil, add mustard seeds and allow to crackle.
7. Pour the seasoning over the mango mixture and set aside for 5 days.
8. Place a thin cloth dipped in oil and turmeric powder over the mouth of the jar before placing the lid over it.
9. The pickle lasts for 1 year. Stir occasionally.

628 Vinegared Tender Mango: Hot

1 kg	tender mango, with soft seeds, keep whole	5 g	asafoetida, roast in oil & powder, combine all evenly
50 ml	vinegar: heat & cool	20 ml	castor oil: for coating mangoes
300 g	salt	100 ml	oil
60 g	coarse chilli powder;	5 g	turmeric powder &
10 g	mustard seeds, sun-dry & powder;	10 ml	oil: for capping
5 g	turmeric powder &		

1. Smear the castor oil over the mangoes. Add the salt and set aside for 5 days.
2. Drain out and strain the salt water given out by the mangoes.
3. Boil the salt water and allow to cool.
4. Grind the spice powders with the cooled salt water. Blend in the vinegar and oil.
5. Add the salted mangoes into the spicy liquid and set aside for 5 more days.
6. Place a thin cloth dipped in oil and turmeric powder over the mouth of the jar before placing the lid over it.
7. The pickle lasts for 1 year. Stir occasionally.

Note: There are different types of **vinegar** like garlic vinegar, herb vinegar, malt vinegar, wine vinegar, white vinegar and red vinegar. Malt vinegar is the preferred vinegar for pickles and chutneys.

629 Spiced Tender Cut Mango : Hot

500 g	salted tender mango, size into lengthy pieces
25 g	dried red chillies &
5 g	mustard seeds, sun-dry & powder coarsely
5 g	turmeric powder
2 g	coriander seeds;
2 g	fenugreek seeds &
2 g	asafoetida, roast all three in oil & powder coarsely
75 ml	oil
5 g	turmeric powder &
10 ml	oil : for capping

1. Stir the mango pieces into the spice mixture and sun for 2 days.
2. Pour over the oil and sun for 2 more days.
3. Ensure that the oil stands a clear 1" over the pickle.
4. Place a thin cloth dipped in oil and turmeric powder over the mouth of the jar before placing the lid over it.
5. The pickle is ready for use after a week. It lasts for 6 months. Sun occasionally.

For an economical pickle, buy mangoes in the season - when they are at their cheapest and tastiest. Salt and dry in the sun for a few days. Use instead of fresh mango and pickle likewise.

630 Tender Mango : Hot

1 kg	tender mango with soft seeds, keep whole
60 g	dried red chillies &
25 g	mustard seeds, sun-dry both & powder together coarsely
5 g	turmeric powder
150 ml	water
300 g	salt
10 ml	castor oil : for coating mangoes
5 g	turmeric powder &
10 ml	oil : for capping

1. Smear the castor oil over the mangoes. Add the salt and set aside for 5 days.
2. Blend the spice mixture in 150ml water.
3. Add the spiced liquid into the salted mangoes, stir thoroughly and set aside for 5 days. Shake twice daily.
4. Place a thin cloth dipped in oil and turmeric powder over the mouth of the jar before placing the lid over it.
5. The pickle is ready for use after 15 days. It lasts for 1 year. Stir frequently.

631 Plain Tender Mango : Watery

1 kg	tender mango with soft seeds, keep whole
40 g	dried red chillies, sun-dry & powder coarsely
225 g	salt
5 g	turmeric powder
15 ml	castor oil : for coating mangoes
5 g	turmeric powder &
10 ml	oil : for capping

1. Smear the castor oil over the mangoes. Add the salt and set aside for 5 days.
2. Drain out and strain the salt water given out by the mangoes.
3. Boil the salt water and allow to cool.
4. Grind the red chillies, turmeric powder with the cooled salted water.
5. Add the salted mangoes into the spicy liquid and set aside for 5 days.
6. Place a thin cloth dipped in oil and turmeric powder over the mouth of the jar before placing the lid over it.
7. The pickle lasts for 1 year. Stir occasionally.

632 Spicy Slit Mango : Watery

1 kg	seeded salted mango, split into 4 without severing
water	sufficient to cover : boil & cool
10	dried red chillies, slit & seed
100 g	dried red chillies &
20 g	asafoetida, roast both in oil & powder
20 g	turmeric powder
50 g	mustard seeds &
20 g	fenugreek seeds: both for seasoning
500 g	salt
500 ml	oil

1. Heat a little oil, add the mustard seeds, fenugreek seeds and allow to crackle.
2. Add in the asafoetida, turmeric powders, dried red chillies, fry for a minute and remove.
3. Blend in the chilli powder and salt to a paste.
4. Stuff the spice paste into the split mango and transfer to the jar. Set aside for 5 days.
5. Pour the cooled water, the remaining oil (after heating & cooling) over the mango mixture and stir thoroughly.
6. The pickle is ready for use. It keeps for 2 weeks.

633 Dried Raw Mango : Salty

1 kg	cut mature sour mango, size medium
100 g	salt

1. Combine the salt with the mangoes in a jar, shake well, cover and set aside.
2. Uncover the jar after a week and toss well.
3. Cover and set aside. Repeat this process after a week.
4. Remove the mango pieces from the salt water and sun till dry yet soft.
5. The pickle lasts for several years.

634 Spiced Dried Mango : Sweet

125 g	dried unsalted cut mango, soak in water overnight	1 g	cummin seeds, dry-roast all three & powder
175 g	sugar	1 g	dried ginger powder
10	peppercorns;		
2	cardamoms, peel &	2 g	black salt
		5 g	salt

1. Grind the soaked mango pieces to a fine paste.
2. Stir in the water used for soaking the mango pieces and heat along with the sugar till the paste thickens.
3. Add in the roasted powders, the salts, ginger powder and mix thoroughly.
4. The pickle is ready for use. It keeps for 10 days and is best refrigerated.

635 Peppered Mango – Ginger : Sweet

500 g	sliced mango, size lengthwise	2 g	cummin seeds &
		2 g	onion seeds, dry-roast all three & powder coarsely
350 g	sugar		
75 ml	water		
30 g	fresh ginger, scrape & chop fine	5 g	chilli powder
		70 ml	vinegar
10 g	peppercorns;	20 g	salt

1. Marinate the mango slices in the salt and sun for 3 hours. Discard the salt water given out by the mangoes.
2. Dissolve the sugar and water over low heat. Add the mango slices, chopped ginger, spice powders and continue heating.
3. When almost dry, add in the vinegar and stir continuously, ensuring the slices remain intact.
4. Remove when dry yet soft.
5. The pickle is ready for use after 4 days. It lasts for 4 months.

636 Preserved Mango – Lime Juice : Sweet

1 kg	peeled large mango, keep whole	1 kg	sugar
		800 ml	water : for pickle
	water sufficient to immerse	30 ml	lime juice

1. Soak the peeled mangoes overnight in sufficient water to which the lime juice has been added.
2. Remove and rinse the mangoes in clean water. Mop out any excess moisture from the mangoes, prick with a fork and dry in the sharp sun for a day.
3. Heat together the sugar with 800ml water till the quantity gets reduced to half.
4. Stir in the whole dried mangoes, cook over low heat till tender and remove when the syrup thickens.
5. The pickle is ready for use after 10 days. It lasts for 1 year.
6. Drain out the syrup and heat over a low flame occasionally.

637 Mango Preserve : Sweet

1 kg	seeded mango, peel & grate	2-1"	sticks of cinnamon, keep both whole
1 kg	sugar		
5	cardamoms &	5 g	salt

1. Squeeze out the water from the grated mango.
2. Combine all the ingredients with the grated mango and cook over low heat till the sugar melts.
3. Continue cooking until the mixture thickens and the mango turns golden.
4. The pickle is ready for use after 2 days. It lasts for 1 year.

638 Spiced Mango : Sweet

500 g	seeded mature mango, peel & grate
750 g	sugar
15 g	chilli powder
5 g	cummin seeds, dry-roast & powder
20 g	salt

1. Combine the grated mango with the spice powders, sugar and salt.
2. Sun the mango mixture for 4 days.
3. The pickle lasts for 4 months.

639 Dried Mango – Date – Raisin : Sweet

500 g	dried unsalted sliced mango water sufficient to immerse	100 g	cleaned tamarind, obtain thick extract using water
500 g	sliced, dried date, stone & slice	10 g	chilli powder
		10 g	cummin seeds & peppercorns, dry-roast both & pound
40 g	seedless raisin, chop	5 g	
2-1"	pieces of fresh ginger, scrape & slice	5 g	mustard seeds: for seasoning
250 g	jaggery, grate	60 g	salt
5 g	turmeric powder	200 ml	oil

1. Soak the dried date and mango in water overnight. Next day discard the water, slice both the date and mango.
2. Heat the oil, add mustard seeds and allow to crackle. Stir in the spice powders and fry for a few seconds.
3. Follow with the sliced date, mango, ginger and stir-fry for a few minutes. Set aside.
4. Heat together the tamarind extract, jaggery, salt and allow to thicken over a high flame.
5. Stir in the mango mixture and raisin.
6. Continue cooking over low heat till the mixture becomes jam-like and leaves the sides of the pan.
7. The pickle is ready for use. Its lasts for 1 month.

640 Mango – Fig – Cashew : Sweet

500 g	seeded large mango, peel & slice thinly
400 g	sugar
1000 ml	vinegar
350 g	cashewnuts, break into bits
250 g	dried figs, slice
40 g	dried red chillies, without seeds, grind using vinegar
40 g	fresh ginger, scrape & slice
60 g	salt

1. Combine all the ingredients including the chilli paste and salt with the vinegar.
2. Bring to the boil and remove when the mixture thickens.
3. The pickle is ready for use after 7 days. It lasts for 1 year.

641 Mango Murabba : Sweet

1 measure	peeled & grated sour mango
3 measures	sugar
2	cardamoms
2	cloves
15 g	salt

1. Heat 200ml water to boiling point.
2. Stir in the grated mango and cook till the mango changes colour.
3. Add in the cardamoms, cloves, sugar, salt and remove.
4. Sun the mango mixture till it attains a two-thread consistency.
5. The pickle is ready for use. It lasts for several years.

642 Sour Spiced Mango – Dry Fruits : Sweet

1 kg	seeded mango, peel & grate
1 kg	sugar
250 ml	water
150 g	dried date, stone & chop
150 g	almond, toast & slice;
120 g	seedless raisin, chop;
60 g	pistachio nuts &
30 ml	lime juice, combine all evenly
20 g	chilli powder
10 g	dried ginger powder
10 g	onion seeds &
5 g	peppercorns, pound both coarsely
5 g	grated nutmeg
5	bay leaves
5	cardamoms;
5	cloves &
2-1"	sticks of cinnamon, keep both whole
200 ml	vinegar
100 g	salt

1. Cook the grated mango and bay leaves in 250ml water to which a teaspoon (5g) salt has been added. Set aside
2. Cook the date in 5ml vinegar till done and allow to cool.
3. Heat the remaining vinegar with the sugar till syrupy.
4. Add in the cooked mango, the remaining ingredients (except the dry fruit mixture) and continue cooking.
5. Allow to thicken over a high flame and add the dry fruit mixture.
6. Continue cooking over low heat and remove when the mixture becomes jam-like.
7. The pickle is ready for use. It lasts for 1 year.

643 Spicy Shredded Mango : Sweet

1 measure	shredded sour mango
2 measures	sugar or jaggery, grate
15 g	chilli powder
10 g	mustard seeds
8	dried red chillies, break into bits
5 g	fenugreek seeds
5 g	cummin seeds
5 g	asafoetida, roast in oil & powder
10 g	salt
200 ml	oil

1. Heat the oil, add the mustard seeds, fenugreek seeds and allow to crackle.
2. Add in the dried red chillies, cummin seeds, asafoetida powder and fry for a minute.
3. Follow with the shredded mango, chilli powder, sugar and cook till the mixture attains a single-thread consistency.
4. Blend in the salt and remove.
5. The pickle is ready for use. It lasts for 1 year.

644 Mango Avakkai – Jaggery : Sweet

1 kg	seeded mango, split into 4 without severing
750 g	jaggery, grate
125 g	chilli powder
50 g	mustard seeds, sun-dry & powder
20 g	fenugreek seeds, roast in oil & powder
5 g	turmeric powder
250 g	salt
750 ml	raw gingelly oil

1. Combine the spice powders, jaggery and the salt with half the oil to a paste.
2. Fill the spice paste into the mangoes and set aside for 3 days.
3. Thereafter sun the spiced mango for 7 days.
4. Simultaneously sun the sauce for 3 days separately.
5. On the 8th day put back the mangoes into the sauce.
6. Pour the remaining oil over the pickle.
7. The pickle is ready for use after 3 weeks. It lasts for 1 year.

645 Mango Ginger – Garlic : Hot

500 g	peeled mango ginger, chop fine
250 g	peeled garlic, chop fine
50 g	chilli powder;
10 g	turmeric powder;
125 ml	lime juice &
75 g	salt, blend all together
10 g	mustard seeds &
5 g	asafoetida, roast in oil & powder : both for seasoning
250 ml	oil

1. Combine the chopped mango ginger and garlic with the spice mixture.
2. Heat the oil, add mustard seeds and allow to crackle.
3. Follow with the asafoetida powder and pour the seasoning over the mango ginger mixture. Blend well.
4. The pickle is ready for use after 2 days. It lasts for 1 month and longer in the refrigerator.

646 Mango Ginger in Lime Juice : Watery

125 g	peeled mango ginger, cut into rings
25 g	tender green chillies, chop fine
5 g	turmeric powder
50 ml	lime juice
18 g	salt
25 ml	oil

1. Combine the turmeric powder and salt with the lime juice.
2. Add in the mango ginger, green chillies and toss well.
3. The pickle is ready for use after a day. It keeps for 10 days and longer in the refrigerator.

647 Mango Ginger : Hot

500 g	peeled mango ginger, chop
50 g	chilli powder
5 g	turmeric powder
5 g	asafoetida, roast in oil & powder
5 g	mustard seeds : for seasoning
175 ml	lime juice
75 g	salt
250 ml	oil

1. Heat a little oil, add mustard seeds and allow to crackle.
2. Add in the sliced mango-ginger and stir-fry for a few minutes over low heat till tender.
3. Stir in all the remaining ingredients (except the reserved oil) and blend well.
4. Pour over the remaining oil after heating and cooling.
5. The pickle is ready for use after 2 days. It lasts for 1 month.

Mango Ginger

Select mango ginger pieces that are unblemished, medium thick with less shoots. When broken, the rings should not appear very pronounced. The ginger should appear ivory coloured. Woody stems indicate toughness. Avoid the decayed and soft ones as they are wasteful.

648 — Mango Ginger – Green Chilli in Tamarind Sauce : Hot

125 g	peeled mango ginger, chop fine
10 g	tender green chillies, chop
15 g	cleaned tamarind, obtain thin extract using water
8 g	chilli powder
3 g	turmeric powder
3 g	asafoetida, roast in oil & powder
25 g	salt
15 ml	oil : heat & cool

1. Combine the chopped mango ginger with the chopped green chilli.
2. Blend in the tamarind extract, chilli, turmeric, asafoetida powders and the salt.
3. Pour over the pre-heated oil and stir thoroughly.
4. The pickle is ready for use after 2 days. It keeps for 10 days and longer in the refrigerator.
5. Sun occasionally and shake daily.

649 — Mango Ginger – Green Pepper in Lime Juice : Hot

125 g	peeled mango ginger, cut into rings
8 g	tender green pepper, string
3 g	chilli powder
30 ml	lime juice
20 g	salt
5 g	mustard seeds &
20 ml	oil : for seasoning

1. Combine the sliced mango ginger with the remaining ingredients.
2. Heat the oil, add mustard seeds and allow to crackle.
3. Pour the seasoning over the mango ginger mixture and blend well.
4. The pickle is ready for use after 2 days. It keeps for 10 days and longer in the refrigerator.

650 — Sour Mango Ginger : Hot

125 g	peeled mango ginger, chop
12 g	chilli powder
25 g	cleaned tamarind, soak in a little water
5 g	jaggery, grate
3	cloves garlic, peel & chop
5 g	mustard seeds
2	dried red chillies, break into bits
3 g	fenugreek seeds &
3 g	asafoetida, roast both in oil & powder
20 g	salt
20 ml	oil

1. Grind together the tamarind with the jaggery coarsely.
2. Add in the remaining ingredients except the seasoning and grind again fine.
3. Heat the oil, add mustard seeds and allow to crackle.
4. Follow with the red chillies, fenugreek, asafoetida powders and fry well.
5. Pour the seasoning over the ground mixture and stir well.
6. The pickle is ready for use. It keeps for 1 week and is best refrigerated.

651 — Mango Ginger Avakkai : Hot

1 kg	peeled mango ginger, cut into rings
200 g	chilli powder
50 g	mustard seeds;
50 g	fenugreek seeds;
10 g	asafoetida &
10 g	cummin seeds, dry-roast all & powder together
400 ml	lime juice
150 g	salt
500 ml	raw gingelly oil

Spice Powders: The quantities of mustard, fenugreek & cummin seeds and asafoetida powder may be varied to suit the individual taste and preference.

1. Combine the spice powders with the salt evenly.
2. Dip the sliced mango ginger first in the oil and squeeze out the excess oil.
3. Thereafter roll in the spice mixture and arrange in a jar.
4. Sprinkle over some spice mixture and pour over a little oil.
5. Repeat this process until all the mango ginger is exhausted.
6. Cover and set aside for 3 days. On the 4th day pour over the remaining oil to cover.
7. The pickle is ready for use after 3 weeks. It lasts for 1 year.

652 Mint – Ginger - Onion : Hot

125 g	mint leaves, wash & air-dry;
1-1"	piece of fresh ginger, scrape &
60 g	onion, peel, chop all three & grind together
20 g	cleaned tamarind, obtain thick extract using water
25 g	jaggery, grate
25 g	dried red chillies;
15 g	split husked black gram;
5 g	mustard seeds &
5 g	asafoetida, roast all in oil & powder
40 g	salt
75 ml	oil

1. Stir-fry the mint-ginger paste in a little oil and set aside.
2. In the same pan heat some more oil, add the onion mixture and fry for a few minutes.
3. Pour in the tamarind extract, jaggery and bring to the boil. Allow to thicken over a high flame.
4. Add in the fried paste, spice powders, salt, the remaining oil and stir thoroughly.
5. Continue cooking over low heat until the mixture becomes jam-like and the oil separates.
6. The pickle is ready for use. It keeps for 15 days in the refrigerator.

653 Mint – Onion in Tamarind Sauce : Hot

125 g	mint leaves, wash, air-dry & chop;
75 g	onion, peel & chop;
25 g	cleaned tamarind;
35 g	dried red chillies &
50 g	salt, grind all to a paste
75 g	small onion, peel & chop fine
25 g	jaggery, grate
6	cloves garlic, peel & chop
5 g	split husked black gram;
5 g	mustard seeds &
3 g	asafoetida, roast in oil & powder : all three for seasoning
30 ml	oil

1. Heat the oil, add mustard seeds and allow to crackle. Add in the black gram, asafoetida powder and fry for a few minutes till done.
2. Add in the chopped onion, garlic and stir-fry for a few minutes.
3. Follow with the ground paste, jaggery and continue cooking over low heat.
4. Remove when the mixture becomes jam-like and leaves the sides of the pan.
5. The pickle is ready for use. It keeps for 15 days in the refrigerator.

Multifaceted Mint

A highly aromatic plant, mint contains plenty of vitamins and is rich in several minerals. It is valued as a carminative - which relieves gastic discomfort, a stimulant, an antispasmodic - which relieves muscle strain and a stomachic for improving the appetite. Peppermint is the most popular of all mints. It contains menthol and is well known for treating colds. It is an effective remedy for colic and flatulence. Dried powder mint is prepared by drying mint leaves in the shade and then powdering them.

654 Mint – Garlic in Tamarind Sauce : Hot

500 g	mint leaves, wash, air-dry & chop;
100 g	dried red chillies &
100 g	peeled garlic, peel & chop, grind all three to a paste
250 g	cleaned tamarind, obtain thick extract using water
60 g	jaggery, grate
10 g	asafoetida, roast in oil & powder
10 g	turmeric powder
10 g	mustard seeds : for seasoning
160 g	salt
250 ml	oil

1. Heat a little oil, add mustard seeds and allow to crackle.
2. Stir in the mint-chilli-garlic paste, fry for a few minutes and set aside.
3. In the same pan heat some more oil, add the tamarind extract, jaggery, turmeric powder, salt and bring to the boil. Allow to thicken over a high flame.
4. Stir in the fried paste, asafoetida powder and the remaining oil.
5. Continue cooking over low heat until the mixture becomes jam-like and the oil separates.
6. The pickle is ready for use. It lasts for 6 months.

655 Mint in Tamarind Sauce : Hot

125 g	mint leaves, wash, air-dry & chop
10 g	green chillies, chop
20 g	cleaned tamarind
5 g	dried red chillies, break into bits
5 g	split husked black gram
5 g	asafoetida, roast in oil & powder
3 g	turmeric powder
3 g	fenugreek seeds
15 g	salt
20 ml	oil

1. Stir-fry the mint leaves in a little oil till tender.
2. Heat the remaining oil, add in the black gram, fenugreek seeds, asafoetida, green chillies, red chillies and fry for a few minutes.
3. Grind the fried ingredients with the mint leaves, tamarind, turmeric powder and the salt to a fine paste with a little water.
4. The pickle is ready for use. It keeps for 1 week in the refrigerator.

656 Mixed Fruit in Spiced Vinegar : Sweet

500 g	fruit pieces : choice – peach, pear, cherry, ber or grape, singly or combined, peel, core, seed, stone & chop as required
400 g	sugar
5 g	chilli powder
5	cloves &
2-1"	sticks of cinnamon, keep both whole
150 ml	vinegar
20 g	salt

1. Bring the sugar and vinegar to the boil. Drop in the prepared fruit and cook till almost tender.
2. Remove the cooked fruit from the juice with a perforated spoon and arrange in a jar.
3. Add the chilli powder, whole spices, salt into the juice and boil until the juice becomes syrupy.
4. Remove and pour the spicy syrup over the fruit.
5. The pickle is ready for use after 4 days. It lasts for 2 months.

657 Mixed Fruit in Lime – Pineapple Juice : Sweet

250 g	ripe malabar banana, peel & cut
100 g	chopped cooking apple &
100 g	chopped pear, peel & core both
75 g	shelled pomegranate
75 g	seeded mango, peel & chop
750 g	sugar
100 ml	water
100 ml	lime juice
100 ml	pineapple juice
15 g	chilli powder
3 ml	rose water
30 g	salt

1. Heat 100ml water in a pan. Add in the sugar, stir to dissolve and heat for 10 minutes.
2. Add half the lime juice and remove. Strain and cool the contents.
3. Stir in the pineapple juice and the remaining lime juice.
4. Follow with the rose water and stir well.
5. The mixture will now have a transparent, yellowish appearance.
6. Add in the chopped fruit, chilli powder, salt and mix thoroughly. Remove and allow to cool.
7. The pickle is ready for use. It keeps for 15 days in the refrigerator. Stir frequently.

658 Sour Mint – Raisin : Sweet

125 g	mint leaves, wash, air-dry & chop
75 g	sugar candy
25 ml	vinegar
30 g	seedless raisin, chop
10 g	chilli powder
15 g	salt

1. Crush the mint leaves with the salt.
2. Grind together all the ingredients to a fine paste with a little vinegar. Add no water.
3. Blend in the remaining vinegar.
4. The pickle is ready for use. It keeps for 1 week and is best refrigerated.

659 Spicy Mixed Fruit – Jaggery in Vinegar : Sweet

250 g	sliced cooking apple, peel & core
125 g	chopped prune &
125 g	chopped dried apricot, stone both
400 g	jaggery, grate
10 g	dried ginger powder
5 g	chilli powder
5	cloves &
2-1"	stick of cinnamon, keep both whole
200 ml	vinegar
25 g	salt

1. Heat together the vinegar and jaggery.
2. Stir in the chopped prune, apricot, spice powders, whole spices and salt.
3. Bring to the boil and cook for 10 minutes.
4. Add in the chopped apple, simmer until the mixture turns soft and brown.
5. The pickle is ready for use after a day. It lasts for 1 month.

660 Mustard Mixed Fruit : Sweet

500 g	whole dried fruit : choice – apricot, fig, prune, pear, peach, apple or pineapple, singly or combined, peel, core, seed, stone, skin, remove eyes & chop as required
500 g	sugar
30 g	mustard seeds, sun-dry & powder
1000 ml	water
200 ml	vinegar
15 g	salt

1. Combine the mustard powder, sugar, salt with the water and vinegar. Bring to the boil and stir frequently.
2. Remove, add in the dry fruits and stir well. Cover and set aside for 4 hours.
3. Return to the fire and bring gently to the boil. Cook for 10 minutes over low heat and remove.
4. The pickle is ready for use after 3 days. It lasts for 4 months.

661 Sour Apple – Pineapple : Sweet

250 g	chopped cooking apple, peel & core
100 g	pineapple, cut into chunks
75 g	seedless raisin, chop
75 g	halved apricot, stone
5 g	chilli powder
1 g	panch phoran powder
125 g	jaggery, grate
150 ml	vinegar
75 ml	water

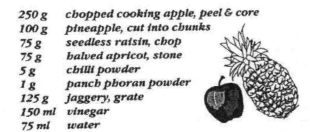

1. Combine the jaggery, spice mixture with the water and vinegar.
2. Cook over low heat till the jaggery dissolves.
3. Boil for 2 minutes. Stir in the pineapple chunks, chopped raisin and cook for 5 minutes.
4. Add in the chopped apple, apricot and cook until the apples become translucent.
5. The pickle is ready for use after 2 days. It lasts for 1 month.

662 Apple – Fig in Vinegar : Sweet

300 g	chopped cooking apple, peel & core
150 g	chopped fig, fresh or dried
50 g	chopped onion, peel
50 g	seedless raisin, chop
5 g	coriander seeds, coarsely crush
5 g	dried ginger powder
5 g	chilli powder
250 g	jaggery, grate
250 ml	vinegar
25 g	salt

1. Combine the chopped onion, fig, raisin, ginger, coriander, chilli powders with the vinegar and salt.
2. Cook for 15 minutes until the apples become partly tender.
3. Add in the jaggery and stir to dissolve.
4. Bring rapidly to the boil until the mixture thickens.
5. Stir frequently and remove if a spoon leaves a burrow when drawn.
6. The pickle is ready for use after 4 days. It lasts for 1 month.

Apple

Apples with a sweet and sour taste are abundantly available in August and September. According to Ayurveds due to its high phosphorus content, it serves as an excellent brain and nerve food. Due to its high pectin content, it heals & cures intestinal diseases and keeps the bowel clean and active. It increases the flow of the bile and is therefore good for those with a sluggish liver.

663 Banana – Date - Raisin : Sweet

250 g	ripe malabar banana, peel & slice
250 g	chopped date, stone
25 g	seedless raisin, chop
50 g	tender green chillies, chop
50 g	grated coconut, dry-roast
25 g	jaggery, grate
10 g	chopped green coriander, wash, air-dry & chop
15 g	sesame seeds, dry-roast & powder
5 g	chilli powder
5 g	turmeric powder
25 g	salt
20 ml	oil

1. Stir-fry the green chillies, chopped coriander in a little oil and set aside.
2. Heat the remaining oil, add 200ml water and bring to the boil.
3. After 2 minutes add in the chopped date, raisin, sesame powder, grated coconut and boil for 15 minutes.
4. Stir in the tamarind extract, jaggery and continue cooking.
5. Add in the sliced banana, fried ingredients, chilli, turmeric powders, salt and allow to thicken over a high flame.
6. Remove when the mixture becomes jam-like.
7. The pickle is ready for use. It lasts for 1 month.

664 Mixed Cauliflower – Potato - Peas : Hot

500 g	cauliflower florets
250 g	baby potato, peel & prick with a fork
250 g	shelled green peas
30 g	salt : for marinating
50 g	tender green chillies &
4	fresh red chillies, chop both
50 g	chilli powder
20 g	mustard seeds, sun-dry & powder
20 g	turmeric powder
10 g	panch phoran powder
250 ml	vinegar
100 g	salt : for pickle
600 ml	oil

1. Blanch the prepared vegetables for 3 minutes in lightly salted water. Drain and sun-dry for a day.
2. Stir in 50g salt, green chillies, red chillies and the oil.
3. Transfer to a jar, cap tight and sun for 3 days.
4. Combine all the spice powders and vinegar with the remaining salt evenly.
5. Add the vinegar mixture into the dried vegetable mixture and sun for a week.
6. The pickle is ready for use. It lasts for 6 months.

665 Vinegared Mixed Vegetable in Lime Juice : Hot

500 g	mixed vegetables : choice – potato, carrot, peas, beans, mango, raw plantain, cluster beans, knol-khol, turnip, singly or combined, peel, shell, scrape, cut or top & tail as required
40 g	chilli powder
5 g	mustard seeds, sun-dry & powder
5 g	turmeric powder
5 g	fenugreek seeds &
5 g	asafoetida, roast both in oil & powder
5 g	sugar
30 ml	vinegar
150 ml	lime juice &
60 g	salt, combine both
250 ml	oil

1. Wash and drain the prepared vegetables in a colander and pat-dry with a towel. Allow to dry indoors on a clean cloth.
2. When dry, combine with the sugar, turmeric powder, toss well and set aside for an hour.
3. Heat the oil, add the spiced vegetables and cook till partly tender.
4. Add in the remaining spice powders, the vinegar and blend well.
5. Stir in the salted lime juice and remove when the mixture begins to bubble.
6. The pickle is ready for use after 3 days. It lasts for 2 months.
7. Sun and stir occasionally.

666 Mixed Cauliflower – Carrot - Peas in Lime Juice : Hot

125 g	cauliflower florets	2 g	asafoetida, roast all three in oil & powder	
125 g	carrot, peel & cube			
100 g	shelled peas			
75 g	beans, top, tail & julienne	15 g	mustard seeds, sun-dry & powder	
75 g	capsicum, cut into chunks	5 g	turmeric powder	
		100 ml	vinegar	
25 g	spring onions, chop	50 ml	lime juice	
40 g	dried red chillies;	70 g	salt	
2 g	fenugreek seeds &	50 ml	oil	

1. Blanch the prepared vegetables in sufficient boiling water for 3 minutes. Drain well and spread to dry on a clean cloth.
2. Heat the oil, add in the dried vegetables, chilli, turmeric powders, salt and cook till tender.
3. Add in the remaining spice powders, lime juice, vinegar and remove when the mixture begins to bubble.
4. The pickle is ready for use after 2 days. It lasts for 2 months.

Mixed Vegetables

Vegetables are valuable in maintaining the alkaline reserve in the body. They are prized mainly for their high content of vitamins and minerals. Vegetables contains Vitamins A, B and C in fair amounts. Deep green vegetables are wonderful sources of carotene. Faulty cooking and prolonged careless storage can destroy these valuable elements.

667 Sour Lady's finger – Snake gourd : Hot

300 g	lady's finger, wash, wipe & slice into thin rounds		
150 g	tender snake gourd;		
80 g	lime, chop & seed;		
50 g	stem greens &		
30	tender green chillies, cut all into small pieces		
25 g	chilli powder;		
5 g	turmeric powder &	150 ml	lime juice
60 g	salt, combine all three evenly	20 ml	oil

1. Wash the prepared vegetables except the lady's finger, drain and air-dry on a clean cloth.
2. Heat the oil to smoking point and remove. When the oil is still lukewarm, stir in the spice mixture and blend well.
3. Pack the vegetables in a jar, add the spiced oil and mix thoroughly.
4. Pour over the lime juice and blend well.
5. The pickle is ready for use after 3 days. It keeps for 1 week and longer if sunned occasionally.

668 Mixed Vegetable – Date – Green Spices : Hot

500 g	mixed vegetables : choice – carrot, peas, cauliflower, beetroot, potato, butter beans, beans, singly or combined, peel, shell, scrape, cut, top, tail & separate into florets as required
15 g	salt : for blanching
100 g	chopped dried date, stone
40 g	tender green chillies, chop
25 g	fresh ginger, scrape & chop
10 g	onion, peel & chop
5	cloves garlic, peel & chop
50 g	mustard seeds;
15 g	dried red chillies;
15 g	peppercorns &
5 g	cummin seeds, sun-dry all & powder
5	cardamoms,
5	cloves &
2-1"	sticks of cinnamon, keep all three whole
150 ml	lime juice
50 ml	vinegar
65 g	salt : for pickle
300 ml	oil : heat & cool

1. Blanch the prepared vegetables in lightly salted boiling water for 2 minutes. Drain and dry.
2. Stir-fry the green chillies, ginger, onion and garlic in a little oil until the onion becomes transluscent.
3. Add in the chopped dates, spice powders, whole spices, salt to the vegetables and cook for a few minutes.
4. Pour over the vinegar and oil to cover and remove.
6. Stir in the lime juice and sun for a week.
7. The pickle is ready for use after 3 days. It lasts for 2 months.
8. Sun and stir occasionally.

669 Mixed Vegetable – Mango – Lime : Hot

500 g	mango &		
200 g	lime, seed, size both into small pieces		
100 g	potato;		
50 g	elephant yam &		
50 g	raw plantain, peel all three & julienne		
50 g	tender snake gourd &		
50 g	tender bitter gourd, scrape, size into thin long pieces		
50 g	beans &		
50 g	cluster beans, top, tail both & julienne		
50 g	brinjal, cube		
50 g	drumstick, cut into 4" lengths		
15 g	salt : for blanching		
100 g	tender green chillies, slit		
30 g	chilli powder		
10 g	turmeric powder		
5 g	fenugreek seeds &		
5 g	asafoetida, roast both in oil & powder		
10 g	mustard seeds : for seasoning		
175 ml	lime juice		
190 g	salt : for pickle	10ml	oil

1. Blanch the prepared vegetables in lightly salted boiling water for 2 minutes. Drain and air-dry.
2. Combine the prepared vegetables, mango, lime pieces with the spice powders, lime juice and salt. Mix well and set aside.
3. Heat the oil, add mustard seeds and allow to crackle.
4. Stir in the green chillies and fry for a few minutes.
5. Pour the seasoning over the pickle.
6. The pickle is ready for use when the vegetables have soaked in the spice powders and lime juice. It lasts for 2 months.

670 Radish – Brinjal : Hot

250 g	radish, peel & chop
250 g	brinjal, cut into small pieces
80 g	cleaned tamarind, obtain thick extract using water
25 g	jaggery, grate
25 g	chilli powder
3 g	fenugreek seeds &
3 g	asafoetida, roast both in oil & powder
3 g	turmeric powder
65 g	salt
150 ml	oil

1. Add the salt and turmeric powder to the radish and brinjal pieces. Shake well and set aside for 2 days.
2. On the 3rd day, remove the vegetable pieces and sun-dry on a clean cloth.
3. Combine the tamarind extract, jaggery and allow to soak for a day.
4. Pound the dried vegetables with the tamarind extract.
5. Heat the oil, add the vegetable mixture and allow to thicken. Stir in all the spice powders thoroughly, remove and transfer to a jar.
6. The pickle is ready for use after a week. It lasts for 6 months. Sun and stir frequently.

671 Mango – Lime - Kalakkai : Hot

150 g	seeded mango, size into small pieces
100 g	lime, split into 4 without severing & seed
100 g	kalakkai, cut into 4 & seed
100 g	fresh ginger, scrape & chop fine
50 g	tender green chillies, slit
50 g	chilli powder
5 g	mustard seeds &
5 g	fenugreek seeds, dry-roast both & powder
5 g	asafoetida, roast in oil & powder
5 g	turmeric powder
5 g	mustard seeds : for seasoning
125 g	salt
50 ml	oil

1. Heat the oil, add mustard seeds, allow to crackle and remove. Add in all the prepared vegetables and mix well.
2. Stir in all the spice powders, salt and blend well.
3. Transfer the mixture to a wide-mouthed jar. Sun and stir the pickle for 10 days. Stir daily.
4. The pickle is ready for use after 2 weeks. It lasts for 6 months.

672 Colocasia – Brinjal : Hot

250 g	colocasia, cook, peel, cut into small pieces & deep-fry
250 g	tiny brinjal, split into 4 without severing & deep-fry
40 g	chilli powder
5 g	mustard seeds, sun-dry & powder
175 ml	lime juice
60 g	salt
400 ml	oil

1. Heat the oil and remove. When the oil is still lukewarm stir in the chilli, mustard powders, salt and mix thoroughly.
2. Dip the fried brinjals in the spiced oil and arrange in a jar. Similarly dip the fried colocasia and arrange in the same jar alternately.
3. Sun the jar with contents for 3 days. Stir in the lime juice and mix well.
4. The pickle is ready for use. It lasts for 1 month. Sun and stir occasionally.

673 Brinjal – Potato : Hot

200 g	brinjal, cube
150 g	potato, peel & cube
150 g	sour tomato &
100 g	onion, peel, chop both & grind to a paste
50 g	tender green chillies, chop
5 g	mustard seeds &
a few	sprigs curry leaves : both for seasoning
3 g	turmeric powder
10 g	sugar
10 ml	lime juice
40 ml	vinegar
50 g	salt
150 ml	oil

Drop chopped brinjal and chopped potato into water to prevent discolouration.

1. Deep-fry the cubed potato and stir-fry the cubed brinjal in a little oil. Set both aside.
2. Heat some more oil, add mustard seeds and allow to crackle. Stir in the curry leaves, onion-tomato paste, green chillies and fry for a few minutes.
3. Add in the fried potato, fried brinjal, turmeric powder, sugar, salt, vinegar, the remaining oil and cook over low heat.
4. Continue cooking until the mixture becomes jam-like and the oil separates.
5. Stir in the lime juice and remove when the mixture begins to bubble.
6. The pickle is ready for use. It lasts for 2 months.

674 Spiced Mixed Vegetable – Lime Strips : Hot

75 g	cauliflower florets
75 g	carrot &
70 g	beetroot, peel & cut into small pieces
70 g	beans, top, tail & julienne
70 g	knol khol, peel & slice
70 g	cucumber, scrub &
70 g	capsicum, cut both into small pieces
40 g	lime, cut into thin strips
30 g	tender green chillies, slit
2-1"	pieces of fresh ginger, scrape & chop fine
15 g	chilli powder
5 g	mustard seeds, sun-dry & powder
5 g	fenugreek seeds &
3 g	asafoetida, roast both in oil & powder
100 ml	vinegar
25 g	citric acid
60 g	salt
50 ml	oil

1. Stir-fry the prepared vegetables in a little oil for 10 minutes and remove.
2. Add in the citric acid and mix well.
3. Mix the spice powders, salt, vinegar and the remaining oil thoroughly.
4. The pickle is ready for use after 1 week. It lasts for 1 month. Sun and stir occasionally.

675 Assorted Vegetables : Hot

200 g	red pumpkin, peel & chop
150 g	radish, peel & chop
150 g	brinjal, cube
25 g	dried red chillies, break into bits
50 g	cleaned tamarind, obtain thick extract using water
5 g	turmeric powder
5 g	cummin seeds &
5 g	mustard seeds: both for seasoning
20 g	sugar
35 g	salt
200 ml	oil

1. Stir-fry the prepared vegetables in a little oil till partly tender and set aside.
2. In the same pan heat the remaining oil, add mustard seeds and allow to crackle. Add in the cummin seeds, dried red chillies and fry for a minute.
3. Pour in the tamarind extract, sugar, salt, turmeric powder and bring to the boil. Allow to thicken over a high flame.
4. Add in the fried vegetables and continue cooking over low heat.
5. Remove when the mixture becomes jam-like and the oil separates.
6. The pickle is ready for use. It lasts for 2 months.

676 Sour & Spied Mixed Vegetable : Hot

100 g	cauliflower florets
75 g	beetroot, peel & julienne
75 g	carrot, peel & julienne
75 g	capsicum, slice fine
75 g	cabbage, thickly shred
50 g	green beans, top, tail & julienne
50 g	shelled peas
30 g	tender green chillies, split
25 g	chilli powder
5 g	turmeric powder
5 g	fenugreek seeds &
5 g	asafoetida, roast both in oil & powder
10 g	mustard seeds &
a few	sprigs curry leaves: both for seasoning
175 ml	lime juice
60 g	salt
100 ml	oil

1. Combine the prepared vegetables, salt, lime juice, fenugreek and asafoetida powders evenly.
2. Heat the oil, add mustard seeds and allow to crackle. Add in the green chillies, curry leaves and fry for a minute.
3. Remove, stir in the chilli, turmeric powders and mix well.
4. Pour the seasoning over the vegetable mixture and stir thoroughly.
5. The pickle is ready for use. It keeps for 10 days and is best refrigerated.

677 Spicy Mixed Vegetable : Hot

175 g	carrot, peel & julienne
175 g	cauliflower florets
150 g	turnip, peel & julienne
30 g	tender green chillies, split
25 g	dried red chillies, break into bits
10 g	aniseeds;
5 g	mustard seeds;
3 g	fenugreek seeds;
2 g	onion seeds &
2 g	coriander seeds, dry-roast all & powder
2 g	garam masala powder
20 ml	acetic acid
60 g	salt
60 ml	oil

1. Add salt to the prepared vegetables, mix well and set aside for 2 days. Stir daily.
2. Heat the oil, add in the green chillies, broken red chillies, spice powders and fry for a few seconds.
3. Add in the vegetables and stir-fry for 2 minutes.
4. Pour over the acetic acid, heat for a few minutes and remove.
5. The pickle is ready for use. It lasts for 3 months. Sun and stir occasionally.

678 Sour Mixed Vegetable in Mustard Sauce : Hot

125 g	cauliflower florets
125 g	cucumber, scrub & cut into chunks
125 g	small red onion, peel & chop
100 g	carrot, peel & chop
75 g	green tomato, cut into chunks
30 g	tender green chillies, chop
25 g	dried red chillies, break into bits
60 g	mustard seeds, sun-dry & powder
5 g	turmeric powder
20 g	refined flour
30 g	sugar
200 ml	vinegar
60 g	salt

1. Sprinkle salt over the prepared vegetables and leave overnight. Drain and rinse the following day.
2. Blend the flour with a little cold water and heat to a sauce consistency.
3. Heat the vinegar with all the ingredients (except the flour and vegetables).
4. Do not boil. Allow to thicken and stir in the salted vegetables.
5. Pour the flour sauce over the vegetable mixture and stir well.
6. The pickle is ready for use after 2 days. It keeps for 15 days in the refrigerator.

679 Mixed Vegetable – Mustard – Garlic : Hot

500 g	mixed vegetables: choice – carrot, beans, cucumber, cabbage, peas, turnip, lady's finger, potato, radish & brinjal, singly or combined, peel, shell, scrape, cut, top & tail as required
25 g	peeled garlic, grind fine
1-1"	piece of fresh ginger, peel, chop & grind
75 g	chilli powder
60 g	jaggery, grate
25 g	mustard seeds, grind fine using vinegar
5 g	cummin seeds, dry-roast & powder
5	cardamoms;
5	cloves &
2-1"	sticks of cinnamon, keep all three whole
200 ml	vinegar
60 g	salt
40 ml	oil

1. Stir-fry the ginger-garlic paste in a little oil for a few minutes.
2. Stir in the chilli, cummin powders, the whole spices, salt and fry for 2 minutes.
3. Add in the prepared vegetables, stir-fry for a minute and remove.
4. When cool, add in the ground mustard, blend well and sun the mixture for 4 days.
5. On the 5th day, separately soak the jaggery in vinegar overnight.
6. Boil the sweetened vinegar the following day and allow to cool.
7. Pour the cooled vinegar over the pickle, cover and sun for 3 days.
8. The pickle is ready for use after 7 days. It lasts for 2 months.

680 Fried Mixed Vegetable in Vinegar : Hot

500 g	mixed vegetables: choice – cauliflower, carrot & turnip, singly or combined, peel, cut, top, tail & separate into florets as required
5	cloves garlic, peel
2-1"	pieces of fresh ginger, scrape & slice
75 g	tender green chillies, split
25 g	chilli powder
5 g	mustard seeds &
3 g	cummin seeds, dry-roast both & powder together
3 g	fenugreek seeds &
2 g	asafoetida, roast both in oil & powder
2 g	turmeric powder
5 g	mustard seeds &
a few	sprigs curry leaves: for seasoning
250 ml	vinegar
75 g	salt
250 ml	oil

1. Heat the oil, add mustard seeds and allow to crackle.
2. Add in the peeled garlic, sliced ginger, slit green chillies and fry for 3 minutes.
3. Stir in the chilli, mustard, cummin, asafoetida, turmeric powders and fry over low heat for a few seconds.
4. Add in the curry leaves and cut vegetables. Stir-fry for a while, add in the salt, vinegar and heat until the oil surfaces.
5. Remove, add in the fenugreek powder and blend well.
6. The pickle is ready for use after 3 days. It lasts for 4 months.

681 Spiced Cauliflower – Carrot : Hot

200 g	cauliflower florets
200 g	carrot, peel & chop
100 g	lady's finger, keep whole
8	cloves garlic, peel
1-1"	piece of fresh ginger, scrape & slice
30 g	tender green chillies, keep whole
25 g	chilli powder
5 g	mustard seeds;
3 g	fenugreek seeds &
3 g	asafoetida, roast all three in oil & powder
2 g	turmeric powder
10 ml	acetic acid
250 ml	water
60 g	sugar
75 g	salt

1. Combine the prepared vegetables, ginger, garlic, green chillies with the salt and turmeric powder.
2. Stir in the spice powders and blend well.
3. Heat together the water with sugar till the sugar dissolves.
4. When the water is still lukewarm pour over the vegetable mixture.
5. Add in the acetic acid and set aside for 3 hours. Store thereafter.
6. The pickle is ready for use after 3 days. It lasts for 3 months.

682 Mixed Vegetable in Tamarind – Vinegar : Hot

100 g	cauliflower florets
200 g	carrot, peel & chop
200 g	turnip, peel & chop
40 g	dried red chillies, break into bits;
40 g	fresh ginger, scrape & chop;
1	clove &
5 g	fenugreek seeds, grind all three to a paste
3 g	turmeric powder
25 g	tamarind, soak in 100 ml vinegar & obtain thick extract
125 g	jaggery, grate
60 g	salt
100 ml	oil

1. Heat a little oil to smoking point and remove. Add the ground spices and stir well.
2. Follow with the prepared vegetables and cook over low heat till partly tender. Set aside.
3. In the same pan heat the remaining oil, add in the vinegar-tamarind extract, jaggery, turmeric powder, salt and bring to the boil. Allow to thicken over a high flame.
4. Stir in the spiced fried vegetables, simmer until the mixture becomes jam-like and the oil separates.
5. The pickle is ready for use. It lasts for 4 months.

683 Mango – Lime : Hot

350 g	seeded mango, peel & chop
150 g	chopped lime, seed
30 g	tender green chillies, chop
25 g	chilli powder
5 g	asafoetida, roast in oil & powder
5 g	turmeric powder
1 g	cardamom powder
80 g	salt
400 ml	oil

1. Combine the prepared vegetables with the salt in a jar and sun for a day.
2. Next day, heat the oil and remove. When the oil is still lukewarm, add in all the spice powders and blend well. Allow to cool.
3. Pour the spiced oil over the salted vegetables and sun for 3 hours every day for 7 days. Shake the jar daily.
4. The pickle is ready for use after 15 days. It lasts for 2 years.

684 Mixed Vegetable in Mustard Sauce : Hot

100 g	shelled peas
75 g	cauliflower florets
75 g	carrot, peel & julienne
75 g	white radish, peel & julienne
75 g	broad white bean, top, tail & julienne
50 g	drumstick inner pith, cook & remove
50 g	potato, peel & cut
50 g	cleaned tamarind, obtain thick extract using water
50 g	jaggery, grate
25 g	dried red chillies &
15 g	mustard seeds, grind both to a paste using water
5 g	panch phoran powder
5 g	turmeric powder
40 g	salt

1. Blanch the prepared vegetables in sufficient boiling water for 3 minutes. Drain well and spread to dry on a clean cloth.
2. Add in the salt, turmeric powder and set aside for half an hour.
3. Combine all the spices with the salted vegetables and transfer to a jar.
4. Pour the oil over the vegetable mixture to cover. Sun for 5 days and keep indoors for 3 days.
5. The pickle keeps for 15 days. Sun occasionally.

685 Cauliflower – Broccoli : Hot

100 g	cauliflower florets
100 g	broccoli florets
100 g	carrot, peel & cube
100 g	radish, peel & cube
100 g	small onion, peel & keep whole
30 g	fresh ginger, scrape & slice
50 g	dried red chillies, break into bits
50 g	jaggery, grate
5 g	peppercorns, keep whole
200 ml	vinegar
60 g	salt

1. Combine the chilli, peppercorns, ginger, vinegar, jaggery and salt evenly.
2. Add in the prepared vegetables, stir well and seal.
3. The pickle is ready for use after 5 days. It lasts for 2 months.

686 Cauliflower – Carrot - Turnip : Hot

200 g	cauliflower florets
150 g	carrot, peel & cube
150 g	turnip, peel & cube
10 g	fresh ginger, scrape &
5	cloves garlic, peel, chop both & grind to a paste
50 g	jaggery, grate
40 g	chilli powder
5 g	garam masala powder
5 g	mustard seeds, sun-dry & powder
100 ml	water
200 ml	vinegar
60 g	salt
100 ml	oil

1. Stir-fry the ginger-garlic paste in a little oil for a few minutes and remove.
2. Bring 100ml water to the boil.
3. Add in the prepared vegetables, spice powders, jaggery, the fried paste, the remaining oil, salt and vinegar.
4. Cook over a high flame until the water evaporates and the oil separates.
5. Sun the pickle for 5 days. Shake daily.
6. The pickle is ready for use after 2 days. It lasts for 6 months.

687 Salted Mango – Loquat : Hot

500 g	cut mango, size into small pieces	25 g	fresh ginger, scrape & slice thinly
50 g	loquat, make cross slits	5 g	panch phoran powder
		5 g	chilli powder;
50 g	noga tenga	25 g	sugar &
50 g	chopped lime, seed	70 g	salt, combine all three evenly
50 g	tender green chillies, chop	100 ml	vinegar
		100 ml	oil

1. Marinate the mango and loquat in salt and transfer to a jar after it has given out water. Sun the jar for 3 days.
2. Combine the lime and ginger with the salt evenly. Sun for 3 days.
3. On the 4th day remove the vegetables from the salt water, rinse thoroughly in water and allow to dry in the shade.
4. When dry, roll the dried vegetables in the powdered spice mixture.
5. Transfer to a jar and sun for 7 days.
6. Heat the oil, add in the panch phoran and vinegar. Cool and pour the seasoning over the pickle.
7. Stir thoroughly and sun for 7 more days.
8. The pickle lasts for 6 months.

688 Mixed Vegetable – Green Chilli in Lime Juice : Hot

1 kg	vegetables : choice – brinjal, cluster beans, snakegourd, stem greens, carrot, singly or combined, peel, scrape, chop, top & tail as required		
30 g	salt : for blanching		
50 g	tender green chillies, chop	10 g	mustard seeds: for seasoning
25 g	chilli powder	350 ml	lime juice
10 g	turmeric powder	135 g	salt
5 g	asafoetida, roast in oil & powder	50 ml	oil

1. Tie the prepared vegetables in a thin cloth. Blanch the vegetable bag in lightly salted boiling water for 5 minutes. Transfer to cold water and remove.
2. Untie the vegetables and sun-dry for an hour.
3. Combine the dried vegetables with the chilli, asafoetida, turmeric powders, salt and stir thoroughly.
4. Stir in the chopped green chillies and the lime juice.
5. Heat the oil, add mustard seeds and allow to crackle.
6. Pour the seasoning over the pickle mixture and blend well.
7. The pickle is ready for use after 2 days. It keeps for 10 days and is best refrigerated.

689 Sour Mixed Vegetable : Hot

200 g	carrot, peel & chop	100 g	cleaned tamarind, obtain thick extract using water
200 g	potato, peel & cube		
200 g	beetroot, peel & chop	60 g	chilli powder
		5 g	turmeric powder
200 g	shelled green peas	5 g	fenugreek seeds & asafoetida, roast both in oil & powder
175 g	turnip, peel & chop	3 g	
100 g	seeded raw mango, peel & chop	10 g	mustard seeds: for seasoning
50 g	fresh ginger, scrape & chop	50 ml	lime juice
50 g	peeled garlic, chop	150 g	salt
		200 ml	oil

1. Marinate the prepared vegetables in a teaspoon (5g) salt for 1 hour.
2. Heat the oil, add mustard seeds and allow to crackle.
3. Add in the chopped ginger, garlic and fry for a few minutes.
4. Pour in the tamarind extract and bring to the boil. Allow to thicken over a high flame.
5. Stir in the chilli, turmeric powders and the salted vegetables.
6. Continue cooking over low heat until the mixture becomes jam-like and the oil separates.
7. Add in the fenugreek, asafoetida powders, salt, lime juice, blend well and remove when the mixture begins to bubble.
8. The pickle is ready for use. It lasts for 1 month.

690 Carrot – Peas - Beans in Lime Juice : Hot

100 g	carrot, peel & chop	10 g	chilli powder
100 g	shelled peas	5 g	mustard seeds : for seasoning
100 g	beans, top, tail & chop		
50 g	onion, peel & halve	100 ml	lime juice
		20 ml	vinegar
4	tender green chillies, chop	50 g	salt
		15 ml	oil

1. Cook the vegetables in vinegar till tender and remove.
2. Stir in the chilli powder and salt.
3. Heat the oil, add mustard seeds and allow to crackle. Stir in the lime juice and heat for 2 minutes.
4. Pour the seasoning over the spiced vegetables and mix thoroughly.
5. The pickle is ready for use. It lasts for 4 months.

691 Cauliflower – Carrot - Peas in Vinegar : Hot

400 g	cauliflower florets
200 g	carrot, peel & chop
200 g	shelled peas
100 g	turnip, peel & chop
100 g	tender beans, top, tail & chop
10 g	salt : for marinating
60 g	tender green chillies, chop
20 g	mustard seeds, sun-dry & powder
20 g	dried red chillies;
5 g	fenugreek seeds &
5 g	asafoetida, roast all three in oil & powder
5 g	turmeric powder
400 ml	vinegar
150 g	salt
150 ml	oil

1. Marinate the prepared vegetables with the salt and turmeric powder for 5 days. Stir daily.
2. Thereafter pour in the vinegar and set aside for 10 days stirring occasionally everyday.
3. Heat the oil, stir in the chilli, mustard, fenugreek, asafoetida powders and blend well.
4. Combine the spice mixture with the vegetable mixture and mix thoroughly. Set aside for 10 days and stir daily.
5. The pickle lasts for 3 months.

692 Mixed Vegetable : Hot

200 g	cauliflower florets		
100 g	carrot, peel & chop		
50 g	beans, top, tail & chop		
50 g	cabbage, shred		
50 g	knol-khol & potato, peel & chop both		
50 g			
200 ml	lime juice		
200 g	chilli powder		
5 g	asafoetida, roast in oil & powder		
5 g	mustard seeds : for seasoning		
50 g	gingelly oil	75 g	salt

1. Wash all the prepared vegetables and dry indoors for a day on a clean cloth.
2. Heat the oil, add mustard seeds and allow to crackle.
3. Blend in the chilli, asafoetida powders and salt.
4. Pour the spice mixture over the vegetable and stir thoroughly.
5. Add in the lime juice and mix well.
6. The pickle is ready for use after 1 day. It lasts for 1 month.

693 Spiced Vegetable in Vinegar : Watery

125 g	cabbage, shred thickly
100 g	cucumber, scrub & slice
100 g	turnip, peel & slice
100 g	carrot, peel & slice
75 g	chopped celery, remove stems & chop
8	peppercorns
5 g	fresh ginger, scrape & slice
2	dried red chillies
3 g	monosodium glutamate
400 ml	water
200 ml	vinegar
60 g	salt

1. Wash and drain the prepared vegetables in a colander and pat-dry with a towel. Allow to dry indoors on a clean cloth.
2. Bring water to the boil, add in all the spices and vinegar. Allow to simmer for a few minutes and remove.
3. Cool and pour the spiced vinegar over the dried vegetables to cover.
4. The pickle is ready for use after 2 days. It lasts for 1 month.

694 Mixed Vegetable in Vinegar : Watery

250 g	cauliflower florets
250 g	onion, peel & chop
25 g	fresh red chillies, slit
750 ml	water
125 ml	water, combine with 10 ml glacial acetic acid
50 g	salt

1. Blanch the prepared vegetables in 750ml boiling water for 2 minutes. Drain well and spread to dry on a clean cloth.
2. Add 50g salt and water sufficient to cover the vegetables. Set aside for a day.
3. Remove the vegetables from the salted water.
4. Add in the glacial acetic acid - water mixture to the brined vegetables and stir well.
5. The pickle is ready for use after 2 days. It lasts for 4 months.

695 Mixed Vegetable : Sweet

75 g	cabbage, shred thickly
75 g	green tomato, cut into chunks
75 g	beans, top, tail & chop
75 g	carrot &
50 g	onion, peel & chop both
50 g	chopped celery, remove stems
50 g	cucumber, scrub &
50 g	capsicum, cut both into chunks
70 g	tender green chillies, slit
10 g	thymol seeds
5 g	chilli powder
5 g	garam masala, keep whole
200 g	sugar
125 ml	vinegar
60 g	salt
50 ml	oil : heat & cool

1. Soak the chopped cucumber, onion, capsicum, tomato, cabbage and celery in water (to which 2 teaspoons (10g) salt has been added) overnight. Wash with water and drain well.
2. Blanch the carrots and beans in sufficient boiling water for 2 minutes. Drain well and set aside.
3. Bring the vinegar, sugar, chilli powder, whole garam masala and thymol seeds to the boil.
4. When the mixture is almost dry stir in the salted vegetables, green chillies, cook for 2 minutes and remove.
5. Cool and pack in a jar. Pour over the pre-heated oil and set aside.
6. The pickle is ready for use after a week. It lasts for 2 months.

> Fibres in **vegetables** especially carrot and cabbage act as mechanical intestinal expanders. They prevent habitual constipation. Fibres in the form of cellulose help in the elimination of colesterol.

696 Mixed Vegetable in Oil : Sweet

200 g	cauliflower florets
150 g	carrot, peel & julienne
150 g	turnip, peel & julienne
10 g	chilli powder
10 g	mustard seeds &
5 g	cummin seeds, sun-dry both & powder
5 g	peppercorns
1-1"	piece of fresh ginger, scrape &
2	cloves garlic, peel, chop both & grind to a paste
1-1"	stick of cinnamon;
1	cardamom &
1	clove, keep all three whole
50 g	sugar
40 g	salt
10 ml	glacial acetic acid
125 ml	oil

1. Blanch the prepared vegetables in 400ml boiling water for 2 minutes. Drain well and spread to dry on a clean cloth.
2. Stir-fry the ginger-garlic paste in oil and remove. Add in all the spice powders, the whole spices and blend well.
3. Heat together the sugar with 20ml water to make a syrup of two-thread consistency.
4. Combine the sugar syrup, fried spiced ginger-garlic, glacial acetic acid and cook for 2 minutes.
5. Stir in the dried vegetables and remove when the oil separates.
6. The pickle is ready for use after 10 days. It lasts for 6 months.

697 Mustard Mixed Vegetable : Sweet

100 g	broccoli florets	15 g	mustard seeds, sun-dry & powder	
100 g	cabbage, shred thickly			
100 g	green tomato, cut into chunks	5 g	turmeric powder	
		5 g	fenugreek seeds &	
100 g	capsicum, cut into chunks	2 g	coriander seeds, dry-roast both & powder	
100 g	spring onion, chop			
100 g	jaggery, grate	250 ml	vinegar	
8	cloves garlic	70 g	salt	
40 g	chilli powder	100 ml	oil	

1. Heat the oil, cook the garlic and the prepared vegetables with the salt till tender.
2. Add in all the remaining spice powders, vinegar, jaggery, blend well and remove.
3. The pickle is ready for use after 2 days. It lasts for 2 months.

698 Spicy Mixed Vegetable – Date : Sweet

250 g	turnip, peel & julienne	60 g	jaggery, grate	
250 g	carrot, peel & julienne	40 g	chilli powder	
100 g	date, stone & chop, soak in 100ml water	15 g	mustard seeds &	
		5 g	cummin seeds, grind both coarsely	
75 g	onion, peel;			
30 g	peeled garlic &	1-1"	stick of cinnamon, keep whole	
30 g	fresh ginger, scrape, chop all three & grind to a paste			
		50 ml	water	
		270 ml	vinegar	
40 g	cleaned tamarind, soak in 100 ml water	75 g	salt	
		250 ml	oil	

1. Fry the onion-ginger-garlic paste in a little oil till golden.
2. Stir in all the remaining ingredients except jaggery. Heat a while and remove.
3. Sun the mixture for 4 days. Stir daily.
4. Make a thick syrup of jaggery with 50ml water.
5. Blend in the dried mixture and sun for 6 days. Stir daily.
6. The pickle is ready for use after 10 days. It lasts for 4 months. Sun and stir occasionally.

699 Sour Small Red Onion : Hot

500 g	small red onion, peel & coarsely grind
200 g	cleaned tamarind, obtain thick extract using water
200 g	fresh ginger, scrape &
50 g	peeled garlic, chop both & grind fine
100 g	chilli powder
5 g	fenugreek seeds, roast in oil & powder
5 g	turmeric powder
5 g	mustard seeds : for seasoning
150 g	salt
400 ml	oil

1. Stir-fry the ginger-garlic paste in a little oil and set aside.
2. In the same pan heat some more oil, add mustard seeds and allow to crackle.
3. Stir in the onion paste and fry for a few minutes till transluscent.
4. Pour in the tamarind extract and bring to the boil. Allow to thicken over a high flame.
5. Add in the chilli, fenugreek, turmeric powders, the ginger-garlic paste, salt and the remaining oil.
6. Continue cooking over low heat for a few minutes until the mixture becomes jam-like and the oil separates.
7. The pickle is ready for use. It lasts for 1 month.

700 Small Red Onion – Green Chilli in Lime Juice : Hot

125 g	small red onion, peel	a few	sprigs curry leaves &	
15 g	green chillies, chop fine	25 ml	oil : all for seasoning	
1/2"	piece of fresh ginger, scrape & chop	40 ml	lime juice	
		20 g	salt	
3 g	turmeric powder			
3 g	asafoetida, roast in oil & powder			
3 g	mustard seeds;			

Add a pinch of salt to the squeezed juice of limes to prevent bitterness.

1. Combine all the ingredients evenly.
2. Heat the oil, add the mustard seeds, curry leaves and allow to crackle.
3. Pour the seasoning over the pickle mixture and stir thoroughly.
4. The pickle is ready for use after 2 hours. It keeps for 3 days and is best refrigerated.

701 Spicy Small Red Onion : Hot

500 g	small red onion, peel & split into 4 without severing	5 g	turmeric powder
		2	cloves;
20 g	salt : for marinating	2	cardamoms &
		2-1"	sticks of cinnamon, keep all three whole
15 g	chilli powder		
10 g	mustard seeds;		
10 g	aniseeds &		
10 g	cummin seeds, sun-dry all three & powder	30 ml	lime juice
		20 g	salt : for pickle
10 g	dried mango powder	5 g	black salt
		150 ml	oil : heat & cool

1. Smear 20g salt into and over the onion. Set aside overnight. Drain out the salt water the following day.
2. Combine the spice powders and whole spices with the lime juice and a little oil.
3. Fill the spice paste into the onion and pack tight into a jar.
4. Pour over the remaining oil, sprinkle over a little salt and set aside for 10 days.
5. The pickle lasts for 2 months.

702 Mustard Onion : Hot

500 g	small red onion, peel & split without severing
35 g	chilli powder
15 g	mustard seeds, sun-dry & powder
10 g	asafoetida, roast in oil & powder
5 g	mustard seeds : for seasoning
60 g	salt
150 ml	oil

1. Smear half the salt into the split onion and set aside for 4 hours.
2. Blend in the spice powders, the remaining salt into and over the onions.
3. Heat the oil, add mustard seeds and allow to crackle.
4. Pour the seasoning over the pickle, stir well and sun for 3 days. Shake daily.
5. The pickle lasts for 1 month. Sun occasionally.

703 Salted Mustard : Watery

500 g	black mustard seeds, sun-dry & powder
10 g	turmeric powder
1500 ml	water : boil & cool
100 g	salt

1. Blend together the mustard, turmeric powders and the salt in water.
2. Keep stirring a while until the mixture gives out a pleasant aroma.
3. Sun for 4 days. The pickle lasts for 3 months.

704 Onion in Spiced Vinegar : Watery

500 g	small onion, unpeeled
500 g	salt, combine with 4500 ml water for brine
2-1"	pieces of fresh ginger, scrape & pound;
5	peppercorns, pound;
3	cardamoms, crush;
1-1"	stick of cinnamon &
1	clove, tie all in a spice bag
175 ml	vinegar

1. Soak the unpeeled onion in the brine and set aside for 12 hours. Drain and peel.
2. Soak the peeled onion in a similar quantity of fresh brine for 36 hours.
3. Drain the onion thoroughly. Pack into jars and cover with the cold spiced vinegar.
4. Cap at once and set aside for 2 months.
5. The pickle lasts for 4 months.

705 Baby Onion in spiced Vinegar : Hot

500 g	white baby onion, peel
250 ml	water
5 g	salt : for marinating
10	peppercorns
5	cloves
5 g	dried red chillies, keep whole
5 g	mustard seeds, sun dry & crush
10 g	sugar
250 ml	vinegar
50 g	salt : for pickle
50 ml	oil

1. Soak the onion in 250ml water to which a teaspoon (5g) salt has been added.
2. Drain the onion and transfer to a jar. Add in the whole red chillies.
3. Heat the oil, add mustard seeds, cool and pour over the onion.
4. Bring the vinegar to boiling along with the sugar, salt, cloves and peppercorns.
5. Simmer for a few minutes, remove and cool. Pour the cooled spiced vinegar over the onion after discarding the spices.
6. The pickle is ready for use after 5 days. It lasts for 1 month.

706 White Onion in Mustard Sauce : Watery

500 g	small white onion, peel & split into 4 without severing
	water sufficient to immerse
40 g	chilli powder;
5 g	turmeric powder &
20 g	mustard seeds, sun-dry & powder, combine all three evenly
75 g	salt
10 g	mustard seeds : for seasoning
150 ml	oil

1. Marinate the onion in half the salt for 4 hours. Rinse in water and pat-dry.
2. Blend the spice mixture and the remaining salt in half the water and oil.
3. Stir in the salted onion and transfer to a jar. Add the remaining water to cover.
4. Heat the remaining oil, add mustard seeds and allow to crackle.
5. Pour the seasoning over the onion mixture, stir well and sun for 5 days. Shake daily.
6. The pickle lasts for 2 months. Sun occasionally.

707 Mustard White Onion : Watery

500 g	small white onion, peel
20 g	mustard seeds, sun-dry, pound & skin
10 g	chilli powder
90 g	salt

1. Combine the onion and mustard powder in a jar with the salt and water sufficient to cover.
2. Add in the chilli powder and stir well.
3. The pickle is ready for use after 3 days. It lasts for 2 months. Stir frequently.

708 Sour Button Onion : Sweet

500 g	button onion, unpeeled
120 g	jaggery, grate
10 g	mustard seeds
1/2"	stick of cinnamon, keep whole
250 ml	vinegar
25 g	salt

1. Drop the onion in sufficient boiling water for 2 minutes. Remove and peel.
2. Bring 30ml vinegar with sufficient water to the boil and blanch the onion for 5 minutes.
3. Drain, pat-dry and pack into a jar.
4. Boil the remaining vinegar with the mustard seeds, jaggery, cinnamon, salt and pour over the onion. Cool and cap tight.
5. The pickle is ready for use after 2 days. It lasts for 2 months.

709 Sour Onion – Aniseed : Hot

500 g	onion, peel & slit crosswise
30 g	chilli powder;
15 g	aniseed, sun-dry & powder;
40 g	salt &
75 ml	lime juice, combine all to a paste
75 ml	vinegar
15 g	sugar
100 ml	oil

1. Smear the spice paste into and over the onion.
2. Heat the oil in a pan. Stir in the spiced onion and fry for a few minutes.
3. Stir in the sugar.
4. Blend in the pre-heated vinegar and remove.
5. The pickle is ready for use after a day. It lasts for 2 months.

710 Stuffed Small Red Onion : Hot

500 g	small red onion, peel & split into 4 without severing
40 g	chilli powder
20 g	mustard seeds, sun-dry & powder
70 g	salt
500 ml	oil

1. Blend the spice powders and salt in a little oil to a paste.
2. Stuff each onion with the spice paste and arrange in a jar.
3. Stir in the remaining spice paste and oil into the jar. Sun for 7 days.
4. The pickle lasts for 1 month. Sun occasionally.

Onions in toto not only fight infections, allergies or are recipes for stamina, but these are essential ingredients in the kitchen. The fresh green one, commonly known as the spring onion, is a tonic and strength builder. Onion gives warmth to the body and thereby increases the body's resistance to diseases and allergies.

711 Onion – Tamarind : Hot

500 g	onion, peel & chop
100 g	cleaned tamarind
40 g	dried red chillies, break into bits
20 g	jaggery, grate
10 g	mustard seeds &
10 g	split husked black gram: both for seasoning
60 g	salt
150 ml	oil

1. Stir-fry the chopped onion, tamarind, dried red chillies and the salt generously in oil. Grind coarsely with the jaggery and set aside.
2. Heat some more oil, add mustard seeds and allow to crackle.
3. Follow with the black gram and fry till golden.
4. Pour the seasoning over the spiced onion paste and grind again but coarsely.
5. Heat the remaining oil, fry the onion paste and remove when the mixture leaves the sides of the pan.
6. The pickle is ready for use. It lasts for 1 month.

712 Spicy Onion : Hot

500 g	big onion, peel & slice lengthwise
50 g	cleaned tamarind, obtain thick extract using water
30 g	jaggery, grate
10	cloves garlic, peel & chop
2-1"	pieces of fresh ginger, scrape & chop
45 g	chilli powder
5 g	turmeric powder
5 g	mustard seeds, sun-dry & powder
5 g	fenugreek seeds;
5 g	asafoetida &
5 g	aniseeds, roast all three in oil & powder
50 g	salt
75 ml	oil

1. Combine the cut onion with the turmeric powder and set aside.
2. Stir-fry the ginger, garlic and onion in a little oil till tender.
3. Heat the remaining oil, add in the tamarind extract, jaggery and bring to the boil. Allow to thicken over a high flame.
4. Stir in the spice powders and the salt.
5. Continue cooking over low heat until the mixture becomes jam-like and the oil separates.
6. The pickle is ready for use. It lasts for 6 months.

Chopping onion
1. Remove skin, cut top off, and then cut onion in half from top to root. Place cut side down on a board, root end to your left.
2. Slice it vertically, lengthwise, almost but not quite to the root.
3. Slice it horizontally, starting at the bottom and working up to the top - but still not through the root.
4. Cut it across, downwards, into dice, starting at right hand end.

713 Spiced Onion – Green Chilli : Hot

500 g	onion, peel, chop & coarsely grind
150 g	green chillies, grind to a paste
65 g	cleaned tamarind, obtain thick extract using water
5 g	turmeric powder
2 g	cummin seeds;
2 g	coriander seeds &
2 g	fenugreek seeds, roast all three in oil & powder
5 g	mustard seeds &
a few	sprigs curry leaves: both for seasoning
45 g	salt
350 ml	oil

1. Heat a little oil, add mustard seeds and allow to crackle. Follow with the curry leaves and fry till crisp.
2. Add in the onion-green chilli paste and fry till translucent.
3. Pour in the tamarind extract, turmeric powder, salt and bring to the boil. Allow to thicken over a high flame.
4. Stir in all the remaining ingredients.
5. Continue cooking over low heat until the oil separates and the mixture attains a jam-like consistency.
6. The pickle is ready for use. It lasts for 2 months.

714 Spiced Onion in Tamarind Sauce : Hot

500 g	onion, peel & grate
30 g	cleaned tamarind, obtain thick extract using water
40 g	chilli powder
5	cloves garlic, peel & grate
15 g	mustard seeds, sun-dry & powder
10 g	aniseeds, dry-roast & powder
5 g	turmeric powder
20 ml	vinegar : heat & cool
40 g	salt
125 ml	oil

1. Stir-fry the grated onion and garlic in a little oil. Set aside.
2. In the same pan heat some more oil, add the tamarind extract and bring to the boil. Allow to thicken over a high flame.
3. Add in the fried onion-garlic, spice powders, salt and the remaining oil.
4. Continue cooking over low heat until the mixture becomes jam-like and the oil separates.
5. Blend in the pre-heated vinegar and remove.
6. The pickle is ready for use. It lasts for 2 months.

715 Small White Onion – Beetroot : Hot

125 g	small white onion, peel
3	dried red chillies, keep whole
25 g	beetroot, parboil & peel
50 ml	vinegar, heat & cool
20 g	salt

1. Pack the onion, chillies and the sliced beetroot in a jar.
2. Sprinkle the salt and pour over the cooled vinegar. Set aside for 5 days.
3. The pickle lasts for 2 months and is best refrigerated.

716 Sour Papaya – Onion : Hot

500 g	raw papaya	10 g	fresh ginger, scrape &
150 g	onion, peel & cut into thin lengthy pieces	10 g	garlic, peel & chop both, grind all fine using vinegar
50 g	green chillies, slit	50 g	sugar
30 g	mustard seeds;	100 ml	vinegar
10 g	dried red chillies;	30 g	salt

1. Dry the papaya and onion pieces on a clean cloth.
2. Heat half the vinegar, add in the papaya, onion pieces, green chillies and cook till tender.
3. Grind the remaining spices in the remaining vinegar.
4. When the vegetables become tender, blend in the spice paste, sugar, salt and remove.
5. The pickle is ready for use after 3 days. It lasts for 2 months.

717 Papaya – Ginger – Garlic : Hot

500 g	raw papaya
60 g	fresh ginger, scrape & slice thinly
50 g	peeled garlic, chop
20	dried red chillies, sun-dry & powder
200 ml	vinegar
30 g	salt

1. Combine the papaya, ginger, garlic with the vinegar and salt. Set aside for 2 days and stir daily.
2. Add in the chilli powder and let stand for 2 more days. Toss daily.
3. The pickle lasts for 1 month. Shake daily.

718 Mustard Papaya : Hot

500 g	raw papaya
50 g	chilli powder
25 g	mustard seeds, sun-dry & powder
15 g	fresh ginger, scrape & slice thinly
10 g	garlic, peel & chop fine
10 g	sugar
30 ml	vinegar sufficient to immerse
20 g	salt

1. Blanch the chopped papaya in boiling water for 5 minutes.
2. Drain the water, add the salt and sun-dry till all the moisture evaporates.
3. Combine all the ingredients with the dried papaya and set aside for 2 days.
4. The pickle lasts for 1 month.

719 Sour & Spicy Papaya : Hot

500 g	raw papaya	50 ml	lime juice
10 g	salt : for marinating	5	dried red chillies, slit & seed
100 ml	water : boil & cool	10	cloves garlic, peel & chop
35 g	chilli powder;	1-1"	piece of fresh ginger, scrape & julienne
1-1"	piece of fresh ginger, scrape & chop;	10 g	mustard seeds & fenugreek seeds : both for seasoning
10	cloves garlic, peel &	3 g	
5 g	fenugreek seeds, grind all to a paste using vinegar	3 g	turmeric powder
10 g	split husked mustard seeds	5 g	sugar
100 ml	vinegar	30 g	salt : for pickle
		200 ml	oil

1. Marinate the papaya pieces with the salt for 1 hour.
2. Heat the oil, add the mustard seeds, fenugreek seeds and allow to crackle.
3. Add in the chopped garlic, ginger and stir-fry for a few minutes till tender.
4. Stir in the ground paste and fry for a few more minutes.
5. Pour in the cooled water and bring to the boil.
6. When the water begins to bubble, stir in the vinegar, sugar and salt.
7. Continue cooking, allow to thicken and remove.
8. Add in the salted papaya, husked mustard seeds and stir well.
9. The pickle is ready for use after 10 days. Stir daily. It lasts for 4 months.

720 Papaya – Raisin – Lime Juice : Sweet

125 g	peeled raw papaya	25 g	sugar
25 g	seedless raisin, chop	10 ml	lime juice
		5 g	salt

1. Cook the chopped papaya in sufficient water.
2. Combine the sugar, water and heat till a thin sugar-syrup is formed.
3. Add in the cooked papaya, raisin, salt and allow the mixture to thicken.
4. Blend in the lime juice and remove when the mixture begins to bubble.
5. The pickle is ready for use. It keeps for 10 days in the refrigerator. Shake daily.

721 Spiced Pear – Tamarind : Hot

500 g	cored pear, peel & grate	5 g	turmeric powder
60 g	cleaned tamarind, obtain thick extract using water	5 g	fenugreek seeds & asafoetida, roast both in oil & powder
35 g	chilli powder	5 g	mustard seeds : for seasoning
10 g	cummin seeds &		
5 g	mustard seeds, sun-dry both & powder	50 g	salt
50 ml	vinegar	200 ml	oil

1. Stir-fry the grated pear in a little oil and set aside.
2. Heat a little oil, add mustard seeds and allow to crackle.
3. Pour in the tamarind extract, jaggery, turmeric powder, salt and bring to the boil. Allow to thicken over a high flame.
4. Stir in the chilli powder, the fried pear and the remaining oil.
5. Continue cooking over low heat until the mixture becomes jam-like and the oil separates.
6. Add in the roasted powders, vinegar and remove.
7. The pickle is ready for use. It lasts for 2 months.

722 Pear – Tamarind : Hot

500 g	cored pear, peel & grate	35 g	chilli powder
60 g	cleaned tamarind, obtain thick extract using water	5 g	mustard seeds : for seasoning
		5 g	turmeric powder
2 g	fenugreek seeds &	50 ml	vinegar
2 g	asafoetida, roast both in oil & powder	50 g	salt
		200 ml	oil

1. Heat a little oil, add mustard seeds and allow to crackle.
2. Add in the grated pear, cook till tender and set aside.
3. In the same pan heat some more oil, pour in the tamarind extract and bring to the boil. Allow to thicken over a high flame.
4. Stir in the pear mixture, spice powders, salt, the remaining oil and cook for a few minutes over low heat.
5. When the oil separates add in the vinegar, heat awhile and remove.
6. The pickle is ready for use. It lasts for 2 months.

723 Spiced Pear : Sweet

500 g	cored pear, peel & chop
500 g	sugar
10 g	aniseeds, dry-roast & powder
5 g	chilli powder
10 g	fenugreek seeds &
5 g	asafoetida, roast both in oil & powder
5 g	turmeric powder
5 g	salt

1. Sprinkle the salt, turmeric powder over the chopped pear and sun-dry on a clean cloth.
2. Heat together the sugar with a little water and stir to dissolve.
3. Add in the salted pear, aniseed, fenugreek, chilli and asafoetida powders.
4. Remove when the pear pieces and water turn red.
5. The pickle is ready for use. It lasts for several months.

724 Sour & Spiced Pear : Sweet

500 g	cored pear, peel & chop
500 g	sugar
10 g	chilli powder
10	peppercorns, sun-dry & powder
2	blades of mace;
2	cloves &
2-1"	sticks of cinnamon, keep all three whole
275 ml	vinegar
20 g	salt

1. Cook the pear pieces in sufficient water till tender.
2. Add in the vinegar, whole spices, sugar, salt and bring to the boil. Allow to thicken over a high flame.
3. Stir in the chilli, pepper powders and continue cooking over low heat until the mixture becomes jam-like.
4. The pickle is ready for use. It lasts for 4 months.

725 Sour Pear : Sweet

500 g	cored pear, peel & chop
300 g	sugar
180 ml	vinegar
2-1"	sticks of cinnamon;
2-1"	pieces of fresh ginger, scrape & chop;
5	dried red chillies;
15	peppercorns;
5	blades of mace &
5	cloves, tie all in a spice bag
pared rind of half a lime	

1. Drop the chopped pear into water to which ½ teaspoon (3g) salt has been added.
2. Bring half the vinegar to the boil with the spice bag for a few minutes.
3. Remove and allow to cool. Squeeze out and discard the spice bag.
4. Combine the spiced vinegar, sugar, lime rind and heat to boiling.
5. Cover and cook over low heat till the pears soften.
6. Remove the pear pieces with a perforated spoon and transfer to a jar.
7. Boil the remaining vinegar rapidly till it is reduced to a third of its original volume.
8. Discard the lime rind and pour the heated vinegar over the pear pieces.
9. Cap tight at once and set aside for 8 weeks.
10. The pickle lasts for 3 months.

726 Pineaapple : Sweet

500 g	ripe pineapple chunks
500 g	sugar
5 g	chilli powder
5 g	aniseeds &
2 g	mustard seeds, dry-roast both & powder
2 g	garam masala powder
2	cardamoms;
2	cloves &
1-1"	stick of cinnamon, keep all three whole
20 ml	lime juice
25 g	salt
20 ml	oil

1. Marinate the pineapple chunks in the salt and set aside till it gives out water.
2. Add in the sugar and set aside overnight.
3. Drain out the sugar syrup from the pineapple the following day.
4. Sun-dry the pineapple (turn over for even drying) and the sugar syrup separately.
5. Heat the oil to smoking point and remove.
6. Add in the dried pineapple chunks, sugar syrup, chilli, mustard, aniseed powders and the whole spices.
7. Bring to the boil and allow to thicken over a high flame.
8. Reduce the heat, stir in the lime juice and continue cooking until the mixture begins to bubble.
9. Blend in the garam masala powder and remove.
10. The pickle is ready for use. It lasts for 2 months. Sun occasionally.

727 Pineapple Preserve : Sweet

500 g	half-ripe pineapple pieces
600 g	sugar
12 g	salt

1. Boil the pineapple pieces in sufficient water along with the salt till partly tender.
2. Heat the sugar with sufficient water until the mixture becomes syrupy.
3. Add in the pineapple pieces, cook till the syrup thickens again and remove.
4. The pickle lasts for 2 months in the refrigerator.

728 Sour Pineapple – Green Chilli : Sweet

500 g	ripe pineapple pieces
600 g	sugar
20 g	green chillies, slit
5 g	mustard seeds : for seasoning
50 ml	vinegar
25 g	salt
150 ml	oil

1. Heat the oil, add mustard seeds and allow to crackle.
2. Add in the pineapple pieces, green chillies and fry till tender. Set aside.
3. Dissolve 600g of sugar in 175ml water.
4. Stir in the vinegar, fried pineapple, chillies, salt and cook until the mixture thickens.
5. The pickle is ready for use. It lasts for 2 months in the refrigerator.

729 Pineapple – Mint - Mango : Sweet

500 g	chopped ripe pineapple
500 g	sugar
300 g	seeded raw mango, peel
5 g	salt : for marinating
50 g	seedless raisin, chop
50 ml	vinegar
10	mint leaves, wash, air-dry & chop
2-1"	pieces of fresh ginger; scrape
2 g	grated nutmeg
25 g	salt

1. Sprinkle 5g salt over the chopped pineapple and set aside overnight.
2. Next day rinse the pineapple pieces and drain well.
3. Combine the chopped pineapple, mango, raisin, mint, ginger, nutmeg with the vinegar and the salt.

4. Cook over low heat till the fruits soften.
5. Stir in the sugar to dissolve and continue cooking over low heat until the mixture becomes jam-like.
6. The pickle is ready for use. It lasts for 2 months.

730 Sour Pineapple – Dry Fruits : Sweet

500 g	ripe pineapple pieces
600 g	sugar
200 ml	water
50 g	date, stone & cut into thin long strips
30 g	seedless raisin, chop
5 g	chilli powder
3	cardamoms, keep whole
2	cloves garlic, peel & chop
50 ml	vinegar
25 g	salt

> **Pineapples** because of their sweet and sour taste, are ideal for sweet pickling. They may also however be used for making hot pickles.

1. Cook the pineapple pieces, date, raisin and garlic in 200ml water.
2. When the water has evaporated, stir in the chilli powder, cardamom, sugar, salt with the vinegar and allow to thicken over a high flame.
3. Continue cooking over low heat until the mixture becomes jam-like.
4. The pickle is ready for use. It lasts for 6 months.

731 Pineapple – Onion : Sweet

500 g	chopped ripe pineapple
250 g	sugar
100 g	onion &
5	cloves garlic, peel & chop both
2-1"	pieces of fresh ginger, scrape & slice
10 g	chilli powder
3 g	garam masala powder
100 ml	vinegar
35 g	salt

1. Cook the chopped pineapple in sufficient water till tender.
2. Add in the sugar, salt and stir to dissolve.
3. Follow with the ginger, garlic, onion and continue cooking until the raw smell disappears.
4. Add in the chilli, garam masala powders and cook for a few more minutes.
5. Pour in the vinegar or glacial acetic acid and allow to thicken again.
6. The pickle is ready for use. It lasts for 2 months.

732 Raw Plantain – Tamarind : Hot

500 g	peeled mature raw plantain, cook & grate
80 g	cleaned tamarind, obtain thick extract using water
40 g	chilli powder
5 g	turmeric powder
5 g	asafoetida, roast in oil & powder
10 g	mustard seeds: for seasoning
80 g	salt
100 ml	oil

1. Stir-fry the grated plantain in a little oil till tender and set aside.
2. Heat a little oil, add mustard seeds and allow to crackle.
3. Pour in the tamarind extract and bring to the boil. Allow to thicken over a high flame.
4. Add in the chilli, asafoetida, turmeric powders, the fried plantain, salt and the remaining oil.
5. Continue cooking over low heat until the mixture becomes jam-like and the oil separates.
6. The pickle is ready for use. It lasts for 2 months.

733 Plantain Flower – Green Chilli – Green Coriander : Hot

500 g	stamen removed plantain flower, chop fine & immerse in thin buttermilk
60 g	green chillies &
30 g	green coriander, wash, air-dry, chop both & grind to a paste
50 g	cleaned tamarind, obtain thick extract using water
20 g	jaggery, grate
5 g	asafoetida, roast in oil & powder
5 g	turmeric powder
35 g	salt
200 ml	oil

1. Stir-fry the dried plantain in a little oil. Follow with the chilli-coriander paste and stir-fry for a few minutes. Set aside.
2. In the same pan heat some more oil, pour in the tamarind extract, jaggery and bring to the boil. Allow to thicken over a high flame.
3. Add in the fried ingredients, asafoetida, turmeric powders and the salt.
4. Continue cooking over low heat until the mixture becomes jam-like and the oil separates.
5. The pickle is ready for use. It lasts for 1 month.

> While cutting **plantain flower**, grease your palm with oil to prevent staining. Ensure that chopped plantain flower is dropped into thin buttermilk or dilute tamarind water to prevent them getting discoloured. Some varieties may be bitter tasting. The bitterness may however be remedied by cooking in lightly salted tamarind water. Discard this water before pickling.

734 Spicy Plantain Flower – Onion – Brinjal : Hot

500 g	chopped plantain flower	12 g	fenugreek seeds	
300 g	small onion, peel & slice	15 g	cummin seeds	
100 g	brinjal, julienne	a few	sprigs curry leaves	
100 g	mustard seeds, grind to a paste using vinegar		skin of 1 lime	
75 g	green chillies	300 ml	vinegar	
5	cloves garlic &	60 g	salt	
1-1"	piece of ginger, peel, chop & grind fine	200 ml	oil	
25 g	coriander seeds, sun-dry & powder			
12 g	chilli powder			

1. Deep-fry the plantain flower, the brinjal slices and the sliced onion separately in a little oil. Set aside.
2. Heat some oil in a pan, add the curry leaves, chilli powder, coriander powder, cummin seeds, the ginger-garlic paste and fry for a minute.
3. Add in the mustard paste and fry for a few more minutes.
4. Bring to the boil, add in all the fried ingredients, blend in the vinegar and remove.
5. The pickle is ready for use and lasts for 1 month.

735 Dried Plum – Raisin – Mango : Hot

500 g	dried plum
100 g	dried mango pieces
100 g	seedless raisin, chop
2-1"	pieces of fresh ginger, scrape & slice thinly
80 g	green chillies, slit
10 g	panch phoran, keep whole
5 g	turmeric powder
80 g	salt
100 ml	oil

1. Wash and soak the dried plums, the mango pieces in sufficient water for 5 hours.
2. Fry the panchphoran in a little oil. Add in the soaked plums and mango pieces along with the water in which they were soaked.
3. Stir in the remaining spices, the remaining oil, salt (except sugar & raisin) and bring to the boil.
4. Add in the raisins, sugar, cook for 10 minutes and remove.
5. The pickle is ready for use. It lasts for 2 months.

736 Plum – Date in Vinegar : Sweet

500 g	plums, seed & extract pulp
200 g	sugar
100 g	date, stone & chop
75 g	onion, peel & chop
10 g	allspice, grind
10 g	chilli powder
10 g	dried ginger powder
250 ml	vinegar
25 g	salt

1. Combine the plum pulp, onion, date and spices in a pan with the vinegar.
2. Bring to the boil and simmer until the plums are thoroughly cooked.
3. Add in the sugar, salt and stir to dissolve. Remove when the mixture becomes jam-like.
4. The pickle is ready for use. It lasts for 4 months.

737 Sour Plum – Dried Ginger : Sweet

500 g	plums, prick all over with a fork
250 g	sugar
2-1"	pieces of dried ginger, pound;
1-1"	stick of cinnamon;
2	blades of mace;
3	cloves &
	pared rind of half a lime, tie all in a spice bag
150 ml	vinegar

1. Heat the vinegar and sugar along with the spice bag to boiling until the sugar dissolves.
2. Add in the plums and continue cooking over low heat till they soften.
3. Remove the plums with a perforated spoon and pack in a jar.
4. Boil the spiced vinegar rapidly for a few minutes. Cool and discard the spice bag after squeezing.
5. Pour over the plums and cover.
6. The pickle is ready for use after a month. It lasts for 3 months.

738 Spiced Ripe Plum in Vinegar : Sweet

500 g	plums, keep whole
500 g	sugar
2	dried red chillies &
5 g	peppercorns, powder together
125 ml	vinegar
1	blade of mace &
4	cloves, keep both whole
10 g	salt

1. Cook together the plums and half the vinegar with all the ingredients (except sugar) till the plums soften.
2. Strain, remove the seeds, skin and return to the fire.
3. Stir in the sugar to dissolve.
4. Add in the remaining vinegar and cook until the mixture becomes jam-like.
5. The pickle is ready for use. It lasts for 3 months.

739 Plum – Apple – Date in Spiced Vinegar : Sweet

500 g	plums, stone & chop
300 g	cored cooking apple, peel and chop
250 g	date, stone and chop
250 g	sugar
200 g	onion, peel & chop
15 g	ground allspice
a pinch	grated nutmeg
a pinch	clove powder
300 ml	vinegar
15 g	salt

1. Combine the plums, apple, onion in half the vinegar and heat until the fruits soften.
2. Add in the raisin, date, spices, salt and continue cooking until the mixture thickens.
3. Stir in the sugar, vinegar and simmer gently until the mixture thickens again.
4. The pickle is ready for use. It lasts for 6 months.

740 Ripe Plum – Jaggery : Sweet

125 g	plums, split and stone
125 g	jaggery, grate
7 g	dried red chillies &
5 g	cummin seeds, sun-dry both & powder
15 g	salt
25 ml	oil

1. Sun-dry the split plums for an hour.
2. Heat the oil and add in the jaggery. When it melts, add in the plums, powdered spices and blend well.
3. The pickle is ready for use. It keeps for 10 days and is best refrigerated.

741 Spicy Potato in Lime Juice : Hot

500 g	potato, peel & julienne
100 g	chilli powder;
50 g	mustard seeds, sun-dry & powder;
30 g	fenugreek seeds, roast in oil & powder;
30 g	dried mango powder;
5 g	turmeric powder &
200 g	salt, combine all evenly
50 g	peeled garlic, chop
5 g	garam masala powder
5 g	asafoetida, roast in oil & powder
5 g	mustard seeds : for seasoning
100 ml	lime juice
250 ml	oil

1. Drop the potato pieces in 2% salt solution to prevent discolouration.
2. Heat half the oil and soak the potato pieces for 15 minutes in a jar.
3. Combine all the spice powders with the salt evenly.
4. Add the spice mixture to the potato pieces and sun for 2 hours every day, for 3 days.
5. On the 4th day stir in the lime juice and blend well.
6. Heat a little oil, add mustard seeds and allow to crackle.
7. Add in the chopped garlic, garam masala and asafoetida powders.
8. Pour the seasoning and the remaining oil over the pickle to cover. Stir thoroughly.
9. Sun the pickle one hour everyday, for 3 days.
10. The pickle is ready for use after 15 days. It lasts for 2 months.

742 Spicy Potato – Peas – Coconut : Hot

500 g	potato, peel, chop, wash & air-dry
500 g	shelled green peas
200 g	grated coconut, dry-roast
200 g	green chillies, chop
50 g	peeled garlic, chop
50 g	fresh ginger, scrape & chop
30 g	green coriander, wash, air-dry & chop
20	peppercorns;
5 g	cummin seeds &
5 g	coriander seeds, sun-dry all three & powder
5 g	turmeric powder
2 g	asafoetida, roast in oil & powder
5 g	mustard seeds : for seasoning
500 ml	lime juice
150 g	salt
400 ml	oil

1. Marinate the chopped potatoes in salt water for one hour.
2. Stir-fry the chopped coriander, ginger, garlic and green chillies in a little oil.
3. Follow with the salted potato, green peas, cook for a few minutes and remove.
4. Stir in the roasted coconut, spice powders, salt at once and mix thoroughly.
5. Heat a litte oil, add mustard seeds and allow to crackle.
6. Pour the seasoning, lime juice and the remaining oil (after heating & cooling) over the vegetable mixture. Stir well.
7. The pickle is ready for use. It lasts for 2 months. Sun occasionally.

743 Sour Spiced Potato – Mustard : Sweet

500 g	potato, peel, cube, wash & air-dry
125 g	cubed jaggery, grate
115 g	chilli powder
75 g	mustard seeds, sun-dry & powder
10 g	fenugreek seeds &
3 g	asafoetida, roast both in oil & powder
3 g	garam masala powder
3 g	turmeric powder
3	cloves garlic, peel & chop
5 g	mustard seeds: for seasoning
250 ml	lime juice
125 g	salt
250 ml	oil

Truly versatile, potatoes come in two types – waxy and mealy, the former being good for frying. A good source of low cost vitamins and minerals especially when cooked in their skins.

1. Stir-fry the cubed potatoes in half the oil.
2. Add in the jaggery and stir to dissolve.
3. Follow with the chilli, fenugreek, mustard, turmeric powders, salt and mix thoroughly.
4. Remove and set aside for 3 days. Shake at least twice daily.
5. Pour over the lime juice and stir well.
6. Heat some more oil, add mustard seeds and allow to crackle.
7. Follow with the chopped garlic, asafoetida powder, stir-fry for a minute and remove.
8. When the oil is still lukewarm blend in the garam masala powder.
9. Pour the spicy oil over the potato mixture and top up with the remaining oil. Sun for a week.
10. The pickle is ready for use after 1 month. It lasts for 6 months. Sun occasionally.

744 Sweet & Sour Pumpkin – Green Coriander : Hot

500 g	peeled pumpkin, chop & seed
50 g	cleaned tamarind, obtain thick extract using water
75 g	jaggery, grate
20 g	green coriander, wash, air-dry & grind coarsely
15 g	dried red chillies &
5 g	asafoetida, roast both in oil & powder
10 g	peppercorns &
5 g	mustard seeds, sun-dry both & powder
60 g	salt
175 ml	oil

1. Stir-fry the chopped pumpkin and green coriander in a little oil till well fried. Set aside.
2. Heat a little oil, add the tamarind extract, jaggery and bring to the boil. Allow to thicken over a high flame.
3. Add in the fried ingredients and cook for a few minutes.
4. Stir in the spice powders, sugar, salt and the remaining oil.
5. Continue cooking over low heat until the mixture becomes jam-like and the oil separates.
6. The pickle is ready for use. It lasts for 1 month.

745 Sour Pumpkin – Raisin : Sweet

500 g	peeled pumpkin, seed & dice
300 g	jaggery, grate
150 g	seedless raisin, chop
40 g	lime, slice thinly & seed
20 g	dried ginger powder
10 g	chilli powder
250 ml	water
200 ml	vinegar
20 g	salt

1. Combine all the ingredients except jaggery in a pan and bring to the boil.
2. Lower the heat and cook till the pumpkin becomes tender.
3. Stir in the jaggery to dissolve.
4. Continue cooking until the mixture becomes thick and jam-like.
5. The pickle is ready for use. It lasts for 1 month.

746 Pumpkin – Raisin in Vinegar : Sweet

500 g	peeled pumpkin, seed & chop
125 g	seedless raisin, chop
30 g	dried red chillies;
10	cloves garlic, peel &
2-1"	pieces of fresh ginger, scrape, chop both & grind all three fine using vinegar
250 g	sugar
200 ml	vinegar
100 ml	water
30 g	salt

1. Cook the chopped pumpkin with a little salt and water till tender. Remove.
2. Combine the spice paste, sugar and the remaining salt with the reserved vinegar. Bring to the boil.
3. Stir in the cooked pumpkin and raisin.
4. Continue cooking over low heat until the mixture becomes thick and jam-like.
5. The pickle is ready for use. It lasts for 1 month.

747 Spicy White Pumpkin – Onion – Tomato : Hot

500 g	peeled pumpkin, seed & grate
200 g	tomato, chop
100 g	onion, peel & chop
30 g	cleaned tamarind, obtain thick extract using water
40 g	jaggery, grate
20 g	green coriander, wash & air-dry;
2-1"	pieces of fresh ginger, scrape &
10	cloves garlic, peel, chop all three & grind fine
50 g	dried red chillies;
10 g	cummin seeds &
5 g	coriander seeds, roast all three in oil & powder
5 g	turmeric powder
10 g	mustard seeds &
a few	sprigs curry leaves : both for seasoning
70 g	salt
300 ml	oil

1. Stir-fry the ginger-garlic-coriander paste in a little oil for 2 minutes and set aside.
2. In the same pan heat some more oil, add mustard seeds and allow to crackle.
3. Add in the curry leaves, chopped tomato, onion, grated pumpkin and fry for a few minutes.
4. Pour in the tamarind extract, jaggery, turmeric powder, salt and continue cooking until the mixture thickens.
5. Stir in the spice powders, fried vegetables, ginger-garlic paste, the remaining oil and stir well.
6. Remove when the mixture becomes jam-like and the oil separates.
7. The pickle is ready for use. It lasts for 1 month.

748 White Pumpkin – Dry Fruits : Sweet

500 g	peeled pumpkin, seed & grate
250 g	sugar
50 g	pistachios &
50 g	almonds, blanch, peel & sliver both
5 g	chilli powder
3 g	grated nutmeg
3	cardamoms, keep whole
10 ml	rosewater
15 g	salt

1. Cook the grated pumpkin with the sugar until transluscent and the moisture evaporates.
2. Add in all the spices, dry fruits, salt, rosewater and stir well. Allow to thicken.
3. The pickle is ready for use. It lasts for 2 months in the refrigerator.

749 Mustard Radish : Hot

500 g	radish, scrape, top, tail & cut into small thin slices
60 g	green chillies, chop
50 g	fresh ginger, scrape &
25 g	peeled garlic, chop both & grind fine
15 g	mustard seeds &
5 g	fenugreek seeds, dry-roast & powder together
60 ml	vinegar
40 ml	lime juice
50 g	salt
60 ml	oil

1. Stir-fry the green chillies in a little oil.
2. Add in the spice paste, fry for a few minutes and remove.
3. Combine the radish slices with the fried ingredients, spice powders, lime juice, vinegar, salt and transfer to a jar.
4. Sun the mixture for 5 days.
5. The pickle lasts for 1 month.

750 Radish – Ginger in Lime Juice : Hot

500 g	white radish, scrape, top, tail & chop fine
50 g	fresh ginger, scrape & chop fine
15 g	chilli powder
5 g	coriander seeds &
5 g	mustard seeds, sun-dry both & powder
5 g	turmeric powder
150 ml	lime juice
50 g	salt

1. Combine all the ingredients except the lime juice in a jar.
2. Shake well and sun the mixture for 7 days.
3. Pour over the lime juice and stir thoroughly.
4. The pickle is ready for use. It lasts for 2 months. Sun occasionally.

751 Spicy Mustard White Radish : Hot

500 g	white radish, scrape, top, tail & chop
30 g	mustard seeds, sun-dry & powder;
30 g	chilli powder &
10 g	turmeric powder, combine all three evenly
25 g	salt
150 ml	oil

1. Marinate the chopped radish in 10g salt for 3 hours.
2. Squeeze out all the water given out by the radish pieces.
3. Blend in the spice mixture, the remaining salt and transfer to a jar.
4. Pour the oil over the pickle to cover. Cap tight and sun for a week.
5. The pickle is ready for use. It lasts for 2 months.

752 White Radish Preserve : Sweet

500 g	white radish scrape, top, tail & cut into chunks water sufficient to immerse	1 kg	sugar, make a syrup with 1000 ml water of single-thread consistency
20 ml	rose water	5 g	salt

1. Prick the radish chunks with a fork, add the water, salt and bring to the boil.
2. Remove after 2 boils and drain.
3. Warm the sugar syrup, add in the radish chunks and cook until the syrup thickens.
4. Continue cooking over low heat till the radish becomes tender and remove.
5. Blend in the rose water.
6. The pickle is ready for use. It lasts for 2 months.

753 Sour Raisin – Date : Sweet

500 g	seedless raisin, chop
500 g	dried date, stone & chop fine
500 g	sugar
50 g	cleaned tamarind, obtain thick extract using water
10 g	chilli powder
40 g	salt

1. Cook the date and raisin in the tamarind extract till tender.
2. Stir in the sugar, salt and chilli powder.
3. Continue cooking over low heat till the mixture becomes thick and jam-like.
4. The pickle is ready for use. It lasts for 6 months and is best refrigerated.

754 Ridge Gourd – Onion : Hot

500 g	peeled tender ridge gourd, grate
100 g	onion, peel & chop;
5	cloves garlic, peel &
2-1"	pieces of fresh ginger, scrape & chop, grind all three to a paste
60 g	dried red chillies, roast in oil & powder
50 g	cleaned tamarind, obtain thick extract using water
10 g	jaggery, grate
5 g	turmeric powder
5 g	asafoetida, roast in oil & powder
10 g	mustard seeds &
a few	sprigs curry leaves : both for seasoning
60 g	salt
100 ml	oil

1. Stir-fry the grated ridge gourd in a little oil till tender.
2. Stir in the onion-ginger-garlic paste, fry for a few minutes till the oil separates and set aside.
3. In the same pan heat some more oil, add mustard seeds and allow to crackle. Add in the curry leaves and fry till crisp.
4. Pour in the tamarind extract, jaggery and bring to the boil. Allow to thicken over a high flame.
5. Stir in the chilli, turmeric, asafoetida powders, salt, fried ingredients and the remaining oil.
6. Continue cooking over low heat until the mixture becomes jam-like and the oil separates.
7. The pickle is ready for use. It lasts for 1 month.

755 Peppered Mahani in Lime Juice : Hot

500 g	mahani, size into small pieces
50 g	chilli powder
50 g	peppercorns, sun-dry & powder
100 ml	lime juice
100 g	salt

1. Soak the mahani pieces in rice-washed water overnight.
2. Drain off the water the next day and wash again in fresh water.
3. Add fresh rice-washed water to immerse the roots.
4. Scrape the roots with a knife, remove the central stem, cut into 2 cm pieces and drop into very thin buttermilk (to prevent discolouration).
5. Add the chilli, pepper powders, salt into the lime juice and stir well. Set aside for half an hour.
6. Pour the spicy sauce over the mahani pieces, blend well and set aside for 10 days.
7. The pickle lasts for 6 months.

756 Mahani in Lime Juice : Watery

1 kg	mahani, cut into 2cm pieces
150 g	chilli powder
200 g	salt, boil with 1600 ml water & cool
40 g	cleaned tamarind, obtain thin extract using water
40 g	mustard seeds, sun-dry & powder
80 ml	lime juice

1. Drop the cut mahani pieces in the thin tamarind extract to avoid discolouration.
2. Drain the root pieces from the tamarind extract and combine all the ingredients with the cooled salt water.
3. The pickle is ready for use after 2 weeks. It lasts for 1 year.

757 Mahani – Green Chilli in Buttermilk : Watery

1 kg	mahani pieces	10 g	chilli powder
1000 ml	sour curd, whip with 2000 ml water & remove cream	10 g	mustard seeds;
		a few	sprigs curry leaves &
20 g	green chillies, chop	20 ml	oil : all three for seasoning
15 g	turmeric powder	50 ml	lime juice
		150 g	salt

1. Soak the mahani pieces in rice-washed water overnight.
2. Drain off the water the next day and wash again in fresh water. Then add fresh rice-washed water to immerse the roots.
3. Scrape the roots with a knife, remove the central stem, cut into small pieces and drop into very thin buttermilk (to prevent discolouration).
4. Combine the salt, whipped curd, turmeric powder and the lime juice.
5. Drain the root pieces from the buttermilk and drop into the curd mixture.
6. Heat the oil, add mustard seeds and allow to crackle. Add in the green chillies, curry leaves and fry for a few minutes.
7. Pour the seasoning over the curd mahani mixture, stir well and set aside for 10 days. Stir twice daily.
8. The pickle is ready for use. It lasts for more than a year.

758 Sesame Seed in Tamarind Sauce : Hot

500 g	sesame seeds, dry-roast & powder coarsely
60 g	cleaned tamarind, obtain thick extract using water
60 g	jaggery, grate
40 g	dried red chillies &
10 g	asafoetida, roast both in oil & powder
10 g	turmeric powder
60 g	salt
300 ml	oil

1. Heat the oil, add the tamarind extract, jaggery, turmeric powder, salt and bring to the boil. Allow to thicken over a high flame.
2. Stir in the chilli, asafoetida powders, continue cooking over low heat until the mixture becomes jam-like and the oil separates.
3. Add in the sesame powder and stir thoroughly.
4. The pickle is ready for use. It lasts for 1 month.

759 Spicy Snake Gourd – Tamarind : Hot

500 g	snake gourd, peel & chop
40 g	cleaned tamarind, obtain thick extract using water
30 g	dried red chillies, break into bits
5	cloves garlic, peel & pound
10 g	jaggery, grate
10 g	asafoetida, roast in oil & powder
10 g	cummin seeds, dry-roast & pound
10 g	mustard seeds;
10 g	split husked black gram;
10 g	split husked bengal gram &
a few	sprigs curry leaves : all for seasoning
5 g	chilli powder
5 g	turmeric powder
30 g	salt
150 ml	oil

1. Stir-fry the chopped snake gourd in a little oil till tender and set aside.
2. Heat some more oil, add mustard seeds and allow to crackle. Stir in the black gram, bengal gram and fry till golden brown.
3. Follow with the curry leaves, dried red chillies, asafoetida powder and fry for a minute.
4. Pour in the tamarind extract, jaggery, chilli, turmeric powders and bring to the boil. Allow to thicken over a high flame.
5. Stir in the fried snake gourd, cummin, garlic, salt and the remaining oil.
6. Continue cooking over low heat until the mixture becomes jam-like and the oil separates.
7. The pickle is ready for use. It lasts for 1 month.

760 Sour Bitterberry : Salty

125 g	bitterberries, halve
100 ml	curd, whip with 50 ml water & remove cream
30 g	salt

1. Blend the bitterberries with the whipped curd and salt. Set aside for 2 days.
2. The pickle is ready for use. It keeps for 3 weeks and longer in the refrigerator. Stir daily.

761 Snake Gourd : Sweet

500 g	chopped snake gourd, slit & seed	3 g	saffron strands, dissolve in 1tsp hot water
300 g	sugar	75 ml	water
5	cardamoms, keep whole	5 g	salt
		30 ml	oil

1. Parboil the chopped snake gourd in sufficient water to which a teaspoon (5g) salt has been added. Drain out the water and set aside.
2. Boil the sugar in suffcient water to prepare a thick syrup.
3. Lower the heat, stir-fry the cooked gourd in the oil till partly fried and remove.
4. Stir in the fried gourd, cardamom and the saffron water into the sugar syrup. Mix thoroughly.
5. The pickle is ready for use after 2 days. It lasts for 6 months.

762 Spicy Star Fruit : Hot

500 g	star fruit, remove ridges, innerstem, seeds & chop	
15 g	chilli powder;	
5 g	ber powder &	
10 g	white mustard seeds, sun-dry & powder, combine all three evenly	
10 g	panch phoran powder	
5 g	dried ginger powder	
2	green chillies, chop	
50 g	sugar	
25 ml	tomato sauce	
50 g	salt	
125 ml	oil	

1. Marinate the star fruit pieces in the salt and sun for a day.
2. Transfer to a jar and set aside for 3 days.
3. On the 4th day remove the fruit pieces and again sun-dry for 3 days.
4. Roll the dried fruit in the spice mixture and pack in a jar. Sun for 4 days till thin and dry.
5. Heat the oil, add in the panch phoran powder, remove and allow to cool.
6. Blend in the tomato sauce and ginger powder.
7. Pack the dried fruit in a jar and pour over the spicy oil.
8. The pickle is ready for use after 3 days. It lasts for 2 months.

763 Sweet & Sour Bitterberry : Hot

500 g	bitterberries, halve	5 g	turmeric powder
30 g	cleaned tamarind, obtain thick extract using water	5 g	mustard seeds &
		5 g	split husked black gram: both for seasoning
40 g	jaggery, grate		
40 g	dried red chillies &		
5 g	asafoetida, roast both in oil & powder	50 g	salt
		150 ml	oil

1. Stir-fry the halved bitterberries in a little oil till partly tender and set aside.
2. In the same pan heat some more oil and add mustard seeds. After they crackle, add in the black gram and fry till golden.
3. Pour in the tamarind extract, jaggery, turmeric powder, salt and bring to the boil. Allow to thicken over a high flame.
4. Lower the heat, stir in the fried bitterberries, chilli, asafoetida powders and the remaining oil.
5. Remove when the mixture becomes jam-like and the oil separates.
6. The pickle is ready for use. It lasts for 2 months.

764 Spiced Bitterberry : Hot

500 g	bitterberries, halve	5 g	coriander seeds &
30 g	cleaned tamarind, obtain thick extract using water	5 g	asafoetida, roast all three in oil & powder
		5 g	turmeric powder
30 g	jaggery, grate		
15	dried red chillies, break into bits	5 g	mustard seeds &
		5 g	fenugreek seeds : both for seasoning
5	cloves garlic, peel & chop		
10 g	chilli powder	60 g	salt
10 g	peppercorns;	150 ml	oil

1. Stir-fry the bitterberries in a little oil and set aside.
2. In the same pan heat some more oil, add the mustard seeds, fenugreek seeds and allow to crackle.
3. Add in the red chillies, garlic and fry for a few minutes.
4. Stir in the tamarind extract, jaggery, turmeric powder and salt.
5. Bring to the boil and allow to thicken over a high flame.

6. Add in the fried bitterberries, chilli, roasted spice powders, salt and the remaining oil.
7. Continue cooking over low heat until the mixture becomes jam-like and the oil separates.
8. The pickle is ready for use. It lasts for 2 months in the refrigerator.

765 Snake Gourd – Onion – Green Spices : Hot

500 g	tender snake gourd, chop	5 g	mustard seeds &
150 g	onion, peel & chop	5 g	turmeric powder, grind all to a paste using water
5	cloves garlic, peel & chop		
10 g	sugar	5 g	mustard seeds
10 g	chilli powder;		
1-1"	piece of fresh ginger, scrape & chop;	3 g	fenugreek seeds
		150 ml	vinegar
5	cloves garlic, peel;	75 g	salt
		50 ml	oil

1. Pressure cook the snake gourd until half tender.
2. Stir-fry the cooked snake gourd in a little oil and set aside.
3. In the same pan heat some more oil, add the mustard seeds, fenugreek seeds and allow to crackle.
4. Follow with the chopped onion, garlic, ginger and fry for a few minutes till tender.
5. Stir in the spice paste and fry for a few minutes.
6. Pour in the vinegar, sugar, salt and the remaining oil.
7. Bring to the boil and allow to thicken over a high flame.
8. Add in the fried snake gourd pieces and continue cooking over low heat until the mixture thickens.
9. The pickle is ready for use. It lasts for 1 month.

766 Spiced Tamarind – Garlic : Hot

500 g	cleaned ripe tamarind	10 g	mustard seeds, roast both in oil & powder
50 g	peeled garlic, keep whole		
50 g	peeled garlic, crush	10 g	turmeric powder
60 g	chilli powder	5 g	mustard seeds: for seasoning
10 g	fenugreek seeds &	125 g	salt
		150 ml	oil

1. Combine the spice powders with the tamarind and sun for 2 days.

2. Heat the oil, add mustard seeds and allow to crackle.
3. Add in the garlic and fry for a few minutes till tender. Allow to cool.
4. Pour the seasoning over the tamarind mixture and stir well.
5. The pickle is ready for use. It lasts for 2 months.

767 Tamarind – Gram – Green Chilli : Hot

500 g	cleaned tamarind, obtain thick extract using water	10 g	asafoetida, roast both in oil & powder
		20 g	peppercorns &
		20 g	mustard seeds, sun-dry both & powder
100 g	green chillies, chop & grind		
10 g	sugar	10 g	turmeric powder
100 g	split husked black gram &	120 g	salt
		150 ml	oil

1. Stir-fry the green chilli paste in a little oil for a few minutes.
2. Pour in the tamarind extract, turmeric powder, sugar and the salt.
3. Bring to the boil and allow to thicken over a high flame.
4. Stir in the ground spices, the remaining oil and continue cooking over low heat.
5. Remove when the mixture becomes jam-like and the oil separates.
6. The pickle is ready for use. It lasts for 2 months.

768 Tamarind – Garlic – Green Coriander : Hot

500 g	cleaned tamarind, obtain thick extract using water
250 g	peeled garlic;
70 g	green chillies &
60 g	green coriander, wash, air-dry, chop all three & grind to a paste
10 g	mustard seeds;
a few	sprigs curry leaves &
100 ml	groundnut oil : all three for seasoning
150 g	salt

1. Heat the oil, add mustard seeds and allow to crackle.
2. Add in the curry leaves and fry till crisp.
3. Stir in the spice paste and continue cooking for a few minutes.
4. Pour in the tamarind extract and bring to the boil.
5. Allow to thicken over a high flame and remove.
6. The pickle is ready for use. It lasts for 1 month.

769 Spicy Tamarind – Cummin Seeds : Sweet

500 g	cleaned tamarind, obtain thick extract using water
500 g	jaggery, grate
30 g	coriander seeds &
20 g	cummin seeds, sun-dry both & powder
20 g	chilli powder
10 g	asafoetida, roast in oil & powder
10 g	dried ginger powder
10 g	black salt, powder
10 g	mint leaves, wash, air-dry & chop
40 g	salt

1. Heat the tamarind extract, jaggery and sufficient water till it is reduced to half.
2. Stir in the remaining ingredients.
3. Continue cooking until the mixture becomes thick and sauce-like.
4. The pickle is ready for use after a day. It lasts for 1 month in the refrigerator.

Cummin seeds
They are yellowish brown in colour with a peculiar, strong and heavy odour. Cummin seeds need roasting over a dry griddle (tawa) to bring out their full flavour. They are done when they turn just a shade darker. They are extensively used in mixed spices and is an important ingredient of curry powder, pickles and chutneys.

770 Sour Tamarind – Raisin : Sweet

500 g	cleaned tamarind, obtain thick extract using vinegar
750 g	sugar
250 g	seedless raisin, chop
50 g	dried red chillies;
30 g	fresh ginger, scrape & chop;
10 g	mustard seeds &
5	cloves garlic, peel, grind all to a paste using vinegar
10 g	turmeric powder
200 ml	vinegar
40 g	salt

1. Combine the ground paste, turmeric powder, vinegar and sugar with the salt.
2. Bring to the boil and set aside.
3. In the same pan, heat the tamarind extract and allow to thicken over a high flame.
4. Stir in the spiced vinegar, raisin and cook over low heat until the mixture thickens again.
5. The pickle is ready for use. It lasts for 6 months.

771 Tamarind – Green Coriander - Jaggery : Sweet

500 g	cleaned tamarind, obtain thick extract using water
500 g	jaggery, grate
60 g	dried red chillies, break into bits
50 g	green coriander, wash, air-dry & chop
10 g	coriander seeds &
5 g	mustard seeds, sun-dry both
5 g	turmeric powder
a few	sprigs curry leaves, string, devein & chop
100 g	salt
200 ml	oil

1. Grind together all the ingredients (except tamarind and jaggery) to a fine paste.
2. Heat a little oil, add the tamarind extract, jaggery and bring to the boil. Allow to thicken over a high flame.
3. Stir in the spice paste and the remaining oil.
4. Continue cooking over low heat until the mixture becomes jam-like and the oil separates.
5. The pickle is ready for use. It lasts for 2 months.

772 Tamarind – Jaggery : Sweet

500 g	cleaned tamarind, obtain thick extract using water
700 g	jaggery, grate
100 g	dried red chillies, break into bits
10	cloves garlic, peel & chop
10 g	mustard seeds : for seasoning
160 g	salt
200 ml	oil

1. Grind together the chillies, garlic and salt to a smooth paste.
2. Heat a little oil, add mustard seeds and allow to crackle.
3. Add in the spice paste and fry for a few minutes.
4. Pour in the tamarind extract, jaggery, the remaining oil and bring to the boil. Allow to thicken over a high flame and remove.
5. The pickle is ready for use. It lasts for 1 month and is best refrigerated.

Variation
Grind together all the ingredients to a fine paste and season with mustard seeds. However while grinding do not soak the tamarind but grind as such.

773 Tapioca in Lime Juice : Hot

125 g	peeled tapioca, cut fine
25 ml	lime juice
10 g	chilli powder;
2 g	peppercorns, sun-dry & powder;
2 g	turmeric powder &
12 g	salt, combine all evenly
3 g	asafoetida, roast in oil & powder
2 g	mustard seeds &
20 ml	oil : both for seasoning

1. Combine the cooked tapioca pieces with the lime juice and the spice mixture evenly.
2. Heat the oil, add mustard seeds and allow to crackle.
3. Stir in the asafoetida powder, tapioca mixture, stir-fry for a few minutes and remove.
4. The pickle is ready for use. It keeps for 1 week and is best refrigerated.

774 Thammatangai in Lime Juice : Hot

125 g	tender thammatangai, cut into 1/2" pieces
8 g	chilli powder
3 g	asafoetida, roast in oil & powder
3 g	mustard seeds : for seasoning
50 ml	lime juice
20 g	salt
20 ml	oil

1. Combine the chilli, asafoetida powders with the salt and lime juice.
2. Add in the cut thammatangai and stir thoroughly.
3. Heat the oil, add mustard seeds and allow to crackle.
4. Pour the seasoning over the thammatangai mixture and blend well.
5. The pickle is ready for use after 1 week. It keeps for 15 days and longer if refrigerated. Stir daily.

775 Thummutikai in Whipped Curd : Watery

500 g	thummutikai
400 ml	curd, whip with 200ml water & remove cream
80 g	salt

1. Blend the thummutikai with the whipped curd and salt. Set aside for 2 days.
2. The pickle is ready for use. It lasts for 1 month and is best refrigerated. Stir daily.

776 Steamed Green Tomato : Hot

500 g	green tomato, cut into lengthy pieces
40 g	dried red chillies;
5 g	fenugreek seeds &
5 g	asafoetida, roast all three in oil & powder
5 g	turmeric powder
5 g	mustard seeds, sun-dry & powder
40 g	salt
200 ml	groundnut oil

1. Smear the salt and turmeric powder over the tomato pieces and steam.
2. Remove and sun-dry.
3. Heat the oil, add the dried tomato pieces and the spice powders. Mix thoroughly and set aside for 4 days.
4. The pickle lasts for 6 months.

777 Green Tomato – Tamarind : Hot

500 g	green tomato, chop
50 g	chilli powder
25 g	cleaned tamarind, obtain thick extract using water
25 g	jaggery, grate
5 g	turmeric powder
5 g	asafoetida &
5 g	fenugreek seeds, roast both in oil & powder
5 g	mustard seeds : for seasoning
40 g	salt
500 ml	oil

1. Stir-fry the chopped tomato in a little oil and set aside.
2. In the same pan heat some more oil, add mustard seeds and allow to crackle.
3. Pour in the tamarind extract, jaggery, salt and bring to the boil. Allow to thicken over a high flame.
4. Lower the heat, add in the chilli, turmeric, fenugreek, asafoetida powders, salt and the fried tomato.
5. Continue cooking over low heat adding the remaining oil a little at a time until the mixture thickens and the oil separates.
7. The pickle is ready for use. It lasts for 2 months.

778 Sour Green Tomato : Sweet

500 g	green tomato, prick each with a fork
400 g	sugar
5	cloves &
1-1"	stick of cinnamon, keep both whole
300 ml	water
300 ml	vinegar
10 g	salt

1. Bring the vinegar, water, sugar, salt and the whole spices to the boil.
2. Drop in the tomatoes and heat thoroughly ensuring they remain firm.
3. Remove the tomatoes with a perforated spoon and pack into jars. Pour over the spiced vinegar, seal and refrigerate for a week.
4. The pickle lasts for 2 months.

779 Green Tomato : Sweet

1 kg	green tomato &
1 kg	large green chillies, chop both
1 kg	jaggery, grate
300 g	onion, peel & slice
30 g	chilli powder
200 ml	vinegar
80 g	salt

1. Arrange a layer of the chopped tomato-chilli mixture in a bowl.
2. Follow with the sliced onion and dust with a layer of salt and chilli powder.
3. Repeat the process until all the vegetables are layered. Set aside overnight.
4. Drain off the salt water. Cook the tomato mixture with the vinegar, jaggery and the remaining salt for 30 minutes, over low heat.
5. Remove and set aside for 5 days. The pickle lasts for 1 year.

780 Sour Green Tomato – Mustard : Sweet

500 g	green tomato, slice,	500 ml	vinegar	
300 g	capsicum, chop fine &	100 g	split husked mustard seeds, crush	
300 g	onion, peel & slice, combine all three	5	cloves, keep whole	
1 kg	jaggery, grate	5 g	allspice	
		150 g	salt	

1. In a bowl arrange a layer of the mixed vegetables.
2. Follow with a sprinkling of salt.
3. Repeat this process until all the vegetables are exhausted. Set aside overnight.
4. Next morning drain off the salt water, add in the remaining spices, jaggery, vinegar and heat gradually to a boil.
5. Simmer for 30 minutes, remove and seal.
6. The pickle is ready for use after 5 days. It lasts for 2 months.

781 Green Tomato in Vinegar : Sweet

500 g	green tomato, chop			
200 g	small onion, peel & chop			
150 g	cored cooking apple, peel & chop			
60 g	seedless raisin, chop			
15 g	dried red chillies, break into bits &			
10 g	dried root ginger, pound, tie both in a spice bag			
		200 ml	vinegar	
125 g	sugar	75 g	salt	

1. Combine the tomato, onion, apple and raisin with half the vinegar in a pan.
2. Drop in the spice bag, heat until the fruits and vegetables soften.
3. Add in the remaining vinegar, salt, sugar and continue heating.
4. Remove when the mixture becomes jam-like after squeezing out the spice bag.
5. The pickle is ready for use. It lasts for 3 months.

> **Raisins** are the dried fruits obtained after dehydration of wine grapes. The outstanding value of raisins in relieving acidosis is because of its high alkalinity. In raisins, three-fourths of the dry weight of the fruit is in the form of pure fruit sugar, emphasizing its importance as a quick energy food.

782 Green Tomato – Sesame – Coconut : Sweet

500 g	green tomato &
50 g	green chillies, chop both & grind fine
60 g	grated coconut, dry-roast & grind
40 g	sesame seeds &
10 g	cummin seeds, sun-dry both & powder
10 g	chilli powder
10 g	asafoetida, roast in oil & powder
10 g	mustard seeds : for seasoning
30 g	jaggery, grate
50 g	salt
200 ml	oil

1. Heat a little oil, add mustard seeds and allow to crackle.
2. Stir in the chilli-tomato paste, coconut paste, jaggery and salt.
3. Bring to the boil, allow to thicken over a high flame, adding the remaining oil little by little.
4. Blend in the roasted powders over low heat and remove when the oil separates.
5. The pickle is ready for use. It lasts for 1 month in the refrigerator.

783 Spicy Tomato : Hot

500 g	ripe tomato, chop;
300	onion, peel & chop &
60 g	green chillies, chop, grind all three
10	cloves garlic, peel & grind
20 g	chilli powder
10 g	turmeric powder
5 g	aniseeds, sun-dry & powder
5	cloves &
1-1"	stick of cinnamon, keep both whole
10 g	mustard seeds &
a few	sprigs curry leaves : both for seasoning
50 g	salt
250 ml	oil

1. Stir-fry the garlic paste in a little oil and set aside.
2. Heat a little oil, add mustard seeds and allow to crackle.
3. Lower the heat, add in the curry leaves, the ground mixture and fry for a while.
4. Stir in the fried paste, chilli, turmeric, aniseed powders, whole spices, salt and the remaining oil.
5. Continue cooking for a few minutes until the mixture becomes jam-like and the oil separates.
6. The pickle is ready for use. It lasts for 1 month and is best refrigerated.

784 Tomato – Asafoetida - Garlic : Hot

500 g	ripe tomato, chop
60 g	dried red chillies, break into bits
40 g	peeled garlic, chop
15 g	asafoetida, roast in oil & powder
10 g	mustard seeds : for seasoning
50 g	salt
200 ml	oil

1. Grind the chopped tomato, red chillies and garlic to a paste with the salt.
2. Heat the oil, add mustard seeds and allow to crackle.
3. Add in the tomato paste, jaggery, salt and bring to the boil. Allow to thicken over a high flame.
4. Sprinkle the asafoetida powder and blend well.
5. Continue cooking over low heat until the mixture becomes jam-like and the oil separates.
6. The pickle is ready for use. It lasts for 1 month and is best refrigerated.

785 Spiced Tomato : Hot

125 g	ripe tomato, chop	3 g	coriander seeds, sun-dry both & powder
10 g	cleaned tamarind, obtain thick extract using water	2 g	asafoetida &
10 g	chilli powder	2 g	fenugreek seeds, roast both in oil & powder
3 g	peppercorns, dry-roast & powder		
2 g	turmeric powder	12 g	salt
3 g	mustard seeds &	60 ml	oil

1. Heat a little oil, add mustard seeds and allow to crackle.
2. Add in the chopped tomato and stir-fry for a few minutes.
3. Pour in the tamarind extract, turmeric powder, jaggery, salt and bring to the boil. Allow to thicken over a high flame.
4. Stir in the powdered spices, chilli powder and the remaining oil.
5. Continue cooking over low heat until the mixture becomes jam-like and the oil separates.
6. The pickle is ready for use. It keeps for 2 weeks and is best refrigerated.

786 Spiced Tomato – Tamarind : Hot

125 g	ripe tomato, chop
30 g	green chillies, chop
10 g	cleaned tamarind
5 g	jaggery, grate
2	cloves garlic, peel & chop fine
2 g	cummin seeds, dry-roast & powder
2 g	asafoetida, roast in oil & powder
10 g	salt
75 ml	oil

1. Stir-fry the green chillies in a little oil.
2. Add in the chopped tomato and cook over low heat till well fried. Allow to cool.
3. Grind the fried ingredients with the tamarind, jaggery and salt. Add no water.
4. Add in the chopped garlic, cummin, asafoetida powders and mix thoroughly.
5. Heat the remaining oil, add mustard seeds and allow to crackle.
6. Stir in the black gram, bengal gram, curry leaves and fry till the gram turns golden.
7. Pour the seasoning over the mixture and blend well.
8. The pickle is ready for use. It keeps for 1 week and is best refrigerated.

787 Sour & Spicy Tomato – Green Spices : Hot

500 g	ripe tomato, chop & cook to half its volume	5 g	fenugreek seeds, soak in little vinegar;	
40 g	cleaned tamarind, soak in 150ml vinegar & obtain thick extract	5 g	cummin seeds &	
		5 g	turmeric powder, grind all to a paste using vinegar	
75 g	green chillies, chop;	5 g	chilli powder	
40 g	peeled garlic, chop;	60 g	salt	
25 g	fresh ginger, scrape & chop;	200 ml	oil	
15 g	mustard seeds;			

1. Heat a little oil, add the spice paste and fry over low heat till the oil separates.
2. In the same pan heat some more oil, stir in the tamarind-vinegar extract, cooked tomato and bring to the boil. Allow to thicken over a high flame.
3. Stir in the chilli powder, salt and the remaining oil.
4. Continue cooking over low heat until the mixture becomes jam-like and the oil separates.
5. The pickle is ready for use. It lasts for 3 months.

788 Tomato – Onion - Ginger : Hot

500 g	ripe tomato, chop	100 g	sugar	
50 g	onion, peel & chop	50 ml	vinegar	
2-1"	pieces of fresh ginger, scrape & chop	40 g	salt	
		30 ml	oil	
10 g	chilli powder			
5	cloves garlic, peel & chop			
5 g	fenugreek seeds			
5 g	onion seeds			
5 g	garam masala powder			

1. Stir-fry the fenugreek seeds, onion seeds, ginger and garlic in a little oil till the fenugreek seeds turn light brown. Set aside.
2. In the same pan stir-fry the chopped onion, tomato, chilli powder, sugar, salt and cook until the mixture thickens. Stir frequently.
3. Add in the vinegar, garam masala powder and the fried ingredients.
4. Continue cooking over low heat until the mixture becomes jam-like and the oil separates.
5. The pickle is ready for use. It lasts for 2 months.

789 Sour & Spicy Tomato : Sweet

500 g	ripe tomato, chop	3	cloves &	
150 g	sugar, dissolve in vinegar	2-1"	sticks of cinnamon, keep all whole	
20 g	dried red chillies &	200 ml	vinegar	
2	bay leaves, break both into bits	40 g	salt	
		50 ml	oil	
5 g	aniseeds			
5 g	fenugreek seeds			
5 g	grated nutmeg;			
2	blades of mace;			

1. Combine all the ingredients (except tomato, sugar, salt & vinegar) evenly.
2. Heat the oil, add the combined spices and fry for a few minutes.
3. Blend in the tomato, sugar, salt and vinegar.
4. Cook over low heat for about 30 minutes and remove when the mixture becomes jam-like.
5. The pickle is ready for use after 1 day. It lasts for 3 months and is best refrigerated.

790 Tomato – Ginger in Mustard Sauce : Hot

500 g	ripe tomato, chop	5 g	turmeric powder	
50 g	fresh ginger, scrape & chop	5 g	cummin seeds : for seasoning	
50 g	green chillies, seed & halve	40 g	sugar, heat with 75ml vinegar	
2	cloves garlic, peel & chop	40 g	salt	
10 g	chilli powder	200 ml	oil	
10 g	mustard seeds, soak in water overnight			

1. Grind the soaked mustard seeds with the ginger and garlic.
2. Fry the cummin seeds in a little oil.
3. Follow with the chopped tomato, chillies and allow to thicken over a high flame.
4. Add in the vinegar mixture and the remaining oil a little at a time.
5. Stir in the chilli and turmeric powders.
6. Continue cooking over low heat until the mixture becomes jam-like and the oil separates.
7. The pickle is ready for use. It lasts for 2 months.

791 Sour & Spicy Traditional Ground Tomato : Hot

1 kg	ripe tomato, size medium
100 g	cleaned tamarind
100 g	chilli powder
50 g	jaggery, grate
10 g	fenugreek seeds &
10 g	asafoetida, roast both in oil & powder
10 g	turmeric powder
10 g	mustard seeds : for seasoning
150 g	salt
300 ml	oil

1. Marinate the tomato pieces in the salt and shake well.
2. Roll the tamarind into a ball and place in the centre making sure it is immersed in the tomato pieces. Cover and set aside for a day.
3. Next day grind the tomato - tamarind mixture along with the jaggery to a fine paste.
4. Spread the ground mixture on a large tray and sun-dry for 3 days. Stir the mixture before sun drying.
5. Heat the oil, add mustard seeds and allow to crackle.
6. Lower the heat, add in the chilli, asafoetida, turmeric, fenugreek powders and stir well.
7. Add in the dried tomato-tamarind mixture and stir thoroughly until the mixture leaves the sides of the pan.
8. The pickle is ready for use. It lasts for 1 year. Sun occasionally.

792 Traditional Ground Tomato : Hot

1 kg	ripe tomato, size medium
60 g	cleaned tamarind
100 g	chilli powder
10 g	fenugreek seeds &
10 g	asafoetida, roast both in oil & powder
10 g	turmeric powder
10 g	mustard seeds, sun-dry & powder
120 g	salt
400 ml	oil

1. Combine the tamarind, turmeric powder and salt with the tomato pieces. Cover and set aside for a day.
2. Next day squeeze out the tomato pieces.
3. Sun-dry the squeezed solids separately and the liquid remaining thereafter separately, for 3 days.
4. Grind together the solids and the liquid without adding water. Stir in the fenugreek and asafoetida powders.
5. Heat the oil to smoking point. When the oil is still lukewarm, blend in the chilli and mustard powders.
6. Stir in the ground mixture and fry until the mixture leaves the sides of the pan.
7. The pickle is ready for use. It lasts for 1 year. Sun occasionally.

793 Ground Tomato : Hot

500 g	ripe tomato, chop;
50 g	cleaned tamarind;
50 g	dried red chillies;
5 g	turmeric powder &
75 g	salt, grind all to a paste using water
5 g	mustard seeds;
5 g	asafoetida &
5 g	fenugreek seeds, roast all three in oil & powder
5 g	mustard seeds : for seasoning
150 ml	oil

1. Heat the oil, add mustard seeds and allow to crackle.
2. Add in the tomato paste and cook until the mixture becomes jam-like.
3. Stir in the powdered spices and remove when the oil separates.
4. The pickle is ready for use after 3 days. It lasts for 3 months.

794 Sour Tomato – Raisin : Sweet

500 g	sour tomato, chop
375 g	sugar
100 g	seedless raisin, chop
5 g	chilli powder
2	cloves garlic, peel &
1-1"	piece of fresh ginger, scrape, chop both & grind to a paste
50 ml	vinegar
12 g	salt

1. Cook together all the ingredients (except vinegar) in a pan over gentle heat, stirring continuously.
2. Conitnue cooking until the tomato becomes tender.
3. Add in the vinegar, heat for a while and remove when well blended.
4. The pickle is ready for use. It lasts for 1 month and is best refrigerated.

795 Mustard Tomato in Groundnut Oil : Hot

500 g	sour tomato, chop
30 g	chilli powder
10 g	fenugreek seeds, roast in oil & powder
15 g	mustard seeds : for seasoning
40 g	salt
250 ml	groundnut oil

1. Marinate the chopped tomato in the salt and sun-dry for 3 days.
2. Remove the skins off the tomatoes (which would have come off by this time), sun-dry, powder and set aside.
3. Sun-dry the peeled tomato for 15 days.
4. Heat the oil, add mustard seeds and allow to crackle.
5. Stir in the peeled dried tomato, powdered tomato skins, the chilli and fenugreek powders.
6. Cook the mixture over low heat until jam-like and remove when the oil separates.
7. The pickle is ready for use. It lasts for 6 months.

796 Sour Tomato – Green Spices : Hot

500 g	sour tomato, size medium
20 g	salt : for marinating
60 g	cleaned tamarind, obtain thick extract using vinegar
50 g	sugar
50 g	green chillies, chop
10	cloves garlic, peel & chop
2-1"	pieces of fresh ginger, scrape & chop
10 g	cummin seeds &
10 g	fenugreek seeds, roast both in oil & powder
5 g	chilli powder
100 ml	vinegar
50 g	salt : for pickle
200 ml	oil

1. Marinate the tomato pieces in 20g salt for 2 hours.
2. Separate the seeds from the tomato pieces and set aside the juice with the seeds.
3. Heat the oil, pour in the tomato juice with the seeds, the tamarind extract and cook for 10 minutes.
4. Stir in the chopped ginger, garlic, green chillies along with the spice powders, salt and sugar.
5. Allow to thicken over a high flame and add in the tomato pieces.
6. Continue cooking over low heat until the mixture becomes jam-like and the oil separates.
7. The pickle is ready for use. It lasts for 3 months.

Oils and Oils

There are several oils used in pickling, ranging from gingelly / sesame oil, mustard oil, peanut / groundnut oil, sunflower oil, olive oil, corn oil and castor oil. Traditionally gingelly oil is the oil used in pickling in South India. Sometimes gingelly oil is used in its raw state as in mango avakkai pickle. It is extracted from black or white gingelly seeds. However, in the northern parts of the country, mustard oil is preferred.

797 Traditional Tomato : Hot

125 g	sour tomato, cut into medium sized pieces
15 g	chilli powder
5	cloves garlic, peel
10 g	cleaned tamarind
10 g	fenugreek seeds, roast in oil & powder
2 g	mustard seeds;
2 g	asafoetida, roast in oil & powder;
2 g	split husked bengal gram &
a few	sprigs curry leaves : all for seasoning
15 g	salt
12 ml	oil

1. Marinate the tomato pieces in salt, cover and set aside for 2 days. Shake twice daily.
2. On the third day squeeze out the juice given out by the tomato and sun for 2 days till dry.
3. On the same day, drop the tamarind into the tomato juice and sun the mixture for a day.
4. Grind together the tamarind, chilli powder and salt coarsely.
5. Add in the tomato and grind once more coarsely.
6. Finally mix in the peeled garlic and fenugreek powder.
7. This basic tomato pickle lasts for 3 months.
8. Whenever desired take the required quantity of the prepared tomato.
9. Heat the oil, add mustard seeds and allow to crackle.
10. Add in the bengal gram, curry leaves, asafoetida powder and fry till the gram turns golden.
11. Pour the seasoning over the prepared tomato and blend well.
12. The pickle is ready for use. It keeps for 10 days.

798 Tomato – Gram – Garlic : Hot

500 g	sour tomato, size medium	20 g	split husked bengal gram;
25 g	peeled garlic	10 g	mustard seeds;
100 g	cleaned tamarind	a few	sprigs curry leaves &
40 g	chilli powder	5 g	asafoetida : all for seasoning
20 g	fenugreek seeds, roast in oil & powder	50 g	salt
		200 ml	oil

1. Stir-fry the tomato pieces in a little oil. The tomato pieces will begin to give out water.
2. Place over a high flame so that the water evaporates and later reduce the flame to medium.
3. Remove from the fire when the tomato gets reduced in volume to three-fourths its original quantity.
4. When it is still hot, arrange the tamarind in the centre of a tray and surround with the cooked tomato.
5. Allow to cool. Grind with the chilli powder, salt and garlic coarsely.
6. Heat the remaining oil and fry the bengal gram, mustard seeds, curry leaves, asafoetida powder till done.
7. Cool and pour the seasoning over the prepared tomato.
8. The pickle is ready for use after 3 days. It lasts for 2 months.

799 Tomato – Onion – Raisin – Plum : Hot

500 g	sour tomato, keep whole	5 g	dried ginger powder
50 g	chilli powder	2	cloves garlic, peel & slice
20 g	onion, peel & slice		
15 g	seedless raisin, chop	2 g	grated nutmeg
15 g	dried plum, chop & seed	25 ml	vinegar
15 g	sugar	40 g	salt

1. Bring the water to boiling. Blanch the tomato in the boiling water for 5 minutes. Peel off the skins and chop.
2. Combine the chopped tomato, onion, garlic, raisin, plum, salt, ginger powder in a pan and cook for 30 minutes.
3. Pass the mixture through a wire-sieve to make a puree.
4. Stir in the chilli powder, nutmeg, vinegar, sugar and cook the mixture over a medium flame until thick.
5. The pickle is ready for use. It lasts for 1 month in the refrigerator.

800 Sour Ground Tomato : Hot

500 g	sour tomato, chop	3 g	fenugreek seeds, roast both in oil & powder
60 g	cleaned new tamarind		
50 g	chilli powder	3 g	mustard seeds
3 g	turmeric powder	50 ml	vinegar
		50 g	salt
3 g	asafoetida &	250 ml	oil

1. Stir-fry the chopped tomato and tamarind in a little oil for a few minutes.
2. Cool and grind the fried ingredients with the salt to a fine paste.
3. Sun-dry the tomato paste in a broad tray for 3 days till the water evaporates. Stir the mixture everyday before sunning.
4. Heat half the oil, add mustard seeds and allow to crackle.
5. Add in the tomato paste and cook for a few minutes.
6. Stir in the chilli, turmeric, fenugreek, asafoetida powders and the remaining oil.
7. Continue cooking over low heat until the mixture leaves the sides of the pan.
8. Pour over the vinegar and blend well.
9. The pickle is ready for use. It lasts for 2 months. Sun occasionally.

801 Tomato – Fenugreek – Mustard : Hot

1 kg	sour tomato, keep whole	80 g	dried red chillies;
35 g	cleaned tamarind, obtain thick extract using water	30 g	fenugreek seeds &
		30 g	mustard seeds, sun-dry all three & powder
10	cloves garlic, peel & crush	50 g	salt
		400 ml	oil

1. Heat a little oil in a pan, fry the tomato until the skin starts shrinking and the juice comes out.
2. Stir in the powdered chillies, fenugreek, mustard powders, crushed garlic and salt. Combine well and set aside.
3. Heat the remaining oil, pour in the tamarind extract and cook till syrupy.
4. Add in the spiced tomato, cook till well blended and remove.
5. The pickle is ready for use. It lasts for 2 months and is best refrigerated.

802 Sour Tomato – Garlic : Hot

1 kg	tomato, keep whole
500 g	dried red chillies &
150 g	peeled garlic, grind to a paste using vinegar
150 ml	vinegar
200 g	salt

1. Blanch tomatoes in boiling water for 4 minutes. Peel off skins and chop the tomatoes.
2. Combine the chopped tomato, spice paste and cook until the juice evaporates.
3. Add vinegar and continue cooking until the mixture becomes thick and jam-like.
4. The pickle is now ready for use. It lasts for 4 months and needs to be refrigerated.

803 Tomato Paste – Tamarind : Hot

1 kg	ripe tomato, chop
100 g	cleaned tamarind
100 g	chilli powder
15 g	fenugreek seeds &
10 g	asafoetida, roast both in oil & powder
10 g	mustard seeds : for seasoning
120 g	salt
200 ml	oil

1. Marinate the tomato pieces in the salt for a day.
2. Squeeze out the tomato pieces from the salt water and sun for 3 days. Separately sun the salt water for 3 days.
3. Add the tamarind to the tomato juice and grind to a paste.
4. Heat a little oil, add mustard seeds and allow to crackle.
5. Add in the dried tomato pieces and stir-fry for a while. Follow with the tamarind paste, the remaining oil and fry for a few more minutes.
6. Stir in the chilli, fenugreek, asafoetida powders, cook over low heat for a few minutes and remove.
7. The pickle is ready for use. It lasts for 1 year.

804 Sour Tomato – Onion - Ginger : Sweet

500 g	sour tomato, keep whole
500 g	sugar
50 g	onion, peel & chop
30 g	fresh ginger, scrape & chop
25 g	chilli powder
5	cloves garlic, peel & chop
5	cardamoms, keep whole
200 ml	vinegar
5 g	salt

1. Bring the water to boiling. Blanch the tomato in the boiling water for 3 minutes. Peel off the skins and chop.
2. Combine the tomato, onion, chilli powder, ginger and garlic in a pan.
3. Cook until thick, stirring frequently.
4. When thick, add in the vinegar, sugar, salt, cardamom and remove when the mixture becomes jam-like.
5. The pickle is ready for use. It lasts for 2 months.

805 Tomato – Raisin - Almond in Vinegar : Sweet

500 g	sour tomato, keep whole
water	sufficient to immerse
40 g	chilli powder
30 g	seedless raisin, chop
10	almonds, blanch & sliver
25 g	onion, peel & chop
1-1"	piece of fresh ginger, scrape & chop
2	cloves garlic, peel & chop
5	big cardamoms, peel & crush seeds
100 g	sugar
200 ml	vinegar
30 g	salt

1. Bring the water to boiling. Blanch the tomato in the boiling water for 3 minutes. Peel off the skins and chop.
2. Combine the tomato, chilli powder, onion, ginger, garlic, salt and cook till tender.
3. When the mixture thickens add in the vinegar, sugar, raisin, almond and cardamom.
4. Continue cooking for 10 minutes and remove.
5. The pickle is ready for use. It lasts for 2 months.

806 Sour & Spiced Tomato – Onion - Capsicum : Sweet

500 g	sour tomato, keep whole
300 g	capsicum, chop
200 g	onion, peel & chop
60 g	chilli powder
10 g	mustard seeds
5 g	thymol seeds : for seasoning
6	dried red chillies, break into bits
4	cloves;
1-1"	stick of cinnamon;
2 g	allspice &
1	bay leaf, keep all whole
400 g	jaggery, grate
400 ml	vinegar
80 g	salt

1. Bring the water to boiling. Blanch the tomato in the boiling water for 3 minutes. Peel off the skins and chop.
2. Combine the tomato, onion, capsicum, chilli powder, salt and cook till tender.
3. When the mixture thickens add in the vinegar, jaggery and the remaining ingredients.
4. Continue cooking for 10 minutes and remove.
5. The pickle is ready for use. It lasts for 2 months.

807 Tudhuvelai Berry in Curd : Watery

500 g	tudhuvelai berry, halve
400 ml	sour curd, whip with 200 ml water & remove cream
80 g	salt

1. Blend the tudhuvelai berries with the whipped curd and salt. Set aside for 2 days.
2. The pickle lasts for 1 month and longer in the refrigerator. Shake daily.

808 Spicy Turnip – Onion : Hot

500 g	turnip, scrape & cut into thin slices
50 g	onion, peel & chop
5	dried date, soak in warm water & chop
15 g	cleaned tamarind
15 g	jaggery, grate & make a thick syrup with water
1-1"	piece of fresh ginger, scrape & shred
20 g	split husked mustard seeds
12 g	chilli powder
5 g	peppercorns, sun-dry & powder
3 g	cummin seeds
1-1"	stick of cinnamon, keep whole
45 g	salt
50 ml	oil : heat & cool

1. Stir-fry the onion, ginger and garlic in a little oil. Set aside.
2. In the same pan heat the tamarind extract and bring to the boil. Allow to thicken and remove.
3. Combine all the ingredients (except jaggery syrup) in a jar and sun the mixture for 4 days.
4. Stir in the cooled jaggery syrup and sun for 3 days.
5. Add in the remaining pre-heated oil and sun for 3 more days.
6. The pickle lasts for 2 months.

809 Sour Turnip – Mustard : Sweet

500 g	turnip, scrape & slice into thin rounds
40 g	dried red chillies
25 g	mustard seeds
5	cloves garlic, peel & chop
1-1"	piece of fresh ginger, scrape & chop
5	cloves, keep whole
2	big cardamoms, keep whole
150 g	jaggery, make a thick syrup with sufficient water
150 ml	vinegar
200 ml	water, combine with 1ml tartaric acid
40 g	salt
100 ml	oil

1. Grind the spices to a fine paste using a little vinegar.
2. Dilute the spice paste with the remaining vinegar and heat for a few minutes.
3. Add the jaggery syrup to the hot spiced vinegar and sun for 7 days.
4. Boil the turnip in the diluted tartaric acid for 5 minutes.
5. Remove the boiled turnip with a perforated spoon and pat-dry on a cloth.
6. Drop into the vinegar mixture and allow to soak for 3 days.
7. Heat the oil, add the garlic, red chillies and fry for a while. Cool and strain the oil.
8. Pour the spiced oil over the pickle mixture and sun for 5 days. The pickle lasts for 2 months.

810 Turnip – Onion – Apple : Sweet

500 g	turnip, scrape & chop water sufficient to immerse		
250 g	onion, peel & chop		
250 g	cored cooking apple, peel & chop		
125 g	date, stone & chop		
125 g	sugar		
10 g	peppercorns &	5 g	turmeric powder
5 g	mustard seeds, sun-dry both & powder	300 ml	vinegar
		50 g	salt

1. Bring the water to a gentle boil. Add in the chopped turnip, cook till tender, drain and set aside.
2. Combine all the remaining ingredients in a little vinegar.
3. Pour in the remaining vinegar and bring to the boil. Allow to thicken over a high flame.
4. Blend in the cooked turnip and remove.
5. The pickle is ready for use. It lasts for 2 months.

811 Spiced Turnip – Ginger - Garlic : Sweet

500 g	turnip, scrape & cut into thin rounds		
50 g	fresh ginger, scrape & chop		
30 g	seedless raisin &		
15	dried date, grind both to a paste		
30 g	peeled garlic, chop		
10 g	chilli powder	120 g	sugar
5 g	peppercorns	150 ml	vinegar
5 g	onion seeds	40 g	salt
5 g	cummin seeds	120 ml	oil

1. Marinate the turnip slices in the salt for 5 hours.
2. Grind together the ginger, chilli powder, peppercorns, onion seeds and cummin seeds with the sugar.
3. Stir-fry the garlic paste in a little oil till golden. Follow with the turnip slices and fry till brown.
4. Add in the vinegar, ground spices, date-raisin paste and the remaining oil. Mix thoroughly.
5. Transfer to a jar and sun the mixture for 5 days.
6. The pickle lasts for 2 months. Sun occasionally.

812 Sweet & Sour Elephant Yam – Green Coriander : Hot

500 g	elephant yam, peel, chop & soak in raw tamarind water
75 g	chilli powder
60 g	green coriander, wash, air-dry & chop;
5 g	coriander seeds, dry-roast &
125 g	salt, grind all three to a paste
120 g	cleaned tamarind, obtain thin extract using water
100 g	jaggery, grate
5 g	turmeric powder
5 g	mustard seeds &
a few	sprigs curry leaves : both for seasoning
250 ml	oil

1. Steam the yam pieces with lightly salted tamarind water till partly tender. Cool and grind to a paste.
2. Stir-fry the yam, green spice paste in a little oil and set aside.
3. Heat some more oil, add mustard seeds and allow to crackle. Add in the curry leaves and allow to turn crisp.
4. Stir in the tamarind extract, jaggery, turmeric powder and bring to the boil. Allow to thicken over a high flame.
5. Add in the yam mixture, chilli powder and the remaining oil.
6. Continue cooking over low heat until the mixture becomes jam-like and the oil separates.
7. The pickle is ready for use. It lasts for 2 months.

813 Spiced Elephant Yam – Onion - Ginger : Hot

500 g	elephant yam, peel, cube & steam till tender
30 g	onion, peel & chop
30 g	fresh ginger, scrape & chop
12 g	chilli powder
12 g	cummin seeds, sun-dry & powder
12 g	mustard seeds, sun-dry
5 g	turmeric powder
8 g	sugar
100 ml	vinegar
40 g	salt
200 ml	oil

1. Roast the cubed elephant yam in a little oil till golden brown and set aside.
2. Grind together the remaining ingredients to a smooth paste using vinegar.
3. Fry the spice paste in a little oil for a few minutes over low heat and remove.
4. Blend in the fried yam, the remaining oil (after heating), the remaining vinegar and remove.
5. Sun the mixture for a week. The pickle lasts for 2 months.

814 Spiced Sour Elephant Yam – Garlic : Hot

500 g	elephant yam, peel, chop & mash
100 g	peeled garlic, chop
75 g	cleaned tamarind, obtain thick extract using water
50 g	chilli powder
15 g	fenugreek seeds, roast in oil & powder
15 g	turmeric powder
15 g	mustard seeds : for seasoning
50 ml	vinegar
100 g	salt
375 ml	oil

1. Stir-fry the mashed elephant yam in half the oil and set aside.
2. In the same pan heat some more oil, add mustard seeds and allow to crackle.
3. Add in the garlic and fry for a minute.
4. Stir in the tamarind extract and bring to the boil. Allow to thicken over a high flame.
5. Add in the fried elephant yam, chilli, fenugreek, turmeric powders, salt and the remaining oil.
6. Continue cooking until the mixture becomes jam-like.
7. Pour over the vinegar and heat for a few minutes till well blended.
8. The pickle is ready for use after 2 days. It lasts for 3 months.

O̲i̲l̲ F̲r̲e̲e̲

recipes

opens up

a staggering variety of

fabulous low-calorie

but tasty delicacies,

injecting

a hot, sweet and sour music

into

any food.

Truly a treat for

the health conscious.

Recipes : Oil - Free

815. Ammatangai in mustard sauce : hot
816. Lime, bamboo shoot : salty
817. Sour bean – onion : sweet
818. Dill bean in vinegar : tender
819. Beetroot in spiced vinegar : salty
820. Spiced capsicum in vinegar : hot
821. Green cardamom in lime juice : watery
822. Cauliflower – lotus stem - onion : hot
823. Cashew – green coriander : instant
824. Carrot – ginger in limejuice : instant
825. Narthangai : hot
826. Narthangai : salty
827. Spiral / sliced narthangai : hot
828. Cocum – date - garlic : instant
829. Spiced cocum – onion : instant
830. Coconut – mango - green coriander : instant
831. Stripped corn – celery in vinegar : watery
832. Stripped corn – mixed vegetable : tender
833. Mustard cucumber : tender
834. Cucumber – green spices : watery
835. Sweet & sour cucumber : watery
836. Curd – green spices : instant
837. Sour date – onion seeds : hot
838. Steamed gooseberry : instant
839. Spice stuffed green chilli : instant
840. Green chilli in vinegar : salty
841. Green chilli – lime - ginger : salty
842. Stuffed green chilli in lime juice : salty
843. Chopped green chilli in vinegar : hot
844. Sour green peas : watery
845. Green pepper – ginger in lime juice : hot
846. Cooked lime whole – green chilli : hot
847. Roasted groundnut – mint - green coriander : instant
848. Stuffed lime : hot
849. Lime mild spicy stuffed : salty
850. Stuffed spicy lime : hot
851. Lime – thymol seeds : hot
852. Spiced lime – ginger - green chilli : hot
853. Gingered lime : hot
854. Fenugreek lime : hot
855. Lime – ginger - date in vinegar : salty
856. Lime – ginger - kalakkai : salty
857. Lime – green chilli : hot
858. Fried lime – green chilli: hot
859. Stuffed lime – sweet spices : salty
860. Unripe lime – fenugreek : salty
861. Sour lime : hot
862. Spiced lime whole in vinegar : watery
863. Mustard lime – green chilli : hot

864. Sunned lime – green spices : hot
865. Lime – mahani - green spices : hot
866. Spicy lime in vinegar : watery
867. Sour & spicy grated mango : watery
868. Sour spiced mango : sweet
869. Grated mango – green chilli : hot
870. Mango – ground spices : instant
871. Spiced mango : salty
872. Stuffed spiced mango in vinegar : watery
873. Mint green coriander – tomato - onion : instant
874. Sour mint – green coriander : instant
875. Sour mint – groundnut - onion : instant
876. Mixed vegetable – lime : hot
877. Bean – onion - papaya : instant
878. Mixed vegetable – garlic in lime juice : watery
879. Sour onion : instant
880. Salted mixed vegetable in vinegar : watery
881. Sour cauliflower – cucumber : sweet
882. Sweet & sour mixed vegetable in vinegar : tender
883. Cauliflower – cucumber - bean : watery
884. Mixed vegetable : watery
885. Mixed vegetable in lime juice : tender
886. Cauliflower – bean : tender
887. Onion in vinegar : salty
888. Small red onion in spiced vinegar : watery
889. Onion – ginger - green chilli : instant
890. Sour peach – raisin - onion : sweet
891. Mustard pineapple – green spices : instant
892. Pineapple – lime juice - vinegar : instant
893. Sour banana : sweet
894. Sweet plum : instant
895. Spiced plum : sweet
896. Pomegranate seed : instant
897. Ground raisin : instant
898. Green tomato – ginger - garlic : instant
899. Sweet tamarind – date : instant
900. Spicy tamarind – cummin : hot
901. Tamarind – cummin : instant
902. Spiced tamarind : sweet
903. Sweet & sour tomato in garlic juice : instant

Pickles automatically conjure up visions of mango / lime or other fruits and vegetables generously smeared with spices and drenched in oil. Pickles can be prepared without oil and without salt as well. A long standing pickle owes its keeping quality to its salt or sugar content, which acts a natural preservative. This being the case, it is not surprising that one can turn out delicious pickles with no oil or salt. A striking example is the *chunndo* – the sweet mango pickle from Gujarat – which is prepared from grated mango with sugar or jaggery.

815 Ammatangai in Mustard Sauce : Hot

500 g	ammatangai, keep whole
20 g	salt, boil in 400ml water
50 g	dried red chillies, sun-dry;
15 g	mustard seeds, sun-dry &
5 g	fenugreek seeds, roast in oil, grind all three together
5 g	turmeric powder
75 g	salt

1. Sun-dry the ammatangai for a day, softly crush with a stone and seed.
2. Drop the seeded ammatangai into the salted boiling water.
3. When almost tender remove from the boiling water and allow to cool.
4. Blend the salt, turmeric powder and the ground spices into the cooled water. Stir in the salted ammatangai.
5. The pickle is ready for use the next day. It lasts for 1 month. Sun occasionally.

816 Lime, Bamboo Shoot : Salty

500 g	fresh tender bamboo shoot pieces, peel
50 g	green chillies, chop
65 g	salt, soak in 150ml lime juice

1. Cook the bamboo shoot pieces in sufficient water till tender. Cool and chop fine.
2. Toss the chopped bamboo shoot with the salted lime juice and green chillies.
3. The pickle is ready for use after 3 days. It lasts for 3 months.

817 Sour Bean – Onion : Sweet

500 g	tender beans, top, tail & julienne
125 g	small onion, peel & chop
125 g	sugar
5 g	salt, combine with 300ml water
10 g	dill seeds
5 g	chilli powder
300 ml	vinegar
75 g	salt : for pickle

1. Cook the beans in 300ml salted boiling water till tender yet crunchy. Drain, air-dry and transfer to a jar.
2. Combine the onion, dill seeds, chilli powder, sugar and salt in vinegar. Bring to the boil and keep stirring till the sugar dissolves.
3. Boil the mixture for 3 minutes, pour over the beans and set the pickle aside for 6 weeks.
4. The pickle lasts for 2 months and needs to be refrigerated on opening.

Note : While choosing **beans**, look for a bright, unblemished colour and a pod firm enough to snap readily. The seeds shoud be only just formed; bulging seeds indicate toughness.

818 Dill Bean in Vinegar : Tender

500 g	tender beans, top, tail & julienne
20 g	dried red chillies, break into bits
20 g	dill
2	cloves garlic, peel & chop
150 ml	vinegar
100 ml	water
50 g	salt

1. Pack the beans in a jar. Throw in the red chillies, garlic and dill.
2. Combine the vinegar, water, salt and bring to the boil.
3. Boil the mixture for 3 minutes, pour over the beans and set the pickle aside for 6 weeks.
4. The pickle lasts for 2 months in the refrigerator.

819 Beetroot in Spiced Vinegar : Salty

500 g	beetroot, steam, peel & chop
10 g	peppercorns
5	cloves
2-1"	sticks of cinnamon
200 ml	vinegar
50 g	salt

1. Combine all the ingredients (except beetroot) and heat well.
2. Stir in the beetroot pieces and set aside.
3. The pickle is ready for use after 3 days. It lasts for 1 month and is best refrigerated.

Choose **beetroots** with deeper colour as they are richer in vitamin A. Should be smooth, free from blemishes, may have some soil on them and preferably medium-sized. Cook whole with the skin intact to hold in all its colour and flavour.

820 Spiced Capsicum in Vinegar : Hot

500 g	ripe capsicum, chop & seed
100 g	onion, peel & chop
2-1"	pieces of dried root ginger, pound;
2	dried red chillies &
5 g	peppercorns, tie all three in a spice bag
30 g	sugar
150 ml	vinegar
5 g	garlic salt
60 g	salt

1. Blanch the capsicum in boiling water for 2 minutes and allow to drain.
2. Bring the sugar, salts, vinegar and the spice bag to boiling. Keep stirring until the sugar dissolves.
3. Add in the capsicum, onion and continue heating till the vegetables are cooked yet crunchy.
4. Remove the vegetables with a perforated spoon and pack into a jar.
5. Squeeze out the spice bag thoroughly and pour the hot vinegar over the pickle.
6. The pickle is ready for use after 2 weeks. It lasts for 2 months.

821 Green Cardamom in Lime Juice : Watery

125 g	fresh green cardamom, remove stems & keep whole
12 g	green pepper
25 g	salt, soak in 40ml lime juice

1. Combine the green cardamom, salted lime juice, green pepper and set aside for 4 days.
2. The pickle lasts for 1 month.

Cardamoms are of two types: small & large, the former having two varieties, viz., the stronger flavoured green cardamoms and the lesser flavoured bleached white ones.

822 Cauliflower – Lotus Stem – Onion : Hot

500 g	cauliflower florets	10	cloves garlic, peel & chop
500 g	small red onion, peel & chop	10	dates, stone & chop
250 g	lotus stem, cut into pieces	5 g	onion seeds
50 g	fresh ginger, scrape & chop	5 g	mustard seeds
40 g	green chillies, chop	2	small cardamoms
15 g	dried red chillies	100 g	jaggery, grate
		600 ml	vinegar
		100 g	salt

1. Boil the lotus stem pieces in water and drain. Allow the lotus stem pieces, chopped ginger and florets to dry for a few hours in the shade on a thick towel.
2. Combine the dried vegetables and salt with the chopped onion and green chillies. Set aside.
3. Simultaneously soak the jaggery in the vinegar and set aside for a day.
4. Strain and pour the sweetened vinegar over the dried vegetables.
5. Stir in all the other ingredients. Mix thoroughly, seal and store.
6. The pickle is ready for use after 2 weeks. It lasts for 1 month. However, refrigerate on opening.

823 Cashew – Green Coriander : Instant

125 g	cashewnuts, chop
20 g	green coriander, wash, air-dry & chop;
10 g	green chillies &
1-1"	piece of fresh ginger, scrape & chop, grind all three to a paste
50 ml	lime juice
10 g	salt

1. Stir-fry the chopped cashewnut in a little oil till the raw taste disappears.
2. Add in the spice paste and fry for a minute.
3. Blend in the salt and lime juice.
4. The pickle is ready for use. It keeps for 1 week in the refrigerator.

824 Carrot – Ginger in Lime Juice : Instant

125 g	carrot, peel & julienne
30 g	fresh ginger, scrape & chop fine
12 g	green chillies, chop fine
50 ml	lime juice
15 g	salt

1. Combine the chopped carrot with the lime juice and salt.
2. Add in the chopped ginger, green chillies and mix thoroughly.
3. The pickle is ready for use. It keeps for 1 week and longer in the refrigerator.

825 Narthangai : Hot

1 kg	narthangai, scrape lightly
60 g	chilli powder
120 g	salt

1. Cut the narthangai into spirals, stuff with the salt and set aside for a week. Shake daily.
2. Sun-dry the narthangai spirals.
3. Add in the chilli powder, mix thoroughly and store.
4. The pickle lasts for more than a year.

826 Narthangai : Salty

1 kg	narthangai, scrape lightly & cut into pieces or spirals
100 g	chilli powder
160 g	salt

1. Pack the narthangai pieces/spirals in a jar. Add in the salt, chilli powder and toss well. Cover and set aside for 10 days. Stir twice daily.
2. Remove the narthangai pieces/spirals from the salt water and dry in mild sunlight. Return to the salt water every night.
3. Repeat this procedure until the entire salt water is absorbed by the narthangai pieces/spirals.
4. The pickle is ready for use when the narthangai pieces/spirals are soft yet dry. It lasts for several years.

827 Spiral / Sliced Narthangai : Hot

1 kg	narthangai, scrape lightly & cut into spirals or slices
60 g	dried red chillies &
5 g	fenugreek seeds, roast both in oil & powder
5 g	turmeric powder
175 g	salt

1. Combine all the spice powders evenly.
2. Stuff the spice mixture into the narthangai spirals / slices and set aside for 2 days. Shake daily.
3. On the 3rd day, remove the narthangai spirals / slices from the salt water and sun-dry.
4. Return to the salt water in the evening. Remove and sun-dry the following day.
5. Repeat this procedure until the entire salt water is absorbed by the narthangai spirals / pieces.
6. The pickle is ready for use when the narthangai spirals / slices are soft yet dry. It lasts for several years.

828 Cocum – Date – Garlic : Hot

500 g	cocum, wash in hot water;
20 g	dried red chillies, break into bits &
60 g	salt, grind all three coarsely
25 g	peeled garlic, chop;
5 g	fenugreek seeds, dry-roast &
100 g	seedless dried date, chop, grind all three coarsely
80 ml	vinegar

1. Blend the spice paste with the cocum paste.
2. Grind the mixture to a fine paste with the vinegar.
3. The pickle is ready for use. It lasts for 1 month in the refrigerator.

829 Spiced Cocum – Onion : Instant

500 g	cocum, wash in hot water;
30 g	dried red chillies, break into bits;
10 g	sugar &
75 g	salt, grind all together coarsely
100 g	small red onion, peel & chop;
10	cloves garlic, peel & chop;
5 g	cummin seeds, dry-roast;
5 g	coriander seeds, dry-roast &
a few	sprigs curry leaves, grind all to a paste
80 ml	vinegar

1. Blend the cocum paste with the spice paste.
2. Grind the mixture to a fine paste with the vinegar.
3. The pickle is ready for use. It lasts for 1 month in the refrigerator.

830 Coconut – Mango – Green Coriander : Instant

125 g	grated coconut, dry roast
60 g	seeded raw mango, peel & chop
30 g	small red onion, peel & chop
30 g	green chillies, chop
15 g	green coriander, wash, air-dry & chop
1-1"	piece of fresh ginger, scrape & chop
25 g	sugar
25 g	salt

1. Stir-fry the chopped mango, onion and green chillies in a little oil and set aside.
2. Grind together all the ingredients to a smooth paste using a little water.
3. The pickle is ready for use. It keeps only for 2 days but longer in the refrigerator.

831 Stripped Corn – Celery in Vinegar : Watery

500 g	stripped corn niblets	175 g	sugar
300 g	celery, chop	5 g	mustard seeds, sun-dry & powder
300 g	ripe red capsicum, seed & dice	3 g	turmeric powder
		400 ml	vinegar
125 g	onion, peel & chop	300 ml	water
		75 g	salt

1. Combine the celery, onion and mustard powder in a pan. Add in the vinegar little by little and bring the mixture gently to the boil.
2. Add in the remaining ingredients. Simmer for 25 minutes until the mixture thickens and the vegetables become tender.
3. Transfer to a jar, seal and set aside.
4. The pickle is ready for use after 3 days. It lasts for 1 month and longer in the refrigerator.

832 Stripped Corn – Mixed Vegetable : Tender

125 g	stripped corn, strip from cob	5 g	mustard seeds, sun-dry & powder
125 g	tomato, chop		
125 g	cucumber &	30 g	sugar
125 g	onion, peel & chop both	75 ml	vinegar : for cooking
50 g	flour	40 ml	vinegar : heat & cool
3 g	turmeric powder	50 g	salt

1. Combine the vinegar, sugar, salt and boil for 20 minutes along with the chopped vegetable.
2. Stir in the mustard, turmeric powders, flour, 40ml cooled vinegar and cook until the mixture thickens.
3. The pickle is ready for use. It lasts for 1 month in the refrigerator.

833 Mustard Cucumber : Tender

500 g	tender cucumber, scrub
50 g	mustard seeds, sun-dry & powder;
20 g	fenugreek seeds, roast in oil & powder;
30 g	chilli powder &
5 g	turmeric powder, combine all evenly
50 g	salt

1. Cut both edges of the cucumbers, apply the salt and set aside overnight.
2. Remove the cucumbers from the salt water and sun-dry. When dry, wash in the salt water.
3. Combine the spice mixture with the prepared cucumber and sun for 3 days.
4. The pickle is ready for use after 15 days. It lasts for 4 months.

834 Cucumber – Green Spices : Watery

500 g	cucumber, scrub & chop	30 g	fresh ginger, scrape & chop
40 g	green chillies, chop	200 ml	vinegar
		50 g	salt

1. Bring the vinegar, 200ml water and the salt to the boil.
2. Lower the heat, add in the chopped cucumber, ginger and cook for a few minutes.
3. Cool, add in the green chillies and set aside for a day.
4. The pickle lasts for 2 months.

835 Sweet & Sour Cucumber : Watery

500 g	cucumber, scrub & keep whole
20 g	powdered alum
400 ml	water
4	dried red chillies;
3	cardamoms;
3	cloves;
2-1"	pieces of fresh ginger, pound &
1-1"	stick of cinnamon, tie all in a spice bag
a few	sprigs of dill
200 ml	vinegar
100 g	sugar
60 g	salt

1. Soak the cucumbers in alum water overnight.
2. Next day rinse in water thoroughly and pack loosely in a jar along with the sprigs of dill.
3. Combine the vinegar, water, sugar, salt, the spice bag and boil for 10 minutes.
4. Remove and squeeze out the spice bag.
5. Pour the spiced vinegar over the cucumber to cover, seal and set aside for 2 weeks.
6. The pickle lasts for 2 months in the refrigerator.

836 Curd – Green Spices : Instant

125 g	curd, whip & remove cream
5 g	green chillies, chop fine
5 g	mint leaves, wash, air-dry & grind fine
3 g	dried mango powder
15 g	salt

1. Combine all the ingredients, blend well and allow to stand for a day.
2. The pickle is ready for use. It keeps for 2 weeks and is best refrigerated.

837 Sour Date – Onion Seeds : Hot

500 g	stoned date, chop fine	10 g	green turmeric, scrape & slice
25 g	green chillies, chop fine	10 g	onion seeds
100 ml	lime juice	40 g	salt

1. Cook the chopped date and turmeric in a little water. Remove and sun-dry for a day.
2. Stir in the chopped green chillies, onion seeds, lime juice and sun-dry for 5 more days.
3. Add in the salt and stir well.
4. The pickle is ready for use. It lasts for 1 month. Sun occasionally.

838 Steamed Gooseberry : Instant

Gooseberry retains its vitamin C content for a long time. For long use dry in the shade and preserve.

1 kg	gooseberry
60 g	dried red chillies;
10 g	fenugreek seeds &
10 g	asafoetida, roast all three in oil & powder
20 g	mustard seeds, sun-dry & powder
10 g	turmeric powder
225 g	salt

1. Pressure cook the gooseberry with the salt. Remove and allow to cool.
2. Fry the gooseberry in a dry pan till the moisture evaporates. Cool, pound coarsely and seed.
3. Combine the spice powders with the pounded gooseberry and mix thoroughly.
4. The pickle is ready for use. It lasts for 1 year. Sun occasionally.

839 Spice Stuffed Green Chilli : Instant

500 g	green chillies, slit
30 g	mustard seeds, sun-dry;
25 g	dried red chillies;
5	cloves garlic, peel;
2-1"	pieces of fresh ginger, scrape, chop &
250 ml	vinegar, grind all to a paste
5 g	turmeric powder
200 g	salt

1. Combine the turmeric powder, salt and the spice paste thoroughly.
2. Stuff the mixture into the green chillies and arrange in a jar.
3. The pickle is ready for use when the vinegar soaks into the green chillies. It lasts for 2 months.

Note : Wash and air-dry the green chillies keeping the stem-end intact. Cut the rear end of the chilli with a scissor and scoop out the seeds with a sharp knife. Pound them together with the required spices and stuff them back into the chillies.

840 Green Chilli in Vinegar : Salty

500 g	green chillies, wash with stem intact	200 g	salt, combine with 500 ml water
		250 ml	vinegar

1. Boil the salt solution. Add in the green chillies. Stir 5 times and remove immediately from the water.
2. Sun-dry the chillies and remove the stems.
3. Transfer to a jar, pour over the vinegar, cap tight and shake well.
4. Sun the pickle for 1½ months.
5. Set aside for another 1½ months indoors.
6. The pickle is ready for use. It lasts for six months.

841 Green Chilli – Lime – Ginger : Salty

125 g	green chillies, cut into lengthwise strips
75 g	lime, chop fine & seed
25 g	fresh ginger, scrape & chop fine
40 g	salt

1. Combine the green chillies, lime and ginger with the salt in a jar. Shake daily.
2. Sun the pickle for 15 days.
3. The pickle is ready for use. It keeps for 10 days. Stir occasionally in mild sunlight.

842 Stuffed Green Chilli in Lime Juice : Salty

500 g	mature long green chillies, slit from lower end & keep stems intact
10 g	mustard seeds, sun-dry & powder;
5 g	fenugreek seeds, roast in oil & powder;
5 g	turmeric powder &
125 g	salt, combine all evenly
125 ml	lime juice

1. Stuff the spice mixture into the chillies.
2. Pack the stuffed chillies in a jar in an upright position and sun for a day.
3. Pour over the lime juice and again sun the pickle for a week.
4. The pickle is ready for use after 2 days. It lasts for 6 months. Sun occasionally.

843 Chopped Green Chilli in Vinegar : Hot

500 g	green chillies, chop
40 g	sugar
300 ml	vinegar
200 g	salt

1. Combine the vinegar, sugar, salt and stir to dissolve.
2. Add in the chopped green chillies and mix well.
3. The pickle is ready for use after 2 days. It lasts for 1 month.

844 Sour Green Peas : Watery

125 g	shelled green peas
5 g	salt : for boiling peas
12 g	green chillies, chop fine
1-1"	piece of fresh ginger, scrape & chop
5 g	asafoetida, roast in oil & powder
40 ml	lime juice
18 g	salt

1. Par-boil the shelled peas in the boiling water to which a teaspoon (5g) salt has been added. Drain, discard the water and pat-dry on a clean cloth.
2. Combine the boiled peas, chopped ginger, green chillies with the asafoetida powder, salt and the lime juice. Set aside for 2 days.
3. The pickle is ready for use. It keeps for 10 days and longer in the refrigerator. Stir frequently.

845 Green Pepper – Ginger in Lime Juice : Hot

1kg	green pepper with string
2-1"	pieces of fresh ginger, scrape & chop
200ml	lime juice
200g	salt

1. Combine the ginger, lime juice, salt with the green pepper & set aside for a week.
2. The pickle lasts for 1 year.

> Green pepper for pickling, should be picked before it gets fully grown, else it will be too pungent. Cut with the stems on, into small bits to retain crunchiness.

846 Cooked Lime Whole – Green Chilli : Hot

1 kg	lime, scrape slightly & prick with a fork
120 g	green chillies, slit
40 g	chilli powder
10 g	mustard seeds, sun-dry & powder
5 g	fenugreek seeds, dry-roast & powder
200 g	salt

1. Combine all the ingredients and cook over low heat.
2. Remove from the fire when the limes turn reddish brown.
3. The pickle is ready for use after 10 days. It lasts for 1 year.

847 Roasted Groundnut – Mint - Green Coriander : Instant

125 g	shelled roasted groundnut, peel		20 g	green chillies, chop
25 g	green coriander &		10 ml	lime juice
25 g	mint leaves, wash, air-dry & chop both		2 g	sugar
			15 g	salt

1. Grind together all the ingredients except lime juice to a coarse paste.
2. Blend in the lime juice.
3. The pickle is ready for use. It keeps only for 2 days but longer if refrigerated.

> **Green Spices**
> Fresh coriander, mint and other green spices used carefully to bring out the flavour of pickles, can add a subtle fragrance and character unlike anything else. Adding too much of it can put people off it for life.

Oil Free

848 Stuffed Lime : Hot

500 g	lime, slit into 4 without severing
40 g	chilli powder;
15 g	fenugreek seeds &
5 g	asafoetida, roast both in oil & powder &
100 g	salt, combine all evenly

1. Stuff the spice mixture into the limes.
2. Set aside for 2 weeks.
3. Stir occasionally.
4. The pickle lasts for 4 months.

Note : Slightly scrape the skin of the **limes** before preparing lime pickles, to reduce their bitterness.

849 Lime Mild Spicy Stuffed : Salty

500 g	lime, slit into 4 without severing
30 g	chilli powder ;
10 g	garam masala powder &
5 g	turmeric powder, combine all three evenly
50 ml	lime juice
125 g	salt

1. Stuff the spice mixture into the limes.
2. Sprinkle a little salt at the bottom of a jar and pack in the stuffed limes. Pour over the lime juice.
3. Sun the pickle for 8 days. Shake daily.
4. The pickle is ready for use after 15 days, when the skins of the limes become soft.
It lasts for 6 months.

850 Stuffed Spicy Lime : Hot

500 g	lime, slit into 4 without severing	5 g	cummin seeds &
100 ml	lime juice	2 g	peppercorns, dry-roast both & powder
50 g	chilli powder	2 g	grated nutmeg
5 g	asafoetida &	5	cardamoms
5 g	coriander seeds, roast both in oil & powder	5	cloves
		1-1"	stick of cinnamon
		8 g	black salt
5 g	dried ginger powder	125 g	salt

1. Combine the spice powders and the salts evenly.
2. Stuff the spice mixture into the limes.
3. Cook the stuffed limes with the lime juice, grated nutmeg and whole spices in a pan over low heat.
4. Remove when the juice begins to bubble and allow to cool.
5. Transfer the cooled spiced limes to a jar and sun for 4 days. Shake daily.
7. The pickle is ready for use after 15 days. It lasts for 3 months.

851 Lime – Thymol Seeds : Hot

1 kg	lime, slit into 4 without severing
50 ml	lime juice
60 g	thymol seeds, dry-roast & powder;
20 g	peppercorns, sun-dry & powder;
80 g	chilli powder &
200 g	salt, combine all three evenly

Ajwain, also called thymol seeds is a spice of the caraway family and has high digestive properties.

1. Stir the spice mixture into the limes and pour over the lime juice.
2. Sun the mixture for 6 days.
3. The pickle is ready for use after 15 days. It lasts for 2 years.

852 Spiced Lime – Ginger - Green Chilli : Hot

500 g	lime, cut into 8 pieces each & seed
60 g	green chillies, chop
40 g	fresh ginger, scrape & slice
10 g	thymol seeds &
5 g	peppercorns, dry-roast both & pound
5 g	asafoetida, roast in oil & powder
40 ml	lime juice
150 g	salt

1. Combine all the spices with the salt evenly.
2. Blend the lime pieces into the spice mixture. Pour over the lime juice and cap tight.
3. Sun the mixture for 20 days. Shake the jar thoroughly everyday.
4. Toss the mixture once every 2 days.
5. The pickle is ready for use after 10 days. It lasts for 6 months.

853 Gingered Lime : Hot

500 g	lime, scrape slightly, keep whole
60 g	green chillies, chop
2-1"	pieces fresh ginger, scrape & chop fine
5 g	turmeric powder
5 g	fenugreek seeds &
5 g	asafoetida, roast both in oil & powder
100 g	salt

1. Soak the whole limes in water for two hours. Wipe, cut into small bits and seed.
2. Pack the lime pieces, chopped green chillies and ginger in a jar.
3. Stir in the turmeric, asafoetida, fenugreek powders, salt and mix thoroughly.
4. The pickle is ready for use after 2 days. It lasts for 6 months. Sun occasionally.

854 Fenugreek Lime : Hot

500 g	lime, cut into small pieces & seed
75 g	dried red chillies;
15 g	fenugreek seeds &
5 g	asafoetida, roast all three in oil & powder coarsely
5 g	turmeric powder
125 g	salt

1. Sprinkle the salt over the lime pieces and set aside for 4 days. Stir twice daily.
2. Combine the powdered spices and turmeric powder with the salt.
3. Blend the spice mixture into the lime pieces and set aside for 10 days. Stir daily.
4. The pickle lasts for 2 months.

855 Lime – Ginger - Date in Vinegar : Salty

500g	lime, cut into small pieces & seed
200g	stoned date, halve
60g	chilli powder
50g	fresh ginger, scrape & slice
2	cloves garlic, peel
500ml	vinegar : heat & cool
150g	salt

1. Drop the lime pieces in a jar along with the salt and set aside for 3 days. Shake daily.
2. Add all the other ingredients except the chilli powder and mix thoroughly.
3. The following day add the chilli powder and set aside for 5 days. Shake daily.
4. The pickle lasts for 6 months.

856 Lime – Ginger - Kalakkai : Salty

500 g	lime, cut into 8 pieces each & seed
125 g	kalakkai,
100 g	fresh ginger, scrape & chop
125 g	tender green chillies, slit
15 ml	lime juice
175 g	salt

1. Marinate the lime pieces and kalakkai in two teaspoons (10g) salt for 3 days.
2. Combine the salted lime, kalakkai with the remaining ingredients and transfer to a jar.
3. Sun the jar with contents for 10 days.
4. The pickle lasts for 6 months.

857 Lime – Green Chilli : Hot

500 g	lime, cut into 8 pieces each & seed
75 g	tender green chillies, slit
10 g	split husked mustard seeds, sun-dry & powder;
5 g	asafoetida, roast in oil & powder;
5 g	fenugreek seeds, roast in oil & powder;
25 g	chilli powder &
125 g	salt, combine all evenly

1. Combine the lime pieces with the slit green chillies.
2. Arrange a layer of the lime-chilli mixture in a jar. Follow with a layer of the spice mixture.
3. Repeat the process till the entire lime-chilli mixture is layered.
4. Ensure that the final layer is that of the spice mixture. Set aside for 3 weeks. Stir thoroughly.
5. The pickle lasts for 6 months. Sun occasionally.

858 Fried Lime – Green Chilli : Hot

1 kg	lime, cut into 8 pieces each & seed
80 g	chilli powder
20 g	green chillies, keep whole
200 g	salt

1. Heat the lime pieces over a low flame till they turn reddish brown and remove.
2. Add in the chilli powder, green chillies, salt and mix thoroughly.
3. The pickle is ready for use after 15 days. It lasts for 2 years.

859 Stuffed Lime – Sweet Spices : Salty

500 g	lime, slit into 4 without severing
10 g	dried red chillies, sun-dry;
5 g	peppercorns, sun-dry;
5 g	cummin seeds, sun-dry;
2 g	asafoetida, roast in oil;
2 g	black cardamom;
2 g	cloves &
100 g	salt, grind all to a paste
40 g	sugar

1. Stuff the spice mixture into the limes.
2. Pack the stuffed limes in a jar and sun the mixture for 4 days till the peels become soft.
3. Stir in the sugar and sun the pickle for 3 more days.
4. The pickle is ready for use after 15 days. It lasts for 3 months.

860 Unripe Lime – Fenugreek : Salty

1 kg	unripe green lime pieces, cut into 8 pieces each & seed
75 g	dried red chillies;
30 g	fenugreek seeds &
10 g	asafoetida, roast all three in oil & powder
10 g	turmeric powder
200 g	salt

1. Combine all the spice powders with the salt evenly.
2. Stir the lime pieces into the spice mixture and blend well. Set aside for 15 days and stir daily.
3. The pickle lasts for 1 year. Stir frequently.

861 Sour Lime : Hot

500 g	lime, cut into 8 pieces each & seed
75 g	green chillies, slit
50 ml	lime juice
50 ml	vinegar : heat & cool
100 g	salt

1. Combine all the ingredients (except lime juice) thoroughly.
2. Pour over the lime juice and sun the mixture for a week or till the limes turn brown.
3. The pickle is ready for use. It lasts for 6 months.

862 Spiced Lime Whole in Vinegar : Watery

500 g	lime, scrape slightly, keep whole
100 ml	water
20 g	green chillies, slit
5	cloves garlic, peel & chop
2-1"	pieces of fresh ginger, scrape & chop fine
100 g	sugar
100 ml	vinegar : heat & cool
75 g	salt

1. Boil the whole limes in 100ml water and salt till tender. Remove.
2. Allow to cool and slit into 4 without severing.
3. Add in the green chillies, garlic and ginger.
4. Stir in the sugar, pre-heated vinegar and set aside for 7 days. Mix daily.
5. The pickle is ready for use. It lasts for 6 months. Stir frequently.

863 Mustard Lime – Green Chilli : Hot

500 g	lime, cut into 8 pieces each & seed
750 g	green chillies, slit twice lengthwise
10 g	turmeric powder
150 g	mustard seeds, sun-dry & powder
20 g	asafoetida, roast in oil & powder
500 ml	lime juice
200 g	salt

1. Combine all the ingredients and the lime juice with half the salt.
2. Separately marinate the lime pieces with the remaining salt and set aside.
3. Arrange a layer of the salted lime pieces in a jar. Pour over a little of the spiced lime juice.
4. Repeat this process until all the lime pieces are layered and salted. Ensure that the final layer is that of the lime pieces.
5. The pickle is ready for use after 10 days. It lasts for 6 months.

864 Sunned Lime – Green Spices : Hot

1 kg	lime, chop & seed
150 g	green chillies, slit
100 g	fresh ginger, scrape & slice
10	cloves garlic, peel & chop
20 g	split husked mustard seeds, sun-dry
10 g	turmeric powder
5 g	fenugreek seeds, roast in oil & powder
200 g	salt

1. Combine all the ingredients in a jar.
2. Sun the mixture for 10 days.
3. The pickle is ready for use after 1 month. It lasts for 1 year.

865 Lime – Mahani – Green Spices : Hot

1 kg	lime, cut into small pieces & seed
100 g	green chillies, chop
60 g	fresh ginger, scrape & chop
30 g	mahani, peel, remove central stem & slice
10 g	peppercorns, keep whole
50 ml	lime juice
275 g	salt

1. Combine all the ingredients and blend in the lime juice.
2. Sun the mixture for a week.
3. The pickle is ready for use. It lasts for 1 year.

866 Spicy Lime in Vinegar : Watery

1 kg	lime, scrape slightly, keep whole	60 g	green chillies, slit, combine all three
500 ml	vinegar : heat & cool	20 g	fenugreek seeds, roast in oil & powder;
60 g	fresh ginger, scrape & slice	150 g	chilli powder &
60 g	peeled garlic, chop &	400 g	salt, combine all thee evenly

1. Bring the water to boiling and remove.
2. Drop in the whole limes, cover and set aside for 2 minutes.
3. Drain, wipe and slit the limes into 4 without severing.
4. Pack the spice mixture into the limes.
5. Arrange a layer of the limes in a jar. Follow with a layer of the ginger mixture.
6. Repeat the process until the lime and ginger mixture are layered.
7. Pour the pre-heated vinegar over the limes to cover. Cap tight and set aside for 15 days.
8. The pickle is ready for use. It lasts for 1 year.

867 Sour & Spicy Grated Mango : Watery

500 g	seeded mango, peel & grate	3 g	turmeric powder, dry-roast all & grind to a paste	
50 g	jaggery, grate			
25 g	chilli powder;	2-1"	sticks of cinnamon;	
5 g	cummin seeds;	2	blades of mace &	
3 g	fenugreek seeds;	1 g	grated nutmeg, combine all three evenly	
3 g	peppercorns;			
3 g	onion seeds;	225 ml	vinegar	
3 g	aniseeds &	75 g	salt	

1. Add the spice paste, jaggery and salt to the grated mango. Mix thoroughly and sun for 3 days.
2. Thereafter pour over the vinegar to cover the pickle.
3. Add in the remaining spices and mix well.
4. The pickle is ready for use after 4 days. It lasts for 4 months.

868 Sour Spiced Mango : Sweet

500 g	seeded mango, size into medium thick slices	2	blades of mace
		1-1"	stick of cinnamon
25 g	chilli powder	1 g	grated nutmeg
5	cloves garlic, peel & chop	65 g	cleaned tamarind, obtain extract using vinegar
5 g	onion seeds, crush		
5 g	cummin powder	125 ml	vinegar
3 g	seedless raisin, chop	125 g	sugar
2 g	dried ginger powder	75 g	salt

1. Smear 25g salt over the mango slices and sun for a day. Next day discard the salt water given out by the mango.
2. Boil the tamarind extract and allow to cool.
3. Combine all the remaining ingredients with the boiled tamarind extract and the salted mango slices thoroughly.
4. The pickle is ready for use after 15 days. It lasts for 6 months. Sun occasionally.

869 Grated Mango – Green Chilli : Hot

500 g	seeded fleshy mango, peel & grate
60 g	green chillies, chop
60 g	salt

1. Grind all the ingredients to a fine paste and set aside.
2. The pickle is ready for use after a month. It lasts for 2 months.

—— Variation : ——

To a small portion of the mixture, add in whipped curd and season with mustard seeds, asafoetida powder, if desired.

870 Mango – Ground Spices : Instant

125 g	cut mango, size into small pieces	5	green chillies, chop & peppercorns, grind all to a paste
10 g	onion, peel & chop;	a few	
1/2"	piece of fresh ginger, scrape & chop;	10 ml	lime juice
		15 g	salt

1. Marinate the mango pieces in the salt for 1 hour.
2. Stir the spice paste and lime juice into the mango pieces.
3. The pickle is ready for use. It keeps for 1 week and is best refrigerated.

871 Spiced Mango : Salty

500 g	cut mango, size into small pieces	5 g	peppercorns, sun-dry all & powder
10 g	chilli powder		
10 g	turmeric powder	5 g	asafoetida, roast in oil & powder
10 g	cummin seeds;		
5 g	mustard seeds &	50 g	salt

1. Smear the cut side of the mango pieces with the salt and set aside for 3 days.
2. Remove the mango pieces from the salt water given out by the mangoes.
3. Reserve the salt water. Allow the mango pieces to dry indoors on a clean cloth.
4. Smear the spice powders evenly on the salted mango and arrange in a jar. Add in the reserved salt water.
5. Cover and sun the mixture for 10 days. Stir well daily.
6. The pickle lasts for 4 months.

> **Note :** Mangoes are at their best during the early hot season. Soak them in water overnight. Wash thoroughly the following day to remove the milky secretion which tends to mar the pickle.

872 Stuffed Spiced Mango in Vinegar : Watery

1 kg	seeded tender mango, split each into 4 without severing	30 g	chilli powder
		2	cardamoms;
		2	blades of mace &
20 g	peppercorns;	2 g	grated nutmeg, keep all three whole
5 g	cummin seeds;		
5 g	fenugreek seeds &		
5 g	onion seeds, dry-roast all & powder together	30 g	sugar
		450 ml	vinegar
		150 g	salt

1. Combine the spice powders with the salt evenly. Stuff the spice mixture into the split mango.
2. Tie the mangoes with a thread to ensure that the spice mixture remains intact.
3. Sun the stuffed mango for 2 days till they shrink.
4. Add in the whole spices, sugar, vinegar and sun the pickle for 7 more days. Shake the contents daily.
5. The pickle is ready for use after 4 days. It lasts for 1 year.

873 Mint, Green Coriander – Tomato - Onion : Instant

125 g	green coriander &
125 g	mint leaves, wash, air-dry & chop both
40 g	onion, peel & chop
40 g	tomato &
30 g	green chillies, chop both
1-1"	piece of fresh ginger, scrape & chop
20 g	cleaned tamarind, obtain thick extract using water
3 g	cummin seeds, dry-roast
25 g	salt

1. Grind together all the ingredients to a fine paste.
2. Add in the tamarind extract and blend well.
3. The pickle is ready for use. It keeps for 1 week in the refrigerator.

874 Sour Mint – Green Coriander : Instant

125 g	green coriander &	10 ml	lime juice
125 g	mint leaves, wash, air-dry & chop	30 g	salt
25 g	green chillies, chop		
10 g	dried mango powder		
5 g	chilli powder		
5 g	cummin seeds, dry-roast		
5 g	asafoetida, roast in oil & powder		

1. Grind together all the ingredients to a fine paste.
2. Stir in the lime juice and blend well.
3. The pickle is ready for use. It keeps for 1 week in the refrigerator.

875 Sour Mint – Groundnut – Onion : Instant

125 g	mint leaves, wash, air-dry & chop
125 g	shelled raw groundnut
50 g	onion, peel & chop
30 g	seeded raw mango, peel & chop
30 g	green chillies, chop
10 g	chilli powder
10 g	sugar
10 ml	lime juice
35 g	salt

1. Stir-fry the chopped mint, mango, onion and chillies in a little oil till tender.
2. Cool and grind with the remaining ingredients. Add no water.
3. Blend in the lime juice.
4. The pickle is ready for use. It keeps for 1 week in the refrigerator.

876 Mixed Vegetable – Lime : Hot

500 g	lime, cut into 8 pieces each & seed
125 g	tender cluster beans, top, tail & cut into 2" lengths
100 g	tender green chillies, chop
50 g	carrot, peel & julienne
40 g	fresh ginger, scrape & slice thinly
8 g	turmeric powder
50 ml	lime juice
100 g	salt

1. Combine the salt and turmeric powder with the lime pieces. Set aside for 4 days. Shake daily.
2. Stir in the chopped green chillies, ginger, carrot and cluster beans.
3. Pour over the lime juice and blend well.
4. The pickle is ready for use after 10 days. It lasts for 2 months.

877 Bean – Onion – Papaya : Instant

100 g	bean, top, tail & julienne
100 g	small red onion, peel
75 g	raw papaya, peel, seed & julienne
75 g	carrot, peel & julienne
75 g	cauliflower florets,
40 g	tender green chillies, slit, seed & grind
10 g	dried red chillies;
1-1"	piece of fresh ginger, scrape & chop;
5	cloves garlic, peel &
5 g	mustard seeds, grind all to a paste using vinegar
2 g	turmeric powder
10 g	sugar
125 ml	vinegar
40 g	salt

1. Cook the prepared vegetables in a little water. When partly tender, remove and discard the water.
2. Heat the remaining vinegar with the chilli paste.
3. When hot, remove, add the spice paste, sugar and stir well.
4. Stir in the cooked vegetables, salt and turmeric powder.
5. Transfer to a jar, cap tight and set aside.
6. The pickle is ready for use when the vinegar and spices are soaked in the vegetable pieces.
7. It lasts for 3 months. Sun and stir frequently.

878 Mixed Vegetable – Garlic in Lime Juice : Watery

200 g	peeled garlic
100 g	carrot, peel & chop
100 g	bitterberry, halve
100 g	tender cluster beans, top, tail & chop
75 g	tender green chillies, chop
175 ml	lime juice
75 g	salt

1. Sprinkle the salt over the prepared vegetables.
2. Pour over the lime juice and toss well.
3. Sun the mixture for 10 days, stirring frequently for even sunning.
4. The pickle is ready for use after a week. It lasts for 2 months. Sun occasionally.

> Wash vegetables throughly to free them from mud and grit. Cook just long enough to get them almost tender. Longer cooking destroys the crispness and freshness of vegetables as well as much of their food value, flavour, texture and colour.

879 Sour Onion : Instant

125 g	onion, peel & slice thinly
10 g	chilli powder
10 ml	lime juice or vinegar
15 g	salt
a pinch	of ajinomoto

1. Sprinkle salt over the sliced onion for 5 minutes. Rinse and drain well.
2. Add in the chilli powder, vinegar, salt and toss well.
3. The pickle is ready for use. It keeps for 1 week in the refrigerator.

880 Salted Mixed Vegetable in Vinegar : Watery

150 g	capsicum, seed & shred	1-1"	piece of fresh ginger, scrape & slice, grind all three fine using vinegar	
150 g	small red onion, peel & keep whole			
100 g	beans, top, tail & slice	10	almonds, soak in water overnight, peel & sliver	
50 g	carrot, peel & slice			
50 g	cucumber, scrub & slice	5 g	turmeric powder	
		150 ml	water	
40	tender green chillies, chop;	30 g	jaggery, grate	
		500 ml	vinegar	
5 g	chilli powder &	90 g	salt	

1. Blanch the prepared vegetables in sufficient boiling water to which a teaspoon (5g) salt and turmeric powder have been added for 2 minutes.
2. Drain well and spread to dry on a clean cloth.
3. Dilute the spice paste with the vinegar and water.
4. Stir in the jaggery, salt and bring to the boil.
5. Add in the blanched vegetables, slivered almonds, cook for 2 minutes and remove.
6. The pickle is ready for use after 2 days. It keeps for 15 days and is best refrigerated.

881 Sour Cauliflower – Cucumber : Sweet

250 g	cauliflower florets,
250 g	cucumber, scrub & cut into chunks
20 g	dried ginger powder
10 g	whole allspice
10 g	mustard seeds, sun-dry & powder
5 g	turmeric powder
20 ml	refined flour
100 g	sugar
200 ml	vinegar
60 g	salt

1. Sprinkle salt over the prepared vegetables and leave overnight. Drain and rinse the following day.
2. Mix the spices with a little vinegar to a paste.
3. Blend the flour with a little cold water and heat to a sauce consistency.
4. Heat the vinegar with all the ingredients including the spice paste (except the flour and vegetables).
5. Do not boil. Allow to thicken and stir in the salted vegetables.
6. Pour the flour sauce over the vegetable mixture and stir well.
7. The pickle is ready for use after 2 days. It keeps for 15 days and is best refrigerated.

882 Sweet & Sour Mixed Vegetable in Vinegar : Tender

100 g	cauliflower florets			
100 g	small red onion, peel & keep whole			
100 g	courgette, cube			
100 g	capsicum, cut into chunks			
100 g	cucumber, scrape lightly & chop			
50 g	french beans, top, tail & julienne			
50 g	chopped celery, remove stems			
25 g	cornflour			
3 g	mustard seeds, sun-dry & powder			
3 g	turmeric powder			
3 g	dried ginger powder	45 g	sugar	
200 ml	vinegar	60 g	salt	

1. Combine the turmeric, mustard, ginger powders, sugar and salt with the vinegar in a pan evenly.
2. Add in the prepared vegetables, bring to the boil and simmer gently for 10 minutes.
3. Remove the vegetables with a perforated spoon and pack into a jar.
4. Dissolve the cornflour in the reserved vinegar and stir into the vinegar mixture in the pan.
5. Boil for 3 minutes, stirring continuously. Pour the vinegar mixture over the vegetables in the jar.
6. The pickle is ready for use after 6 weeks. It lasts for 1 year.

883 Cauliflower – Cucumber - Bean : Watery

200 g	cauliflower florets	20 g	onion, peel & chop
150 g	cucumber, scrub & cube	40 g	dried red chillies, keep whole
150 g	bean, top, tail & julienne	200 ml	vinegar
		60 g	salt

1. Pack the prepared vegetables in a jar.
2. Add in the dried chillies and cover with the cold spiced vinegar. Cap tight at once.
3. The pickle is ready for use after 4 weeks. It lasts for 3 months.

884 Mixed Vegetable : Watery

500 g	vegetables : choice – carrot, turnip, potato, cabbage, beans, pumpkin, singly or combined, peel, shred, scrape, cut, top & tail as required
300 ml	water
1	dried red chilli, break into bits
15 g	sugar
100 ml	vinegar
60 g	salt

1. Marinate the vegetables with the salt for a day in a wide-mouthed jar.
2. Heat together the vinegar, water, sugar and the broken chilli until the sugar dissolves. Remove and allow to cool.
3. Drain out the water from the salted vegetables and transfer to a jar.
4. Pour the spiced vinegar over the vegetable mixture and stir well. Refrigerate for 2 days.
5. The pickle lasts for 1 month in the refrigerator.

885 Mixed Vegetable in Lime Juice : Tender

200 ml	lime juice	100 g	cluster beans, top, tail & julienne
100 g	carrot, peel & chop		
100 g	tender green chillies, chop	5	cloves garlic, peel & chop
100 g	bitterberry, halve	60 g	salt

1. Combine all the prepared vegetables with the garlic, lime juice and salt.
2. Mix thoroughly and sun for 10 days.
3. The pickle is ready for use after 15 days. It lasts for 1 month.

886 Cauliflower – Bean : Tender

250 g	cauliflower florets,
175 g	bean, top, tail & julienne
75 g	button onion, peel
30 g	tender green chillies, slit
75 g	salt, make a solution with 250ml water
5 g	peppercorns &
5 g	husked mustard seeds, sun-dry both & powder
5 g	dried ginger powder;
2	cloves garlic, peel &
2	dried red chillies, break into bits, grind all three fine using vinegar
5 g	turmeric powder
60 g	sugar
200 ml	vinegar

1. Soak the prepared vegetables in the salt solution overnight.
2. Drain in a colander the following day.
3. Blend the pepper and mustard powders in 50ml vinegar. Set aside.
4. Combine the spice paste, turmeric powder, sugar, salt with the remaining vinegar and bring to the boil.
5. Add in the salted vegetables when the mixture begins to bubble.
6. Stir in the pepper-mustard blend and remove before the mixture boils.
7. The pickle is ready for use after 3 days. It lasts for 2 months.

887 Onion in Vinegar : Salty

500 g	onion, peel & keep whole
500 g	salt, make a solution with 5000ml water
250 ml	vinegar
60 g	salt : for pickle

1. Boil the onions in the salt solution and allow to cool.
2. Remove the onions with a perforated spoon. Add the salt and set aside for 3 days.
3. Discard the salt water and arrange the onions in a jar.
4. Pour over the vinegar to cover and set aside for 3 days.
5. The pickle is ready for use. It lasts for 1 month.

888 Small Red Onion in Spiced Vinegar : Watery

500 g	small red onion, peel & keep whole
20 g	chilli powder
20 g	dried red chillies, break into bits
2-1"	pieces of fresh ginger, scrape & chop
5	cloves garlic, peel
10 g	peppercorns, dry-roast & powder
5	cloves, crush
400 ml	vinegar
30 g	salt

1. Apply half the salt and chilli powder over the onion. Set aside for half an hour.
2. Pack the onion and chillies in a jar.
3. Heat the vinegar with all the spices and the remaining salt for 10 minutes over a low flame.
4. Strain, pour the hot spiced vinegar over the onion and cap tight immediately.
5. The pickle is ready for use after 5 days. It lasts for 2 months.

889 Onion – Ginger – Green Chilli : Instant

125 g	tiny big onion, peel & keep whole
8 g	green chillies, chop
1-1"	piece of fresh ginger, scrape & chop
3 g	mustard seeds
3 g	asafoetida, roast in oil & powder
3 g	turmeric powder
10 ml	lime juice
12 g	salt

1. Combine the onion with the chopped green chillies and ginger.
2. Blend in the salt, turmeric powder and the lime juice.
3. Heat the oil, add mustard seeds and allow to crackle. Stir in the asafoetida powder and remove.
4. Pour the seasoning over the vegetable mixture and stir thoroughly.
5. The pickle is ready for use. It keeps for 5 days and longer in the refrigerator.

890 Sour Peach – Raisin – Onion : Sweet

500 g	peach, slice
150 g	onion, peel & chop
125 g	seedless raisin, halve
1-1"	piece of fresh ginger, scrape & chop
5 g	chilli powder
5 g	garam masala powder
200 g	sugar
120 ml	vinegar
5 g	salt

1. Combine the onion, ginger, chilli, garam masala powders with the vinegar and cook for a few minutes.
2. Add in the sliced peaches and continue cooking till almost tender.
3. Stir in the sugar, salt, raisin and cook until the mixture reaches a jam-like consistency.
4. The pickle is ready for use. It lasts for 1 month.

891 Mustard Pineapple – Green Spices : Instant

500 g	cubed ripe pineapple
4	dried red chillies
10 g	garlic, peel & chop
10 g	mustard seeds &
10 g	fresh ginger, scrape & chop, grind all fine using vinegar
10 g	turmeric powder
100 ml	vinegar
30 g	salt

To cube pineapples, cut the crown and peel off the skin thickly. Remove the eyes with a sharp knife and cut into small squares. To preserve the pickle for longer periods, add a few pinches of sodium benzoate.

1. Blend the vinegar, turmeric powder and the salt with the ground paste.
2. Add in the cubed pineapple pieces and stir well.
3. The pickle is ready for use when the vinegar soaks into the pineapple pieces. It lasts for 2 months.

892 Pineapple – Lime Juice – Vinegar : Instant

125 g	cubed ripe pineapple
10 g	chilli powder
1-1"	piece of fresh ginger, scrape & chop;
3 g	mustard seeds &
2	cloves garlic, peel & chop, grind all three fine using vinegar
3 g	sugar
40 ml	vinegar
10 ml	lime juice
12 g	salt

1. Combine all the ingredients (except pineapple) with the vinegar in a jar.
2. Add in the cubed pineapple and stir thoroughly.
3. The pickle is ready for use. It keeps for 15 days and is best refrigerated.

893 Sour Banana : Sweet

125 g	peeled ripe malabar banana, chop
12 g	seedless raisin, chop
12 g	kashmiri dried red chillies, roast in oil & powder coarsely
12 g	cleaned tamarind, obtain thick extract using water
20 g	sugar
5 g	cummin seeds, dry-roast & powder
1-1"	piece of fresh ginger, peel & grate
5 ml	lime juice
4 g	salt

1. Combine the chopped banana and raisin with the lime juice. Set aside.
2. Heat the tamarind extract, sugar and stir till the sugar dissolves.
3. Stir in the banana mixture, ginger, spice powders, salt and remove.
4. The pickle is ready for use. It keeps for 4 days and longer in the refrigerator.

894 Sweet Plum : Instant

125 g	chopped plum, stone
25 g	cleaned tamarind, obtain thick extract using water
50 g	sugar
12 ml	water
5 g	chilli powder
2 g	cummin seeds, sun-dry & powder
12 g	salt

1. Bring the tamarind extract, sugar and water to the boil. Heat till thick and syrupy.
2. Remove and blend in the chopped plum, spice powders and salt.
3. The pickle is ready for use. It keeps for 7 days and is best refrigerated.

895 Spiced Plum : Sweet

500 g	firm ripe plum, prick all over with a fork
250 g	sugar
3	dried red chillies;
2-1"	sticks of cinnamon;
3	cloves &
2	blades of mace, dry-roast all & powder
250 ml	vinegar
10 g	salt

1. Combine all the spice powders with the salt evenly.
2. Pack the pricked plums in a jar and sprinkle over the spice mixture.
3. Boil the vinegar with the sugar for a few minutes and pour over the plums.
4. Seal and store for a month before use.
5. The pickle lasts for 6 months.

896 Pomegranate Seed – Raisin : Instant

250 g	pomegranate seeds
60 g	seedless raisin, chop
1/2"	piece of fresh ginger, scrape & chop
3 g	chilli powder
2 g	thymol seeds
2 g	sugar
1	clove, keep whole
10 ml	lime juice
10 g	salt

1. Soak the pomegranate seeds in sufficient water overnight.
2. Grind all the ingredients (except clove) to a fine paste. Blend in the clove and lime juice.
3. The pickle is ready for use. It keeps for 5 days in the refrigerator.

897 Ground Raisin : Instant

125 g	seedless raisin, chop
10 g	green chillies, chop
1/2"	piece of fresh ginger, scrape & chop
25 ml	lime juice
3 g	salt

1. Grind together all the ingredients to a smooth paste with the salt.
2. Stir in the lime juice and blend well.
3. The pickle is ready for use. It keeps for 5 days and is best refrigerated.

898 Green Tomato – Ginger - Garlic : Instant

125 g	green tomato, chop
3 g	salt : for marinating
125 g	sugar
5 g	dried red chillies;
3 g	mustard seeds;
3	cloves garlic, peel &
2-1"	pieces of fresh ginger, scrape & chop, grind all to a paste using vinegar
25 ml	vinegar
5 g	salt : for pickle

1. Marinate the tomato in salt overnight.
2. Cook the salted tomato pieces with the vinegar till tender.
3. Add in the remaining ingredients and stir well.
4. Continue cooking over low heat until the mixture reaches a jam-like consistency.
5. The pickle is ready for use. It keeps for 3 weeks and is best refrigerated.

Oil Free

899 Sweet Tamarind – Date : Instant

125 g	cleaned tamarind, obtain thick extract using water
75 g	jaggery, grate
75 g	date, stone & grind fine with jaggery
15 g	chilli powder
5 g	cummin seeds, sun-dry & powder
5 g	garam masala powder
25 g	salt

1. Combine the ingredients with the salt evenly.
2. The pickle is ready for use. It keeps only for 2 days but longer if refrigerated.

> As regards all **tamarind** based pickles, if the salt content is high and the oil stands a clear 2" above the pickle, the pickle will last for as long as 6 months to 1 year.

---

900 Spicy Tamarind – Cummin : Hot

500 g	cleaned tamarind
250 g	jaggery, grate
15 g	black cummin seeds ;
15 g	cummin seeds ;
10 g	fenugreek seeds &
10 g	aniseeds, roast all in oil & powder
60 g	chilli powder
125 g	salt

1. Combine the tamarind pieces with the spice powders and salt.
2. Bring the jaggery to the boil with sufficient water, allow to thicken and remove.
3. Stir in the tamarind mixture and set aside for 2 days.
4. Sun the pickle for 5 days.
5. The pickle lasts for 1 month.

---

901 Tamarind – Cummin : Instant

125 g	cleaned tamarind, obtain thick extract using water
50 g	jaggery, grate
10 g	chilli powder
5 g	cummin seeds, dry-roast & powder
15 g	black salt

1. Combine the tamarind extract, jaggery, cummin and chilli powders with the salt.
2. Bring to the boil, allow to thicken and remove.
3. The pickle is ready for use. It keeps for 1 week and longer in the refrigerator.

Variation : Can be prepared similarly without heating for a different taste.

---

902 Spiced Tamarind : Sweet

500 g	cleaned tamarind
250 g	jaggery, grate, make a syrup of one-string consistency with 200 ml water
30 g	chilli powder
10 g	fenugreek seeds;
10 g	cummin seeds &
10 g	aniseeds, dry-roast all three & powder
50 g	salt

1. Combine the powdered spices with the chilli powder and salt evenly.
2. Blend the spice mixture with the tamarind pieces thoroughly.
3. Pour the jaggery syrup into the spiced tamarind mixture and heat till well blended.
4. Sun the pickle for 2 days. It lasts for 2 months.

---

903 Sweet & Sour Tomato in Garlic Juice : Instant

500 g	sour tomato, keep whole
100 g	onion, peel & chop
2-1"	pieces of fresh ginger, scrape & chop
50 g	green chillies, chop
20 g	seedless raisin, chop
10	almonds, blanch & cut into slivers
15 ml	garlic juice
5 g	cummin seeds, sun-dry & powder
2	cardamoms, keep whole
60 g	sugar
100 ml	vinegar
50 g	salt

1. Blanch the tomato in boiling water for 3 minutes. Peel and mash well.
2. Combine the mashed tomato, chopped onion, ginger, garlic juice and green chillies in a pan.
3. Heat till the vegetables soften and are well blended. Allow to thicken over a medium flame.
4. Add in the cummin powder, cardamom, sliced almond, raisin, sugar, vinegar and cook for 10 minutes over low heat.
5. Remove when the mixture becomes thick and well blended.
6. The pickle is ready for use. It lasts for 1 month in the refrigerator.

ALL ABOUT PRESSURE COOKING

Why pressure cook?

Vegetables are an essential part of our diet. Fresh vegetables do need a certain amount of preparation, but by cooking them in a pressure cooker (either in the separators as the accompaniment to the main course, or as a dish on their own) there is an enormous saving both in time and fuel consumption. Another plus factor for using the pressure cooker for vegetables is that by cooking them in the absence of light and air and in steam as opposed to water they retain colour, flavour, texture and nutritive values. Even when cooking a selection of different vegetables simultaneously, there is no danger of the flavours becoming intermingled.

Be selective when purchasing vegetables and reject ones which are limp, shrivelled and looking decidedly antique. Remember that a pressure cooker cannot wave a magic wand over stale vegetables and turn them into fresh ones!

Advantages :

- Foods cooked under pressure obviously cook more quickly resulting in, over the long term, a tremendous fuel saving.
- Further economies can be achieved as more than one type of food-even complete meals – may be cooked simultaneously.
- A pressure cooker can be used in conjunction with other kitchen equipment.
- With all types of cooking there is inevitably some loss of nutritive value but with the comparatively short pressure cooking time, small amount of liquid used and the absence of light and air, this nutritive loss is certainly cut down to a minimum.
- A pressure cooker is equally suitable for the family and for bachelor cooks.
- A pressure cooker is a splendid piece of equipment to take on a self-catering holiday.
- Some foods do have a somewhat unpleasant aroma. Both the steam and cooking smells are sealed in the pressure cooker until the end of the cooking time.

RULES FOR PRESSURE COOKING

Fresh Vegetables :

- Prepare the vegetables according to kind.
- Pour the necessary amount of liquid into the cooker – check with the manufacturer's leaflet.
- Place the trivet in the base of the cooker. Add the prepared vegetables either in the separators, or they may be placed directly on the trivet. Add a *sprinkling* of salt – beware of adding as much salt as you would if cooking the vegetables in an ordinary pan.

  Do not fill the cooker more than two-thirds full of vegetables if you are cooking them on the trivet and not using the separators. The steam must have sufficient room to circulate.

- Bring to high pressure and cook for the calculated time.
- At the end of the cooking time reduce the pressure with cold water. This should be done immediately to prevent the vegetables becoming overcooked. Reducing the pressure at room temperature would lead to the same results – overcooked, unappetising vegetables.
- Tip the vegetables from the separators (no draining is necessary) into a serving dish. If they have been cooked on the trivet, remove them with a spoon.
- Do not waste the cooking liquor in the bottom of the cooker – utilise it in sauces, gravies or in stock, soups or stews.

Dried Vegetables :

- Strain and keep the soaking water from the vegetables. Make it up to 1 litre for every 450 g of vegetables. Pour the measured amount of water into the cooker with the trivet removed.
- Bring to the boil and add the vegetables, making sure that the cooker is not more than half full. Season with salt and pepper and add a bouquet garni if liked. Bring back to the boil and, with a slotted draining spoon, remove the scum that rises.
- Lower the heat, secure the lid, and weight and bring to high pressure. (It is necessary to bring to pressure with the source of heat turned low, so that the vegetables and water do not rise up during the cooking.)
- Cook for the calculated time and allow the pressure to reduce at room temperature.

VEGETABLE	COOKING TIME
Butter beans	20 minutes
Haricot beans (large/small)	30/20 minutes
Lentils	15 minutes
Split peas	15 minutes
Whole peas	20 minutes

Dietary

pickles

are

full of

the goodness of

vitamin & mineral-rich

fruits and vegetables,

skillfully combined

with spices

to tone up the system

and

whet the appetite.

Recipes : Dietary

904. Spiced apple – onion : sweet [stomach]
905. Apricot in vinegar : sweet [anaemia]
906. Asparagus in spicy curd : watery [blood acidity]
907. Sour beetroot – apple - date : sweet [skin]
908. Sweet ber : hot [cold]
909. Bel preserve in jaggery : sweet [ulcer]
910. Bilimbi – dry fruit in spiced vinegar : sweet [piles]
911. Bitter gourd – ginger in lime juice : hot
912. Spicy bitter gourd – onion : hot [diabetes]
913. Stuffed bitter gourd in tamarind : hot [diabetes]
914. Sour bottle gourd : hot [kidney]
915. Sour brinjal pulp : hot [asthma]
916. Red cabbage : watery [bones / muscles]
917. Carrot – onion - green spices : hot [eye]
918. Carrot in lime juice : hot [eye / liver]
919. Garlic, green coriander – tamarind : hot [immunity]
920. Cucumber whole : salty [laxitive]
921. Curry lime – fenugreek : hot [liver]
922. Date – green turmeric : sweet [heart]
923. Banana – date : sweet [anaemia]
924. Spicy dry fruit in vinegar : sweet [mouth ulcer]
925. Sour spiced banana : sweet [ulcer]
926. Spicy garlic in lime juice : hot [cholestrol]
927. Garlic in soya sauce : sweet [blood pressure]
928. Spiced ginger : hot [low blood pressure]
929. Sweet & spiced ginger : hot [cough / cold]
930. Cooked gooseberry : hot [rheumatism / t b]
931. Dry fried gooseberry : hot [diabetes]
932. Salted gooseberry : watery [ageing]
933. Hibiscus flower : sweet [heart]
934. Spicy kashmiri red chilli – stuffed : hot [immunity]
935. Spiced raw jackfruit – onion : hot [cramps]
936. Lime pulp : hot [liver]
937. Spicy lime in lime juice : hot [peptic ulcer /bones]
938. Lime – fenugreek leaves : salty [rheumatism]
939. Raw makoy berry : watery [mouth ulcer]
940. Mango – onion : hot [cooling]
941. Sunned mango – jaggery : sweet [blood disorder]

942. Mustard mango in vinegar : hot [sinusitis]
943. Mango ginger in curd : watery [stomach]
944. Sour mint – green pepper : hot [nausea]
945. Mint – green coriander : hot [bronchitis]
946. Apple, pear, plum & cherry : sweet [constipation]
947. Vellarai keerai – black gram : instant [memory]
948. Dry fruits – fresh ginger : sweet [anaemia]
949. Cabbage – carrot - sprouted gram : hot [weight loss]
950. Drumstick – gooseberry : hot [pox]
951. Green tomato – horse radish : salty [piles]
952. Mixed vegetable – gram : tender [weight loss]
953. Cabbage – tomato in vinegar : sweet [constipation]
954. Small red onion whole : hot [piles]
955. Spiced small red onion in vinegar : hot [insomnia]
956. Sweet & sour neem flower : hot [malaria]
957. Small white onion : watery [blood pressure]
958. Papaya – raisin : sweet [kidney stone]
959. Sour pear – ginger - raisin : sweet [bladder stone]
960. Pineapple – raisin : sweet [lung]
961. Spiced pineapple : sweet [bronchitis]
962. Plantain stem in lime juice : hot [diabetes]
963. Potato in mustard sauce : salty [kidney stone]
964. Baby potato preserve : sweet [weight loss]
965. Pumpkin – cabbage - tamarind : hot [worms]
966. Radish preserve – honey : sweet [cough]
967. Radish – green spices : hot [nerves]
968. Mahani in curd : watery [blood purifier]
969. Bitterberry in buttermilk : watery [acidity]
970. Spicy tamarind – coriander - jaggery : sweet [heat]
971. Tomato – garlic in vinegar : sweet [arthritis]
972. Tomato – tender bitterberries : hot [obesity]
973. Tudhuvelai leaf : instant [lung]
974. Dry Fruits – nuts in honey : sweet [ageing]

Contrary to popular belief, pickles are preserved naturally without additives or refrigeration, provided adequate quantities of salt and spices are used.

904 Spiced Apple – Onion : Sweet
(Stomach)

500 g	cored cooking apple, peel & slice
75 g	onion, peel & chop
30 g	fresh ginger, scrape & grate
10	cloves garlic, peel & chop
10 g	chilli powder
10 g	cummin seeds, dry roast & powder
150 g	sugar
125 ml	vinegar
20 ml	lime juice
30 g	salt

1. Cook the onion, chilli powder, ginger and garlic in sufficient water till tender.
2. Add in the sliced apple and continue cooking until they soften.
3. Stir in the sugar, salt, vinegar and cummin powder.
4. Heat until the mixture reaches a jam-like consistency.
5. Blend in the lime juice and set aside.
6. The pickle is ready for use. It lasts for 1 month and is best refrigerated.

905 Apricot in Vinegar : Sweet
[Anaemia]

500 g	dried apricot, stone & chop
	water sufficient to cover
350 g	sugar ;
2-1"	pieces of fresh ginger, scrape & chop;
15 g	chilli powder &
30 g	salt, grind all together fine
375 ml	vinegar

1. Soak the chopped apricot in sufficient water overnight. Boil the mixture until the apricot becomes tender.
2. Combine the cooked apricot with the spice paste and cook until the mixture attains a jam-like consistency.
3. Stir in the vinegar and continue cooking until the mixture thickens again.
4. The pickle is ready for use. It lasts for 1 month.

906 Asparagus in Spicy Curd :
Watery [Blood / Acidity]

1 kg	asparagus root pieces
1000 ml	curd, whip with 500 ml water & remove cream
40 g	green chillies, chop
20 g	chilli powder
20 g	mustard seeds, sun-dry & powder
10 g	asafoetida, roast in oil & powder
150 g	salt

1. Chop the asparagus roots and drop into rice-washed water to prevent discolouration.
2. Blend the spice powders into the whipped curd.
3. Drain the chopped asparagus from the water, stir into the spiced curd and set aside for 15 days. Stir twice daily.
4. The pickle lasts for 1 year.

907 Sour Beetroot – Apple-Date :
Sweet [Skin]

500 g	beetroot, parboil, peel & cube
200 g	cored cooking apple, peel & chop
200 g	date, stone & chop
150 g	onion, peel & chop
150 ml	water
30 g	fresh ginger, scrape & grind
300 g	sugar
400 ml	vinegar
75 g	salt

1. Cook the onion in 150ml water with a little vinegar until soft.
2. Add in the chopped apple, date and continue cooking till almost tender.
3. Follow with the parboiled beetroot, ginger, salt and the remaining vinegar.
4. Stir in the sugar, the remaining vinegar and continue cooking over low heat until the mixture thickens again.
5. The pickle is ready for use. It lasts for 4 months.

908 Sweet Ber : Hot (Cold)

1 kg	ripe ber, remove stems
150 g	jaggery, grate
40 g	dried red chillies
20 g	peppercorns &
10 g	aniseeds, sun-dry both & powder
5	cardamoms
1"	stick of cinnamon
150 g	salt
300 ml	oil

1. Lightly pound the bers with the chilli, salt and jaggery.
2. Blend in all the ingredients, shape into small round / flat balls and sun-dry for 4 days.
3. The pickle lasts for 2 years. Expose to mild sunlight occasionally.

909 Bel Preserve in Jaggery : Sweet *(Ulcer)*

500 g	sliced ripe bel, break shell & remove kernel
500 g	jaggery, grate
10 g	salt

1. Boil the bel slices in lightly salted water till tender. Drain and allow to dry.
2. Add 50ml water to the jaggery and heat till syrupy.
3. Drop in the bel slices, cook for a few minutes over low heat and remove.
4. The pickle is ready for use after 15 days. It lasts for 2 months. Sun occasionally.

> **Bel**
> There are several varieties of bel, of which the pale green ones with a thinner rind and colour are the best. Ensure that there are no perforations in them; else air through these might have oxidised the pulp, making it discolour and decay.

910 Bilimbi – Dry Fruit in Spiced Vinegar : Sweet *(Piles)*

500 g	dried bilimbi, sun-dry & soak in 50ml vinegar
150 g	seedless raisin, chop
75 g	date, stone, chop & grind
1-1"	piece of fresh ginger, scrape & chop
20 g	chilli powder
250 g	sugar
50 g	salt, boil with 100ml water & cool
200 ml	vinegar
50 ml	oil

1. Stir-fry the chopped ginger in a little oil.
2. Add in the date paste, bilimbi, chopped raisin, chilli powder, sugar, salt solution and the remaining vinegar.
3. Bring to the boil and remove when the mixture begins to bubble.
4. The pickle is ready for use after 15 days. It lasts for 6 months.

911 Bitter gourd – Ginger in Lime Juice : Hot *[Diabetes]*

500 g	bitter gourd, scrape lightly, cut into thin rounds & seed
100 g	chilli powder
2-1"	pieces of fresh ginger, scrape & chop
10	cloves garlic, peel & chop
5 g	mustard seeds, sun-dry & powder
5 g	asafoetida, roast in oil & powder
200 ml	lime juice
150 g	salt
200 ml	oil, heat & cool

1. Blanch the bitter gourd rounds in boiling water for 5 minutes till partly tender and drain.
2. Sprinkle salt over the blanched bitter gourd and set in the sun for 1 hour.
3. Squeeze out the salt water from the bitter gourd.
4. Dry the bitter gourd and the chopped ginger in the shade for 3 hours.
5. Dissolve the salt in the lime juice.
6. Add in the mustard powder, oil, the dried bitter gourd, chopped ginger and blend well. Allow to soak for 3 days.
7. Stir in the chopped garlic, chilli and asafoetida powders. Mix thoroughly.
8. The pickle is ready for use after 3 days. It lasts for 2 months.

912 Spicy Bitter gourd – Onion : Hot *[Diabetes]*

500 g	bitter gourd, scrape lightly, cut into rounds & seed
175 g	small red onion, peel & chop
125 g	fresh ginger, scrape & chop
125 g	peeled garlic, slice
100 g	green chillies, chop
100 g	jaggery, grate (less if desired)
50 g	chilli powder
10 g	mustard seeds;
a few	sprigs curry leaves &
250 ml	vinegar
90 ml	lime juice
175 g	salt

1. Heat the oil, add mustard seeds and allow to crackle. Add in the curry leaves and allow to turn crisp.
2. Stir in the bitter gourd, onion, chillies, ginger, garlic and fry till the onion becomes translucent.
3. Add in the chilli powder, vinegar, salt and continue cooking till the bitter gourd becomes tender.
4. Stir in the sugar and the jaggery.
5. When it has dissolved, pour over the lime juice and remove when the mixture begins to bubble.
6. The pickle is ready for use after 3 days. It lasts for 2 months.

913 Stuffed Bitter gourd in Tamarind : Hot [Diabetes]

500 g	bitter gourd, scrape lightly, slit three-fourths & seed
150 g	cleaned tamarind, obtain thick extract using water
50 g	chilli powder;
5 g	turmeric powder &
5 g	mustard seeds, sun-dry & powder, combine all three with oil to a paste
100 g	salt
250 ml	oil : heat & cool

1. Add salt to the slit bitter gourd, sun-dry for half an hour and rinse thoroughly.
2. Squeeze-dry and boil for 5 minutes in tamarind water to which a teaspoon (5g) salt has been added.
3. Drain out the water, pat-dry with a cloth and allow to cool.
4. Fill the spice mixture into the slit bitter gourd, close and coat the remaining spice mixture on the outside.
5. Sun the spiced bitter gourd for 5 days.
6. Pour the cooled oil over the sunned bitter gourd and store.
7. The pickle is ready for use. It lasts for 2 months. Sun occasionally.

914 Sour Bottle gourd : Hot [Kidney]

125g	bottle gourd, peel, chop & air-dry
15g	cleaned tamarind
10g	fresh red chillies, chop
2	cloves garlic, peel & chop
1g	cummin seeds &
1g	fenugreek seeds, dry-roast both
15g	salt
25ml	oil

1. Grind the chopped bottle gourd with the red chillies, salt, tamarind very coarsely and set aside for 3 days.
2. On the 4th day pound together the cummin seeds, fenugreek seeds and garlic.
3. Grind together both the mixtures, keeping the texture of the final mixture coarse.
4. This basic pickle lasts for 6 months.
5. For instant use, take the desired quantity of the basic pickle and season with mustard seeds. Blend well.
6. The pickle is ready for use. It keeps for 1 week.

915 Sour Brinjal Pulp : Hot [Asthma]

125 g	seedless brinjal, cut into small pieces
15 g	dried red chillies, powder coarsely
20 g	cleaned tamarind
5 g	jaggery, grate
3 g	turmeric powder
3 g	mustard seeds : for seasoning
2 g	asafoetida, roast in oil & powder
5 ml	vinegar
10 g	salt
125 ml	oil

1. Combine the brinjal pieces with the salt, chilli, turmeric powders, tamarind and jaggery. Set aside for 5 hours.
2. Grind together without adding water.
3. Heat the oil, add mustard seeds and allow to crackle.
4. Stir in the brinjal mixture, asafoetida powder, vinegar and cook till the mixture leaves the sides of the pan.
5. The pickle is ready for use. It keeps for 1 week and longer in the refrigerator.

916 Red Cabbage : Watery [Bones / Muscles]

500 g	red cabbage, cut into fine strips
10	peppercorns;
2 g	dried ginger powder;
2	cardamoms;
1	clove &
1	bay leaf, tie all in a spice bag
75 g	salt
250 ml	vinegar

Note : Choose tightly formed **red cabbages** with firm, unblemished outer leaves. If boiled in water it turns an unappetizing blue. Addition of vinegar, balances its flavour and preserves its colour.

1. Bring the vinegar along with the spice bag to the boil. Lower the heat, allow to simmer for 30 minutes and remove.
2. Squeeze out and discard the spice bag. Allow the spiced vinegar to cool.
3. Sprinkle the salt over the cabbage strips and set aside overnight.
4. Squeeze-dry the cabbage strips from the salt water and pack in a jar.
5. Cover with the cold spiced vinegar.
6. The pickle is ready for use after 3 days. It lasts for 2 months. Stir frequently.

917 Carrot – Onion – Green Spices : Hot [Eye]

500 g	carrot, peel & grate
200 g	onion, peel & chop
70 g	green chillies, chop;
2-1"	pieces of fresh ginger, scrape & chop;
20 g	green coriander &
10 g	mint leaves, wash, air-dry & chop both, grind all to a paste
50 g	cleaned tamarind, obtain thick extract using water
10 g	chilli powder
5 g	turmeric powder
60 g	salt
250 ml	oil

1. Stir-fry the chopped onion in a little oil till translucent.
2. Follow with the spice paste, cook for a few minutes and set aside.
3. Pour in the remaining oil, tamarind extract, chilli, turmeric powders, salt and bring to the boil. Alllow to thicken over a high flame.
4. Add in the carrot, fried spice paste and stir well.
5. Continue cooking over low heat until the mixture becomes jam-like and the oil separates.
6. The pickle is ready for use. It lasts for 2 months.

918 Carrot in Lime Juice : Hot [Eye / Liver]

125 g	carrot, peel & chop
12 g	chilli powder
3 g	mustard seeds, dry-roast & powder
3 g	turmeric powder
3 g	asafoetida, roast in oil & powder
40 ml	lime juice
15 g	salt
40 ml	oil

1. Combine the chilli, mustard, asafoetida and turmeric powders with the salt evenly.
2. Add in the carrot and stir thoroughly.
3. Heat the oil, add the lime juice, allow to bubble for a few seconds and remove.
4. Pour the heated lime juice over the spiced carrot and mix thoroughly.
5. The pickle is ready for use after 3 days. It keeps for 2 weeks in the refrigerator.

919 Garlic, Green Coriander – Tamarind : Hot [Immunity]

500 g	green coriander, wash, air-dry & chop;
80 g	peeled garlic;
75 g	green chillies &
50 g	dried red chillies, grind all three to a paste
200 g	cleaned tamarind, obtain thick extract using water
80 g	jaggery, grate
5 g	asafoetida, roast in oil & powder
5 g	turmeric powder
5 g	mustard seeds : for seasoning
175 g	salt
300 ml	oil

1. Heat a little oil, add mustard seeds and allow to crackle.
2. Stir in the coriander-chilli-garlic paste, stir-fry for a few minutes and set aside.
3. In the same pan heat some more oil, add in the tamarind extract, jaggery and bring to the boil. Allow to thicken over a high flame.
4. Stir in the fried spice paste, asafoetida, turmeric powders, salt and the remaining oil.
5. Continue cooking over low heat until the mixture becomes jam-like and the oil separates.
6. The pickle is ready for use. It lasts for 6 months.

920 Cucumber Whole : Salty [Laxative]

500 g	cucumber, scrub & keep whole
5 g	salt : for marinating
400 ml	water
200 ml	vinegar
40 g	sugar
60 g	salt : for pickle

Note : Cucumbers have a sweetish, rather elusive flavour and a high water content. They are at their best when very small, bright in colour, smooth-skinned and firm.

1. Marinate the cucumbers in water to which a teaspoon (5g) salt has been added overnight.
2. Drain and pack in a jar.
3. Combine the water, vinegar, sugar and salt.
4. Bring to the boil.
5. Pour the spicy liquid over the vegetables.
6. The pickle is ready for use after a day. It lasts for 1 month in the refrigerator.

921 Curry Lime - Fenugreek : Hot [Liver]

1 kg	chopped curry lime, scrape lightly, chop & seed
100 g	dried red chillies;
50 g	fenugreek seeds &
20 g	asafoetida, roast all three in oil & powder
10 g	turmeric powder
200 g	salt
400 ml	oil

1. Marinate the chopped curry lime in salt overnight.
2. Next day remove the lime pieces from the salt water and sun-dry for 2 days. Reserve the salt water.
3. Heat some oil and stir-fry the dried curry lime, a little at a time. Remove before the lime pieces change colour.
4. Add in all the powdered spices, turmeric powder, the salt water and stir well.
5. Heat the remaining oil, cool and pour over the mixture.
6. The pickle is ready for use after 1 week. It lasts for 1 year.

922 Date – Green Turmeric : Sweet [Heart]

500 g	date, slit, stone & chop fine
250 g	sugar
15 g	green turmeric, scrape & chop fine
5 g	chilli powder
5 g	mustard seeds, sun-dry & powder
5	cardamoms
1-1"	stick of cinnamon
50 ml	lime juice
25 g	salt

1. Cook the chopped date and turmeric in a little water. Remove and sun-dry for a day.
2. Stir in the chilli, mustard powders, whole spices, lime juice, sugar and sun-dry for 5 more days.
3. Add in the salt and stir well.
4. The pickle is ready for use. It lasts for 1 month.

Fruit Pickling

Pour the sweetened spiced vinegar into a saucepan. Add the fruit and simmer until tender. Remove the fruit with a perforated spoon and pack into hot, clean jars, leaving about 1" headspace. Boil the vinegar rapidly, uncovered, until it is reduced by one third. Fill the jars with the hot, syrupy vinegar, covering the fruit by at least 1/2". Cover with airtight, vinegar-proof lids.

923 Banana – Date : Sweet [Anaemia]

500 g	ripe malabar banana, peel & slice
200 g	date, slit, stone & chop
150 ml	sugar syrup
75 g	crystallised ginger, chop
5 g	chilli powder
2 g	garam masala powder
200 ml	vinegar
20 g	salt

1. Combine the banana and date with the vinegar. Bring to the boil and allow to thicken.
2. Add in the spices, the sugar syrup and heat until the mixture thickens again. Cover and set aside.
3. The pickle is ready for use after 1 week. It lasts for 2 months.

924 Spicy Dry Fruit in Vinegar : Sweet [Mouth Ulcer]

250 g	dried fig, chop
100 g	carrot, peel & chop
100 g	seedless raisin, chop
150 g	ripe mango pulp
50 g	date, stone & chop
500 g	jaggery, grate
10 g	dried red chillies, keep whole
10 g	mustard seeds &
5 g	cummin seeds, sun-dry both & powder
3	cardamoms,
3	cloves &
1-1"	stick of cinnamon, keep all three whole
400 ml	vinegar
30 g	salt

1. Wash the fruits in 100ml vinegar.
2. Heat another 200ml vinegar along with the chillies, jaggery, spice powders (except the mustard powder), whole spices and the salt.
3. After the jaggery melts, add in the chopped fig, raisin, date, carrot and the mango pulp.
4. Continue heating until the fruit is cooked and the gravy thickens. Allow to cool.
5. Blend the mustard powder into the remaining vinegar and stir into the cold pickle mixture.
6. The pickle is ready for use after 2 days. It lasts for 2 months.

925 Sour Spiced Banana : Sweet [Ulcer]

500 g	peeled banana, chop	2	big cardamoms, keep all three whole
300 g	sugar		
20 g	seedless raisin, chop	75 ml	vinegar
15 g	almonds, halve & blanch	10 g	salt
3 g	chilli powder		
1-1"	stick of cinnamon;		
2	cloves &		

1. Combine the banana with the vinegar, sugar and cook over low heat until well blended.
2. Stir in the salt, chilli powder, whole spices, raisin, almond and continue cooking until the mixture thickens.
3. The pickle is ready for use after 2 days. It lasts for 2 months and is best refrigerated.

926 Spicy Garlic in Lime Juice : Hot [Cholestrol]

- 500 g peeled garlic
- 100 g kashmiri red chillies &
- 20 g fenugreek seeds, roast both in oil & powder
- 150 ml lime juice
- 60 g salt
- 200 ml oil : heat & cool

1. Marinate the garlic with the salt and lime juice in a jar for 4 days.
2. Stir in the powdered spices and pre-heated oil. Set aside for 4 more days.
3. The pickle is ready for use. It lasts for 2 months.

927 Garlic in Soya Sauce : Sweet [Blood Pressure]

- 500 g large peeled garlic
- 500 ml soya sauce
- 500 ml vinegar
- 200 g sugar
- 20 g salt

1. Combine all the ingredients and set aside for 3 days.
2. Remove the garlic cloves from the liquid and transfer to a jar.
3. Bring the liquid alone to the boil. Lower the heat and simmer until the liquid is reduced to half.
4. Pour the reduced liquid over the garlic cloves. Allow to cool and set aside for a month.
5. The pickle lasts for 2 months.

928 Spiced Ginger : Hot [Low Blood Pressure]

500 g	fresh ginger, scrape & chop;	120 g	cleaned tamarind, grind both to a paste
50 g	chilli powder;	5 g	mustard seeds : for seasoning
10 g	mustard seeds, dry-roast &	5 g	asafoetida, roast in oil & powder
5 g	fenugreek seeds, dry-roast, grind all to a paste	5 g	turmeric powder
		120 g	salt
30 g	jaggery, grate &	200 ml	oil

1. Heat a little oil, add mustard seeds and allow to crackle.
2. Add in the ginger paste and stir-fry for a few minutes.
3. Stir in the tamarind paste and the remaining spice powders.
4. Continue cooking over low heat, adding the remaining oil little by little, until the mixture leaves the sides of the pan.
5. The pickle is ready for use. It lasts for 1 month.

929 Sweet & Spiced Ginger : Hot [Cough / Cold]

500 g	fresh ginger, scrape & chop fine		golden & powder
		3 g	mustard seeds, sun-dry & powder
125 g	cleaned tamarind, obtain thick extract using water	3 g	turmeric powder
		2 g	fenugreek seeds &
125 g	jaggery, grate	2 g	asafoetida, roast both in oil & powder
40 g	chilli powder		
5 g	split husked black gram, fry in oil till	120 g	salt
		200 ml	oil

Note : Ginger can be used in its fresh and dried form, although dried ginger is more suitable for treating digestive and respiratory disorders.

1. Stir-fry the chopped ginger in a little oil and set aside.
2. In the same pan, heat some more oil, pour in the tamarind extract, jaggery, turmeric powder and salt. Allow to thicken over a high flame.
3. Stir in the fried ginger, chilli, mustard, fenugreek, asafoetida and gram powders.
4. Continue cooking over low heat, adding the remaining oil little by little, until the mixture becomes jam-like and the oil separates.
5. The pickle is ready for use. It lasts for 2 months.

930 Cooked Gooseberry : Hot
[Rheumatism / Tuberculosis]

500 g	gooseberry, keep whole
50 g	chilli powder
5 g	mustard seeds;
5 g	coriander seeds &
5 g	cummin seeds, dry-roast all three & powder
5 g	turmeric powder
110 g	salt
200 ml	oil

1. Cook the gooseberry in a little water. Remove from the water, sun-dry and seed.
2. Stir-fry the gooseberry pieces in a little oil for a few minutes.
3. Add in the spice powders, salt, the remaining oil and cook over low heat for a few more minutes, till well blended.
4. The pickle is ready for use. It lasts for 6 months. Sun occasionally.

931 Dry Fried Gooseberry : Hot
[Diabetes]

500 g	gooseberry, keep whole
50 g	chilli powder
10 g	asafoetida, roast in oil & powder
10 g	mustard seeds : for seasoning
110 g	salt
200 ml	oil

1. Heat a little oil, add mustard seeds and allow to crackle.
2. Add in the gooseberries and cook over low heat until tender.
3. Stir in the chilli, asafoetida powders, salt and the remaining oil.
4. Continue cooking for a few minutes till dry and remove.
5. The pickle is ready for use. It lasts for 6 months.

932 Salted Gooseberry : Watery
[Ageing]

500 g	gooseberry, keep whole	50 g	chilli powder
		10 g	turmeric powder
2000 ml	water	150 g	salt

1. Boil the water and cool partly. Add in the whole gooseberry, chilli, turmeric powders, salt and stir well.
2. Allow the gooseberries to soak in the spicy liquid for about a month.
3. The pickle is ready for use. It lasts for few months, provided the gooseberries are immersed in the liquid.

933 Hibiscus Flower : Sweet
[Heart]

100 g	red hibiscus flower, chop fine	10 g	cleaned tamarind, obtain thick extract using water
2 g	chilli powder		
2	green chillies, chop fine	25 ml	honey
1-1"	piece of fresh ginger, scrape & chop fine	25 g	jaggery, grate
		a pinch of salt	
		25 ml	oil

1. Heat a little oil, add the chopped green chillies, ginger and fry for a few minutes over low heat.
2. Add in the chopped hibiscus, cook till tender and set aside.
3. In the same pan heat some more oil, add the tamarind extract, jaggery, turmeric powder, salt and bring to the boil. Allow to thicken over a high flame.
4. Add in the fried ingredients, chilli powder and continue cooking over low heat.
5. Pour in the honey and remove when the mixture leaves the sides of the pan.
6. The pickle is ready for use. It lasts for 1 month.

934 Spicy Kashmiri Red Chilli – Stuffed : Hot [Immunity]

500 g	fresh kashmiri red chillies
150 g	dried mango powder
12 g	onion seeds;
10 g	mustard seeds;
8 g	coriander seeds;
8 g	aniseeds;

5 g	fenugreek seeds;
5 g	turmeric powder &
5 g	thymol seeds, dry-roast all & powder
5 g	asafoetida, roast in oil & powder
175 g	salt
250 ml	oil

1. Combine the spice powders with a little oil to a paste.
2. Stuff the spice paste into the chillies with the help of a toothpick and sun for 4 days.
3. Transfer to a jar and cover with oil.
4. The pickle is ready for use. It lasts for 2 months. Sun occasionally.

935 Spiced Raw Jackfruit – Onion : Hot [Cramps]

500 g	mature raw jackfruit, wash, peel & chop
30 g	onion, peel & chop
1-1"	piece of fresh ginger, scrape & chop
5	cloves garlic, peel & chop
15 g	mustard seeds, sun-dry & powder
10 g	chilli powder
3 g	cummin seeds
3	cloves
3	cardamoms
1-1"	stick of cinnamon
150 g	sugar
100 ml	vinegar
50 g	salt

1. Stir-fry the ginger, garlic, onion in a little oil till golden and set aside.
2. Combine the spice powders and whole spices with the fried ingredients (except the sugar and vinegar).
3. Add to the jackfruit pieces, mix thoroughly and sun for 4 days.
4. Dissolve the sugar, stir in the vinegar and sun the pickle for 4 more days.
5. The pickle lasts for 3 months.

936 Lime Pulp : Hot [Liver]

500 g	lime pieces, cut into 8 pieces each & seed thoroughly
100 g	salt &
10 g	turmeric powder, combine evenly
60 g	chilli powder
5 g	asafoetida, roast in oil & powder
10 g	mustard seeds &
200 ml	oil : both for seasoning

1. Add the salt-turmeric mixture to the lime pieces and set aside for 7 days.
2. Grind the salted lime pieces to a coarse paste.
3. Heat the oil, add mustard seeds and allow to crackle.
4. Stir in the lime paste and cook over low heat, adding the remaining oil a little at a time.
5. Add in the chilli, asafoetida powders and continue cooking until the mixture leaves the sides of the pan.
6. The pickle is ready for use after 2 days. It lasts for 4 months.

937 Spicy Lime in Lime Juice : Hot [Peptic Ulcer / Bones]

250 g	lime pieces, cut into small pieces & seed
250 g	lime, extract juice & chop peels
50 g	chilli powder
10 g	mustard seeds;
5 g	peppercorns;
5 g	cummin seeds &
5 g	thymol seeds, dry-roast all & powder
5 g	asafoetida, roast in oil & powder
5 g	turmeric powder
2	cloves
1-1"	stick of cinnamon
100 g	salt
200 ml	oil

1. Combine the lime pieces with the lime peels and set aside.
2. Mix all the spice powders evenly.
3. Blend the lime juice with the spice mixture and the whole spices to make a paste.
4. Stir the spice paste into the lime mixture and mix thoroughly.
5. Add in the salt, the oil and stir well. Sun the mixture for 4 days.
6. The pickle is ready for use after 15 days. It lasts for 6 months.

938 Lime – Fenugreek Leaves : Salty [Rhuematism]

500 g	lime pieces, cut into small pieces & seed
20 g	dried fenugreek leaves, chop
10 g	chilli powder
5 g	turmeric powder
100 g	salt
150 ml	oil

1. Combine all the ingredients except oil with the lime pieces.
2. Arrange in a jar and pour over the oil to cover.
3. The pickle is ready for use after 10 days. It lasts for 6 months.

939 Raw Makoy Berry : Watery
[Mouth Ulcer]

125 g	raw makoy berry
100 ml	sour curd, whip with 50ml water & remove cream
30 g	salt

1. Blend the makoy berries with the whipped curd and salt. Set aside for 2 days.
2. The pickle is ready for use. It keeps for 3 weeks and longer in the refrigerator. Shake daily.

940 Mango – Onion : Hot [Cooling]

500 g	cut large sour mango, size into small pieces
250 g	small red onion, peel & chop fine
25 g	chilli powder
25 g	jaggery, grate
3 g	fenugreek seeds &
3 g	asafoetida, roast both in oil & powder
3 g	mustard seeds &
a few	sprigs curry leaves : both for seasoning
75 g	salt
200 ml	oil

1. Heat a little oil, add the mustard seeds, curry leaves and allow to crackle.
2. Add in the chopped onion and stir-fry until they become translucent.
3. Follow with the chopped mango and cook for a few minutes.
4. Stir in the spice powders, jaggery, salt and the remaining oil. Allow to thicken.
5. Remove when the mixture becomes jam-like and the oil separates.
6. The pickle is ready for use. It lasts for 2 months.

> **Note :** Immerse **Mangoes** in cold water for some time before peeling them. This hastens the process of peeling and makes it rather neat too!

941 Sunned Mango – Jaggery : Sweet [Blood Disorder]

500 g	seeded mango, peel & grate
275 g	jaggery, grate
25 g	chilli powder
5 g	turmeric powder &
40 g	salt, combine evenly
150 ml	oil

1. Arrange a layer of the grated mango in a wide-mouthed shallow jar.
2. Sprinkle over a handful of jaggery. Follow with a little of the salt-turmeric mixture.
3. Repeat this process until all the ingredients are layered. Mix thoroughly and set aside for 2 days.
4. On the 3 rd day stir well from the bottom of the jar.
5. Squeeze out the salt water from the mangoes. Store the salt water in a closed jar.
6. Sun the squeezed mango for 4 days and combine thereafter with the salt water.
7. Heat the oil to smoking point. Reduce the heat, add in the chilli powder and stir well.
8. Pour the spiced oil over the salted mango and mix thoroughly. Stir daily.
9. The pickle is ready for use after 10 days. It lasts for 6 months.

942 Mustard Mango in Vinegar : Hot [Sinusitis]

500 g	seeded mango, chop	5 g	turmeric powder
30 g	chilli powder	50 ml	vinegar
15 g	mustard seeds, sun-dry & powder	60 g	salt
		200 ml	oil

1. Blend the mustard powder with a little vinegar.
2. Combine the chopped mango, chilli, turmeric powders with the salt and the oil.
3. Stir the mustard sauce and the remaining vinegar into the mango mixture. Mix thoroughly.
4. The pickle is ready for use after 3 days. It lasts for 6 months. Sun occasionally.

943 Mango Ginger in Curd : Watery [Stomach]

500 g	peeled mango ginger, cut into rings	10 g	turmeric powder
500 ml	sour curd, whip with 375 ml water & remove cream	10 g	mustard seeds : for seasoning
		40 g	salt
25 g	chilli powder	50 ml	oil

1. Drop the mango ginger rings into the whipped curd.
2. Heat the oil, add mustard seeds and allow to crackle.
3. Blend in the chilli, turmeric powders and the salt.
4. Pour the spiced oil over the mango ginger mixture and blend well.
5. The pickle is ready for use after 4 days. It lasts for 1 month and longer in the refrigerator.

944 Sour Mint – Green Pepper : Hot [Nausea]

500 g	mint leaves, wash, air-dry & chop
100 g	green pepper, string & mince
100 g	cleaned tamarind, obtain thick extract using water
60 g	jaggery, grate
10 g	asafoetida, roast in oil & powder
10 g	turmeric powder
10 g	mustard seeds : for seasoning
200 ml	lime juice
50 ml	vinegar
160 g	salt
250 ml	oil

1. Heat a little oil, add mustard seeds and allow to crackle.
2. Add in the chopped mint, the minced green pepper, fry for a few minutes and set aside.
3. In the same pan heat some more oil, pour in the tamarind extract, jaggery and bring to the boil. Allow to thicken over a high flame.
4. Stir in the fried ingredients, lime juice, vinegar, asafoetida, turmeric powders, salt and the remaining oil.
5. Continue cooking over low heat until the mixture becomes jam-like and the oil separates.
6. The pickle is ready for use. It lasts for 2 months.

945 Mint – Green Corriander : Hot [Bronchitis]

125 g	mint leaves, wash & air-dry;
40 g	green chillies;
25 g	green coriander, wash & airdry, chop all three fine
20 g	cleaned tamarind, obtain thick extract using water
20 g	jaggery, grate
5 g	chilli powder
5 g	turmeric powder
5 g	split husked black gram;
5 g	mustard seeds &
a few	sprigs curry leaves : all three for seasoning
40 g	salt
50 ml	oil

1. Stir-fry the chopped ingredients in a little oil and set aside.
2. In the same pan heat some more oil, add mustard seeds and allow to crackle.
3. Add in the curry leaves, blackgram and fry till golden.
4. Pour in the tamarind extract, jaggery, turmeric powder and the salt.
5. Bring to the boil and allow to thicken over a high flame.
6. Stir in the chilli powder, fried paste and the remaining oil.
6. Continue cooking over low heat until the mixture becomes jam-like and the oil separates.
7. The pickle is ready for use. It keeps for 15 days in the refrigerator.

946 Apple, Pear, Plum & Cherry : Sweet [Constipation]

125 g	cored cooking apple &	10 g	chilli powder
125 g	cored chopped pear, peel both	3	cloves garlic, peel & chop
125 g	chopped plum &	2 g	peppercorns &
125 g	chopped cherry, stone both	2 g	caraway seeds, pound both
125 g	seedless raisin, chop	2 g	garam masala powder
100 g	onion, peel & slice	250 ml	vinegar
350 g	sugar	10 g	salt

1. Combine the fruit pieces, seedless raisin with the vinegar and cook over low heat for 45 minutes.
2. Add in all the remaining ingredients and simmer for one hour.
3. The pickle is ready for use after 3 days. It lasts for 2 months.

Note : Pear is a sub-acid fruit. If eaten without the skin, it has a constipating effect.

947 Vellarai Keerai – Black Gram : Instant [Memory]

125 g	vellarai keerai, wash, wipe, air-dry & chop
20 g	split husked black gram;
10	peppercorns &
15 g	cleaned tamarind, dry-roast
15 g	salt

1. Grind together all the ingredients with the salt using a little water.
2. The pickle is ready for use. It keeps for 5 days in the refrigerator.

Dried Fruits

Dried fruits include currants, dates, prunes, raisins, sultanas, etc.

Currants: are very small, seedless, sweet dried grapes.

Dates: are from the date palm.

Prunes: are dried plums with a particularly high sugar content and firm flesh.

Raisins: are special variety of grapes, dried in the sun or by artificial heat and so preserves them.

Sultanas: are also a special variety of grape; seedless, golden yellow and very sweet.

948 Dry Fruits – Fresh Ginger : Sweet [Anaemia]

250 g	*dried apricot, soak overnight in water & seed*
50 g	*almond, blanch, peel & sliver*
50 g	*date, stone, chop & soak overnight in water*
20 g	*fresh ginger, scrape & chop*
20 g	*chilli powder*
3	*cardamoms, keep whole*
250 g	*sugar*
250 ml	*vinegar*
20 g	*salt*

1. Grind the soaked apricot with the water in which they were soaked until smooth.
2. Heat together the almond, date, ginger, chilli powder, cardamom with the vinegar, sugar and salt. Cook over low heat until the sugar dissolves.
3. When the mixture becomes syrupy, add in the apricot paste and cook for 15 minutes until thick.
4. The pickle is ready for use. It lasts for 6 months.

949 Cabbage – Carrot-Sprouted Gram : Hot [Weight loss]

125 g	*cabbage, shred thickly*
125 g	*carrot, peel & chop*
60 g	*big seedless brinjal, chop*
15 g	*salt : for marinating*
150 g	*sour tomato, chop;*
100 g	*onion, peel, chop &*
40 g	*dried red chillies, grind all three to a paste*
50 g	*cleaned tamarind, obtain thick extract using water*
20 g	*sprouted whole bengal gram*
5 g	*asafoetida, roast in oil & powder*
65 g	*salt : for pickle*
150 ml	*oil*

1. Soak the prepared vegetables in lightly salted water for a few hours.
2. Rinse and sun-dry for an hour, turning them over once or twice.
3. Stir-fry the dried vegetables in a little oil and set aside.
4. Heat the oil, add the bengal gram sprouts and stir-fry for a while.
5. Add in the tomato-onion-chilli paste, salt and cook for a few minutes.
6. Pour over the tamarind extract and continue cooking till the mixture thickens.
7. Stir in the fried vegetables and the asafoetida powder.
8. Continue cooking until the mixture becomes jam-like and the oil separates.
9. The pickle is ready for use. It lasts for 2 months.

950 Drumstick – Gooseberry : Hot [Pox]

250 g	*cooked drumstick inner pith*
250 g	*gooseberry, cook & seed*
35 g	*dried red chillies, break into bits*
20 g	*cleaned tamarind, obtain thick extract using water*
50 g	*jaggery, grate*
5 g	*asafoetida, roast in oil & powder*
5 g	*mustard seeds &*
a few	*sprigs curry leaves : both for seasoning*
1	*dried spice ball*
80 g	*salt*
150 ml	*oil*

1. Fry the chillies, dried spice ball, asafoetida powder in a little oil and set aside.
2. In the same pan heat some more oil, stir-fry the cooked drumstick pith and the gooseberry pieces for a few minutes.
3. Cool and grind together all the fried ingredients.
4. Heat the remaining oil, add the mustard seeds, curry leaves and allow to crackle.
5. Pour in the tamarind extract, jaggery and bring to the boil. Allow to thicken over a high flame.
6. Stir in the spice paste and continue cooking over low heat.
7. Remove when the mixture becomes jam-like and the oil separates.
8. The pickle is ready for use. It lasts for 2 months.

951 Green Tomato – Horse Radish : Salty [Piles]

500 g	green tomato, cut into chunks
20 g	horse radish, peel & cube
15 g	dried red chillies, keep whole
10 g	mustard seeds, sun-dry & powder
175 ml	vinegar
50 g	salt

Green tomatoes for pickling should be fully grown yet green and firm. Leave the stalks on to prevent ripening. The seedless ones are less bitter and therefore preferred.

1. Pack the prepared vegetables in a jar.
2. Bring the spices, salt and vinegar to the boil. Simmer gently for 10 minutes and remove.
3. Pour the boiling spiced vinegar over the pickle to cover.
4. The pickle is ready for use after 1 month.
   It lasts for 4 months.

---

952 Mixed Vegetable – Gram : Tender [Weight loss]

500 g	vegetables : choice – carrot, beetroot, cabbage, potato, fresh cow peas, pumpkin; singly or combined; peel, shell, shred, scrape & cut as required
100 g	bengal gram whole;
100 g	green gram whole;
100 g	dried field beans, whole;
100 g	dried cow peas, whole &
100 g	raw groundnut, soak all for 2hrs & pressure cook
20 g	almonds &
20 g	cashewnuts, chop both & roast in oil
50 g	chilli powder
5 g	turmeric powder
20 g	mustard seeds;
5	tender green chillies, chop &
a few	sprigs curry leaves all three for seasoning
350 ml	lime juice
150 g	salt
150 ml	oil

1. Drain and discard the water from the cooked cereal. Allow to dry in the shade for 3 hours.
2. Heat the oil, add mustard seeds and allow to crackle.
3. Add in the chillies, curry leaves, the prepared vegetable, dried cereal and stir-fry until dry.
4. Stir in the chilli, turmeric powders, almond, cashewnut, salt, lime juice and remove when the mixture begins to bubble.
5. The pickle is ready for use. It lasts for 1 month in the refrigerator. Sun occasionally.

---

953 Cabbage – Tomato in Vinegar : Sweet [Constipation]

250 g	cabbage, shred thickly
125 g	green tomato, cut into chunks
25 g	capsicum, chop
60 g	salt, make a solution with 15ml water
100 g	onion, peel & chop
20 g	peeled garlic, chop
5 g	thymol seeds, crush
3 g	mustard seeds, sun-dry & powder
3 g	turmeric powder
125 g	sugar
200 ml	vinegar
20 ml	oil

1. Bring the salt solution to the boil.
2. Blanch the prepared vegetables in the salted boiling water for 2 minutes. Drain well and spread to dry on a clean cloth.
3. Heat the oil to smoking point. Reduce the heat, fry the onions and garlic till golden brown.
4. Add in the sugar, vinegar and stir to dissolve.
5. Stir in the remaining spices, vegetables and remove immediately.
6. The pickle is ready for use after 2 days. It lasts for 6 months. Sun and stir occasionally.

---

954 Small Red Onion Whole : Hot [Piles]

500 g	small red onion, peel & slit crosswise
20 g	mustard seeds, sun-dry & powder;
25 g	chilli powder &
40 g	salt, combine all three evenly
200 ml	oil

1. Soak the onions in hot water overnight and wipe-dry the following day.
2. Apply the spice mixture into and over them.
3. Pack in a jar and sun for 2 days.
4. The pickle is ready for use. It lasts for 2 months. Sun occasionally.

955 Spiced Small Red Onion in Vinegar : Hot [Insomnia]

500 g	small red onion, peel
10 g	green chillies, split lengthwise
5 g	peppercorns, dry-roast & powder
5	cloves garlic, peel & chop
2-1"	sticks of cinnamon
10 g	sugar
200 ml	vinegar
40 g	salt
25 ml	oil

1. Marinate the onion in salt for a day. Drain the salt water.
2. Combine all the ingredients and bring to the boil.
3. Lower the heat and continue cooking till tender. Remove and cool.
4. The pickle is ready for use. It lasts for 1 month.

956 Sweet & Sour Neem Flower : Hot [Malaria]

500 g	neem flower, fry for 30 seconds in a dry pan
80 g	cleaned tamarind, obtain thick extract using water
80 g	jaggery, grate
80 g	split husked black gram
40 g	chilli powder
10 g	turmeric powder
10 g	asafoetida, roast in oil & powder
10 g	mustard seeds : for seasoning
80 g	salt
200 ml	oil

1. Heat the oil, add mustard seeds and allow to crackle. Stir in the black gram & fry till golden.
2. Pour in the tamarind extract, jaggery and bring to the boil. Allow to thicken over a high flame.
3. Stir in the chilli, asafoetida, turmeric powders and the salt.
4. Add in the fried neem flower, cook for a few minutes over low heat until the mixture becomes jam-like and the oil separates.
5. The pickle is ready for use. It lasts for 1 month.

Note : Neem flowers though very bitter have high medicinal value. Both the fresh flowers and dried ones are used in pickling.

957 Small White Onion : Watery [Blood Pressure]

500 g	small white onion, unpeeled
250 ml	boiling water
20 g	dried red chillies, break into bits
20 g	sugar
5 g	aniseeds
5 g	allspice
1	bay leaf
60 g	salt, boil with 200 ml water & 120 ml vinegar

1. Pour 250ml boiling water over the onion and allow to stand for 2 minutes.
2. Drain the water and peel the onion.
3. Boil 60g salt in 200ml water. Pour the salt solution over the onion and let stand overnight.
4. Drain the onion, cover with cold water and let stand for 1 hour.
5. Remove, pack the onion in a jar along with the red chillies and the bay leaf.
6. Bring the vinegar to boil with the sugar, aniseeds, allspice and simmer gently for 15 minutes.
7. Pour the boiling vinegar over the onion, cool and cap tight.
8. The pickle is ready for use after 2 days. It lasts for 2 months.

958 Papaya – Raisin : Sweet [Kidney stone]

125 g	peeled raw papaya, chop fine
25 g	seedless raisin, chop
25 g	sugar
10 g	cleaned tamarind, obtain thick extract using water
10 g	chilli powder
3 g	turmeric powder
3 g	panch phoran powder
10 ml	lime juice
5 g	salt
50 ml	oil

1. Heat a little oil to smoking point, reduce the heat, add in the panch phoran, fry for a minute and remove.
2. In the same pan heat some more oil, add all the remaining ingredients except the ginger juice and raisin.
3. Cook over low heat till the mixture thickens, adding the remaining oil a little by little.
4. Stir in the ginger juice, raisin, mix thoroughly and remove.
5. The pickle is ready for use. It keeps for 5 days in the refrigerator.

959 Sour Pear – Ginger – Raisin : Sweet [Bladder stone]

500 g	cored pear, peel & chop
500 g	sugar
100 g	seedless raisin, chop
75 g	fresh ginger, scrape & chop
100 ml	lime juice
20 g	salt

1. Combine the chopped pear, raisin, ginger and cook till tender.
2. Stir in the sugar to dissolve and allow the mixture to thicken.
3. Add in the lime juice, salt and remove when the mixture becomes jam-like.
4. The pickle is ready for use. It lasts for 1 month and is best refrigerated.

Raisins
Highly alkaline in nature, raisins are very effective in relieving acidosis. Because of its pure fructose content, it is also considered a quick energy food.

960 Pineapple – Raisin : Sweet [Lung]

500 g	grated half-ripe pineapple
600 g	sugar
200 ml	water
100 g	seedless raisin, chop
2-1"	pieces of fresh ginger, scrape & grate
5 g	chilli powder
5 g	mustard seeds : for seasoning
25 g	salt
15 ml	oil

1. Heat the oil, add mustard seeds and allow to crackle.
2. Stir in the grated pineapple, ginger, raisin, chilli powder, sugar, salt, 200ml water and bring to the boil.
3. Lower the heat, cover and continue cooking until the pineapple pieces soften.
4. Remove when the mixture becomes thick and jam-like.
5. The pickle is ready for use. It lasts for 2 months.

961 Spiced Pineapple : Sweet [Bronchitis]

500 g	half-ripe pineapple pieces
600 g	sugar
5 g	chilli powder
5 g	peppercorns, dry-roast & powder
3 g	garam masala powder
25 g	salt

1. Add the sugar to the pineapple pieces and cook till done.
2. Stir in the chilli, pepper, garam masala powders, salt and cook for a few minutes.
3. Remove when the mixture becomes thick and jam-like.
4. The pickle is ready for use after a day. It lasts for 2 months.

962 Plantain Stem in Lime Juice : Hot [Diabetes]

125 g	tender plantain stem
8 g	green chillies, chop fine
3 g	green coriander, wash, air-dry & chop
3 g	mustard seeds &
a few	sprigs curry leaves : both for seasoning
25 ml	lime juice
10 g	salt
25 ml	oil

1. Remove the fibres of the plantain stem, cut into thin small bits and drop into weak buttermilk solution. Drain after a few minutes and pat-dry.
2. Combine the dried plantain stem pieces with the green chilli, lime juice and salt.
3. Heat the oil, add mustard seeds and allow to crackle. Add in the curry leaves, chopped coriander and fry for a few minutes.
4. Blend the seasoning into the mixture.
5. The pickle is ready for use after 1 hour. It keeps for 1 week in the refrigerator.

963 Potato in Mustard Sauce : Salty [Kidney stone]

125 g	potato, peel, cube & parboil
12 g	mustard seeds, grind a paste with 250ml water
3 g	turmeric powder
5 g	salt
12 ml	oil

1. Heat the oil to smoking point and remove.
2. When the oil is still lukewarm, blend in the mustard paste, turmeric powder and the salt.
3. Stir in the parboiled potato, mix thoroughly and sun for 2 days.
4. The pickle keeps for 15 days.

964 Baby Potato Preserve : Sweet [Weight loss]

500 g	baby potatoes, peel & prick with a fork
250 g	sugar, make a syrup of one-string consistency with 50ml water
3	cardamoms, keep whole
2 g	saffron strands, soak in a little warm water
150 ml	lime juice

1. Boil the pricked potatoes in water to which 75ml lime juice has been added. Remove, allow to cool and drain.
2. Add the remaining lime juice to the sugar syrup, cook until the syrup thickens and remove.
3. When cool, stir in the cardamom and saffron.
4. The pickle is ready for use. It lasts for 2 months.

965 Pumpkin – Cabbage – Tamarind : Hot [Worms]

500g	peeled pumpkin, seed & shred
500g	cabbage, shred thickly
10g	jaggery, grate
40g	split husked black gram;
40g	dried red chillies, break into bits &
5g	asafoetida, roast all three in oil & powder
5g	turmeric powder
5g	mustard seeds : for seasoning
50ml	lime juice
50ml	vinegar
100g	salt
300ml	oil

1. Stir-fry the shredded cabbage and pumpkin in a little oil. Set aside.
2. Heat a little oil, add mustard seeds and allow to crackle.
3. Stir in the fried cabbage, pumpkin, powdered spices, turmeric powder, salt and the remaining oil.
4. Continue cooking over low heat until the mixture becomes jam-like.
5. Pour in the lime juice, vinegar and remove when the mixture begins to bubble.
6. The pickle is ready for use. It lasts for 2 months.

966 Radish Preserve – Honey : Sweet [Cough]

500 g	red radish &
500 g	white radish, scrape, top, tail & slice both
10 g	salt
240 g	almond, soak in water overnight & cut into slivers
1800 ml	honey
2-1"	pieces of fresh ginger, scrape & chop
60 ml	lime juice

Honey is a rich concentrated food, high in calories and slightly laxative. While it is generally more readily digested than sugar and its effect in cooking is very similar, its flavour is more distinctive than most types of sugar. Because it dominates the flavour of other ingredients, honey's use in pickling is quite limited.

1. Parboil the sliced radish in sufficient boiling water to which two teaspoons (10g) salt has been added. Drain and allow to dry.
2. Combine all the ingredients except the lime juice and cook for 10 minutes till well blended.
3. Blend in the lime juice immediately.
4. The pickle is ready for use. It lasts for 1 month and is best refrigerated.

967 Radish – Green Spices : Hot [Nerves]

500 g	radish, peel & grate		thick extract using water
50 g	onion, peel & chop	10 g	jaggery, grate
30 g	green coriander, clean, air-dry & chop fine	5 g	dried mango powder
3	green chillies, chop fine	3 g	garam masala powder
60 g	cleaned tamarind, obtain	2 g	turmeric powder
		30 g	chilli powder
		25 g	salt
		50 ml	oil

1. Stir-fry the radish pieces, chopped onion, coriander, chillies in a little oil and set aside.
2. Heat the remaining oil, add the tamarind extract, jaggery and salt.
3. Bring to the boil and allow to thicken over a high flame.
4. Add in the spice powders, fried ingredients and continue cooking over low heat.
5. Remove when the mixture becomes jam-like and the oil separates.
6. The pickle is ready for use. It lasts for 2 months.

Note : Green spices should preferably be plucked leaf by leaf rather than chopped, in order to preserve their juices.

968 Mahani in Curd : Watery
[Blood Purifier]

> The Mahani Root is glorified as "a sweet refreshing nervine tonic". It destroys poison, removes indigestion and increases strength and vitality.

500g	mahani root pieces
500ml	sour curd, whip with 400 ml water & remove cream
40g	chilli powder
10g	turmeric powder
100g	salt

1. Cut the mahani into small pieces and drop into very thin buttermilk to prevent discolouration.
2. Combine the chilli, turmeric powders and the salt with the whipped curd.
3. Remove the root pieces from the buttermilk, drop into the spiced curd and stir thoroughly. Shake daily.
4. The pickle is ready for use after 10 days. It lasts for 2 months.

969 Bitterberry in Buttermilk : Watery *[Acidity]*

125 g	bitterberry, prick with fork or halve
150 ml	curd, whip with 150ml water & remove cream
15 g	chilli powder
5 g	mustard seeds, sun-dry & powder
3 g	turmeric powder
50 g	salt

1. Drop the berries in rice-washed water for a day. Drain out the water and add fresh rice-washed water.
2. Repeat this process three times to remove the bitterness from the berries.
3. Combine the spice powders, salt and blend with the buttermilk.
4. Stir in the berries and set aside for 2 days. Shake daily.
5. The pickle is ready for use. It keeps for 3 weeks in the refrigerator.

Buttermilk
Free of any fat content or remnants of butter, buttermilk is considered one of the best health foods, as it wards off innumerable diseases. Cow's buttermilk helps to cure cough, anaemia, piles and skin diseases.

970 Spicy Tamarind – Coriander - Jaggery : Sweet *[Heat]*

500 g	cleaned tamarind, obtain thick extract using water
500 g	jaggery, grate
30 g	coriander seeds &
20 g	cummin seeds, sun-dry both & powder
20 g	chilli powder
10 g	asafoetida, roast in oil & powder
10 g	dried ginger powder
10 g	black salt, powder
10 g	mint leaves, wash, air-dry & chop
40 g	salt

1. Heat the tamarind extract, jaggery and sufficient water till it is reduced to half.
2. Stir in the remaining ingredients.
3. Continue cooking until the mixture becomes thick and sauce-like.
4. The pickle is ready for use after a day. It lasts for 1 month in the refrigerator.

Note : To get the maximum quantity of juice from **tamarind**, soak the required quantity of tamarind in lukewarm water for 10 minutes before squeezing. Alternatively it may be blended in the mixer.

971 Tomato – Garlic in Vinegar : Sweet *[Arthritis]*

500 g	ripe tomato, blanch, skin & chop
300 g	sugar
2-1"	pieces of fresh ginger, scrape &
10	cloves garlic, peel, chop both & grind to a paste
10 g	chilli powder
5 g	mustard seeds;
5 g	cummin seeds &
5 g	fenugreek seeds, soak in vinegar, grind all three fine
200 ml	vinegar
40 g	salt
200 ml	oil

1. Fry the ginger-garlic paste and the mustard mixture in a little oil for a few minutes.
2. Stir in the remaining oil, chopped tomato, sugar, salt and allow to thicken over a high flame.
3. Add in the vinegar and chilli powder.
4. Continue cooking over low heat until the mixture becomes jam-like and the oil separates.
5. The pickle is ready for use. It lasts for 1 month and is best refrigerated.

972 Tomato – Tender Bitterberries : Hot [Obesity]

500 g	green tomato	2 g	grated nutmeg		
50 g	tender bitterberry, halve	25 ml	vinegar		
30 g	chilli powder	40 g	salt		
20 g	onion, peel & slice				
5 g	fenugreek seeds, roast in oil & powder				
5 g	dried ginger powder				
2	cloves garlic, peel & slice				

1. Bring the water to boiling. Blanch the tomato in the boiling water for 5 minutes. Peel off the skins and chop.
2. Combine the chopped tomato, onion, garlic, salt, ginger powder in a pan and cook for 30 minutes.
3. Pass the mixture through a wire-sieve to make a puree.
4. Stir in the chilli powder, fenugreek powder, nutmeg, vinegar, sugar, bitterberry and cook the mixture over a medium flame until thick.
5. The pickle is ready for use. It lasts for 1 month in the refrigerator.

973 Thuduvelai Leaf : Instant [Lung]

- 125 g thuduvelai leaves, wash, air-dry & chop
- 20 g cleaned tamarind
- 20 g split husked black gram &
- 5 g peppercorns, dry-roast all three
- 12 g salt
- a pinch of sugar

1. Grind together all the ingredients with the salt using a little water.
2. The pickle is ready for use. It keeps for 5 days in the refrigerator.

974 Dry Fruits – Nuts in Honey : Sweet [Ageing]

- 150 g seedless raisin, chop
- 75 g almond, slice
- 75 g date, stone & chop
- 50 g cashewnuts, halve
- 50 g pine nuts
- 50 g shelled walnuts, chop
- 50 g pistachios, slice
- 20 g tender green chillies, slit
- 20 g chilli powder
- 15 g peppercorns, sun-dry & powder
- 250 ml honey
- 150 g sugar
- 250 ml vinegar
- 20 ml lime juice
- 50 g salt

Honey
Honey's flavour, aroma, quality and consistency vary according to the type of flavours most widespread in the region where it is gathered. Honey is full of powerful anti-bacterial properties.

1. Combine the dried fruit with the spice powders, salt and green chillies.
2. Heat the vinegar, add in the sugar and stir to dissolve.
3. Remove and allow to cool. Stir in the honey and lime juice.
4. Blend in the spiced dried fruits.
5. The pickle is ready for use after 2 days. It lasts for 3 months.

Wherever oil is mentioned use gingelly oil or refined oil unless specifically stated. Refined oil is more suitable if the pickle has to be preserved for longer periods. If gingelly oil is kept for too long it tends to get a rancid smell and taste.

A lot more oil is required for pickles with garlic as an ingredient in it, for it is highly susceptible to bacterial activity. The extra oil on top will inhibit the growth of bacteria.

THE OIL RANGE

The range of oils used in Indian cooking and pickling is varied, starting from the most preferred gingelly oil/mustard oil to the least preferred castor oil. Its advantage lies in the fact that, on frying it doesn't congeal on fried or roast foods served cold.

The flavour of an oil is to some extent dependent on the refining process. The more highly refined the oil is, the less flavour and odour it will have – that's why it pays to buy a good one. The level of refining is set by a manufacturer's specifications, so of course even the same types of oil can and do vary.

You can use oil to make cakes, but you can't beat butter for a cake – the flavour is better, and the texture lighter.

Give your wooden kitchen and dining room possessions an occasional rub with a tissue lightly soaked in oil, to feed the wood and keep them shiny – salad bowl and servers, cheeseboard, breadboard, butter dishes, sugar bowl, toast rack or what have-you. They all like a face-lift.

COCONUT OIL

Coconut oil has a delicate flavour and is used mostly in the southern parts of India, especially in Kerala. It is extracted from the dried coconut kernel called *copra*.

CORN OIL

Comes from the germs of the maize kernel – and it takes approximately 25 kilograms of maize to produce approximately 900 ml of a top quality oil – no wonder it is so expensive.

You can use good quality corn oil for anything and everything – shallow or deep fat frying, preferring it to olive oil because it is lighter and flavourless.

The shelf life of an unopened bottle of pure corn oil is about 12 months, in practice probably quite a lot longer.

GINGELLY OIL

Gingelly oil / sesame oil is used mainly in southern and western India. Both the light and dark versions of this oil are used in Indian cooking.

The lighter version is preferred in pickling as it is less pungent although expensive. However, if the pickles are preserved for too long they develop a rancid taste.

GROUNDNUT OIL.

Comes from peanuts/monkey-nuts, which are better known as groundnuts. They are the oily edible seeds of a trailing plant, ripening underground in very brittle pods – hence their names.

Due to its strong flavour it is not commonly used by many in pickling.

MUSTARD OIL

Mustard oil has a strong aroma and is used mainly in northern India. In Bengal fish and vegetable dishes are prepared in mustard oil. Because of its preservative qualities, Portuguese cooking uses mustard oil in its famous vindaloo dishes and seafood pickles.

OLIVE OIL

Olive oil, like wines vary according to the country and area of origin, as well as from season to season. Among all fats though, olive oil is closest in chemical composition to the fat in mother's milk, making it the most easily digested of all fats and oils. Its high content of unsaturated fat means no cholesterol.

Olive oil is unsuitable for deep fat frying because – quite apart from its cost – it has too low a *smoke point*. Besides it has a tendency to *go off*.

SOYA OIL

From the soya bean, this is one of the cheapest oils in the market. It has rather a marked back taste, a flavour always associated with soya which is difficult even in refining. This explains why it is somewhat unsuitable for sale as a pure oil but often forms part of blended cooking oils.

SUNFLOWER OIL

Is being used more and more, and is good for deep fat frying as well as for shallow, because it has a fairly high *smoke point*. Use it in salad dressings and baked products too, as long as you don't dislike its flavour.

Sunflower oil is good for pickling as it is flavourless and therefore brings out the true aroma of the pickled vegetable or fruit.

VEGETABLE OILS

Usually a blend of various oils chosen by the manufacturer and may include sunflower, groundnut, soya and rapeseed oil but not usually corn oil because of its high price. Blended oils aren't necessarily highly refined as this would add to their cost. For some, the usage is restricted largely to frying, as their back taste would be unacceptable.

Anti Waste

*pickles

are

unforgettable, tasty, tangy,

nutritious morsels

combining

skins, peels, rinds and seeds,

with aromatic spices ;

creating

choicest delicacies

from

humble origins.*

Recipes : Anti - Waste

975. Spiced bottle gourd peel : hot
976. Bottle gourd seed – black gram : hot
977. Cauliflower stem – green spices : hot
978. Cauliflower stem : hot
979. Spicy drumstick leaf – fenugreek leaf paste : hot
980. Jackfruit seed – tamarind : hot
981. Spiced jackfruit seed : hot
982. Jackfruit seed – green spices : instant
983. Kumquat leaf – green coriander - gram : instant
984. Lime leaf – green coriander - gram : instant
985. Lime peel paste : hot
986. Lime peel : watery
987. Sour mango skin : sweet
988. Mango leaf in tamarind sauce : hot
989. Mixed vegetable peel in nut paste : hot
990. Sour & spicy raw plantain skin : hot
991. Raw plantain skin – raisin : sweet
992. Spicy ridge gourd peel – gram : hot
993. Steamed ridge gourd peel : instant
994. Sweet & sour mahani peel : hot
995. Spicy snake gourd seed – gram : hot
996. Tender tamarind leaves : instant
997. Watermelon rind – onion - tamarind : instant
998. Spiced watermelon rind : instant
999. Sweet & sour watermelon rind : instant
1000. Watermelon rind in spiced vinegar : instant

PREPARATION OF SPICE POWDERS

ASAFOETIDA POWDER
Prepared by breaking the asafoetida lump into small bits and deep frying in hot oil till done. Cool and then finely powder in a mixer. Asafoetida powder sold in the shops not only has less aroma and flavour than home-ground asafoetida, but is also less economical. More of it has to be used in pickling.

CHILLI POWDER
Can be made by buying bright, red, plump chillies and getting it coarsely ground in your local mill or home mixer. Before grinding sun-dry the chillies. This helps to preserve the chilli powder for longer periods as well as makes for easier grinding. Best results are obtained by home grinding.

FENUGREEK POWDER
Best prepared at home. Roast with or without oil in a heavy pan (kadai) over low heat, till light brown. Cool and finely powder in a mixer. If over roasted, the powder will taste bitter. It is safer to roast the seeds a little less than more.

MUSTARD POWDER
Must be prepared at home. Sun-dry the mustard seeds. Cool and then finely powder in a mixer. Mustard powder should be freshly prepared, just before pickling or at best a day earlier. Powdered mustard tends to get rancid with time. However, for mango avakkai pickle the mustard seeds should not be roasted in a pan but should be sun-dried and powdered.

TURMERIC POWDER
Can be made buying the long, thin variety of turmeric sticks (viral manjal). Sun-dry the turmeric sticks and grind at your local mill. Do not grind it at home as the mixer blade may break or wear off.

975 Spiced Bottle Gourd Peel : Hot

125 g	chopped bottle gourd peel
20 g	split husked black gram
10 g	dried red chillies, break into bits
10 g	cleaned tamarind
5 g	asafoetida
5 g	mustard seeds &
a few	sprigs curry leaves : both for seasoning
10 g	salt
30 ml	oil

1. Stir-fry the bottle gourd peel in a little oil and set aside.
2. In the same pan fry the black gram, red chillies and asafoetida in a little oil till done.
3. Cool the fried ingredients and grind together coarsely with the sauted peel.
4. Add in the tamarind, salt and grind again coarsely.
5. Heat oil, add the mustard seeds, curry leaves and allow to crackle.
6. Blend the seasoning into the ground mixture.
7. The pickle is ready for use. It keeps for 1 week and is best refrigerated.

976 Bottle Gourd Seed – Black Gram : Hot

125 g	mature bottle gourd seed, husk
15 g	split husked blackgram
10 g	cleaned tamarind
6 g	dried red chillies, break into bits
5 g	mustard seeds
5 g	asafoetida, roast in oil & powder
10 g	salt
30 ml	oil

1. Heat a little oil, fry the bottle gourd seeds till light brown and set aside.
2. In the same pan fry the blackgram, mustard seeds, red chillies in the remaining oil and set aside.
3. Grind both the roasted ingredients with the tamarind, asafoetida powder and salt using a little water.
4. The pickle is ready for use. It keeps for 2 weeks and is best refrigerated.

977 Cauliflower Stem – Green Spices : Hot

250 g	cauliflower stem, slice	4	green chillies, grind fine
10 ml	curd &	4	dried red chillies, break into bits
10 g	salt : both for marinating	3	cloves garlic, peel & chop fine
35 g	onion, peel & chop	2-1"	pieces of fresh ginger, scrape, chop & grind fine
15 g	green coriander, clean, air-dry, chop & grind		
15 g	dried mango powder	35 g	salt : for pickle
5 g	chilli powder	50 ml	oil

1. Marinate the sliced cauliflower stems in salt and curd.
2. Heat the oil and fry the red chillies till done. Follow with the chopped onion and cook till translucent.
3. Add in the marinated cauliflower stems, chopped garlic and cook till partly tender.
4. Stir in the ginger, coriander, green chilli pastes, dried mango powder, garam masala, chilli powders and salt.
5. Cook till well blended and remove.
6. The pickle is ready for use. It lasts for 1 month in the refrigerator.

978 Cauliflower Stem : Hot

500 g	cauliflower stem, slice thinly	5 g	dried mango powder
5 g	salt : for marinating	3 g	garam masala powder
20 g	green coriander, clean, air-dry & chop	4	green chillies, chop fine
20 g	peeled garlic &	4	dried red chillies, break into small bits
2-1"	pieces of fresh ginger, scrape & chop, grind both to a paste	200 ml	curd, whip with 100ml water & remove cream
		30 g	salt : for pickle
5 g	chilli powder	50 ml	oil

1. Blanch the sliced cauliflower stems in boiling water for 2 minutes.
2. Drain, pat-dry and marinate in the salt and curd for 30 minutes.
3. Stir-fry the green chillies and red chillies in a little oil.
4. Follow with the ginger-garlic paste and fry for a few minutes over low heat till done.
5. Stir in the remaining oil, the marinated cauliflower stem, dried mango, garam masala, chilli powders, chopped coriander, heat till well blended and remove.
6. The pickle is ready for use. It keeps for 1 week in the refrigerator.

979 Spicy Drumstick Leaf – Fenugreek Leaf paste : Hot

125 g	drumstick leaves;
15 g	fenugreek leaves &
15 g	green coriander, grind all three to a paste
40 g	onion, peel &
20 g	tomato, chop & grind to a paste
25 g	cleaned tamarind, obtain thick extract using water
25 g	jaggery, grate
1	green chilli, chop
5 g	chilli powder
5 g	turmeric powder
5 g	peppercorns;
5 g	coriander seeds &
3 g	cummin seeds, roast all three in oil & powder
2	cloves garlic, peel &
1"	piece of fresh ginger, scrape, chop both & grind fine
1	clove &
1"	stick of cinnamon, keep both whole
15 g	salt
100 ml	oil

1. Stir-fry the whole spices in a little oil. Add in the onion-tomato paste, ginger-garlic paste, and fry for a few minutes.
2. Add in the slit green chillies, the leaf paste and fry for a while over low heat. Set aside.
3. In the same pan, heat the remaining oil, stir in the tamarind extract, jaggery and bring to the boil. Allow to thicken over a high flame.
4. Stir in the fried spice pastes, the spice powders and salt.
5. Remove when the mixture becomes jam-like and the oil separates.
6. The pickle is ready for use. It lasts for 2 months.

980 Jackfruit Seed – Tamarind : Hot

500 g	jackfruit seeds, peel & wash
10 g	salt : for marinating
60 g	cleaned tamarind, obtain thick extract using water
50 g	dried red chillies &
10 g	mustard seeds, sun-dry both & powder
5 g	turmeric powder
75 g	salt : for pickle
100 ml	oil

1. Boil the jackfruit seeds in water to which two teaspoons (10g) salt has been added. Peel, halve, drain and air-dry.
2. Combine the spices with a little oil to a paste.
3. Stir in the cooked jackfruit seeds and sun for 4 days.
4. Pour over the remaining oil to cover.
5. The pickle is ready for use after 3 days. Stir daily. It lasts for 1 month. Sun occasionally.

981 Spiced Jackfruit Seed : Hot

500 g	jackfruit seeds, skin, steam-cook with salt & cut lengthwise into thin pieces
20 g	chilli powder
10 g	coriander seeds &
10 g	mustard seeds, sun-dry both & powder
30 g	salt
100 ml	oil

1. Combine the jackfruit pieces, chilli powder, salt and oil in a jar.
2. Sun the spiced jackfruit for 7 days.
3. On the 8th day blend in the coriander and mustard powders.
4. The pickle is ready for use after a week. It lasts for 2 months.

982 Jackfruit Seed – Green Spices : Instant

125 g	jackfruit seeds, peel outer skin & halve
25 g	grated coconut;
15 g	green chillies, chop &
10 g	green coriander, wash, air-dry & chop, grind all three with salt
3 g	mustard seeds;
3 g	split husked black gram &
a few	sprigs curry leaves, all three for seasoning
20 ml	lime juice
15 g	salt
15 ml	oil

1. Steam the jackfruit seeds with the salt till tender. Allow to cool, peel and crumble.
2. Combine the crumbled seeds with the green chilli-coconut paste.
3. Heat the oil, add the mustard seeds, black gram, curry leaves and fry till done.
4. Follow with the spiced crumbled jackfruit and cook over low heat for a few minutes.
5. Blend in the lime juice and remove when the mixture begins to bubble.
6. The pickle is ready for use. It keeps for 5 days and is best refrigerated.

983 Kumquat Leaf – Green Coriander – Gram : Instant

125 g	kumquat leaf &
250 g	green coriander, wash, air-dry & chop both
250 g	split husked black gram;
125 g	dried red chillies, break into bits &
125 g	cleaned tamarind, dry-roast all three separately
10 g	mustard seeds : for seasoning
75 g	salt
125 ml	oil

1. Heat a little oil, add mustard seeds and allow to crackle.
2. Add in the chopped kumquat leaf, green coriander and stir-fry for a few minutes.
3. Grind the fried leaves with the roasted ingredients and salt to a smooth paste.
4. Blend in the remaining oil after heating and cooling.
5. The pickle is ready for use. It keeps for 1 week.

984 Lime Leaf – Green Coriander – Gram : Instant

125 g	lime leaves &
250 g	green coriander, wash, air-dry & chop both
250 g	split husked black gram;
250 g	dried red chillies, break into bits &
125 g	cleaned tamarind, dry-roast all three & powder
10 g	asafoetida, roast in oil & powder
75 g	salt
150 ml	oil

1. Stir-fry the chopped lime leaf and coriander in oil. Remove and allow to cool.
2. Grind the fried leaves with the roasted ingredients and salt to a smooth paste.
3. The pickle is ready for use. It keeps for 1 week and is best refrigerated.

985 Lime Peel Paste : Hot

500 g	ground lime peel
75 g	jaggery, grate
50 g	chilli powder
5 g	fenugreek seeds &
5 g	asafoetida, roast both in oil & powder
5 g	turmeric powder
5 g	mustard seeds : for seasoning
100 g	salt
200 ml	groundnut oil : heat & cool

1. Add 50g salt to the lime peels and soak in the 5% citric acid solution for 20 days till the peels soften. Sun every day to speed up the process.
2. Grind the peels to a pulp.
3. Heat a little oil, add mustard seeds and allow to crackle. Add in the lime peel pulp and stir-fry for a few minutes.
4. Stir in the spice powders, jaggery, the remaining salt and oil.
5. Continue cooking over low heat until the mixture becomes jam-like and leaves the sides of the pan.
6. The pickle is ready for use. It lasts for 2 months.

986 Lime Peel : Watery

250 g	lime peel pieces
50 g	salt, make a solution with 600ml water
5 g	black salt
10 g	cummin seeds, dry-roast

1. Combine the lime pieces with the salt solution. Stir in the black salt.
2. Sun the mixture for 5 days.
3. Stir in the roasted cummin and set aside for a day.
4. The pickle is ready for use. It lasts for 1 month. Sun occasionally

987 Sour Mango Skin : Sweet

500 g	mango skins, chop
400 g	jaggery, grate
15 g	chilli powder
2-1"	pieces of fresh ginger, scrape & pound
120 ml	vinegar
30 g	salt

1. Boil the mango skins in sufficient water till tender and almost dry.
2. Lower the heat, stir in the chilli powder, jaggery, salt, ginger and vinegar.
3. Cook till the jaggery dissolves and the mixture reaches a single-thread consistency.
4. The pickle is ready for use after 3 days. It lasts for 1 month.

Leaves are always best when they are young and tender, but small size is not always an index of age; tender leaves of one variety may be larger than the fully grown leaves of another.

988 Mango Leaf in Tamarind Sauce : Hot

500 g	tender mango leaves, devein, wash & air-dry
60 g	cleaned tamarind, obtain thick extract using water
40 g	jaggery, grate
40 g	dried red chillies, dry-roast & powder
10 g	mustard seeds : for seasoning
10 g	turmeric powder
5 g	asafoetida, roast in oil & powder
60 g	salt
80 ml	oil

1. Stir-fry the mango leaves in a little oil. Allow to cool, grind coarsely and set aside.
2. Heat some more oil, add mustard seeds and allow to crackle.
3. Pour in the tamarind extract, jaggery, turmeric powder and the salt.
4. Bring to the boil and allow to thicken over a high flame.
5. Stir in the ground mango leaves, chilli, asafoetida powders and the remaining oil.
6. Continue cooking over low heat until the mixture becomes jam-like and the oil separates.
7. The pickle is ready for use. It lasts for 1 month.

> Young leaves are glossy, so avoid leaves that have developed the dull surface of maturity: and of course, reject specimens that are discoloured or limp.

989 Mixed Vegetable Peel in Nut Paste : Hot

100 g	pea pods, chop fine
100 g	carrot peel, chop fine
100 g	bottle gourd peel, chop fine
100 g	sweet potato peel, chop fine
100 g	turnip peel, chop fine
100 g	onion, peel & chop
20 g	cashewnut, halve;
15 g	poppy seeds, soak in warm water for 10 minutes &
20 g	shelled walnut, grind all three to a paste
100 g	tomato, chop
20 g	chilli powder
5 g	turmeric powder
5 g	garam masala powder
2-1"	pieces of fresh ginger, scrape &
3	cloves garlic, peel, chop both & grind to a paste
35 g	salt
150 ml	oil

1. Heat a little oil, add the ginger-garlic, nut pastes and fry for a few minutes. Set aside.
2. In the same pan, heat the remaining oil and fry the chopped onion till translucent.
3. Follow with the tomato, the chopped peels and cook till the mixture thickens.
4. Add in the chilli, turmeric, garam masala powders and the fried paste.
5. Remove when the mixture becomes jam-like and the oil separates.
6. The pickle is ready for use. It lasts for 1 month.

990 Sour & Spicy Raw Plantain Skin : Hot

500 g	raw plantain skins, cut into slivers
50 g	cleaned tamarind, obtain thick extract using water
30 g	jaggery, grate
40 g	onion, peel & chop
3	cloves garlic, peel
1-1"	piece of fresh ginger, scrape & chop
2	green chillies, chop
20 g	chilli powder
5 g	garam masala powder
5 g	turmeric powder
10 ml	lime juice
40 g	salt
50 ml	oil

1. Cook the slivered plantain skins with the tamarind extract over low heat till tender. Cool and grind to a paste.
2. Grind the onion, garlic, ginger and green chillies to a coarse paste.
3. Combine the plantain skin paste and the green spice paste with the chilli, garam masala, turmeric powders, jaggery and salt. Cook over low heat till well blended.
4. Stir in the lime juice and remove when the mixture begins to bubble.
5. The pickle is ready for use. It lasts for 1 month in the refrigerator.

991 Raw Plantain Skin – Raisin : Sweet

500 g	raw plantain skin, cut into slivers
500 g	seedless raisin, chop fine
500 g	jaggery, grate
20 g	chilli powder
2	cloves garlic, peel & slice
400 ml	vinegar
30 g	salt

1. Cook the slivered plantain skins over low heat, in water to which a teaspoon (5g) salt has been added, till tender. Drain and allow to dry.
2. Combine the chilli powder, garlic, jaggery, vinegar, salt with the cooked plantain skins. Cook over low heat till well blended.
3. Add in the raisin, stir well and remove.
4. The pickle is ready for use. It lasts for 3 months in the refrigerator.

992 Spicy Ridge Gourd Peel – Gram : Hot

500 g	ridge gourd peel, chop
50 g	green coriander, wash, air-dry & chop
50 g	split husked black gram
40 g	split husked bengal gram
40 g	cleaned tamarind, obtain thick extract using water
40 g	jaggery, grate
20 g	dried red chillies, break into bits
20 g	green chillies, chop
10 g	mustard seeds : for seasoning
10 g	asafoetida
60 g	salt
150 ml	oil

1. Dry-roast the gram, mustard seeds, asafoetida, red chillies, green chillies and set aside.
2. Stir-fry the green chilly, the chopped ridge gourd peel and the coriander in a little oil. Set aside.
3. Grind together the roasted spices with the fried ingredients and the salt.
4. Heat the remaining oil, add mustard seeds and allow to crackle.
5. Follow with the tamarind extract, jaggery and bring to the boil. Allow to thicken over a high flame.
6. Stir in the ground mixture and continue cooking over low heat. Remove when the mixture becomes jam-like and the oil separates.
7. The pickle is ready for use. It lasts for 2 months.

993 Steamed Ridge Gourd Peel : Instant

125 g	ridge gourd peel, chop
10 g	cleaned tamarind
10 g	jaggery, grate
7 g	green chillies, chop
5 g	dried red chillies, break into bits
3 g	asafoetida, roast in oil & powder
3 g	fenugreek seeds
3 g	split husked black gram
3 g	mustard seeds : for seasoning
12 g	salt
10 ml	groundnut oil

1. Steam the ridgegourd peel and allow to dry indoors on a clean cloth.
2. Stir-fry the steamed peel in a little oil and set aside.
3. In the same pan heat some more oil, add mustard seeds and allow to crackle. Add in the black gram and fry till golden.
4. Follow with the fenugreek seeds, chopped green chillies, broken red chillies, fry for a while and set aside.
5. Grind together all the ingredients with the asafoetida powder, tamarind, jaggery and salt coarsely.
6. The pickle is ready for use. It keeps for 2 weeks and longer in the refrigerator.

994 Sweet & Sour Mahani Peel : Hot

500 g	mahani peel
60 g	chilli powder
50 g	cleaned tamarind, obtain thick extract using water
100 g	jaggery, grate
20 ml	vinegar
100 g	salt
150 ml	oil

1. Soak the mahani pieces in rice-washed water overnight.
2. Drain out the water the next day and wash again in fresh water. Add in fresh rice-washed water to immerse the roots.
3. Remove the outer skin and discard. Peel the reddish skin and grind coarsely.
4. Heat the oil, add mustard seeds and allow to crackle.
5. Stir in the ground peel and fry for a few minutes.
6. Pour in the tamarind extract, jaggery, salt and bring to the boil.
7. Allow to thicken and add in the vinegar.
8. Remove when the mixture becomes jam-like and the oil separates.
9. The pickle is ready for use. It lasts for 2 months.

995 Spicy Snake Gourd Seed – Gram : Hot

500 g	snake gourd seeds, chop & roast in oil
50 g	green coriander, wash, air-dry & chop
50 g	split husked black gram
40 g	split husked bengal gram
40 g	jaggery, grate
30 g	cleaned tamarind, obtain thick extract using water
20 g	dried red chillies, break into bits
20 g	green chillies, chop
10 g	asafoetida, roast in oil & powder
10 g	mustard seeds : for seasoning
80 g	salt
200 ml	oil

1. Dry-roast the gram, asafoetida, red chillies, green chillies and set aside.
2. Stir-fry the chopped coriander in a little oil and set aside.
3. Grind together the roasted ingredients and the fried coriander with the roasted snake gourd seeds.
4. Heat the remaining oil, add mustard seeds and allow to crackle.
5. Pour in the tamarind extract, jaggery, salt and bring to the boil.
6. Allow to thicken over a high flame and stir in the ground mixture.
7. Continue cooking until the mixture becomes jam-like and the oil separates.
8. The pickle is ready for use. It lasts for 2 months.

Seeds
Within seeds are stored proteins, carbohydrates and minerals necessary to nourish embryonic plants. Much of their appeal has always been the ease with which they can be dried for storing.
Soak seeds overnight, drain and allow to dry on a thick towel. At short notice they may be soaked in warm water. However, wash the seeds thoroughly to remove any toxic chemicals. Take care to discard the stones and the decayed seeds carefully, before soaking.

996 Tender Tamarind Leaves : Instant

500 g	fresh tender tamarind leaves, wash & air-dry
50 g	chilli powder
5 g	fenugreek seeds &
3 g	asafoetida, roast both in oil & powder
3 g	turmeric powder
12 g	mustard seeds;
12 g	split husked black gram;
12 g	split husked bengal gram;
3	dried red chillies &
125 ml	oil : all for seasoning
100 g	salt

1. Stir-fry the tamarind leaves in a dry pan and set aside.
2. Grind the fried leaves with the chilli, turmeric, fenugreek, asafoetida powders and salt to a coarse paste.
3. Heat the oil, add mustard seeds and allow to crackle.
4. Add in the broken chillies, black gram, bengal gram and fry till the gram turns golden.
5. Pour the seasoning over the leaf mixture and blend well.
6. The pickle is ready for use. It lasts for 3 months.

997 Watermelom Rind – Onion - Tamarind : Instant

500 g	watermelon rind, peel & cut white portion into tiny bits
120 g	small onion, peel & chop
50 g	dried red chillies &
10 g	split husked black gram, dry-roast both & powder
20 g	cleaned tamarind, obtain thick extract using water
10 g	mustard seeds : for seasoning
5 g	tumeric powder
30 g	salt
100 ml	oil

1. Heat a little oil, add mustard seeds and allow to crackle.
2. Stir in the chopped onion, watermelon pieces and fry for a few minutes.
3. Pour in the tamarind extract and bring to the boil. Allow to thicken over a high flame.
4. Blend in the powdered spices, turmeric powder, salt and the remaining oil.
5. Continue cooking over low heat until the mixture becomes jam-like and the oil separates.
6. The pickle is ready for use. It lasts for 2 months.

998 Spiced Watermelon Rind : Instant

125 g	peeled watermelon rind, chop fine	2 g	garam masala powder;	
5 g	chilli powder;	2 g	turmeric powder &	
10 g	mustard seeds, sun-dry & powder;	2 g	asafoetida, roast in oil & powder, combine all evenly	
2 g	aniseeds, sun-dry both & powder;	25 ml	vinegar	
		10 g	salt	
		50 ml	oil	

1. Heat the oil and stir-fry the chopped rind till partly tender.
2. Stir in the spice mixture, salt and the vinegar.
3. Bring to the boil.
4. Continue cooking over low heat until the mixture leaves the sides of the pan.
5. The pickle is ready for use. It keeps for 1 week in the refrigerator.

999 Sweet & Sour Watermelon Rind : Instant

500 g	peeled watermelon rind, chop fine water sufficient to immerse
250 g	sugar
2	limes, slice thinly & seed
2	cloves, keep whole
1-1"	stick of cinnamon, keep whole
250 ml	vinegar
20 ml	lime juice
30 g	salt

1. Marinate the chopped rind in the salt overnight. Rinse and drain well.
2. Combine the lime juice, sugar and whole spices with the vinegar in a pan and bring to the boil.
3. Allow to simmer for 5 minutes, remove the spices and set aside.
4. Cook the salted rind in sufficient water until the rind becomes translucent.
5. Add in the lime slices, spiced vinegar, cook for 10 more minutes and remove.
6. The pickle is ready for use. It lasts for 2 months.

1000 Watermelon Rind in Spiced Vinegar : Instant

500 g	peeled watermelon rind, chop fine
10 g	salt : for marinating
500 g	sugar
250 ml	vinegar
20	peppercorns;
10 g	mustard seeds &
5	cloves, tie all three in a bag
30 g	salt : for pickle

1. Marinate the chopped rind in two teaspoons (10g) salt overnight. Rinse and drain well.
2. Heat the vinegar, sugar and salt along with the spice bag. Bring to the boil and allow to thicken.
3. Add in the salted rind and allow to simmer for 5 minutes.
4. Discard the spice bag after squeezing thoroughly.
5. The pickle is ready for use. It lasts for 2 months.

This is a reading and reference book on pickling.
For good measure, there are hundreds of hints, pickling basics and techniques –
in short, innumerable ways to transform pickle-making from a task to an adventure.

Appendix

Glossary

Index

Acknowledgements

Appendix

Adulterants Chart

FOOD STUFF	ADULTERANT	METHOD OF DETECTION
1) Asafoetida	Soapstone or other earthy matter	Shake with water. Soapstone or other earthy matter will settle down at the bottom. **Caution:** In compounded hing, due to the presence of starch (a certain percentage of starch is permissible by law), a slightly turbid solution may be produced. However, this will settle down after you keep the mixture aside for some time. b) Add tincture of iodine, indication of blue colour shows the presence of starch.
2) Black pepper	Dried seeds of papaya fruits	Papaya seeds are shrunken, oval in shape and greenish-brown or brownish-black in colour. They are also repulsive in flavour and quite distinct from the bite of black pepper.
3) Cardamom	Talcum powder	On rubbing, the talcum will stick to the fingers. On tasting, if hardly any aromatic taste is present, it indicates removal of essential oil.
4) Chilli powder	Brick powder, salt powder or talcum powder	Put a teaspoonful of chilli powder in a glass of water. Coloured water extract will show the presence of artificial colour. Any grittiness that may be felt on rubbing the sediment at the bottom of the glass confirms the presence of brick powder or sand. Soapy and smooth touch of the white residue at the bottom indicates the presence of soap-stone. **Caution:** This test is only for earthy material.
5) Cinnamon	Cassia bark	Added colour may come off in water.
6) Cummin seeds	Coloured grass seeds with charcoal dust	If rubbed in the hand, the fingers will turn black.
7) Gur (Jaggery)	Metanil yellow	Hydrochloric acid added to the jaggery will turn it a magenta red.
8) Edible oils	Argemone or poppy oil	Add concentrated nitric acid and shake carefully. Red to Reddish brown colour in the acid layer indicates the presence of argemone oil. **Caution:** Colourless (not yellowish) nitric acid may be used. Artifical colour, if present, will usually be a bright shade of colour, generally red or pink. The test therefore may sometimes give misleading results.

	Mineral oil	Take 2ml. edible oil and add an equal quantity of N/2 Alcoholic potash. Heat in a boiling water bath for about 15 minutes and add 10ml water. Any turbidity shows the presence of mineral oil. **Caution :** This test is not for minute traces.
	Castor oil	Dissolve some oil in petroleum in a test-tube and cool in ice-salt mixture. Presence of turbidity within five minutes indicates the presence of castor oil. **Caution :** This test is not for minute traces.
9) Lentils (Dals)	Kesari dal	Add 50ml of dilute hydrochloric acid to the lentils and keep on simmering in water for about 15 minutes. If pink colour develops it indicates that the presence of kesari dal. **Caution :** Metanil yellow, If present, will give similar colour immediately without simmering.
	Clay, stones, gravel, etc.,	Visual examination will reveal these adulterants.
	Lead chromate yellow	Shake 5 grams of dal with 5ml of water and add a few drops of hydrochloric acid. A pink colour shows the presence of colour.
10) Saffron (Kesari)	Dyed tendrils of maize cob	Genuine saffron will not break easily. Artifical saffron is prepared by soaking maize cob in sugar and colouring it with coal-tar dye, which dissolves in water.
11) Sugar	Chalk powder	Dissolve in a glass of water. Chalk will settle at the bottom.
12) Turmeric powder	Metanil yellow	Put a teaspoonful of turmeric powder in a test tube. Add a few drops of concentrated hydrochloric acid to it. The instant appearance of violet colour, which disappears on dilution with water, shows the presence of turmeric. If the colour persists, metanil yellow is indicated.
13) Wheat, bajra & other foodgrains	Ergot (a fungus)	Purple-black longer-sized grains in bajra show the presence of ergots. ii) Put some grains in a glass containing 20 per cent salt solution. Ergot floats over the surface while sound grains settle down.
	Dhatura seeds	Dhatura seeds resemble chilli seeds with blackish-brown colour. They can be separated by close examination.

Cooking Methods Chart

METHOD	WHAT IT IS	USED FOR	EFFECT ON NUTRIENTS
DRY HEAT			
Baking	Cooking in hot air, in a closed oven, wherein hot air circulates around the food placed in it.	Breads, cakes, biscuits, cookies, pies, pastries, puddings, eggs, au-gratins, vegetables like stuffed tomatoes etc.	
Grilling/Broiling	Cooking by radiant or direct heat under a grill or over a hot-fire. Also used as a final step to brown dishes as in au-gratins (where the dish is covered with sauce, bread crumbs or cheese and then baked or grilled).	Good quality meats, steaks, chops, fish, liver, kidney, chicken, vegetables like tomato, muhrooms etc.	
Roasting	Food is brought in contact with direct heat, from a flame or any source of radiant heat. The three ways it is done are : (a) in a pit (tandoor); (b) in an oven; or (c) in a thick heavy pan, with occasional basting (to moisten the food with melted fat or drippings). Barbecue or roasting food on skewers is also included in this. Roasting is also used as preliminary step (as in making of bharta) or as a final process (roasting potatoes).	Good quality meats, chicken, vegetables like potato, sweet potato and brinjal, cereals like broken wheat, vermicelli, naan, cooked in tandoor, etc.	B-Complex vitamins like thiamine and vitamin C are usually destroyed due to exposure to air and heat. However starch in foods, becomes easier to digest as it is broken down to dextrin which lends the brown colour to foods like chappatis, naans etc. Another advantage is that very little fat or oil is used in most dry heat methods. So it is the best for low calorie cooking.
FRYING			
Deep-fat frying	Cooking food in heated oil or fat. Frying food in a large amount of fat in a deep pan.	Puris, kachories, koftas, cutlets, pakoras, samosas, gujias, mathris, wadas, chips, fish, etc.	B-Complex and vitamin C are destroyed due to high temperature. Foods absorb lot of oil or fat and are therefore high in calories.

METHOD	WHAT IT IS	USED FOR	EFFECT ON NUTRIENTS
Sauteing	Frying and tossing food in a small amount of hot fat in a frying pan with rounded sides.	Vegetables like cabbage, beans, carrot, capsicum, beans, sprouts, onion, tomato, noodles etc.	Here there is less destruction of vitamins. Also best conserved, as foods are cooked in their own juices. Also low calorie foods can be made.
Shallow-fat frying	It is done in just enough fat to prevent sticking.	Eggs, parathas, dosas, pancakes, chillas, tikkis, naans, etc.	Same as above. Except where less fat is used in non-stick cookware. So foods could be low calorie as compared to deep fried.
MOIST HEAT			
Boiling	Cooking food in boiling water. The food is then allowed to simmer till done. Temperature of boiling is 100°C and that of simmering is between 80°-90°C. Boiling should be done in a covered pan of correct size using a minimum amount of water, sufficient to cover the food.	Vegetables like potato, cauliflower, etc eggs, rice, pasta, noodles, spagetti, etc.	If the food is boiled continuously, water is evaporated quickly, the structure and texture of the food product is affected adversely (damaged) and the loss of heat liable nutrients (vitamins C and B - complex) is increased. Low calorie nourishing food can be prepared if minimum amount of water and time is used and the pan is covered.
Steaming (a) Direct	Cooking food by surrounding with plenty of steam from fast boiling water. Done in an ordinary steamer or by putting food in a metal sieve over a pan of boiling water and keeping it covered.	Dhoklas, idlis, peas, carrot, sprouts etc.	Steaming, pressure cooking and stewing are the best methods for conserving nutrients. Also these are most nutritious with a low calorie benefit and easy to digest. In preparations like steamed sprouts, dhoklas, idlis, where fermentation is a prior step; nutrients like B-Complex and vitamins are enhanced in quantity and quality.
(b) Indirect	Steamed by having the food in a covered dish placed in a steam or boiling water. Cooking in aluminium foils also comes under this.	Steamed pudding and custards, chicken, meat, fish etc.	

METHOD	WHAT IT IS	USED FOR	EFFECT ON NUTRIENTS
Pressure Cooking	A form of steaming in which water is boiled under pressure, thus raising the temperature and reducing the cooking time.	Tough cuts of meat, chicken, vegetables and fruits.	
Stewing	Cooking in a covered pan using only a small quantity of liquid, which is kept simmering.	Tough cuts of meat, chicken, vegetables and fruits.	
COMBINATION METHOD			
Braising	Where roasting and stewing are combined.	Various meats, vegetables, upma etc.	Low calorie, nutritious food can be prepared. Less loss of nutrients.
MICROWAVE OVEN COOKING			
Microwave	Involves the use of high frequency electromagnetic waves (microwaves) which penetrate the food and produce functional heat by setting up vibrations within the food.	All types of food	Two advantages: (1) Quick method (within minutes) (2) Absence of heat in the oven. Less loss of nutrients. Low calorie food is prepared in less time and retention of the original colour of the food are added benefits.

Substitutes

- 250ml honey = 250g sugar in 75ml water
- Instead of tamarind, you can use slices of raw mango.
- When tomatoes are very expensive, use a dash of tomato sauce to give body and colour.
- The nearest substitute to jaggery or unrefined cane sugar is molasses.
- 3ml vinegar = 5ml lime juice
- Garlic powder can be used instead of fresh garlic. 1/4 teaspoon garlic powder is equal to 4 cloves of garlic.
- One teaspoon dried ginger powder is equivalent to 2 teaspoons fresh ginger (but soak dried ginger in ¼ cup of water).

Goodness Chart

CONSTITUENTS	SOURCES	FUNCTIONS	DEFICIENCY
Calcium	Nuts, green vegetables, woodapple, spinach, fenugreek leaves, etc.	Mainly required as a building material for strong bones and teeth. Essential element for several life processes	Heart contraction, muscle contraction will be impaired and the blood will not clot
Carbohydrates	Dry fruits, honey, potato, sugar, sweet potato, tapioca, wheat, etc.	It supplies the body with the normal daily energy requirement and is important when the body needs quick supplies of energy	Lack of energy, tendency to constipation
Fats	Nuts, soya bean, oils, dry fruits, etc.	It greatly adds to the calorific value of the diet. Its supply of energy is gradual and sustained. It builds up stores of energy, makes tissues firm and protects certain delicate organs from injury	Brings down resistance power
Iodine	Common salt, salt water, etc.	It is a constituent of thyroid hormones and is required in small amounts by the body	Causes goitre, a disease characterised by swelling of the thyroid gland in the neck
Iron	Celery, cucumber, lettuce, onion, pulses, spinach, tomato, whole wheat, spinach, fenugreek leaves, carrot, bitter gourd, etc.	It is essential for the body in the manufacture of haemoglobin	Causes anaemia
Phosphorous	Beans, grams, nuts, oilseeds, etc.	Its essential role is the assimilation of carbohydrates and fats	Causes improper bone development
Proteins	Amaranth leaves, beans, gram, fenugreek leaves, nuts, peas, wheat, etc.	It is derived from animal and vegetable sources and are important as body builders. It builds up flesh during years of growth and keeps the body in a state of good health throughout our lives	Causes natural breakdown of body tissues

CONSTITUENTS	SOURCES	FUNCTIONS	DEFICIENCY
Vitamin A	Apricot, cabbage, carrot, green leaves, drumstick, green peas, lettuce, ripe mango, papaya, peach, prunes, yellow pumpkin, spinach, tomato, etc.	Required for normal growth of the skeletal system, for a healthy skin. Necessary for good vision, protects the body against diseases - especially of the respiratory tract	Night blindness, impaired vision, leading ultimately to xerophthalmia (total blindness), skin disorders
Vitamin B/ Thiamine	Cabbage, celery, grams, green leafy vegetables like fenugreek leaves, turnip greens & beet greens, lettuce, nuts, pulses, pumpkin, tomato, spinach, whole grains (wheat), legumes (beans & peas) raisin, apple, plum, date, pomegranate, etc.	Essential for normal functioning of the nervous system. Required for carbohydrate metabolism	Deficiency is called 'Beri-beri'. Severe impairment of the nervous system, mental depression, weakness of the heart, loss of weight
Vitamin B2/ Riboflavin	Cereal, leafy vegetables, nuts, etc.	Essential for overall health, is an important component of coenzymes (which help the enzymes to act) like flavanoids, thereby assisting in many biochemical reactions	Inflammation of the tongue, inflammation of the mouth, eczema, cracking at the sides of the mouth
Vitamin B3/ Niacin/Nicotinic acid	Peanuts, cereal, whole grain, tomato, potato, banana, fig, etc.	Component of important coenzymes which regulate carbohydrate, fat and protein metabolism. Required for normal functioning of the nervous system	Deficiency is called 'Pellagra'. Diarrhoea, dermatitis, insomnia, dementia and death in extreme cases
Vitamin B6/ Pyridoxine	Avocado, banana, green leafy vegetables, whole grain, legumes, potato, etc.	Helps in the digestion and absorption of fats and proteins. Required for a normal nervous system and skin	Anaemia, dermatitis, mental depression, skin disorders, cardiac diseases, insomnia
Vitamin B12/ Cyanocobalamin	Soya bean milk, milk products, etc.	Essential for maturation of red blood cells. Also essential for several metabolic and enzymatic processes	Pernicious anaemia, degenerative changes of the nervous system

CONSTITUENTS	SOURCES	FUNCTIONS	DEFICIENCY
Vitamin C / Ascorbic acid	Bitter gourd, gooseberry, cabbage, cashew fruit, citrus fruits like orange, lemon, lime, grapefruit, drumstick, green pepper, green walnut, guava, onion, papaya, potato, spinach, sprouted pulses, strawberry, tomato, black currants, etc.	Essential for normal growth and maintenance of body tissues especially those of joints, bones, teeth and gums. Protects against infections, helps in iron absorption, in folic acid metabolism and perhaps cholesterol metabolism	Deficiency is called 'Scurvy'. Symptoms include loose teeth, bleeding gums, haemorrhagic tendency, anaemia, slow healing of wounds, premature ageing, growth retardation in infants / children
Vitamin D / Calciferols	Dairy produce, sunlight, etc.	Essential for proper formation of bones and teeth, for the absorption and metabolism of calcium and phosphorus	Deficiency is called 'Rickets'. Also there is tooth decay, pyorrhoea, osteomalacia (adult rickets), gross deficiencies of bones and muscular weakness
Vitamin E / Tocopherols	Vegetable oils, green leafy vegetables, whole grains, soya bean, nuts, dairy products, etc.	Potent anti-oxidant (protects vitamin A, polyunsaturated fatty acids, etc from oxidation) and plays a role in red blood cell generation. Influences utilization of sex hormones, cholesterol and vitamin D	Increased breakdown of red blood cells leading to anaemia. In animals, deficiency results in reproductive failure, anaemia and muscular degeneration
Vitamin K / Phylioquinone	Beetroot, carrot, green leafy vegetables, spinach, cereal, soya bean, etc.	Necessary for normal blood clotting	Increased tendency to haemorrhage, leading to anaemia

Eat fruits whole as they contain much more fibre than fruit juices. If taking fruit juices, do so without straining. Eat fruits with their peels. Peels are rich in vitamins and fibres. Fibre prevents constipation, thus flushing toxins safely out of the body before they can do any harm. Fibre is found not only in fruits but also in grain, seeds and vegetables. Fibre helps insulate the bowel wall from potential carcinogens.

Foodstuff Multi-Language Chart

ENGLISH	HINDI	TAMIL	TELUGU	MALAYALAM	KANNADA	BENGALI	GUJARATI	MARATHI	ORIYA	BOTANICAL NAME
Agathi grandiflora	Basna or Agasti	Ahathikai	Avasinara or Agise	Agathi	Agase or Agasthi	Buko or Bakful	Agathio	Basna or Agasti	Agasti	Sesbania grandiflora
Almond	Badam	Badam	Badam pappu	Badam	Badam	Badam	Bilati badam	Badam	Badam	Prunus amygdalus
Allspice or Pimenta		Kattukkaruva		Kappalmulaku	Gandamenasu					Pimenta officinalis
Amaranth leaves	Chaulai sag	Keera thandu	Thota koora	Cheru cheera	Dantu	Notya		Math-che-deth	Khada	Amaranthus gangeticus
		Ammantangal								
Apple	Seb	Apple pazham			Sebu	Sebu	Safarjan	Safar chand	Sev	Malus sylvestris
Apricot	Khoomani								Jardalu	Prunus armeniaca
Apricot, dried	Jardaloo								Kharikh	Prunus armeniaca
Asafoetida	Hing	Perungayam	Inguva	Perungayam	Hinger	Hing	Hing	Hing	Hingu	Ferula assafoetida
Asparagus root	Shatavar	Thaneer vitta kilangu	Challagadda	Shathaveri or Chataveli	Shatavari	Shatamuli	Satavar	Satavari muli		Asparagus officinalis
Bamboo shoot	Bans	Moongil Kuruthu	Veduru Chiguru	Mulan koombu		Bansher ankur	Vasasni kupal	Kalkipan	Baunsa gaja	Bambusa bambos
Banana ripe	Kela	Vazhapazham	Arati pandu	Vazha pazham	Bale hannu	Kala	Kela	Kele	Champa kadali	Musa paradisiaca
Basil	Tulsi, ram	Elumichan tulasi	Bhutulesi	Tulsi, rama	Tulasi, kari	Tulsi	Damaro	Marva, Sabza	Dhala tulasi	Ocimum sanctum
Bay leaf	Tej pat	Talishappattairi	Talisapatri		Bevina elae			Kaddhee nimbu		Cinnamomum tamala
Beans, broad	Bakla, sem	Avarai	Pedda chikkudi	Amarakka	Chapparadavare	Makhan sim	Fafda papdi	Valpapdi	Simba	Dolichos lablab
Beetroot	Chukandar	Beet	Beet	Beet	Beet	Bit palang	Beet	Beet	Bita	Beta vulgaris
Bel fruit	Bel or siriphal	Vilvam or Bilva pazham	Bilambu	Kuvalam pazham	Bilwapatre	Bel or siriphal	Bilwa phal		Bela	Aegle marmelos
Bengal gram, whole	Chana sabut	Kothukadalai	Sanagalu	Kadala	Kandale	Chola	Chana	Harbara	Buta	Cicer arietinum
Bengal gram	Chane-ki-dal	Kadalai paruppu	Sanaga pappu	Kadala parippu	Kadale bele	Cholar dal		Harbara dal		Cicer arietinum
Bengal gram, roasted	Chana sabut	Pottukadalai	Putnalu pappu	Varutha kadala	Huri kadale	Chola bhaja	Phutana	Phutana	Bhajabuta	Cicer arietinum
Bengal quince	Bel or siriphal	Vilwa pazham	Maredu pandu	Kuvvalam or Kulukam	Belapatri	Bel	Bil	Bel		Aegle marmelos
Bilimbi	Bilimbi	Pulithikal	Bilumbi	Bilimbi	Kamaleku	Kamranga	Bilimbu		Kamranga	Averrhoa bilimbi
Bitter gourd	Karela	Pavakkai	Kakara kayi	Kaipakka	Hagalkai	Karala	Karela	karle	Kalara	Monordica charantia
Bitter gourd, small	Chotta karela	Nila pavakkai								Monordica species
Bitterberry	Asheta	Sundakkai	Ustni kayi	Chundakka	Sondekai	Titbaigum				Solanum torvum
Blackberry	Jaman or jamoon	Naval pazham	Neredu pandu	Nthyaaval	Neralae	Kalojam	Jambudo	Jambhool	Jamukoli	Rubus fruticosus
Black cummin seeds	Kalajira or kalunji	Karun jiragam	Nullajilakara	Karunshiragam		Kalijira		Kalanjire		Nigella sativa
Black gram	Urd dal	Ulutham paruppu	Minapa pappu	Uzhunnu parippu	Uddina bele	Mashkalair dal	Aalad	Uddachi dal	Biri	Phaseolus mungo

ENGLISH	HINDI	TAMIL	TELUGU	MALAYALAM	KANNADA	BENGALI	GUJARATI	MARATHI	ORIYA	BOTANICAL NAME
Black grapes	Kala darakh	Kodi mundiri		Karuthu munthiringa						Citrus paradisi
Blacknightshade leaves	Makoy	Manathakkali Keerai	Kamanchi	Manathakkali cherra	Ganika	Kakmachi	Piludi			Solanum nigrum
Black salt	Kala namak									
Bottle gourd	Dodhi or Lauki	Suraikai	Anapakaya	Churakka	Sorekai	Lau or kodulau	Dudhi	Pandhara Bhopala	Lau	Lagenaria sicerana
Brinjal or Aubergine	Baingan or Vengna	Kathiri	Venkaya	Vazhuthininga	Doddabadane	Begun	Ringna	Vange	Baigen	Solanum melongena
Broccoli										Brassica oleracea var.
Brussels sprouts	Chotee goobee	Kalakose			Mara kosu	Bilati bandhakopi			Chota bandha kobi	Brassica oleracea var.
Buttermilk	Lassi	Moru	Majjiga	Moru	Majjige	Ghol	Chhas	Tak	Ghola dahi	
Cabbage	Bandh gobi	Muttaikose	Goskoora	Muttagose	Kosu	Bandhakopee	Kobi	Kobi	Bandha kopee	Brassica oleracea var.
Capsicum	Barra mirch	Koda milagai	Mirappakaya	Unda mulagu	Menssina kayi	Lanka bilathi	Marcha	Bhopli mirch	Lanka	Capsicum annuum
Caraway seeds	Siya jeera	Seema sombu	Sima jirakala	Seema jeeragum	Shime jeerige	Jeera	Safed jiraum	Wilayati zira		Carum carvi
Caradamom	Chhoti elaichi	Elakkai	Elakkayi	Elathari or Elakka	Yalakki	Choti elaichi	Elaychi	Veldoda or Velchi	Alaichi	Elettaria Cardamomum
Canssa carandas	Karonda	Kalakkai	Vaka	Karakka	Karikayi	Karomja		Kandya cha bean		Carissa carandas
Carrot	Gajar		Gajjara gadda		Gajjare	Gajar	Gajar	Gajar	Gajara	Daucus carrots
Cashewnut	Kaju	Mundiri paruppu	Jeedi pappu	Kasu andi	Geru beeja	Hijli badam	Kaji	Kaji	Lanka ambu manji	Anacardium occidentale
Cashew fruit	kaju phal	Mundiri pazham	Jeedi pandu	Kasu manga	Geru hanna	Hijli badam	Kaju phal	Kaju phal	Lanka amba	Anacardium occidentale
Cauliflower	Phool gobee	Kovippu	Khosu povvu		Hukosu	Kash or Phool kopi	Kash	Kash	Kash	Brassica oleracea var.
Celery seeds or thymol seeds	Shalari or Ajmud	Ajmoda		Ajmothakkam		Bandhuri or Chanu	Bodiajmoda	Ajmoda		Apium graveolens
Celery leaves	Ajwan-ka-patta					Randhuni sag	Ajmana pan		Juani patra	Apium graveolens
Cereal	Anna	Paruppu		Dhanyam		Anna		Kad dhanya		
Cherry	Aelche	Cherry pazham	Cherry pandu	Cherry pazham				Cheri		Prunus cerasus
Chilli Powder	Pissa hua lal mirch	Molgapodi	Mirapapodi	Molagu Podu		Lankar gooro		Lal thikhat		Capsicum annum
Choyote		Seemai kathirikai	Seemai venkayi		Seeme badame				Phuti kakudi	Sechium edule
Cinnamon	Dalchini	Lavanga pattai	Lavanga patta	Lavanga pattai	Dalchini	Dalchini	Dalchini	Dalhcini	Dalhcini	Cinnamomum Zeylanicum
Citron, sour	Bara nimbu	Kadarangai	Lungamu	Vadu naranga		Bara nimbu		Gitam limbu		Citrus medica
Citron, bitter	Khatta	Narthangai	Mellikanarangi	Kama						Citrus Aurantium
	Mitha nebu	Kolumichangai	Gajanimma			Mitha nebu				Citrus limettioides
Cloves	Lavang	Lavangam or Krambu	Lavangulu	Krambu	Lavanga	Lawang	Lavang	Luvang	Labang	Syzygium aromaticum

ENGLISH	HINDI	TAMIL	TELUGU	MALAYALAM	KANNADA	BENGALI	GUJARATI	MARATHI	ORIYA	BOTANICAL NAME
Cluster beans	Gavarphali	Kothavarankai	Gorchikudi	Kothavara		Jharsim	Govar	Govari	Guanra chhuta	Cyamopsis tetragonoloba
Coconut	Naryal	Thenga	Kobbari	Thenga	Thengini kai	Narkel	Nariyal	Naral	Nadia	Cocos nucifera
Coconut, dried	Copra	Copra		Copra		Copra		Suke khobra		Cocos nucifera
Cocum	Cocum or kokum	Mergal		Punampuli or Kodumpuli	Murgala	Kokam	Kokan	Amsol, kokam		Garcinia indica
Coleus	Panjiri-ka-pat	Karpuravalli	Karpuravalli	Paturkurkka		Paterchur				Coleus amboinicus
Colocasia or yam	Arbi, kachaki	Seppam kizhangu	Chana dumpa	Chembu	Samagadde	Kochu	Alvi	Alu kandu	Saru	Colocasia esculenta
Colocasia leaves	Arvi-ka-sag	Seppam ilaigal	Chama akulu	Chembu ilegal	Shamagadde yele	Kochu sag		Alu pan	Sarue	Colocasia esculenta
Cooking apple	Khatta seb							Safar chand		Malus sylvestris
Coriander leaves	Hara dhania	Kothamalli	Kothimiri	Kothamalli	Kothambari soppu	Dhane sag	Kothmer	Kothimbir	Dhania	Coriandrum sativum
Coriander powder	Pissa sukha dhania	Kothamalli Podi		Malli Podi		Guro dhane		Dhania chi pud		Coriandrum sativum
Coriander seeds	Sukha Dhania	Kothamalli Vidhai	Dhaniyalu	Kothambalari bija	Kothambari	Aasto dhane	Libdhana	Dhane	Dhania	Coriandrum sativum
Corn-on-the-cob	Makkai buttha	Makka cholam	Mokka junna	Makka cholam	Musukina jola	Butta	Makai	Jondla	Makka	Zea mays
Cow peas	Bora or Lobia	Thattapayeru	Alchandalu	Thattapayeru	Alasanda	Barbali		Chali	Bargada or Chani	Vigna sinensis
Cucumber	Khira or kakri	Kakkarikai or Vellarikai	Dosakayi	Vellarikai	Sou te kayi	Sasha or soshi	Kakdi	Kakadi	Kakudi	Cucumis sativus
Cummin seeds	Safed jeera	Jeerakum	Jeelakarra	Jeerakum	Jeerage	Jira	Jiru	Zerigire	Jira	Cuminum cyminum
Curd	Dahi	Thayir	Perugu	Thayir	Mosaru	Doyi	Dahi	Dahin	Dahi	
Curry leaves	Gandhela	Kariveppilai	Karivepaku	Kariveppilai	Karibevu	Bursunga	Kadhi limbdo	Kadhi limb	Bursunga	Murraya koenigi
Curry lime			Gajanimma	Vadugapuli						
Currants	Kismis or Angur		Munthri or draaksha		Onadrakshee	Angur	Mudraka	Manuka	Angura	
Custard apple	Andoos or Sitaphul	Sitappalam	Sitaapandu	Atha chakka	Sita phala	Aata phol		Sitaphal		Anona squamosa
Date	Khajoor	Pericham pazham	Kharjoora pandu	Eethapazham	Kajjuradha hannu	Khejur	Khajur	Khajur	Khajuri	Phoenix dactylifera
Date, dried immature	Kharak	Pericham pinju		Eethapazham				Kharik		Phoenix dactylifera
Dill leaves	Soya or sowa	Sata kuppi sompa	Sabasige	Sata kuppa	Sabasige	Sowa, soya	Surva	Surva, shepu		Anethum sowa
		Tuduvalai	Tellavuste	Tutavalam	Mullumusta					Solanum trilobatum
Dried red chilli	Sabta lal mirch	Milagai vatral	Enda mirapakayalu	Chuvanna mulagu		Sukno lanka		Lal mirchi		Capsicum annum
Drumstick	Saijan-ki-phali	Muringakkai	Mulaga kada	Muringakkai	Nugge kayi	Sajna danta	Saragavo	Shevangya chi sheng	Sajana chhuin	Moringa oleifera
Drumstick flower	Saijan-ki-phool	Muringarpoo		Muringapoovu		Sajne phool		Shevangya chi puul		Moringa oleifera
Drumstick leaves	Saijan patta	Murungai keerai	Mulaga akulu	Muringa ela	Negge yele	Sajna sag	Saragavo	Shevangya chi pala	Sajna sag	Moringa oleifera
Elephant apple										

ENGLISH	HINDI	TAMIL	TELUGU	MALAYALAM	KANNADA	BENGALI	GUJARATI	MARATHI	ORIYA	BOTANICAL NAME
Elephant yam	Zaminkand	Senai kizhangu	Kanda dumpa	Chena, valuthu	Suvarna gadde	Ol kochu or Suran	Suran	Suran	Hathi khojla alu	Amorphophallus campanulatus
Fennel seeds	Saunf	Sombu	Pedda jilakara	Perum jeeragum or Shombu	Badi sompu	Muhuri	Anisi or Sowa	Badi shep		Foeniculum vulgare
Fenugreek leaves	Methi sag	Venthiya keerai	Menth koora	Uluva ila	Menthiina soopu	Methi sag	Methi	Methi chi patta	Methi sag	Trigonella foenum graecum
Fenugreek seeds	Methi Ka Beej	Venthayam	Menthulu	Uluva	Menthe	Methi	Methi	Methi	Methi	Trigonella foenum graecum
Fig, wild	Gular	Athi	Athi	Athi	Athi	Oummur	Umbaro	Umbar or Rumbadi	Dimure	Ficus carica
Fig, dried	Sookha anjeer	Atti pazham	Athi pallu	Atti pazham	Anjura	Dumoor	Anjeer	Anjeer	Dimiri	Ficus carica
French beans	Rajmah or Bakla		Barigalu		Tingalanari	Barbati	Phanasi	Shravangheveda		Phaseolus vulgaris
Garlic	Lehsan	Ulli poondu	Vellulli	Vellulli	Bellulli	Rashun	Lasan	Lasoon	Rasuna	Allium sativum
Gherkins	Tendli	Kaavai or koovarai	Kaki donda	Kova or kovel	Thonde kayi	Telakucha		Thendlee	Kunduri	
Ginger, fresh	Adhrak	Inji	Altam	Inji	Shunti	Ada	Adu	Ale	Ada	Zingiber officinale
Ginger, dried	Saunt	Chuchoo	Sonti	Chukku				Sunte		Zingiber officinale
Gingelly seeds	Til	Ellu	Nuvvulu	Ellu	Acchellu	Til	Taj	Til	Rasi	Sesamum indicum
Gooseberry, Indian	Amla	Nellikai	Usirikayi	Nellikai	Nellikai	Amlaki	Amla	Aavla	Amla	Emblica officinalis
Gooseberry, star	Hartarowrie	Aranelli	Racha usirikayi	Aranelli	Aranelli	Hariphal		Rai avala		Phyllanthus acidus
Grapes	Angoor or Darakh	Draksha	Draksha	Mundiringa	Draksha	Angoor	Draksha	Draksha	Fbada angur	Vitis vinifera
Green chillies	Hari mirch	Pacha milagai		Pacha milagu		Kaacha lanka		Hirvi mirchi		Capsicum annum
Green gram, whole	Sabut mung	Pasipayir	Pesalu	Cheru payaru	Hesara kalu	Aasto sabooj chola	Mug	Mung	Muga	Phaseolus aureus
Green gram	Dhuli mung dal	Payatham paruppu	Pesara pappu	Cheru payar parippu	Hesara bele	Sabooj mung dal		Mug dal		Phaseolus aureus
Green pepper	Gol Hari Mirch	Pacha Milagu		Pacha kuru mulagu				Hirvi mire		Piper nigrum
Green tomato, raw	Haras tomato	Pacha thakkali		Pacha thakkali		Kaacha tomato		Hirvi tomato		Trachyspermun ammi
Green tamarind, raw	Imli or amli	Puli	Chinthakayi			Kaacha te tool		Hirvi chinch		Tamarindus indica
Groundnut	Moong phali	Nilakkadalai	Verusanaga	Nilakkadalai	Kadale kayi	China badam	Bhoising	Shend dane	China badam	Arachis hypogaea
Guava	Amrud or Peru	Koya pazham	Jami pandu	Perakka	Seeba	Payra	Jam phal	Peru	Pijuli	Psidium guajava
Guntur sour orange			Kichilikai							Citrus maderaspatana
Honey	Shaid	Then	Thene	Then	Tenthuppa	Mou		Pend or madh		
Horse gram	Kulthi	Kollu	Ulavalu	Muthira	Huruie	Kulthi kalai	Kuleeth	Kuleeth	Kolatha	Dolichos biflorus
Horse radish	Sufaid moolae			Mullanki		Saada moole		Saled mula		Cochlearia armoracia
Indian pennywort	Brahma manduki	Vallarai or ollarai	Manduka brahma	Kodangal or Kudakam	Ondelaga	Tholkhuri or thankuni	Karbbrahmi	Karivana or Brahmi	Thalakudi	Centella asiatica
Jackfruit, ripe	Kathal	Pala pazham	Panasa	Chakka	Halasu	Kanthal	Phanas	Fanasa	Panasa	Artocarpus heterophyllus
Jackfruit seeds	Kathal-ka-beej	Pala kottai		Chakka kuri				Fanasa chi bean		Artocarpus heterophyllus

ENGLISH	HINDI	TAMIL	TELUGU	MALAYALAM	KANNADA	BENGALI	GUJARATI	MARATHI	ORIYA	BOTANICAL NAME
Jackfruit, tender	Fannas or Katahal	Pila pinchu	Panasa	Idichakka	Halasu, yela	Eechor	Kawla phanas	Fanasa	Panasa katha	Artocarpus heterophyllus
Jaggery	Gur	Vellum	Bellum	Vellam	Bhella	Gud or gur	Gol	Gul	Guda	
Jerusalem artichoke	Hatichok									Helianthus tuberosus
Jujube or Indian plum	Ber	Elandapazham	Regu pandu	Elandapazham	Yelachi	Kool	Bor	Boor	Barakoli	Zizyphus jujuba
Knol kohl	Ganth gobi	Knol khol	Knol khol	Knol khol		Ol kopi	Nol kol	Nol kol	Ulkobi	Brassica oleracea
	Keduri or kanduri	Kovakkai or koval	Donda kaya	Kovakkai	Tondekayi	Telakucha	Ghole gluru	Tondale	Kunduru	Coccinia indica
Lady's finger or okra	Bhindi or Bheenda	Vendakkai	Benda kayi	Vendakkai	Bende	Dherash	Bhinda	Bhendi	Bhendi	Abelmoschus esculentus
Lentil	Masur dal	Mysore paruppu	Misur pappu	Masur Parippu	Masur bele	Musoorir dal	Masur dal	Masur dal	Masura	
Lettuce leaves	Salad patta or kahu	Saladhu	Kavu	Uvar cheera		Salad pata	Salat	Lettuce		Lactuca sativa
Litchi	Lichi	Ilichi				Lichu		Litchi		Litchi chinensis
Lime	Neembu	Elumichai	Nimma pandu	Cherunaranga	Nimbe	Lebu	Kagzi limbu	Limbu	Gangakulia lembu	Citrus aurantifolia
Lime leaves	Nimbu-ka-patha	Narthella		Cherunaranga ela		Lebur paata		Limbu chi paan		Citrus aurantifolia
Lime peel	Neebu ka chilka	Elumicham thol	Nimma thokku	Charu naranga tholi	Nimbe sippal	Lebur khosa	Limbuni chal	Limbsal	Lembri chopa	Citrus medica var acida
Loquat	Lokat	Lakot pazham	Lokat	Lakot pazham	Laquot			Lukat		Eriobotrya japonica
Lotus stem	Kamal kakri	Thamara thandu	Thamara kadu	Thamara thandu				Kamala cha denta		Nelumbium nelumbo
Lotus root	Kamal ke jadh	Thamara kizhangu	Thamara dumpa	Thamara kizhangu	Kamla dambu					Nelumbium nelumbo
Love-lovi				Lololikka						
Mace	Javitri	Jathipatri	Japathiri	Jathipatri	Japathri	Jaytri	Jaypatri	Jaypatri	Jayitri	Myristica fragranse
Mango, ripe	Aam, paka	Mam pazham	Mamidi pandu	Mam pazham	Mavina hannu	Aam, pake	Keri	Amba, pikiela	Amba, pachila	Mangifera indica
Mango ginger	Am hatdi	Ma inji	Mamidi allam	Manga inji	Mavina hasisunthi	Amada		Ambehaldi		Curcuma amada
Mango powder	Amchoor	Mangai podi		Manga podi				Amchur		Mangifera indica
Mango, raw	Am	Manga	Mamidi kayi	Manga, pacha	Mavinakayi	Am, kancha	Ambo	Kairi	Ambu, kancha	Mangifera indica
Mango, tender		Vadumangai		Kanni manga						Mangifera indica
Mango leaves	Amchoor patta	Mavilai	Mamidi	Mavila	Mavu	Aam saraa		Amba chi paan		Mangifera indica
Marjoram, sweet	Marwa or Ban tulsi	Maruvu or Maru		Maruvamu	Maruga	Murru				Majorana hortensis
Marrow	Safed kaddu				Dilpasand	Dhudul or kakri		Kashi bhopla	Golu phuti kakuri	Cucurbita pepo
Mint leaves	Pudinah	Puthina	Pudina	Putiyana	Chetni maragu	Pudina sag	Pudina	Pudina	Podana patra	Mentha arvensis
Moth	Moth	Narippayir					Mut	Matid		Phaseolus aconitifolius
	Kanphuti	Mudukottan keerai	Budda kakara			Sibjhul	Karolis	Kapat phodi		Cardiospermum halicacabum
Mulberry	Shainture or thuth	Musukkottai pazham	Reshmichettu	Yusham	Hipnerle	Thuth	Shalur	Thuth		Morus acedosa

ENGLISH	HINDI	TAMIL	TELUGU	MALAYALAM	KANNADA	BENGALI	GUJARATI	MARATHI	ORIYA	BOTANICAL NAME
Mushroom	Goochi or Guchian	Kalaan	Kukka godugu	Koon				Kuthra chi chatri		
Mustard greens	Sarson-ka-sag	Kadugu ilai	Ava akulu	Kadugu ila	Sasuva yele	Sorisa sag		Mohari-chi pan		Brassica species
Mustard seeds	Rai or Sarson	Kadugu	Avalu	Kadugu	Sasuve	Sorsu	Rai	Mohori	Sorisa	Brassica nigra
Mustard seeds, wild	Halhal or hurhut	Nayikadugu	Kukhavomanta	Ariavila		Hurhuria				Cleome icosandra
		Naravalikai								
Neem leaves, margosa	Neem-ke-patte	Veppilai	Vepa akulu	Arya veppila	Bevu	Neem pata	Limdo limba	Kadu limb	Nima patra	Azadirachta indica
Neem flower	Neem-ka-phool	Vepampoo		Arya veppin poovu		Neemer phool		Kadi limba cha phut		Azadirachta indica
Malabar banana		Malabar vazhai pazham		Nendran						Musa paradisiaca
		Nilathavarai poovoo								
Noga tanga - Assam										
Nutmeg	Jaiphal	Jadhikai	Jajikaya	Jadhikai	Jaggi kayi	Jaiphal	Jaiphal	Jaiphal	Jaiphal	Myristica fragrans
Nutringgets										
Olive, raw	Jaithun or Jalpal					Jalpai				Olea europaea
Olive, ripe	Jaithun					Jalpai, paka				Olea europaea
Onion	Pyaz or kanda	Vengayam	Neerulli	Ulli	Nirulli	Pyaz	Kande	Kanda	Piaja	Allium cepa
Onion, spring	Hara pyaj	Vengaya thandu	Ulli kadalu	Ulli thandu	Eerulli soppu	Piysz kali	Dungline dakkadi	Kandya chi path	Piaja sandha	Allium cepa
Orange	Narangi	Kichili pazham	Kamala pandu	Madhura naranga	Kithilai	Kamala lebu	Santra	Santre	Kamala	Citrus aurantium
Orange peel	Narangi-ka-chilka	Orange thol		Madhura narenga thol		Kamala lebur khasa		Santra chi saal		
Papaya, raw green	Kacha papita	Pappaikkai	Boppaykayi	Pacha omakai	Parangi	Kacha pepe	Papayi	Papayi		Carica papaya
Papaya, ripe	Papita	Pappali pazham	Boppayi pandu	Omakai	Pharangi	Pope paka	Papaya	Pcpai	Amrut bhanda	Carica papaya
Peach	Aarhoo				Marasebu			Peach	Piccuu	Prunus persica
Pears	Nashpati	Berikai	Berikai	Sabaraja	Berikai	Nashpati	Nashpati	Naspati	Nashpati	Pyrus communis
Peas	Matar	Pattani	Batani	Pattani	Batani	Matar	Vatana	Matar	Matora	Pisum sativum
Peppercorns	Gol kali mirch	Milagu	Miriyalu	Kurumulagu	Kari menasu	Golmarich	Kala mari	Mire	Golmarich	Piper nigrum
Pineapple	Ananas	Anasi pazham	Anasa pandu	Kaytha chakka	Ananas	Anarash	Ananas	Ananas	Sapuri Anasianas	Ananas comosus
Pistachio nuts	Pista	Pista	Pista	Pista	Pista	Pesta	Pista	Piste	Pista	Pistacia vera
Plantain, raw	Kela or Kera, raw	Vazhakkai	Arati kayi	Vazhakkai	Bale kayi	Kola, kanchi	Kela	Kele	Bantala kadali	Musa sapientum
Plantain flower	Kele ka phool	Vazhaipoo	Arati puvvu	Vazhapoo	Bale motho	Mocha	Kel phool	Kel phool	Kadali bhanda	Musa sapientum
Plantain skin	Kele ka chilka	Vazhai thol		Vazha thol		Kalar chaal		Kal phoot chi sal pat		Musa sapientum
Plantain stem	Kele ka tana	Vazhai thandu	Arati doota	Unni pindi	Dinda	Thor	Kelanu thed	Kelicha khunt	Kadali manja	Musa sapientum

ENGLISH	HINDI	TAMIL	TELUGU	MALAYALAM	KANNADA	BENGALI	GUJARATI	MARATHI	ORIYA	BOTANICAL NAME
Plums	Alubokhara	Alpagoda	Alpagoda			Alubokhara				Prunus domestica
Pomegranate	Anar	Mathalam pazham	Danimma pandu	Mathalam pazham	Dalimbari	Dalim	Dalamb	Dalimb	Dalimba	Punica granatum
Pomegranate seeds	Anardana	Madhulai vidai				Bedana		Dalimba chi dana		Punica granatum
Pommellos	Chakotra	Bombilimas	Pampara panasa	Bombilimas	Chakkota	Batabi lebu	Papnas	Papanas	Batapi lembu	Citrus maxima
Poppy seeds	Khus khus	Khasakhasa	Gasagasalu	Khasa khasa	Gasgase	Posto or kaskash	Khuskhush	Khaskhas		Papaver somniferum
Potato	Aloo or batata	Urulai kizhangu	Alu gaddalu	Urula kizhangu	Allu gadda	Gol alu	Batata	Batata	Alu	Solanum tuberosum
Prunes, dried	Alubokhara									
Pumpkin seeds		Pusani vithai	Gummadi ginjalu	Mathan vithugal		Kumdar dana		Bhoplya chi bean		Cucurbita maxima
Pumpkin, red	Koru or kaddu	Parangikai	Gummadi kayi	Mathanga	Kumbola	Kumra	Kohlu	Lal bhopla	Kakharu	Cucurbita maxima
Pumpkin, white or Ashgourd	Petha	Pocsinikai	Boodida gummudi	Kumbalanga	Budagumbala	Chalkumra	Vherukohlu	Kohala	Panikakharu	Benincasa hispida
Radish, white	Moolee or moora	Vella Mullangi	Mullangi	Mullangi	Moolangi	Mulo	Mula	Phandra mule	Mula	Raphanus sativus
Radish, red	Lal moolee	Sigappu mullangi				Laal mulo		Lal mule		Raphanus sativus
Raisin	Kishmish	Drakshai	Yendu dhaksha	Vonagidha dracshi	Drakshi	Kishmish	Kishmish	Bedana	Kishmish	Vitis vanifera
Raspberry	Rashbary									
Red gram	Arhar dal	Turvaram paruppu	Kandi pappu	Tarvara parippu	Thugare bele	Arhar dal	Tuver	Mosur chi dal	Harada	Cajanus cajan
Red chillies, fresh	Lal mirch	Milagai pazham		Chuvanna mulago		Lanka, paka		Thazi lal mirchi		Capsicum annum
Rhubarb	Revandchini	Revalchini	Revalchiani			Revanchini				Rheum emodi
Ridge gourd	Tooria or Toori	Peerkangai	Beera kayi	Peechinga	Heeraikai	Jhinga	Teria	Dodka	Janchi	Luffa acutangula
Ridge gourd skin	Toori-ka-chilka	Peerkangal thol						Dodkya chi seal		Luffa acutangula
Rose apple	Sufaid jambhul	Pannirkoyya	Gulab jamen	Jambakka	Panneeralai hannu	Jamrul	Gulab jambu	jambhool	Chota pijuli	Syzygium jambos
Rosemary	Rusmary									Rosmarinus officinalis
Saffron	Kesar or zafran	Kunkuma poo	Kumkumpuvvu	Kesaram or kumkum	Kunkuma kesari	Jafran	Keshar	Keshar		Crocus sativus
Sage	Salvia or sefakuss									Salvia officinalis
Salt	Namak	Uppu	Uppu Podi	Uppu		Noon		Meet		
Sarasaparilla root	Choochini	Mahani kizhangu	Sugandhi pala	Nannari kizhangu	Makali beru	Kumarika		Ghotvel or uparsari	Kumbatas	Decalepis hamiltonii
Sesame seeds	Til	Ellu	Navvulu	Ellu	Acchellu	Til	Tal	Til	Rasi	Sesamum indicum
Snake gourd	Padwal or Chochega	Podalangai	Potle kayi	Padavalanga	Padavala	Chichinga or potol	Pandola	Padwal	Chachinda or Potala	Trichosanthes anguina
Sodium benzoate	Mestha soda					Khabar soda				
Sorrel leaves or Red roselle	Lal ambadi	Puiicha keerai	Gonkura			Mestapal		Ambaadi		Hibiscus cannabinus
Soya bean										Glycine max merr
Spinach	Palak or kash	Pasalai keerai	Bachchali Koora	Basala cheera	Palang sag	Palak or shak	Palak	Palak sag	Palang sag	Spinacia oleracea

ENGLISH	HINDI	TAMIL	TELUGU	MALAYALAM	KANNADA	BENGALI	GUJARATI	MARATHI	ORIYA	BOTANICAL NAME
Star anise	Anasphal	Anashuppu, anasipu	Anaspuvu					Badian		Illicium verum
Star fruit	Kamrakh									Averrhoa carambola
Sugar	Shakur	Chakeray	Panchasara	Panchasara	Sakkari	Chini		Saakhar		
Sugar candy		Kalkandu	Kalakanda		Kal sakkare					
Sugarcane	Ganna or Sherdi	Karumbu	Cheraku	Karimbu	Ikshu	Ganna				Saccharum officinarum
Sultanas	Kismis or munakka			Munthiringa		Baro kismis		Menuka		Vitis vinifera
Sweet potato	Sakar kund	Sakaravalli kizhangi	Chilagada dumpa	Sakaravalli kizhangu	Genasa	Ranga alu	Sakkaria	Ratalu or rataali	Kandamula	Ipomoea batatas
Tamarind	Imli	Puliyankai	Chintapandu	Puli	Hunise hannu	Tetul	Amli	Chinch	Tentuli	Tamarindus indica
Tamarind leaves	Imli patte	Puli ilaigal	Chinta chiguru	Puli ilaigal	Hunise chiguru	Tetul pata		Chinchecha pala		Tamarindus indica
Tamarind ripe	Imli	Puli				Paaka tetul		Chinch		Tamarindus indica
Tapioca or sago	Sabudhana	Maravalli kizhangu	Karrapendalamu	Marachini	Mara genasu	Simla alu or sabu			Kathakanda	Manihot esculenta
Tarragon										Arpemisia dracunculus
Tekheda - Aassam										
		Thammatangai								
		Thethangkottai								Strychnos potatorum
Thymol seeds	Ajwain	Omam	Vamu	Omum	Oma	Jowan	Yavan	Onva	Juani	Trachyspermum ammi
Tomato ripe	Tamatar	Thakkali		Thakkali pazham		Tomato		Lal tomato		Lycopersicon esculentum
Turmeric	Haldi	Manjal	Pasupu Podi	Manjal	Arishina	Holud	Haldhar	Halad	Haladi	Curcuma longa
Turnip	Shalgam or ghogroo					Shalgam		Shalgam or Naval kol		Brassica rapa
	Hadjora	Pirandal	Nalleru	Changaperanda	Sundu balli	Horjora			Siji	Vitis quadrangularis
Vinegar	Sirka	Gadi								
Walnut	Akhrot	Akrottu	Nettu akoti vittu	Akrotu or nettumchadi	Akrodu or Akrodaa	Akhrot	Akhrot	Akroda or akrrod	Akhoot	Juglans regia
Watercress	Jal kumhi	Alli ilai			Alvi		Asalia	Ahliv	Brahmi sag	Nasturtium fontanum
Watermelon	Tarbus or kalingar	Darbusini	Puchakayi	Thannir mathan	Kallan gadi	Tarmuj	Tarbuj	Kalingad	Tarvuja	Citrullus vulgaris
Water melon, rind						Tarmujer khosa				
Wheat	Gehoon	Godumal	Godhumalu	Godhambu	Godhi	Gorn	Ghau	Gahu	Gahama	Triticum aestivum
White gourd or Round gourd	Tinda					Tinda	Tadabuch			Citrullus vulgaris
Winged beans		Chatura avarai		Chaturanchikdikai						Psophocarpus tetragonolobus
Woodapple, raw	Kaith	Vilam pazham	Velaga pandu	Vilam pazham	Baelada hannu	Kath bael	Kotha	Kavath kavat	Kaintha	Feronia limonia
Woodapple, ripe						Kathbel or paaka		Pikela kavat		
Yam		Pidikarnai								

Glossary

PICKLING VOCABULARY

Pickling vocabulary identifies and clarifies cooking terms frequently used in this book with particular reference to pickling, this being a rather specialised area.

Some of the words like cook, cool, cut may seem rather simple but some as for instance, julienne, puree, seed, smoking point etc., may require more than a working knowledge of the English language.

It would be worthwhile to go through these terms before embarking on pickling, as exactness and accuracy comes with a proper appreciation of the instructions spelt out in the recipe.

AIR-DRY
- To dry by exposure to air.

BLANCH
- To dip in boiling water in order to remove the skin. To cover tomato or whatever fruit or vegetable you want to blanch with cold water and bring to the boil. Reduce heat and simmer gently till you find the skin of that which you are blanching wrinkly. Remove from the heat at once. Drain and cover with cold water, then peel off the skin.

- Kernels of nuts like almonds and pistachios are put into boiling water for 2-3 minutes. They are then transferred to cold water and their skins peeled off. Soaking in cold water prevents shrivelling.

BLEND
- To combine or mix two or more ingredients thoroughly till smooth.

BOIL
- To cook in boiling water and drain off. To heat a liquid until bubbles appear on the surface and the vapour starts rising.

BRINE
- A salt and water solution for pickling.

BRUSH
- To apply oil, buttermilk etc lightly.

CHOP FINE
- To cut into fine particles or pieces eg. onions.

CHUNKS
- A thick mass or lump of anything eg. chunks of pineappple.

COARSE
- Composed of relatively large particles and rough in texture.

COMBINE
- To mix two or more ingredients together.

CONSISTENCY
- The back of a spoon after it is dipped in a mixture and remvoed quickly.

COOK
- To prepare (food) by the action of heat as by boiling, baking, roasting etc.

COOL
- Moderately cold; neither warm nor cold.

CORE
- To remove the inner portion of an apple, pear etc.

CRUSH
- Mash dry food to a coarse powder.

CUBE
- A solid bounded by 6 equal squares. To cut into small equal pieces usually about ¼" in a size.

CUT
- To penetrate or divide something as with a sharp instrument.

DEEP-FRY
- To fry in plenty of fat, say ghee or oil.

DICE
- To cut into ½" or smaller cubes eg. carrots.

DISCARD
- To cast aside or throw out eg. the spice bag.

DISSOLVE
- To mix a dry substance like sugar into a concentrated watery solution or an extract like cochineal colouring into water.

DRAIN
- To free a food completely from liquid.

DRY-ROAST
- Generally means frying the seed in a pan over dry heat without any cooking medium. eg. cummin seeds.

FRY
- To cook food in ghee or oil till it turns brown.

FLAKE
- Peel-off into chip like pieces.

GRATE
- To rub food into small pieces on a rough perforted plate or grater.

GRIND
- To reduce food to a paste.

HALVE
- To divide into halves. eg. bitter berries

JULIENNE
- Cut into thin strips or small, match-like pieces. eg. carrots.

MARINATE
- To let stand in a mixture - such as oil, vinegar, lime juice and seasonings - called a marinade. The process brings out the flavour.

MASH
- To crush or pound, to pulp any soft substance (eg. potato). To break down by using hands or a masher.

Glossary

MINCE
- To chop food as finely as possible.

PARBOIL
- Just as it sounds, to partly cook by boiling, (taking usually 1/3rd the time) prior to completing the cooking by another method.

PARE
- Simply another word for peel – to remove the outer skin from fruits and vegetables. Strips of lime peel or orange peel are best taken off with a potato peeler, to take the minimum of the bitter pith with the rind.

PASTE
- Soft thick and slightly moist compound produced by grinding or mixing together a number of ingredients. Smooth blend of dry ingredients with liquid.

PAT-DRY
- To strike gently or lightly as with the palm of the hand eg. to pat-dry on a wet cloth.

PINCH
- A pinch of any dry ingredient is the amount which you can pick between the thumb and forefinger.

POUND
- To beat into fine pieces / powder.

PUREE
- Pulp of cooked fruit or vegetable obtained through a sieve.

REDUCE
- Boiling a liquid down rapidly in an uncovered pan to thicken the consistency and concentrate the flavour in a very small amount of liquid. Any salt you add will become concentrated, so go lightly with that until after the liquid is reduced.

SAUTE
- To fry lightly in a small amount of fat over a medium fire. Also called pan-frying.

SCRAPE
- To free the outer layer of a fruit or vegetable eg. scrape ginger.

SCRUB
- To free the outer layer of a fruit or vegetable by rubbing with the hand, a brush or a cloth eg. to scrub a carrot, potato etc.

SEASON
- To add spices.

SEED
- To remove seeds from fruit.

SHELL
- To remove from the ear or husk eg. shell peas.

SHRED
- To cut into fine strips or small, long or narrow strips. eg. cabbage.

SIMMER
- To boil very slowly in a covered pan on top of the cooker or in a covered dish in a very slow oven, the liquid showing only the slightest movement on the surface.

SMOKING POINT
- The temperature at which oils and fats begin to break down and give off a blue vapour. The temperature varies according to the type of fat, and the more refined it is, the higher the smoking point will be.

SKIN
- To remove the peel of a fruit or vegetable eg. skin bananas.

SLICE
- A thin, broad flat piece cut from something.

SLIT
- To cut apart or open along a line eg. chillies.

SLIVER
- A small slender piece, cut off, usually lengthwise eg. slivered almonds.

SMEAR
- To spread or daub an oily or wet substance on or over something eg. smear a spice paste.

SOAK
- To lie in and become saturated or permeated with water or some other liquid. eg. soak in vinegar or lime juice. To cover food with liquid.

SPLIT
- To break apart, to divide or to separate into four, end to end eg. split mango.

SPRIG
- A few strands from a bunch.

SPRINKLE
- To scatter, to disperse or distribute here and there eg. sprinkle fenugreek seeds etc.

STIRRING
- Mixing foods with a suitable tool such as a spoon or ladle, by a circular motion in contact with the pan.

SQUEEZE
- To drain out the liquid by crushing or pressing by your hands.

STEAM
- To cook by means of steam generated by boiling water. The food does not come in contact with the water. To cook by heat with steam as the surrounding medium. The steam may be applied directly to the food or to the container (as in a double boiler).

STEEP
- Soak in liquid.

STIR
- A fairly brisk movement, to mix with the spoon etc. (a wooden spoon is the best thing to use) using a rotary motion.

STONE
- To remove stones (seeds) from fruit eg. stone plums, apricots etc.

SUN-DRY
- To dry vegetable or fruit in the sun eg. mango pieces, raisins etc.

TOAST
- To brown by exposure to heat.

TOP
- To cover up the food with liquid like oil, water or vinegar.

TOSS
- To stir or mix lightly and gently until the ingredients are coated with the dressing.

Index

RECIPE : CATEGORY

CATEGORY	RECIPE NO.
Amaranth leaves	
Amaranth leaves in tamarind sauce : hot	190
Amaranth leaves – peppered : hot	191
Ammatangai	
Ammatangai in mustard sauce : hot	815
Anbazhanga	
Garlic, ginger – spicy anbazhanga : hot	335
Mustard anbazhanga : hot	116
Mustard anbazhanga in vinegar : hot	334
Salted anbazhanga : watery	337
Spiced anbazhanga : hot	336
Apple	
Apple – date & raisin : sweet	339
Apple : sweet	338
Sour & spiced apple : sweet	340
Sour apple - dry fruit : sweet	341
Spiced apple - onion : sweet	904
Apricot	
Apricot in spiced vinegar : sweet	342
Apricot in vinegar : sweet	905
Sour apricot - dry fruits : sweet	118
Atichoke	
Arthichoke in vinegar : watery	117
Artichoke – capsicum-tomato : watery	067
Asparagus	
Asparagus in buttermilk : watery	068
Asparagus in spicy curd : watery	906
Spicy asparagus : hot	343
Bamboo shoot	
Bamboo shoot in curd : hot	069
Cummin, bamboo shoot - onion : hot	344
Garlic, ginger – bamboo shoot : hot	119
Lime, bamboo shoot : salty	816
Spiced bamboo shoot in vinegar : sweet	039
Sweet & sour bamboo shoot : hot	347
Banana	
Sour banana : sweet	893
Sour spiced banana : sweet	925
Bean	
Bean in tamarind sauce : hot	346
Cluster bean in tamarind sauce : hot	349
Dill bean in vinegar : tender	818
Four angled beans in lime juice : hot	120
Sour & spiced bean : sweet	345
Sour bean - onion : sweet	817

CATEGORY	RECIPE NO.
Spicy bean sprouts – onion : hot	121
Spiced broad bean : hot	348
Beetroot	
Beetroot – ginger : hot	350
Beetroot – gram : hot	354
Beetroot in spiced vinegar : salty	819
Beetroot – onion - tomato in tamarind sauce : hot	351
Lime, beet root - tomato - onion : hot	352
Sour beetroot - apple - date : sweet	907
Spicy beetroot in vinegar : hot	353
Bel	
Bel murabba : sweet	123
Bel preserve in jaggery : sweet	909
Ber	
Ber – ginger : sweet	122
Sweet & sour ber : hot	356
Sweet ber : hot	908
Bilimbi	
Bilimbi – dry fruit in spiced vinegar : sweet	910
Bilimbi : hot	358
Dried bilimbi – raisin : hot	359
Fried bilimbi – gram : hot	124
Bitterberry	
Bitterberry in buttermilk : watery	969
Sour bitterberry : salty	760
Spiced bitterberry : hot	764
Sweet & sour bitterberry : hot	763
Bitter gourd	
Bitter gourd – bean sprouts-onion : hot	070
Bitter gourd – ginger in lime juice : hot	911
Bitter gourd in ground spices : hot	364
Bitter gourd in lime juice : hot	360
Bitter gourd in vinegar : hot	361
Bitter gourd – mango-raisin : sweet	072
Bitter gourd – onion : hot	126
Small bitter gourd – green spices : hot	127
Sour bitter gourd - ginger : hot	366
Sour bitter gourd : hot	363
Sour, ripe bitter gourd : hot	125
Spicy bitter gourd in lime juice : hot	365
Spicy bitter gourd in tamarind sauce : hot	362
Spicy bitter gourd - onion : hot	912
Sprout stuffed bitter gourd : hot	071
Stuffed bitter gourd in tamarind : hot	913
Bottle gourd	
Bottle gourd – raw mango : hot	367

CATEGORY	RECIPE NO.
Bottle gourd seed – black gram : hot	976
Sour bottle gourd : hot	914
Spiced bottle gourd peel : hot	975

Brinjal

CATEGORY	RECIPE NO.
Brinjal – green coriander – onion - tomato : hot	378
Brinjal – green spices : hot	376
Brinjal – lime strips : hot	372
Brinjal – mango : hot	369
Brinjal – onion - tomato : hot	384
Brinjal – potato : hot	673
Fried spiced brinjal : hot	375
Mustard brinjal : watery	383
Pounded brinjal – tamarind : hot	380
Sour & spicy brinjal : hot	368
Sour brinjal – cashew : sweet	385
Sour brinjal – green spices : hot	381
Sour brinjal pulp : hot	915
Sour, oven toasted brinjal : hot	128
Sour, toasted brinjal : hot	371
Spiced brinjal in tamarind sauce : hot	012
Spiced brinjal in vinegar : hot	370
Spicy brinjal – fresh red chilli : hot	377
Spicy brinjal : hot	382
Spicy brinjal in tamarind suace : hot	379
Stuffed brinjal : hot	373
Sweet & sour brinjal – raisin : hot	374

Cabbage

CATEGORY	RECIPE NO.
Cabbage – carrot - green spices : hot	390
Cabbage – carrot - sprouted gram : hot	949
Cabbage in lime juice : salty	193
Cabbage in tamarind sauce : hot	386
Cabbage in vinegar : watery	194
Cabbage – lime : hot	388
Cabbage – onion - tomato : hot	389
Cabbage – tomato in vinegar : sweet	953
Red cabbage : watery	916
Sour cabbage – ground spices : hot	391

Capsicum

CATEGORY	RECIPE NO.
Capsicum – bitter gourd - mango stuffing : hot	129
Capsicum – green chilli in tamarind sauce : hot	195
Capsicum – green spices : hot	130
Capsicum in tamarind sauce : hot	393
Capsicum in vinegar : watery	387
Sour & spicy capsicum : hot	392
Sour capsicum – bean sprout : hot	073
Sour capsicum – brinjal : sweet	394
Spiced capsicum in vinegar : hot	820
Spiced capsicum – onion in vinegar : sweet	395

Carrot

CATEGORY	RECIPE NO.
Aniseed, mustard-carrot : hot	398
Carrot – ginger in lime juice : instant	824
Carrot – green chilli in lime juice : hot	197
Carrot in lime juice : hot	918
Carrot in spicy mahani liquid : watery	295
Carrot in tamarind sauce : sweet	196
Carrot – onion - green spices : hot	917
Carrot – walnut : sweet	400
Ginger, garlic - carrot : hot	397
Mustard carrot – garlic : hot	133
Red carrot in vinegar : watery	198
Sour & spicy carrot - peas : sweet	200
Sour carrot – onion : hot	199
Sour carrot – raisin : sweet	401
Spiced baby carrot : watery	134
Spicy carrot – date : sweet	399
Spicy carrot – dry fruit : sweet	402
Sweet & sour carrot : hot	396

Cashew

CATEGORY	RECIPE NO.
Cashew – green coriander : instant	823

Cauliflower

CATEGORY	RECIPE NO.
Cauliflower – almond - date : hot	405
Cauliflower – cummin - mango : hot	407
Cauliflower – date - onion : hot	132
Cauliflower – gram in lime juice : hot	203
Cauliflower in lime juice : hot	403
Cauliflower in tamarind sauce : tender	201
Cauliflower – lime strips : tender	202
Cauliflower – lotus stem - onion : hot	822
Cauliflower – spring onion : hot	408
Cauliflower stem – green spices : hot	977
Cauliflower stem : hot	978
Mustard cauliflower – lime : watery	047
Mustard cauliflower : watery	409
Sour cauliflower – mango : hot	404
Spicy cauliflower – carrot : hot	406
Spicy cauliflower : watery	410
Sweet & sour cauliflower : instant	016

Celery

CATEGORY	RECIPE NO.
Celery in vinegar : salty	205

Cereal

CATEGORY	RECIPE NO.
Sour & spiced cereal mango : hot	207
Spicy cereal – green coriander : tender	214

Chambakai

CATEGORY	RECIPE NO.
Sour chambakai : hot	075

Cherry

CATEGORY	RECIPE NO.
Cherry in vinegar : sweet	412
Sour cherry in lime juice : hot	411
Sour cherry in tamarind sauce : hot	136

Chilli

CATEGORY	RECIPE NO.
Chopped green chilli in vinegar : hot	843
Dried red chilli in lime juice : hot	227
Fresh red chilli in tomato sauce : hot	457
Fresh red chilli – fenugreek : hot	458
Fresh red chilli – tamarind - garlic : hot	229
Fried green chilli in vinegar : hot	502
Green chilli – garlic : hot	513
Green chilli – ginger blend : hot	521

CATEGORY	RECIPE NO.
Green chilli – ginger – garlic vinegared : hot	236
Green chilli in curd : salty	143
Green chilli – lime – ginger : salty	841
Green chilli in mustard sauce : hot	043
Green chilli in tamarind sauce : hot	503
Green chilli in vinegar : salty	840
Green chilli – mango – mustard : hot	507
Green chilli – mango – thymol seeds : hot	508
Green chilli – mustard – mango stuffed : hot	520
Green chilli – onion : hot	506
Green chilli spice stuffed : hot	511
Green chilli – tamarind : sweet	526
Ground green chilli : hot	505
Sesame – green chilli – tamarind : hot	235
Sour & spicy green chlli : hot	501
Sour & spicy green chilli – tamarind : hot	523
Sour fresh red chilli : hot	230
Sour green chilli – green spices : hot	518
Sour green chilli – ginger : sweet	515
Spice stuffed green chilli : instant	839
Spiced fresh red chilli – grated mango : hot	455
Spiced fresh red chilli – tamarind : hot	454
Spicy stuffed fresh red chilli : hot	141
Spicy green chilli – mint : hot	519
Spicy kashmiri red chilli stuffed : hot	934
Stuffed fresh red chilli (burvan lal mirch) : hot	061
Stuffed green chilli in lime juice : salty	842
Stuffed kashmiri red chilli : hot	456
Stuffed mustard green chilli : hot	525
Stuffed spicy green chilli : hot	524
Sweet & sour green chilli – green coriander : hot	504
Sweet & sour green chilli : hot	014
Sweet & sour green chilli – sesame : hot	510
Sweet & sour green chilli – tamarind : hot	516
Sweet & sour mustard green chilli : hot	509
Large green chilli in mustard oil : hot	512
Large green chilli – mango – green coriander stuffed : hot	514
Tanjore green chilli in tamarind sauce : hot	522

Chow chow
Chow chow – green spices : hot	137
Chow chow in lime juice : hot	414
Chow chow in tamarind sauce : hot	413

Coconut
Coconut – green coriander : hot	422
Coconut – mango – green coriander : instant	830
Coconut – mango – green spices : tender	219
Coconut – tamarind : hot	215
Flavoury coconut – mango : salty	217
Spicy coconut – mango : hot	216

Cocum
Cocum – date – garlic : instant	828
Sour cocum : sweet	218

CATEGORY	RECIPE NO.
Spiced cocum – onion : instant	829

Colocasia
Sour & spiced colocasia : hot	424
Sour colocasia : hot	017
Spiced colocasia : hot	423

Coriander
Coriander seeds – grated coconut : hot	425
Green coriander – ginger – garlic : hot	426
Green coriander – green chilli : hot	020
Green coriander – sesame : hot	220
Sour green coriander – dried red chilli : hot	427
Spiced green coriander – onion : hot	429
Sweet & sour green coriander – ginger : hot	430

Corn
Baby corn in vinegar : hot	428
Corn – ginger : hot	077
Spicy corn – onion-sprouts : hot	138
Stripped corn – celery in vinegar : watery	831
Stripped corn – mixed vegetable : tender	832

Cucumber :
Cucumber Avakkai (Dosakkai) : hot	035
Cucumber – dill : salty	435
Cucumber – green spices : watery	834
Cucumber in lime juice : watery	223
Cucumber in tamarind sauce : hot	437
Cucumber – celery-onion in vinegar : sweet	441
Cucumber in spiced vinegar : watery	440
Cucumber in vinegar : sweet	442
Cucumber whole : salty	920
Garlic – cucumber in vinegar : watery	221
Ginger – cucumber in vinegar : salty	222
Ginger, garlic – cucumber : hot	433
Grated cucumber – poppy seeds : hot	434
Mustard cucumber : tender	833
Pounded cucumber – green coriander : hot	431
Sour & spicy cucumber : hot	438
Sour cucumber – spring onion : hot	078
Spicy cucumber – onion : hot	436
Sweet & sour cucumber : watery	835
Sweet & sour cucumber : watery	439
Toasted cucumber in tamarind sauce : hot	432

Curd
Curd – green spices : instant	836
Spiced curd – tamarind : sweet	443
Spicy curd – mango : oilless	079
Spicy curd : watery	224

Curry leaf
Curry leaf – coconut : hot	225
Curry leaf – green coriander : hot	445
Curry leaf in tamarind sauce : hot	024
Curry leaf seed : hot	080
Spiced curry leaf – green chilli : hot	444

CATEGORY	RECIPE NO.
Date	
Date – green turmeric : sweet	922
Date in tamarind sauce : sweet	449
Date – raisin in lime juice : sweet	451
Sour & spicy date : sweet	139
Sour date – onion seeds : hot	837
Spiced date : sweet	226
Spicy date in vinegar : sweet	446
Dry fruit	
Dry fruit in tamarind sauce : sweet	157
Dry fruits - nuts in honey : sweet	974
Spicy dry fruit in vinegar : sweet	924
Drumstick	
Drumstick avakkai : hot	452
Drumstick – gooseberry : hot	950
Drumstick – green spices : hot	453
Drumstick pith : hot	007
Drumstick pith – green chilli : hot	081
Spicy drumstick leaf – fenugreek leaf paste : hot	979
Elephant apple	
Spiced elephant apple (tekheda) : salty	041
Fenugreek	
Sour fenugreek leaf – green spices : hot	140
Sprouted fenugreek in tamarind sauce : hot	082
Garlic	
Garlic, green coriander tamarind : hot	919
Garlic in soya sauce : sweet	927
Garlic, mustard – green chilli : hot	517
Garlic – pepper – tamarind : hot	461
Green garlic in lime juice : hot	083
Peppered sour garlic : hot	462
Sour & spicy garlic : watery	464
Sour garlic – coconut : salty	056
Spiced garlic : hot	463
Spicy hill garlic in lime juice : hot	460
Spicy garlic in lime juice : hot	926
Steamed spicy garlic in lime juice : watery	232
Sweet & sour garlic : hot	009
Gherkin	
Gherkin in mustard oil : hot	465
Perky Gherkin : oilless	142
Ginger :	
Dry fruits – fresh ginger : sweet	948
Ginger – green chilli in lime juice : hot	467
Ginger in lime juice : watery	233
Ginger in raw tamarind sauce : salty	234
Ginger in sweet vinegar : watery	471
Ginger in tamarind : sweet	052
Gingered – lime : hot	853
Ginger preserve : sweet	472
Sour cut ginger – green spices : hot	470
Sour ginger : hot	466
Sour mango ginger : hot	650

CATEGORY	RECIPE NO.
Sour mango ginger – garlic : hot	005
Spiced ginger : hot	928
Spicy ginger in tamarind sauce : hot	010
Sweet & sour ginger : hot	468
Sweet & sour ginger – garlic : hot	469
Sweet & spiced ginger : hot	929
Gonkura	
Fenugreek sorrel leaves (gonkura) : hot	036
Gonkura – coriander seeds : hot	475
Gonkura – garlic – green chilli : hot	476
Gonkura – green chilli : instant	011
Gonkura – onion : hot	474
Spiced gonkura : hot	473
Gooseberry	
Cooked goosberry : hot	930
Cooked gooseberry in lime juice : hot	480
Curd gooseberry – green chilli : watery	490
Cut gooseberry avakkai : hot	477
Dry fried gooseberry : hot	931
Fried gooseberry in spicy sauce : watery	492
Fried gooseberry whole in oil : hot	486
Fried star gooseberry : instant	013
Gooseberry avakkai in tamarind sauce : hot	482
Gooseberry – ginger – garlic : hot	488
Gooseberry honeyed : sweet	497
Gooseberry preserve : sweet	492
Gooseberry – tamarind : hot	478
Gooseberry whole : watery	489
Grated gooseberry : sweet	495
Ground gooseberry : hot	481
Ground star gooseberry : hot	499
Pounded gooseberry : hot	004
Salted gooseberry : watery	932
Sour cut gooseberry : hot	483
Sour gooseberry : hot	485
Sour gooseberry – onion – raisin : sweet	497
Sour gooseberry – onion : sweet	498
Sour ground raw gooseberry : hot	237
Spiced gooseberry : sweet	494
Spicy fried gooseberry : hot	479
Spicy steamed gooseberry in curd : hot	493
Steamed gooseberry – garlic : hot	484
Steamed gooseberry : instant	838
Star gooseberry – green chilli : hot	500
Star gooseberry sauce : hot	487
Star gooseberry : sweet	084
Grams	
Black gram – tamarind : hot	192
Bengal gram – mango : hot	357
Fried gram – mango : hot	231
Green gram – mango : hot	527
Mixed gram in tamarind : salty	204
Mixed gram sprouts : hot	135
Sour & spiced bengal gram : hot	355

CATEGORY	RECIPE NO.
Sour spiced sprouted bengal gram : salty	076
Sour & spicy sprouted green gram : hot	145
Sour gram : hot	208
Spicy sprouted pulses – onion : tender	299
Spiced horse gram – onion : hot	148
Spiced red gram – tamarind : hot	291
Sprouted green gram – cocum : hot	144
Sprouted green gram : hot	085
Grapes	
Green grape : hot	239
Ripe black grapes : sweet	528
Unripe grape – coconut – green coriander : salty	238
Green cardamom	
Green cardamom in lime juice : watery	821
Green pepper	
Green – pepper – ginger in lime juice : hot	845
Green pepper in lime juice : watery	015
Groundnut	
Gram groundnut in tamarind : hot	206
Raw groundnut – coconut – mango : hot	529
Raw groundnut – cummin : hot	241
Roasted groundnut – chilli – garlic : hot	146
Roasted groundnut – ginger : salty	244
Roasted groundnut – mint – green coriander : instant	847
Roasted groundnut – tamarind : hot	242
Sour raw groundnut – green coriander : tender	243
Spiced raw groundnut – coconut – mango : hot	530
Guava	
Guava in tamarind sauce : hot	531
Guava – tomato : watery	245
Sour guava : hot	147
Gunda	
Gunda : hot	048
Hibiscus	
Hibiscus flower : sweet	933
Irumban puli	
Spicy irumban puli : watery	086
Jack fruit	
Jackfruit seed – green spices : instant	982
Jackfruit seed – tamarind : hot	980
Mustard jackfruit : hot	533
Raw jackfruit in lime juice : hot	087
Ripe jackfruit – mustard – aniseed : hot	532
Sour & spiced ripe jackfruit : sweet	246
Spiced jackfruit seed : hot	981
Spiced raw jackfruit – onion : hot	935
Spicy jackfruit : sweet	535
Steamed raw jackfruit : hot	534
Tender raw jackfruit – mango powder : hot	149
Jaggery	
Jaggery – black gram : sweet	247

CATEGORY	RECIPE NO.
Kalakkai	
Salted small kalakkai : watery	538
Small kalakkai – cummin seed : hot	248
Small kalakkai : hot	540
Small kalakkai in buttermilk : watery	541
Small kalakkai : salty	539
Spiced Kalakkai : hot	003
Spicy kalakkai : sweet	536
Spicy small kalakkai : hot	537
Stuffed kalakkai chain : oilless	074
Kichilikai	
Spicy kichilikai : hot	209
Kidarangai	
Boiled kidarangai : salty	213
Fried kidarangai : hot	418
Kidarangai – ginger : hot	212
Kidarangai : hot	006
Kidarangai in tamarind sauce : hot	419
Khol-rabi	
Khol rabi – aniseed – mustard : hot	542
Khol rabi – capsicum : hot	543
Kolumichai	
Spiced kolumichai : salty	415
Kovakkai :	
Kovakkai in buttermilk : watery	545
Kovakkai – onion – gram : hot	150
Spicy kovakkai – green chilli : hot	544
Kumquat	
Flavoury kumquat : hot	421
Kumquat leaf – green coriander – gram : instant	983
Sweet & sour kumquat : hot	089
Spiced kumquat – mango ginger : hot	088
Lady's finger	
Lady's finger in lime juice : hot	546
Spice stuffed lady's finger in lime juice : hot	151
Spiced lady's finger – raw mango : hot	549
Stuffed lady's finger – ginger : hot	548
Lime	
Economical dried lime : hot	550
Aromatic – lime – lime juice : salty	572
Aromatic lime whole : salty	571
Cabbage strips – stuffed lime : oilless	131
Cooked lime whole – green chilli : hot	846
Curry lime – fenugreek : hot	921
Economical spiced lime : hot	557
Fenugreek – lime : hot	854
Fried lime – green chilli : hot	858
Fried lime : hot	249
Ground lime peel : hot	591
Lime – green coriander – coconut : tender	250
Lime – coriander seeds : sweet	586
Lime – date – jaggery : sweet	583
Lime – fenugreek leaves : salty	938

CATEGORY	RECIPE NO.
Lime – fenugreek – mustard : hot	551
Lime – ginger – date in vinegar : salty	855
Lime – ginger – green chilli : hot	252
Lime – ginger – green chilli in vinegar : hot	567
Lime – ginger – green chilli stuffed : hot	566
Lime – ginger – green chilli : watery	576
Lime – ginger : hot	562
Lime – ginger – kalakkai : salty	856
Lime – green chilli : hot	857
Lime – green chilli paste : hot	553
Lime – green pepper – garlic : hot	564
Lime in oil : sweet	578
Lime in spiced vinegar : watery	577
Lime in spicy sauce : watery	575
Lime in vinegar : hot	558
Lime leaf – curry leaves : instant	092
Lime leaf – green coriander – gram : instant	984
Lime – mahani – green spices : hot	865
Lime mild spicy stuffed : salty	849
Lime peel paste : hot	985
Lime peel : watery	986
Lime preserve – jaggery : sweet	589
Lime pulp : hot	936
Lime : sweet	581
Lime – thymol seeds : hot	851
Lime whole : salty	570
Malta lime – mustard – garlic : hot	568
Mustard lime – green chilli : hot	863
Peeled lime – raisin : sweet	584
Peppered lime – ginger : sweet	580
Sambaara lime : hot	090
Sliced lime : sweet	579
Sour & spicy curry lime – garlic : hot	447
Sour lime : hot	861
Sour lime – raisin : sweet	587
Sour lime – thymol seeds : sweet	547
Sour peeled lime : sweet	593
Sour spiced garlic : hot	459
Spice stuffed lime : hot	556
Spiced lime – fresh red chillies : watery	152
Spiced lime – fresh red chilli-ginger : hot	552
Spiced lime – ginger – garlic : hot	561
Spiced lime – ginger – green chilli : hot	852
Spiced lime : hot	002
Spiced lime – jaggery : sweet	590
Spiced lime strips : sweet	592
Spiced lime (metha nimbu) : sweet	045
Spiced lime – vinegar : sweet	585
Spiced lime whole : hot	559
Spiced lime whole in vinegar : watery	862
Spiced stuffed boiled lime : watery	251
Spicy curry lime : hot	448
Spicy curry lime – onion : hot	450
Spicy lime – date : hot	554
Spicy lime – fenugreek : sweet	588

CATEGORY	RECIPE NO.
Spicy lime in groundnut oil : hot	555
Spicy lime in lime juice : hot	937
Spicy lime in vinegar : watery	866
Steamed lime : hot	563
Steamed lime in spicy vinegar : hot	565
Stuffed fenugreek lime : hot	055
Stuffed lime – green chilli : hot	560
Stuffed lime – sweet spices : salty	859
Stuffed lime : hot	848
Stuffed lime : salty	573
Stuffed lime : sweet	582
Stuffed spicy lime : hot	850
Sunned lime – green spices : hot	864
Sweet & sour lime : watery	569
Sweet & sour lime whole – thymol seeds : watery	574
Unripe lime – fenugreek : salty	860
Loquat	
Loquat preserve : sweet	595
Spiced loquat – jaggery : sweet	594
Lotus stem	
Cooked lotus stem : hot	596
Lotus stem – mustard – aniseed : hot	181
Steamed lotus stem : hot	154
Stuffed lotus stem : hot	155
Love-lovi	
Dried love-lovi – garlic – ginger : sweet	599
Dried love-lovi in vinegar : sweet	598
Love-lovi – mustard – ginger spiced : hot	597
Spiced love-lovi : hot	156
Mahani	
Mahani – green chilli in buttermilk : watery	757
Mahani in buttermilk : watery	034
Mahani in curd : watery	968
Mahani in lime juice : watery	756
Peppered mahani in lime juice : hot	755
Sweet & sour mahani peel : hot	994
Makoy	
Raw makoy berry : watery	939
Sour makoy leaves : hot	600
Mango	
Aniseed – mango : hot	062
Aromatic mango : hot	607
Cooked mango : hot	255
Cooked mango preserve : sweet	254
Cut mango : hot	602
Dried mango – onion – garlic : hot	626
Dried mango – date – raisin : sweet	639
Dried raw mango : salty	633
Fenugreek – mango (vendhaya mangai) : hot	066
Grated mango – green chilli : hot	869
Grated mango pachadi : hot	262
Grated spiced mango : watery	063
Half-ripe mango – coconut : hot	267

CATEGORY	RECIPE NO.
Half-ripe mango – onion : hot	266
Juicy mango : hot	613
Mango avakkai – bengal gram : hot	603
Mango avakkai – garlic (new method) : hot	019
Mango avakkai – garlic (old method) : hot	018
Mango avakkai – ginger : tender	164
Mango avakkai – jaggery : sweet	644
Mango avakkai – mustard - sesame : hot	161
Mango avakkai (old method) : hot	022
Mango – bengal gram – fenugreek : hot	616
Mango – bengal gram : hot	261
Mango – brinjal : instant	158
Mango – cabbage : hot	259
Mango – curry leaf : tender	258
Mango – fig - cashew : sweet	640
Mango – gooseberry – onion : hot	159
Mango – green chilli :tender	163
Mango – green coriander : tender	256
Mango – green gram : hot	260
Mango – green spices : hot	612
Mango – ground spices : instant	870
Mango – groundnut pachadi : hot	263
Mango (kadu manga) : tender	050
Mango – lime juice : hot	622
Mango – mint : tedner	257
Mango murabba : sweet	641
Mango – mustard - garlic : hot	608
Mango – onion : hot	940
Mango pachadi : hot	253
Mango preserve : sweet	637
Mango – tamarind avakkai : hot	160
Mild mango : salty	268
Mustard mango in vinegar : hot	942
Mustard mango (kadugu manga) : tender	053
Peeled spiced mango (Maagaya) : hot	037
Peppered mango -ginger : sweet	635
Peppered mango : hot	625
Plain tender mango : watery	631
Pounded mango : hot	619
Preserved mango – lime juice : sweet	636
Raw mango in oil (mangai curry) : hot	054
Salted baby mango : tender	620
Sambaara mango : hot	091
Seasoned spiced tender mango : hot	627
Sliced tender spicy mango : hot	614
Small mango avakkai : tender	618
Sour & spicy grated mango : watery	867
Sour cut mango : hot	601
Sour mango – green chilli : instant	044
Sour mango : hot	606
Sour mango skin : sweet	987
Sour spiced grated mango (kaduikash) : salty	064
Sour spiced mango – dry fruit : sweet	642
Sour spiced mango : sweet	868
Spice stuffed mango : hot	623

CATEGORY	RECIPE NO.
Spiced ada manga : hot	051
Spiced dried mango : sweet	634
Spiced grated mango (chhundo) : sweet	046
Spiced mango : hot	001
Spiced peeled mango : hot	610
Spiced mango : salty	871
Spiced mango : sweet	638
Spiced ripe mango in vinegar : hot	265
Spiced ripe mango :sweet	264
Spiced sliced mango : sweet	269
Spicy cooked mango : watery	165
Spicy grated mango : instant	021
Spicy mango (avakkai) : hot	038
Spicy mango – coriander seeds : hot	624
Spicy mango – garlic : tender	162
Spicy mango in oil (ennai mangai) : hot	065
Spicy mango – mustard : hot	604
Spicy shredded mango : sweet	643
Spicy slit mango : watery	632
Spicy stuffed mango : hot	611
Spicy tender mango : hot	615
Split mango in mustard oil : hot	609
Spiced tender cut mango : hot	629
Stuffed spiced mango in vinegar : watery	872
Sunned mango – jaggery : sweet	941
Sweet & sour spiced mango : hot	605
Tender mango : hot	630
Tender mango – ginger-green chilli : hot	621
Treated mango : hot	617
Whole ripe mango (Buffena) : sweet	059
Vinegared tender mango : hot	628
Mango leaf in tamarind sauce : hot	988

Mango ginger

CATEGORY	RECIPE NO.
Mango ginger Avakkai : hot	651
Mango ginger – garlic : hot	645
Mango ginger – green chilli in tamarind sauce : hot	648
Mango ginger – green pepper in lime juice : hot	649
Mango ginger – green spices : salty	023
Mango ginger : hot	647
Mango ginger in curd : watery	943
Mango ginger in lime juice : hot	271
Mango ginger in lime juice : watery	646
Mango ginger in tamarind sauce : hot	093
Mango ginger – lime: hot	270

Mint

CATEGORY	RECIPE NO.
Mint – dried red chilli - tamarind : hot	025
Mint – garlic in tamarind sauce : hot	654
Mint – ginger - onion : hot	652
Mint – green coriander : hot	945
Mint, green coriander – onion – mango powder : tender	240
Mint, green coriander – tomato – onion : instant	873
Mint in tamarind sauce : hot	655
Mint – onion in tamarind sauce : hot	653
Mint – onion - mango : tender	272

Index

CATEGORY	RECIPE NO.
Sour mint – green coriander : instant	874
Sour mint – green pepper : hot	944
Sour mint – ground nut – onion : instant	875
Sour mint – raisin : sweet	658
Mixed fruit	
Apple – fig in vinegar : sweet	662
Apple, pear, plum & cherry : sweet	946
Banana – date – raisin : sweet	663
Banana – date : sweet	923
Mixed fruit in lime – pineapple juice : sweet	657
Mixed fruit in spiced vinegar : sweet	656
Mustard mixed fruit : sweet	660
Plum – apple – date in spiced vinegar : sweet	739
Plum – date in vinegar : sweet	736
Sour apple – pineapple : sweet	661
Spicy mixed fruits – jaggery in vinegar : sweet	659
Mixed vegetable	
Assorted vegetables : hot	675
Bean – onion – papaya : instant	877
Carrot – peas – bean in lime juice : hot	690
Cauliflower – bean : tender	886
Cauliflower – cucumber – bean ; watery	883
Cauliflower – broccoli : hot	685
Cauliflower – carrot – turnip : hot	686
Cauliflower – carrot – peas in vinegar : watery	691
Colocasia – brinjal : hot	672
Fried Mixed vegetable in vinegar : hot	680
Mango – lime : hot	683
Mango – lime – kalakkai : hot	671
Mixed cauliflower – carrot – peas in lime juice : hot	666
Mixed cauliflower – potato – peas : hot	664
Mixed vegetable – date – green spices : hot	668
Mixed vegetable – garlic in lime juice : hot	166
Mixed vegetable – garlic in lime : watery	878
Mixed vegetable – gram : tender	952
Mixed vegetable – green spices : watery	168
Mixed vegetable : hot	692
Mixed vegetable – green chilli in lime juice : hot	688
Mixed vegetable in lime juice : tender	885
Mixed vegetable in lime juice : watery	276
Mixed vegetable in mustard sauce : hot	684
Mixed vegetable in oil : sweet	696
Mixed vegetable in tamarind sauce : hot	280
Mixed vegetable in tamarind – vinegar : hot	682
Mixed vegetable in vinegar : sweet	167
Mixed vegetable in vinegar : watery	694
Mixed vegetable – lime : hot	876
Mixed vegetable – mango – lime : hot	669
Mixed vegetable – mustard – garlic : hot	679
Mixed vegetable peel in nut paste : hot	989
Mixed vegetable : sweet	695
Mixed vegetable : watery	884

CATEGORY	RECIPE NO.
Mustard mixed vegetable – onion – ginger : hot	060
Mustard mixed vegetable : sweet	697
Radish – brinjal : hot	670
Salted mango – loquat : hot	687
Salted mixed vegetable in vinegar : watery	880
Sour & spiced mixed vegetable : hot	676
Sour cauliflower – cucumber : sweet	881
Sour lady's finger – snake gourd : hot	667
Sour mixed vegetbale : hot	689
Sour Mixed vegetable – garlic : watery	277
Sour mixed vegetable in mustard sauce : hot	678
Spiced cauliflower – carrot : hot	681
Spiced mixed vegetable – ginger : hot	275
Spiced mixed vegetable – lime strips : hot	674
Spiced vegetable in vinegar : watery	693
Spiced carrot – peas in lime juice : watery	026
Spicy mixed vegetable – date : sweet	698
Spicy mixed vegetable : hot	677
Sweet & sour mixed vegetable in vinegar : tender	882
Vinegared mixed vegetable in lime juice : hot	665
Moth	
Sour sprouted moth – thymol seeds : hot	094
Mudukottan leaf	
Mudukottan leaf in tamarind sauce : hot	095
Mulberry	
Mulberry : hot	096
Mushroom	
Button mushroom : watery	274
Button mushroom – green spices : tender	278
Button mushroom – ginger – onion : oilless	170
Mushroom – bamboo shoot – water chestnut : sweet	099
Mushroom in tamarind sauce : hot	169
Mustard mushroom in vinegar : instant	097
Sour mushroom – spring onion : salty	098
Sour spiced button mushroom : watery	279
Spicy mushroom : hot	100
Mustard	
Salted mustard : watery	703
Wild mustard – grated coconut : instant	184
Naravallikai	
Sour naravallikai : hot	101
Narthangai	
Fried narthangai : hot	210
Narthangai : hot	825
Narthangai : salty	826
Sour narthangai : sweet	211
Spiced narthangai : hot	416
Spiced narthangai in tamarind : hot	417
Spiced narthangai in tomato juice : hot	420
Spiral / sliced narthangai : hot	827

CATEGORY	RECIPE NO.
Neem flower	
Sweet & sour neem flower : hot	956
Ugadi tamarind – neem – mango : sweet	308
Nogatenga	
Sour noga tenga : sweet	040
Nutmeg	
Sweet / spiced nutmeg : hot	102
Nutrinuggets :	
Spicy nutrinuggets – capsicum : hot	171
Olive	
Ripe olive – frenugreek – onion seeds : hot	172
Omavalli	
Aromatic omavalli : hot	103
Onion	
Baby onion in spiced vinegar : hot	705
Mustard onion : hot	702
Mustard white onion : watery	707
Onion – ginger – green chilli : instant	889
Onion – green spices : hot	029
Onion in spiced vinegar : watery	704
Onion in vinegar : salty	887
Onion – tamarind : hot	711
Sour button onion : sweet	708
Sour onion – aniseed : hot	709
Sour onion : instant	879
Spiced onion – green chilli : hot	713
Spiced onion in tamarind sauce : hot	714
Spicy onion : hot	712
Small red onion – green chilli in lime juice : hot	700
Small red onion in spiced vinegar : watery	888
Small red onion in tamarind sauce : hot	027
Small red onion whole : hot	954
Small white onion – beetroot : hot	715
Small white onion in mustard oil : hot	174
Small white onion : watery	957
Sour small red onion : hot	699
Spiced small red onion in vinegar : hot	955
Spicy small red onion : hot	701
Sour spring onion – honey – green chilli : sweet	281
Spring onion – green chilli : hot	028
Stuffed small red onion : hot	710
White onion in mustard sauce : watery	706
Orange	
Sweet & sour orange peel : hot	030
Papaya	
Mustard papaya : hot	718
Papaya – ginger – garlic : hot	717
Papaya – raisin – lime juice : sweet	720
Papaya – raisin : sweet	958
Papaya preserve : sweet	173
Sour & spicy papaya : hot	719
Sour papaya – onion : hot	716

CATEGORY	RECIPE NO.
Peach	
Sour peach – raisin – onion : sweet	890
Pear	
Pear – tamarind : hot	722
Pear – tomato – onion : sweet	282
Sour & spiced pear : sweet	724
Sour pear – ginger – raisin : sweet	959
Sour pear : sweet	725
Spiced pear : sweet	723
Spiced pear – tamarind : hot	721
Peas	
Green peas in tamarind sauce : hot	175
Sour & spicy green peas : hot	104
Sour green peas : watery	844
Pine apple	
Mustard pineapple – green spices : instant	891
Perky pineapple : sweet	283
Pineapple – lime juice – vinegar : instant	892
Pineapple – mint – mango : sweet	729
Pineapple – onion : sweet	731
Pineapple preserve : sweet	727
Pineapple – raisin : sweet	960
Pineapple : sweet	726
Sour pineapple – dry fruits : sweet	730
Sour pineapple – fruit & nut : sweet	105
Sour pineapple – green chilli : sweet	728
Sour pineapple : sweet	176
Spiced pineapple : sweet	961
Pirandal	
Pirandai – gram : hot	284
Plantain	
Plantain flower : hot	032
Plantain flower – green chilli – green coriander : hot	733
Plantain flower in tamarind sauce : hot	177
Plantain stem : hot	107
Plantain stem in lime juice : hot	962
Raw plantain – tamarind : hot	732
Raw plantain – gram – green chilli : hot	178
Raw plantain skin – raisin : sweet	991
Sour & spicy plantain flower : hot	106
Sour & spicy raw plantain skin : hot	990
Sour spiced raw plantain : sweet	285
Spicy plantain flower – onion – brinjal : hot	734
Plum	
Dried plum – raisin – mango : hot	735
Ripe plum – jaggery : sweet	740
Sour plum – dried ginger : sweet	737
Spiced plum : sweet	895
Spiced ripe plum in vinegar : sweet	738
Sweet plum : instant	894
Pomegranate seed	
Pomegranate seed : instant	896

CATEGORY	RECIPE NO.
Poppy seed	
Poppy seed – garlic - green chilli : hot	287
Sweet & sour poppy seeds in curd : watery	286
Potato	
Potato avakkai : hot	179
Potato – green coriander in lime juice : hot	108
Potato in mustard sauce : salty	963
Baby Potato preserve : sweet	964
Sour spiced potato – mustard : sweet	743
Spicy potato in lime juice : hot	741
Spicy potato – peas - coconut : hot	742
Pumpkin	
Pumpkin – cabbage - tamarind : hot	965
Pumpkin – raisin in vinegar :sweet	746
Sour pumpkin – raisin : sweet	745
Sour red pumpkin : sweet	109
Spicy white pumpkin – onion - tomato : hot	747
Sweet & sour pumpkin – green coriander : hot	744
White pumpkin – dry fruits : sweet	748
Radish	
Mustard radish : hot	749
Radish – ginger in lime juice : hot	750
Radish – green spices : hot	967
Radish – lentils : hot	288
Radish preserve - honey : sweet	966
Spicy mustard – white radish : hot	751
White radish preserve : sweet	752
Raisin	
Black raisin in lime juice : sweet	289
Ground raisin : instant	897
Raisin – almond - pistachio : sweet	273
Raisin – green spices : tender	290
Sour raisin – date : sweet	753
Sweet & sour raisin : hot	180
Rhubarb	
Rhubarb – date - onion : watery	292
Ridge gourd	
Ridge gourd – onion : hot	754
Spiced ridge gourd – gram : hot	294
Spicy ridge gourd – lentils : hot	293
Spicy ridge gourd peel – gram : hot	992
Steamed ridge gourd peel : instant	993
Round gourd	
Spiced round gourd : instant	110
Sesame	
Sesame – gram - green chilli : hot	296
Sesame – groundnut - green spices : tender	297
Sesame seed in tamarind sauce : hot	758

CATEGORY	RECIPE NO.
Snake gourd	
Snake gourd – onion - green spices : hot	760
Snake gourd : sweet	761
Spicy snake gourd seed – gram : hot	995
Spicy snake gourd – tamarind : hot	759
Spices	
Spice ball – coconut : instant	153
Spinach	
Spiced spinach : hot	112
Spinach – green spices : tender	298
Star fruit	
Spicy star fruit : hot	762
Star fruit in tamarind sauce : hot	111
Sugarcane :	
Spicy sugarcane juice – dry fruits : sweet	300
Sweet potato	
Boiled sweet potato – mango : instant	058
Raw sweet potato – mango : hot	301
Tamarind	
Green tamarind – green chilli : hot	302
Green tamarind – gram - red chilli : hot	182
Fenugreek greens – tamarind : tender	228
Peppered tamarind - cucumber seeds : sweet	309
Salted tamarind : hot	312
Sour tamarind – raisin : sweet	770
Spiced green tamarind : tender	033
Spiced tamarind (imli chutney) : sweet	057
Spiced tamarind : sweet	902
Spiced tamarind – garlic : hot	766
Spicy tamarind – cummin seeds : sweet	769
Spicy tamarind – cummin-jaggery : sweet	310
Spicy tamarind – green chilli : hot	307
Spicy tamarind – jaggery (tetular achar) : sweet	042
Spicy tamarind – raisin : sweet	314
Spicy tamarind – cummin : hot	900
Spicy tamarind : sweet	303
Spicy tamarind – coriander-jaggery : sweet	970
Sunned spiced tamarind : sweet	315
Sweet tamarind – date : instant	899
Sweet tamarind – ginger - garlic : hot	305
Tamarind – cummin : instant	901
Tamarind – garlic - green coriander : hot	768
Tamarind – ginger - garlic - date : hot	313
Tamarind – ginger - green chilli : hot	304
Tamarind – gram - green chilli : hot	767
Tamarind – green chilli : salty	306
Tamarind – green coriander - jaggery: sweet	771
Tamarind – jaggery : sweet	772
Tamarind – mint-dried ginger : sweet	311
Tender tamarind leaves : instant	996

CATEGORY	RECIPE NO.
Tapioca	
Tapioca in lime juice : hot	773
Thammatankai	
Thammatankai in lime juice : hot	774
Tudhuvelai	
Tudhuvelai berry / leaf tamarind : instant	113
Tudhuvelai berry in curd : watery	807
Tudhuvelai berry in lime juice : hot	189
Tudhuvelai leaf : instant	973
Thummutikai	
Thummutikai in whipped curd : watery	775
Tomato	
Green tomato – ginger - garlic : instant	898
Green tomato – horse radish : salty	951
Green tomato in vinegar : sweet	781
Green tomato – jaggery : sweet	325
Green tomato – sesame - coconut : sweet	782
Green tomato : sweet	779
Green tomato – tamarind : hot	777
Ground tomato – aniseed : hot	323
Ground tomato : hot	793
Mustard tomato in groundnut oil : hot	795
Ripe tomato – garlic - ginger : sweet	321
Sesame – green tomato : hot	316
Sour & spiced tomato – onion - capsicum : sweet	806
Sour & spicy green tomato : hot	187
Sour & spicy tomato – green spices : hot	787
Sour & spicy tomato : sweet	789
Sour & spicy traditional ground tomato : hot	791
Sour green tomato – mustard : sweet	780
Sour green tomato : sweet	778
Sour ground tomato : hot	800
Sour tomato – garlic : hot	802
Sour tomato – gram - garlic : hot	327
Sour tomato – green coriander : tender	317
Sour tomato – green spices : hot	796
Sour tomato – onion - ginger : sweet	804
Sour tomato – onion : watery	324
Sour tomato – raisin - apricot : sweet	328
Sour tomato – raisin : sweet	794
Spiced ripe tomato : sweet	319
Spiced tomato : hot	785
Spiced tomato – tamarind : hot	786
Spicy tomato – dry fruits : sweet	326
Spicy tomato : hot	783
Steamed green tomato : hot	776
Sweet & sour tomato in garlic juice : instant	903
Tomato – asafoetida - garlic : hot	784
Tomato – fenugreek - mustard : hot	801
Tomato – garlic in vinegar : sweet	971

CATEGORY	RECIPE NO.
Tomato – ginger in mustard sauce : hot	790
Tomato – gram - garlic : hot	798
Tomato – green spices : tender	318
Tomato – onion - ginger : hot	788
Tomato – onion - raisin - plum : hot	799
Tomato paste – tamarind : hot	803
Tomato – raisin - almond in vinegar : sweet	805
Tomato – raisin : sweet	322
Tomato – tamarind : hot	031
Tomato – tender bitterberries : hot	972
Tomato – onion - green chilli : hot	320
Traditional ground tomato : hot	792
Traditional tomato : hot	797
Tulsi	
Tulsi – gram - green chilli : instant	114
Turmeric	
Green turmeric in lime juice : oilless	185
Turnip	
Sour turnip – mustard : sweet	809
Spiced turnip – ginger - garlic : sweet	811
Spicy turnip – onion : hot	808
Turnip in mustard sauce : watery	329
Turnip – onion - apple : sweet	810
Vellarai keerai	
Vellarai keerai – black gram : instant	947
Walnut	
Green walnuts in spiced vinegar : watery	049
Watermelon	
Spiced watermelon rind : instant	998
Sweet & sour watermelon rind : instant	999
Watermelon rind in spiced viengar : instant	1000
Watermelon rind – onion - tamarind : instant	997
Wheat	
Wheat sprout – bengal gram sprout : hot	115
Wheat – coconut : instant	186
Woodapple	
Woodapple – ginger : sweet	188
Woodapple – tamarind : hot	333
Yam	
Elephant yam in tamarind sauce : hot	008
Sour elephant yam – garlic : hot	331
Sour grated elephant yam – tamarind : hot	330
Spiced elephant yam – onion - ginger : hot	813
Spiced sour elephant yam – garlic : hot	814
Spicy elephant yam – mustard : hot	332
Sweet & sour elephant yam – green coriander : hot	812
Sweet & sour pidikarnai : instant	183

Acknowledgements

The author is truly grateful to all the people who made this book possible and particularly wish to thank –

husband, PRABHAKHARAN : for his total faith and inspiration

son, PRAJNESH : for his unconditional love and patience

sister, SHEELA RANI CHUNKATH : for the total confidence reposed

brother-in-law MOHAN VERGHESE CHUNKATH : for the wonderful words of encouragement and suggestions

neice, ANUTTAMA : for her constructive criticism and enthusiastic comments

MOM & DAD : for being the motivation behind this work

PRABHAKHARAN'S parents : for having helped to recognise talent

ART PRINT : for their painstaking effort, extreme patience and cooperation

SUDARSAN GRAPHICS : for their quality work and time-sense

SUN TV Viewers for their words of appreciation

SWAMI RAMACHANDRANANDA : for his creativity, constant support and motivation

and other innumerable friends and well-wishers for their assistance and comments

This book takes you through an exciting journey into Pickleland where you will encounter pickles of all kinds: the sweet, sour, hot and spicy varieties — suitable to every palate. More importantly, they are naturally preserved by the use of spices, without artificial additives to increase their shelf life.

Usha R Prabakaran must be commended for meticulously gathering, selecting, standardising, testing and cataloguing the recipes into her book *Usha's* PICKLE DIGEST using her reputed skills and knowledge in this field.

Padmashree Thangam, E. Philip in her Foreword

Usha's PICKLE DIGEST is not a fancy coffee-table book on pickling. It demolishes the myth that pickling is difficult, cumbersome and time-consuming.

In simple and straight-forward language Usha presents 1000 mouth-watering pickle delicacies on a variety of vegetables and fruits, guaranteed to make even the connoisseur marvel. The author demonstrates that the fascinating world of Indian pickling is rich in variety and sophistication, and is in a class of its own.

This book of 1000 usual and unusual pickle recipes, covers the whole gamut of the Indian pickling repetoire. The recipes have been adapted to suit various palates, without sacrificing authenticity.

Usha R Prabakaran, an Economics and Law Graduate, born in 1955, was a practising lawyer for several years before entering the corporate sector. After heading the legal division of a major corporate, she took to pickling research.

During her sustained research in cookery, especially pickling, for more than a decade, the author has drawn on both traditional knowledge and modern science to create hundreds of new varieties of pickles.

She has contributed a number of articles on pickle recipes to The Hindu and various Tamil magazines like Mangayar Malar, Kumudam, Kalki, etc. She has shared her exclusive knowledge of pickling on the TV, demonstrating the ease with which pickles may be prepared in the average kitchen using everyday ingredients.

Usha is married and has a son, Prajnesh. Her husband Prabhakharan, S.G. is a lawyer turned businessman.

Usha's PICKLE DIGEST

Rs. 460/-

Made in the USA
Middletown, DE
11 January 2020